Learn Java 17 Programming

Second Edition

Learn the fundamentals of Java Programming
with this updated guide with the latest features

Nick Samoylov

BIRMINGHAM—MUMBAI

Learn Java 17 Programming
Second Edition

Publishing Product Manager: Gebin George

Senior Editor: Kinnari Chohan

Technical Editor: Pradeep Sahu

Copy Editor: Safis Editing

Project Coordinator: Manisha Singh

Proofreader: Safis Editing

Indexer: Manju Arasan

Production Designer: Vijay Kamble

Marketing Coordinator: Pooja Yadav

Business Development Executive: Kriti Sharma

First published: April 2019

Second edition: July 2022

Production reference: 1060722

Published by Packt Publishing Ltd.

Livery Place

35 Livery Street

Birmingham

B3 2PB, UK.

ISBN 978-1-80324-143-2

www.packt.com

To my wife, Luda, a software developer too, who was the source of my inspiration and the sound technical advice for this book.

– Nick Samoylov

Contributors

About the author

Nick Samoylov graduated from Moscow Institute of Physics and Technology, working as a theoretical physicist and learning to program as a tool for testing his mathematical models. After the demise of the USSR, Nick created and successfully ran a software company, but was forced to close it under the pressure of governmental and criminal rackets. In 1999, with his wife Luda and two daughters, he emigrated to the USA and has been living in Colorado since then, working as a Java programmer. In his free time, Nick likes to write and hike in the Rocky Mountains.

About the reviewers

Alain Trottier loves to drive struggling people, processes, and products to their better versions. He finds immense joy in taking the efforts to help a person find their version 2.0. He believes that there's a thrill in taking a jackhammer to an industrial process and building a more effective version in its place. He finds it invigorating to deconstruct a product or service to reveal key principles and then innovate something way better. He finds delight in smashing everything that makes a client feel awful and turning them into family. These all, he believes are ways to manhandle technology into doing what is right and best.

Fabrizio Marmitt has been a software development engineer for the past 15 years, building web applications as a full-stack software development engineer, from setting up servers to styling frontends. He currently works at Epic Games.

Table of Contents

2

Java Object-Oriented Programming (OOP)

3

Java Fundamentals

Part 2: Building Blocks of Java

4

Exception Handling

5

Strings, Input/Output,and Files

6

Data Structures, Generics, and Popular Utilities

7

Java Standard and External Libraries

8
Multithreading and Concurrent Processing

9
JVM Structure and Garbage Collection

10

Managing Data in a Database

11

Network Programming

12

Java GUI Programming

Part 3: Advanced Java

13

Functional Programming

14

Java Standard Streams

15
Reactive Programming

16
Java Microbenchmark Harness

17

Best Practices for Writing High-Quality Code

Assessments

Index

Other Books You May Enjoy

Preface

The purpose of this book is to equip the readers with a solid understanding of Java fundamentals and to lead them through a series of practical steps from the basics to the actual real programming. The discussion and examples aim to stimulate the growth of the reader's professional intuition by using proven programming principles and practices. The book starts with the basics and brings the readers up to the latest programming technologies, considered on a professional level.

After finishing this book, you will be able to do the following:

- Install and configure your Java development environment.

- Install and configure your Integrated Development Environment (IDE)–essentially, your editor.

- Write, compile, and execute Java programs and tests.

- Understand and use Java language fundamentals.

- Understand and apply object-oriented design principles.

- Master the most frequently used Java constructs.

- Learn how to access and manage data in the database from Java application.

- Enhance your understanding of network programming.

- Learn how to add graphical user interface for better interaction with your application.

- Become familiar with the functional programming.

- Understand the most advanced data processing technologies—streams, including parallel and reactive streams.

- Learn and practice creating microservices and building a reactive system.

- Learn the best design and programming practices.

- Envision Java's future and learn how you can become part of it.

Who this book is for

This book is for those who would like to start a new career in the modern Java programming profession, as well as those who do it professionally already and would like to refresh their knowledge of the latest Java and related technologies and ideas.

What this book covers

Chapter 1, Getting Started with Java 17, begins with the basics, first explaining what "Java" is and defining its main terms, then going on to how to install the necessary tools to write and run (execute) a program. This chapter also describes the basic Java language constructs, illustrating them with examples that can be executed immediately.

Chapter 2, Java Object-Oriented Programming (OOP), presents the concepts of object-oriented programming and how they are implemented in Java. Each concept is demonstrated with specific code examples. The Java language constructs of class and interface are discussed in detail, as well as overloading, overriding, hiding, and use of the final keyword. The last section of the chapter is dedicated to presenting the power of polymorphism.

Chapter 3, Java Fundamentals, presents to the reader a more detailed view of Java as a language. It starts with the code organization in packages and a description of the accessibility levels of classes (interfaces) and their methods and properties (fields). The reference types as the main types of Java's object-oriented nature are presented in much detail, followed by a list of reserved and restricted keywords and a discussion of their usage. The chapter ends with the methods of conversion between primitive types, and from a primitive type to the corresponding reference type and back.

Chapter 4, Exception Handling, tells the reader about the syntax of the Java constructs related to exception handling and the best practices to address (handle) exceptions. The chapter ends with the related topic of the assertion statement that can be used to debug the application code in production.

Chapter 5, Strings, Input/Output, and Files, discusses the String class methods, as well as popular string utilities from standard libraries and the Apache Commons project. An overview of Java input/output streams and related classes of the java.io package follow along with some classes of the org.apache.commons.io package. The file-managing classes and their methods are described in a dedicated section.

Chapter 6, Data Structures, Generics, and Popular Utilities, presents the Java collections framework and its three main interfaces, List, Set, and Map, including discussion and demonstration of generics. The `equals()` and `hashCode()` methods are also discussed in the context of Java collections. Utility classes for managing arrays, objects, and time/date values have corresponding dedicated sections, too.

Chapter 7, Java Standard and External Libraries, provides an overview of the functionality of the most popular packages of Java Class Library (JCL): java.lang, java.util, java.time, java.io and java.nio, java.sql and javax.sql, java.net, java.lang.math, java.math, java.awt, javax.swing, and javafx. The most popular external libraries are represented by the org. junit, org.mockito, org.apache.log4j, org.slf4j, and org.apache.commons packages. This chapter helps the reader to avoid writing custom code in cases where such functionality already exists and can be just imported and used out of the box.

Chapter 8, Multithreading and Concurrent Processing, presents the ways to increase Java application performance by using workers (threads) that process data concurrently. It explains the concept of Java threads and demonstrates their usage. It also talks about the difference between parallel and concurrent processing, and how to avoid unpredictable results caused by the concurrent modification of a shared resource.

Chapter 9, JVM Structure and Garbage Collection, provides the readers with an overview of JVM's structure and behavior, which are more complex than we usually expect. One of the service threads, called garbage collection, performs an important mission of releasing the memory from unused objects. After reading this chapter, the readers will understand better what constitutes Java application execution, Java processes inside JVM, garbage collection, and how JVM works in general.

Chapter 10, Managing Data in a Database, explains and demonstrates how to manage— that is, insert, read, update, and delete–data in a database from a Java application. It also provides a short introduction to the SQL language and basic database operations: how to connect to a database, how to create a database structure, how to write a database expression using SQL, and how to execute them.

Chapter 11, Network Programming, describes and discusses the most popular network protocols, User Datagram Protocol (UDP), Transmission Control Protocol (TCP), HyperText Transfer Protocol (HTTP), and WebSocket, and their support for JCL. It demonstrates how to use these protocols and how to implement client-server communication in Java code. The APIs reviewed include URL-based communication and the latest Java HTTP Client API.

Chapter 12, Java GUI Programming, provides an overview of Java GUI technologies and demonstrates how the JavaFX kit can be used to create a GUI application. The latest versions of JavaFX not only provide many helpful features, but also allow preserving and embedding legacy implementations and styles.

Chapter 13, Functional Programming, explains what a functional interface is, provides an overview of functional interfaces that come with JDK, and defines and demonstrates lambda expressions and how to use them with functional interfaces, including using method reference.

Chapter 14, Java Standard Streams, talks about the processing of data streams, which are different from the I/O streams reviewed in *Chapter 5, Strings, Input/Output, and Files*. It defines what data streams are, how to process their elements using methods (operations) of the java.util.stream.Stream object, and how to chain (connect) stream operations in a pipeline. It also discusses the stream's initialization and how to process the stream in parallel.

Chapter 15, Reactive Programming, introduces the Reactive Manifesto and the world of reactive programming. It starts with defining and discussing the main related concepts – "asynchronous", "non-blocking", "responsive", and so on. Using them, it then defines and discusses reactive programming, the main reactive frameworks, and talks about RxJava in more details.

Chapter 16, Java Microbenchmark Harness, presents the Java Microbenchmark Harness (JMH) project that allows us to measure various code performance characteristics. It defines what JMH is, how to create and run a benchmark, what the benchmark parameters are, and outlines supported IDE plugins. The chapter ends with some practical demo examples and recommendations.

Chapter 17, Best Practices for Writing High-Quality Code, introduces Java idioms and the most popular and useful practices for designing and writing application code.

To get the most out of this book

Read the chapters systematically and answer the quiz questions at the end of each chapter. Clone or just download the source code repository (see the following sections) and run all the code samples that demonstrate the discussed topics. For getting up to speed in programming, there is nothing better than executing the provided examples, modifying them, and trying your own ideas. Code is truth.

If you are using the digital version of this book, we advise you to type the code yourself or access the code from the book's GitHub repository (a link is available in the next section). Doing so will help you avoid any potential errors related to the copying and pasting of code.

Download the example code files

You can download the example code files for this book from GitHub at `https://github.com/PacktPublishing/Learn-Java-17-Programming`. If there's an update to the code, it will be updated in the GitHub repository.

We also have other code bundles from our rich catalog of books and videos available at `https://github.com/PacktPublishing/`. Check them out!

Download the color images

We also provide a PDF file that has color images of the screenshots and diagrams used in this book. You can download it here: `https://packt.link/CQqKD`.

Conventions used

There are a number of text conventions used throughout this book.

`Code in text`: Indicates code words in text, database table names, folder names, filenames, file extensions, pathnames, dummy URLs, user input, and Twitter handles. Here is an example: "When an exception is thrown inside a `try` block, it redirects control flow to the first `catch` clause."

A block of code is set as follows:

```
void someMethod(String s){
    try {
        method(s);
    } catch (NullPointerException ex){
        //do something
    } catch (Exception ex){
        //do something else
    }
}
```

When we wish to draw your attention to a particular part of a code block, the relevant lines or items are set in bold:

```
class TheParentClass {
    private int prop;
    public TheParentClass(int prop){
        this.prop = prop;
    }
    // methods follow
}
```

Any command-line input or output is written as follows:

```
--module-path /path/JavaFX/lib \
          :-add-modules=javafx.controls,javafx.fxml
```

Bold: Indicates a new term, an important word, or words that you see onscreen. For instance, words in menus or dialog boxes appear in **bold**. Here is an example: "Select a value for **Project SDK** (java version 12, if you have installed JDK 12 already) and click **Next**".

> **Tips or important notes**
> Appear like this.

Get in touch

Feedback from our readers is always welcome.

General feedback: If you have questions about any aspect of this book, email us at customercare@packtpub.com and mention the book title in the subject of your message.

Errata: Although we have taken every care to ensure the accuracy of our content, mistakes do happen. If you have found a mistake in this book, we would be grateful if you would report this to us. Please visit www.packtpub.com/support/errata and fill in the form.

Piracy: If you come across any illegal copies of our works in any form on the internet, we would be grateful if you would provide us with the location address or website name. Please contact us at copyright@packt.com with a link to the material.

If you are interested in becoming an author: If there is a topic that you have expertise in and you are interested in either writing or contributing to a book, please visit authors. packtpub.com.

Share Your Thoughts

Once you've read *Learn Java 17 Programming*, we'd love to hear your thoughts! Scan the QR code below to go straight to the Amazon review page for this book and share your feedback.

https://packt.link/r/1-803-24143-8

Your review is important to us and the tech community and will help us make sure we're delivering excellent quality content.

Part 1: Overview of Java Programming

Get up and running with fundamental concepts of Java and OOP with practical examples and sample programs. This will build a base, which will help the readers get started with some core/advanced concepts of Java.

This part contains the following chapters:

- *Chapter 1, Getting Started with Java 17*
- *Chapter 2, Java Object-Oriented Programming (OOP)*
- *Chapter 3, Java Fundamentals*

1
Getting Started with Java 17

This chapter is about how to start learning Java 17 and Java in general. We will begin with the basics, first explaining what Java is and its main terms, followed by how to install the necessary tools to write and run (execute) a program. In this respect, Java 17 is not much different from the previous Java versions, so this chapter's content applies to the older versions too.

We will describe and demonstrate all the necessary steps for building and configuring a Java programming environment. This is the bare minimum that should have on your computer to start programming. We also describe the basic Java language constructs and illustrate them with examples that can be executed immediately.

The best way to learn a programming language—or any language, for that matter—is to use it, and this chapter guides readers on how they can do this with Java. We will cover the following topics in this chapter:

- How to install and run Java
- How to install and run an **integrated development environment (IDE)**
- Java primitive types and operators

- String types and literals
- **Identifiers** (**IDs**) and variables
- Java statements

Technical requirements

To be able to execute the code examples provided in this chapter, you will need the following:

- A computer with a Microsoft Windows, Apple macOS, or Linux operating system
- Java SE version 17 or later
- An IDE or your preferred code editor

The instructions for how to set up a Java **Standard Edition** (**SE**) and IntelliJ IDEA editor will be provided later in this chapter. The files with the code examples for this chapter are available on GitHub in the `https://github.com/PacktPublishing/Learn-Java-17-Programming.git` repository, in the `examples/src/main/java/com/packt/learnjava/ch01_start` folder.

How to install and run Java

When somebody says "*Java*", they may mean quite different things. They could be referring to any of the following:

- **Java programming language**: A high-level programming language that allows an intent (a program) to be expressed in a human-readable format that can be translated into binary code that is executable by a computer
- **Java compiler**: A program that can read a text written in the Java programming language and translate it into bytecode that can be interpreted by the **Java Virtual Machine** (**JVM**) into binary code that is executable by a computer
- **JVM**: A program that reads bytecode of the compiled Java program and interprets it into binary code that is executable by a computer
- **Java Development Kit** (**JDK**): A collection of programs (tools and utilities), including the Java compiler, the JVM, and supporting libraries, which allow the compilation and execution of a program written in the Java language

The following section walks you through the installation of the JDK of Java 17 and the basic related terms and commands.

What is the JDK and why do we need it?

As we have mentioned already, the JDK includes a Java compiler and the JVM. The task of the compiler is to read a .java file that contains the text of a program written in Java (called source code) and transform (compile) it into bytecode stored in a .class file. The JVM can then read the .class file, interpret the bytecode into binary code, and send it to the operating system for execution. Both the compiler and the JVM have to be invoked explicitly from the command line.

The hierarchy of languages used by Java programs goes like this:

- You write Java code (.java file).

- The compiler converts your Java code into bytecode (.class file).

- The JVM converts the bytecode into machine-level assembly instructions (run on hardware).

Have a look at the following example:

```
int a = b + c;
```

When you write the preceding code, the compiler adds the following bytecode to the .class file:

```
ILOAD b
ILOAD c
IADD
ISTORE a
```

Write once, run anywhere is the most famous programming marketing jingle driving worldwide adoption. Oracle claims more than 10 million developers use Java, which runs on 13 billion devices. You write Java and compile it into bytecode in .class files. There is a different JVM for Windows, Mac, Unix, Linux, and more, but the same .class file works on all of them.

To support the .java file compilation and its bytecode execution, the JDK installation also includes standard Java libraries called the **Java Class Library** (**JCL**). If the program uses a third-party library, it has to be present during compilation and execution. It has to be referred from the same command line that invokes the compiler, and later when the bytecode is executed by the JVM. JCL, on the other hand, does not need to be referred to explicitly. It is assumed that the standard Java libraries reside in the default location of the JDK installation so that the compiler and the JVM know where to find them.

If you do not need to compile a Java program and would like to run only the already compiled `.class` files, you can download and install the **Java Runtime Environment** (**JRE**). For example, it consists of a subset of the JDK and does not include a compiler.

Sometimes, the JDK is referred to as a **software development kit** (**SDK**), which is a general name for a collection of software tools and supporting libraries that allow the creation of an executable version of source code written using a certain programming language. So, the JDK is an SDK for Java. This means it is possible to call the JDK an SDK.

You may also hear the terms *Java platform* and *Java edition* applied to the JDK. A typical platform is an operating system that allows a software program to be developed and executed. Since the JDK provides its own operating environment, it is called a platform too. An edition is a variation of a Java platform (JDK) assembled for a specific purpose. There are four Java platform editions, as listed here:

- **Java Platform SE (Java SE)**: This includes the JVM, JCL, and other tools and utilities.

- **Java Platform Enterprise Edition (Java EE)**: This includes Java SE, servers (computer programs that provide services to the applications), JCL, other libraries, code samples, tutorials, and other documentation for developing and deploying large-scale, multi-tiered, and secure network applications.

- **Java Platform Micro Edition (Java ME)**: This is a subset of Java SE with some specialized libraries for developing and deploying Java applications for embedded and mobile devices, such as phones, personal digital assistants, TV set-top boxes, printers, and sensors. A variation of Java ME (with its own JVM implementation) is called the Android SDK, which was developed by Google for Android programming.

- **Java Card**: This is the smallest of the Java editions and is intended for developing and deploying Java applications onto small embedded devices such as smart cards. It has two editions: Java Card Classic Edition, for smart cards, (based on **International Organization for Standardization (ISO)** *7816* and ISO *14443* communication), and Java Card Connected Edition, which supports a web application model and **Transmission Control Protocol/Internet Protocol (TCP/IP)** as a basic protocol and runs on high-end secure microcontrollers.

- So, to install Java means to install the JDK, which also means to install the Java platform on one of the listed editions. In this book, we are going to talk about and use only Java SE (which includes the JVM, JCL, and other tools and utilities necessary to compile your Java program into bytecode, interpret it into binary code, and automatically send it to your operating system for execution).

Installing Java SE

All the recently released JDKs are listed on the official Oracle page at `https://www.oracle.com/java/technologies/downloads/#java17` (we will call this the *installation home page* for further references in later chapters).

Here are the steps that need to be followed to install Java SE:

1. Select the Java SE tab with your operating system.

2. Click on the link to the installer that fits your operating system and the format (extension) you are familiar with.

3. If in doubt, click the **Installation Instructions** link below and read the installation instructions for your operating system.

4. Follow the steps that correspond to your operating system.

5. The JDK is installed successfully when the `java -version` command on your computer displays the correct Java version, as demonstrated in the following example screenshot:

```
→  ~
→  ~ java -version
java version "17" 2021-09-14 LTS
Java(TM) SE Runtime Environment (build 17+35-LTS-2724)
Java HotSpot(TM) 64-Bit Server VM (build 17+35-LTS-2724, mixed mode, sharing)
→  ~
→  ~
```

Commands, tools, and utilities

If you follow the installation instructions, you may have noticed a link (**Installed Directory Structure** of the JDK) given under **Table of Contents**. This brings you to a page that describes the location of the installed JDK on your computer and the content of each directory of the JDK root directory. The `bin` directory contains all executables that constitute Java commands, tools, and utilities. If the `bin` directory is not added to the `PATH` environment variable automatically, consider doing so manually so that you can launch a Java executable from any directory.

In the previous section, we have already demonstrated the `java -version` Java command. A list of the other Java executables available (commands, tools, and utilities) can be found in the Java SE documentation (`https://www.oracle.com/technetwork/java/javase/documentation/index.html`) by clicking the **Java Platform Standard Edition Technical Documentation** site link, and then the **Tools Reference link** on the next page. You can learn more about each executable tool by clicking its link.

You can also run each of the listed executables on your computer using one of the following options:

`-?`, `-h`, `--help`, or `-help`

These will display a brief description of the executable and all its options.

The most important Java commands are listed here:

- `javac`: This reads a `.java` file, compiles it, and creates one or more corresponding `.class` files, depending on how many Java classes are defined in the `.java` file.
- `java`: This executes a `.class` file.

These are the commands that make programming possible. Every Java programmer must have a good understanding of their structure and capabilities, but if you are new to Java programming and use an IDE (see the *How to install and run an IDE* section), you do not need to master these commands immediately. A good IDE hides them from you by compiling a `.java` file automatically every time you make a change to it. It also provides a graphical element that runs the program every time you click it.

Another very useful Java tool is jcmd. This facilitates communication with, and diagnosis of, any currently running Java processes (JVM) and has many options. But in its simplest form, without any option, it lists all currently running Java processes and their **process IDs (PIDs)**. You can use it to see whether you have runaway Java processes. If you have, you can then kill such a process using the PID provided.

How to install and run an IDE

What used to be just a specialized editor that allowed checking the syntax of a written program the same way a Word editor checks the syntax of an English sentence gradually evolved into an IDE. This bears its main function in the name. It integrates all the tools necessary for writing, compiling, and then executing a program under one **graphical user interface (GUI)**. Using the power of Java compiler, the IDE identifies syntax errors immediately and then helps to improve code quality by providing context-dependent help and suggestions.

Selecting an IDE

There are several IDEs available for a Java programmer, such as NetBeans, Eclipse, IntelliJ IDEA, BlueJ, DrJava, JDeveloper, JCreator, jEdit, JSource, and jCRASP, to name a few. You can read a review of the top Java IDEs and details about each by following this link: `https://www.softwaretestinghelp.com/best-java-ide-and-online-compilers`. The most popular ones are NetBeans, Eclipse, and IntelliJ IDEA.

NetBeans development started in 1996 as a Java IDE student project at Charles University in Prague. In 1999, the project and the company created around the project were acquired by Sun Microsystems. After Oracle acquired Sun Microsystems, NetBeans became open source, and many Java developers have since contributed to the project. It was bundled with JDK 8 and became an official IDE for Java development. In 2016, Oracle donated it to the Apache Software Foundation.

There is a NetBeans IDE for Windows, Linux, Mac, and Oracle Solaris. It supports multiple programming languages and can be extended with plugins. As of the time of writing, NetBeans is bundled only with JDK 8, but NetBeans 8.2 can work with JDK 9 too and uses features introduced with JDK 9 such as Jigsaw, for example. On `netbeans.apache.org`, you can read more about the NetBeans IDE and download the latest version, which is 12.5 as of the time of this writing.

Eclipse is the most widely used Java IDE. The list of plugins that add new features to the IDE is constantly growing, so it is not possible to enumerate all the IDE's capabilities. The Eclipse IDE project has been developed since 2001 as **open source software (OSS)**. A non-profit, member-supported corporation Eclipse Foundation was created in 2004 to provide the infrastructure (**version control systems (VCSs)**, code review systems, build servers, download sites, and so on) and a structured process. None of the 30-something employees of the Eclipse Foundation is working on any of the 150 Eclipse-supported projects.

The sheer number and variety of Eclipse IDE plugins create a certain challenge for a beginner because you have to find your way around different implementations of the same—or similar—features that can, on occasion, be incompatible and may require deep investigation, as well as a clear understanding of all the dependencies. Nevertheless, the Eclipse IDE is very popular and has solid community support. You can read about the Eclipse IDE and download the latest release from `www.eclipse.org/ide`.

IntelliJ IDEA has two versions: a paid one and a free community edition. The paid version is consistently ranked as the best Java IDE, but the community edition is listed among the three leading Java IDEs too. The JetBrains software company that develops the IDE has offices in Prague, Saint Petersburg, Moscow, Munich, Boston, and Novosibirsk. The IDE is known for its deep intelligence that is "*giving relevant suggestions in every context: instant and clever code completion, on-the-fly code analysis, and reliable refactoring tools*", as stated by the authors while describing the product on their website (`www.jetbrains.com/idea`). In the *Installing and configuring IntelliJ IDEA* section, we will walk you through the installation and configuration of IntelliJ IDEA's community edition.

Installing and configuring IntelliJ IDEA

These are the steps you need to follow in order to download and install IntelliJ IDEA:

1. Download an installer of the IntelliJ community edition from `www.jetbrains.com/idea/download`.

2. Launch the installer and accept all the default values.

3. Select `.java` on the **Installation Options** screen. We assume you have installed the JDK already, so you do not check the **Download and install JRE** option.

4. The last installation screen has a **Run IntelliJ IDEA** checkbox that you can check to start the IDE automatically. Alternatively, you can leave the checkbox unchecked and launch the IDE manually once the installation is complete.

5. When the IDE starts for the first time, it provides you with an **Import IntelliJ IDEA settings** option. Check the **Do not import settings** checkbox if you have not used IntelliJ IDEA before.

6. The next couple of screens ask whether you accept the **JetBrains Privacy Policy** and whether you would like to pay for the license or prefer to continue to use the free community edition or free trial (this depends on the particular download you get).

7. Answer the questions whichever way you prefer, and if you accept the privacy policy, the **Customize IntelliJ IDEA** screen will ask you to choose a theme: **white (IntelliJ)** or **dark (Darcula)**.

8. Accept the default settings.

9. If you decide to change the set values, you can do so later by selecting from the topmost menu, **File | Settings**, on Windows, or **Preferences** on Linux and macOS.

Creating a project

Before you start writing your program, you need to create a project. There are several ways to create a project in IntelliJ IDEA, which is the same for any IDE, as follows:

1. **New Project**: This creates a new project from scratch.
2. **Open**: This facilitates reading of the existing project from the filesystem.
3. **Get from VCS**: This facilitates reading of the existing project from the VCS.

In this book, we will walk you through the first option only—using the sequence of guided steps provided by the IDE. Options *2* and *3* include many settings that are automatically set by importing an existing project that has those settings. Once you have learned how to create a new project from scratch, the other ways to bring up a project in the IDE will be very easy for you.

Start by clicking the **New Project** link and proceed further as follows:

1. Select **Maven** in the left panel and a value for **Project SDK** (Java Version 17, if you have installed JDK 17 already), and click **Next**.
2. Maven is a project configuration tool whose primary function is to manage project dependencies. We will talk about it shortly. For now, we will use its other responsibility: to define and hold the project code identity using three **Artifact Coordinates** properties (see next).
3. Type the project name—for example, `myproject`.
4. Select the desired project location in the **Location field** setting (this is where your new code will reside).
5. Click **Artifact Coordinates**, and the following properties will appear:

    *   `GroupId`: This is the base package name that identifies a group of projects within an organization or an open source community. In our case, l et's type `com.mywork`.

    *   `ArtifactId`: To identify a particular project within the group. Leave it as `myproject`.

    *   `Version`: To identify the version of the project. Leave it as `1.0-SNAPSHOT`.

The main goal is to make the identity of a project unique among all projects in the world. To help avoid a `GroupId` clash, the convention requires that you start building it from the organization domain name in reverse. For example, if a company has a `company.com` domain name, the `GroupId` properties of its projects should start with `com.company`. That is why for this demonstration we use `com.mywork`, and for the code in this book, we use the `com.packt.learnjava` GroupID value.

6.   Click **Finish**.

7.   You will see the following project structure and generated `pom.xml` file:

Now, if somebody would like to use the code of your project in their application, they would refer to it by the three values shown, and Maven (if they use it) will bring it in (if you upload your project to the publicly shared Maven repository, of course). Read more about Maven at `https://maven.apache.org/guides`. Another function of the `GroupId` value is to define the root directory of the folders tree that holds your project code. The `java` folder under `main` will hold the application code, while the `java` folder under `test` will hold the test code.

Let's create our first program using the following steps:

1. Right-click on `java`, select **New**, and then click **Package**, as illustrated in the following screenshot:

2. In the **New Package window** provided, type `com.mywork.myproject` and press *Enter*.

    You should see in the left panel the following set of new folders:

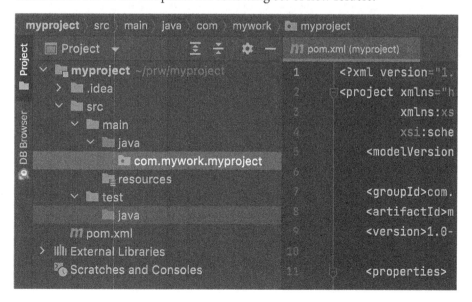

3. Right-click on `com.mywork.myproject`, select **New**, and then click **Java Class**, as illustrated in the following screenshot:

4. In the input window provided, type `HelloWorld`, as follows:

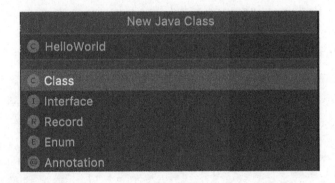

5. Press *Enter* and you will see your first Java class, `HelloWorld`, created in the `com.`
    `mywork.myproject` package, as illustrated in the following screenshot:

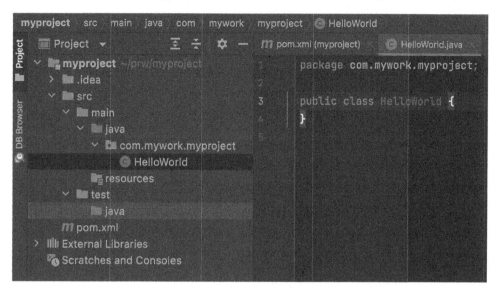

The package reflects the Java class location in the filesystem. We will talk about this more
in *Chapter 2, Java Object-Oriented Programming (OOP)*. Now, in order to run a program,
we create a `main()` method. If present, this method can be executed to serve as an entry
point into the application. It has a certain format, as shown here:

This has to have the following attributes:

- `public`: Freely accessible from outside the package

- `static`: Should be able to be called without creating an object of the class it
  belongs to

It should also have the following:

- Return `void` (nothing)

Accept a `String` array as an input, or `varargs`, as we have done. We will talk about `varargs` in *Chapter 2, Java Object-Oriented Programming (OOP)*. For now, suffice to say that `String[] args` and `String... args` essentially define the same input format.

We explain how to run the `main` class using a command line in the *Executing examples from the command line* section. You can read more about Java command-line arguments in the official Oracle documentation at `https://docs.oracle.com/javase/tutorial/essential/environment/cmdLineArgs.html`. It is also possible to run the examples from IntelliJ IDEA.

Notice the two green triangles to the left in the screenshot shown next. By clicking any of them, you can execute the `main()` method. For example, let's display `Hello, world!`.

In order to do this, type the following line inside the `main()` method:

```
System.out.println("Hello, world!");
```

The following screenshot shows how the program should look afterward:

```
package com.mywork.myproject;

public class HelloWorld {
    public static void main(String... args){
        System.out.println("Hello, world!");
    }
}
```

Then, click one of the green triangles, and you should get the following output in the Terminal area:

```
Hello, world!
```

From now on, every time we are going to discuss code examples, we will run them the same way, by using the `main()` method. While doing this, we will not capture a screenshot but put the result in comments, because such a style is easier to follow. For example, the following code snippet displays how the previous code demonstration would look in this style:

```
System.out.println("Hello, world!"); //prints: Hello, world!
```

It is possible to add a comment (any text) to the right of the code line separated by a double slash `//`. The compiler does not read this text and just keeps it as it is. The presence of a comment does not affect performance and is used to explain the programmer's intent to humans.

Importing a project

We are going to demonstrate project importing using the source code for this book. We assume that you have Maven installed (`https://maven.apache.org/install.html`) on your computer and that you have Git (`https://gist.github.com/derhuerst/1b15ff4652a867391f03`) installed too, and can use it. We also assume that you have installed JDK 17, as was described in the *Installing Java SE* section.

To import the project with the code examples for this book, follow these steps:

1. Go to the source repository (`https://github.com/PacktPublishing/Learn-Java-17-Programming`) and click the **Code** drop-down menu, as shown in the following screenshot:

2. Copy the provided **Uniform Resource Locator (URL)** (click the *copy* symbol to the right of the URL), as illustrated in the following screenshot:

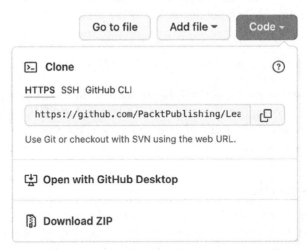

3. Select a directory on your computer where you would like the source code to be placed and then run the `git clone https://github.com/PacktPublishing/Learn-Java-17-Programming.git` Git command and observe similar output to that shown in the following screenshot:

```
→  prw git clone https://github.com/PacktPublishing/Learn-Java-17-Programming.git
Cloning into 'Learn-Java-17-Programming'...
remote: Enumerating objects: 31, done.
remote: Counting objects: 100% (31/31), done.
remote: Compressing objects: 100% (16/16), done.
remote: Total 31 (delta 2), reused 28 (delta 2), pack-reused 0
Unpacking objects: 100% (31/31), done.
```

4. A new `Learn-Java-17-Programming` folder is created.

    Alternatively, instead of cloning, you can download the source as a `.zip` file using the `Download ZIP` link shown in the screenshot just before. Unarchive the downloaded source in a directory on your computer where you would like the source code to be placed, and then rename the newly created folder by removing the `-master` suffix from its name, making sure that the folder's name is `Learn-Java-17-Programming`.

5. The new `Learn-Java-17-Programming` folder contains the Maven project with all the source code from this book. If you prefer, you can rename this folder however you like. In our case, we renamed it `LearnJava` for brevity.

6. Now, run IntelliJ IDEA and click **Open**. Navigate to the location of the project and select the just-created folder (`LearnJava`, in our case), then click the **Open** button.

7. If the following popup shows in the bottom-right corner, click **Load**:

8. Also, click **Trust project...**, as shown in the following screenshot:

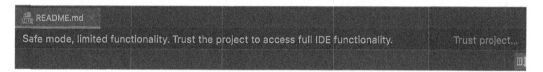

9. Then, click the **Trust Project** button on the following popup:

10. Now, go to **Project Structure** (cogwheel symbol in the upper-right corner) and make sure that Java 17 is selected as an SDK, as shown in the following screenshot:

11. Click **Apply** and make sure that the default **Project SDK** is set to Java **version 17** and **Project language level** is set to **17**, as in the following screenshot:

12. Click **Apply** and then (optionally) remove the `LearnJava` module by selecting it and clicking " - ", as follows:

13. Confirm the `LearnJava` module removal on the popup by clicking **Yes**, as follows:

14. Here's how the final list of modules should look:

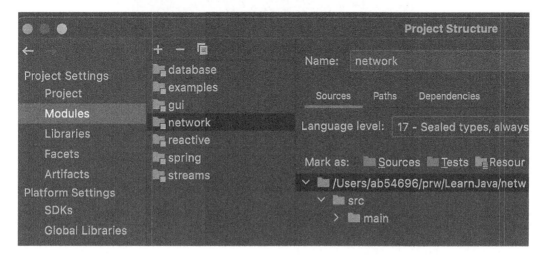

Click **OK** in the bottom-right corner and get back to your project. Click examples in the left pane and continue going down the source tree until you see the following list of classes:

Click on the green arrow in the right pane and execute the `main()` method of any class you want. For example, let's execute the `main()` method of the `PrimitiveTypes` class. The result you will be able to see in the **Run** window should be similar to this:

Executing examples from the command line

To execute the examples from the command line, go to the `examples` folder, where the `pom.xml` file is located, and run the `mvn clean package` command. If the command is executed successfully, you can run any `main()` method in any of the programs in the `examples` folder from the command line. For example, to execute the `main()` method in the `ControlFlow.java` file, run the following command as one line:

```
java -cp target/examples-1.0-SNAPSHOT.jar    com.packt.
learnjava.ch01_start.ControlFlow
```

You will see the following results:

```
→  examples git:(main) x
→  examples git:(main) x java -cp target/examples-1.0-SNAPSHOT.jar com.packt.learnjava.ch01_start.ControlFlow

Selection statements:
1 or 3

Iteration statements:
0 1 2 3 4
0 1 2 3 4
0 1 2
0 1 2
```

This way, you can run any class that has the `main()` method in it. The content of the `main()` method will be executed.

Java primitive types and operators

With all the main programming tools in place, we can start talking about Java as a language. The language syntax is defined by the *Java Language Specification*, which you can find at `https://docs.oracle.com/javase/specs`. Don't hesitate to refer to it every time you need some clarification—it is not as daunting as many people assume.

All the values in Java are divided into two categories: reference types and primitive types. We start with primitive types and operators as the natural entry point to any programming language. In this chapter, we will also discuss one reference type called `String` (see the *String types and literals* section).

All primitive types can be divided into two groups: Boolean types and numeric types.

Boolean types

There are only two Boolean type values in Java: `true` and `false`. Such a value can only be assigned to a variable of a `boolean` type, as in the following example:

```
boolean b = true;
```

A `boolean` variable is typically used in control flow statements, which we are going to discuss in the *Java statements* section. Here is one example:

```
boolean b = x > 2;
if(b){
    //do something
}
```

In the preceding code, we assign to the b variable the result of the evaluation of the x > 2 expression. If the value of x is greater than 2, the b variable gets the assigned value, true. Then, the code inside the braces ({ }) is executed.

Numeric types

Java numeric types form two groups: integral types (byte, char, short, int, and long) and floating-point types (float and double).

Integral types

Integral types consume the following amount of memory:

- byte: 8 bits
- char: 16 bits
- short: 16 bits
- int: 32 bits
- long: 64 bits

The char type is an unsigned integer that can hold a value (called a code point) from 0 to 65,535 inclusive. It represents a Unicode character, which means there are 65,536 Unicode characters. Here are three records from the basic Latin list of Unicode characters:

Code point	Unicode escape	Printable symbol	Description
33	\u0021	!	Exclamation mark
50	\u0032	2	Digit two
65	\u0041	A	Latin capital letter "A"

The following code demonstrates the properties of the char type (execute the main() method of the com.packt.learnjava.ch01_start.PrimitiveTypes class—see the charType() method):

```
char x1 = '\u0032';
System.out.println(x1);  //prints: 2

char x2 = '2';
System.out.println(x2);  //prints: 2
x2 = 65;
```

```
System.out.println(x2);    //prints: A

char y1 = '\u0041';
System.out.println(y1);    //prints: A

char y2 = 'A';
System.out.println(y2);    //prints: A
y2 = 50;
System.out.println(y2);    //prints: 2

System.out.println(x1 + x2);    //prints: 115
System.out.println(x1 + y1);    //prints: 115
```

The last two lines from the preceding code example explain why the char type is considered an integral type because char values can be used in arithmetic operations. In such a case, each char value is represented by its code point.

The range of values of other integral types is shown here:

- byte: from -128 to 127 inclusive

- short: from -32,768 to 32,767 inclusive

- int: from -2.147.483.648 to 2.147.483.647 inclusive

- long: from -9,223,372,036,854,775,808 to 9,223,372,036,854,775,807 inclusive

You can always retrieve the maximum and minimum value of each primitive type from a corresponding Java constant, as follows (execute the main() method of the com.packt.learnjava.ch01_start.PrimitiveTypes class—see the minMax() method):

```
System.out.println(Byte.MIN_VALUE);        //prints: -128
System.out.println(Byte.MAX_VALUE);        //prints:  127
System.out.println(Short.MIN_VALUE);       //prints: -32768
System.out.println(Short.MAX_VALUE);       //prints:  32767
System.out.println(Integer.MIN_VALUE);     //prints: -2147483648
System.out.println(Integer.MAX_VALUE);     //prints:  2147483647
System.out.println(Long.MIN_VALUE);
                                 //prints: -9223372036854775808
System.out.println(Long.MAX_VALUE);
```

```
                                  //prints: 9223372036854775807
System.out.println((int)Character.MIN_VALUE); //prints: 0
System.out.println((int)Character.MAX_VALUE); //prints: 65535
```

The construct (int) in the last two lines is an example of cast operator usage. It forces the conversion of a value from one type to another in cases where such a conversion is not always guaranteed to be successful. As you can see from our examples, some types allow bigger values than other types. But a programmer may know that the value of a certain variable can never exceed the maximum value of the target type, and the cast operator is the way the programmer can force their opinion on the compiler. Otherwise, without a cast operator, the compiler would raise an error and would not allow the assignment. However, the programmer may be mistaken and the value may become bigger. In such a case, a runtime error will be raised during execution time.

There are types that, in principle, cannot be cast to other types, though, or at least not to all types—for example, a Boolean type value cannot be cast to an integral type value.

Floating-point types

There are two types in this group of primitive types—float and double. These consume the following amount of memory:

- float: 32 bit

- double: 64 bit

Their positive maximum and minimum possible values are shown here (execute the main() method of the com.packt.learnjava.ch01_start.PrimitiveTypes class—see the minMax() method):

```
System.out.println(Float.MIN_VALUE);   //prints: 1.4E-45
System.out.println(Float.MAX_VALUE);   //prints: 3.4028235E38
System.out.println(Double.MIN_VALUE);  //prints: 4.9E-324
System.out.println(Double.MAX_VALUE);
                            //prints: 1.7976931348623157E308
```

The maximum and minimum negative values are the same as those just shown, only with a minus sign (-) in front of them. So, effectively, the Float.MIN_VALUE and Double. MIN_VALUE values are not the minimal values, but the precision of the corresponding type. A zero value can be either 0.0 or -0.0 for each of the floating-point types.

A special feature of the floating-point type is the presence of a dot (.) that separates integer and fractional parts of the number. By default, in Java, a number with a dot is assumed to be a double type. For example, the following is assumed to be a double value:

42.3

This means that the following assignment causes a compilation error:

```
float f = 42.3;
```

To indicate that you would like it to be treated as a float type, you need to add either f or F. For example, the following assignments do not cause an error (execute the main() method of the com.packt.learnjava.ch01_start.PrimitiveTypes class—see the casting() method):

```
float f = 42.3f;
float d = 42.3F;

double a = 42.3f;
double b = 42.3F;

float x = (float)42.3d;
float y = (float)42.3D;
```

As you may have noticed from the preceding example, d and D indicate a double type, but we were able to cast them to the float type because we are confident that 42.3 is well inside the range of possible float-type values.

Default values of primitive types

In some cases, a variable has to be assigned a value even when a programmer did not want to do that. We will talk about such cases in *Chapter 2, Java Object-Oriented Programming (OOP)*. The default primitive type value in such cases is outlined here:

- byte, short, int, and long types have a default value of 0.
- The char type has a default value of \u0000, with the code point 0.
- float and double types have a default value of 0.0.
- The boolean type has a default value of false.

Literals of primitive types

The representation of a value is called a literal. The `boolean` type has two literals: `true` and `false`. Literals of `byte`, `short`, `int`, and `long` integral types have an `int` type by default, as illustrated here:

```
byte b = 42;
short s = 42;
int i = 42;
long l = 42;
```

In addition, to indicate a literal of a `long` type, you can append the letter l or L to the end, like this:

```
long l1 = 42l;
long l2 = 42L;
```

The letter l can be easily confused with the number 1, so using L (instead of l) for this purpose is a good practice.

So far, we have expressed integral literals in a decimal number system. Meanwhile, literals of `byte`, `short`, `int`, and `long` types can also be expressed in binary (base 2, digits 0-1), octal (base 8, digits 0-7), and hexadecimal (base 16, digits 0-9, and a-f) number systems. A binary literal starts with 0b (or 0B), followed by the value expressed in a binary system. For example, the decimal 42 is expressed as 101010 = $2^0 \ast 0 + 2^1 \ast 1 + 2^2 \ast 0 + 2^3 \ast 1 + 2^4 \ast 0 + 2^5 \ast 1$ (we start from the right 0). An octal literal starts with 0, followed by the value expressed in an octal system, so 42 is expressed as 52 = $8^0 \ast 2 + 8^1 \ast 5$. A hexadecimal literal starts with 0x (or with 0X), followed by a value expressed in a hexadecimal system. So, 42 is expressed as 2a = $16^0 \ast a + 16^1 \ast 2$ because, in the hexadecimal system, the symbols a to f (or A to F) map to the decimal values 10 to 15. Here is the demonstration code (execute the `main()` method of the `com.packt.learnjava.ch01_start.PrimitiveTypes` class—see the `literals()` method):

```
int i = 42;
System.out.println(Integer.toString(i, 2));      // 101010
System.out.println(Integer.toBinaryString(i));   // 101010
System.out.println(0b101010);                    // 42

System.out.println(Integer.toString(i, 8));      // 52
System.out.println(Integer.toOctalString(i));    // 52
```

```
System.out.println(052);                              // 42

System.out.println(Integer.toString(i, 10));          // 42
System.out.println(Integer.toString(i));              // 42
System.out.println(42);                               // 42

System.out.println(Integer.toString(i, 16));          // 2a
System.out.println(Integer.toHexString(i));           // 2a
System.out.println(0x2a);                             // 42
```

As you can see, Java provides methods that convert decimal system values to systems with different bases. All these expressions of numeric values are called literals.

One feature of numeric literals makes them human-friendly. If the number is large, it is possible to break it into triples separated by an underscore (_) sign. Observe the following, for example:

```
int i = 354_263_654;
System.out.println(i);    //prints: 354263654

float f = 54_436.98f;
System.out.println(f);    //prints: 54436.98

long l = 55_763_948L;
System.out.println(l);    //prints: 55763948
```

The compiler ignores an embedded underscore sign.

The char type has two kinds of literals: a single character or an escape sequence. We have seen examples of char-type literals when discussing numeric types, and you can see some others here:

```
char x1 = '\u0032';
char x2 = '2';
char y1 = '\u0041';
char y2 = 'A';
```

As you can see, the character has to be enclosed in single quotes.

An escape sequence starts with a backslash (\) followed by a letter or another character. Here is a full list of escape sequences:

- \b: backspace BS, Unicode escape \u0008
- \t: horizontal tab HT, Unicode escape \u0009
- \n: line feed LF, Unicode escape \u000a
- \f: form feed FF, Unicode escape \u000c
- \r: carriage return CR, Unicode escape \u000d
- \": double quote ", Unicode escape \u0022
- \': single quote ', Unicode escape \u0027
- \\: backslash \, Unicode escape \u005c

From the eight escape sequences, only the last three are represented by a symbol. They are used when this symbol cannot be otherwise displayed. Observe the following, for example:

```
System.out.println("\"");    //prints: "
System.out.println('\'');    //prints: '
System.out.println('\\');    //prints: \
```

The rest are used more as control codes that direct the output device to do something, as in the following example:

```
System.out.println("The back\bspace");
                                    //prints: The backspace
System.out.println("The horizontal\ttab");
                                    //prints: The horizontal tab
System.out.println("The line\nfeed");
                                    //prints: The line feed
System.out.println("The form\ffeed");
                                    //prints: The form feed
System.out.println("The carriage\rreturn");//prints: return
```

As you can see, \b deletes a previous symbol, \t inserts a tab space, \n breaks the line and begins the new one, \f forces the printer to eject the current page and to continue printing at the top of another, and \r starts the current line anew.

New compact number format

The java.text.NumberFormat class presents numbers in various formats. It also allows formats to be adjusted to those provided, including locales. A new feature added to this class in Java 12 is called a compact or short number format.

It represents a number in a locale-specific, human-readable form. Observe the following, for example (execute the main() method of the com.packt.learnjava.ch01_ start.PrimitiveTypes class—see the newNumberFormat() method):

```
NumberFormat fmt = NumberFormat.
getCompactNumberInstance(Locale.US, NumberFormat.Style.SHORT);
System.out.println(fmt.format(42_000));          //prints: 42K
System.out.println(fmt.format(42_000_000));      //prints: 42M

NumberFormat fmtP = NumberFormat.getPercentInstance();
System.out.println(fmtP.format(0.42));           //prints: 42%
```

As you can see, to access this capability, you have to acquire a particular instance of the NumberFormat class, sometimes based on the locale and style provided.

Operators

There are 44 operators in Java. These are listed in the following table:

Operators	Description
`+` `-` `*` `/` `%`	Arithmetic unary and binary operators
`++` `--`	Increment and decrement unary operators
`==` `!=`	Equality operators
`<` `>` `<=` `>=`	Relational operators
`!` `&` `|`	Logical operators
`&&` `||` `?:`	Conditional operators
`=` `+=` `-=` `*=` `/=` `%=`	Assignment operators
`&=` `|=` `^=` `<<=` `>>=` `>>>=`	Assignment operators
`&` `|` `~` `^` `<<` `>>` `>>>`	Bitwise operators
`->` `::`	Arrow and method reference operators
`New`	Instance creation operator
`.`	Field access/method invocation operator
`Instanceof`	Type comparison operator
`(target type)`	Cast operator

We will not describe the not-often-used `&=`, `|=`, `^=`, `<<=`, `>>=`, `>>>=` assignment operators and bitwise operators, but you can read about them in the Java specification (`https://docs.oracle.com/javase/specs`). Arrow (`->`) and method reference (`::`) operators will be described in *Chapter 14, Java Standard Streams*. The new instance creation operator, the `.` field access/method invocation operator, and the `instanceof` type comparison operator will be discussed in *Chapter 2, Java Object-Oriented Programming (OOP)*. As for the cast operator, we have already described it in the *Integral types* section.

Arithmetic unary (+ and -) and binary (+, -, *, /, and %) operators

Most of the arithmetic operators and positive and negative signs (unary operators) are quite familiar to us. The modulus operator (%) divides the left-hand operand by the right-hand operand and returns the remainder, as follows (execute the main() method of the com.packt.learnjava.ch01_start.Operators class—see the integerDivision() method:

```java
int x = 5;
System.out.println(x % 2);    //prints: 1
```

It is also worth mentioning that the division of two integer numbers in Java loses the fractional part because Java assumes the result should be an integer number 2, as follows:

```java
int x = 5;
System.out.println(x / 2);    //prints: 2
```

If you need the fractional part of the result to be preserved, convert one of the operands into a floating-point type. Here are a few ways (among many) in which to do this:

```java
int x = 5;
System.out.println(x / 2.);               //prints: 2.5
System.out.println((1. * x) / 2);         //prints: 2.5
System.out.println(((float)x) / 2);       //prints: 2.5
System.out.println(((double) x) / 2);     //prints: 2.5
```

Increment and decrement unary operators (++ and --)

The ++ operator increases the value of an integral type by 1, while the -- operator decreases it by 1. If placed before the variable (prefix), it changes its value by 1 before the variable value is returned. But when placed after the variable (postfix), it changes its value by 1 after the variable value is returned. Here are a few examples (execute the main() method of the com.packt.learnjava.ch01_start.Operators class—see the incrementDecrement() method):

```java
int i = 2;
System.out.println(++i);    //prints: 3
System.out.println(i);      //prints: 3
System.out.println(--i);    //prints: 2
System.out.println(i);      //prints: 2
System.out.println(i++);    //prints: 2
```

```
System.out.println(i);        //prints: 3
System.out.println(i--);      //prints: 3
System.out.println(i);        //prints: 2
```

Equality operators (== and !=)

The `==` operator means equals, while the `!=` operator means not equals. They are used to compare values of the same type and return a `true` Boolean value if the operand's values are `equal`, or `false` otherwise. Observe the following, for example (execute the `main()` method of the `com.packt.learnjava.ch01_start.Operators`, class—see the `equality()` method):

```
int i1 = 1;
int i2 = 2;
System.out.println(i1 == i2);         //prints: false
System.out.println(i1 != i2);         //prints: true
System.out.println(i1 == (i2 - 1));   //prints: true
System.out.println(i1 != (i2 - 1));   //prints: false
```

Exercise caution, though, while comparing values of floating-point types, especially when you compare the results of calculations. Using relational operators (`<`, `>`, `<=`, and `>=`) in such cases is much more reliable, because calculations such as 1/3—for example—result in a never-ending fractional part 0.33333333... and ultimately depend on precision implementation (a complex topic that is beyond the scope of this book).

Relational operators (<, >, <=, and >=)

Relational operators compare values and return a Boolean value. Observe the following, for example (execute the `main()` method of the `com.packt.learnjava.ch01_start.Operators` class—see the `relational()` method):

```
int i1 = 1;
int i2 = 2;
System.out.println(i1 > i2);          //prints: false
System.out.println(i1 >= i2);         //prints: false
System.out.println(i1 >= (i2 - 1));   //prints: true
System.out.println(i1 < i2);          //prints: true
System.out.println(i1 <= i2);         //prints: true
System.out.println(i1 <= (i2 - 1));   //prints: true
```

```
float f = 1.2f;
System.out.println(i1 < f);              //prints: true
```

Logical operators (!, &, and |)

Logical operators can be defined as follows:

- The ! binary operator returns true if the operand is false; otherwise, it returns false.

- The & binary operator returns true if both of the operands are true.

- The | binary operator returns true if at least one of the operands is true.

Here is an example (execute the main() method of the com.packt.learnjava. ch01_start.Operators class—see the logical() method):

```
boolean b = true;
System.out.println(!b);        //prints: false
System.out.println(!!b);       //prints: true
boolean c = true;
System.out.println(c & b); //prints: true
System.out.println(c | b); //prints: true
boolean d = false;
System.out.println(c & d); //prints: false
System.out.println(c | d); //prints: true
```

Conditional operators (&&, ||, and ? :)

The && and || operators produce the same results as the & and | logical operators we have just demonstrated, as follows (execute the main() method of the com.packt. learnjava.ch01_start.Operators class—see the conditional() method):

```
boolean b = true;
boolean c = true;
System.out.println(c && b); //prints: true
System.out.println(c || b); //prints: true
boolean d = false;
System.out.println(c && d); //prints: false
System.out.println(c || d); //prints: true
```

The difference is that the `&&` and `||` operators do not always evaluate the second operand. For example, in the case of the `&&` operator, if the first operand is `false`, the second operand is not evaluated because the result of the whole expression will be `false` anyway. Similarly, in the case of the `||` operator, if the first operand is `true`, the whole expression will be clearly evaluated to `true` without evaluating the second operand. We can demonstrate this in the following code snippet:

```
int h = 1;
System.out.println(h > 3 && h++ < 3);   //prints: false
System.out.println(h);                  //prints: 2
System.out.println(h > 3 && h++ < 3);   //prints: false
System.out.println(h);                  //prints: 2
```

The `?  :` operator is called a ternary operator. It evaluates a condition (before the ? sign), and if it results in `true`, assigns to a variable the value calculated by the first expression (between the ? and : signs); otherwise, it assigns a value calculated by the second expression (after the : sign), as illustrated in the following code snippet:

```
int n = 1, m = 2;
float k = n > m ? (n * m + 3) : ((float)n / m);
System.out.println(k);              //prints: 0.5
```

Assignment operators (=, +=, -=, *=, /=, and %=)

The = operator just assigns a specified value to a variable, like this:

```
x = 3;
```

Other assignment operators calculate a new value before assigning it, as follows:

- `x += 42` assigns to x the result of the `x = x + 42` addition operation.
- `x -= 42` assigns to x the result of the `x = x - 42` subtraction operation.
- `x *= 42` assigns to x the result of the `x = x * 42` multiplication operation.
- `x /= 42` assigns to x the result of the `x = x / 42` division operation.
- `x %= 42` assigns the remainder of the `x = x + x % 42` division operation.

Here is how these operators work (execute the `main()` method of the `com.packt.learnjava.ch01_start.Operators` class—see the `assignment()` method):

```
float a = 1f;
a += 2;
System.out.println(a); //prints: 3.0
a -= 1;
System.out.println(a); //prints: 2.0
a *= 2;
System.out.println(a); //prints: 4.0
a /= 2;
System.out.println(a); //prints: 2.0
a %= 2;
System.out.println(a); //prints: 0.0
```

String types and literals

We have just described the primitive value types of the Java language. All the other value types in Java belong to a category of reference types. Each reference type is a more complex construct than just a value. It is described by a class, which serves as a template for creating an object, and a memory area that contains values and methods (the processing code) defined in the class. An object is created by the new operator. We will talk about classes and objects in more detail in *Chapter 2, Java Object-Oriented Programming (OOP)*.

In this chapter, we will talk about one of the reference types called `String`. It is represented by the `java.lang.String` class, which belongs, as you can see, to the most foundational package of the JDK, `java.lang`. The reason we're introducing the `String` class so early is that it behaves in some respects very similar to primitive types, despite being a reference type.

A reference type is so-called because, in the code, we do not deal with values of this type directly. A value of a reference type is more complex than a primitive-type value. It is called an object and requires more complex memory allocation, so a reference-type variable contains a memory reference. It points (refers) to the memory area where the object resides, hence the name.

This nature of the reference type requires particular attention when a reference-type variable is passed into a method as a parameter. We will discuss this in more detail in *Chapter 3, Java Fundamentals*. For now, we will see how String, being a reference type, helps to optimize memory usage by storing each String value only once.

String literals

The String class represents character strings in Java programs. We have seen several such strings. We have seen Hello, world!, for example. That is a String literal.

Another example of a literal is null. Any reference class can refer to a null literal. It represents a reference value that does not point to any object. In the case of a String type, it looks like this:

```
String s = null;
```

But a literal that consists of characters enclosed in double quotes ("abc", "123", and "a42%$#", for example) can only be of a String type. In this respect, the String class, being a reference type, has something in common with primitive types. All String literals are stored in a dedicated section of memory called a string pool, and two literals are equally spelled to represent the same value from the pool (execute the main() method of the com.packt.learnjava.ch01_start.StringClass class—see the compareReferences() method):

```
String s1 = "abc";
String s2 = "abc";
System.out.println(s1 == s2);     //prints: true
System.out.println("abc" == s1); //prints: true
```

The JVM authors have chosen such an implementation to avoid duplication and improve memory usage. The previous code examples look very much like operations involving primitive types, don't they? But when a String object is created using a new operator, the memory for the new object is allocated outside the string pool, so references of two String objects—or any other objects, for that matter—are always different, as we can see here:

```
String o1 = new String("abc");
String o2 = new String("abc");
System.out.println(o1 == o2);     //prints: false
System.out.println("abc" == o1); //prints: false
```

If necessary, it is possible to move the string value created with the new operator to the string pool using the intern() method, like this:

```
String o1 = new String("abc");
System.out.println("abc" == o1);           //prints: false
System.out.println("abc" == o1.intern()); //prints: true
```

In the previous code snippet, the intern() method attempted to move the newly created "abc" value into the string pool but discovered that such a literal exists there already, so it reused the literal from the string pool. That is why the references in the last line in the preceding example are equal.

The good news is that you probably will not need to create String objects using the new operator, and most Java programmers never do this. But when a String object is passed into your code as an input and you have no control over its origin, comparison by reference only may cause an incorrect result (if the strings have the same spelling but were created by the new operator). That is why, when the equality of two strings by spelling (and case) is necessary, to compare two literals or String objects, the equals() method is a better choice, as illustrated here:

```
String o1 = new String("abc");
String o2 = new String("abc");
System.out.println(o1.equals(o2));         //prints: true
System.out.println(o2.equals(o1));         //prints: true
System.out.println(o1.equals("abc"));      //prints: true
System.out.println("abc".equals(o1));      //prints: true
System.out.println("abc".equals("abc")); //prints: true
```

We will talk about the equals() method and other methods of the String class shortly.

Another feature that makes String literals and objects look like primitive values is that they can be added using the + arithmetic operator, like this (execute the main() method of the com.packt.learnjava.ch01_start.StringClass class—see the operatorAdd() method):

```
String s1 = "abc";
String s2 = "abc";
String s = s1 + s2;
System.out.println(s);                 //prints: abcabc
System.out.println(s1 + "abc");        //prints: abcabc
```

```
System.out.println("abc" + "abc");    //prints: abcabc

String o1 = new String("abc");
String o2 = new String("abc");
String o = o1 + o2;
System.out.println(o);                //prints: abcabc
System.out.println(o1 + "abc");       //prints: abcabc
```

No other arithmetic operator can be applied to a String literal or an object.

A new String literal, called a text block, was introduced with Java 15. It facilitates the preservation of indents and multiple lines without adding white spaces in quotes. For example, here is how a programmer would add indentation before Java 15 and use \n to break the line:

```
String html = "<html>\n" +
       "    <body>\n" +
       "        <p>Hello World.</p>\n" +
       "    </body>\n" +
       "</html>\n";
```

And here is how the same result is achieved with Java 15:

```
String html = """
              <html>
                  <body>
                      <p>Hello World.</p>
                  </body>
              </html>
              """;
```

To see how it works, execute the main() method of the com.packt.learnjava. ch01_start.StringClass class—see the textBlock() method.

String immutability

Since all String literals can be shared, the JVM authors make sure that, once stored, a String variable cannot be changed. This helps not only avoid the problem of concurrent modification of the same value from different places of the code but also prevents unauthorized modification of a String value, which often represents a username or password.

The following code looks like a String value modification:

```
String str = "abc";
str = str + "def";
System.out.println(str);        //prints: abcdef
str = str + new String("123");
System.out.println(str);        //prints: abcdef123
```

But, behind the scenes, the original "abc" literal remains intact. Instead, a few new literals were created: "def", "abcdef", "123", and "abcdef123". To prove this, we have executed the following code:

```
String str1 = "abc";
String r1 = str1;
str1 = str1 + "def";
String r2 = str1;
System.out.println(r1 == r2);        //prints: false
System.out.println(r1.equals(r2)); //prints: false
```

As you can see, the r1 and r2 variables refer to different memories, and the objects they refer to are spelled differently too.

We will talk more about strings in *Chapter 5, Strings, Input/Output, and Files.*

IDs and variables

From our school days, we have an intuitive understanding of what a variable is. We think of it as a name that represents a value. We solve problems using such variables as x gallons of water or n miles of distance, and similar. In Java, the name of a variable is called an ID and can be constructed by certain rules. Using an ID, a variable can be declared (defined) and initialized.

ID

According to the *Java Language Specification* (`https://docs.oracle.com/javase/specs`), an ID (a variable name) can be a sequence of Unicode characters that represent letters, digits 0-9, a dollar sign ($), or an underscore (_).

Other limitations are outlined here:

- The first symbol of an ID cannot be a digit.
- An ID cannot have the same spelling as a keyword (see the *Java keywords* section of *Chapter 3, Java Fundamentals*).
- It cannot be spelled as a `true` or `false` Boolean literal or as a `null` literal.
- And since Java 9, an ID cannot be just an underscore (_).

Here are a few unusual but legal examples of IDs:

```
$
_42
αρετη
String
```

Variable declaration (definition) and initialization

A variable has a name (an ID) and a type. Typically, it refers to the memory where a value is stored, but may refer to nothing (`null`) or not refer to anything at all (then, it is not initialized). It can represent a class property, an array element, a method parameter, and a local variable. The last one is the most frequently used kind of variable.

Before a variable can be used, it has to be declared and initialized. In some other programming languages, a variable can also be defined, so Java programmers sometimes use the word *definition* as a synonym of declaration, which is not exactly correct.

Here is a terminology review with examples:

```
int x;      //declaration of variable x
x = 1;      //initialization of variable x
x = 2;      //assignment of variable x
```

Initialization and assignment look the same. The difference is in their sequence: the first assignment is called initialization. Without an initialization, a variable cannot be used.

Declaration and initialization can be combined in a single statement. Observe the following, for example:

```
float $ = 42.42f;
String _42 = "abc";
int αρετη = 42;
double String = 42.;
```

var type holder

In Java 10, a sort of type holder, `var`, was introduced. The *Java Language Specification* defines it thus: "*var is not a keyword, but an identifier with special meaning as the type of a local variable declaration.*"

In practical terms, it lets a compiler figure out the nature of the declared variable, as follows (see the `var()` method in the `com.packt.learnjava.ch01_start. PrimitiveTypes` class):

```
var x = 1;
```

In the preceding example, the compiler can reasonably assume that x has the `int` primitive type.

As you may have guessed, to accomplish that, a declaration on its own would not suffice, as we can see here:

```
var x;      //compilation error
```

That is, without initialization, the compiler cannot figure out the type of the variable when `var` is used.

Java statements

A Java statement is a minimal construct that can be executed. It describes an action and ends with a semicolon (;). We have seen many statements already. For example, here are three statements:

```
float f = 23.42f;
String sf = String.valueOf(f);
System.out.println(sf);
```

The first line is a declaration statement combined with an assignment statement. The second line is also a declaration statement combined with an assignment statement and method invocation statement. The third line is just a method invocation statement.

Here is a list of Java statement types:

- An empty statement that consists of only one symbol, `;` (semicolon)
- A class or interface declaration statement (we will talk about this in *Chapter 2, Java Object-Oriented Programming (OOP)*)
- A local variable declaration statement: `int x;`
- A synchronized statement: this is beyond the scope of this book
- An expression statement
- A control flow statement

An expression statement can be one of the following:

- A method invocation statement: `someMethod();`
- An assignment statement: `n = 23.42f;`
- An object creation statement: `new String("abc");`
- A unary increment or decrement statement: `++x ;` or `--x;` or `x++;` or `x--;`

We will talk more about expression statements in the *Expression statements* section.

A control flow statement can be one of the following:

- A selection statement: `if-else` or `switch-case`
- An iteration statement: `for,` or `while,` or `do-while`
- An exception-handling statement: `throw, try-catch,` or `try-catch-finally`
- A branching statement: `break, continue,` or `return`

We will talk more about control statements in the *Control flow statements* section.

Expression statements

An expression statement consists of one or more expressions. An expression typically includes one or more operators. It can be evaluated, which means it can produce a result of one of the following types:

- A variable: `x = 1`, for example
- A value: `2*2`, for example

It returns nothing when the expression is an invocation of a method that returns `void`. Such a method is said to produce only a side effect: `void someMethod()`, for example.

Consider the following expression:

```
x = y++;
```

The preceding expression assigns a value to an x variable and has a side effect of adding 1 to the value of the y variable.

Another example would be a method that prints a line, like this:

```
System.out.println(x);
```

The `println()` method returns nothing and has a side effect of printing something.

By its form, an expression can be one of the following:

- A primary expression: a literal, a new object creation, a field or method access (invocation).
- A unary operator expression: x++, for example.
- A binary operator expression: x*y, for example.
- A ternary operator expression: `x > y ? true : false`, for example.
- A lambda expression: `x -> x + 1` (see *Chapter 14, Java Standard Streams*).
- If an expression consists of other expressions, parentheses are often used to identify each of the expressions clearly. This way, it is easier to understand and to set the expressions' precedence.

Control flow statements

When a Java program is executed, it is executed statement by statement. Some statements have to be executed conditionally, based on the result of an expression evaluation. Such statements are called control flow statements because, in computer science, a control flow (or flow of control) is the order in which individual statements are executed or evaluated.

A control flow statement can be one of the following:

- A selection statement: `if-else` or `switch-case`
- An iteration statement: `for`, `while`, or `do-while`
- An exception-handling statement: `throw`, `try-catch`, or `try-catch-finally`
- A branching statement: `break`, `continue`, or `return`

Selection statements

Selection statements are based on an expression evaluation and have four variations, as outlined here:

- `if` (expression) {do something}
- `if` (expression) {do something} `else` {do something else}
- `if` (expression) {do something} `else` `if` {do something else} `else` {do something else}
- `switch...case` statement

Here are some examples of `if` statements:

```
if(x > y){
    //do something
}

if(x > y){
    //do something
} else {
    //do something else
}

if(x > y){
    //do something
```

```
} else if (x == y) {
    //do something else
} else {
    //do something different
}
```

A switch...case statement is a variation of an if...else statement, as illustrated here:

```
switch(x) {
    case 5:                    //means: if(x = 5)
        //do something
        break;
    case 7:
        //do something else
        break;
    case 12:
        //do something different
        break;
    default:
        //do something completely different
        //if x is not 5, 7, or 12
}
```

As you can see, the switch...case statement forks the execution flow based on the value of the variable. The break statement allows the switch...case statement to be executed. Otherwise, all the following cases would be executed.

In Java 14, a new switch...case statement has been introduced in a less verbose form, as illustrated here:

```
void switchStatement(int x) {
    switch (x) {
        case 1, 3 -> System.out.print("1 or 3");
        case 4    -> System.out.print("4");
        case 5, 6 -> System.out.print("5 or 6");
        default   -> System.out.print("Not 1,3,4,5,6");
```

```
    }
    System.out.println(": " + x);
}
```

As you can see, it uses an arrow (->) and does not use a break statement.

Execute the main() method of the com.packt.learnjava.ch01_
start.ControlFlow class—see the selection() method that calls the
switchStatement() method with different parameters, as follows:

```
switchStatement(1);    //prints: 1 or 3: 1
switchStatement(2);    //prints: Not 1,3,4,5,6: 2
switchStatement(5);    //prints: 5 or 6: 5
```

You can see the results from the comments.

If several lines of code have to be executed in each case, you can just put braces ({ })
around the block of code, as follows:

```
switch (x) {
    case 1, 3 -> {
                    //do something
            }
    case 4     -> {
                    //do something else
            }
    case 5, 6 -> System.out.println("5 or 6");
    default    -> System.out.println("Not 1,3,4,5,6");
}
```

The Java 14 switch...case statement can even return a value, thus becoming in
effect a switch expression. For example, here is a case when another variable has to be
assigned based on the switch...case statement result:

```
void switchExpression1(int i){
    boolean b = switch(i) {
        case 0, 1 -> false;
        case 2 -> true;
        default -> false;
    };
```

```
        System.out.println(b);
    }
```

If we execute the switchExpression1() method (see the selection() method of the com.packt.learnjava.ch01_start.ControlFlow class), the results are going to look like this:

```
    switchExpression1(0);     //prints: false
    switchExpression1(1);     //prints: false
    switchExpression1(2);     //prints: true
```

The following example of a switch expression is based on a constant:

```
    static final String ONE = "one", TWO = "two", THREE = "three",
                   FOUR = "four", FIVE = "five";
    void switchExpression2(String number){
        var res = switch(number) {
            case ONE, TWO -> 1;
            case THREE, FOUR, FIVE -> 2;
            default -> 3;
        };
        System.out.println(res);
    }
```

If we execute the switchExpression2() method (see the selection() method of the com.packt.learnjava.ch01_start.ControlFlow class), the results are going to look like this:

```
    switchExpression2(TWO);          //prints: 1
    switchExpression2(FOUR);         //prints: 2
    switchExpression2("blah");       //prints: 3
```

Here's yet another example of a switch expression, this time based on the enum value:

```
    enum Num { ONE, TWO, THREE, FOUR, FIVE }
    void switchExpression3(Num number){
        var res = switch(number) {
            case ONE, TWO -> 1;
            case THREE, FOUR, FIVE -> 2;
```

```
    };
    System.out.println(res);
}
```

If we execute the `switchExpression3()` method (see the `selection()` method of the `com.packt.learnjava.ch01_start.ControlFlow` class), the results are going to look like this:

```
switchExpression3(Num.TWO);          //prints: 1
switchExpression3(Num.FOUR);         //prints: 2
//switchExpression3("blah"); //does not compile
```

In case a block of code has to be executed based on a particular input value, it is not possible to use a `return` statement because it is reserved already for the returning value from a method. That is why, to return a value from a block, we have to use a `yield` statement, as shown in the following example:

```
void switchExpression4(Num number){
    var res = switch(number) {
        case ONE, TWO -> 1;
        case THREE, FOUR, FIVE -> {
            String s = number.name();
            yield s.length();
        }
    };
    System.out.println(res);
}
```

If we execute the `switchExpression4()` method (see the `selection()` method of the `com.packt.learnjava.ch01_start.ControlFlow` class), the results are going to look like this:

```
switchExpression4(Num.TWO);          //prints: 1
switchExpression4(Num.THREE);        //prints: 5
```

Iteration statements

An iteration statement can take one of the following three forms:

- A while statement
- A do...while statement
- A for statement, also called a loop statement

A while statement looks like this:

```
while (boolean expression) {
      //do something
}
```

Here is a specific example (execute the main() method of the com.packt.
learnjava.ch01_start.ControlFlow class—see the iteration() method):

```
int n = 0;
while(n < 5){
  System.out.print(n + " "); //prints: 0 1 2 3 4
  n++;
}
```

In some examples, instead of the println() method, we use the print() method, which does not feed another line (does not add a line feed control at the end of its output). The print() method displays the output in one line.

A do...while statement has a very similar form, as we can see here:

```
do {
      //do something
} while (boolean expression)
```

It differs from a while statement by always executing the block of statements at least once before evaluating the expression, as illustrated in the following code snippet:

```
int n = 0;
do {
    System.out.print(n + " ");    //prints: 0 1 2 3 4
    n++;
} while(n < 5);
```

As you can see, it behaves the same way when the expression is `true` at the first iteration. But if the expression evaluates to `false`, the results are different, as we can see here:

```java
int n = 6;
while (n < 5) {
    System.out.print(n + " ");    //prints nothing
    n++;
}


n = 6;
do {
    System.out.print(n + " ");    //prints: 6
    n++;
} while (n < 5);
```

`for` statement syntax looks like this:

```java
for (init statements; boolean expression; update statements) {
  //do what has to be done here
}
```

Here is how a `for` statement works:

1. `init` statements initialize a variable.

2. A Boolean expression is evaluated using the current variable value: if `true`, the block of statements is executed; otherwise, the `for` statement exits.

3. `update` statements update the variable, and the Boolean expression is evaluated again with this new value: if `true`, the block of statements is executed; otherwise, the `for` statement exits.

4. Unless exited, the final step is repeated.

As you can see here, if you aren't careful, you can get into an infinite loop:

```java
for (int x = 0; x > -1; x++) {
    System.out.print(x + " ");  //prints: 0 1 2 3 4 5 6 ...
}
```

So, you have to make sure that the Boolean expression guarantees eventual exit from the loop, like this:

```java
for (int x = 0; x < 3; x++){
    System.out.print(x + " ");  //prints: 0 1 2
}
```

The following example demonstrates multiple initialization and `update` statements:

```java
for (int x = 0, y = 0; x < 3 && y < 3; ++x, ++y){
    System.out.println(x + " " + y);
}
```

And here is a variation of the preceding code for statements for demonstration purposes:

```java
for (int x = getInitialValue(), i = x == -2 ? x + 2 : 0,
              j = 0; i < 3 || j < 3 ; ++i, j = i) {
  System.out.println(i + " " + j);
  }
```

If the `getInitialValue()` method is implemented like int `getInitialValue()` { `return -2;` }, then the preceding two `for` statements produce exactly the same results.

To iterate over an array of values, you can use an array index, like so:

```java
int[] arr = {24, 42, 0};
for (int i = 0; i < arr.length; i++){
    System.out.print(arr[i] + " ");  //prints: 24 42 0
}
```

Alternatively, you can use a more compact form of a `for` statement that produces the same result, as follows:

```java
int[] arr = {24, 42, 0};
for (int a: arr){
    System.out.print(a + " ");  //prints: 24 42 0
}
```

This last form is especially useful with a collection, as shown here:

```
List<String> list = List.of("24", "42", "0");
for (String s: list){
    System.out.print(s + " ");   //prints: 24 42 0
}
```

We will talk about collections in *Chapter 6, Data Structures, Generics, and Popular Utilities*.

Exception-handling statements

In Java, there are classes called exceptions that represent events that disrupt the normal execution flow. They typically have names that end with Exception: NullPointerException, ClassCastException, ArrayIndexOutOfBoundsException, to name but a few.

All the exception classes extend the java.lang.Exception class, which, in turn, extends the java.lang.Throwable class (we will explain what this means in *Chapter 2, Java Object-Oriented Programming (OOP)*). That's why all exception objects have common behavior. They contain information about the cause of the exceptional condition and the location of its origination (line number of the source code).

Each exception object can be generated (thrown) either automatically by the JVM or by the application code, using the throw keyword. If a block of code throws an exception, you can use a try-catch or try-catch-finally construct to capture the thrown exception object and redirect the execution flow to another branch of code. If the surrounding code does not catch the exception object, it propagates all the way out of the application into the JVM and forces it to exit (and abort the application execution). So, it is good practice to use try-catch or try-catch-finally in all the places where an exception can be raised and you do not want your application to abort execution.

Here is a typical example of exception handling:

```
try {
    //x = someMethodReturningValue();
    if(x > 10){
        throw new RuntimeException("The x value is out
                                    of range: " + x);
    }
    //normal processing flow of x here
} catch (RuntimeException ex) {
```

```
      //do what has to be done to address the problem
 }
```

In the preceding code snippet, normal processing flow will be not executed in the case of x > 10. Instead, the do what has to be done block will be executed. But, in the x <= 10 case, the normal processing flow block will be run and the do what has to be done block will be ignored.

Sometimes, it is necessary to execute a block of code anyway, whether an exception was thrown/caught or not. Instead of repeating the same code block in two places, you can put it in a finally block, as follows (execute the main() method of the com.packt.learnjava.ch01_start.ControlFlow class—see the exception() method):

```
 try {
     //x = someMethodReturningValue();
     if(x > 10){
         throw new RuntimeException("The x value is out
                                     of range: " + x);
     }
     //normal processing flow of x here
 } catch (RuntimeException ex) {
    System.out.println(ex.getMessage());
    //prints: The x value is out of range: ...
    //do what has to be done to address the problem
 } finally {
    //the code placed here is always executed
 }
```

We will talk about exception handling in more detail in *Chapter 4, Exception Handling*.

Branching statements

Branching statements allow breaking of the current execution flow and continuation of execution from the first line after the current block or from a certain (labeled) point of the control flow.

A branching statement can be one of the following:

- `break`

- `continue`

- `return`

We have seen how `break` was used in `switch-case` statements. Here is another example (execute the `main()` method of the `com.packt.learnjava.ch01_start.ControlFlow` class—see the `branching()` method):

```java
String found = null;
List<String> list = List.of("24", "42", "31", "2", "1");
for (String s: list){
    System.out.print(s + " ");            //prints: 24 42 31
    if(s.contains("3")){
        found = s;
        break;
    }
}
System.out.println("Found " + found);   //prints: Found 31
```

If we need to find the first list element that contains `"3"`, we can stop executing as soon as the `s.contains("3")` condition is evaluated to `true`. The remaining list elements are ignored.

In a more complicated scenario, with nested `for` statements, it is possible to set a label (with a `:` column) that indicates which `for` statement has to be exited, as follows:

```java
String found = null;
List<List<String>> listOfLists = List.of(
        List.of("24", "16", "1", "2", "1"),
        List.of("43", "42", "31", "3", "3"),
        List.of("24", "22", "31", "2", "1")
);
exit: for(List<String> l: listOfLists){
    for (String s: l){
        System.out.print(s + " "); //prints: 24 16 1 2 1 43
        if(s.contains("3")){
            found = s;
```

```
            break exit;
        }
    }
}
System.out.println("Found " + found);    //prints: Found 43
```

We have chosen a label name of exit, but we could call it any other name too.

A continue statement works similarly, as follows:

```
String found = null;
List<List<String>> listOfLists = List.of(
                List.of("24", "16", "1", "2", "1"),
                List.of("43", "42", "31", "3", "3"),
                List.of("24", "22", "31", "2", "1")
);
String checked = "";
cont: for(List<String> l: listOfLists){
        for (String s: l){
            System.out.print(s + " ");
                //prints: 24 16 1 2 1 43 24 22 31
            if(s.contains("3")){
                continue cont;
            }
            checked += s + " ";
        }
}
System.out.println("Found " + found);    //prints: Found 43
System.out.println("Checked " + checked);
                        //prints: Checked 24 16 1 2 1 24 22
```

It differs from break by stating which of the for statements need to continue and not exit.

A `return` statement is used to return a result from a method, as follows:

```
String returnDemo(int i){
    if(i < 10){
        return "Not enough";
    } else if (i == 10){
        return "Exactly right";
    } else {
        return "More than enough";
    }
}
```

As you can see, there can be several `return` statements in a method, each returning a different value in different circumstances. If the method returns nothing (`void`), a `return` statement is not required, although it is frequently used for better readability, as follows:

```
void returnDemo(int i){
    if(i < 10){
        System.out.println("Not enough");
        return;
    } else if (i == 10){
        System.out.println("Exactly right");
        return;
    } else {
        System.out.println("More than enough");
        return;
    }
}
```

Execute the `returnDemo()` method by running the `main()` method of the `com. packt.learnjava.ch01_start.ControlFlow` class (see the `branching()` method). The results are going to look like this:

```
String r = returnDemo(3);
System.out.println(r);        //prints: Not enough
r = returnDemo(10);
System.out.println(r);        //prints: Exactly right
```

```
r = returnDemo(12);
System.out.println(r);         //prints: More than enough
```

Statements are the building blocks of Java programming. They are like sentences in English—complete expressions of intent that can be acted upon. They can be compiled and executed. Programming is like expressing an action plan in statements.

With this, the explanation of the basics of Java is concluded. Congratulations on getting through it!

Summary

This chapter introduced you to the exciting world of Java programming. We started with explaining the main terms, and then explained how to install the necessary tools—the JDK and the IDE—and how to configure and use them.

With a development environment in place, we have provided readers with the basics of Java as a programming language. We have described Java primitive types, the `String` type, and their literals. We have also defined what an ID is and what a variable is and finished with a description of the main types of Java statements. All the points of the discussion were illustrated by specific code examples.

In the next chapter, we are going to talk about the **object-oriented** (**OO**) aspects of Java. We will introduce the main concepts, explain what a class is, what an interface is, and the relationship between them. The terms *overloading*, *overriding*, and *hiding* will also be defined and demonstrated in code examples, as well as usage of the `final` keyword.

Quiz

1. What does JDK stand for?

    A. Java Document Kronos

    B. June Development Karate

    C. Java Development Kit

    D. Java Developer Kit

2. What does JCL stand for?

    A. Java Classical Library

    B. Java Class Library

    C. Junior Classical Liberty

    D. Java Class Libras

3. What does Java SE stand for?

    A. Java Senior Edition

    B. Java Star Edition

    C. Java Structural Elections

    D. Java Standard Edition

4. What does IDE stand for?

    A. Initial Development Edition

    B. Integrated Development Environment

    C. International Development Edition

    D. Integrated Development Edition

5. What are Maven's functions?

    A. Project building

    B. Project configuration

    C. Project documentation

    D. Project cancellation

6. Which of the following are Java primitive types?

    A. `boolean`

    B. `numeric`

    C. `integer`

    D. `string`

7. Which of the following are Java numeric types?

   A. `long`
   B. `bit`
   C. `short`
   D. `byte`

8. What is a *literal*?

   A. A letter-based string
   B. A number-based string
   C. A variable representation
   D. A value representation

9. Which of the following are literals?

   A. `\\`
   B. `2_0`
   C. `2__0f`
   D. `\f`

10. Which of the following are Java operators?

    A. `%`
    B. `$`
    C. `&`
    D. `->`

11. What does the following code snippet print?

    ```
    int i = 0; System.out.println(i++);
    ```

    A. `0`
    B. `1`
    C. `2`
    D. `3`

12. What does the following code snippet print?

```
boolean b1 = true;
 boolean b2 = false;
 System.out.println((b1 & b2) + " " + (b1 && b2));
```

A. false true

B. false false

C. true false

D. true true

13. What does the following code snippet print?

```
int x = 10;
 x %= 6;
 System.out.println(x);
```

A. 1

B. 2

C. 3

D. 4

14. What is the result of the following code snippet?

```
System.out.println("abc" - "bc");
```

A. a

B. abc-bc

C. Compilation error

D. Execution error

15. What does the following code snippet print?

```
System.out.println("A".repeat(3).lastIndexOf("A"));
```

A. 1

B. 2

C. 3

D. 4

16. Which of the following are correct IDs?

    A. int ___ (two underscores)

    B. 2a

    C. a2

    D. $

17. What does the following code snippet print?

```
for (int i=20, j=-1; i < 23 && j < 0; ++i, ++j){
        System.out.println(i + " " + j + " ");

}
```

    A. 20 -1 21 0

    B. Endless loop

    C. 21 0

    D. 20 -1

18. What does the following code snippet print?

```
int x = 10;
try {
    if(x++ > 10){
        throw new RuntimeException("The x value is out of
the range: " + x);
    }
    System.out.println("The x value is within the range:
" + x);
} catch (RuntimeException ex) {
    System.out.println(ex.getMessage());
}
```

    A. Compilation error

    B. The x value is out of the range: 11

    C. The x value is within the range: 11

    D. Execution time error

19. What does the following code snippet print?

```
int result = 0;
List<List<Integer>> source = List.of(
        List.of(1, 2, 3, 4, 6),
        List.of(22, 23, 24, 25),
        List.of(32, 33)
);
cont: for(List<Integer> l: source){
    for (int i: l){
        if(i > 7){
            result = i;
            continue cont;
        }
    }
}
System.out.println("result=" + result);
```

    A. result = 22

    B. result = 23

    C. result = 32

    D. result = 33

20. Select all the following statements that are correct:

    A. A variable can be declared.

    B. A variable can be assigned.

    C. A variable can be defined.

    D. A variable can be determined.

21. Select all the correct Java statement types from the following:

    A. An executable statement

    B. A selection statement

    C. A method end statement

    D. An increment statement

2
Java Object-Oriented Programming (OOP)

Object-Oriented Programming (OOP) was born out of the necessity for better control over the concurrent modification of shared data, which was the curse of pre-OOP programming. The core of the idea was not to allow direct access to data and instead, do it only through a dedicated layer of code. Since data needs to be passed around and modified in the process, the concept of an object was conceived. In the most general sense, an *object* is a set of data that can be passed around and accessed only through the set of methods passed along too. This data is said to compose an **object state**, while the methods constitute the **object behavior**. The object state is hidden (**encapsulated**) from direct access.

Each object is constructed based on a certain template called a **class**. In other words, a class defines a class of objects. Each object has a certain **interface**, a formal definition of the way other objects can interact with it. Originally, one object would send a message to another object by calling its method. But this terminology did not hold, especially after actual message-based protocols and systems were introduced.

To avoid code duplication, a parent-child relationship between objects was introduced – one class can inherit behavior from another class. In such a relationship, the first class is called a **child class**, or **subclass**, while the second is called a **parent**, **base class**, or **superclass**.

Another form of relationship was defined between classes and interfaces – a class can *implement* an interface. Since an interface describes how you can interact with an object but not how an object responds to the interaction, different objects can behave differently while implementing the same interface.

In Java, a class can have only one direct parent but can implement many interfaces.

The ability to behave like any of its ancestors and adhere to multiple interfaces is called **polymorphism**.

In this chapter, we will look at these OOP concepts and how they are implemented in Java. The topics discussed include the following:

- OOP concepts
- Class
- Interface
- Overloading, overriding, and hiding
- The final variable, method, and class
- Record and sealed classes
- Polymorphism in action

Technical requirements

To be able to execute the code examples provided in this chapter, you will need the following:

- A computer with a Microsoft Windows, Apple macOS, or Linux operating system
- Java SE version 17 or later
- An IDE or code editor that you prefer

The instructions for how to set up a Java SE and IntelliJ IDEA editor were provided in *Chapter 1, Getting Started with Java 17*, of this book. The files with the code examples for this chapter are available in the GitHub repository at `https://github.com/PacktPublishing/Learn-Java-17-Programming.git` in the `examples/src/main/java/com/packt/learnjava/ch02_oop` folder.

OOP concepts

As we have already stated in the introduction, the main OOP concepts are as follows:

- **Class**: This defines the properties and behavior (methods) of objects that are created based on this class.

- **Object**: This defines a state (data) as values of its properties, adds behavior (methods) taken from a class, and holds them together.

- **Inheritance**: This propagates behavior down the chain of classes connected via parent-child relationships.

- **Interface**: This describes how object data and behavior can be accessed. It isolates (abstracts) an object's appearance from its implementations (behavior).

- **Encapsulation**: This hides the state and details of the implementation.

- **Polymorphism**: This allows an object to assume an appearance of implemented interfaces and behave like any of the ancestor classes.

Object/class

In principle, you can create a very powerful application with minimal usage of classes and objects. It became even easier to do this after functional programming was added to Java 8, to a JDK, which allowed you to pass around behavior as a function. Yet passing data (state) still requires classes/objects. This means that the position of Java as an OOP language remains intact.

A class defines the types of all internal object properties that hold the object state. A class also defines object behavior expressed by the code of the methods. It is possible to have a class/object without a state or behavior. Java also has a provision for making the behavior accessible statically – without creating an object. But these possibilities are no more than just additions to the object/class concept that was introduced for keeping the state and behavior together.

To illustrate this concept, a `Vehicle` class, for example, defines the properties and behavior of a vehicle in principle. Let's make the model simple and assume that a vehicle has only two properties – weight and engine of a certain power. It also can have a certain behavior – it can reach a certain speed in a certain period of time, depending on the values of its two properties. This behavior can be expressed in a method that calculates the speed the vehicle can reach in a certain period of time. Every object of the `Vehicle` class will have a specific state (the values of its properties) and the speed calculation will result in a different speed in the same time period.

All Java code is contained inside methods. A **method** is a group of statements that have (optional) input parameters and a return a value (also optional). In addition, each method can have side effects – it can display a message or write data into the database, for example. Class/object behavior is implemented in the methods.

To follow our example, speed calculations can reside in a `double` `calculateSpeed(float seconds)` method, for instance. As you can guess, the name of the method is `calculateSpeed`. It accepts a number of seconds (with a fractional part) as a parameter and returns the speed value as `double`.

Inheritance

As we have mentioned already, objects can establish a parent-child relationship and share properties and behavior this way. For example, we can create a `Car` class that inherits properties (weight, for example) and behavior (speed calculation) of the `Vehicle` class. In addition, the `child` class can have its own properties (the number of passengers, for example) and car-specific behavior (soft shock absorption, for example). But if we create a `Truck` class as the vehicle's child, its additional truck-specific property (payload, for example) and behavior (hard shock absorption) will be different.

It is said that each object of the `Car` or `Truck` class has a parent object of the `Vehicle` class. But objects of the `Car` and `Truck` class do not share the specific `Vehicle` object (every time a child object is created, a new parent object is created first). They share only the parent's behavior. That is why all child objects can have the same behavior but different states. This is one way to achieve code reusability, but it may not be flexible enough when object behavior has to change dynamically. In such cases, object composition (bringing behavior from other classes) or functional programming is more appropriate (see *Chapter 13, Functional Programming*).

It is possible to make a child behave differently than the inherited behavior would do. To achieve it, the method that captures the behavior can be re-implemented in the `child` class. It is said that a child can *override* inherited behavior. We will explain how to do it shortly (see the *Overloading, overriding, and hiding* section). If, for example, the `Car` class has its own method for speed calculation, the corresponding method of the `Vehicle` parent class is not inherited, and the new speed calculation, implemented in the `child` class, is used instead.

Properties of a parent class can be inherited (but not overridden) too. However, class properties are typically declared private; they cannot be inherited – that's the point of encapsulation. See the description of various access levels – `public`, `protected`, `default`, and `private` – in the *Access modifiers* section of *Chapter 3, Java Fundamentals*.

If the parent class inherits some behavior from another class, the child class acquires (inherits) this behavior too, unless, of course, the parent class overrides it. There is no limit to how long the chain of inheritance can be.

The parent-child relationship in Java is expressed using the extends keyword:

```
class A { }
class B extends A { }
class C extends B { }
class D extends C { }
```

In this code, the A, B, C, and D classes have the following relationships:

- The D class inherits from the A, B, and C classes.
- The C class inherits from the A and B classes.
- The B class inherits from the A class.

All non-private methods of the A class are inherited (if not overridden) by the B, C, and D classes.

All non-private methods of the B class are inherited (if not overridden) by the C and D classes.

All non-private methods of the C class are inherited (if not overridden) by the D class.

Abstraction/interface

The name of a method and the list of its parameter types is called a **method signature**. It describes how the behavior of an object (of Car or Truck, in our example) can be accessed. Such a description together with a return type is presented as an interface. It does not say anything about the code that does calculations – only about the method name, the parameters' types, their position in the parameter list, and the result type. All the implementation details are hidden (encapsulated) within the class that *implements* this interface.

As we have mentioned already, a class can implement many different interfaces. But two different classes (and their objects) can behave differently even when they implement the same interface.

Similarly to classes, interfaces can have a parent-child relationship using the `extends` keyword too:

```
interface A { }
interface B extends A {}
interface C extends B {}
interface D extends C {}
```

In this code, the A, B, C, and D interfaces have the following relationships:

- The D interface inherits from the A, B, and C interfaces.
- The C interface inherits from the A and B interfaces.
- The B interface inherits from the A interface.

All non-private methods of the A interface are inherited by the B, C, and D interfaces.

All non-private methods of the B interface are inherited by the C and D interfaces.

All non-private methods of the C interface are inherited by the D interface.

Abstraction/interface also reduces dependency between different sections of the code, thus increasing its maintainability. Each class can be changed without the need to coordinate it with its clients, as long as the interface stays the same.

Encapsulation

Encapsulation is often defined either as data hiding or a bundle of publicly accessible methods and privately accessible data. In a broad sense, encapsulation is controlled access to an object's properties.

The snapshot of values of object properties is called an **object state**. This is data that is encapsulated. So, encapsulation addresses the main issue that motivated the creation of object-oriented programming – better management of concurrent access to shared data, such as the following:

```
class A {
  private String prop = "init value";
  public void setProp(String value){
    prop = value;
  }
  public String getProp(){
```

```
        return prop;
    }
}
```

As you can see, to read or modify the value of the `prop` property, we cannot access it directly because of the `private` access modifier. Instead, we can do it only via the `setProp(String value)` and `getProp()` methods.

Polymorphism

Polymorphism is the ability of an object to behave as an object of a different class or as an implementation of a different interface. It owes its existence to all the concepts that have been mentioned previously – inheritance, interface, and encapsulation. Without them, polymorphism would not be possible.

Inheritance allows an object to acquire or override the behaviors of all its ancestors. An interface hides from the client code the name of the class that implemented it. The encapsulation prevents exposing the object state.

In the following sections, we will demonstrate all these concepts in action and look at the specific usage of polymorphism in the *Polymorphism in action* section.

Class

A Java program is a sequence of statements that express an executable action. The statements are organized in methods, and methods are organized in classes. One or more classes are stored in `.java` files. They can be compiled (transformed from the Java language into a bytecode) by the `javac` Java compiler and stored in `.class` files. Each `.class` file contains one compiled class only and can be executed by JVM.

A `java` command starts JVM and tells it which class is the `main` one, the class that has the method called `main()`. The `main` method has a particular declaration – it has to be `public static`, must return `void`, has the name `main`, and accepts a single parameter of an array of a `String` type.

JVM loads the main class into memory, finds the `main()` method, and starts executing it, statement by statement. The `java` command can also pass parameters (arguments) that the `main()` method receives as an array of `String` values. If JVM encounters a statement that requires the execution of a method from another class, that class (its `.class` file) is loaded into the memory too and the corresponding method is executed. So, a Java program flow is all about loading classes and executing their methods.

Here is an example of the `main` class:

```
public class MyApp {
  public static void main(String[] args){
    AnotherClass an = new AnotherClass();
    for(String s: args){
      an.display(s);
    }
  }
}
```

It represents a very simple application that receives any number of parameters and passes them, one by one, into the `display()` method of the `AnotherClass` class. As JVM starts, it loads the `MyApp` class from the `MyApp.class` file first. Then, it loads the `AnotherClass` class from the `AnotherClass.class` file, creates an object of this class using the `new` operator (which we will talk about shortly), and calls the `display()` method on it.

Here is the `AnotherClass` class:

```
public class AnotherClass {
  private int result;
  public void display(String s){
    System.out.println(s);
  }
  public int process(int i){
    result = i *2;
    return result;
  }
  public int getResult(){
    return result;
  }
}
```

As you can see, the display() method is used for its side effect only – it prints out the passed-in value and returns nothing (void). The AnotherClass class has other two methods:

- The process() method doubles the input integer, stores it in its result property, and returns the value to the caller.
- The getResult() method allows you to get the result from the object at any time later.

These two methods are not used in our demo application. We have shown them just to show that a class can have properties (result, in this case) and many other methods.

The private keyword makes the value accessible only from inside the class, from its methods. The public keyword makes a property or a method accessible by any other class.

Method

As we have stated already, Java statements are organized as methods:

```
<return type> <method name>(<list of parameter types>){
    <method body that is a sequence of statements>
}
```

We have seen a few examples already. A method has a name, a set of input parameters or no parameters at all, a body inside { } brackets, and a return type or void keyword that indicates that the method does not return any value.

The method name and the list of parameter types together are called the **method signature**. The number of input parameters is called an **arity**.

> **Important Note**
> Two methods have the same *signature* if they have the same name, the same arity, and the same sequence of types in the list of input parameters.

The following two methods have the same signature:

```
double doSomething(String s, int i){
    //some code goes here
}
```

```
double doSomething(String i, int s){
    //some code other code goes here
}
```

The code inside the methods may be different even if the signature is the same.

The following two methods have different signatures:

```
double doSomething(String s, int i){
    //some code goes here
}


double doSomething(int s, String i){
    //some code other code goes here
}
```

Just a change in the sequence of parameters makes the signature different, even if the method name remains the same.

Varargs

One particular type of parameter requires a mention because it is quite different from all the others. It is declared a type followed by three dots. It is called **varargs**, which stands for **variable arguments**. But, first, let's briefly define what an array is in Java.

An **array** is a data structure that holds elements of the same type. The elements are referenced by a numerical index. That's all we need to know, for now. We will talk about arrays in more detail in *Chapter 6, Data Structures, Generics, and Popular Utilities*.

Let's start with an example. Let's declare method parameters using `varargs`:

```
String someMethod(String s, int i, double... arr){
  //statements that compose method body
}
```

When the `someMethod` method is called, the Java compiler matches the arguments from left to right. Once it gets to the last `varargs` parameter, it creates an array of the remaining arguments and passes it to the method. Here is a demo code:

```
public static void main(String... args){
    someMethod("str", 42, 10, 17.23, 4);
```

```
    }

    private static String someMethod(
            String s, int i, double... arr){
        System.out.println(arr[0] + ", " + arr[1] + ", " + arr[2]);
                                    //prints: 10.0, 17.23, 4.0
        return s;
    }
```

As you can see, the `varargs` parameter acts like an array of the specified type. It can be listed as the last or the only parameter of a method. That is why, sometimes, you can see the `main` method declared, as in the preceding example.

Constructor

When an object is created, JVM uses a **constructor**. The purpose of a constructor is to initialize the object state to assign values to all the declared properties. If there is no constructor declared in the class, JVM just assigns default values to the properties. We have talked about the default values for primitive types – it is 0 for integral types, 0.0 for floating-point types, and `false` for Boolean types. For other Java reference types (see *Chapter 3, Java Fundamentals*), the default value is `null`, which means that the property of a reference type is not assigned any value.

> **Important Note**
> When there is no constructor declared in a class, it is said that the class has a default constructor without parameters provided by the JVM.

If necessary, it is possible to declare any number of constructors explicitly, each taking a different set of parameters to set the initial state. Here is an example:

```
class SomeClass {
    private int prop1;
    private String prop2;
    public SomeClass(int prop1){
        this.prop1 = prop1;
    }
    public SomeClass(String prop2){
        this.prop2 = prop2;
    }
```

```
    public SomeClass(int prop1, String prop2){
        this.prop1 = prop1;
        this.prop2 = prop2;
    }
    // methods follow
}
```

If a property is not set by a constructor, the default value of the corresponding type is going to be assigned to it automatically.

When several classes are related along the same line of succession, the parent object is created first. If the parent object requires the setting of non-default initial values to its properties, its constructor must be called as the first line of the child constructor using the super keyword, as follows:

```
class TheParentClass {
    private int prop;
    public TheParentClass(int prop){
        this.prop = prop;
    }
    // methods follow
}


class TheChildClass extends TheParentClass{
    private int x;
    private String prop;
    private String anotherProp = "abc";
    public TheChildClass(String prop){
        super(42);
        this.prop = prop;
    }
    public TheChildClass(int arg1, String arg2){
        super(arg1);
        this.prop = arg2;
    }
    // methods follow
}
```

In the preceding code example, we added two constructors to `TheChildClass` – one that always passes `42` to the constructor of `TheParentClass`, and another that accepts two parameters. Note that the x property is declared but not initialized explicitly. It is going to be set to value 0, the default value of the `int` type, when an object of `TheChildClass` is created. Also, note that the `anotherProp` property is initialized explicitly to the value of `"abc"`. Otherwise, it would be initialized to the `null` value, the default value of any reference type, including `String`.

Logically, there are three cases when an explicit definition of a constructor in the class is not required:

- When neither the object nor any of its parents have properties that need to be initialized
- When each property is initialized along with the type declaration (`int x = 42`, for example)
- When default values for the properties' initialization are good enough

Nevertheless, it is possible that a constructor is still implemented even when all three conditions (mentioned in the list) are met. For example, you may want to execute some statements that initialize some external resource – a file or another database – that the object will need as soon as it is created.

As soon as an explicit constructor is added, the default constructor is not provided and the following code generates an error:

```
class TheParentClass {
    private int prop;
    public TheParentClass(int prop){
        this.prop = prop;
    }
    // methods follow
}

class TheChildClass extends TheParentClass{
    private String prop;
    public TheChildClass(String prop){
        //super(42);   //No call to the parent's constructor
        this.prop = prop;
    }
```

```
    // methods follow
}
```

To avoid the error, either add a constructor without parameters to `TheParentClass` or call an explicit constructor of the parent class as the first statement of the child's constructor. The following code does not generate an error:

```java
class TheParentClass {
    private int prop;
    public TheParentClass() {}
    public TheParentClass(int prop){
        this.prop = prop;
    }
    // methods follow
}

class TheChildClass extends TheParentClass{
    private String prop;
    public TheChildClass(String prop){
        this.prop = prop;
    }
    // methods follow
}
```

One important aspect to note is that constructors, although they look like methods, are not methods or even members of the class. A constructor doesn't have a return type and always has the same name as the class. Its only purpose is to be called when a new instance of the class is created.

The new operator

The `new` operator creates an object of a class (it also can be said that it **instantiates a class** or **creates an instance of a class**) by allocating memory for the properties of the new object and returning a reference to that memory. This memory reference is assigned to a variable of the same type as the class used to create the object or the type of its parent:

```java
TheChildClass ref1 = new TheChildClass("something");
TheParentClass ref2 = new TheChildClass("something");
```

Here is an interesting observation. In the code, both the `ref1` and `ref2` object references provide access to the methods of `TheChildClass` and `TheParentClass`. For example, we can add methods to these classes, as follows:

```
class TheParentClass {
    private int prop;
    public TheParentClass(int prop){
        this.prop = prop;
    }
    public void someParentMethod(){}
}


class TheChildClass extends TheParentClass{
    private String prop;
    public TheChildClass(int arg1, String arg2){
        super(arg1);
        this.prop = arg2;
    }
    public void someChildMethod(){}
}
```

Then, we can call them using any of the following references:

```
TheChildClass ref1 = new TheChildClass("something");
TheParentClass ref2 = new TheChildClass("something");
ref1.someChildMethod();
ref1.someParentMethod();
((TheChildClass) ref2).someChildMethod();
ref2.someParentMethod();
```

Note that, to access the child's methods using the parent's type reference, we had to cast it to the child's type. Otherwise, the compiler generates an error. That is possible because we have assigned the reference to the child's object to the parent's type reference.
That is the power of polymorphism. We will talk more about it in the *Polymorphism in action* section.

Naturally, if we had assigned the parent's object to the variable of the parent's type, we would not be able to access the child's method even with casting, as the following example shows:

```
TheParentClass ref2 = new TheParentClass(42);
((TheChildClass) ref2).someChildMethod();  //compiler's error
ref2.someParentMethod();
```

The area where memory for the new object is allocated is called **heap**. The JVM has a process called **garbage collection** that watches for the usage of this area and releases memory for usage as soon as an object is not needed anymore. For example, look at the following method:

```
void someMethod(){
    SomeClass ref = new SomeClass();
    ref.someClassMethod();
    //other statements follow
}
```

As soon as the execution of the someMethod() method is completed, the object of SomeClass is not accessible anymore. That's what the garbage collector notices, and it releases the memory occupied by this object. We will talk about the garbage collection process in *Chapter 9, JVM Structure and Garbage Collection*.

Class java.lang.Object

In Java, all classes are children of the Object class by default, even if you do not specify it implicitly. The Object class is declared in the java.lang package of the standard JDK library. We will define what a *package* is in the *Packages, importing, and access* section and describe libraries in *Chapter 7, Java Standard and External Libraries*.

Let's look back at the example we provided in the *Inheritance* section:

```
class A { }
class B extends A {}
class C extends B {}
class D extends C {}
```

All classes, A, B, C, and D, are children of the `Object` class, which has 10 methods that every class inherits:

- `public String toString()`
- `public int hashCode()`
- `public boolean equals (Object obj)`
- `public Class getClass()`
- `protected Object clone()`
- `public void notify()`
- `public void notifyAll()`
- `public void wait()`
- `public void wait(long timeout)`
- `public void wait(long timeout, int nanos)`

The first three, `toString()`, `hashCode()`, and `equals()`, are the most-used methods and often re-implemented (overridden). The `toString()` method is typically used to print the state of the object. Its default implementation in JDK looks like this:

```
public String toString() {
    return getClass().getName()+"@"+
                     Integer.toHexString(hashCode());
}
```

If we use it on the object of the `TheChildClass` class, the result will be as follows:

```
TheChildClass ref1 = new TheChildClass("something");
System.out.println(ref1.toString());
//prints: com.packt.learnjava.ch02_oop.
//Constructor$TheChildClass@72ea2f77
```

By the way, there is no need to call `toString()` explicitly while passing an object into the `System.out.println()` method and similar output methods because they do it inside the method anyway, and `System.out.println(ref1)`, in our case, produces the same result.

So, as you can see, such an output is not human-friendly, so it is a good idea to override the toString() method. The easiest way to do it is by using an IDE. For example, in IntelliJ IDEA, right-click inside TheChildClass code, as shown in the following screenshot:

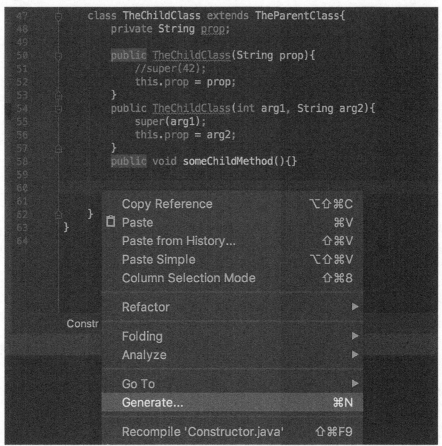

Select and click **Generate...**, and then select and click **toString()**, as shown in the following screenshot:

```
46
47    class TheChildClass extends TheParentClass{
48        private String prop;
49
50        public TheChildClass(String prop){
51            //super(42);
52            this.prop = prop;
53        }
54        public TheChildClass(int arg1, String arg2){
55            super(arg1);
56            this.prop = arg2;
57        }
58        public void someChildMethod(){}
59
60
61
62                        Generate
63
64        Constructor
            Getter
            Setter
            Getter and Setter
            equals() and hashCode()
            toString()
            Override Methods...      ^O
            Delegate Methods...
            Copyright

tor$TheChildClass@72ea2f77
```

The new pop-up window will enable you to select the properties you wish to include in the `toString()` method. Select only the properties of `TheChildClass`, as follows:

```
● ● ●                     Generate toString()

Template:   String concat (+)                          ▼     Settings

↓ᵃ  Ⓒ  ⊠  ⊡

▼ Ⓒ com.packt.learnjava.ch02_oop.Constructor.TheChildClass
      ⓕ    prop:String
▼ Ⓒ com.packt.learnjava.ch02_oop.Constructor.TheParentClass
      ⓕ ⓔ  prop:int
```

After you click the **OK** button, the following code will be generated:

```java
@Override
public String toString() {
    return "TheChildClass{" +
            "prop='" + prop + '\'' +
            '}';
}
```

If there were more properties in the class and you had selected them, more properties and their values would be included in the method output. If we print the object now, the result will be this:

```java
TheChildClass ref1 = new TheChildClass("something");
System.out.println(ref1.toString());
                        //prints: TheChildClass{prop='something'}
```

That is why the toString() method is often overridden and even included in the services of an IDE.

We will talk about the hashCode() and equals() methods in more detail in *Chapter 6, Data Structures, Generics, and Popular Utilities*.

The getClass() and clone() methods are not used as often. The getClass() method returns an object of the Class class that has many methods that provide various system information. The most used method is the one that returns the name of the class of the current object. The clone() method can be used to copy the current object. It works just fine as long as all the properties of the current object are of primitive types. But, if there is a reference type property, the clone() method has to be re-implemented so that the copy of the reference type can be done correctly. Otherwise, only the reference will be copied, not the object itself. Such a copy is called a **shallow copy**, which may be good enough in some cases. The protected keyword indicates that only children of the class can access it. See the *Packages, importing, and access* section.

The last five of the class Object methods are used for communication between threads – the lightweight processes for concurrent processing. They are typically not re-implemented.

Instance and static properties and methods

So far, we have seen mostly methods that can be invoked only on an object (instance) of a class. Such methods are called **instance methods**. They typically use the values of the object properties (the object state). Otherwise, if they do not use the object state, they can be made `static` and invoked without creating an object. An example of such a method is the `main()` method. Here is another example:

```
class SomeClass{
    public static void someMethod(int i){
        //do something
    }
}
```

This method can be called as follows:

```
SomeClass.someMethod(42);
```

> **Important Note**
>
> Static methods can be called on an object too, but it is considered bad practice, as it hides the static nature of the method from a human trying to understand the code. Besides, it raises a compiler warning and, depending on the compiler implementation, may even generate a compiler error.

Similarly, a property can be declared static and thus accessible without creating an object, such as the following:

```
class SomeClass{
    public static String SOME_PROPERTY = "abc";
}
```

This property can be accessed directly via class too, as follows:

```
System.out.println(SomeClass.SOME_PROPERTY);   //prints: abc
```

Having such a static property works against the idea of state encapsulation and may cause all the problems of concurrent data modification because it exists as a single copy in JVM memory, and all the methods that use it share the same value. That is why a static property is typically used for two purposes:

- To store a constant – a value that can be read but not modified (also called a **read-only value**)

- To store a stateless object that is expensive to create or that keeps read-only values

A typical example of a constant is a name of a resource:

```
class SomeClass{
    public static final String INPUT_FILE_NAME = "myFile.csv";
}
```

Note the final keyword in front of the static property. It tells the compiler and JVM that this value, once assigned, cannot change. An attempt to do it generates an error. It helps to protect the value and express clearly the intent to have this value as a constant. When a human tries to understand how the code works, such seemingly small details make the code easier to understand.

That said, consider using interfaces for such a purpose. Since Java 1.8, all the fields declared in an interface are implicitly static and final, so there is less chance you'll forget to declare a value to be final. We will talk about interfaces shortly.

When an object is declared a static final class property, it does not mean all its properties become final automatically. It only protects the property from assigning another object of the same type. We will discuss the complicated procedure of concurrent access of an object property in *Chapter 8, Multithreading and Concurrent Processing*. Nevertheless, programmers often use static final objects to store the values that are read-only just by the way they are used in the application. A typical example would be application configuration information. Once created after reading from a disk, it is not changed, even if it could be. Also, caching of data is obtained from an external resource.

Again, before using such a class property for this purpose, consider using an interface that provides more default behavior that supports a read-only functionality.

Similar to static properties, static methods can be invoked without creating an instance of the class. Consider, for example, the following class:

```
class SomeClass{
    public static String someMethod() {
        return "abc";
    }
}
```

We can call the preceding method by using just a class name:

```
System.out.println(SomeClass.someMethod()); //prints: abc
```

Interface

In the *Abstraction/interface* section, we talked about an interface in general terms. In this section, we are going to describe a Java language construct that expresses it.

An interface presents what can be expected of an object. It hides the implementation and exposes only method signatures with return values. For example, here is an interface that declares two abstract methods:

```
interface SomeInterface {
    void method1();
    String method2(int i);
}
```

Here is a class that implements it:

```
class SomeClass implements SomeInterface{
    public void method1(){
        //method body
    }
    public String method2(int i) {
        //method body
        return "abc";
    }
}
```

An interface cannot be instantiated. An object of an interface type can be created only by creating an object of a class that *implements* this interface:

```
SomeInterface si = new SomeClass();
```

If not all of the abstract methods of the interface have been implemented, the class must be declared abstract and cannot be instantiated. See the *Interface versus abstract class* section.

An interface does not describe how the object of the class can be created. To discover that, you must look at the class and see what constructors it has. An interface also does not describe the static class methods. So, an interface is a public face of a class instance (object) only.

With Java 8, an interface acquired the ability to have not just abstract methods (without a body) but really implemented ones. According to the Java Language Specification, *"the body of an interface may declare members of the interface, that is, fields, methods, classes, and interfaces."* Such a broad statement brings up the question, what is the difference between an interface and a class? One principal difference that we have pointed out already is this – an interface cannot be instantiated; only a class can be instantiated.

Another difference is that a non-static method implemented inside an interface is declared `default` or `private`. By contrast, a `default` declaration is not available for the class methods.

Also, fields in an interface are implicitly public, static, and final. By contrast, class properties and methods are not static or final by default. The implicit (default) access modifier of a class itself, its fields, methods, and constructors are package-private, which means it is visible only within its own package.

Default methods

To get an idea about the function of default methods in an interface, let's look at an example of an interface and a class that implements it, as follows:

```
interface SomeInterface {
    void method1();
    String method2(int i);
    default int method3(){
        return 42;
    }
}
```

```
}

class SomeClass implements SomeInterface{
    public void method1(){
        //method body
    }
    public String method2(int i) {
        //method body
        return "abc";
    }
}
```

We can now create an object of the SomeClass class and make the following call:

```
SomeClass sc = new SomeClass();
sc.method1();
sc.method2(22);   //returns: "abc"
System.out.println(sc.method2(22)); //prints: abc
sc.method3();      //returns: 42
System.out.println(sc.method3());    //prints: 42
```

As you can see, method3() is not implemented in the SomeClass class, but it looks as if the class has it. That is one way to add a new method to an existing class without changing it – by adding the default method to the interface the class implements.

Let's now add the method3() implementation to the class too, as follows:

```
class SomeClass implements SomeInterface{
    public void method1(){
        //method body
    }
    public String method2(int i) {
        //method body
        return "abc";
    }
    public int method3(){
        return 15;
    }
}
```

Now, the interface implementation of method3() will be ignored:

```
SomeClass sc = new SomeClass();
sc.method1();
sc.method2(22);   //returns: "abc"
sc.method3();     //returns: 15
System.out.println(sc.method3());        //prints: 15
```

> **Important Note**
>
> The purpose of the default method in an interface is to provide a new method to the classes (that implement this interface) without changing them. But the interface implementation is ignored as soon as a class implements the new method too.

Private methods

If there are several default methods in an interface, it is possible to create private methods accessible only by the default methods of the interface. They can be used to contain common functionality, instead of repeating it in every default method:

```
interface SomeInterface {
    void method1();
    String method2(int i);
    default int method3(){
        return getNumber();
    }
    default int method4(){
        return getNumber() + 22;
    }
    private int getNumber(){
        return 42;
    }
}
```

This concept of private methods is not different from private methods in classes (see the *Packages, importing, and access* section). The private methods cannot be accessed from outside the interface.

Static fields and methods

Since Java 8, all the fields declared in an interface are implicitly public, static, and final constants. That is why an interface is a preferred location for the constants. You do not need to add `public static final` to their declarations.

As for the static methods, they function in an interface in the same way as in a class:

```
interface SomeInterface{
    static String someMethod() {
        return "abc";
    }
}
```

Note that there is no need to mark the interface method as `public`. All non-private interface methods are public by default.

We can call the preceding method by using just an interface name:

```
System.out.println(SomeInetrface.someMethod()); //prints: abc
```

Interface versus abstract class

We have mentioned already that a class can be declared `abstract`. It may be a regular class that we do not want to be instantiated, or it may be a class that contains (or inherits) abstract methods. In the last case, we must declare such a class as `abstract` to avoid a compilation error.

In many respects, an abstract class is very similar to an interface. It forces every `child` class that extends it to implement the abstract methods. Otherwise, the child cannot be instantiated and has to be declared abstract itself.

However, a few principal differences between an interface and abstract class make each of them useful in different situations:

- An abstract class can have a constructor, while an interface cannot.
- An abstract class can have a state, while an interface cannot.
- The fields of an abstract class can be `public`, `private`, or `protected`, `static` or not, and `final` or not, while, in an interface, fields are always `public`, `static`, and `final`.

- The methods in an abstract class can be `public`, `private`, or `protected`, while the interface methods can be `public` or `private` only.

- If the class you would like to amend extends another class already, you cannot use an abstract class, but you can implement an interface because a class can extend only one other class but can implement multiple interfaces.

You will see an example of abstract usage in the *Polymorphism in action* section.

Overloading, overriding, and hiding

We have already mentioned overriding in the *Inheritance* and *Abstraction/interface* sections. It is a replacement of a non-static method implemented in a parent class with the method of the same signatures in the `child` class. The default method of an interface also can be overridden in the interface that extends it. Hiding is similar to overriding but applies only to static methods and static, as well as properties of the instance.

Overloading is creating several methods with the same name and different parameters (thus, different signatures) in the same class or interface.

In this section, we will discuss all these concepts and demonstrate how they work for classes and interfaces.

Overloading

It is not possible to have two methods in the same interface or a class with the same signature. To have a different signature, the new method has to have either a new name or a different list of parameter types (and the sequence of the type does matter). Having two methods with the same name but a different list of parameter types constitutes overloading. Here are a few examples of a legitimate method of overloading in an interface:

```
interface A {
    int m(String s);
    int m(String s, double d);
    default int m(String s, int i) { return 1; }
    static int m(String s, int i, double d) { return 1; }
}
```

Note that no two of the preceding methods have the same signature, including the default and static methods. Otherwise, a compiler's error would be generated. Neither designation as default nor static plays any role in the overloading. A return type does not affect the overloading either. We use `int` as a return type everywhere just to make the examples less cluttered.

Method overloading is done similarly in a class:

```
class C {
    int m(String s){ return 42; }
    int m(String s, double d){ return 42; }
    static int m(String s, double d, int i) { return 1; }
}
```

And it does not matter where the methods with the same name are declared. The following method overloading is not different from the previous example, as follows:

```
interface A {
    int m(String s);
    int m(String s, double d);
}
interface B extends A {
    default int m(String s, int i) { return 1; }
    static int m(String s, int i, double d) { return 1; }
}
class C {
    int m(String s){ return 42; }
}
class D extends C {
    int m(String s, double d){ return 42; }
    static int m(String s, double d, int i) { return 1; }
}
```

A private non-static method can be overloaded only by a non-static method of the same class.

> **Important Note**
> Overloading happens when methods have the same name but a different list of parameter types and belong to the same interface (or class) or to different interfaces (or classes), one of which is an ancestor to another. A private method can be overloaded only by a method in the same class.

Overriding

In contrast to overloading, which happens with the static and non-static methods, method overriding happens only with non-static methods and only when they have *exactly the same signature* and *belong to different interfaces (or classes)*, one of which is an ancestor to another.

> **Important Note**
> The overriding method resides in the child interface (or class), while the overridden method has the same signature and belongs to one of the ancestor interfaces (or classes). A private method cannot be overridden.

The following are examples of a method overriding an interface:

```java
interface A {
    default void method(){
        System.out.println("interface A");
    }
}
interface B extends A{
    @Override
    default void method(){
        System.out.println("interface B");
    }
}
class C implements B { }
```

If we call the method() using the C class instance, the result will be as follows:

```
C c = new C();
c.method();        //prints: interface B
```

Please note the usage of the @Override annotation. It tells the compiler that the programmer thinks that the annotated method overrides a method of one of the ancestor interfaces. This way, the compiler can make sure that the overriding does happen and generates an error if it doesn't. For example, a programmer may misspell the name of the method, as follows:

```
interface B extends A{
    @Override
    default void method(){
        System.out.println("interface B");
    }
}
```

If that happens, the compiler generates an error because there is no metod() method to override. Without the @Overrride annotation, this mistake may go unnoticed by the programmer, and the result would be quite different:

```
C c = new C();
c.method();        //prints: interface A
```

The same rules of overriding apply to the class instance methods. In the following example, the C2 class overrides a method of the C1 class:

```
class C1{
    public void method(){
        System.out.println("class C1");
    }
}
class C2 extends C1{
    @Override
    public void method(){
        System.out.println("class C2");
    }
}
```

The result is as follows:

```
C2 c2 = new C2();
c2.method();        //prints: class C2
```

It does not matter how many ancestors are between the class or interface with the overridden method and the class or interface with the overriding method:

```
class C1{
    public void method(){
        System.out.println("class C1");
    }
}
class C3 extends C1{
    public void someOtherMethod(){
        System.out.println("class C3");
    }
}
class C2 extends C3{
    @Override
    public void method(){
        System.out.println("class C2");
    }
}
```

The result of the preceding method's overriding will still be the same.

Hiding

Hiding is considered by many to be a complicated topic, but it should not be, and we will try to make it look simple.

The name *hiding* came from the behavior of static properties and methods of classes and interfaces. Each static property or method exists as a single copy in the JVM's memory because they are associated with the interface or class, not with an object. An interface or class exists as a single copy. That is why we cannot say that the child's static property or method overrides the parent's static property or method with the same name. All static properties and methods are loaded into the memory only once when the class or interface is loaded and stay there, not being copied anywhere. Let's look at an example.

Let's create two interfaces that have a parent-child relationship and static fields and methods with the same name:

```
interface A {
    String NAME = "interface A";
    static void method() {
        System.out.println("interface A");
    }
}
interface B extends A {
    String NAME = "interface B";
    static void method() {
        System.out.println("interface B");
    }
}
```

Please note the capital case for an identifier of an interface field. That's the convention often used to denote a constant, whether it is declared in an interface or a class. Just to remind you, a constant in Java is a variable that, once initialized, cannot be re-assigned another value. An interface field is a constant by default because any field in an interface is *final* (see the *Final properties, methods, and classes* section).

If we print NAME from the B interface and execute its method(), we get the following result:

```
System.out.println(B.NAME);    //prints: interface B
B.method();                    //prints: interface B
```

It looks very much like overriding, but, in fact, it is just that we call a particular property or a method associated with this particular interface.

Similarly, consider the following classes:

```
public class C {
    public static String NAME = "class C";
    public static void method(){
        System.out.println("class C");
    }
    public String name1 = "class C";
}
```

```
public class D extends C {
    public static String NAME = "class D";
    public static void method(){
        System.out.println("class D");
    }
    public String name1 = "class D";
}
```

If we try to access the static members of the D class using the class itself, we will get what we asked for:

```
System.out.println(D.NAME);   //prints: class D
D.method();                   //prints: class D
```

The confusion appears only when a property or a static method is accessed using an object:

```
C obj = new D();

System.out.println(obj.NAME);            //prints: class C
System.out.println(((D) obj).NAME);      //prints: class D

obj.method();                            //prints: class C
((D)obj).method();                       //prints: class D

System.out.println(obj.name1);           //prints: class C
System.out.println(((D) obj).name1);     //prints: class D
```

The obj variable refers to the object of the D class, and the casting proves it, as you can see in the preceding example. But, even if we use an object, trying to access a static property or method brings us the members of the class that was used as the declared variable type. As for the instance property in the last two lines of the example, the properties in Java do not conform to polymorphic behavior, and we get the name1 property of the parent C class, instead of the expected property of the child D class.

> **Important Note**
> To avoid confusion with static members of a class, always access them using the class, not an object. To avoid confusion with instance properties, always declare them private and access them via methods.

To illustrate the last tip, consider the following classes:

```
class X {
    private String name = "class X";
    public String getName() {
        return name;
    }
    public void setName(String name) {
        this.name = name;
    }
}
class Y extends X {
    private String name = "class Y";
    public String getName() {
        return name;
    }
    public void setName(String name) {
        this.name = name;
    }
}
```

If we run the same test for the instance properties as we did for the C and D classes, the result will be this:

```
X x = new Y();
System.out.println(x.getName());        //prints: class Y
System.out.println(((Y)x).getName()); //prints: class Y
```

Now, we access instance properties using methods, which are subjects for an overriding effect and do not have unexpected results anymore.

To conclude the discussion of hiding in Java, we would like to mention another type of hiding, namely when a local variable hides the instance or static property with the same name. Here is a class that does it:

```
public class HidingProperty {
    private static String name1 = "static property";
    private String name2 = "instance property";
```

```
public void method() {
    var name1 = "local variable";
    System.out.println(name1);        //prints: local variable

    var name2 = "local variable";   //prints: local variable
    System.out.println(name2);

    System.out.println(HidingProperty.name1);
                                    //prints: static property
    System.out.println(this.name2);
                                    //prints: instance property
    }
}
```

As you can see, the name1 local variable hides the static property with the same name, while the name2 local variable hides the instance property. It is possible still to access the static property using the class name (see HidingProperty.name1). Please note that, despite being declared private, it is accessible from inside the class.

The instance property can always be accessed by using the this keyword, which means the **current object**.

The final variable, method, and classes

We have mentioned a final property several times in relation to the notion of a constant in Java, but that is only one case of using the final keyword. It can be applied to any variable in general. Also, a similar constraint can be applied to a method and even a class too, thus preventing the method from being overridden and the class from being extended.

The final variable

The final keyword placed in front of a variable declaration makes this variable immutable after the initialization, such as the following:

```
final String s = "abc";
```

The initialization can even be delayed:

```
final String s;
s = "abc";
```

In the case of an object property, this delay can last only until the object is created. This means that the property can be initialized in the constructor, such as the following:

```
class A {
    private final String s1 = "abc";
    private final String s2;
    private final String s3;    //error
    private final int x;        //error

    public A() {
        this.s1 = "xyz";        //error
        this.s2 = "xyz";
    }
}
```

Note that, even during the object construction, it is not possible to initialize the property twice – during declaration and in the constructor. It is also interesting to note that a final property has to be initialized explicitly. As you can see from the preceding example, the compiler does not allow the initialization of the final property to a default value.

It is also possible to initialize a final property in an initialization block:

```
class B {
    private final String s1 = "abc";
    private final String s2;
    {
        s1 = "xyz"; //error
        s2 = "abc";
    }
}
```

In the case of a `static` property, it is not possible to initialize it in a constructor, so it has to be initialized either during its declaration or in a static initialization block:

```java
class C {
    private final static String s1 = "abc";
    private final static String s2;
    static {
        s1 = "xyz"; //error
        s2 = "abc";
    }
}
```

In an interface, all fields are always final, even if they are not declared as such. Since neither a constructor nor an initialization block is not allowed in an interface, the only way to initialize an interface field is during declaration. Failing to do it results in a compilation error:

```java
interface I {
    String s1;  //error
    String s2 = "abc";
}
```

Final method

A method declared `final` cannot be overridden in a `child` class or hidden in the case of a static method. For example, the `java.lang.Object` class, which is the ancestor of all classes in Java, has some of its methods declared `final`:

```java
public final Class getClass()x
public final void notify()
public final void notifyAll()
public final void wait() throws InterruptedException
public final void wait(long timeout)
                        throws InterruptedException
public final void wait(long timeout, int nanos)
                        throws InterruptedException
```

All the private methods and uninherited methods of a `final` class are effectively final because you cannot override them.

Final class

A final class cannot be extended. It cannot have children, which makes all the methods of the class effectively final too. This feature is used for security or when a programmer would like to make sure the class functionality cannot be overridden, overloaded, or hidden because of some other design considerations.

The record class

The record class was added to the SDK in Java 16. It was a long-awaited Java feature. It allows you to avoid writing boilerplate code in a case when you need an immutable class (with getters only), which looks similar to the following Person class (see the Record class in the ch02_oop folder):

```java
final class Person {
    private int age;
    private String name;
    public Person(int age, String name) {
        this.age = age;
        this.name = name;
    }
    public int age() { return age; }
    public String name() { return name; }
    @Override
    public boolean equals(Object o) {
        //implementation not shown for brevity
    }
    @Override
    public int hashCode() {
        //implementation not shown for brevity
    }
    @Override
    public String toString() {
        //implementation not shown for brevity
    }
```

Please note that the getters in the preceding above do not have the `get` prefix. It is done deliberately because, in the case of immutable class, there is no need to distinguish between getters and setters, as setters do not and should not exist if we want to have the class truly immutable. And that is the principal difference between such a class and JavaBeans, which are mutable and have both – setters and getters.

The `record` class allows you to replace the preceding implementation with the following one line only:

```
record Person(int age, String name){}
```

We can demonstrate it with the following code:

```
record PersonR(int age, String name){} //We added suffix "R"
                //to distinguish this class from class Person

Person person = new Person(25, "Bill");
System.out.println(person);
                            //prints: Person{age=25, name='Bill'}
System.out.println(person.name());              //prints: Bill


Person person1 = new Person(25, "Bill");
System.out.println(person.equals(person1));    //prints: true


PersonR personR = new PersonR(25, "Bill");
System.out.println(personR);
                            //prints: PersonR{age=25, name='Bill'}
System.out.println(personR.name());             //prints: Bill


PersonR personR1 = new PersonR(25, "Bill");
System.out.println(personR.equals(personR1)); //prints: true

System.out.println(personR.equals(person));    //prints: false
```

In addition to being `final` (not extendable) and immutable, `record` cannot extend another class because it already extends `java.lang.Record`, but it can implement another interface, as shown in the following example:

```
interface Student{
    String getSchoolName();
```

```
}
record StudentImpl(String name, String school) implements
Student{
    @Override
    public String getSchoolName() { return school(); }
}
```

It is possible to add a `static` method to `record`, as shown in the following code snippet:

```
record StudentImpl(String name, String school) implements
Student{
    public static String getSchoolName(Student student) {
        return student.getSchoolName();
    }
}
```

A `static` method does not and cannot access instance properties and can utilize only the values passed into it as parameters.

`record` can have another constructor, which can be added, for example, as follows:

```
record StudentImpl(String name, String school) implements
Student{
    public StudentImpl(String name) {
        this(name, "Unknown");
    }
}
```

As you may have noticed, it is not possible to add another property or a setter to `record`, while all additional getters have to use only getters provided already by `record`.

Sealed classes and interfaces

A `final` class cannot be extended, while a non-public class or interface has limited access. Yet, there are times when a class or interface needs to be accessible from anywhere but be extendable only by a certain class or interface, or, in the case of an interface, be implemented only by certain classes. That was the motivation for `sealed` classes and interfaces being added to the SDK in Java 17.

The difference between a `sealed` class or interface and a `final` one is that a `sealed` class or interface always has a `permits` keyword, followed by the list of the existing direct subtypes that are allowed to extend the `sealed` class or interface, or, in the case of the interface, implement it. Please note the word *existing*. The subtypes listed after the `permits` keyword must exist at compilation time in the same module as the sealed class or in the same package if in the default (unnamed) module.

A subtype of a `sealed` class must be marked either `sealed`, `final`, or `non-sealed`. A subtype of a `sealed` interface must be marked either `sealed` or `non-sealed`, since an interface cannot be `final`.

Let's look at an example of a `sealed` interface first:

```java
sealed interface Engine permits EngineBrand {
    int getHorsePower();
}
sealed interface EngineBrand extends Engine permits Vehicle {
    String getBrand();
}
non-sealed class Vehicle implements EngineBrand {
    private final String make, model, brand;
    private final int horsePower;
    public Vehicle(String make, String model,
                   String brand, int horsePower) {
        this.make = make;
        this.model = model;
        this.brand = brand;
        this.horsePower = horsePower;
    }
    public String getMake() { return make; }
    public String getModel() { return model; }
    public String getBrand() { return brand; }
    public int getHorsePower() { return horsePower; }
}
```

As you can see, the EngineBrand interface extends the Engine interface and allows (permits) the Vehicle implementation. Alternatively, we can allow the Vehicle class to implement the Engine interface directly, as shown in the following example:

```
sealed interface Engine permits EngineBrand, Vehicle {
    int getHorsePower();
}
sealed interface EngineBrand extends Engine permits Vehicle {
    String getBrand();
}
non-sealed class Vehicle implements Engine, EngineBrand {...}
```

Now, let's look at an example of a sealed class:

```
sealed class Vehicle permits Car, Truck {
    private final String make, model;
    private final int horsePower;
    public Vehicle(String make, String model, int horsePower) {
        this.make = make;
        this.model = model;
        this.horsePower = horsePower;
    }
    public String getMake() { return make; }
    public String getModel() { return model; }
    public int getHorsePower() { return horsePower; }
}
```

The following is an example of the Car and Truck permitted subtypes of the Vehicle sealed class:

```
final class Car extends Vehicle {
    private final int passengerCount;
    public Car(String make, String model, int horsePower,
        int passengerCount) {
        super(make, model, horsePower);
        this.passengerCount = passengerCount;
    }
    public int getPassengerCount() { return passengerCount; }
```

```
}

non-sealed class Truck extends Vehicle {
    private final int payloadPounds;
    public Truck(String make, String model, int horsePower,
      int payloadPounds) {
        super(make, model, horsePower);
        this.payloadPounds = payloadPounds;
    }
    public int getPayloadPounds() { return payloadPounds; }
}
```

In support sealed classes, the Java Reflections API in Java 17 has two new methods, isSealed() and getPermittedSubclasses(). The following is an example of their usage:

```
Vehicle vehicle = new Vehicle("Ford", "Taurus", 300);
System.out.println(vehicle.getClass().isSealed());
                                            //prints: true
System.out.println(Arrays.stream(vehicle.getClass()
                .getPermittedSubclasses())
              .map(Objects::toString).toList());
                        //prints list of permitted classes

Car car = new Car("Ford", "Taurus", 300, 4);
System.out.println(car.getClass().isSealed());  //prints: false
System.out.println(car.getClass().getPermittedSubclasses());
                                            //prints: null
```

The sealed interface integrates well with record because record is final and can be listed as a permittable implementation.

Polymorphism in action

Polymorphism is the most powerful and useful feature of OOP. It uses all the other OOP concepts and features we have presented so far. It is the highest conceptual point on the way to mastering Java programming. After discussing it, the rest of the book will be mostly about Java language syntax and JVM functionality.

As we stated in the *OOP concepts* section, polymorphism is the ability of an object to behave as an object of different classes or as an implementation of different interfaces. If you search the word *polymorphism* on the internet, you will find that it is *the condition of occurring in several different forms*. Metamorphosis is *a change of the form or nature of a thing or person into a completely different one, by natural or supernatural means*. So, **Java polymorphism** is the ability of an object to behave as if going through a metamorphosis and to exhibit completely different behaviors under different conditions.

We will present this concept in a practical hands-on way, using an **object factory** – a specific programming implementation of a factory, which is a *method that returns objects of a varying prototype or class* (https://en.wikipedia.org/wiki/Factory_ (object-oriented_programming).

The object factory

The idea behind the object factory is to create a method that returns a new object of a certain type under certain conditions. For example, look at the `CalcUsingAlg1` and `CalcUsingAlg2` classes:

```
interface CalcSomething{ double calculate(); }
class CalcUsingAlg1 implements CalcSomething{
    public double calculate(){ return 42.1; }
}
class CalcUsingAlg2 implements CalcSomething{
    private int prop1;
    private double prop2;
    public CalcUsingAlg2(int prop1, double prop2) {
        this.prop1 = prop1;
        this.prop2 = prop2;
    }
    public double calculate(){ return prop1 * prop2; }
}
```

As you can see, they both implement the same interface, `CalcSomething`, but use different algorithms. Now, let's say that we decided that the selection of the algorithm used will be done in a `property` file. Then, we can create the following object factory:

```java
class CalcFactory{
    public static CalcSomething getCalculator(){
        String alg = getAlgValueFromPropertyFile();
        switch(alg){
            case "1":
                return new CalcUsingAlg1();
            case "2":
                int p1 = getAlg2Prop1FromPropertyFile();
                double p2 = getAlg2Prop2FromPropertyFile();
                return new CalcUsingAlg2(p1, p2);
            default:
                System.out.println("Unknown value " + alg);
                return new CalcUsingAlg1();
        }
    }
}
```

The factory selects which algorithm to use based on the value returned by the `getAlgValueFromPropertyFile()` method. In the case of the second algorithm, it also uses the `getAlg2Prop1FromPropertyFile()` methods and `getAlg2Prop2FromPropertyFile()` to get the input parameters for the algorithm. But this complexity is hidden from the client:

```java
CalcSomething calc = CalcFactory.getCalculator();
double result = calc.calculate();
```

We can add new algorithm variations, and change the source for the algorithm parameters or the process of the algorithm selection, but the client will not need to change the code. And that is the power of polymorphism.

Alternatively, we can use inheritance to implement polymorphic behavior. Consider the following classes:

```java
class CalcSomething{
    public double calculate(){ return 42.1; }
}
```

```java
class CalcUsingAlg2 extends CalcSomething{
    private int prop1;
    private double prop2;
    public CalcUsingAlg2(int prop1, double prop2) {
        this.prop1 = prop1;
        this.prop2 = prop2;
    }
    public double calculate(){ return prop1 * prop2; }
}
```

Then, our factory may look as follows:

```java
class CalcFactory{
    public static CalcSomething getCalculator(){
        String alg = getAlgValueFromPropertyFile();
        switch(alg){
            case "1":
                return new CalcSomething();
            case "2":
                int p1 = getAlg2Prop1FromPropertyFile();
                double p2 = getAlg2Prop2FromPropertyFile();
                return new CalcUsingAlg2(p1, p2);
            default:
                System.out.println("Unknown value " + alg);
                return new CalcSomething();
        }
    }
}
```

But the client code does not change:

```java
CalcSomething calc = CalcFactory.getCalculator();
double result = calc.calculate();
```

Given a choice, an experienced programmer uses a common interface for the implementation. It allows for a more flexible design, as a class in Java can implement multiple interfaces but can extend (inherit from) one class.

The instanceof operator

Unfortunately, life is not always that easy, and once in a while, a programmer has to deal with code that is assembled from unrelated classes, even coming from different frameworks. In such a case, using polymorphism may be not an option. However, you can hide the complexity of an algorithm selection and even simulate polymorphic behavior using the `instanceof` operator, which returns `true` when an object is an instance of a certain class.

Let's assume we have two unrelated classes:

```java
class CalcUsingAlg1 {
    public double calculate(CalcInput1 input){
        return 42. * input.getProp1();
    }
}


class CalcUsingAlg2{
    public double calculate(CalcInput2 input){
        return input.getProp2() * input.getProp1();
    }
}
```

Each of the classes expects as an input an object of a certain type:

```java
class CalcInput1{
    private int prop1;
    public CalcInput1(int prop1) { this.prop1 = prop1; }
    public int getProp1() { return prop1; }
}

class CalcInput2{
    private int prop1;
    private double prop2;
    public CalcInput2(int prop1, double prop2) {
        this.prop1 = prop1;
        this.prop2 = prop2;
    }
}
```

```
        public int getProp1() { return prop1; }
        public double getProp2() { return prop2; }
}
```

And let's assume that the method we implement receives such an object:

```
void calculate(Object input) {
    double result = Calculator.calculate(input);
    //other code follows
}
```

We still use polymorphism here because we describe our input as the Object type. We can do it because the Object class is the base class for all Java classes.

Now, let's look at how the Calculator class is implemented:

```
class Calculator{
    public static double calculate(Object input){
        if(input instanceof CalcInput1 calcInput1){
            return new CalcUsingAlg1().calculate(calcInput1);
        } else if (input instanceof CalcInput2 calcInput2){
            return new CalcUsingAlg2().calculate(calcInput2);
        } else {
            throw new RuntimeException("Unknown input type " +
                        input.getClass().getCanonicalName());
        }
    }
}
```

As you can see, it uses the instanceof operator for selecting the appropriate algorithm. By using the Object class as an input type, the Calculator class takes advantage of polymorphism too, but most of its implementation has nothing to do with it. Yet, from the outside, it looks polymorphic, and it is, but only to a degree.

Summary

This chapter introduced you to the concepts of OOP and how they are implemented in Java. It provided an explanation of each concept and demonstrated how to use it in specific code examples. The Java language constructs of `class` and `interface` were discussed in detail. You also learned what overloading, overriding, and hiding are and how to use the `final` keyword to protect methods from being overridden.

In the *Polymorphism in action* section, you learned about the powerful Java feature of polymorphism. This section brought all the presented material together and showed how polymorphism stays at the center of OOP.

In the next chapter, you will become familiar with the Java language syntax, including packages, importing, access modifiers, reserved and restricted keywords, and some aspects of Java reference types. You will also learn how to use the `this` and `super` keywords, what widening and narrowing conversions of primitive types are, boxing and unboxing, primitive and reference type assignment, and how the `equals()` method of a reference type works.

Quiz

1. Select all the correct OOP concepts from the following list:

    A. Encapsulation

    B. Isolation

    C. Pollination

    D. Inheritance

2. Select all the correct statements from the following list:

    A. A Java object has status.

    B. A Java object has behavior.

    C. A Java object has state.

    D. A Java object has methods.

3. Select all the correct statements from the following list:

    A. A Java object behavior can be inherited.

    B. A Java object behavior can be overridden.

    C. A Java object behavior can be overloaded.

    D. A Java object behavior can be overwhelmed.

4. Select all the correct statements from the following list:

    A. Java objects of different classes can have the same behavior.

    B. Java objects of different classes share a parent object state.

    C. Java objects of different classes have as a parent an object of the same class.

    D. Java objects of different classes can share behavior.

5. Select all the correct statements from the following list:

    A. The method signature includes the return type.

    B. The method signature is different if the return type is different.

    C. The method signature changes if two parameters of the same type switch positions.

    D. The method signature changes if two parameters of different types switch positions.

6. Select all the correct statements from the following list:

    A. Encapsulation hides the class name.

    B. Encapsulation hides behavior.

    C. Encapsulation allows access to data only via methods.

    D. Encapsulation does not allow direct access to the state.

7. Select all the correct statements from the following list:

    A. The class is declared in the `.java` file.

    B. The class bytecode is stored in the `.class` file.

    C. The parent class is stored in the `.base` file.

    D. The `child` class is stored in the `.sub` file.

8. Select all the correct statements from the following list:

    A. A method defines an object state.

    B. A method defines object behavior.

    C. A method without parameters is marked as `void`.

    D. A method can have many `return` statements.

9. Select all the correct statements from the following list:

    A. Varargs is declared as a var type.

    B. Varargs stands for *various arguments*.

    C. Varargs is a String array.

    D. Varargs can act as an array of the specified type.

10. Select all the correct statements from the following list:

    A. A constructor is a method that creates a state.

    B. The primary responsibility of a constructor is to initialize a state.

    C. JVM always provides a default constructor.

    D. The parent class constructor can be called using the parent keyword.

11. Select all the correct statements from the following list:

    A. The new operator allocates memory to an object.

    B. The new operator assigns default values to the object properties.

    C. The new operator creates a parent object first.

    D. The new operator creates a child object first.

12. Select all the correct statements from the following list:

    A. An Object class belongs to the java.base package.

    B. An Object class belongs to the java.lang package.

    C. An Object class belongs to a package of the Java Class Library.

    D. An Object class is imported automatically.

13. Select all the correct statements from the following list:

    A. An instance method is invoked using an object.

    B. A static method is invoked using a class.

    C. An instance method is invoked using a class.

    D. A static method is invoked using an object.

14. Select all the correct statements from the following list:

   A. Methods in an interface are implicitly `public`, `static`, and `final`.

   B. An interface can have methods that can be invoked without being implemented in a class.

   C. An interface can have fields that can be used without any class.

   D. An interface can be instantiated.

15. Select all the correct statements from the following list:

   A. The default method of an interface is always invoked by default.

   B. The private method of an interface can be invoked only by the default method.

   C. The interface static method can be invoked without being implemented in a class.

   D. The default method can enhance a class that implements the interface.

16. Select all the correct statements from the following list:

   A. An `Abstract` class can have a default method.

   B. An `Abstract` class can be declared without an `abstract` method.

   C. Any class can be declared abstract.

   D. An interface is an `abstract` class without a constructor.

17. Select all the correct statements from the following list:

   A. Overloading can be done only in an interface.

   B. Overloading can be done only when one class extends another.

   C. Overloading can be done in any class.

   D. The overloaded method must have the same signature.

18. Select all the correct statements from the following list:

   A. Overriding can be done only in a `child` class.

   B. Overriding can be done in an interface.

   C. The overridden method must have the same name.

   D. No method of an `Object` class can be overridden.

19. Select all the correct statements from the following list:

    A. Any method can be hidden.

    B. A variable can hide a property.

    C. A static method can be hidden.

    D. A public instance property can be hidden.

20. Select all the correct statements from the following list:

    A. Any variable can be declared final.

    B. A public method cannot be declared final.

    C. A protected method can be declared final.

    D. A class can be declared protected.

21. Select all the correct statements from the following list:

    A. Polymorphic behavior can be based on inheritance.

    B. Polymorphic behavior can be based on overloading.

    C. Polymorphic behavior can be based on overriding.

    D. Polymorphic behavior can be based on an interface.

3
Java Fundamentals

This chapter presents to you a more detailed view of Java as a language. It starts with code organization in packages and a description of accessibility levels of classes (interfaces) and their methods and properties (fields). Reference types, as the main types of a Java object-oriented nature, are also presented in detail, followed by a list of reserved and restricted keywords and a discussion of their usage. The chapter ends with the methods of conversion between different primitive types and from a primitive type to a corresponding reference type and back.

These are the fundamental terms and features of the Java language. The importance of understanding them cannot be overstated. Without them, you cannot write any Java program. So, try not to rush through this chapter and make sure you understand everything presented.

The following topics will be covered in this chapter:

- Packages, importing, and access
- Java reference types
- Reserved and restricted keywords
- Usage of the `this` and `super` keywords
- Converting between primitive types
- Converting between primitive and reference types

Technical requirements

To be able to execute the code examples provided in this chapter, you will need the following:

- A computer with a Microsoft Windows, Apple macOS, or Linux operating system

- Java SE version 17 or later

- An IDE or a code editor you prefer

The instructions for how to set up a Java SE and an IntelliJ IDEA editor were provided in *Chapter 1*, *Getting Started with Java 17*, of this book. The files with the code examples for this chapter are available in the GitHub repository at `https://github.com/ PacktPublishing/Learn-Java-17-Programming.git` in the `examples/src/ main/java/com/packt/learnjava/ch03_fundamentals` folder.

Packages, importing, and access

As you already know, a package name reflects a directory structure, starting with the project directory that contains the `.java` files. The name of each `.java` file has to be the same as the name of the top-level class declared in it (this class can contain other classes). The first line of the `.java` file is the package statement that starts with the `package` keyword, followed by the actual package name – the directory path to this file in which slashes are replaced with dots.

A package name and the class name together compose a **fully qualified class name**. It uniquely identifies the class but tends to be too long and inconvenient to use. This is when **importing** comes to the rescue by allowing specification of the fully qualified name only once, and then referring to the class only by the class name.

Invoking a method of a class from the method of another class is possible only if a caller has access to that class and its methods. The `public`, `protected`, and `private` access modifiers define the level of accessibility and allow (or disallow) some methods, properties, or even the class itself to be visible to other classes.

All these aspects will be discussed in detail in the current section.

Packages

Let's look at the class we called `Packages`:

```
package com.packt.learnjava.ch03_fundamentals;
import com.packt.learnjava.ch02_oop.hiding.C;
```

```
import com.packt.learnjava.ch02_oop.hiding.D;
public class Packages {
    public void method(){
        C c = new C();
        D d = new D();
    }
}
```

The first line in the `Packages` class is a package declaration that identifies the class location on the source tree or, in other words, the `.java` file location in a filesystem. When the class is compiled and its `.class` file with bytecode is generated, the package name also reflects the `.class` file location in the filesystem.

Importing

After the package declaration, the `import` statements follow. As you can see from the previous example, they allow you to avoid using the fully qualified class (or interface) name anywhere else in the current class (or interface). When many classes (or interfaces) from the same package are imported, it is possible to import all classes and interfaces from the same package as a group, using the * symbol. In our example, it would look as follows:

```
import com.packt.learnjava.ch02_oop.hiding.*;
```

But that is not a recommended practice as it hides away the imported class (or interface) location when several packages are imported as a group. For example, look at this code snippet:

```
package com.packt.learnjava.ch03_fundamentals;
import com.packt.learnjava.ch02_oop.*;
import com.packt.learnjava.ch02_oop.hiding.*;
public class Packages {
    public void method(){
        C c = new C();
        D d = new D();
    }
}
```

In the preceding code, can you guess the package to which class C or class D belongs? Also, it is possible that two classes in different packages have the same name. If that is the case, group importing can create a degree of confusion or even a problem that's difficult to nail down.

It is also possible to import an individual static class (or interface) members. For example, if SomeInterface has a NAME property (as a reminder, interface properties are public and static by default), you can typically refer to it as follows:

```java
package com.packt.learnjava.ch03_fundamentals;
import com.packt.learnjava.ch02_oop.SomeInterface;
public class Packages {
    public void method(){
        System.out.println(SomeInterface.NAME);
    }
}
```

To avoid using even the interface name, you can use a static import:

```java
package com.packt.learnjava.ch03_fundamentals;
import static com.packt.learnjava.ch02_oop.SomeInterface.NAME;
public class Packages {
    public void method(){
        System.out.println(NAME);
    }
}
```

Similarly, if SomeClass has a public static property, someProperty, and a public static method, someMethod(), it is possible to import them statically too:

```java
package com.packt.learnjava.ch03_fundamentals;
import com.packt.learnjava.ch02_oop.StaticMembers.SomeClass;
import com.packt.learnjava.ch02_oop.hiding.C;
import com.packt.learnjava.ch02_oop.hiding.D;
import static com.packt.learnjava.ch02_oop.StaticMembers
                                      .SomeClass.someMethod;
import static com.packt.learnjava.ch02_oop.StaticMembers
                                      .SomeClass.SOME_PROPERTY;
public class Packages {
    public static void main(String... args){
```

```
        C c = new C();
        D d = new D();

        SomeClass obj = new SomeClass();
        someMethod(42);
        System.out.println(SOME_PROPERTY);    //prints: abc
    }
}
```

But this technique should be used wisely, since it may create the impression that a statically imported method or property belongs to the current class.

Access modifiers

We have already used in our examples the three access modifiers –`public`, `protected`, and `private` – which regulate access to the classes, interfaces, and their members from outside – from other classes or interfaces. There is also a fourth implicit one (also called the **default modifier package-private**) that is applied when none of the three explicit access modifiers is specified.

The effect of their usage is pretty straightforward:

- `public`: Accessible to other classes and interfaces of the current and other packages
- `protected`: Accessible only to other members of the same package and children of the class
- no access modifier: Accessible only to other members of the same package
- `private`: Accessible only to members of the same class

From inside the class or an interface, all the class or interface members are always accessible. Besides, as we have stated several times already, all interface members are public by default, unless declared as `private`.

Also, please note that class accessibility supersedes the class members' accessibility because, if the class itself is not accessible from somewhere, no change in the accessibility of its methods or properties can make them accessible.

When people talk about access modifiers for classes and interfaces, they mean the classes and interfaces that are declared inside other classes or interfaces. The encompassing class or interface is called a top-level class or interface, while those inside them are called inner classes or interfaces. The static inner classes are also called static nested classes.

It does not make sense to declare a top-level class or interface `private` because it will not be accessible from anywhere. And the Java authors decided against allowing the top-level class or interface to be declared `protected` too. It is possible, though, to have a class without an explicit access modifier, thus making it accessible only to members of the same package.

Here is an example:

```
public class AccessModifiers {
    String prop1;
    private String prop2;
    protected String prop3;
    public String prop4;

    void method1(){ }
    private void method2(){ }
    protected void method3(){ }
    public void method4(){ }

    class A1{ }
    private class A2{ }
    protected class A3{ }
    public class A4{ }

    interface I1 {}
    private interface I2 {}
    protected interface I3 {}
    public interface I4 {}
}
```

Please note that static nested classes do not have access to other members of the top-level class.

Another particular feature of an inner class is that it has access to all, even private members, of the top-level class, and vice versa. To demonstrate this feature, let's create the following private properties and methods in the top-level class and in a `private` inner class:

```
public class AccessModifiers {
    private String topLevelPrivateProperty =
                                "Top-level private value";
    private void topLevelPrivateMethod(){
        var inner = new InnerClass();
        System.out.println(inner.innerPrivateProperty);
        inner.innerPrivateMethod();
    }


    private class InnerClass {
        //private static String PROP = "Inner static"; //error
        private String innerPrivateProperty =
                                "Inner private value";
        private void innerPrivateMethod(){
            System.out.println(topLevelPrivateProperty);
        }
    }


    private static class InnerStaticClass {
        private static String PROP = "Inner private static";
        private String innerPrivateProperty =
                                "Inner private value";
        private void innerPrivateMethod(){
            var top = new AccessModifiers();
            System.out.println(top.topLevelPrivateProperty);
        }
    }
}
```

As you can see, all the methods and properties in the previous classes are private, which means that normally, they are not accessible from outside the class. And that is true for the `AccessModifiers` class – its private methods and properties are not accessible for other classes that are declared outside of it. But the `InnerClass` class can access the private members of the top-level class, while the top-level class can access the private members of its inner classes. The only limitation is that a non-static inner class cannot have static members. By contrast, a static nested class can have both static and non-static members, which makes a static nested class much more usable.

To demonstrate all the possibilities described, we will add the following `main()` method to the `AccessModifiers` class:

```java
public static void main(String... args){
    var top = new AccessModifiers();
    top.topLevelPrivateMethod();
    //var inner = new InnerClass();   //compiler error
    System.out.println(InnerStaticClass.PROP);
    var inner = new InnerStaticClass();
    System.out.println(inner.innerPrivateProperty);
    inner.innerPrivateMethod();
}
```

Naturally, a non-static inner class cannot be accessed from a static context of the top-level class, hence the `compiler error` comment in the preceding code. If we run it, the result will be as follows:

```
Inner private value
Top-level private value
Inner private static
Inner private value
Top-level private value
```

The first two lines of the output come from `topLevelPrivateMethod()`, and the rest from the `main()` method. As you can see, an inner- and a top-level class can access each other's private state, inaccessible from outside.

Java reference types

A `new` operator creates an object of a class and returns the reference to the memory where the object resides. From a practical standpoint, the variable that holds this reference is treated in the code as if it is the object itself. Such a variable can be a class, an interface, an array, or a `null` literal that indicates that no memory reference is assigned to the variable. If the type of reference is an interface, it can be assigned either `null` or a reference to the object of the class that implements this interface because the interface itself cannot be instantiated.

A JVM watches for all the created objects and checks whether there are references to each of them in the currently executed code. If there is an object without any reference to it, JVM removes it from the memory in a process called **garbage collection**. We will describe this process in *Chapter 9, JVM Structure and Garbage Collection*. For example, an object was created during a method execution and was referred to by the local variable. This reference will disappear as soon as the method finishes its execution.

You have seen the examples of custom classes and interfaces, and we have talked about the `String` class already (see *Chapter 1, Getting Started with Java 17*). In this section, we will also describe two other Java reference types – array and enum – and demonstrate how to use them.

Class and interface

A variable of a class type is declared using the corresponding class name:

```
<Class name> identifier;
```

The value that can be assigned to such a variable can be one of the following:

- A `null` literal reference type (which means the variable can be used but does not refer to any object)
- A reference to an object of the same class or any of its descendants (because a descendant inherits the types of all of its ancestors)

This last type of assignment is called a **widening assignment** because it forces a specialized reference to become less specialized. For example, since every Java class is a subclass of `java.lang.Object`, the following assignment can be done for any class:

```
Object obj = new AnyClassName();
```

Such an assignment is also called an **upcasting** because it moves the type of the variable up on the line of inheritance (which, like any family tree, is usually presented with the oldest ancestor at the top).

After such an upcasting, it is possible to make a narrowing assignment using a `(type)` cast operator:

```
AnyClassName anyClassName = (AnyClassName)obj;
```

Such an assignment is also called **downcasting** and allows you to restore the descendant type. To apply this operation, you have to be sure that the identifier in fact refers to a descendant type. If in doubt, you can use the `instanceof` operator (see *Chapter 2, Java Object-Oriented Programming (OOP)*) to check the reference type.

Similarly, if a class implements a certain interface, its object reference can be assigned to this interface or any ancestor of the interface:

```
interface C {}
interface B extends C {}
class A implements B { }
B b = new A();
C c = new A();
A a1 = (A)b;
A a2 = (A)c;
```

As you can see, as in the case with class reference upcasting and downcasting, it is possible to recover the original type of the object after its reference was assigned to a variable of one of the implemented interface types.

The material of this section can also be viewed as another demonstration of Java polymorphism in action.

Array

An **array** is a reference type and, as such, extends the `java.lang.Object` class too. The array elements have the same type as the declared array type. The number of elements may be zero, in which case the array is said to be an empty array. Each element can be accessed by an index, which is a positive integer or zero. The first element has an index of zero. The number of elements is called an array length. Once an array is created, its length never changes.

The following are examples of an array declaration:

```
int[] intArray;
float[][] floatArray;
String[] stringArray;
SomeClass[][][] arr;
```

Each bracket pair indicates another dimension. The number of bracket pairs is the nesting depth of the array:

```
int[] intArray = new int[10];
float[][] floatArray = new float[3][4];
String[] stringArray = new String[2];
SomeClass[][][] arr = new SomeClass[3][5][2];
```

The new operator allocates memory for each element that can be assigned (filled with) a value later. But in my case, the elements of an array are initialized to the default values at creation time, as the following example demonstrates:

```
System.out.println(intArray[3]);        //prints: 0
System.out.println(floatArray[2][2]);   //prints: 0.0
System.out.println(stringArray[1]);     //prints: null
```

Another way to create an array is to use an array initializer – a comma-separated list of values enclosed in braces for each dimension, such as the following:

```
int[] intArray = {1,2,3,4,5,6,7,8,9,10};
float[][] floatArray ={{1.1f,2.2f,3,2},{10,20.f,30
.f,5},{1,2,3,4}};
String[] stringArray = {"abc", "a23"};

System.out.println(intArray[3]);        //prints: 4
System.out.println(floatArray[2][2]);   //prints: 3.0
System.out.println(stringArray[1]);     //prints: a23
```

A multidimensional array can be created without declaring the length of each dimension. Only the first dimension has to have the length specified:

```
float[][] floatArray = new float[3][];
System.out.println(floatArray.length);  //prints: 3
System.out.println(floatArray[0]);      //prints: null
```

```
System.out.println(floatArray[1]);          //prints: null
System.out.println(floatArray[2]);          //prints: null
//System.out.println(floatArray[3]);        //error
//System.out.println(floatArray[2][2]);     //error
```

The missing length of other dimensions can be specified later:

```
float[][] floatArray = new float[3][];
floatArray[0] = new float[4];
floatArray[1] = new float[3];
floatArray[2] = new float[7];
System.out.println(floatArray[2][5]);       //prints: 0.0
```

This way, it is possible to assign a different length to different dimensions. Using the array initializer, it is also possible to create dimensions of different lengths:

```
float[][] floatArray ={{1.1f},{10,5},{1,2,3,4}};
```

The only requirement is that a dimension has to be initialized before it can be used.

Enum

The **enum** reference type class extends the `java.lang.Enum` class, which, in turn, extends `java.lang.Object`. It allows the specification of a limited set of constants, each of them an instance of the same type. The declaration of such a set starts with the enum keyword. Here is an example:

```
enum Season { SPRING, SUMMER, AUTUMN, WINTER }
```

Each of the listed items – SPRING, SUMMER, AUTUMN, and WINTER – is an instance of a Season type. They are the only four instances the Season class can have. They are created in advance and can be used everywhere as a value of a Season type. No other instance of the Season class can be created, and that is the reason for the creation of the enum type – it can be used for cases when the list of instances of a class has to be limited to the fixed set.

The enum declaration can also be written in title case:

```
enum Season { Spring, Summer, Autumn, Winter }
```

However, the all-capitals style is used more often because, as we mentioned earlier, there is a convention to express the static final constant's identifier in a capital case. It helps to distinguish constants from variables. The enum constants are implicitly static and final.

Because the enum values are constants, they exist uniquely in a JVM and can be compared by reference:

```
Season season = Season.WINTER;
boolean b = season == Season.WINTER;
System.out.println(b);    //prints: true
```

The following are the most frequently used methods of the java.lang.Enum class:

- name(): Returns the enum constant's identifier as it is spelled when declared (WINTER, for example).

- toString(): Returns the same value as the name() method by default but can be overridden to return any other String value.

- ordinal(): Returns the position of the enum constant when declared (the first in the list has a 0 ordinal value).

- valueOf(Class enumType, String name): Returns the enum constant object by its name, expressed as a String literal.

- values(): A static method, described in the documentation of the valueOff() method as follows: "All the constants of an enum class can be obtained by calling the implicit public static T[] values() method of that class."

To demonstrate the preceding methods, we are going to use the already familiar enum, Season:

```
enum Season { SPRING, SUMMER, AUTUMN, WINTER }
```

And here is the demo code:

```
System.out.println(Season.SPRING.name());        //prints: SPRING
System.out.println(Season.WINTER.toString());    //prints: WINTER
System.out.println(Season.SUMMER.ordinal());        //prints: 1
Season season = Enum.valueOf(Season.class, "AUTUMN");
System.out.println(season == Season.AUTUMN);        //prints: true

for(Season s: Season.values()){
    System.out.print(s.name() + " ");
```

```
                              //prints: SPRING SUMMER AUTUMN WINTER
}
```

To override the `toString()` method, let's create the `Season1` enum:

```java
enum Season1 {
    SPRING, SUMMER, AUTUMN, WINTER;
    public String toString() {
        return this.name().charAt(0) +
                this.name().substring(1).toLowerCase();
    }
}
```

Here is how it works:

```java
for(Season1 s: Season1.values()){
    System.out.print(s.toString() + " ");
                              //prints: Spring Summer Autumn Winter
}
```

It is possible to add any other property to each enum constant. For example, let's add an average temperature value to each enum instance:

```java
Enum Season2 {
    SPRING(42), SUMMER(67), AUTUMN(32), WINTER(20);
    private int temperature;
    Season2(int temperature){
    this.temperature = temperature;
    }
    public int getTemperature(){
        return this.temperature;
    }
    public String toString() {
        return this.name().charAt(0) +
            this.name().substring(1).toLowerCase() +
                "(" + this.temperature + ")";
    }
}
```

If we iterate over values of the Season2 enum, the result will be as follows:

```
for(Season2 s: Season2.values()){
    System.out.print(s.toString() + " ");
            //prints: Spring(42) Summer(67) Autumn(32) Winter(20)
}
```

In the standard Java libraries, there are several enum classes – for example, java.time. Month, java.time.DayOfWeek, and java.util.concurrent.TimeUnit.

Default values and literals

As we have already seen, the default value of a reference type is null. Some sources call it a **special type null**, but the Java language specification qualifies it as a literal. When an instance property or an array of a reference type is initialized automatically (when a value is not assigned explicitly), the assigned value is null.

The only reference type that has a literal other than the null literal is the String class. We discussed strings in *Chapter 1, Getting Started with Java 17*.

A reference type as a method parameter

When a primitive type value is passed into a method, we use it. If we do not like the value passed into the method, we change it as we see fit and do not think twice about it:

```
void modifyParameter(int x){
    x = 2;
}
```

We have no concerns that the variable value outside the method may change:

```
int x = 1;
modifyParameter(x);
System.out.println(x);   //prints: 1
```

It is not possible to change the parameter value of a primitive type outside the method because a primitive type parameter is passed into the method by value. This means that the copy of the value is passed into the method, so even if the code inside the method assigns a different value to it, the original value is not affected.

Another issue with a reference type is that even though the reference itself is passed by value, it still points to the same original object in the memory, so the code inside the method can access the object and modify it. To demonstrate it, let's create a `DemoClass` and the method that uses it:

```
class DemoClass{
    private String prop;
    public DemoClass(String prop) { this.prop = prop; }
    public String getProp() { return prop; }
    public void setProp(String prop) { this.prop = prop; }
}
void modifyParameter(DemoClass obj){
    obj.setProp("Changed inside the method");
}
```

If we use the preceding method, the result will be as follows:

```
DemoClass obj = new DemoClass("Is not changed");
modifyParameter(obj);
System.out.println(obj.getProp());
                      //prints: Changed inside the method
```

That's a big difference, isn't it? So, you have to be careful not to modify the passed-in object in order to avoid an undesirable effect. However, this effect is occasionally used to return the result. But it does not belong to the list of best practices because it makes code less readable. Changing the passed-in object is like using a secret tunnel that is difficult to notice. So, use it only when you have to.

Even if the passed-in object is a class that wraps a primitive value, this effect still holds (we will talk about the primitive values wrapping type in the *Converting between primitive and reference types* section). Here is `DemoClass1` and an overloaded version of the `modifyParameter()` method:

```
class DemoClass1{
    private Integer prop;
    public DemoClass1(Integer prop) { this.prop = prop; }
```

```
    public Integer getProp() { return prop; }
    public void setProp(Integer prop) { this.prop = prop; }
}
void modifyParameter(DemoClass1 obj){
    obj.setProp(Integer.valueOf(2));
}
```

If we use the preceding method, the result will be as follows:

```
DemoClass1 obj = new DemoClass1(Integer.valueOf(1));
modifyParameter(obj);
System.out.println(obj.getProp());   //prints: 2
```

The only exception to this behavior of reference types is an object of the String class. Here is another overloaded version of the modifyParameter() method:

```
void modifyParameter(String obj){
    obj = "Changed inside the method";
}
```

If we use the preceding method, the result will be as follows:

```
String obj = "Is not changed";
modifyParameter(obj);
System.out.println(obj); //prints: Is not changed

obj = new String("Is not changed");
modifyParameter(obj);
System.out.println(obj); //prints: Is not changed
```

As you can see, whether we use a literal or a new String object, the result remains the same – the original String value is not changed after the method that assigns another value to it. That is exactly the purpose of the String value immutability feature we discussed in *Chapter 1, Getting Started with Java 17.*

equals() method

The equality operator (==), when applied to the variables of reference types, compares the references themselves, not the content (the state) of the objects. But two objects always have different memory references even if they have identical content. Even when used for String objects, the operator (==) returns false if at least one of them is created using a new operator (see the discussion about String value immutability in *Chapter 1*, *Getting Started with Java 17*).

To compare content, you can use the equals() method. Its implementation in the String class and numerical type wrapper classes (Integer, Float, and so on) does exactly that – compare the content of the objects.

However, the equals() method implementation in the java.lang.Object class compares only references, which is understandable because the variety of possible content the descendants can have is huge, and the implementation of the generic content comparison is just not feasible. This means that every Java object that needs to have the equals() method comparing the object's content – not just references – has to re-implement the equals() method and, thus, override its implementation in the java.lang.Object class, which appears as follows:

```
public boolean equals(Object obj) {
    return (this == obj);
}
```

By contrast, look at how the same method is implemented in the Integer class:

```
private final int value;
public boolean equals(Object obj) {
    if (obj instanceof Integer) {
        return value == ((Integer)obj).intValue();
    }
    return false;
}
```

As you can see, it extracts the primitive int value from the input object and compares it to the primitive value of the current object. It does not compare object references at all.

The String class, on the other hand, compares the references first and, if the references are not the same value, compares the content of the objects:

```
private final byte[] value;
public boolean equals(Object anObject) {
```

```
    if (this == anObject) {
        return true;
    }
    if (anObject instanceof String) {
        String aString = (String)anObject;
        if (coder() == aString.coder()) {
            return isLatin1() ? StringLatin1.equals(value,
                aString.value)
                            : StringUTF16.equals(value,
                aString.value);
        }
    }
    return false;
}
```

The `StringLatin1.equals()` and `StringUTF16.equals()` methods compare the values character by character, not just references.

Similarly, if the application code needs to compare two objects by their content, the `equals()` method in the corresponding class has to be overridden. For example, let's look at the familiar `DemoClass` class:

```
class DemoClass{
    private String prop;
    public DemoClass(String prop) { this.prop = prop; }
    public String getProp() { return prop; }
    public void setProp(String prop) { this.prop = prop; }
}
```

We can add to it the `equals()` method manually, but the IDE can help us to do this, as follows:

1. Right-click inside the class just before the closing brace (`}`).

2. Select **Generate** and then follow the prompts.

Eventually, two methods will be generated and added to the class:

```
@Override
public boolean equals(Object o) {
    if (this == o) return true;
```

```
    if (!(o instanceof DemoClass)) return false;
    DemoClass demoClass = (DemoClass) o;
    return Objects.equals(getProp(), demoClass.getProp());
}


@Override
public int hashCode() {
    return Objects.hash(getProp());
}
```

Looking at the generated code, focus your attention on the following points:

- The usage of the `@Override` annotation – this ensures that the method does override a method (with the same signature) in one of the ancestors. With this annotation in place, if you modify the method and change the signature (by mistake or intentionally), the compiler (and your IDE) will immediately raise an error, telling you that there is no method with such a signature in any of the ancestor classes. So, it helps to detect an error early.

- The usage of the `java.util.Objects` class – this has quite a few very helpful methods, including the `equals()` static method that not only compares references but also uses the `equals()` method:

  ```
  public static boolean equals(Object a, Object b) {
      return (a == b) || (a != null && a.equals(b));
  }
  ```

  As we have demonstrated earlier, the `equals()` method, implemented in the `String` class, compares strings by their content and serves this purpose because the `getProp()` method of `DemoClass` returns a string.

The `hashCode()` method – the integer returned by this method uniquely identifies this particular object (but please do not expect it to be the same between different runs of the application). It is not necessary to have this method implemented if the only method needed is `equals()`. Nevertheless, it is recommended to have it just in case the object of this class is going to be collected in `Set` or another collection based on a hash code (we are going to talk about Java collections in *Chapter 6*, *Data Structures, Generics, and Popular Utilities*).

Both these methods are implemented in `Object` because many algorithms use the `equals()` and `hashCode()` methods, and your application may not work without these methods implemented. Meanwhile, your objects may not need them in your application. However, once you decide to implement the `equals()` method, it is a good idea to implement the `hasCode()` method too. Besides, as you have seen, an IDE can do this without any overhead.

Reserved and restricted keywords

The **keywords** are the words that have particular meaning for a compiler and cannot be used as identifiers. As of Java 17, there are 52 reserved keywords, 5 reserved identifiers, 3 reserved words, and 10 restricted keywords. The reserved keywords cannot be used as identifiers anywhere in the Java code, while the restricted keywords cannot be used as identifiers only in the context of a module declaration.

Reserved keywords

The following is a list of all Java-reserved keywords:

abstract	assert	boolean	break	byte
case	catch	char	class	const
continue	default	do	double	else
enum	extends	final	finally	float
for	goto	if	implements	import
instanceof	int	interface	long	native
new	non-sealed	package	private	protected
public	return	short	strictfp	super
super	switch	synchronized	this	throw
throws	transient	try	void	volatile
while	_ (underscore)			

By now, you should feel at home with most of the preceding keywords. By way of an exercise, you can go through the list and check how many of them you remember. Up until now, we have not discussed the following eight keywords:

- `const` and `goto` are reserved but not used, so far.

- The `assert` keyword is used in an `assert` statement (we will talk about this in *Chapter 4, Exception Handling*).

- The `synchronized` keyword is used in concurrent programming (we will talk about this in *Chapter 8, Multithreading and Concurrent Processing*).

- The `volatile` keyword makes the value of a variable uncacheable.

- The `transient` keyword makes the value of a variable not serializable.

- The `strictfp` keyword restricts floating-point calculations, making it the same result on every platform while performing operations in the floating-point variable.

- The `native` keyword declares a method implemented in platform-dependent code, such as C or C++.

Reserved identifiers

The five reserved identifiers in Java are as follows:

- `permits`
- `record`
- `sealed`
- `var`
- `yield`

Reserved words for literal values

The three reserved words in Java are as follows:

- `true`
- `false`
- `null`

Restricted keywords

The 10 restricted keywords in Java are as follows:

- `open`
- `module`
- `requires`
- `transitive`

- exports
- opens
- to
- uses
- provides
- with

They are called *restricted* because they cannot be identifiers in the context of a module declaration, which we will not discuss in this book. In all other places, it is possible to use them as identifiers, such as the following:

```
String to = "To";
String with = "abc";
```

Although you can, it is a good practice not to use them as identifiers, even outside module declaration.

Usage of the this and super keywords

The this keyword provides a reference to the current object. The super keyword refers to the parent class object. These keywords allow us to refer to a variable or method that has the same name in the current context and the parent object.

Usage of the this keyword

Here is the most popular example:

```
class A {
    private int count;
    public void setCount(int count) {
        count = count;           // 1
    }
    public int getCount(){
        return count;            // 2
    }
}
```

The first line looks ambiguous, but, in fact, it is not – the local variable, `int count`, hides the `int count` private property instance. We can demonstrate this by running the following code:

```
A a = new A();
a.setCount(2);
System.out.println(a.getCount());        //prints: 0
```

Using the `this` keyword fixes the problem:

```
class A {
    private int count;
    public void setCount(int count) {
        this.count = count;          // 1
    }
    public int getCount(){
        return this.count;           // 2
    }
}
```

Adding `this` to line 1 allows the value to be assigned the instance property. Adding `this` to line 2 does not make a difference, but it is good practice to use the `this` keyword every time with the `instance` property. It makes the code more readable and helps avoid difficult-to-trace errors, such as the one we have just demonstrated.

We have also seen the `this` keyword usage in the `equals()` method:

```
@Override
public boolean equals(Object o) {
    if (this == o) return true;
    if (!(o instanceof DemoClass)) return false;
    DemoClass demoClass = (DemoClass) o;
    return Objects.equals(getProp(), demoClass.getProp());
}
```

And, just to remind you, here are the examples of a constructor that we presented in *Chapter 2, Java Object-Oriented Programming (OOP)*:

```
class TheChildClass extends TheParentClass{
    private int x;
    private String prop;
```

```
    private String anotherProp = "abc";
    public TheChildClass(String prop){
        super(42);
        this.prop = prop;
    }
    public TheChildClass(int arg1, String arg2){
        super(arg1);
        this.prop = arg2;
    }
    // methods follow
}
```

In the preceding code, you can see not only the this keyword but also the usage of the super keyword, which we are going to discuss next.

Usage of the super keyword

The super keyword refers to the parent object. We saw its usage in the *Usage of the this keyword* section in a constructor already, where it has to be used only in the first line because the parent class object has to be created before the current object can be created. If the first line of the constructor is not super(), this means the parent class has a constructor without parameters.

The super keyword is especially helpful when a method is overridden and the method of the parent class has to be called:

```
class B  {
    public void someMethod() {
        System.out.println("Method of B class");
    }
}
class C extends B {
    public void someMethod() {
        System.out.println("Method of C class");
    }
    public void anotherMethod() {
        this.someMethod();     //prints: Method of C class
        super.someMethod();    //prints: Method of B class
```

```
    }
}
```

As we progress through this book, we will see more examples of using the `this` and `super` keywords.

Converting between primitive types

The maximum numeric value that a numeric type can hold depends on the number of bits allocated to it. The following are the number of bits for each numeric type of representation:

- `byte`: 8 bits
- `char`: 16 bits
- `short`: 16 bits
- `int`: 32 bits
- `long`: 64 bits
- `float`: 32 bits
- `double`: 64 bits

When a value of one numeric type is assigned to a variable of another numeric type and the new type can hold a bigger number, such a conversion is called a **widening conversion**. Otherwise, it is a **narrowing conversion**, which usually requires typecasting, using a `cast` operator.

Widening conversion

According to the Java Language Specification, there are 19 widening primitive type conversions:

- `byte` to `short`, `int`, `long`, `float`, or `double`
- `short` to `int`, `long`, `float`, or `double`
- `char` to `int`, `long`, `float`, or `double`
- `int` to `long`, `float`, or `double`
- `long` to `float` or `double`
- `float` to `double`

During widening conversion between integral types, and from some integral types to a floating-point type, the resulting value matches the original one exactly. However, conversion from int to float, from long to float, or from long to double may result in a loss of precision. The resulting floating-point value may be correctly rounded using IEEE 754 round-to-nearest mode, according to the Java Language Specification. Here are a few examples that demonstrate the loss of precision:

```java
int i = 123456789;
double d = (double)i;
System.out.println(i - (int)d);        //prints: 0


long l1 = 12345678L;
float f1 = (float)l1;
System.out.println(l1 - (long)f1);     //prints: 0


long l2 = 123456789L;
float f2 = (float)l2;
System.out.println(l2 - (long)f2);     //prints: -3


long l3 = 1234567891111111L;
double d3 = (double)l3;
System.out.println(l3 - (long)d3);     //prints: 0


long l4 = 12345678999999999L;
double d4 = (double)l4;
System.out.println(l4 - (long)d4);     //prints: -1
```

As you can see, conversion from int to double preserves the value, but long to float, or long to double, may lose precision. It depends on how big the value is. So, be aware and allow for some loss of precision if it is important for your calculations.

Narrowing conversion

The Java Language Specification identifies 22 narrowing primitive conversions:

- short to byte or char
- char to byte or short
- int to byte, short, or char

- `long` to `byte`, `short`, `char`, or `int`
- `float` to `byte`, `short`, `char`, `int`, or `long`
- `double` to `byte`, `short`, `char`, `int`, `long`, or `float`

Similar to the widening conversion, a narrowing conversion may result in a loss of precision, or even in a loss of the value magnitude. The narrowing conversion is more complicated than a widening one, and we are not going to discuss it in this book. It is important to remember that before performing a narrowing, you must make sure that the original value is smaller than the maximum value of the target type. Otherwise, you can get a completely different value (with lost magnitude). Look at the following example:

```
System.out.println(Integer.MAX_VALUE); //prints: 2147483647
double d1 = 1234567890.0;
System.out.println((int)d1);           //prints: 1234567890

double d2 = 12345678909999999999999.0;
System.out.println((int)d2);           //prints: 2147483647
```

As you can see from the examples, without checking first whether the target type can accommodate the value, you can get the result just equal to the maximum value of the target type. The rest will be just lost, no matter how big the difference is.

> **Important Note**
> Before performing a narrowing conversion, check whether the maximum value of the target type can hold the original value.

Please note that the conversion between the `char` type and the `byte` or `short` types is an even more complicated procedure because the `char` type is an unsigned numeric type, while the `byte` and `short` types are signed numeric types, so some loss of information is possible even when a value may look as though it fits in the target type.

Methods of conversion

In addition to the casting, each primitive type has a corresponding reference type (called a **wrapper class**) that has methods that convert the value of this type to any other primitive type, except `boolean` and `char`. All the wrapper classes belong to the `java.lang` package:

- `java.lang.Boolean`
- `java.lang.Byte`

- `java.lang.Character`
- `java.lang.Short`
- `java.lang.Integer`
- `java.lang.Long`
- `java.lang.Float`
- `java.lang.Double`

Each of them – except the `Boolean` and `Character` classes – extends the `java.lang.Number` abstract class, which has the following abstract methods:

- `byteValue()`
- `shortValue()`
- `intValue()`
- `longValue()`
- `floatValue()`
- `doubleValue()`

Such design forces the descendants of the `Number` class to implement all of them. The results they produce are the same as the `cast` operator in the previous examples:

```
int i = 123456789;
double d = Integer.valueOf(i).doubleValue();
System.out.println(i - (int)d);            //prints: 0


long l1 = 12345678L;
float f1 = Long.valueOf(l1).floatValue();
System.out.println(l1 - (long)f1);         //prints: 0


long l2 = 123456789L;
float f2 = Long.valueOf(l2).floatValue();
System.out.println(l2 - (long)f2);         //prints: -3


long l3 = 1234567891111111L;
double d3 = Long.valueOf(l3).doubleValue();
System.out.println(l3 - (long)d3);         //prints: 0
```

```
long 14 = 12345678999999999L;
double d4 = Long.valueOf(14).doubleValue();
System.out.println(14 - (long)d4);        //prints: -1


double d1 = 1234567890.0;
System.out.println(Double.valueOf(d1)
                            .intValue());  //prints: 1234567890


double d2 = 12345678909999999999999.0;
System.out.println(Double.valueOf(d2)
                            .intValue());  //prints: 2147483647
```

In addition, each of the wrapper classes has methods that allow the conversion of the String representation of a numeric value to the corresponding primitive numeric type or reference type, such as the following:

```
byte b1 = Byte.parseByte("42");
System.out.println(b1);                   //prints: 42
Byte b2 = Byte.decode("42");
System.out.println(b2);                   //prints: 42


boolean b3 = Boolean.getBoolean("property");
System.out.println(b3);                //prints: false
Boolean b4 = Boolean.valueOf("false");
System.out.println(b4);                //prints: false


int i1 = Integer.parseInt("42");
System.out.println(i1);                //prints: 42
Integer i2 = Integer.getInteger("property");
System.out.println(i2);                //prints: null


double d1 = Double.parseDouble("3.14");
System.out.println(d1);                //prints: 3.14
Double d2 = Double.valueOf("3.14");
System.out.println(d2);                //prints: 3.14
```

In the examples, please note the two methods that accept the `property` parameter. These two and similar methods of other wrapper classes convert a system property (if one exists) to the corresponding primitive type.

Each of the wrapper classes has the `toString(primitive value)` static method to convert the primitive type value to its `String` representation, such as the following:

```
String s1 = Integer.toString(42);
System.out.println(s1);            //prints: 42
String s2 = Double.toString(3.14);
System.out.println(s2);            //prints: 3.14
```

The wrapper classes have many other useful methods of conversion from one primitive type to another and to different formats. So, if you need to do something such as that, look into the corresponding wrapper class first.

Converting between primitive and reference types

The conversion of a primitive type value to an object of the corresponding wrapper class is called **boxing**. Also, the conversion from an object of a wrapper class to the corresponding primitive type value is called **unboxing**.

Boxing

The boxing of a primitive type can be done either automatically (called **autoboxing**) or explicitly using the `valueOf()` method available in each wrapper type:

```
int i1 = 42;
Integer i2 = i1;            //autoboxing
//Long l2 = i1;            //error
System.out.println(i2);     //prints: 42


i2 = Integer.valueOf(i1);
System.out.println(i2);     //prints: 42


Byte b = Byte.valueOf((byte)i1);
System.out.println(b);      //prints: 42
```

```
Short s = Short.valueOf((short)i1);
System.out.println(s);         //prints: 42


Long l = Long.valueOf(i1);
System.out.println(l);         //prints: 42


Float f = Float.valueOf(i1);
System.out.println(f);         //prints: 42.0


Double d = Double.valueOf(i1);
System.out.println(d);         //prints: 42.0
```

Note that autoboxing is only possible in relation to a corresponding wrapper type. Otherwise, the compiler generates an error.

The input value of the `valueOf()` method of the `Byte` and `Short` wrappers required casting because it was a narrowing of a primitive type we discussed in the previous section.

Unboxing

Unboxing can be accomplished using methods of the `Number` class implemented in each wrapper class:

```
Integer i1 = Integer.valueOf(42);
int i2 = i1.intValue();
System.out.println(i2);        //prints: 42


byte b = i1.byteValue();
System.out.println(b);         //prints: 42


short s = i1.shortValue();
System.out.println(s);         //prints: 42


long l = i1.longValue();
System.out.println(l);         //prints: 42


float f = i1.floatValue();
System.out.println(f);         //prints: 42.0
```

```
double d = i1.doubleValue();
System.out.println(d);         //prints: 42.0


Long l1 = Long.valueOf(42L);
long l2 = l1;                  //implicit unboxing
System.out.println(l2);        //prints: 42


double d2 = l1;                //implicit unboxing
System.out.println(d2);        //prints: 42.0


long l3 = i1;                  //implicit unboxing
System.out.println(l3);        //prints: 42


double d3 = i1;                //implicit unboxing
System.out.println(d3);        //prints: 42.0
```

As you can see from the comment in the example, the conversion from a wrapper type to the corresponding primitive type is not called **auto-unboxing**; it is called **implicit unboxing** instead. In contrast to autoboxing, it is possible to use implicit unboxing even between wrapping and primitive types that do not match.

Summary

In this chapter, you learned what Java packages are and the role they play in organizing code and class accessibility, including the `import` statement and access modifiers. You also became familiar with reference types – classes, interfaces, arrays, and enums. The default value of any reference type is `null`, including the `String` type.

You should now understand that the reference type is passed into a method by reference and how the `equals()` method is used and can be overridden. You also had an opportunity to study the full list of reserved and restricted keywords and learned the meaning and usage of the `this` and `super` keywords.

The chapter concluded by describing the process and methods of conversion between primitive types, wrapping types, and `String` literals.

In the next chapter, we will talk about the Java exceptions framework, checked and unchecked (runtime) exceptions, `try-catch-finally` blocks, `throws` and `throw` statements, and the best practices of exception handling.

Quiz

1. Select all the statements that are correct:

    A. The `Package` statement describes the class or interface location.

    B. The `Package` statement describes the class or interface name.

    C. `Package` is a fully qualified name.

    D. The `Package` name and class name compose a fully qualified name of the class.

2. Select all the statements that are correct:

    A. The `Import` statement allows the use of the fully qualified name.

    B. The `Import` statement has to be the first in the `.java` file.

    C. The `Group import` statement brings in the classes (and interfaces) of one package only.

    D. The `Import statement` allows the use of the fully qualified name to be avoided.

3. Select all the statements that are correct:

    A. Without an access modifier, the class is accessible only by other classes and interfaces of the same package.

    B. The private method of a private class is accessible to other classes declared in the same `.java` file.

    C. The public method of a private class is accessible to other classes not declared in the same `.java` file but from the same package.

    D. The protected method is accessible only to the descendants of the class.

4. Select all the statements that are correct:

    A. Private methods can be overloaded but not overridden.

    B. Protected methods can be overridden but not overloaded.

    C. Methods without an access modifier can be both overridden and overloaded.

    D. Private methods can access private properties of the same class.

5. Select all the statements that are correct:

    A. Narrowing and downcasting are synonyms.

    B. Widening and downcasting are synonyms.

    C. Widening and upcasting are synonyms.

    D. Widening and narrowing have nothing in common with upcasting
        and downcasting.

6. Select all the statements that are correct:

    A. `Array` is an object.

    B. `Array` has a length that is a number of the elements it can hold.

    C. The first element of an array has the index 1.

    D. The second element of an array has the index 1.

7. Select all the statements that are correct:

    A. Enum contains constants.

    B. Enum always has a constructor, either default or explicit.

    C. An enum constant can have properties.

    D. Enum can have constants of any reference type.

8. Select all the statements that are correct:

    A. Any reference type passed in as a parameter can be modified.

    B. A new `String()` object passed in as a parameter can be modified.

    C. An object reference value passed in as a parameter cannot be modified.

    D. An array passed in as a parameter can have elements assigned to
        different values.

9. Select all the statements that are correct:

    A. Reserved keywords cannot be used.

    B. Restricted keywords cannot be used as identifiers.

    C. A reserved `identifier` keyword cannot be used as an identifier.

    D. A reserved keyword cannot be used as an identifier.

10. Select all the statements that are correct:

   A. The this keyword refers to the current class.

   B. The super keyword refers to the super class.

   C. The this and super keywords refer to objects.

   D. The this and super keywords refer to methods.

11. Select all the statements that are correct:

   A. The widening of a primitive type makes the value bigger.

   B. The narrowing of a primitive type always changes the type of the value.

   C. The widening of a primitive type can be done only after narrowing a conversion.

   D. Narrowing makes the value smaller.

12. Select all the statements that are correct:

   A. Boxing puts a limit on the value.

   B. Unboxing creates a new value.

   C. Boxing creates a reference-type object.

   D. Unboxing deletes a reference-type object.

Part 2: Building Blocks of Java

This section will give you a deeper understanding of core programming concepts with a sample program. This will enable to advance to the next step of building projects in Java.

This part contains the following chapters:

4

Exception Handling

In *Chapter 1, Getting Started with Java 17*, we briefly introduced exceptions. In this chapter, we will treat this topic more systematically. There are two kinds of exceptions in Java: checked and unchecked. We'll demonstrate each of them, and the differences between the two will be explained. Additionally, you will learn about the syntax of the Java constructs related to exception handling and the best practices to address (that is, handle) those exceptions. The chapter will end on the related topic of assertion statements, which can be used to debug the code in production.

In this chapter, we will cover the following topics:

- The Java exceptions framework
- Checked and unchecked (runtime) exceptions
- The try, catch, and finally blocks
- The throws statement
- The throw statement
- The assert statement
- Best practices of exception handling

So, let's begin!

Technical requirements

To be able to execute the code examples that are provided in this chapter, you will need the following:

- A computer with a Microsoft Windows, Apple macOS, or Linux operating system
- Java SE version 17, or later
- An IDE or code editor that you prefer

The instructions for how to set up a Java SE and IntelliJ IDEA editor were provided in *Chapter 1, Getting Started with Java 17*. The files with the code examples for this chapter are available on GitHub in the `https://github.com/PacktPublishing/Learn-Java-17-Programming.git` repository. Please search in the `examples/src/main/java/com/packt/learnjava/ch04_exceptions` folder.

The Java exceptions framework

As described in *Chapter 1, Getting Started with Java 17*, an unexpected condition can cause the **Java Virtual Machine** (**JVM**) or the application code to create and throw an exception object. As soon as that happens, the control flow is transferred to the `catch` clause, that is, if the exception was thrown inside a `try` block. Let's look at an example. Consider the following method:

```
void method(String s){
    if(s.equals("abc")){
        System.out.println("Equals abc");
    } else {
        System.out.println("Not equal");
    }
}
```

If the input parameter value is `null`, you could expect to see the output as `Not equal`. Unfortunately, that is not the case. The `s.equals("abc")` expression calls the `equals()` method on an object referred to by the `s` variable; however, if the `s` variable is `null`, it does not refer to any object. Let's see what happens next.

Let's run the following code (that is, the `catchException1()` method in the Framework class):

```
try {
    method(null);
```

```
} catch (Exception ex){
    System.out.println("catchException1():");
    System.out.println(ex.getClass().getCanonicalName());
                        //prints: java.lang.NullPointerException
    waitForStackTrace();
    ex.printStackTrace();  //prints: see the screenshot
    if(ex instanceof NullPointerException){
        //do something
    } else {
        //do something else
    }
}
}
```

The preceding code includes the `waitForStackTrace()` method, allowing you to wait a bit until the stack trace has been generated. Otherwise, the output would be out of sequence. The output of this code appears as follows:

```
catchException1():
java.lang.NullPointerException
java.lang.NullPointerException: Cannot invoke "String.
equals(Object)" because "s" is null
    at com.packt.learnjava.ch04_exceptions.Framework.
method(Framework.java:14)
    at com.packt.learnjava.ch04_exceptions.Framework.
catchException1(Framework.java:24)
    at com.packt.learnjava.ch04_exceptions.Framework.
main(Framework.java:8)
```

As you can see, the method prints the name of the exception class, followed by a **stack trace**. The name of **stack trace** comes from the way the method calls are stored (as a stack) in JVM memory: one method calls another, which, in turn, calls another, and so on. After the most inner method returns, the stack is walked back, and the returned method (**stack frame**) is removed from the stack. We will talk about the JVM memory structure, in more detail, in *Chapter 9, JVM Structure and Garbage Collection*. When an exception happens, all the stack content (such as the stack frames) is returned as the stack trace. This allows us to track down the line of code that caused the problem.

In the preceding code example, different blocks of code were executed depending on the type of the exception. In our case, it was `java.lang.NullPointerException`. If the application code does not catch it, this exception would propagate through the stack of the called methods into the JVM, which will then stop executing the application. To avoid this happening, the exception can be caught and code can be executed to recover from the exceptional condition.

The purpose of the exception handling framework in Java is to protect the application code from an unexpected condition and, if possible, recover from it. In the following sections, we will dissect this concept in more detail and rewrite the given example using the framework capability.

Checked and unchecked exceptions

If you look up the documentation of the `java.lang` package API, you will discover that the package contains almost three dozen exception classes and a couple of dozen error classes. Both groups extend the `java.lang.Throwable` class, inherit all the methods from it, and do not add other methods. The methods that are most often used in the `java.lang.Throwable` class include the following:

- `void printStackTrace()`: This outputs the stack trace (stack frames) of the method calls.

- `StackTraceElement[] getStackTrace()`: This returns the same information as `printStackTrace()` but allows programmatic access of any frame of the stack trace.

- `String getMessage()`: This retrieves the message that often contains a user-friendly explanation of the reason for the exception or error.

- `Throwable getCause()`: This retrieves an optional object of `java.lang.Throwable` that was the original reason for the exception (but the author of the code decided to wrap it in another exception or error).

All errors extend the `java.lang.Error` class, which, in turn, extends the `java.lang.Throwable` class. Typically, an error is thrown by JVM and, according to the official documentation, *indicates serious problems that a reasonable application should not try to catch*. Here are a few examples:

- `OutOfMemoryError`: This is thrown when the JVM runs out of memory and cannot clean the memory using garbage collection.

- `StackOverflowError`: This is thrown when the memory allocated for the stack of the method calls is not enough to store another stack frame.

- `NoClassDefFoundError`: This is thrown when the JVM cannot find the definition of the class requested by the currently loaded class.

The authors of the framework assumed that an application cannot recover from these errors automatically, which proved to be a largely correct assumption. That is why programmers, typically, do not catch errors, but that is beyond the scope of this book.

On the other hand, exceptions are typically related to application-specific problems and often do not require us to shut down the application and allow recovery. Usually, that is why programmers catch them and implement an alternative (to the main flow) path of the application logic, or at least report the problem without shutting down the application. Here are a few examples:

- `ArrayIndexOutOfBoundsException`: This is thrown when the code tries to access the element by the index that is equal to, or bigger than, the array length (remember that the first element of an array has an index of 0, so the index is equal to the array length points outside of the array).

- `ClassCastException`: This is thrown when the code casts a reference to a class or an interface not associated with the object referred to by the variable.

- `NumberFormatException`: This is thrown when the code tries to convert a string into a numeric type, but the string does not contain the necessary number format.

All exceptions extend the `java.lang.Exception` class, which, in turn, extends the `java.lang.Throwable` class. That is why, by catching an object of the `java.lang.Exception` class, the code catches an object of any exception type. In the *The Java exceptions framework* section, we demonstrated this by catching `java.lang.NullPointerException` in the same way.

One of the exceptions is `java.lang.RuntimeException`. The exceptions that extend it are called **runtime exceptions** or **unchecked exceptions**. We have already mentioned some of them: `NullPointerException`, `ArrayIndexOutOfBoundsException`, `ClassCastException`, and `NumberFormatException`. The reason they are called runtime exceptions is clear; the reason they are called unchecked exceptions will become clear next.

Those exceptions that do not have `java.lang.RuntimeException` among their ancestors are called **checked exceptions**. The reason for such a name is that the compiler makes sure (checks) that these exceptions have either been caught or listed in the `throws` clause of the method (please refer to the *The throws statement* section). This design forces the programmer to make a conscious decision, either to catch the checked exception or inform the client of the method that this exception might be thrown by the method and has to be processed (handled) by the client. Here are a few examples of checked exceptions:

- `ClassNotFoundException`: This is thrown when an attempt to load a class using its string name with the `forName()` method of the `Class` class has failed.

- `CloneNotSupportedException`: This is thrown when the code tries to clone an object that does not implement the `Cloneable` interface.

- `NoSuchMethodException`: This is thrown when there is no method called by the code.

Not all exceptions reside in the `java.lang` package. Many other packages contain exceptions related to the functionality that is supported by the package. For example, there is a `java.util.MissingResourceException` runtime exception and a `java.io.IOException` checked exception.

Despite not being forced, programmers often catch runtime (unchecked) exceptions to have better control of the program flow, making the behavior of an application more stable and predictable. By the way, all errors are also runtime (unchecked) exceptions. However, as we mentioned already, typically, it is not possible to handle them programmatically, so there is no point in catching descendants of the `java.lang.Error` class.

The try, catch, and finally blocks

When an exception is thrown inside a `try` block, it redirects the control flow to the first `catch` clause. If there is no `catch` block that can capture the exception (but the `finally` block has to be in place), the exception propagates up and out of the method. If there is more than one `catch` clause, the compiler forces you to arrange them so that the child exception is listed before the parent exception. Let's look at the following example:

```
void someMethod(String s){
    try {
       method(s);
    } catch (NullPointerException ex){
       //do something
```

```
    } catch (Exception ex){
        //do something else
    }
}
```

In the preceding example, a `catch` block with `NullPointerException` is placed before the block with `Exception` because `NullPointerException` extends `RuntimeException`, which, in turn, extends `Exception`. We could even implement this example, as follows:

```
void someMethod(String s){
    try {
        method(s);
    } catch (NullPointerException ex){
        //do something
    } catch (RuntimeException ex){
        //do something else
    } catch (Exception ex){
        //do something different
    }
}
```

Note that the first `catch` clause only catches `NullPointerException`. Other exceptions that extend `RuntimeException` will be caught by the second `catch` clause. The rest of the exception types (that is, all of the checked exceptions) will be caught by the last `catch` block. Note that errors will not be caught by any of these `catch` clauses. To catch them, you should add a `catch` clause for `Error` (in any position) or `Throwable` (after the last `catch` clause in the previous example). However, usually, programmers do not do it and allow errors to propagate into the JVM.

Having a `catch` block for each exception type allows us to provide specific exception type processing. However, if there is no difference in the exception processing, you can simply have one `catch` block with the `Exception` base class to catch all types of exceptions:

```
void someMethod(String s){
    try {
        method(s);
    } catch (Exception ex){
        //do something
```

```
        }
    }
```

If none of the clauses catch the exception, it is thrown further up until it is either handled by a `try...catch` statement in one of the method callers or propagates all the way out of the application code. In such a case, the JVM terminates the application and exits.

Adding a `finally` block does not change the described behavior. If present, it is always executed, whether an exception has been generated or not. Usually, a `finally` block is used to release the resources, to close a database connection, a file, or similar. However, if the resource implements the `Closeable` interface, it is better to use the `try-with-resources` statement, which allows you to release the resources automatically. The following demonstrates how it can be done with Java 7:

```
try (Connection conn = DriverManager
                .getConnection("dburl", "username", "password");
     ResultSet rs = conn.createStatement()
                .executeQuery("select * from some_table")) {
    while (rs.next()) {
        //process the retrieved data
    }
} catch (SQLException ex) {
    //Do something
    //The exception was probably caused
    //by incorrect SQL statement
}
```

The preceding example creates the database connection, retrieves data and processes it, and then closes (calls the `close()` method) the `conn` and `rs` objects.

Java 9 enhances the `try-with-resources` statement's capabilities by allowing the creation of objects that represent resources outside the `try` block, along with the use of them in a `try-with-resources` statement, as follows:

```
void method(Connection conn, ResultSet rs) {
    try (conn; rs) {
        while (rs.next()) {
            //process the retrieved data
        }
    } catch (SQLException ex) {
```

```
    //Do something
    //The exception was probably caused
    //by incorrect SQL statement
  }
}
```

The preceding code looks much cleaner, although, in practice, programmers prefer to create and release (close) resources in the same context. If that is your preference too, consider using the `throws` statement in conjunction with the `try-with-resources` statement.

The throws statement

We have to deal with `SQLException` because it is a checked exception, and the `getConnection()`, `createStatement()`, `executeQuery()`, and `next()` methods declare it in their `throws` clause. Here is an example:

```
Statement createStatement() throws SQLException;
```

This means that the method's author warns the method's users that it might throw such an exception, forcing them to either catch the exception or to declare it in the `throws` clause of their methods. In our preceding example, we have chosen to catch it using two `try...catch` statements. Alternatively, we can list the exception in the `throws` clause and, thus, remove the clutter by effectively pushing the burden of the exception handling onto the users of our method:

```
void throwsDemo() throws SQLException {
    Connection conn =
      DriverManager.getConnection("url","user","pass");
    ResultSet rs = conn.createStatement().executeQuery(
      "select * ...");
    try (conn; rs) {
        while (rs.next()) {
            //process the retrieved data
        }
    } finally {
        try {
            if(conn != null) {
                conn.close();
```

```
        }
    } finally {
        if(rs != null) {
            rs.close();
        }
    }
}
```

We got rid of the catch clause, but we need the finally block to close the created conn and rs objects.

Please, notice how we included code that closes the conn object in a try block and we included the code that closes the rs object in the finally block. This way we make sure that an exception during closing of the conn object will not prevent us from closing the rs object.

This code looks less clear than the try-with-resources statement we demonstrated in the previous section. We show it just to demonstrate all the possibilities and how to avoid possible danger (of not closing the resources) if you decide to do it yourself, not letting the try-with-resources statement do it for you automatically.

But let us get back to the discussion of the throws statement.

The throws clause allows but does not require us to list unchecked exceptions. Adding unchecked exceptions does not force the method's users to handle them.

Finally, if the method throws several different exceptions, it is possible to list the base Exception exception class instead of listing all of them. That will make the compiler happy; however, this is not considered a good practice because it hides the details of particular exceptions that a method's user might expect.

Please note that the compiler does not check what kind of exception the code in the method's body can throw. So, it is possible to list any exception in the throws clause, which might lead to unnecessary overhead. If, by mistake, a programmer includes a checked exception in the throws clause that is never actually thrown by the method, the method's user could write a catch block for it that is never executed.

The throw statement

The throw statement allows the throwing of any exception that a programmer deems necessary. You can even create your own exception. To create a checked exception, extend the java.lang.Exception class as follows:

```
class MyCheckedException extends Exception{
    public MyCheckedException(String message){
        super(message);
    }
    //add code you need to have here
}
```

Also, to create an unchecked exception, extend the java.lang.RunitmeException class, as follows:

```
class MyUncheckedException extends RuntimeException{
    public MyUncheckedException(String message){
        super(message);
    }
    //add code you need to have here
}
```

Notice the *add code you need to have here* comment. You can add methods and properties to the custom exception as with any other regular class, but programmers rarely do it. In fact, the best practices explicitly recommend avoiding the use of exceptions for driving business logic. Exceptions should be what the name implies, covering only exceptional or very rare situations.

However, if you need to announce an exceptional condition, use the throw keyword and the new operator to create and trigger the propagation of an exception object. Here are a few examples:

```
throw new Exception("Something happened");
throw new RuntimeException("Something happened");
throw new MyCheckedException("Something happened");
throw new MyUncheckedException("Something happened");
```

It is even possible to throw null, as follows:

```
throw null;
```

The result of the preceding statement is the same as the result of this one:

```
throw new NullPointerException;
```

In both cases, an object of an unchecked NullPointerException exception begins to propagate through the system, until it is caught either by the application or the JVM.

The assert statement

Once in a while, a programmer needs to know whether a particular condition has happened in the code, even after the application has already been deployed to production. At the same time, there is no need to run this check all the time. That is where the assert branching statement comes in handy. Here is an example:

```
public someMethod(String s){
    //any code goes here
    assert(assertSomething(x, y, z));
    //any code goes here
}
boolean assertSomething(int x, String y, double z){
    //do something and return boolean
}
```

In the preceding code, the assert() method takes input from the assertSomething() method. If the assertSomething() method returns false, the program stops executing.

The assert() method is executed only when the JVM is run using the -ea option. The -ea flag should not be used in production, except maybe temporarily for testing purposes. This is because it creates an overhead that affects the application performance.

Best practices of exception handling

Checked exceptions were designed to be used for recoverable conditions when an application can do something automatically to amend or work around the problem. In practice, this doesn't happen very often. Typically, when an exception is caught, the application logs the stack trace and aborts the current action. Based on the logged information, the application support team modifies the code to address the condition that is unaccounted for or to prevent it from occurring in the future.

Each application is different, so best practices depend on the particular application requirements, design, and context. In general, it seems that there is an agreement in the development community to avoid using checked exceptions and to minimize their propagation in the application code. The following is a list of a few other recommendations that have proved to be useful:

- Always catch all checked exceptions that are close to the source.
- If in doubt, catch unchecked exceptions that are also close to the source.
- Handle the exception as close to the source as possible because that is where the context is the most specific and where the root cause resides.
- Do not throw checked exceptions unless you have to because you force the building of extra code for a case that might never happen.
- Convert third-party checked exceptions into unchecked ones by re-throwing them as `RuntimeException` with the corresponding message if you have to.
- Do not create custom exceptions unless you have to.
- Do not drive business logic by using the exception handling mechanism unless you have to.
- Customize generic `RuntimeException` exceptions by using the system of messages and, optionally, the `enum` type instead of using the exception type to communicate the cause of the error.

There are many other possible tips and recommendations; however, if you follow these, you are probably going to be fine in the vast majority of situations. With that, we conclude this chapter.

Summary

In this chapter, you were introduced to the Java exception handling framework, and you learned about two kinds of exceptions—checked and unchecked (runtime)—and how to handle them using `try-catch-finally` and `throws` statements. Also, you learned how to generate (throw) exceptions and how to create your own (custom) exceptions. The chapter concluded with the best practices of exception handling which, if followed consistently, will help you to write clean and clear code, which is pleasant to write and easy to understand and maintain.

In the next chapter, we will talk about strings and their processing in detail, along with input/output streams and file reading and writing techniques.

Quiz

1. What is a stack trace? Select all that apply:

    A. A list of classes currently loaded

    B. A list of methods currently executing

    C. A list of code lines currently executing

    D. A list of variables currently used

2. What kinds of exceptions are there? Select all that apply:

    A. Compilation exceptions

    B. Runtime exceptions

    C. Read exceptions

    D. Write exceptions

3. What is the output of the following code?

    ```
    try {
        throw null;
    } catch (RuntimeException ex) {
        System.out.print("RuntimeException ");
    } catch (Exception ex) {
        System.out.print("Exception ");
    } catch (Error ex) {
        System.out.print("Error ");
    } catch (Throwable ex) {
        System.out.print("Throwable ");
    } finally {
        System.out.println("Finally ");
    }
    ```

    A. A RuntimeException error

    B. Exception Error Finally

    C. RuntimeException Finally

    D. Throwable Finally

4. Which of the following methods will compile without an error?

```
void method1() throws Exception { throw null; }
void method2() throws RuntimeException { throw null; }
void method3() throws Throwable { throw null; }
void method4() throws Error { throw null; }
```

A. method1()

B. method2()

C. method3()

D. method4()

5. Which of the following statements will compile without an error?

```
throw new NullPointerException("Hi there!"); //1
throws new Exception("Hi there!");           //2
throw RuntimeException("Hi there!");         //3
throws RuntimeException("Hi there!");        //4
```

A. 1

B. 2

C. 3

D. 4

6. Assuming that int x = 4, which of the following statements will compile without an error?

```
assert (x > 3); //1
assert (x = 3); //2
assert (x < 4); //3
assert (x = 4); //4
```

A. 1

B. 2

C. 3

D. 4

7. Which are the best practices from the following list?

    A. Always catch all exceptions and errors.

    B. Always catch all exceptions.

    C. Never throw unchecked exceptions.

    D. Try not to throw checked exceptions unless you have to.

5
Strings, Input/Output, and Files

In this chapter, you will be presented with the `String` class methods in more detail. We will also discuss popular string utilities from standard libraries and the Apache Commons project. An overview of Java input/output streams and the related classes of the `java.io` packages will follow, along with some classes of the `org.apache.commons.io` package. The file-managing classes and their methods are described in a dedicated section. After completing this chapter, you will be able to write code that processes strings and files, using standard Java API and Apache Commons utilities.

The following topics will be covered in this chapter:

- String processing
- I/O streams
- File management
- Apache Commons' `FileUtils` and `IOUtils` utilities

Technical requirements

To be able to execute the code examples provided in this chapter, you will need the following:

- A computer with a Microsoft Windows, Apple macOS, or Linux operating system

- Java SE version 17 or later

- An IDE or code editor you prefer

The instructions for how to set up a Java SE and IntelliJ IDEA editor were provided in *Chapter 1*, *Getting Started with Java 17*, in this book. The files with the code examples for this chapter are available in the GitHub repository at `https://github.com/PacktPublishing/Learn-Java-17-Programming.git` in the `examples/src/main/java/com/packt/learnjava/ch05_stringsIoStreams` folder.

String processing

In mainstream programming, `String` probably is the most popular class. In *Chapter 1*, *Getting Started with Java 17*, we learned about this class, its literals, and its specific feature called **string immutability**. In this section, we will explain how a string can be processed using the `String` class methods and utility classes from the standard library, and the `StringUtils` class from the `org.apache.commons.lang3` package in particular.

Methods of the String class

The `String` class has more than 70 methods that enable analyzing, modifying, and comparing strings, and converting numeric literals into the corresponding string literals. To see all the methods of the `String` class, please refer to the Java API online at `https://docs.oracle.com/en/java/javase`.

String analysis

The `length()` method returns the number of characters in the string, as shown in the following code:

```
String s7 = "42";
System.out.println(s7.length());      //prints: 2
System.out.println("0 0".length()); //prints: 3
```

The following `isEmpty()` method returns `true` when the length of the string (count of characters) is `0`:

```
System.out.println("".isEmpty());    //prints: true
System.out.println(" ".isEmpty());   //prints: false
```

The `indexOf()` and `lastIndexOf()` methods return the position of the specified substring in the string shown in this code snippet:

```
String s6 = "abc42t%";
System.out.println(s6.indexOf(s7));              //prints: 3
System.out.println(s6.indexOf("a"));             //prints: 0
System.out.println(s6.indexOf("xyz"));           //prints: -1
System.out.println("ababa".lastIndexOf("ba"));   //prints: 3
```

As you can see, the first character in the string has a position (index) of `0`, and the absence of the specified substring results in the index `-1`.

The `matches()` method applies the regular expression (passed as an argument) to the string as follows:

```
System.out.println("abc".matches("[a-z]+"));    //prints: true
System.out.println("ab1".matches("[a-z]+"));    //prints: false
```

Regular expressions are outside the scope of this book. You can learn about them at `https://www.regular-expressions.info`. In the preceding example, the `[a-z]+` expression matches one or more letters only.

String comparison

In *Chapter 3*, *Java Fundamentals*, we talked about the `equals()` method that returns `true` only when two `String` objects or literals are spelled exactly the same way. The following code snippet demonstrates how it works:

```
String s1 = "abc";
String s2 = "abc";
String s3 = "acb";
System.out.println(s1.equals(s2));       //prints: true
System.out.println(s1.equals(s3));       //prints: false
System.out.println("abc".equals(s2));    //prints: true
System.out.println("abc".equals(s3));    //prints: false
```

Another `String` class, the `equalsIgnoreCase()` method, does a similar job but ignores the difference in the characters' case, as follows:

```
String s4 = "aBc";
String s5 = "Abc";
System.out.println(s4.equals(s5));             //prints: false
System.out.println(s4.equalsIgnoreCase(s5)); //prints: true
```

The `contentEquals()` method acts similar to the `equals()` method, as shown here:

```
String s1 = "abc";
String s2 = "abc";
System.out.println(s1.contentEquals(s2));       //prints: true
System.out.println("abc".contentEquals(s2)); //prints: true
```

The difference is that the `equals()` method checks whether both values are represented by the `String` class, while `contentEquals()` compares only the characters (content) of the character sequence. The character sequence can be represented by `String`, `StringBuilder`, `StringBuffer`, `CharBuffer`, or any other class that implements a `CharSequence` interface. Nevertheless, the `contentEquals()` method will return `true` if both sequences contain the same characters, while the `equals()` method will return `false` if one of the sequences is not created by the `String` class.

The `contains()` method returns `true` if the `string` contains a certain substring, as follows:

```
String s6 = "abc42t%";
String s7 = "42";
String s8 = "xyz";
System.out.println(s6.contains(s7));       //prints: true
System.out.println(s6.contains(s8));       //prints: false
```

The `startsWith()` and `endsWith()` methods perform a similar check but only at the start of the string or the end of the string value, as shown in the following code:

```
String s6 = "abc42t%";
String s7 = "42";

System.out.println(s6.startsWith(s7));       //prints: false
System.out.println(s6.startsWith("ab"));     //prints: true
```

```
System.out.println(s6.startsWith("42", 3)); //prints: true


System.out.println(s6.endsWith(s7));         //prints: false
System.out.println(s6.endsWith("t%"));       //prints: true
```

The compareTo() and compareToIgnoreCase() methods compare strings lexicographically – based on the Unicode value of each character in the strings. They return the value 0 if the strings are equal, a negative integer value if the first string is lexicographically less (has a smaller Unicode value) than the second string, and a positive integer value if the first string is lexicographically greater than the second string (has a bigger Unicode value), as shown here:

```
String s4 = "aBc";
String s5 = "Abc";
System.out.println(s4.compareTo(s5));             //prints: 32
System.out.println(s4.compareToIgnoreCase(s5));   //prints: 0
System.out.println(s4.codePointAt(0));            //prints: 97
System.out.println(s5.codePointAt(0));            //prints: 65
```

From this code snippet, you can see that the compareTo() and compareToIgnoreCase() methods are based on the code points of the characters that compose the strings. The reason the s4 string is bigger than the s5 string by 32 is because the code point of the a character (97) is bigger than the code point of the A character (65) by 32.

The given example also shows that the codePointAt() method returns the code point of the character located in the string at the specified position. The code points were described in the *Integral types* section of *Chapter 1, Getting Started with Java 17*.

String transformation

The substring() method returns the substring, starting with the specified position (index), as follows:

```
System.out.println("42".substring(0));    //prints: 42
System.out.println("42".substring(1));    //prints: 2
System.out.println("42".substring(2));    //prints:
System.out.println("42".substring(3));
                              //error: index out of range: -1
```

```
String s6 = "abc42t%";
System.out.println(s6.substring(3));       //prints: 42t%
System.out.println(s6.substring(3, 5));  //prints: 42
```

The format() method uses the passed-in first argument as a template and inserts the other arguments in the corresponding position of the template sequentially. The following code example prints the sentence Hey, Nick! Give me 2 apples, please! three times:

```
String t = "Hey, %s! Give me %d apples, please!";
System.out.println(String.format(t, "Nick", 2));
String t1 = String.format(t, "Nick", 2);
System.out.println(t1);
System.out.println(String.format("Hey,
               %s! Give me %d apples, please!", "Nick", 2));
```

The %s and %d symbols are called **format specifiers**. There are many specifiers and various flags that allow a programmer to fine-control the result. You can read about them in the API of the java.util.Formatter class.

The concat() method works the same way as the arithmetic operator (+), as shown here:

```
String s7 = "42";
String s8 = "xyz";
String newStr1 = s7.concat(s8);
System.out.println(newStr1);     //prints: 42xyz


String newStr2 = s7 + s8;
System.out.println(newStr2);     //prints: 42xyz
```

The following join() method acts similarly but allows the addition of a delimiter:

```
String newStr1 = String.join(",", "abc", "xyz");
System.out.println(newStr1);          //prints: abc,xyz


List<String> list = List.of("abc","xyz");
String newStr2 = String.join(",", list);
System.out.println(newStr2);          //prints: abc,xyz
```

The following group of the `replace()`, `replaceFirst()`, and `replaceAll()` methods replace certain characters in the string with the provided ones:

```
System.out.println("abcbc".replace("bc","42"));
                                                //prints: a4242
System.out.println("abcbc".replaceFirst("bc", "42"));
                                                //prints: a42bc
System.out.println("ab11bcd".replaceAll("[a-z]+", "42"));
                                                //prints: 421142
```

The first line of the preceding code replaces all the instances of `"bc"` with `"42"`. The second replaces only the first instance of `"bc"` with `"42"`, and the last one replaces all the substrings that match the provided regular expression with `"42"`.

The `toLowerCase()` and `toUpperCase()` methods change the case of the whole string, as shown here:

```
System.out.println("aBc".toLowerCase());    //prints: abc
System.out.println("aBc".toUpperCase());    //prints: ABC
```

The `split()` method breaks the string into substrings, using the provided character as the delimiter, as follows:

```
String[] arr = "abcbc".split("b");
System.out.println(arr[0]);    //prints: a
System.out.println(arr[1]);    //prints: c
System.out.println(arr[2]);    //prints: c
```

There are several `valueOf()` methods that transform the values of a primitive type to a `String` type, such as the following:

```
float f = 23.42f;
String sf = String.valueOf(f);
System.out.println(sf);            //prints: 23.42
```

There are also the () and getChars() methods that transform a string to an array of a corresponding type, while the chars() method creates an IntStream of characters (their code points). We will talk about streams in *Chapter 14, Java Standard Streams*.

Methods added with Java 11

Java 11 introduced several new methods in the String class.

The repeat() method allows you to create a new String value based on multiple concatenations of the same string, as shown in the following code:

```
System.out.println("ab".repeat(3)); //prints: ababab
System.out.println("ab".repeat(1)); //prints: ab
System.out.println("ab".repeat(0)); //prints:
```

The isBlank() method returns true if the string has a length of 0 or consists of white spaces only, such as the following:

```
System.out.println("".isBlank());        //prints: true
System.out.println("  ".isBlank());      //prints: true
System.out.println(" a ".isBlank());     //prints: false
```

The stripLeading() method removes leading white spaces from the string, the stripTrailing() method removes trailing white spaces, and the strip() method removes both, as shown here:

```
String sp = "   abc   ";
System.out.println("'" + sp + "'");
                                        //prints: '   abc   '
System.out.println("'" + sp.stripLeading() + "'");
                                        //prints: 'abc   '
System.out.println("'" + sp.stripTrailing() + "'");
                                        //prints: '   abc'
System.out.println("'" + sp.strip() + "'");
                                        //prints: 'abc'
```

And finally, the `lines()` method breaks the string by line terminators and returns a `Stream<String>` of resulting lines. A line terminator is an escape sequence line feed (`\n`) (`\u000a`), a carriage return (`\r`) (`\u000d`), or a carriage return followed immediately by a line feed (`\r\n`) (`\u000d\u000a`), such as the following:

```
String line = "Line 1\nLine 2\rLine 3\r\nLine 4";
line.lines().forEach(System.out::println);
```

The output of the preceding code is as follows:

We will talk about streams in *Chapter 14, Java Standard Streams*.

String utilities

In addition to the `String` class, there are many other classes that have methods that process the `String` values. Among the most useful is the `StringUtils` class of the `org.apache.commons.lang3` package from a project called an **Apache Commons**, maintained by an open source community of programmers called the **Apache Software Foundation**. We will talk more about this project and its libraries in *Chapter 7, Java Standard and External Libraries*. To use it in your project, add the following dependency in the `pom.xml` file:

```
<dependency>
    <groupId>org.apache.commons</groupId>
    <artifactId>commons-lang3</artifactId>
    <version>3.8.1</version>
</dependency>
```

The `StringUtils` class is the favorite of many programmers. It complements methods of the `String` class by providing the following null-safe operations (when a method is implemented in such a way – by checking the values for null, for example – that it does not throw `NullPointerException`):

- `isBlank(CharSequence cs)`: Returns `true` if the input value is white space, empty (`""`), or `null`

- `isNotBlank(CharSequence cs)`: Returns `false` when the preceding method returns `true`

- `isEmpty(CharSequence cs)`: Returns `true` if the input value is empty (`""`) or `null`

- `isNotEmpty(CharSequence cs)`: Returns `false` when the preceding method returns `true`

- `trim(String str)`: Removes leading and trailing white space from the input value and processes `null`, empty (`""`), and white space, as follows:

```
System.out.println("'" + StringUtils.trim(" x ")+"'");
                                            //prints: 'x'
System.out.println(StringUtils.trim(null));
                                            //prints: null
System.out.println("'" + StringUtils.trim("") + "'");
                                            //prints: ''
System.out.println("'" + StringUtils.trim("   ")+"'");
                                            //prints: ''
```

- `trimToNull(String str)`: Removes leading and trailing white space from the input value and processes `null`, empty (`""`), and white space, as follows:

```
System.out.println("'"+StringUtils.trimToNull(" x ")+"'");
                                            // prints: 'x'
System.out.println(StringUtils.trimToNull(null));
                                            //prints: null
System.out.println(StringUtils.trimToNull(""));
                                            //prints: null
System.out.println(StringUtils.trimToNull("   "));
                                            //prints: null
```

- `trimToEmpty(String str)`: Removes leading and trailing white space from the input value and processes `null`, empty (`""`), and white space, as follows:

```
System.out.println("'" +
        StringUtils.trimToEmpty(" x ") + "'");   // 'x'
System.out.println("'" +
        StringUtils.trimToEmpty(null) + "'");    // ''
System.out.println("'" +
        StringUtils.trimToEmpty("") + "'");      // ''
System.out.println("'" +
        StringUtils.trimToEmpty("   ") + "'");   // ''
```

- `strip(String str)`, `stripToNull(String str)`, and `stripToEmpty(String str)`: Produces the same result as the preceding `trim(String str)`, `trimToNull(String str)`, and `trimToEmpty(String str)` methods but uses a more extensive definition of white space (based on `Character.isWhitespace(int codepoint)`) and thus removes the same characters as the `trim(String str)`, `trimToNull(String str)`, and `trimToEmpty(String str)` methods do, and more

- `strip(String str, String stripChars)`, `stripAccents(String input)`, `stripAll(String... strs)`, `stripAll(String[] strs, String stripChars)`, `stripEnd(String str, String stripChars)`, and `stripStart(String str, String stripChars)`: Removes particular characters from particular parts of `String` or `String[]` array elements

- `startsWith(CharSequence str, CharSequence prefix)`, `startsWithAny(CharSequence string, CharSequence... searchStrings)`, `startsWithIgnoreCase(CharSequence str, CharSequence prefix)`, and similar `endsWith*()` methods: Checks whether a `String` value starts (or ends) with a certain prefix (or suffix)

- `indexOf`, `lastIndexOf`, `contains`: Checks an index in a null-safe manner

- `indexOfAny`, `lastIndexOfAny`, `indexOfAnyBut`, `lastIndexOfAnyBut`: Returns an index

- `containsOnly`, `containsNone`, and `containsAny`: Checks whether the value contains certain characters or not

- `substring`, `left`, `right`, and `mid`: Returns a substring in a null-safe manner

- `substringBefore`, `substringAfter`, `substringBetween`: Returns a substring from a relative position

- `split` or `join`: Splits or joins a value (respectively)

- `remove` and `delete`: Eliminates a substring

- `replace` and `overlay`: Replaces a value

- `chomp` and `chop`: Removes the end

- `appendIfMissing`: Adds a value if not present

- `prependIfMissing`: Prepends a prefix to the start of the `String` value if not present

- `leftPad`, `rightPad`, `center`, and `repeat`: Adds padding

- `upperCase`, `lowerCase`, `swapCase`, `capitalize`, and `uncapitalize`: Changes the case

- `countMatches`: Returns the number of the substring occurrences

- `isWhitespace`, `isAsciiPrintable`, `isNumeric`, `isNumericSpace`, `isAlpha`, `isAlphaNumeric`, `isAlphaSpace`, and `isAlphaNumericSpace`: Checks the presence of a certain type of characters

- `isAllLowerCase` and `isAllUpperCase`: Checks the case

- `defaultString`, `defaultIfBlank`, and `defaultIfEmpty`: Returns a default value if `null`

- `rotate`: Rotates characters using a circular shift

- `reverse` and `reverseDelimited`: Reverses characters or delimited groups of characters

- `abbreviate` and `abbreviateMiddle`: Abbreviates a value using an ellipsis or another value

- `difference`: Returns the differences in values

- `getLevenshteinDistance`: Returns the number of changes needed to transform one value into another

As you can see, the `StringUtils` class has a very rich (we have not listed everything) set of methods for string analysis, comparison, and transformation that complements the methods of the `String` class.

I/O streams

Any software system has to receive and produce some kind of data that can be organized as a set of isolated input/output or as a stream of data. A stream can be limited or endless. A program can read from a stream (which is called an **input stream**) or write to a stream (which is called an **output stream**). The Java I/O stream is either byte-based or character-based, meaning that its data is interpreted either as raw bytes or as characters.

The `java.io` package contains classes that support many, but not all, possible data sources. It is built for the most part around input from and to files, network streams, and internal memory buffers. It does not contain many classes necessary for network communication. They belong to `java.net`, `javax.net`, and other packages of a Java networking API. Only after the networking source or destination is established (a network socket, for example) can a program read and write data using the `InputStream` and `OutputStream` classes of the `java.io` package.

The classes of the `java.nio` package have pretty much the same functionality as the classes of `java.io` packages. But, in addition, they can work in *non-blocking* mode, which can substantially increase performance in certain situations. We will talk about non-blocking processing in *Chapter 15, Reactive Programming*.

Stream data

Input data has to be binary – expressed in 0s and 1s – at the very least because that is the format a computer can read. Data can be read or written one byte at a time or an array of several bytes at a time. These bytes can remain binary or can be interpreted as characters.

In the first case, they can be read as bytes or byte arrays by the descendants of the `InputStream` and `OutputStream` classes, such as (omitting the package name if the class belongs to the `java.io` package) `ByteArrayInputStream`, `ByteArrayOutputStream`, `FileInputStream`, `FileOutputStream`, `ObjectInputStream`, `ObjectOutputStream`, `javax.sound.sampled.AudioInputStream`, and `org.omg.CORBA.portable.OutputStream`; which one you use depends on the source or destination of the data. The `InputStream` and `OutputStream` classes themselves are abstract and cannot be instantiated.

In the second case, data that can be interpreted as characters is called **text data**, and there are character-oriented reading and writing classes based on `Reader` and `Writer`, which are abstract classes too. Examples of their sub-classes are `CharArrayReader` and `CharArrayWriter`, `InputStreamReader` and `OutputStreamWriter`, `PipedReader` and `PipedWriter`, and `StringReader` and `StringWriter`.

You may have noticed that we listed the classes in pairs. But not every input class has a matching output specialization – for example, there are the `PrintStream` and `PrintWriter` classes that support output to a printing device, but there is no corresponding input partner, not by name at least. However, there is a `java.util.Scanner` class that parses input text in a known format.

There is also a set of buffer-equipped classes that help to improve performance by reading or writing a bigger chunk of data at a time, especially in cases when access to a source or destination takes a long time.

In the rest of this section, we will review classes of the `java.io` package and some popular related classes from other packages.

The InputStream class and its subclasses

In the Java Class Library, the `InputStream` abstract class has the following direct implementations: `ByteArrayInputStream`, `FileInputStream`, `ObjectInputStream`, `PipedInputStream`, `SequenceInputStream`, `FilterInputStream`, and `javax.sound.sampled.AudioInputStream`.

All of them can be used as they are or override the following methods of the `InputStream` class:

- `int available()`: Returns the number of bytes available for reading
- `void close()`: Closes the stream and releases the resources
- `void mark(int readlimit)`: Marks a position in the stream and defines how many bytes can be read
- `boolean markSupported()`: Returns `true` if the marking is supported
- `static InputStream nullInputStream()`: Creates an empty stream
- `abstract int read()`: Reads the next byte in the stream
- `int read(byte[] b)`: Reads data from the stream into the b buffer
- `int read(byte[] b, int off, int len)`: Reads len or fewer bytes from the stream into the b buffer
- `byte[] readAllBytes()`: Reads all the remaining bytes from the stream
- `int readNBytes(byte[] b, int off, int len)`: Reads len or fewer bytes into the b buffer at the off offset
- `byte[] readNBytes(int len)`: Reads len or fewer bytes into the b buffer
- `void reset()`: Resets the reading location to the position where the mark() method was last called
- `long skip(long n)`: Skips n or fewer bytes of the stream; returns the actual number of bytes skipped
- `long transferTo(OutputStream out)`: Reads from the input stream and writes to the provided output stream byte by byte; returns the actual number of bytes transferred

`abstract int read()` is the only method that has to be implemented, but most of the descendants of this class override many of the other methods too.

ByteArrayInputStream

The `ByteArrayInputStream` class allows reading a byte array as an input stream. It has the following two constructors that create an object of the class and define the buffer used to read the input stream of bytes:

- `ByteArrayInputStream(byte[] buffer)`
- `ByteArrayInputStream(byte[] buffer, int offset, int length)`

The second of the constructors allows you to set, in addition to the buffer, the offset and the length of the buffer too. Let's look at an example and see how this class can be used. We will assume there is a source of the `byte[]` array with data:

```
byte[] bytesSource(){
    return new byte[]{42, 43, 44};
}
```

Then, we can write the following:

```
byte[] buffer = bytesSource();
try(ByteArrayInputStream bais = new
ByteArrayInputStream(buffer)){
    int data = bais.read();
    while(data != -1) {
        System.out.print(data + " ");    //prints: 42 43 44
        data = bais.read();
    }
} catch (Exception ex){
    ex.printStackTrace();
}
```

The `bytesSource()` method produces the array of bytes that fills the buffer that is passed into the constructor of the `ByteArrayInputStream` class as a parameter. The resulting stream is then read byte by byte using the `read()` method until the end of the stream is reached (and the `read()` method returns `-1`). Each new byte is printed out (without a line feed and with white space after it, so all the read bytes are displayed in one line separated by the white space).

The preceding code is usually expressed in a more compact form, as follows:

```
byte[] buffer = bytesSource();
try(ByteArrayInputStream bais = new
ByteArrayInputStream(buffer)){
    int data;
    while ((data = bais.read()) != -1) {
        System.out.print(data + " ");    //prints: 42 43 44
    }
} catch (Exception ex){
    ex.printStackTrace();
}
```

Instead of just printing the bytes, they can be processed in any other manner necessary, including interpreting them as characters, such as the following:

```
byte[] buffer = bytesSource();
try(ByteArrayInputStream bais =
                        new ByteArrayInputStream(buffer)){
  int data;
  while ((data = bais.read()) != -1) {
      System.out.print(((char)data) + " ");    //prints: * + ,
  }
} catch (Exception ex){
    ex.printStackTrace();
}
```

But, in such a case, it is better to use one of the Reader classes that are specialized for character processing. We will talk about them in the *Reader and writer classes and their subclasses* section.

FileInputStream

The FileInputStream class gets data from a file in a filesystem – the raw bytes of an image, for example. It has the following three constructors:

- FileInputStream(File file)
- FileInputStream(String name)
- FileInputStream(FileDescriptor fdObj)

Each constructor opens the file specified as the parameter. The first constructor accepts the `File` object; the second, the path to the file in the filesystem; and the third, the file descriptor object that represents an existing connection to an actual file in the filesystem. Let's look at the following example:

```
String file =  classLoader.getResource("hello.txt").getFile();
try(FileInputStream fis = new FileInputStream(file)){
    int data;
    while ((data = fis.read()) != -1) {
        System.out.print(((char)data) + " ");
                                        //prints: H e l l o !
    }
} catch (Exception ex){
    ex.printStackTrace();
}
```

In the `src/main/resources` folder, we have created the `hello.txt` file that has only one line in it – `Hello!`. The output of the preceding example looks as follows:

```
H e l l o !
```

After reading bytes from the `hello.txt` file, we decided, for demo purposes, to cast each `byte` to `char` so that you can see that the code does read from the specified file, but the `FileReader` class is a better choice for text file processing (we will discuss it shortly). Without the cast, the result would be the following:

```
System.out.print((data) + " ");
                                //prints: 72 101 108 108 111 33
```

By the way, because the `src/main/resources` folder is placed by the IDE (using Maven) on the classpath, a file placed in it can also be accessed via a class loader that creates a stream using its own `InputStream` implementation:

```
try(InputStream is = InputOutputStream.class.
getResourceAsStream("/hello.txt")){
    int data;
    while ((data = is.read()) != -1) {
        System.out.print((data) + " ");
            //prints: 72 101 108 108 111 33
    }
}
```

```
} catch (Exception ex){
    ex.printStackTrace();
}
```

The InputOutputStream class in the preceding example is not a class from some library. It is just the main class we used to run the example. The InputOutputStream. class.getResourceAsStream() construct allows you to use the same classloader that has loaded the InputOutputStream class for the purpose of finding a file on the classpath and creating a stream that contains its content. In the *File management* section, we will present other ways of reading a file too.

ObjectInputStream

The set of methods of the ObjectInputStream class is much bigger than the set of methods of any other InputStream implementation. The reason for that is that it is built around reading the values of the object fields that can be of various types. In order for ObjectInputStream to be able to construct an object from the input stream of data, the object has to be *deserializable*, which means it has to be *serializable* in the first place – that is, to be convertible into a byte stream. Usually, it is done for the purpose of transporting objects over a network. At the destination, the serialized objects are deserialized, and the values of the original objects are restored.

Primitive types and most Java classes, including the String class and primitive type wrappers, are serializable. If a class has fields of custom types, they have to be made serializable by implementing java.io.Serizalizable. How to do that is outside the scope of this book. For now, we are going to use only the serializable types. Let's look at this class:

```
class SomeClass implements Serializable {
    private int field1 = 42;
    private String field2 = "abc";
}
```

We have to tell the compiler that it is serializable. Otherwise, the compilation will fail. It is done in order to make sure that, before stating that the class is serializable, the programmer either reviewed all the fields and made sure they are serializable or has implemented the methods necessary for the serialization.

Before we can create an input stream and use `ObjectInputStream` for deserialization, we need to serialize the object first. That is why we first use `ObjectOutputStream` and `FileOutputStream` to serialize an object and write it into the `someClass.bin` file. We will talk more about them in the *The OutputStream class and its subclasses* section. Then, we read from the file using `FileInputStream` and deserialize the file content using `ObjectInputStream`:

```
String fileName = "someClass.bin";
try (ObjectOutputStream oos = new ObjectOutputStream(new
FileOutputStream(fileName));
     ObjectInputStream ois = new ObjectInputStream(new
                            FileInputStream(fileName))){
    SomeClass obj = new SomeClass();
    oos.writeObject(obj);
    SomeClass objRead = (SomeClass) ois.readObject();
    System.out.println(objRead.field1);   //prints: 42
    System.out.println(objRead.field2);   //prints: abc
} catch (Exception ex){
    ex.printStackTrace();
}
```

Note that the file has to be created first before the preceding code is run. We will show how it can be done in the *Creating files and directories* section. And, as a reminder, we have used the `try-with-resources` statement because `InputStream` and `OutputStream` both implement the `Closeable` interface.

PipedInputStream

A piped input stream has a very particular specialization; it is used as one of the mechanisms of communication between threads. One thread reads from a `PipedInputStream` object and passes data to another thread that writes data to a `PipedOutputStream` object. Here is an example:

```
PipedInputStream pis = new PipedInputStream();
PipedOutputStream pos = new PipedOutputStream(pis);
```

Alternatively, data can be moved in the opposite direction when one thread reads from a `PipedOutputStream` object and another thread writes to a `PipedInputStream` object as follows:

```
PipedOutputStream pos = new PipedOutputStream();
PipedInputStream pis = new PipedInputStream(pos);
```

Those who work in this area are familiar with the message, `Broken pipe`, which means that the supplying data pipe stream has stopped working.

The piped streams can also be created without any connection and connected later, as shown here:

```
PipedInputStream pis = new PipedInputStream();
PipedOutputStream pos = new PipedOutputStream();
pos.connect(pis);
```

As an example, here are two classes that are going to be executed by different threads – first, the `PipedOutputWorker` class, as follows:

```
class PipedOutputWorker implements Runnable{
    private PipedOutputStream pos;
    public PipedOutputWorker(PipedOutputStream pos) {
        this.pos = pos;
    }
    @Override
    public void run() {
        try {
            for(int i = 1; i < 4; i++){
                pos.write(i);
            }
            pos.close();
        } catch (Exception ex) {
            ex.printStackTrace();
        }
    }
}
```

The `PipedOutputWorker` class has the `run()` method (because it implements a `Runnable` interface) that writes into the stream the three numbers 1, 2, and 3, and then closes. Now, let's look at the `PipedInputWorker` class, as shown here:

```java
class PipedInputWorker implements Runnable{
    private PipedInputStream pis;
    public PipedInputWorker(PipedInputStream pis) {
        this.pis = pis;
    }
    @Override
    public void run() {
        try {
            int i;
            while((i = pis.read()) > -1){
                System.out.print(i + " ");
            }
            pis.close();
        } catch (Exception ex) {
            ex.printStackTrace();
        }
    }
}
```

It also has a `run()` method (because it implements a `Runnable` interface) that reads from the stream and prints out each byte until the stream ends (indicated by `-1`). Now, let's connect these pipes and execute a `run()` method of these classes:

```java
PipedOutputStream pos = new PipedOutputStream();
PipedInputStream pis = new PipedInputStream();
try {
    pos.connect(pis);
    new Thread(new PipedOutputWorker(pos)).start();
    new Thread(new PipedInputWorker(pis)).start();
                                        //prints: 1 2 3
} catch (Exception ex) {
    ex.printStackTrace();
}
```

As you can see, the objects of the workers were passed into the constructor of the `Thread` class. The `start()` method of the `Thread` object executes the `run()` method of the passed in `Runnable`. And we see the results as expected –`PipedInputWorker` prints all the bytes written to the piped stream by `PipedOutputWorker`. We will go into more detail about threads in *Chapter 8, Multithreading and Concurrent Processing.*

SequenceInputStream

The `SequenceInputStream` class concatenates input streams passed into one of the following constructors as parameters:

- `SequenceInputStream(InputStream s1, InputStream s2)`
- `SequenceInputStream(Enumeration<InputStream> e)`

Enumeration is a collection of objects of the type indicated in the angle brackets, called **generics**, meaning *of type T*. The `SequenceInputStream` class reads from the first input string until it ends, whereupon it reads from the second one, and so on, until the end of the last of the streams. As an example, let's create a `howAreYou.txt` file (with the text, `How are you?`) in the `resources` folder next to the `hello.txt` file. The `SequenceInputStream` class can then be used as follows:

```
String file1 = classLoader.getResource("hello.txt").getFile();
String file2 = classLoader.getResource("howAreYou.txt").
getFile();
try(FileInputStream fis1 =
                    new FileInputStream(file1);
    FileInputStream fis2 =
                    new FileInputStream(file2);
    SequenceInputStream sis=
            new SequenceInputStream(fis1, fis2)){
    int i;
    while((i = sis.read()) > -1){
        System.out.print((char)i);
                                    //prints: Hello!How are you?

    }
} catch (Exception ex) {
    ex.printStackTrace();

}
```

Similarly, when an enumeration of input streams is passed in, each of the streams is read (and printed in our case) until the end.

FilterInputStream

The `FilterInputStream` class is a wrapper around the `InputStream` object passed as a parameter in the constructor. Here is the constructor and the two `read()` methods of the `FilterInputStream` class:

```
protected volatile InputStream in;
protected FilterInputStream(InputStream in) { this.in = in; }
public int read() throws IOException { return in.read(); }
public int read(byte b[]) throws IOException {
    return read(b, 0, b.length);
}
```

All the other methods of the `InputStream` class are overridden similarly; the function is delegated to the object assigned to the `in` property.

As you can see, the constructor is protected, which means that only the child has access to it. Such a design hides from the client the actual source of the stream and forces the programmer to use one of the `FilterInputStream` class extensions: `BufferedInputStream`, `CheckedInputStream`, `DataInputStream`, `PushbackInputStream`, `javax.crypto.CipherInputStream`, `java.util.zip.DeflaterInputStream`, `java.util.zip.InflaterInputStream`, `java.security.DigestInputStream`, or `javax.swing.ProgressMonitorInputStream`. Alternatively, you can create a custom extension. But, before creating your own extension, look at the listed classes and see if one of them fits your needs. Here is an example of using a `BufferedInputStream` class:

```
String file = classLoader.getResource("hello.txt").getFile();
try(FileInputStream  fis = new FileInputStream(file);
    FilterInputStream filter = new BufferedInputStream(fis)){
    int i;
    while((i = filter.read()) > -1){
        System.out.print((char)i);       //prints: Hello!
    }
} catch (Exception ex) {
    ex.printStackTrace();
}
```

The `BufferedInputStream` class uses the buffer to improve performance. When the bytes from the stream are skipped or read, the internal buffer is automatically refilled with as many bytes as necessary at the time, from the contained input stream.

The `CheckedInputStream` class adds a checksum of the data being read that allows the verification of the integrity of the input data using the `getChecksum()` method.

The `DataInputStream` class reads and interprets input data as primitive Java data types in a machine-independent way.

The `PushbackInputStream` class adds the ability to push back the read data using the `unread()` method. It is useful in situations when the code has the logic of analyzing the just-read data and deciding to unread it, so it can be reread at the next step.

The `javax.crypto.CipherInputStream` class adds `Cipher` to the `read()` methods. If `Cipher` is initialized for decryption, `javax.crypto.CipherInputStream` will attempt to decrypt the data before returning.

The `java.util.zip.DeflaterInputStream` class compresses data in the deflate compression format.

The `java.util.zip.InflaterInputStream` class uncompresses data in the deflate compression format.

The `java.security.DigestInputStream` class updates the associated message digest using the bits going through the stream. The `on (boolean on)` method turns the `digest` function on or off. The calculated digest can be retrieved using the `getMessageDigest()` method.

The `javax.swing.ProgressMonitorInputStream` class provides a monitor of the progress of reading from `InputStream`. The monitor object can be accessed using the `getProgressMonitor()` method.

javax.sound.sampled.AudioInputStream

The `AudioInputStream` class represents an input stream with a specified audio format and length. It has the following two constructors:

- `AudioInputStream (InputStream stream, AudioFormat format, long length)`: Accepts the stream of audio data, the requested format, and the length in sample frames

- `AudioInputStream (TargetDataLine line)`: Accepts the target data line indicated

The `javax.sound.sampled.AudioFormat` class describes audio-format properties such as channels, encoding, frame rate, and similar. The `javax.sound.sampled.TargetDataLine` class has the `open()` method that opens the line with the specified format and the `read()` method that reads audio data from the data line's input buffer.

There is also the `javax.sound.sampled.AudioSystem` class, and its methods handle `AudioInputStream` objects. They can be used for reading from an audio file, a stream, or a URL, and they write to an audio file. They also can be used to convert an audio stream to another audio format.

The OutputStream class and its subclasses

The `OutputStream` class is a peer of the `InputStream` class that writes data instead of reading. It is an abstract class that has the following direct implementations in the **Java Class Library** (**JCL**): `ByteArrayOutputStream`, `FilterOutputStream`, `ObjectOutputStream`, `PipedOutputStream`, and `FileOutputStream`.

The `FileOutputStream` class has the following direct extensions: `BufferedOutputStream`, `CheckedOutputStream`, `DataOutputStream`, `PrintStream`, `javax.crypto.CipherOutputStream`, `java.util.zip.DeflaterOutputStream`, `java.security.DigestOutputStream`, and `java.util.zip.InflaterOutputStream`.

All of them can be used as they are or override the following methods of the `OutputStream` class:

- `void close()`: Closes the stream and releases the resources
- `void flush()`: Forces the remaining bytes to be written out
- `static OutputStream nullOutputStream()`: Creates a new `OutputStream` that writes nothing
- `void write(byte[] b)`: Writes the provided byte array to the output stream
- `void write(byte[] b, int off, int len)`: Writes `len` bytes of the provided byte array, starting at the `off` offset, to the output stream
- `abstract void write(int b)`: Writes the provided byte to the output stream

The only method that has to be implemented is `abstract void write(int b)`, but most of the descendants of the `OutputStream` class override many of the other methods too.

After learning about the input streams in the *The InputStream class and its subclasses* section, all of the OutputStream implementations, except the PrintStream class, should be intuitively familiar to you. So, we will discuss here only the PrintStream class.

PrintStream

The PrintStream class adds to another output stream the ability to print data as characters. We have actually used it already many times. The System class has an object of the PrintStream class set as a System.out public static property. This means that every time we print something using System.out, we are using the PrintStream class:

```
System.out.println("Printing a line");
```

Let's look at another example of the PrintStream class usage:

```
String fileName = "output.txt";
try(FileOutputStream  fos = new FileOutputStream(fileName);
    PrintStream ps = new PrintStream(fos)){
    ps.println("Hi there!");
} catch (Exception ex) {
    ex.printStackTrace();
}
```

As you can see, the PrintStream class takes the FileOutputStream object and prints the characters generated by it. In this case, it prints out all the bytes that FileOutputStream writes to the file. By the way, there is no need to create the destination file explicitly. If absent, it will be created automatically inside the FileOutputStream constructor. If we open the file after the preceding code is run, we will see one line in it – "Hi there!".

Alternatively, the same result can be achieved using another PrintStream constructor that takes the File object, as follows:

```
String fileName = "output.txt";
File file = new File(fileName);
try(PrintStream ps = new PrintStream(file)){
    ps.println("Hi there!");
} catch (Exception ex) {
    ex.printStackTrace();
}
```

An even simpler solution can be created using the third variation of the `PrintStream` constructor that takes the filename as a parameter:

```
String fileName = "output.txt";
try(PrintStream ps = new PrintStream(fileName)){
    ps.println("Hi there!");
} catch (Exception ex) {
    ex.printStackTrace();
}
```

The previous two examples are possible because the `PrintStream` constructor uses the `FileOutputStream` class behind the scenes, exactly as we did it in the first example of the `PrintStream` class usage. So, the `PrintStream` class has several constructors just for convenience, but all of them essentially have the same functionality:

- `PrintStream(File file)`
- `PrintStream(File file, String csn)`
- `PrintStream(File file, Charset charset)`
- `PrintStream(String fileName)`
- `PrintStream(String fileName, String csn)`
- `PrintStream(String fileName, Charset charset)`
- `PrintStream(OutputStream out)`
- `PrintStream(OutputStream out, boolean autoFlush)`
- `PrintStream(OutputStream out, boolean autoFlush, String encoding)`
- `PrintStream(OutputStream out, boolean autoFlush, Charset charset)`

Some of the constructors also take a `Charset` instance or just its name (`String csn`), which allows you to apply a different mapping between sequences of 16-bit Unicode code units and sequences of bytes. You can see all available charsets by just printing them out, as shown here:

```
for (String chs : Charset.availableCharsets().keySet()) {
    System.out.println(chs);
}
```

Other constructors take `boolean autoFlush` as a parameter. This parameter indicates (when `true`) that the output buffer should be flushed automatically when an array is written or the symbol end-of-line is encountered.

Once an object of `PrintStream` is created, it provides a variety of methods, as listed here:

- `void print(T value)`: Prints the value of any `T` primitive type passed in without moving to another line

- `void print(Object obj)`: Calls the `toString()` method on the passed in object and prints the result without moving to another line; does not generate `NullPointerException` in case the passed-in object is `null` and prints `null` instead

- `void println(T value)`: Prints the value of any `T` primitive type passed in and moves to another line

- `void println(Object obj)`: Calls the `toString()` method on the passed-in object, prints the result, and moves to another line; does not generate `NullPointerException` in case the passed-in object is `null` and prints `null` instead

- `void println()`: Just moves to another line

- `PrintStream printf(String format, Object... values)`: Substitutes the placeholders in the provided `format` string with the provided `values` and writes the result into the stream

- `PrintStream printf(Locale l, String format, Object... args)`: The same as the preceding method but applies localization using the provided `Local` object; if the provided `Local` object is `null`, no localization is applied, and this method behaves exactly like the preceding one

- `PrintStream format(String format, Object... args)` and `PrintStream format(Locale l, String format, Object... args)`: Behaves the same way as `PrintStream printf(String format, Object... values)` and `PrintStream printf(Locale l, String format, Object... args)` (already described in the list), such as the following:

```
System.out.printf("Hi, %s!%n", "dear reader");
                                    //prints: Hi, dear reader!
System.out.format("Hi, %s!%n", "dear reader");
                                    //prints: Hi, dear reader!
```

In the preceding example, (%) indicates a formatting rule. The following symbol (s) indicates a `String` value. Other possible symbols in this position can be (d) (decimal), (f) (floating-point), and so on. The symbol (n) indicates a new line (the same as the (\n) escape character). There are many formatting rules. All of them are described in the documentation for the `java.util.Formatter` class.

- `PrintStream append(char c)`, `PrintStream append(CharSequence c)`, and `PrintStream append(CharSequence c, int start, int end)`: Appends the provided character to the stream, such as the following:

```
System.out.printf("Hi %s", "there").append("!\n");
                                        //prints: Hi there!
System.out.printf("Hi ")
            .append("one there!\n two", 4, 11);
                                        //prints: Hi there!
```

With this, we conclude the discussion of the `OutputStream` subclass and now turn our attention to another class hierarchy – the `Reader` and `Writer` classes and their subclasses from the JCL.

The Reader and Writer classes and their subclasses

As we mentioned several times already, the `Reader` and `Writer` classes are very similar in their function to the `InputStream` and `OutputStream` classes but specialize in processing texts. They interpret stream bytes as characters and have their own independent `InputStream` and `OutputStream` class hierarchy. It is possible to process stream bytes as characters without `Reader` and `Writer` or any of their subclasses. We have seen such examples in the preceding sections describing the `InputStream` and `OutputStream` classes. However, using the `Reader` and `Writer` classes makes text processing simpler and code easier to read.

Reader and its subclasses

The `Reader` class is an abstract class that reads streams as characters. It is an analog to `InputStream` and has the following methods:

- `abstract void close()`: Closes the stream and other used resources

- `void mark(int readAheadLimit)`: Marks the current position in the stream

- `boolean markSupported()`: Returns `true` if the stream supports the `mark()` operation

- `static Reader nullReader()`: Creates an empty `Reader` that reads no characters

- `int read()`: Reads one character

- `int read(char[] buf)`: Reads characters into the provided `buf` array and returns the count of the read characters

- `abstract int read(char[] buf, int off, int len)`: Reads the `len` characters into an array starting from the `off` index

- `int read(CharBuffer target)`: Attempts to read characters into the provided `target` buffer

- `boolean ready()`: Returns `true` when the stream is ready to be read

- `void reset()`: Resets the mark; however, not all streams support this operation, with some supporting it but not supporting a mark being set in the first place

- `long skip(long n)`: Attempts to skip the n characters; returns the count of skipped characters

- `long transferTo(Writer out)`: Reads all characters from this reader and writes the characters to the provided `Writer` object

As you can see, the only methods that need to be implemented are the two abstract `read()` and `close()` methods. Nevertheless, many children of this class override other methods too, sometimes for better performance or different functionality. The `Reader` subclasses in the JCL are `CharArrayReader`, `InputStreamReader`, `PipedReader`, `StringReader`, `BufferedReader`, and `FilterReader`. The `BufferedReader` class has a `LineNumberReader` subclass, and the `FilterReader` class has a `PushbackReader` subclass.

Writer and its subclasses

The abstract `Writer` class writes to character streams. It is an analog to `OutputStream` and has the following methods:

- `Writer append(char c)`: Appends the provided character to the stream

- `Writer append(CharSequence c)`: Appends the provided character sequence to the stream

- `Writer append(CharSequence c, int start, int end)`: Appends a subsequence of the provided character sequence to the stream

- `abstract void close()`: Flushes and closes the stream and related system resources

- `abstract void flush()`: Flushes the stream

- `static Writer nullWriter()`: Creates a new `Writer` object that discards all characters

- `void write(char[] c)`: Writes an array of c characters

- `abstract void write(char[] c, int off, int len)`: Writes the `len` elements of an array of c characters, starting from the `off` index

- `void write(int c)`: Writes one character

- `void write(String str)`: Writes the provided string

- `void write(String str, int off, int len)`: Writes a substring of the `len` length from the provided `str` string, starting from the `off` index

As you can see, the three abstract methods, `write(char[], int, int)`, `flush()`, and `close()`, must be implemented by the children of this class. They also typically override other methods too.

The `Writer` subclasses in the JCL are `CharArrayWriter`, `OutputStreamWriter`, `PipedWriter`, `StringWriter`, `BufferedWriter`, `FilterWriter`, and `PrintWriter`. The `OutputStreamWriter` class has a `FileWriter` subclass.

Other classes of the java.io package

Other classes of the `java.io` package include the following:

- `Console`: Allows interaction with the character-based console device, associated with the current Java Virtual Machine instance

- `StreamTokenizer`: Takes an input stream and parses it into `tokens`

- `ObjectStreamClass`: The serialization's descriptor for classes

- `ObjectStreamField`: A description of a serializable field from a serializable class

- `RandomAccessFile`: Allows random access for reading from and writing to a file, but its discussion is outside the scope of this book

- `File`: Allows creating and managing files and directories; described in the *File management* section

Console

There are several ways to create and run a **Java Virtual Machine** (**JVM**) instance that executes an application. If the JVM is started from a command line, a console window is automatically opened. It allows you to type on the display from the keyboard; however, the JVM can be started by a background process too. In such a case, a console is not created.

To check programmatically whether a console exists, you can invoke the System. console() static method. If no console device is available, then an invocation of that method will return null. Otherwise, it will return an object of the Console class that allows interaction with the console device and the application user.

Let's create the following ConsoleDemo class:

```
package com.packt.learnjava.ch05_stringsIoStreams;
import java.io.Console;
public class ConsoleDemo {
    public static void main(String... args)  {
        Console console = System.console();
        System.out.println(console);
    }
}
```

If we run it from the IDE, as we usually do, the result will be as follows:

```
null
```

That is because the JVM was not launched from the command line. In order to do it, let's compile our application and create a .jar file by executing the mvn clean package Maven command in the root directory of the project. (We assume that you have Maven installed on your computer.) It will delete the target folder, then recreate it, compile all the .java files to the corresponding .class files in the target folder, and then archive them in a .jar file, learnjava-1.0-SNAPSHOT.jar.

Now, we can launch the ConsoleDemo application from the same project root directory using the following command:

```
java -cp ./target/examples-1.0-SNAPSHOT.jar
        com.packt.learnjava.ch05_stringsIoStreams.ConsoleDemo
```

The preceding –cp command option depicts a classpath, so in our case, we tell the JVM to look for the classes in the .jar file in the folder target. The command is shown in two lines because the page width cannot accommodate it. But if you want to run it, make sure you do it as one line. The result will be as follows:

```
java.io.Console@70dea4e
```

This tells us that we have the Console class object now. Let's see what we can do with it. The class has the following methods:

- String readLine(): Waits until the user hits the *Enter* key and reads the line of text from the console

- String readLine(String format, Object... args): Displays a prompt (the message produced after the provided format had the placeholders substituted with the provided arguments), waits until the user hits the *Enter* key, and reads the line of text from the console; if no arguments (args) are provided, it displays the format as the prompt

- char[] readPassword(): Performs the same function as the readLine() function but without echoing the typed characters

- char[] readPassword(String format, Object... args): Performs the same function as readLine(String format, Object... args) but without echoing the typed characters

To run each of the following code sections individually, you need to comment out the console1() call in the main method and uncomment console2() or console3(), recompile using mvn package, and then rerun the java command shown previously.

Let's demonstrate the preceding methods with the following example (the console2() method):

```
Console console = System.console();

System.out.print("Enter something 1: ");
String line = console.readLine();
System.out.println("Entered 1: " + line);
line = console.readLine("Enter something 2: ");
System.out.println("Entered 2: " + line);
line = console.readLine("Enter some%s", "thing 3: ");
System.out.println("Entered 3: " + line);
```

```java
System.out.print("Enter password: ");
char[] password = console.readPassword();
System.out.println("Entered 4: " + new String(password));
password = console.readPassword("Enter password 5: ");
System.out.println("Entered 5: " + new String(password));
password = console.readPassword("Enter pass%s", "word 6: ");
System.out.println("Entered 6: " + new String(password));
```

The result of the preceding example is as follows:

```
abc
Entered 1: abc
Enter something 2: xyz
Entered 2: xyz
Enter something 3: 123
Entered 3: 123

Entered 4: abc
Enter password 5:
Entered 5: xyz
Enter password 6:
Entered 6: 123
```

Some IDEs cannot run these examples and throw `NullPointerException`. If that is the case, run the console-related examples from the command line, as described previously. Don't forget to run the `maven package` command every time you change code.

Another group of `Console` class methods can be used in conjunction with the previously demonstrated methods:

- `Console format(String format, Object... args)`: Substitutes the placeholders in the provided `format` string with the provided `args` values and displays the result

- `Console printf(String format, Object... args)`: Behaves the same way as the `format()` method

As an example, look at the following line:

```java
String line = console.format("Enter some%s", "thing:").
readLine();
```

It produces the same result as this line:

```
String line = console.readLine("Enter some%s", "thing:");
```

And finally, the last three methods of the Console class are as follows:

- PrintWriter writer(): Creates a PrintWriter object associated with this console that can be used for producing an output stream of characters
- Reader reader(): Creates a Reader object associated with this console that can be used for reading the input as a stream of characters
- void flush(): Flushes the console and forces any buffered output to be written immediately

Here is an example of their usage (the console3() method):

```
try (Reader reader = console.reader()){
    char[] chars = new char[10];
    System.out.print("Enter something: ");
    reader.read(chars);
    System.out.print("Entered: " + new String(chars));
} catch (IOException e) {
    e.printStackTrace();
}

PrintWriter out = console.writer();
out.println("Hello!");

console.flush();
```

The result of the preceding code looks as follows:

```
Enter something: Hi!
Entered: Hi!
Hello!
```

Reader and PrintWriter can also be used to create other Input and Output streams that we have been talking about in this section.

StreamTokenizer

The `StreamTokenizer` class parses the input stream and produces tokens. Its `StreamTokenizer(Reader r)` constructor accepts a `Reader` object that is the source of the tokens. Every time the `int nextToken()` method is called on the `StreamTokenizer` object, the following happens:

1. The next token is parsed.

2. The `StreamTokenizer` instance field, `ttype`, is populated by the value that indicates the token type:

   - The `ttype` value can be one of the following integer constants: `TT_WORD`, `TT_NUMBER`, `TT_EOL` (end-of-line), or `TT_EOF` (end-of-stream).

   - If the `ttype` value is `TT_WORD`, the `StreamTokenizer` instance, the `sval` field, is populated by the `String` value of the token.

   - If the `ttype` value is `TT_NUMBER`, the `StreamTokenizer` instance field, `nval`, is populated by the `double` value of the token.

3. The `lineno()` method of the `StreamTokenizer` instance returns the current line number.

Let's look at an example before talking about other methods of the `StreamTokenizer` class. Let's assume that, in the project `resources` folder, there is a `tokens.txt` file that contains the following four lines of text:

```
There
happened
42
events.
```

The following code will read the file and tokenize its content (the `streamTokenizer()` method of the `InputOutputStream` class):

```
String file =  classLoader.
                          getResource("tokens.txt").getFile();
try(FileReader fr = new FileReader(file);
   BufferedReader br = new BufferedReader(fr)){
   StreamTokenizer st = new StreamTokenizer(br);
   st.eolIsSignificant(true);
   st.commentChar('e');
   System.out.println("Line " + st.lineno() + ":");
```

```
int i;
while ((i = st.nextToken()) != StreamTokenizer.TT_EOF) {
  switch (i) {
      case StreamTokenizer.TT_EOL:
          System.out.println("\nLine " + st.lineno() + ":");
          break;
      case StreamTokenizer.TT_WORD:
          System.out.println("TT_WORD => " + st.sval);
          break;
      case StreamTokenizer.TT_NUMBER:
          System.out.println("TT_NUMBER => " + st.nval);
          break;
      default:
          System.out.println("Unexpected => " + st.ttype);
      }
  }
} catch (Exception ex){
    ex.printStackTrace();
}
```

If we run this code, the result will be the following:

```
Line 1:
TT_WORD => Th

Line 2:
TT_WORD => happ

Line 3:
TT_NUMBER => 42.0

Line 4:
```

We have used the BufferedReader class, which is a good practice for higher efficiency, but in our case, we can easily avoid it, like this:

```
FileReader fr = new FileReader(filePath);
StreamTokenizer st = new StreamTokenizer(fr);
```

The result would not change. We also used the following three methods that we have not described yet:

- `void eolIsSignificant(boolean flag)`: Indicates whether the end-of-line should be treated as a token

- `void commentChar(int ch)`: Indicates which character starts a comment, so the rest of the line is ignored

- `int lineno()`: Returns the current line number

The following methods can be invoked using the `StreamTokenizer` object:

- `void lowerCaseMode(boolean fl)`: Indicates whether a word token should be lowercase

- `void ordinaryChar(int ch)`, `void ordinaryChars(int low, int hi)`: Indicate a specific character or the range of characters that have to be treated as *ordinary* (not as a comment character, word component, string delimiter, white space, or number character)

- `void parseNumbers()`: Indicates that a word token that has the format of a double-precision floating-point number has to be interpreted as a number, rather than a word

- `void pushBack()`: Forces the `nextToken()` method to return the current value of the `ttype` field

- `void quoteChar(int ch)`: Indicates that the provided character has to be interpreted as the beginning and the end of the string value that has to be taken as-is (as a quote)

- `void resetSyntax()`: Resets this tokenizer's syntax table so that all characters are *ordinary*

- `void slashSlashComments(boolean flag)`: Indicates that C++-style comments have to be recognized

- `void slashStarComments(boolean flag)`: Indicates that C-style comments have to be recognized

- `String toString()`: Returns the string representation of the token and the line number

- `void whitespaceChars(int low, int hi)`: Indicates the range of characters that have to be interpreted as white space

- `void wordChars(int low, int hi)`: Indicates the range of characters that have to be interpreted as a word

As you can see, using the wealth of the preceding methods allows you to fine-tune the text interpretation.

ObjectStreamClass and ObjectStreamField

The ObjectStreamClass and ObjectStreamField classes provide access to the serialized data of a class loaded in the JVM. The ObjectStreamClass object can be found/created using one of the following lookup methods:

- static ObjectStreamClass lookup(Class cl): Finds the descriptor of a serializable class

- static ObjectStreamClass lookupAny(Class cl): Finds the descriptor for any class, whether serializable or not

After ObjectStreamClass is found and the class is serializable (implementing the Serializable interface), it can be used to access the ObjectStreamField objects, each containing information about one serialized field. If the class is not serializable, there is no ObjectStreamField object associated with any of the fields.

Let's look at an example. Here is the method that displays information obtained from the ObjectStreamClass and ObjectStreamField objects:

```
void printInfo(ObjectStreamClass osc) {
    System.out.println(osc.forClass());
    System.out.println("Class name: " + osc.getName());
    System.out.println("SerialVersionUID: " +
                                    osc.getSerialVersionUID());
    ObjectStreamField[] fields = osc.getFields();
    System.out.println("Serialized fields:");
    for (ObjectStreamField osf : fields) {
        System.out.println(osf.getName() + ": ");
        System.out.println("\t" + osf.getType());
        System.out.println("\t" + osf.getTypeCode());
        System.out.println("\t" + osf.getTypeString());
    }
}
```

To demonstrate how it works, we will create a serializable `Person1` class:

```
package com.packt.learnjava.ch05_stringsIoStreams;
import java.io.Serializable;
public class Person1 implements Serializable {
    private int age;
    private String name;
    public Person1(int age, String name) {
        this.age = age;
        this.name = name;
    }
}
```

We did not add methods because only the object state is serializable, not the methods. Now, let's run the following code:

```
ObjectStreamClass osc1 =
        ObjectStreamClass.lookup(Person1.class);
printInfo(osc1);
```

The result will be as follows:

```
class com.packt.learnjava.ch05_stringsIoStreams.Person1
Class name: com.packt.learnjava.ch05_stringsIoStreams.Person1
SerialVersionUID: -2546904836625458265
Serialized fields:
age:
    int
    I
    null
name:
    class java.lang.String
    L
    Ljava/lang/String;
```

As you can see, there is information about the class name and all field names and types. There are also two other methods that can be called using the `ObjectStreamField` object:

- `boolean isPrimitive()`: Returns `true` if this field has a primitive type
- `boolean isUnshared()`: Returns `true` if this field is unshared (private or accessible only from the same package)

Now, let's create a non-serializable `Person2` class:

```
package com.packt.learnjava.ch05_stringsIoStreams;
public class Person2 {
    private int age;
    private String name;
    public Person2(int age, String name) {
        this.age = age;
        this.name = name;
    }
}
```

This time, we will run the code that only looks up the class, as follows:

```
ObjectStreamClass osc2 =
            ObjectStreamClass.lookup(Person2.class);
System.out.println("osc2: " + osc2);     //prints: null
```

As expected, the non-serializable object was not found using the `lookup()` method. In order to find a non-serializable object, we need to use the `lookupAny()` method:

```
ObjectStreamClass osc3 =
            ObjectStreamClass.lookupAny(Person2.class);
printInfo(osc3);
```

If we run the preceding example, the result will be as follows:

```
class com.packt.learnjava.ch05_stringsIoStreams.Person2
Class name: com.packt.learnjava.ch05_stringsIoStreams.Person2
SerialVersionUID: 0
Serialized fields:
```

From a non-serializable object, we were able to extract information about the class but not about the fields.

The java.util.Scanner class

The `java.util.Scanner` class is typically used to read input from a keyboard but can also read text from any object that implements the `Readable` interface (this interface only has the `int read(CharBuffer buffer)` method). It breaks the input value by a delimiter (white space is a default delimiter) into tokens that are processed using different methods.

For example, we can read an input from `System.in` – a standard input stream, which typically represents keyboard input:

```
Scanner sc = new Scanner(System.in);
System.out.print("Enter something: ");
while(sc.hasNext()){
    String line = sc.nextLine();
    if("end".equals(line)){
        System.exit(0);
    }
    System.out.println(line);
}
```

It accepts many lines (each line ends after the *Enter* key is pressed) until the line end is entered, as follows:

```
Enter something: type
type
one line
one line
at a time
at a time
end

Process finished with exit code 0
```

Alternatively, `Scanner` can read lines from a file:

```
String file =  classLoader.getResource("tokens.txt").getFile();
try(Scanner sc = new Scanner(new File(file))){
    while(sc.hasNextLine()){
        System.out.println(sc.nextLine());
    }
} catch (Exception ex){
    ex.printStackTrace();
}
```

As you can see, we have used the `tokens.txt` file again. The results are as follows:

```
There
happened
42
events.
```

To demonstrate `Scanner` breaking the input by a delimiter, let's run the following code:

```
String input = "One two three";
Scanner sc = new Scanner(input);
while(sc.hasNext()){
    System.out.println(sc.next());
}
```

The result is as follows:

To use another delimiter, it can be set as follows:

```
String input = "One,two,three";
Scanner sc = new Scanner(input).useDelimiter(",");
while(sc.hasNext()){
    System.out.println(sc.next());
}
```

The result remains the same:

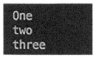

It is also possible to use a regular expression for extracting the tokens, but that topic is outside the scope of this book.

The `Scanner` class has many other methods that make its usage applicable to a variety of sources and required results. The `findInLine()`, `findWithinHorizon()`, `skip()`, and `findAll()` methods do not use the delimiter; they just try to match the provided pattern. For more information, refer to the Scanner documentation (`https://docs.oracle.com/en/java/javase/17/docs/api/java.base/java/util/Scanner.html`).

File management

We have already used some methods for finding, creating, reading, and writing files using the JCL classes. We had to do it in order to support a demo code of input/output streams. In this section, we are going to talk about file management using the JCL in more detail.

The `File` class from the `java.io` package represents the underlying filesystem. An object of the `File` class can be created with one of the following constructors:

- `File(String pathname)`: Creates a new `File` instance based on the provided pathname

- `File(String parent, String child)`: Creates a new `File` instance based on the provided parent pathname and a child pathname

- `File(File parent, String child)`: Creates a new `File` instance based on the provided parent `File` object and a child pathname

- `File(URI uri)`: Creates a new `File` instance based on the provided `URI` object that represents the pathname

We will now see some examples of the constructors' usage while talking about creating and deleting files.

Creating and deleting files and directories

To create a file or directory in the filesystem, you need first to construct a new `File` object using one of the constructors listed in the *File management* section. For example, assuming that the filename is `FileName.txt`, the `File` object can be created as new `File("FileName.txt")`. If the file has to be created inside a directory, then either a path has to be added in front of the filename (when it is passed into the constructor) or one of the other three constructors has to be used, such as the following (see the `createFile2()` method in the `Files` class):

```
String path = "demo1" + File.separator +
                         "demo2" + File.separator;
String fileName = "FileName.txt";
File f = new File(path + fileName);
```

Note the usage of `File.separator` instead of the slash symbols, (/) or (\). That is because `File.separator` returns the platform-specific slash symbol. Here is an example of another `File` constructor usage:

```
String path = "demo1" + File.separator +
                          "demo2" + File.separator;
String fileName = "FileName.txt";
File f = new File(path, fileName);
```

Yet another constructor can be used as follows:

```
String path = "demo1" + File.separator +
                          "demo2" + File.separator;
String fileName = "FileName.txt";
File f = new File(new File(path), fileName);
```

However, if you prefer or have to use a **Universal Resource Identifier (URI)**, you can construct a `File` object like this:

```
String path = "demo1" + File.separator +
                          "demo2" + File.separator;
String fileName = "FileName.txt";
URI uri = new File(path + fileName).toURI();
File f = new File(uri);
```

Then, one of the following methods has to be invoked on the newly created `File` object:

- `boolean createNewFile()`: If a file with this name does not yet exist, creates a new file and returns `true`; otherwise, returns `false`

- `static File createTempFile(String prefix, String suffix)`: Creates a file in the temporary-file directory

- `static File createTempFile(String prefix, String suffix, File directory)`: Creates the directory; the provided prefix and suffix are used to generate the directory name

If the file you would like to create has to be placed inside a directory that does not exist yet, one of the following methods has to be used first, invoked on the `File` object that represents the filesystem path to the file:

- `boolean mkdir()`: Creates the directory with the provided name

- `boolean mkdirs()`: Creates the directory with the provided name, including any necessary but nonexistent parent directories

Before we look at a code example, we need to explain how the `delete()` method works:

- `boolean delete()`: Deletes the file or empty directory, which means you can delete the file but not all of the directories, as follows:

```
String path = "demo1" + File.separator +
                          "demo2" + File.separator;
String fileName = "FileName.txt";
File f = new File(path + fileName);
f.delete();
```

Let's look at how to overcome this limitation in the following example:

```
String path = "demo1" + File.separator +
                          "demo2" + File.separator;
String fileName = "FileName.txt";
File f = new File(path + fileName);
try {
    new File(path).mkdirs();
    f.createNewFile();
    f.delete();
    path = StringUtils
            .substringBeforeLast(path, File.separator);
    while (new File(path).delete()) {
        path = StringUtils
            .substringBeforeLast(path, File.separator);
    }
} catch (Exception e) {
    e.printStackTrace();
}
```

This example creates and deletes a file and all related directories. Notice our usage of the `org.apache.commons.lang3.StringUtils` class, which we discussed in the *String utilities* section. It allowed us to remove from the path the just-deleted directory and to continue doing it until all the nested directories are deleted, and the top-level directory is deleted last.

Listing files and directories

The following methods can be used for listing directories and the files in them:

- `String[] list()`: Returns the names of the files and directories in the directory
- `File[] listFiles()`: Returns the `File` objects that represent the files and directories in the directory
- `static File[] listRoots()`: Lists the available filesystem roots

In order to demonstrate the preceding methods, let's assume we have created the directories and two files in them, as follows:

```
String path1 = "demo1" + File.separator;
String path2 = "demo2" + File.separator;
String path = path1 + path2;
File f1 = new File(path + "file1.txt");
File f2 = new File(path + "file2.txt");
File dir1 = new File(path1);
File dir = new File(path);
dir.mkdirs();
f1.createNewFile();
f2.createNewFile();
```

After that, we should be able to run the following code:

```
System.out.print("\ndir1.list(): ");
for(String d: dir1.list()){
    System.out.print(d + " ");
}
System.out.print("\ndir1.listFiles(): ");
for(File f: dir1.listFiles()){
    System.out.print(f + " ");
}
```

```
System.out.print("\ndir.list(): ");
for(String d: dir.list()){
    System.out.print(d + " ");
}
System.out.print("\ndir.listFiles(): ");
for(File f: dir.listFiles()){
    System.out.print(f + " ");
}
System.out.print("\nFile.listRoots(): ");
for(File f: File.listRoots()){
    System.out.print(f + " ");
}
```

The result should be as follows:

```
dir1.list(): demo2
dir1.listFiles(): demo1/demo2
dir.list(): file1.txt file2.txt
dir.listFiles(): demo1/demo2/file1.txt demo1/demo2/file2.txt
File.listRoots(): /
```

The demonstrated methods can be enhanced by adding the following filters to them so that they will list only the files and directories that match the filter:

- `String[] list(FilenameFilter filter)`
- `File[] listFiles(FileFilter filter)`
- `File[] listFiles(FilenameFilter filter)`

However, a discussion of the file filters is outside the scope of this book.

Apache Commons' FileUtils and IOUtils utilities

A popular companion of JCL is the Apache Commons project (https://commons.apache.org), which provides many libraries that complement the JCL functionality. The classes of the org.apache.commons.io package are contained in the following root package and sub-packages:

- The org.apache.commons.io root package contains utility classes with static methods for common tasks, such as the popular FileUtils and IOUtils classes, described in the *FileUtils class* and *Class IOUtils class* sections respectively.

- The `org.apache.commons.io.input` package contains classes that support input based on the `InputStream` and `Reader` implementations, such as `XmlStreamReader` or `ReversedLinesFileReader`.

- The `org.apache.commons.io.output` package contains classes that support output based on the `OutputStream` and `Writer` implementations, such as `XmlStreamWriter` or `StringBuilderWriter`.

- The `org.apache.commons.io.filefilter` package contains classes that serve as file filters, such as `DirectoryFileFilter` or `RegexFileFilter`.

- The `org.apache.commons.io.comparator` package contains various implementations of `java.util.Comparator` for files such as `NameFileComparator`.

- The `org.apache.commons.io.serialization` package provides a framework for controlling the deserialization of classes.

- The `org.apache.commons.io.monitor` package allows monitoring filesystems, checking for a directory, and file creating, updating, or deleting. You can launch the `FileAlterationMonitor` object as a thread and create an object of `FileAlterationObserver` that performs a check of the changes in the filesystem at a specified interval.

Refer to the Apache Commons project documentation (`https://commons.apache.org/`) for more details.

The FileUtils class

The popular `org.apache.commons.io.FileUtils` class allows you to do all possible operations with files, as follows:

- Writing to a file
- Reading from a file
- Making a directory, including parent directories
- Copying files and directories
- Deleting files and directories
- Converting to and from a URL
- Listing files and directories by filter and extension
- Comparing file content

- Getting a file last-changed date
- Calculating a checksum

If you plan to manage files and directories programmatically, it is imperative that you study the documentation of this class on the Apache Commons project website (`https://commons.apache.org/proper/commons-io/javadocs/api-2.7/org/apache/commons/io/FileUtils.html`).

The IOUtils class

`org.apache.commons.io.IOUtils` is another very useful utility class that provides the following general I/O stream manipulation methods:

- The `closeQuietly` methods that close a stream, ignoring nulls and exceptions
- The `toXxx`/`read` methods that read data from a stream
- The `write` methods that write data to a stream
- The `copy` methods that copy all the data from one stream to another
- The `contentEquals` methods that compare the content of two streams

All the methods in this class that read a stream are buffered internally, so there is no need to use the `BufferedInputStream` or `BufferedReader` class. The `copy` methods all use `copyLarge` methods behind the scenes that substantially increase their performance and efficiency.

This class is indispensable for managing the I/O streams. See more details about this class and its methods on the Apache Commons project website (`https://commons.apache.org/proper/commons-io/javadocs/api-2.7/org/apache/commons/io/IOUtils.html`).

Summary

In this chapter, we have discussed the `String` class methods that allow analyzing, comparing, and transforming strings. We have also discussed popular string utilities from the JCL and the Apache Commons project. Two big sections of this chapter were dedicated to the input/output streams and the supporting classes in the JCL and the Apache Commons project. The file-managing classes and their methods were also discussed and demonstrated in specific code examples. Now, you should be able to write code that processes strings and files, using standard Java API and Apache Commons utilities.

In the next chapter, we will present the Java Collections framework and its three main interfaces, List, Set, and Map, including discussion and demonstration of generics. We will also discuss utility classes for managing arrays, objects, and time/date values.

Quiz

1. What does the following code print?

    ```
    String str = "&8a!L";
    System.out.println(str.indexOf("a!L"));
    ```

    A. 3

    B. 2

    C. 1

    D. 0

2. What does the following code print?

    ```
    String s1 = "x12";
    String s2 = new String("x12");
    System.out.println(s1.equals(s2));
    ```

    A. Error

    B. Exception

    C. true

    D. false

3. What does the following code print?

    ```
    System.out.println("%wx6".substring(2));
    ```

    A. wx

    B. x6

    C. %w

    D. Exception

4. What does the following code print?

```
System.out.println("ab"+"42".repeat(2));
```

A. `ab4242`

B. `ab42ab42`

C. `ab422`

D. `Error`

5. What does the following code print?

```
String s = "   ";
System.out.println(s.isBlank()+" "+s.isEmpty());
```

A. `false false`

B. `false true`

C. `true true`

D. `true false`

6. Select all correct statements:

A. A stream can represent a data source.

B. An input stream can write to a file.

C. A stream can represent a data destination.

D. An output stream can display data on a screen.

7. Select all correct statements about the classes of the `java.io` package:

A. Reader extends `InputStream`.

B. Reader extends `OutputStream`.

C. Reader extends `java.lang.Object`.

D. Reader extends `java.lang.Input`.

8. Select all correct statements about the classes of the `java.io` package:

A. Writer extends `FilterOutputStream`.

B. Writer extends `OutputStream`.

C. Writer extends `java.lang.Output`.

D. Writer extends `java.lang.Object`.

9. Select all correct statements about the classes of the `java.io` package:

    A. `PrintStream` extends `FilterOutputStream`.

    B. `PrintStream` extends `OutputStream`.

    C. `PrintStream` extends `java.lang.Object`.

    D. `PrintStream` extends `java.lang.Output`.

10. What does the following code do?

```
String path = "demo1" + File.separator + "demo2" + File.
separator;
String fileName = "FileName.txt";
File f = new File(path, fileName);
try {
    new File(path).mkdir();
    f.createNewFile();
} catch (Exception e) {
    e.printStackTrace();
}
```

    A. Creates two directories and a file in the demo2 directory

    B. Creates one directory and a file in it

    C. Does not create any directory

    D. Exception

6

Data Structures, Generics, and Popular Utilities

This chapter presents the Java collections framework and its three main interfaces, `List`, `Set`, and `Map`, including a discussion and demonstration of generics. The `equals()` and `hashCode()` methods are also discussed in the context of Java collections. Utility classes for managing arrays, objects, and time/date values have corresponding dedicated sections too. After studying this chapter, you will be able to use all the main data structures in your programs.

The following topics will be covered in this chapter:

- `List`, `Set`, and `Map` interfaces
- `Collections` utilities
- `Arrays` utilities
- `Object` utilities
- The `java.time` package

Let's begin!

Technical requirements

To be able to execute the code examples provided in this chapter, you will need the following:

- A computer with a Microsoft Windows, Apple macOS, or Linux operating system

- Java **Standard Edition** (**SE**) version 17 or later

- An **integrated development environment** (**IDE**) or your preferred code editor

Instructions on how to set up a Java SE and IntelliJ IDEA editor were provided in *Chapter 1* of this book, *Getting Started with Java 17*. The files with code examples for this chapter are available on GitHub in the `https://github.com/PacktPublishing/Learn-Java-17-Programming.git` repository, in the `examples/src/main/java/com/packt/learnjava/ch06_collections` folder.

List, Set, and Map interfaces

The **Java collections framework** consists of classes and interfaces that implement a collection data structure. Collections are similar to arrays in that they can hold references to objects and can be managed as a group. The difference is that arrays require their capacity to be defined before they can be used, while collections can increase and decrease their size automatically as needed. You just add or remove an object reference to a collection, and the collection changes its size accordingly. Another difference is that collections cannot have their elements be primitive types, such as `short`, `int`, or `double`. If you need to store such type values, the elements must be of a corresponding wrapper type, such as `Short`, `Integer`, or `Double`.

Java collections support various algorithms for storing and accessing elements of a collection: an ordered list, a unique set, a dictionary (called a **map** in Java), a **stack**, a **queue**, and some others. All classes and interfaces of the Java collections framework belong to the `java.util` package of the **Java Class Library** (**JCL**). The `java.util` package contains the following:

- Interfaces that extend the `Collection` interface: `List`, `Set`, and `Queue`, to name the most popular ones

- Classes that implement the previously listed interfaces: `ArrayList`, `HashSet`, `Stack`, `LinkedList`, and some others

- The `Map` interface and its `ConcurrentMap` and `SortedMap` sub-interfaces, to name a couple

- Classes that implement `Map`-related interfaces: `HashMap`, `HashTable`, and `TreeMap`, to name the three most frequently used

Reviewing all the classes and interfaces of the `java.util` package would require a dedicated book. So, in this section, we will just have a brief overview of the three main interfaces—`List`, `Set`, and `Map`—and one implementation class for each of them—`ArrayList`, `HashSet`, and `HashMap`. We start with methods that are shared by the `List` and `Set` interfaces. The principal difference between `List` and `Set` is that `Set` does not allow the duplication of elements. Another difference is that `List` preserves the order of elements and also allows them to be sorted.

To identify an element inside a collection, the `equals()` method is used. To improve performance, classes that implement the `Set` interface often use the `hashCode()` method too. This facilitates rapid calculation of an integer (called a **hash value** or **hash code**) that is most of the time (but not always) unique to each element. Elements with the same hash value are placed in the same *bucket*. While establishing whether there is already a certain value in the set, it is enough to check the internal hash table and see whether such a value has already been used. If not, the new element is unique. If yes, then the new element can be compared (using the `equals()` method) with each of the elements with the same hash value. Such a procedure is faster than comparing a new element with each element of the set one by one.

That is why we often see that the name of a class has a `hash` prefix, indicating that the class uses a hash value, so the element must implement the `hashCode()` method. While doing this, you must make sure that it is implemented so that every time the `equals()` method returns `true` for two objects, the hash values of these two objects returned by the `hashCode()` method are equal too. Otherwise, the just-described algorithm of using the hash value will not work.

And finally, before talking about `java.util` interfaces, a few words about generics.

Generics

You can see these most often in declarations such as these:

```
List<String> list = new ArrayList<String>();
Set<Integer> set  = new HashSet<Integer>();
```

In the preceding examples, **generics** are element nature declarations surrounded by angle brackets. As you can see, they are redundant, as they are repeated in the left- and right-hand sides of the assignment statement. That is why Java allows replacement of the generics on the right side with empty brackets (`<>`) called a **diamond**, as illustrated in the following code snippet:

```
List<String> list = new ArrayList<>();
Set<Integer> set = new HashSet<>();
```

Generics inform the compiler about the expected type of collection elements. This way, the compiler can check whether an element a programmer tries to add to a declared collection is of a compatible type. Observe the following, for example:

```
List<String> list = new ArrayList<>();
list.add("abc");
list.add(42);    //compilation error
```

This helps to avoid runtime errors. It also tips off the programmer (because an IDE compiles the code when a programmer writes it) about possible manipulations of collection elements.

We will also see these other types of generics:

- `<? extends T>` means *a type that is either* `T` *or a child of* `T`, where `T` is the type used as the generics of a collection.

- `<? super T>` means *a type* `T` *or any of its base (parent) class*, where `T` is the type used as the generics of a collection.

With that, let's start with how an object of a class that implements the `List` or `Set` interface can be created—or, in other words, the `List` or `Set` type of variable can be initialized. To demonstrate the methods of these two interfaces, we will use two classes: `ArrayList` (implements `List`) and `HashSet` (implements `Set`).

How to initialize List and Set

Since Java 9, the `List` or `Set` interfaces have static `of()` factory methods that can be used to initialize a collection, as outlined here:

- `of()`: Returns an empty collection.

- `of(E... e)`: Returns a collection with as many elements as are passed in during the call. They can be passed in a comma-separated list or as an array.

Here are a few examples:

```
//Collection<String> coll
//          = List.of("s1", null); //does not allow null
Collection<String> coll = List.of("s1", "s1", "s2");
//coll.add("s3");          //does not allow add element
//coll.remove("s1");    //does not allow remove element
//((List<String>) coll).set(1, "s3");
                          //does not allow modify element
System.out.println(coll);        //prints: [s1, s1, s2]

//coll = Set.of("s3", "s3", "s4");
                          //does not allow duplicate
//coll = Set.of("s2", "s3", null);
                          //does not allow null
coll = Set.of("s3", "s4");
System.out.println(coll);
                    //prints: [s3, s4] or [s4, s3]

//coll.add("s5");         //does not allow add element
//coll.remove("s2");    //does not allow remove element
```

As you might expect, the factory method for Set does not allow duplicates, so we have commented the line out (otherwise, the preceding example would stop running at that line). What is less expected is that you cannot have a null element, and you cannot add/remove/modify elements of a collection after it was initialized using one of the of() methods. That's why we have commented out some lines of the preceding example. If you need to add elements after a collection is initialized, you have to initialize it using a constructor or some other utilities that create a modifiable collection (we will see an example of Arrays.asList() shortly).

The Collection interface provides two methods for adding elements to an object that implements Collection (the parent interface of List and Set) that look like this:

- boolean add(E e): This attempts to add the provided element e to the collection; it returns true in case of success, and false in case of not being able to accomplish it (for example, when such an element already exists in the Set interface).

- `boolean addAll(Collection<? extends E> c)`: This attempts to add all of the elements in the provided collection to the collection; it returns `true` if at least one element was added, and `false` in case of not being able to add an element to the collection (for example, when all elements of the provided collection c already exist in the Set interface).

Here's an example of using the `add()` method:

```java
List<String> list1 = new ArrayList<>();
list1.add("s1");
list1.add("s1");
System.out.println(list1);        //prints: [s1, s1]


Set<String> set1 = new HashSet<>();
set1.add("s1");
set1.add("s1");
System.out.println(set1);         //prints: [s1]
```

And here is an example of using the `addAll()` method:

```java
List<String> list1 = new ArrayList<>();
list1.add("s1");
list1.add("s1");
System.out.println(list1);         //prints: [s1, s1]


List<String> list2 = new ArrayList<>();
list2.addAll(list1);
System.out.println(list2);         //prints: [s1, s1]


Set<String> set = new HashSet<>();
set.addAll(list1);
System.out.println(set);           //prints: [s1]
```

Here is an example of the `add()` and `addAll()` methods' functionality:

```java
List<String> list1 = new ArrayList<>();
list1.add("s1");
list1.add("s1");
```

```
System.out.println(list1);        //prints: [s1, s1]


List<String> list2 = new ArrayList<>();
list2.addAll(list1);
System.out.println(list2);        //prints: [s1, s1]


Set<String> set = new HashSet<>();
set.addAll(list1);
System.out.println(set);          //prints: [s1]


Set<String> set1 = new HashSet<>();
set1.add("s1");


Set<String> set2 = new HashSet<>();
set2.add("s1");
set2.add("s2");


System.out.println(set1.addAll(set2)); //prints: true
System.out.println(set1);                 //prints: [s1, s2]
```

Notice how, in the last example in the preceding code snippet, the set1.addAll(set2)
method returns true, although not all elements were added. To see the case of the add()
and addAll() methods returning false, look at the following example:

```
Set<String> set = new HashSet<>();
System.out.println(set.add("s1"));     //prints: true
System.out.println(set.add("s1"));     //prints: false
System.out.println(set);               //prints: [s1]


Set<String> set1 = new HashSet<>();
set1.add("s1");
set1.add("s2");


Set<String> set2 = new HashSet<>();
set2.add("s1");
set2.add("s2");
```

```
System.out.println(set1.addAll(set2)); //prints: false
System.out.println(set1);               //prints: [s1, s2]
```

The `ArrayList` and `HashSet` classes also have constructors that accept a collection, as illustrated in the following code snippet:

```
Collection<String> list1 = List.of("s1", "s1", "s2");
System.out.println(list1);        //prints: [s1, s1, s2]

List<String> list2 = new ArrayList<>(list1);
System.out.println(list2);        //prints: [s1, s1, s2]

Set<String> set = new HashSet<>(list1);
System.out.println(set);          //prints: [s1, s2]

List<String> list3 = new ArrayList<>(set);
System.out.println(list3);        //prints: [s1, s2]
```

Now, after we have learned how a collection can be initialized, we can turn to other methods in the `List` and `Set` interfaces.

java.lang.Iterable interface

The `Collection` interface extends the `java.lang.Iterable` interface, which means that classes that implement the `Collection` interface—directly or not—also implement the `java.lang.Iterable` interface. There are only three methods in the `Iterable` interface, as outlined here:

- `Iterator<T> iterator()`: This returns an object of a class that implements the `java.util.Iterator` interface; it allows the collection to be used in FOR statements, as in this example:

  ```
  Iterable<String> list = List.of("s1", "s2", "s3");
  System.out.println(list);        //prints: [s1, s2, s3]

  for(String e: list){
      System.out.print(e + " ");  //prints: s1 s2 s3
  }
  ```

- `default void forEach (Consumer<? super T> function):`
This applies the provided function of the `Consumer` type to each element of
the collection until all elements have been processed or the function throws
an exception. We will discuss what a function is in *Chapter 13, Functional
Programming*; for now, we will just provide an example here:

```
Iterable<String> list = List.of("s1", "s2", "s3");
System.out.println(list);    //prints: [s1, s2, s3]
list.forEach(e -> System.out.print(e + " "));
                             //prints: s1 s2 s3
```

- `default Spliterator<T> splititerator():` This returns an object
of a class that implements the `java.util.Spliterator` interface; it is used
primarily for implementing methods that allow parallel processing and is outside
the scope of this book.

Collection interface

As we have mentioned already, the `List` and `Set` interfaces extend the `Collection`
interface, which means that all methods of the `Collection` interface are inherited by
`List` and `Set`. These methods are listed here:

- `boolean add(E e):` This attempts to add an element to the collection.

- `boolean addAll(Collection<? extends E> c):` This attempts to add all
elements in the collection provided.

- `boolean equals(Object o):` This compares the collection with the o object
provided. If the object provided is not a collection, this object returns `false`;
otherwise, it compares the composition of the collection with the composition of
the collection provided (as an o object). In the case of `List`, it also compares the
order of elements. Let's illustrate this with a few examples, as follows:

```
Collection<String> list1 = List.of("s1", "s2", "s3");
System.out.println(list1);     //prints: [s1, s2, s3]


Collection<String> list2 = List.of("s1", "s2", "s3");
System.out.println(list2);     //prints: [s1, s2, s3]


System.out.println(list1.equals(list2));
```

```
                                                  //prints: true

Collection<String> list3 = List.of("s2", "s1", "s3");
System.out.println(list3);        //prints: [s2, s1, s3]


System.out.println(list1.equals(list3));
                                                  //prints: false


Collection<String> set1 = Set.of("s1", "s2", "s3");
System.out.println(set1);
            //prints: [s2, s3, s1] or different order


Collection<String> set2 = Set.of("s2", "s1", "s3");
System.out.println(set2);
            //prints: [s2, s1, s3] or different order


System.out.println(set1.equals(set2));
                                                  //prints: true


Collection<String> set3 = Set.of("s4", "s1", "s3");
System.out.println(set3);
            //prints: [s4, s1, s3] or different order


System.out.println(set1.equals(set3));
                                                  //prints: false
```

- `int hashCode()`: This returns the hash value for the collection; it is used in the case where the collection is an element of a collection that requires the `hashCode()` method implementation.

- `boolean isEmpty()`: This returns `true` if the collection does not have any elements.

- `int size()`: This returns the count of elements of the collection; when the `isEmpty()` method returns `true`, this method returns 0.

- `void clear()`: This removes all elements from the collection; after this method is called, the `isEmpty()` method returns `true`, and the `size()` method returns 0.

- `boolean contains(Object o)`: This returns `true` if the collection contains the provided o object. For this method to work correctly, each element of the collection and the provided object must implement the `equals()` method, and, in the case of `Set`, the `hashCode()` method should be implemented.

- `boolean containsAll(Collection<?> c)`: This returns `true` if the collection contains all elements in the collection provided. For this method to work correctly, each element of the collection and each element of the collection provided must implement the `equals()` method, and, in the case of `Set`, the `hashCode()` method should be implemented.

- `boolean remove(Object o)`: This attempts to remove the specified element from this collection and returns `true` if it was present. For this method to work correctly, each element of the collection and the object provided must implement the `equals()` method, and, in the case of `Set`, the `hashCode()` method should be implemented.

- `boolean removeAll(Collection<?> c)`: This attempts to remove from the collection all elements of the collection provided; similar to the `addAll()` method, this method returns `true` if at least one of the elements was removed; otherwise, it returns `false`. For this method to work correctly, each element of the collection and each element of the collection provided must implement the `equals()` method, and, in the case of `Set`, the `hashCode()` method should be implemented.

- `default boolean removeIf(Predicate<? super E> filter)`: This attempts to remove from the collection all elements that satisfy the given predicate; it is a function we are going to describe in *Chapter 13, Functional Programming*. It returns `true` if at least one element was removed.

- `boolean retainAll(Collection<?> c)`: This attempts to retain in the collection just the elements contained in the collection provided. Similar to the `addAll()` method, this method returns `true` if at least one of the elements is retained; otherwise, it returns `false`. For this method to work correctly, each element of the collection and each element of the collection provided must implement the `equals()` method, and, in the case of `Set`, the `hashCode()` method should be implemented.

- `Object[] toArray()`, `T[] toArray(T[] a)`: This converts the collection to an array.

- `default T[] toArray(IntFunction<T[]> generator)`: This converts the collection to an array, using the function provided. We are going to explain functions in *Chapter 13, Functional Programming*.

- `default Stream<E> stream()`: This returns a `Stream` object (we talk about streams in *Chapter 14, Java Standard Streams*).

- `default Stream<E> parallelStream()`: This returns a possibly parallel `Stream` object (we talk about streams in *Chapter 14, Java Standard Streams*).

List interface

The `List` interface has several other methods that do not belong to any of its parent interfaces, as outlined here:

- Static factory `of()` methods, described in the *How to initialize List and Set* subsection.

- `void add(int index, E element)`: This inserts the element provided at the provided position in the list.

- `static List<E> copyOf(Collection<E> coll)`: This returns an unmodifiable `List` interface containing the elements of the given `Collection` interface and preserves their order. The following code snippet demonstrates the functionality of this method:

```
Collection<String> list = List.of("s1", "s2", "s3");
System.out.println(list);    //prints: [s1, s2, s3]


List<String> list1 = List.copyOf(list);
//list1.add("s4");                    //run-time error
//list1.set(1, "s5");                 //run-time error
//list1.remove("s1");                 //run-time error


Set<String> set = new HashSet<>();
System.out.println(set.add("s1"));
System.out.println(set);             //prints: [s1]


Set<String> set1 = Set.copyOf(set);
//set1.add("s2");                     //run-time error
//set1.remove("s1");                  //run-time error


Set<String> set2 = Set.copyOf(list);
System.out.println(set2);    //prints: [s1, s2, s3]
```

- `E get(int index)`: This returns the element located at the position specified in the list.

- `List<E> subList(int fromIndex, int toIndex)`: Extracts a sublist between `fromIndex` (inclusive) and `toIndex` (exclusive).

- `int indexOf(Object o)`: This returns the first index (position) of a specified element in the list; the first element in the list has an index (position) of 0.

- `int lastIndexOf(Object o)`: This returns the last index (position) of a specified element in the list; the final element in the list has a `list.size()` - 1 index position.

- `E remove(int index)`: This removes the element located at a specified position in the list; it returns the element removed.

- `E set(int index, E element)`: This replaces the element located at a position specified in the list; it returns the element replaced.

- `default void replaceAll(UnaryOperator<E> operator)`: This transforms the list by applying the function provided to each element. The `UnaryOperator` function will be described in *Chapter 13, Functional Programming*.

- `ListIterator<E> listIterator()`: Returns a `ListIterator` object that allows the list to be traversed backward.

- `ListIterator<E> listIterator(int index)`: Returns a `ListIterator` object that allows the sublist (starting from the provided position) to be traversed backward. Observe the following, for example:

```
List<String> list = List.of("s1", "s2", "s3");
ListIterator<String> li = list.listIterator();
while(li.hasNext()){
    System.out.print(li.next() + " ");
                                //prints: s1 s2 s3
}
while(li.hasPrevious()){
    System.out.print(li.previous() + " ");
                                //prints: s3 s2 s1
}
ListIterator<String> li1 = list.listIterator(1);
while(li1.hasNext()){
    System.out.print(li1.next() + " ");
                                //prints: s2 s3
```

```
    }
    ListIterator<String> li2 = list.listIterator(1);
    while(li2.hasPrevious()){
        System.out.print(li2.previous() + " ");
                                            //prints: s1

    }
```

- `default void sort(Comparator<? super E> c)`: This sorts the list according to the order generated by the `Comparator` interface provided. Observe the following, for example:

```
    List<String> list = new ArrayList<>();
    list.add("S2");
    list.add("s3");
    list.add("s1");
    System.out.println(list);      //prints: [S2, s3, s1]


    list.sort(String.CASE_INSENSITIVE_ORDER);
    System.out.println(list);       //prints: [s1, S2, s3]


    //list.add(null);      //causes NullPointerException
    list.sort(Comparator.naturalOrder());
    System.out.println(list);      //prints: [S2, s1, s3]


    list.sort(Comparator.reverseOrder());
    System.out.println(list);      //prints: [s3, s1, S2]


    list.add(null);
    list.sort(Comparator.nullsFirst(Comparator
                                    .naturalOrder()));
    System.out.println(list);
                            //prints: [null, S2, s1, s3]


    list.sort(Comparator.nullsLast(Comparator
                                    .naturalOrder()));
    System.out.println(list);
```

```
                                //prints: [S2, s1, s3, null]


Comparator<String> comparator =
       (s1, s2) -> s1 == null ? -1 : s1.compareTo(s2);
list.sort(comparator);
System.out.println(list);
                                //prints: [null, S2, s1, s3]


Comparator<String> comparator = (s1, s2) ->
  s1 == null ? -1 : s1.compareTo(s2);
list.sort(comparator);
System.out.println(list);
                                //prints: [null, S2, s1, s3]
```

There are principally two ways to sort a list, as follows:

- Using a `Comparable` interface implementation (called **natural order**)

- Using a `Comparator` interface implementation

The `Comparable` interface only has a `compareTo()` method. In the preceding example, we have implemented the `Comparator` interface basing it on the `Comparable` interface implementation in the `String` class. As you can see, this implementation provided the same sort order as `Comparator.nullsFirst(Comparator.naturalOrder())`. This style of implementation
is called **functional programming**, which we will discuss in more detail in *Chapter 13, Functional Programming*.

Set interface

The `Set` interface has the following methods that do not belong to any of its
parent interfaces:

- Static `of()` factory methods, described in the *How to initialize List and Set* subsection.

- The `static Set<E> copyOf(Collection<E> coll)` method: This returns an unmodifiable `Set` interface containing elements of the given `Collection`; it works the same way as the `static <E> List<E> copyOf(Collection<E> coll)` method described in the *List interface* section.

Map interface

The `Map` interface has many methods similar to the `List` and `Set` methods, as listed here:

- `int size()`

- `void clear()`

- `int hashCode()`

- `boolean isEmpty()`

- `boolean equals(Object o)`

- `default void forEach(BiConsumer<K,V> action)`

- Static factory methods: `of()`, `of(K, V v)`, `of(K k1, V v1, K k2, V v2)`, and many other methods besides

The `Map` interface, however, does not extend `Iterable`, `Collection`, or any other interface, for that matter. It is designed to be able to store **values** by their **keys**. Each key is unique, while several equal values can be stored with different keys on the same map. The combination of key and value constitutes `Entry`, which is an internal interface of `Map`. Both `value` and `key` objects must implement the `equals()` method. A `key` object must also implement the `hashCode()` method.

Many methods of the `Map` interface have exactly the same signature and functionality as in the `List` and `Set` interfaces, so we are not going to repeat them here. We will only walk through the `Map`-specific methods, as follows:

- `V get(Object key)`: This retrieves the value according to the key provided; it returns `null` if there is no such key.

- `Set<K> keySet()`: This retrieves all keys from the map.

- `Collection<V> values()`: This retrieves all values from the map.

- `boolean containsKey(Object key)`: This returns `true` if the key provided exists in the map.

- `boolean containsValue(Object value)`: This returns `true` if the value provided exists in the map.

- `V put (K key, V value)`: This adds the value and its key to the map; it returns the previous value stored with the same key.

- `void putAll (Map<K,V> m)`: This copies from the map provided all the key-value pairs.

- `default V putIfAbsent (K key, V value)`: This stores the value provided and maps to the key provided if such a key is not already used by the map. It returns the value mapped to the key provided—either an existing or a new one.

- `V remove (Object key)`: This removes both the key and value from the map; it returns a value or `null` if there is no such key, or if the value is `null`.

- `default boolean remove (Object key, Object value)`: This removes the key-value pair from the map if such a pair exists in the map.

- `default V replace (K key, V value)`: This replaces the value if the key provided is currently mapped to the value provided. It returns the old value if it was replaced; otherwise, it returns `null`.

- `default boolean replace (K key, V oldValue, V newValue)`: This replaces the `oldValue` value with the `newValue` value provided if the key provided is currently mapped to the `oldValue` value. It returns `true` if the `oldValue` value was replaced; otherwise, it returns `false`.

- `default void replaceAll (BiFunction<K,V,V> function)`: This applies the function provided to each key-value pair in the map and replaces it with the result, or throws an exception if this is not possible.

- `Set<Map.Entry<K,V>> entrySet ()`: This returns a set of all key-value pairs as objects of `Map.Entry`.

- `default V getOrDefault (Object key, V defaultValue)`: This returns the value mapped to the key provided or the `defaultValue` value if the map does not have the key provided.

- `static Map.Entry<K,V> entry (K key, V value)`: This returns an unmodifiable `Map.Entry` object with the `key` object and `value` object provided in it.

- `static Map<K,V> copy (Map<K,V> map)` : This converts the `Map` interface provided to an unmodifiable one.

The following Map methods are much too complicated for the scope of this book, so we are just mentioning them for the sake of completeness. They allow multiple values to be combined or calculated and aggregated in a single existing value in the Map interface, or a new one to be created:

- `default V merge(K key, V value, BiFunction<V,V,V> remappingFunction)`: If the provided key-value pair exists and the value is not `null`, the provided function is used to calculate a new value; it removes the key-value pair if the newly calculated value is `null`. If the key-value pair provided does not exist or the value is `null`, the non-`null` value provided replaces the current one. This method can be used for aggregating several values; for example, it can be used for concatenating the following string values: `map.merge(key, value, String::concat)`. We will explain what `String::concat` means in *Chapter 13, Functional Programming.*

- `default V compute(K key, BiFunction<K,V,V> remappingFunction)`: This computes a new value using the function provided.

- `default V computeIfAbsent(K key, Function<K,V> mappingFunction)`: This computes a new value using the function provided only if the provided key is not already associated with a value, or the value is `null`.

- `default V computeIfPresent(K key, BiFunction<K,V,V> remappingFunction)`: This computes a new value using the function provided only if the provided key is already associated with a value and the value is not `null`.

This last group of *computing* and *merging* methods is rarely used. The most popular, by far, are the `V put(K key, V value)` and `V get(Object key)` methods, which allow the use of the main Map function of storing key-value pairs and retrieving the value using the key. The `Set<K> keySet()` method is often used for iterating over the map's key-value pairs, although the `entrySet()` method seems a more natural way of doing that. Here is an example:

```
Map<Integer, String> map = Map.of(1, "s1", 2, "s2", 3, "s3");

for(Integer key: map.keySet()){
    System.out.print(key + ", " + map.get(key) + ", ");
                                    //prints: 3, s3, 2, s2, 1, s1,
}
for(Map.Entry e: map.entrySet()){
    System.out.print(e.getKey() + ", " + e.getValue() + ", ");
```

```
                                        //prints: 2, s2, 3, s3, 1, s1,
}
```

The first of the `for` loops in the preceding code example uses a more widespread way to access the key-pair values of a map by iterating over the keys. The second `for` loop iterates over the set of entries, which (in our opinion) is a more natural way to do it. Notice that the printed-out values are not in the same order we have put them in the map. That is because, since Java 9, unmodifiable collections (that is, what `of()` factory methods produce) have added randomization to the order of `Set` elements, which changes the order of elements between different code executions. Such a design was done to make sure a programmer does not rely on a certain order of `Set` elements, which is not guaranteed for a set.

Unmodifiable collections

Please note that collections produced by `of()` factory methods used to be called **immutable** in Java 9, and **unmodifiable** since Java 10. That is because immutable implies that you cannot change anything in collections, while, in fact, collection elements can be changed if they are modifiable objects. For example, let's build a collection of objects of the `Person1` class, as follows:

```
class Person1 {
    private int age;
    private String name;
    public Person1(int age, String name) {
        this.age = age;
        this.name = name == null ? "" : name;
    }
    public void setName(String name){ this.name = name; }
    @Override
    public String toString() {
        return "Person{age=" + age +
                ", name=" + name + "}";
    }
}
```

In the following code snippet, for simplicity, we will create a list with one element only and will then try to modify the element:

```
Person1 p1 = new Person1(45, "Bill");
List<Person1> list = List.of(p1);
//list.add(new Person1(22, "Bob"));
                         //UnsupportedOperationException
System.out.println(list);
                //prints: [Person{age=45, name=Bill}]
p1.setName("Kelly");
System.out.println(list);
                //prints: [Person{age=45, name=Kelly}]
```

As you can see, although it is not possible to add an element to the list created by the of() factory method, its element can still be modified if a reference to the element exists outside the list.

Collections utilities

There are two classes with static methods handling collections that are very popular and helpful, as follows:

- java.util.Collections
- org.apache.commons.collections4.CollectionUtils

The fact that the methods are static means they do not depend on the object state, so they are also called **stateless methods** or **utility methods**.

java.util.Collections class

Many methods in the `Collections` class manage collections and analyze, sort, and compare them. There are more than 70 of them, so we won't have a chance to talk about all of them. Instead, we are going to look at the ones most often used by mainstream application developers, as follows:

- `static copy(List<T> dest, List<T> src)`: This copies elements of the `src` list to the `dest` list and preserves the order of elements and their position in the list. The `dest` list size has to be equal to, or bigger than, the `src` list size, otherwise a runtime exception is raised. Here is an example of this method's usage:

```
List<String> list1 = Arrays.asList("s1","s2");
List<String> list2 = Arrays.asList("s3", "s4", "s5");
Collections.copy(list2, list1);
System.out.println(list2);     //prints: [s1, s2, s5]
```

- `static void sort(List<T> list)`: This sorts the list in order according to the `compareTo(T)` method implemented by each element (called **natural ordering**). It only accepts lists with elements that implement the `Comparable` interface (which requires implementation of the `compareTo(T)` method). In the example that follows, we use `List<String>` because the `String` class implements `Comparable`:

```
//List<String> list =
       //List.of("a", "X", "10", "20", "1", "2");
List<String> list =
     Arrays.asList("a", "X", "10", "20", "1", "2");
Collections.sort(list);
System.out.println(list);
                     //prints: [1, 10, 2, 20, X, a]
```

Note that we could not use the `List.of()` method to create a list because the list would be unmodifiable and its order could not be changed. Also, look at the resulting order: numbers come first, then capital letters, followed by lowercase letters. That is because the `compareTo()` method in the `String` class uses code points of the characters to establish the order. Here is the code that demonstrates this:

```
List<String> list =
          Arrays.asList("a", "X", "10", "20", "1", "2");
Collections.sort(list);
System.out.println(list);  //prints: [1, 10, 2, 20, X, a]
list.forEach(s -> {
```

```
        for(int i = 0; i < s.length(); i++){
            System.out.print(" " +
                                Character.codePointAt(s, i));
        }
        if(!s.equals("a")) {
            System.out.print(",");
                    //prints: 49, 49 48, 50, 50 48, 88, 97
        }
    });
```

As you can see, the order is defined by the value of the code points of the characters that compose the string.

- `static void sort(List<T> list, Comparator<T> comparator)`:
  This sorts the order of the list according to the `Comparator` object provided, irrespective of whether the list elements implement the `Comparable` interface or not. As an example, let's sort a list that consists of objects in the `Person` class, as follows:

```
class Person {
    private int age;
    private String name;
    public Person(int age, String name) {
        this.age = age;
        this.name = name == null ? "" : name;
    }
    public int getAge() { return this.age; }
    public String getName() { return this.name; }
    @Override
    public String toString() {
        return "Person{name=" + name +
                    ", age=" + age + "}";
    }
}
```

- And here is the `Comparator` class to sort the list of `Person` objects:

```
class ComparePersons implements Comparator<Person> {
    public int compare(Person p1, Person p2){
        int result = p1.getName().compareTo(p2.
getName());
        if (result != 0) { return result; }
        return p1.age - p2.getAge();
    }
}
```

Now, we can use the `Person` and `ComparePersons` classes, as follows:

```
List<Person> persons =
    Arrays.asList(new Person(23, "Jack"),
                    new Person(30, "Bob"),
                    new Person(15, "Bob"));
Collections.sort(persons, new ComparePersons());
System.out.println(persons);
                //prints: [Person{name=Bob, age=15},
                //          Person{name=Bob, age=30},
                //          Person{name=Jack, age=23}]
```

As we have mentioned already, there are many more utilities in the `Collections` class, so we recommend you look through the related documentation at least once and understand all its capabilities.

CollectionUtils class

The `org.apache.commons.collections4.CollectionUtils` class in the *Apache Commons* project contains static stateless methods that complement the methods of the `java.util.Collections` class. They help to search, process, and compare Java collections.

To use this class, you would need to add the following dependency to the Maven pom. xml configuration file:

```
<dependency>
    <groupId>org.apache.commons</groupId>
    <artifactId>commons-collections4</artifactId>
    <version>4.4</version>
</dependency>
```

There are many methods in this class, and more methods will probably be added over time. These utilities are created in addition to Collections methods, so they are more complex and nuanced and do not fit the scope of this book. To give you an idea of the methods available in the CollectionUtils class, here is a brief description of the methods, grouped according to their functionality:

- Methods that retrieve an element from a collection
- Methods that add an element or a group of elements to a collection
- Methods that merge Iterable elements into a collection
- Methods that remove or retain elements with or without criteria
- Methods that compare two collections
- Methods that transform a collection
- Methods that select from, and filter, a collection
- Methods that generate the union, intersection, or difference of two collections
- Methods that create an immutable empty collection
- Methods that check collection size and emptiness
- A method that reverses an array

This last method should probably belong to the utility class that handles arrays, and that is what we are going to discuss now.

Arrays utilities

There are two classes with static methods handling collections that are very popular and helpful, as follows:

- `java.util.Arrays`
- `org.apache.commons.lang3.ArrayUtils`

We will briefly review each of them.

java.util.Arrays class

We have already used the `java.util.Arrays` class several times. It is the primary utility class for array management. This utility class used to be very popular because of the `asList(T...a)` method. It was the most compact way of creating and initializing a collection and is shown in the following snippet:

```
List<String> list = Arrays.asList("s0", "s1");
Set<String> set = new HashSet<>(Arrays.asList("s0", "s1");
```

It is still a popular way of creating a modifiable list—we used it, too. However, after a `List.of()` factory method was introduced, the `Arrays` class declined substantially.

Nevertheless, if you need to manage arrays, then the `Arrays` class may be a big help. It contains more than 160 methods, and most of them are overloaded with different parameters and array types. If we group them by the method name, there will be 21 groups, and if we further group them by functionality, only the following 10 groups will cover all the `Arrays` class functionality:

- `asList()`: This creates an `ArrayList` object based on the provided array or comma-separated list of parameters.
- `binarySearch()`: This searches an array or only a specified part of it (according to the range of indices).
- `compare()`, `mismatch()`, `equals()`, and `deepEquals()`: These compare two arrays or their elements (according to the range of indices).
- `copyOf()` and `copyOfRange()`: This copies all arrays or only a specified (according to the range of indices) part of them.
- `hashcode()` and `deepHashCode()`: This generates a hash code value based on the array provided.
- `toString()` and `deepToString()`: This creates a `String` representation of an array.

- `fill()`, `setAll()`, `parallelPrefix()`, and `parallelSetAll()`: This sets a value (fixed or generated by the function provided) for every element of an array or those specified according to a range of indices.

- `sort()` and `parallelSort()`: This sorts elements of an array or only part of it (specified according to a range of indices).

- `splititerator()`: This returns a `Splititerator` object for parallel processing of an array or part of it (specified according to a range of indices).

- `stream()`: This generates a stream of array elements or some of them (specified according to a range of indices); see *Chapter 14, Java Standard Streams*.

All of these methods are helpful, but we would like to draw your attention to the `equals(a1, a2)` and `deepEquals(a1, a2)` methods. They are particularly helpful for array comparison because an `array` object cannot implement an `equals()` custom method and uses the implementation of the `Object` class instead (which compares only references). The `equals(a1, a2)` and `deepEquals(a1, a2)` methods allow a comparison of not just `a1` and `a2` references, but use the `equals()` method to compare elements as well. Here is a code example to demonstrate how these methods work:

```
String[] arr1 = {"s1", "s2"};
String[] arr2 = {"s1", "s2"};
System.out.println(arr1.equals(arr2));    //prints: false
System.out.println(Arrays.equals(arr1, arr2));
                                          //prints: true
System.out.println(Arrays.deepEquals(arr1, arr2));
                                          //prints: true


String[][] arr3 = {{"s1", "s2"}};
String[][] arr4 = {{"s1", "s2"}};
System.out.println(arr3.equals(arr4));    //prints: false
System.out.println(Arrays.equals(arr3, arr4));
                                          //prints: false
System.out.println(Arrays.deepEquals(arr3, arr4));
                                          //prints: true
```

As you can see, `Arrays.deepEquals()` returns `true` every time two equal arrays are compared when every element of one array equals the element of another array in the same position, while the `Arrays.equals()` method does the same, but for **one-dimensional (1D)** arrays only.

ArrayUtils class

The `org.apache.commons.lang3.ArrayUtils` class complements the `java.util.Arrays` class by adding new methods to the array managing the toolkit and the ability to handle `null` in cases when, otherwise, `NullPointerException` could be thrown. To use this class, you would need to add the following dependency to the Maven `pom.xml` configuration file:

```
<dependency>
    <groupId>org.apache.commons</groupId>
    <artifactId>commons-lang3</artifactId>
    <version>3.12.0</version>
</dependency>
```

The `ArrayUtils` class has around 300 overloaded methods that can be collected in the following 12 groups:

- `add()`, `addAll()`, and `insert()`: These add elements to an array.
- `clone()`: This clones an array, similar to the `copyOf()` method of the `Arrays` class and the `arraycopy()` method of `java.lang.System`.
- `getLength()`: This returns an array length or `0` when the array itself is `null`.
- `hashCode()`: This calculates the hash value of an array, including nested arrays.
- `contains()`, `indexOf()`, and `lastIndexOf()`: These search an array.
- `isSorted()`, `isEmpty`, and `isNotEmpty()`: These check an array and handle `null`.
- `isSameLength()` and `isSameType()`: These compare arrays.
- `nullToEmpty()`: This converts a `null` array to an empty one.
- `remove()`, `removeAll()`, `removeElement()`, `removeElements()`, and `removeAllOccurances()`: These remove certain or all elements.
- `reverse()`, `shift()`, `shuffle()`, and `swap()`: These change the order of array elements.

- `subarray()`: This extracts part of an array according to a range of indices.

- `toMap()`, `toObject()`, `toPrimitive()`, `toString()`, and `toStringArray()`: These convert an array to another type and handle `null` values.

Objects utilities

The following two utilities are described in this section:

- `java.util.Objects`

- `org.apache.commons.lang3.ObjectUtils`

They are especially useful during class creation, so we will concentrate largely on methods related to this task.

java.util.Objects class

The `Objects` class has only 17 methods that are all static. Let's look at some of them while applying them to the `Person` class. Let's assume this class will be an element of a collection, which means it has to implement the `equals()` and `hashCode()` methods. The code is illustrated in the following snippet:

```
class Person {
    private int age;
    private String name;
    public Person(int age, String name) {
        this.age = age;
        this.name = name;
    }
    public int getAge(){ return this.age; }
    public String getName(){ return this.name; }
    @Override
    public boolean equals(Object o) {
        if (this == o) return true;
        if (o == null) return false;
        if(!(o instanceof Person)) return false;
        Person = (Person)o;
        return age == person.getAge() &&
                Objects.equals(name, person.getName());
```

```
    }
    @Override
    public int hashCode(){
        return Objects.hash(age, name);
    }
}
```

Notice that we do not check the name property for null because Object.equals() does not break when any of the parameters is null. It just does the job of comparing objects. If only one of them is null, it returns false. If both are null, it returns true.

Using Object.equals() is a safe way to implement the equals() method; however, if you need to compare objects that may be arrays, it is better to use the Objects. deepEquals() method because it not only handles null, as the Object.equals() method does, but also compares values of all array elements, even if the array is multidimensional, as illustrated here:

```
String[][] x1 = {{"a","b"},{"x","y"}};
String[][] x2 = {{"a","b"},{"x","y"}};
String[][] y =  {{"a","b"},{"y","y"}};


System.out.println(Objects.equals(x1, x2));
                                        //prints: false
System.out.println(Objects.equals(x1, y));
                                        //prints: false
System.out.println(Objects.deepEquals(x1, x2));
                                        //prints: true
System.out.println(Objects.deepEquals(x1, y));
                                        //prints: false
```

The Objects.hash() method handles null values too. One important thing to remember is that the list of properties compared in the equals() method has to match the list of properties passed into Objects.hash() as parameters. Otherwise, two equal Person objects will have different hash values, which makes hash-based collections work incorrectly.

Another thing worth noticing is that there is another hash-related `Objects.`
`hashCode()` method that accepts only one parameter, but the value it generates is not
equal to the value generated by `Objects.hash()` with only one parameter. Observe the
following, for example:

```
System.out.println(Objects.hash(42) ==
               Objects.hashCode(42));      //prints: false
System.out.println(Objects.hash("abc") ==
               Objects.hashCode("abc")); //prints: false
```

To avoid this caveat, always use `Objects.hash()`.

Another potential source of confusion is demonstrated in the following code snippet:

```
System.out.println(Objects.hash(null));      //prints: 0
System.out.println(Objects.hashCode(null));  //prints: 0
System.out.println(Objects.hash(0));         //prints: 31
System.out.println(Objects.hashCode(0));     //prints: 0
```

As you can see, the `Objects.hashCode()` method generates the same hash value for
`null` and 0, which can be problematic for some algorithms based on the hash value.

`static <T> int compare (T a, T b, Comparator<T> c)` is another
popular method that returns 0 (if the arguments are equal); otherwise, it returns the
result of `c.compare(a, b)`. It is very useful for implementing the `Comparable`
interface (establishing a natural order for custom object sorting). Observe the following,
for example:

```
class Person implements Comparable<Person> {
    private int age;
    private String name;
    public Person(int age, String name) {
        this.age = age;
        this.name = name;
    }
    public int getAge(){ return this.age; }
    public String getName(){ return this.name; }
    @Override
    public int compareTo(Person p){
```

```
        int result = Objects.compare(name, p.getName(),
                                Comparator.naturalOrder());
        if (result != 0) {
            return result;
        }
        return Objects.compare(age, p.getAge(),
                                Comparator.naturalOrder());
    }
}
```

This way, you can easily change the sorting algorithm by setting the `Comparator.reverseOrder()` value or by adding `Comparator.nullFirst()` or `Comparator.nullLast()`.

Also, the `Comparator` implementation we used in the previous section can be made more flexible by using the `Objects.compare()` method, as follows:

```
class ComparePersons implements Comparator<Person> {
    public int compare(Person p1, Person p2){
        int result = Objects.compare(p1.getName(),
            p2.getName(), Comparator.naturalOrder());
        if (result != 0) {
            return result;
        }
        return Objects.compare(p1.getAge(), p2.getAge(),
                            Comparator.naturalOrder());
    }
}
```

Finally, the last two methods of the `Objects` class that we are going to discuss are methods that generate a string representation of an object. They come in handy when you need to call a `toString()` method on an object but are not sure whether the object reference is `null`. Observe the following, for example:

```
List<String> list = Arrays.asList("s1", null);
for(String e: list){
    //String s = e.toString();  //NullPointerException
}
```

In the preceding example, we know the exact value of each element; however, imagine a scenario where the list is passed into the method as a parameter. Then, we are forced to write something like this:

```
void someMethod(List<String> list){
    for(String e: list){
        String s = e == null ? "null" : e.toString();
    }
```

This doesn't seem to be a big deal. But after writing such code a dozen times, a programmer naturally thinks about some kind of utility method that does all of that, and that is when the following two methods of the Objects class help:

- `static String toString(Object o)`: This returns the result of calling `toString()` on the parameter when it is not `null` and returns `null` when the parameter value is `null`.

- `static String toString(Object o, String nullDefault)`: This returns the result of calling `toString()` on the first parameter when it is not `null` and returns the second `nullDefault` parameter value when the first parameter value is `null`.

The following code snippet demonstrates these two methods:

```
List<String> list = Arrays.asList("s1", null);
for(String e: list){
    String s = Objects.toString(e);
    System.out.print(s + " ");              //prints: s1 null
}
for(String e: list){
    String s = Objects.toString(e, "element was null");
    System.out.print(s + " ");
                                     //prints: s1 element was null

}
```

As of the time of writing, the Objects class has 17 methods. We recommend you become familiar with them so as to avoid writing your own utilities in the event that the same utility already exists.

ObjectUtils class

The last statement of the previous section applies to the `org.apache.commons.lang3.ObjectUtils` class of the `Apache Commons` library that complements the methods of the `java.util.Objects` class described in the preceding section. The scope of this book and its allotted size does not allow for a detailed review of all the methods under the `ObjectUtils` class, so we will describe them briefly in groups according to their related functionality. To use this class, you would need to add the following dependency to the Maven `pom.xml` configuration file:

```
<dependency>
    <groupId>org.apache.commons</groupId>
    <artifactId>commons-lang3</artifactId>
    <version>3.12.0</version>
</dependency>
```

All the methods of the `ObjectUtils` class can be organized into seven groups, as follows:

- Object cloning methods
- Methods that support a comparison of two objects
- The `notEqual()` method, which compares two objects for inequality, where either one or both objects may be `null`
- Several `identityToString()` methods that generate a `String` representation of the provided object as if produced by `toString()`, which is a default method of the `Object` base class and, optionally, append it to another object
- The `allNotNull()` and `anyNotNull()` methods, which analyze an array of objects for `null`
- The `firstNonNull()` and `defaultIfNull()` methods, which analyze an array of objects and return the first not-`null` object or default value
- The `max()`, `min()`, `median()`, and `mode()` methods, which analyze an array of objects and return the one that corresponds to the method name

The java.time package

There are many classes in the `java.time` package and its sub-packages. They were introduced as a replacement for other (older packages) that handled date and time. The new classes are thread-safe (hence, better suited for multithreaded processing), and what is also important is that they are more consistently designed and easier to understand. Also, the new implementation follows **International Organization for Standardization (ISO)** standards as regards date and time formats, but allows any other custom format to be used as well.

We will describe the following five main classes and demonstrate how to use them:

- `java.time.LocalDate`
- `java.time.LocalTime`
- `java.time.LocalDateTime`
- `java.time.Period`
- `java.time.Duration`

All these and other classes of the `java.time` package, as well as its sub-packages, are rich in various functionality that covers all practical cases. But we are not going to discuss all of them; we will just introduce the basics and the most popular use cases.

LocalDate class

The `LocalDate` class does not carry time. It represents a date in *ISO 8601* format (`yyyy-MM-dd`) and is shown in the following code snippet:

```
System.out.println(LocalDate.now());
                    //prints: current date in format yyyy-MM-dd
```

That is the current date in this location at the time of writing. The value was picked up from the computer clock. Similarly, you can get the current date in any other time zone using that static `now(ZoneId zone)` method. A `ZoneId` object can be constructed using the static `ZoneId.of(String zoneId)` method, where `String zoneId` is any of the string values returned by the `ZoneId.getAvailableZoneIds()` method, as illustrated in the following code snippet:

```
Set<String> zoneIds = ZoneId.getAvailableZoneIds();
for(String zoneId: zoneIds){
    System.out.println(zoneId);
}
```

The preceding code prints almost 600 time zone **identifiers** (**IDs**). Here are a few of them:

```
Asia/Aden
Etc/GMT+9
Africa/Nairobi
America/Marigot
Pacific/Honolulu
Australia/Hobart
Europe/London
America/Indiana/Petersburg
Asia/Yerevan
Europe/Brussels
GMT
Chile/Continental
Pacific/Yap
CET
Etc/GMT-1
Canada/Yukon
Atlantic/St_Helena
Libya
US/Pacific-New
Cuba
Israel
GB-Eire
GB
Mexico/General
Universal
Zulu
Iran
Navajo
Egypt
Etc/UTC
SystemV/AST4ADT
Asia/Tokyo
```

Let's try to use `"Asia/Tokyo"`, for example, as follows:

```
ZoneId = ZoneId.of("Asia/Tokyo");
System.out.println(LocalDate.now(zoneId));
            //prints: current date in Tokyo in format yyyy-MM-dd
```

A `LocalDate` object can represent any date in the past, or in the future too, using the following methods:

- `LocalDate parse(CharSequence text)`: This constructs an object from a string in *ISO 8601* format (`yyyy-MM-dd`).

- `LocalDate parse(CharSequence text, DateTimeFormatter formatter)`: This constructs an object from a string in a format specified by the `DateTimeFormatter` object that has a rich system of patterns and many predefined formats as well—here are a few of them:

  - `BASIC_ISO_DATE`—for example, `20111203`

  - `ISO_LOCAL_DATE ISO`—for example, `2011-12-03`

  - `ISO_OFFSET_DATE`—for example, `2011-12-03+01:00`

  - `ISO_DATE`—for example, `2011-12-03+01:00; 2011-12-03`

  - `ISO_LOCAL_TIME`—for example, `10:15:30`

  - `ISO_OFFSET_TIME`—for example, `10:15:30+01:00`

  - `ISO_TIME`—for example, `10:15:30+01:00; 10:15:30`

  - `ISO_LOCAL_DATE_TIME`—for example, `2011-12-03T10:15:30`

- `LocalDate of(int year, int month, int dayOfMonth)`: This constructs an object from a year, month, and day.

- `LocalDate of(int year, Month, int dayOfMonth)`: This constructs an object from a year, month (enum constant), and day.

- `LocalDate ofYearDay(int year, int dayOfYear)`: This constructs an object from a year and day-of-year.

The following code snippet demonstrates the methods listed in the preceding bullets:

```
LocalDate lc1 = LocalDate.parse("2023-02-23");
System.out.println(lc1);            //prints: 2023-02-23


LocalDate lc2 = LocalDate.parse("20230223",
                    DateTimeFormatter.BASIC_ISO_DATE);
System.out.println(lc2);            //prints: 2023-02-23


DateTimeFormatter frm =
            DateTimeFormatter.ofPattern("dd/MM/yyyy");
LocalDate lc3 =  LocalDate.parse("23/02/2023", frm);
System.out.println(lc3);            //prints: 2023-02-23


LocalDate lc4 =  LocalDate.of(2023, 2, 23);
System.out.println(lc4);            //prints: 2023-02-23


LocalDate lc5 =  LocalDate.of(2023, Month.FEBRUARY, 23);
System.out.println(lc5);            //prints: 2023-02-23


LocalDate lc6 = LocalDate.ofYearDay(2023, 54);
System.out.println(lc6);            //prints: 2023-02-23
```

A `LocalDate` object can provide various values, as illustrated in the following code snippet:

```
LocalDate lc = LocalDate.parse("2023-02-23");
System.out.println(lc);                     //prints: 2023-02-23
System.out.println(lc.getYear());           //prints: 2023
System.out.println(lc.getMonth());          //prints: FEBRUARY
System.out.println(lc.getMonthValue());     //prints: 2
System.out.println(lc.getDayOfMonth());     //prints: 23
System.out.println(lc.getDayOfWeek());      //prints: THURSDAY
System.out.println(lc.isLeapYear());        //prints: false
System.out.println(lc.lengthOfMonth());     //prints: 28
System.out.println(lc.lengthOfYear());      //prints: 365
```

A `LocalDate` object can be modified, like this:

```
LocalDate lc = LocalDate.parse("2023-02-23");
System.out.println(lc.withYear(2024));        //prints: 2024-02-23
System.out.println(lc.withMonth(5));          //prints: 2023-05-23
System.out.println(lc.withDayOfMonth(5));     //prints: 2023-02-05
System.out.println(lc.withDayOfYear(53));     //prints: 2023-02-22
System.out.println(lc.plusDays(10));          //prints: 2023-03-05
System.out.println(lc.plusMonths(2));         //prints: 2023-04-23
System.out.println(lc.plusYears(2));          //prints: 2025-02-23
System.out.println(lc.minusDays(10));         //prints: 2023-02-13
System.out.println(lc.minusMonths(2));        //prints: 2022-12-23
System.out.println(lc.minusYears(2));         //prints: 2021-02-23
```

A `LocalDate` object can be compared, like this:

```
LocalDate lc1 = LocalDate.parse("2023-02-23");
LocalDate lc2 = LocalDate.parse("2023-02-22");
System.out.println(lc1.isAfter(lc2));         //prints: true
System.out.println(lc1.isBefore(lc2));        //prints: false
```

There are many other helpful methods in the `LocalDate` class. If you have to work with dates, we recommend that you read the **application programming interface (API)** of this class and other classes of the `java.time` package and its sub-packages.

LocalTime class

The `LocalTime` class contains time without a date. It has similar methods to the methods of the `LocalDate` class. Here is how an object of the `LocalTime` class can be created:

```
System.out.println(LocalTime.now()); //prints: 21:15:46.360904

ZoneId = ZoneId.of("Asia/Tokyo");
System.out.println(LocalTime.now(zoneId));
                                    //prints: 12:15:46.364378

LocalTime lt1 =  LocalTime.parse("20:23:12");
```

```
System.out.println(lt1);                          //prints: 20:23:12


LocalTime lt2 = LocalTime.of(20, 23, 12);
System.out.println(lt2);                          //prints: 20:23:12
```

Each component of time value can be extracted from a LocalTime object, as follows:

```
LocalTime lt2 =  LocalTime.of(20, 23, 12);
System.out.println(lt2);                          //prints: 20:23:12
System.out.println(lt2.getHour());                //prints: 20
System.out.println(lt2.getMinute());              //prints: 23
System.out.println(lt2.getSecond());              //prints: 12
System.out.println(lt2.getNano());                //prints: 0
```

An object of the LocalTime class can be modified, as follows:

```
LocalTime lt2 = LocalTime.of(20, 23, 12);
System.out.println(lt2.withHour(3));         //prints: 03:23:12
System.out.println(lt2.withMinute(10));      //prints: 20:10:12
System.out.println(lt2.withSecond(15));      //prints: 20:23:15
System.out.println(lt2.withNano(300));
                              //prints: 20:23:12.000000300
System.out.println(lt2.plusHours(10));       //prints: 06:23:12
System.out.println(lt2.plusMinutes(2));      //prints: 20:25:12
System.out.println(lt2.plusSeconds(2));      //prints: 20:23:14
System.out.println(lt2.plusNanos(200));
                              //prints: 20:23:12.000000200
System.out.println(lt2.minusHours(10));      //prints: 10:23:12
System.out.println(lt2.minusMinutes(2));     //prints: 20:21:12
System.out.println(lt2.minusSeconds(2));     //prints: 20:23:10
System.out.println(lt2.minusNanos(200));
                              //prints: 20:23:11.999999800
```

And two objects of the `LocalTime` class can also be compared, as follows:

```
LocalTime lt2 =  LocalTime.of(20, 23, 12);
LocalTime lt4 =  LocalTime.parse("20:25:12");
System.out.println(lt2.isAfter(lt4));       //prints: false
System.out.println(lt2.isBefore(lt4));      //prints: true
```

There are many other helpful methods in the `LocalTime` class. If you have to work with dates, we recommend that you read the API of this class and other classes of the `java. time` package and its sub-packages.

LocalDateTime class

The `LocalDateTime` class contains both the date and time and has all the methods the `LocalDate` and `LocalTime` classes have, so we are not going to repeat them here. We will only show how an object of the `LocalDateTime` class can be created, as follows:

```
System.out.println(LocalDateTime.now());
                    //prints: 2019-03-04T21:59:00.142804


ZoneId = ZoneId.of("Asia/Tokyo");
System.out.println(LocalDateTime.now(zoneId));
                    //prints: 2019-03-05T12:59:00.146038


LocalDateTime ldt1 =
          LocalDateTime.parse("2020-02-23T20:23:12");
System.out.println(ldt1);  //prints: 2020-02-23T20:23:12


DateTimeFormatter formatter =
    DateTimeFormatter.ofPattern("dd/MM/yyyy HH:mm:ss");
LocalDateTime ldt2 =
  LocalDateTime.parse("23/02/2020 20:23:12", formatter);
System.out.println(ldt2);  //prints: 2020-02-23T20:23:12


LocalDateTime ldt3 =
              LocalDateTime.of(2020, 2, 23, 20, 23, 12);
System.out.println(ldt3);  //prints: 2020-02-23T20:23:12
```

```
LocalDateTime ldt4 =
  LocalDateTime.of(2020, Month.FEBRUARY, 23, 20, 23, 12);
System.out.println(ldt4);  //prints: 2020-02-23T20:23:12


LocalDate ld = LocalDate.of(2020, 2, 23);
LocalTime lt = LocalTime.of(20, 23, 12);
LocalDateTime ldt5 = LocalDateTime.of(ld, lt);
System.out.println(ldt5); //prints: 2020-02-23T20:23:12
```

There are many other helpful methods in the LocalDateTime class. If you have to work with dates, we recommend that you read the API of this class and other classes of the java.time package and its sub-packages.

Period and Duration classes

The java.time.Period and java.time.Duration classes are designed to contain an amount of time, as outlined here:

- A Period object contains an amount of time in units of years, months, and days.

- A Duration object contains an amount of time in hours, minutes, seconds, and nanoseconds.

The following code snippet demonstrates their creation and usage using the LocalDateTime class, but the same methods exist in the LocalDate (for Period) and LocalTime (for Duration) classes:

```
LocalDateTime ldt1 = LocalDateTime.parse("2023-02-
23T20:23:12");
LocalDateTime ldt2 = ldt1.plus(Period.ofYears(2));
System.out.println(ldt2);        //prints: 2025-02-23T20:23:12
```

The following methods work the same way as the methods of the LocalTime class:

```
LocalDateTime ldt = LocalDateTime.parse("2023-02-23T20:23:12");
ldt.minus(Period.ofYears(2));
ldt.plus(Period.ofMonths(2));
ldt.minus(Period.ofMonths(2));
ldt.plus(Period.ofWeeks(2));
ldt.minus(Period.ofWeeks(2));
ldt.plus(Period.ofDays(2));
```

```
ldt.minus(Period.ofDays(2));
ldt.plus(Duration.ofHours(2));
ldt.minus(Duration.ofHours(2));
ldt.plus(Duration.ofMinutes(2));
ldt.minus(Duration.ofMinutes(2));
ldt.plus(Duration.ofMillis(2));
ldt.minus(Duration.ofMillis(2));
```

Some other methods of creating and using `Period` objects are demonstrated in the following code snippet:

```
LocalDate ld1 =  LocalDate.parse("2023-02-23");
LocalDate ld2 =  LocalDate.parse("2023-03-25");
Period = Period.between(ld1, ld2);
System.out.println(period.getDays());        //prints: 2
System.out.println(period.getMonths());       //prints: 1
System.out.println(period.getYears());        //prints: 0
System.out.println(period.toTotalMonths()); //prints: 1
period = Period.between(ld2, ld1);
System.out.println(period.getDays());        //prints: -2
```

`Duration` objects can be similarly created and used, as illustrated in the following code snippet:

```
LocalTime lt1 =  LocalTime.parse("10:23:12");
LocalTime lt2 =  LocalTime.parse("20:23:14");
Duration = Duration.between(lt1, lt2);
System.out.println(duration.toDays());        //prints: 0
System.out.println(duration.toHours());       //prints: 10
System.out.println(duration.toMinutes());     //prints: 600
System.out.println(duration.toSeconds());     //prints: 36002
System.out.println(duration.getSeconds());    //prints: 36002
System.out.println(duration.toNanos());
                                        //prints: 36002000000000
System.out.println(duration.getNano());       //prints: 0.
```

There are many other helpful methods in `Period` and `Duration` classes. If you have to work with dates, we recommend that you read the API of this class and other classes of the `java.time` package and its sub-packages.

Period of day

Java 16 includes a new time format that shows a period of the day as AM, in the morning, and similar. The following two methods demonstrate usage of the DateTimeFormatter.ofPattern() method with the LocalDateTime and LocalTime classes:

```
void periodOfDayFromDateTime(String time, String pattern){
    LocalDateTime date = LocalDateTime.parse(time);
    DateTimeFormatter frm =
            DateTimeFormatter.ofPattern(pattern);
    System.out.print(date.format(frm));
}
void periodOfDayFromTime(String time, String pattern){
    LocalTime date = LocalTime.parse(time);
    DateTimeFormatter frm =
            DateTimeFormatter.ofPattern(pattern);

    System.out.print(date.format(frm));
}
```

The following code demonstrates the effect of "h a" and "h B" patterns:

```
periodOfDayFromDateTime("2023-03-23T05:05:18.123456",
          "MM-dd-yyyy h a"); //prints: 03-23-2023 5 AM
periodOfDayFromDateTime("2023-03-23T05:05:18.123456",
        "MM-dd-yyyy h B"); //prints: 03-23-2023 5 at night
periodOfDayFromDateTime("2023-03-23T06:05:18.123456",
                "h B");    //prints: 6 in the morning
periodOfDayFromTime("11:05:18.123456", "h B");
                          //prints: 11 in the morning
periodOfDayFromTime("12:05:18.123456", "h B");
                    //prints: 12 in the afternoon
periodOfDayFromTime("17:05:18.123456", "h B");
                    //prints: 5 in the afternoon
periodOfDayFromTime("18:05:18.123456", "h B");
                    //prints: 6 in the evening
periodOfDayFromTime("20:05:18.123456", "h B");
```

```
                                    //prints: 8 in the evening
    periodOfDayFromTime("21:05:18.123456", "h B");
                                    //prints: 9 at night
```

You can use `"h a"` and `"h B"` patterns to make the time presentation more user-friendly.

Summary

This chapter introduced you to the Java collections framework and its three main interfaces: `List`, `Set`, and `Map`. Each of the interfaces was discussed and its methods were demonstrated with one of the implementing classes. The generics were explained and demonstrated as well. The `equals()` and `hashCode()` methods have to be implemented in order for an object to be capable of being handled by Java collections correctly.

The `Collections` and `CollectionUtils` utility classes have many useful methods for collection handling and were presented in examples, along with the `Arrays`, `ArrayUtils`, `Objects`, and `ObjectUtils` classes.

The class methods of the `java.time` package allow time/date values to be managed and were demonstrated in specific practical code snippets.

You can now use all the main data structures we talked about in this chapter in your programs.

In the next chapter, we will overview JCL and some external libraries, including those that support testing. Specifically, we will explore the `org.junit`, `org.mockito`, `org.apache.log4j`, `org.slf4j`, and `org.apache.commons` packages and their sub-packages.

Quiz

1.   What is the Java collections framework? Select all that apply:

   A. A collection of frameworks

   B. Classes and interfaces of the `java.util` package

   C. `List`, `Set`, and `Map` interfaces

   D. Classes and interfaces that implement a collection data structure

2. What is meant by *generics* in a collection? Select all that apply:

    A. A collection structure definition

    B. An element type declaration

    C. A type generalization

    D. A mechanism that provides compile-time safety

3. What are the limitations of the collection of `of()` factory methods? Select all that apply:

    A. They do not allow a `null` element.

    B. They do not allow elements to be added to the initialized collection.

    C. They do not allow modification of elements in relation to the initialized collection.

4. What does the implementation of the `java.lang.Iterable` interface allow? Select all that apply:

    A. It allows elements of the collection to be accessed one by one.

    B. It allows the collection to be used in `FOR` statements.

    C. It allows the collection to be used in `WHILE` statements.

    D. It allows the collection to be used in `DO...WHILE` statements.

5. What does the implementation of the `java.util.Collection` interface allow? Select all that apply:

    A. Addition to the collection of elements from another collection

    B. Removal from the collection of objects that are elements of another collection

    C. Modification of just those elements of the collection that belong to another collection

    D. Removal from the collection of objects that do not belong to another collection

6. Select all the correct statements pertaining to `List` interface methods:

    A. `z get(int index)`: This returns the element at a specified position in the list.

    B. `E remove(int index)`: This removes the element at a specified position in the list; it returns the removed element.

    C. `static List<E> copyOf(Collection<E> coll)`: This returns an unmodifiable `List` interface containing elements of the given `Collection` interface and preserves their order.

    D. `int indexOf(Object o)`: This returns the position of a specified element in the list.

7. Select all the correct statements pertaining to `Set` interface methods:

    A. `E get(int index)`: This returns the element at a specified position in the list.

    B. `E remove(int index)`: This removes the element at a specified position in the list; it returns the removed element.

    C. `static Set<E> copyOf(Collection<E> coll)`: This returns an unmodifiable `Set` interface containing elements of the given `Collection` interface.

    D. `int indexOf(Object o)`: This returns the position of a specified element in the list.

8. Select all the correct statements pertaining to `Map` interface methods:

    A. `int size()`: This returns the count of key-value pairs stored in the map; when the `isEmpty()` method returns `true`, this method returns `0`.

    B. `V remove(Object key)`: This removes both the key and value from the map; returns `value` or `null` if there is no such key or the value is `null`.

    C. `default boolean remove(Object key, Object value)`: This removes the key-value pair if such a pair exists in the map; returns `true` if the value is removed.

    D. `default boolean replace(K key, V oldValue, V newValue)`: This replaces the `oldValue` value with the `newValue` value provided if the key provided is currently mapped to the `oldValue` value—it returns `true` if the `oldValue` value was replaced; otherwise, it returns `false`.

9. Select all correct statements pertaining to the `static void sort(List<T> list, Comparator<T> comparator)` method of the `Collections` class:

A. It sorts the list's natural order if list elements implement the `Comparable` interface.

B. It sorts the list's order according to the `Comparator` object provided.

C. It sorts the list's order according to the `Comparator` object provided if list elements implement the `Comparable` interface.

D. It sorts the list's order according to the provided `Comparator` object irrespective of whether the list elements implement the `Comparable` interface.

10. What is the outcome of executing the following code?

```
List<String> list1 = Arrays.asList("s1","s2", "s3");
List<String> list2 = Arrays.asList("s3", "s4");
Collections.copy(list1, list2);
System.out.println(list1);
```

A. [s1, s2, s3, s4]

B. [s3, s4, s3]

C. [s1, s2, s3, s3, s4]

D. [s3, s4]

11. What is the functionality of `CollectionUtils` class methods? Select all that apply:

A. It matches the functionality of `Collections` class methods, but by handling `null`

B. It complements the functionality of `Collections` class methods

C. It searches, processes, and compares Java collections in a way that `Collections` class methods do not do

D. It duplicates the functionality of `Collections` class methods

12. What is the result of executing the following code?

```
Integer [] [] ar1 = {{42}};
Integer [] [] ar2 = {{42}};
System.out.print (Arrays.equals (ar1, ar2) + " ");
System.out.println (Arrays.deepEquals (arr3, arr4));
```

A. false true

B. false

C. true false

D. true

13. What is the result of executing the following code?

```
String [] arr1 = { "s1", "s2" };
String [] arr2 = { null };
String [] arr3 = null;
System.out.print (ArrayUtils.getLength (arr1) + " ");
System.out.print (ArrayUtils.getLength (arr2) + " ");
System.out.print (ArrayUtils.getLength (arr3) + " ");
System.out.print (ArrayUtils.isEmpty (arr2) + " ");
System.out.print (ArrayUtils.isEmpty (arr3));
```

A. 1 2 0 false true

B. 2 1 1 false true

C. 2 1 0 false true

D. 2 1 0 true false

14. What is the result of executing the following code?

```
String str1 = "";
String str2 = null;
System.out.print((Objects.hash(str1) ==
                Objects.hashCode(str2)) + " ");
System.out.print(Objects.hash(str1) + " ");
System.out.println(Objects.hashCode(str2) + " ");
```

A. true 0 0

B. Error

C. false -1 0

D. false 31 0

15. What is the result of executing the following code?

```
String[] arr = {"c", "x", "a"};
System.out.print(ObjectUtils.min(arr) + " ");
System.out.print(ObjectUtils.median(arr) + " ");
System.out.println(ObjectUtils.max(arr));
```

A. c x a

B. a c x

C. x c a

D. a x c

16. What is the result of executing the following code?

```
LocalDate lc = LocalDate.parse("1900-02-23");
System.out.println(lc.withYear(21));
```

A. 1921-02-23

B. 21-02-23

C. 0021-02-23

D. Error

17. What is the result of executing the following code?

```
LocalTime lt2 = LocalTime.of(20, 23, 12);
System.out.println(lt2.withNano(300));
```

A. `20:23:12.000000300`

B. `20:23:12.300`

C. `20:23:12:300`

D. `Error`

18. What is the result of executing the following code?

```
LocalDate ld = LocalDate.of(2020, 2, 23);
LocalTime lt = LocalTime.of(20, 23, 12);
LocalDateTime ldt = LocalDateTime.of(ld, lt);
System.out.println(ldt);
```

A. `2020-02-23 20:23:12`

B. `2020-02-23T20:23:12`

C. `2020-02-23:20:23:12`

D. `Error`

19. What is the result of executing the following code?

```
LocalDateTime ldt =
              LocalDateTime.parse("2020-02-23T20:23:12");
System.out.print(ldt.minus(Period.ofYears(2)) + " ");
System.out.print(ldt.plus(Duration.ofMinutes(12)) + " ");
System.out.println(ldt);
```

A. `2020-02-23T20:23:12 2020-02-23T20:23:12`

B. `2020-02-23T20:23:12 2020-02-23T20:35:12`

C. `2018-02-23T20:23:12 2020-02-23T20:35:12 2020-02-23T20:23:12`

D. `2018-02-23T20:23:12 2020-02-23T20:35:12 2018-02-23T20:35:12`

7
Java Standard and External Libraries

It is not possible to write a Java program without using the standard libraries, also called the **Java Class Library** (**JCL**). That is why a solid familiarity with such libraries is as vital for successful programming as knowing the language itself.

There are also the non-standard libraries, which are called external libraries or third-party libraries because they are not included in the **Java Development Kit** (**JDK**) distribution. Some of them have long become a permanent fixture of any programmer's toolkit.

Keeping track of all the functionality that's available in these libraries is not easy. This is because an **integrated development environment** (**IDE**) gives you a hint about the language's possibilities, but it cannot advise you about the functionality of a package that hasn't been imported yet. The only package that is imported automatically is `java.lang`.

The purpose of this chapter is to provide you with an overview of the functionality of the most popular packages of JCL, as well as external libraries.

In this chapter, we will cover the following topics:

- **Java Class Library** (**JCL**)
- External libraries

Technical requirements

To be able to execute the code examples in this chapter, you will need the following:

- A computer with Microsoft Windows, Apple macOS, or the Linux operating system
- Java SE version 17 or later
- An IDE or code editor of your choice

The instructions on how to set up a Java SE and IntelliJ IDEA editor were provided in *Chapter 1*, *Getting Started with Java 17*. The files that contain the code examples for this chapter are available on GitHub in the `https://github.com/PacktPublishing/Learn-Java-17-Programming.git` repository, in the `examples/src/main/java/com/packt/learnjava/ch07_libraries` folder.

Java Class Library (JCL)

JCL is a collection of packages that implement the language. In simpler terms, it is a collection of the `.class` files that are included in the JDK and ready to be used. Once you have installed Java, you get them as part of the installation and can start building your application code up using the JCL classes as building blocks, which take care of a lot of the low-level plumbing. The richness and ease of use of JCL have substantially contributed to Java's popularity.

To use a JCL package, you can import it without adding a new dependency to the `pom.xml` file. Maven adds JCL to the classpath automatically. And that is what separates the standard library and external libraries; if you need to add a library (typically, a `.jar` file) as a dependency in the Maven `pom.xml` configuration file, this library is an external one. Otherwise, it is a standard library or JCL.

Some JCL package names start with `java`. Traditionally, they are called *core Java packages*, while those that start with `javax` used to be called *extensions*. This was done because the extensions were thought to be optional and maybe even released independently of JDK. There was also an attempt to promote the former extension library to become a core package. But that would require changing the package name from `java` to `javax`, which would break the already existing applications that used the `javax` package. Therefore, the idea was abandoned, so the distinction between the core package and extensions gradually disappeared.

That is why, if you look at the official Java API on the Oracle website, you will see listed as standard not only the `java` and `javax` packages, but also `jdk`, `com.sun`, `org.xml`, and some other packages too. These extra packages are primarily used by the tools of other specialized applications. In this book, we will concentrate mostly on mainstream Java programming and talk only about the `java` and `javax` packages.

java.lang

This package is so fundamental that it doesn't need to be imported for you to use it. The JVM authors decided to import it automatically. It contains the most often used classes of JCL:

- `Object`: The base class of any other Java class.
- `Class`: Carries metadata of every loaded class at runtime.
- `String`, `StringBuffer`, and `StringBuilder`: Supports operations of the `String` type.
- The wrapper classes of all primitive types: `Byte`, `Boolean`, `Short`, `Character`, `Integer`, `Long`, `Float`, and `Double`.
- `Number`: The base class for the wrapper classes of the numeric primitive types – all the previously listed classes, except `Boolean`.
- `System`: Provides access to important system operations and the standard input and output (we have used the `System.out` object in every code example in this book).
- `Runtime`: Provides access to the execution environment.
- The `Thread` and `Runnable` interfaces: Fundamental for creating Java threads.
- The `Iterable` interface: Used by the iteration statements.
- `Math`: Provides methods for basic numeric operations.
- `Throwable`: The base class for all exceptions.
- `Error`: This is an `exception` class since all its children are used to communicate system errors that can't be caught by an application.
- `Exception`: This class and its direct children represent checked exceptions.
- `RuntimeException`: This class and its children represent unchecked exceptions, also called runtime exceptions.

- `ClassLoader`: This class reads the `.class` files and puts (loads) them into memory; it also can be used to build a customized class loader.

- `Process` and `ProcessBuilder`: These classes allow you to create other JVM processes.

Many other useful classes and interfaces are available as well.

java.util

Most of the content of the `java.util` package is dedicated to supporting Java collections:

- The `Collection` interface: The base interface of many other interfaces of collections, it declares all the basic methods that are necessary to manage collection elements; for example, `size()`, `add()`, `remove()`, `contains()`, `stream()`, and others. It also extends the `java.lang.Iterable` interface and inherits its methods, including `iterator()` and `forEach()`, which means that any implementation of the `Collection` interface or any of its children – `List`, `Set`, `Queue`, `Deque`, and others – can be used in iteration statements too, such as `ArrayList`, `LinkedList`, `HashSet`, `AbstractQueue`, `ArrayDeque`, and others.

- The `Map` interface and the classes that implement it: `HashMap`, `TreeMap`, and others.

- The `Collections` class: This class provides many static methods that are used to analyze, manipulate, and convert collections.

Many other collection interfaces, classes, and related utilities are also available.

We talked about Java collections and saw examples of their usage in *Chapter 6, Data Structures, Generics, and Popular Utilities*.

The `java.util` package also includes several other useful classes:

- `Objects`: Provides various object-related utility methods, some of which we looked at in *Chapter 6, Data Structures, Generics, and Popular Utilities*.

- `Arrays`: Contains 160 static methods to manipulate arrays, some of which we looked at in *Chapter 6, Data Structures, Generics, and Popular Utilities*.

- `Formatter`: This allows you to format any primitive type, including `String`, `Date`, and other types; we learned how to use it in *Chapter 6, Data Structures, Generics, and Popular Utilities*.

- `Optional`, `OptionalInt`, `OptionalLong`, and `OptionalDouble`: These classes help avoid `NullPointerException` by wrapping the actual value that can be null or not.

- `Properties`: Helps read and create key-value pairs that are used for application configuration and similar purposes.

- `Random`: Complements the `java.lang.Math.random()` method by generating streams of pseudo-random numbers.

- `StringTokenizer`: Breaks the `String` object into tokens that are separated by the specified delimiter.

- `StringJoiner`: Constructs a sequence of characters that are separated by the specified delimiter. Optionally, it is surrounded by the specified prefix and suffix.

Many other useful utility classes are available, including the classes that support internationalization and Base64-encoding and decoding.

java.time

The `java.time` package contains classes for managing dates, times, periods, and durations. The package includes the following:

- The `Month` enum.

- The `DayOfWeek` enum.

- The `Clock` class, which returns the current instant, date, and time using a time zone.

- The `Duration` and `Period` classes represent and compare amounts of time in different time units.

- The `LocalDate`, `LocalTime`, and `LocalDateTime` classes represent dates and times without a time zone.

- The `ZonedDateTime` class represents the date and time with a time zone.

- The `ZoneId` class identifies a time zone such as America/Chicago.

- The `java.time.format.DateTimeFormatter` class allows you to present the date and time as per the **International Standards Organization (ISO)** formats, such as the *YYYY-MM-DD* pattern.

- Some other classes that support date and time manipulation.

We discussed most of these classes in *Chapter 6, Data Structures, Generics, and Popular Utilities.*

java.io and java.nio

The `java.io` and `java.nio` packages contain classes and interfaces that support reading and writing data using streams, serialization, and filesystems. The difference between these two packages is as follows:

- The `java.io` package classes allow you to read/write data as it comes without caching it (as we discussed in *Chapter 5, Strings, Input/Output, and Files*), while classes of the `java.nio` package create buffers that allow you to move back and forth along the populated buffer.

- The `java.io` package classes block the stream until all the data is read or written, while classes of the `java.nio` package are implemented in a non-blocking style (we will talk about the non-blocking style in *Chapter 15, Reactive Programming*).

java.sql and javax.sql

These two packages compose the **Java Database Connectivity** (**JDBC**) API, which allows you to access and process data that's stored in a data source, typically a relational database. The `javax.sql` package complements the `java.sql` package by providing support for the following:

- The `DataSource` interface as an alternative to the `DriverManager` class
- Connections and statements pooling
- Distributed transactions
- Rowsets

We will talk about these packages and see code examples in *Chapter 10, Managing Data in a Database*.

java.net

The `java.net` package contains classes that support application networking at the following two levels:

- **Low-level networking**, based on the following:

  - IP addresses
  - Sockets, which are basic bidirectional data communication mechanisms
  - Various network interfaces

- **High-level networking**, based on the following:

  - **Universal Resource Identifier (URI)**

  - **Universal Resource Locator (URL)**

  - Connections to the resource being pointed to by URLs

We will talk about this package and see code examples of it in *Chapter 11, Network Programming*.

java.lang.math and java.math

The `java.lang.math` package contains methods for performing basic numeric operations, such as calculating the minimum and maximum of two numeric values, the absolute value, the elementary exponential, logarithms, square roots, trigonometric functions, and many other mathematical operations.

The `java.math` package complements Java primitive types and wrapper classes of the `java.lang` package as you can work with much bigger numbers using the `BigDecimal` and `BigInteger` classes.

java.awt, javax.swing, and javafx

The first Java library that supported building a **graphical user interface (GUI)** for desktop applications was the **Abstract Window Toolkit (AWT)** in the `java.awt` package. It provided an interface to the native system of the executing platform that allowed you to create and manage windows, layouts, and events. It also had the basic GUI widgets (such as text fields, buttons, and menus), provided access to the system tray, and allowed you to launch a web browser and email a client from the Java code. Its heavy dependence on the native code made the AWT-based GUI look different on different platforms.

In 1997, Sun Microsystems and Netscape Communications Corporation introduced Java Foundation Classes, later called Swing, and placed them in the `javax.swing` package. The GUI components that were built with Swing were able to emulate the look and feel of some native platforms but also allowed you to plug in a look and feel that did not depend on the platform it was running on. It expanded the list of widgets the GUI could have by adding tabbed panels, scroll panes, tables, and lists. Swing components are lightweight because they do not depend on the native code and are fully implemented in Java.

In 2007, Sun Microsystems announced the creation of JavaFX, which eventually became a software platform for creating and delivering desktop applications across many different devices. It was intended to replace Swing as the standard GUI library for Java SE. The JavaFX framework is located in the packages that start with `javafx` and supports all major desktop **operating systems** (**OSs**) and multiple mobile OSs, including Symbian OS, Windows Mobile, and some proprietary real-time OSs.

JavaFX has added support for smooth animation, web views, audio and video playback, and styles to the arsenal of a GUI developer, based on **Cascading Style Sheets** (**CSS**). However, Swing has more components and third-party libraries, so using JavaFX may require creating custom components and plumbing that was implemented in Swing a long time ago. That's why, although JavaFX is recommended as the first choice for desktop GUI implementation, Swing will remain part of Java for the foreseeable future, according to the official response on the Oracle website (`http://www.oracle.com/technetwork/java/javafx/overview/faq-1446554.html#6`). So, it is possible to continue using Swing, but, if possible, it's better to switch to JavaFX.

We will talk about JavaFX and see code examples of it in *Chapter 12, Java GUI Programming*.

External libraries

Different lists of the most used third-party non-JCL libraries include between 20 and 100 libraries. In this section, we are going to discuss those libraries that are included in the majority of such lists. All of them are open source projects.

org.junit

The `org.junit` package is the root package of an open source testing framework's JUnit. It can be added to the project as the following `pom.xml` dependency:

```
<dependency>
    <groupId>junit</groupId>
    <artifactId>junit</artifactId>
    <version>4.13.2</version>
    <scope>test</scope>
</dependency>
```

The `scope` value in the preceding dependency tag tells Maven to include the library `.jar` file, but only when the test code is going to be run, not in the production `.jar` file of the application. With the dependency in place, you can create a test. You can write the code yourself or let the IDE do it for you by doing the following:

1. *Right-click* on the class name you would like to test.
2. Select **Go To**.
3. Select **Test**.
4. Click **Create New Test**.
5. Click the checkbox for the methods of the class you would like to test.
6. Write code for the generated test methods with the `@Test` annotation.
7. Add methods with the `@Before` and `@After` annotations if necessary.

Let's assume we have the following class:

```
public class Class1 {
    public int multiplyByTwo(int i){
        return i * 2;
    }
}
```

If you follow the preceding steps, the following test class will be created under the test source tree:

```
import org.junit.Test;
public class Class1Test {
    @Test
    public void multiplyByTwo() {
    }
}
```

Now, you can implement the `void multiplyByTwo()` method, as follows:

```
@Test
public void multiplyByTwo() {
    Class1 class1 = new Class1();
    int result = class1.multiplyByTwo(2);
    Assert.assertEquals(4, result);
}
```

A unit is a minimal piece of code that can be tested, thus the name. The best testing practices consider a method as a minimal testable unit. That's why a unit test usually tests a method.

org.mockito

One of the problems a unit test often faces is the need to test a method that uses a third-party library, a data source, or a method of another class. While testing, you want to control all the inputs so that you can predict the expected result of the tested code. That is where the technique of simulating or mocking the behavior of the objects the tested code interacts with comes in handy.

The open source Mockito framework (the org.mockito root package name) allows you to do just that – create mock objects. Using it is quite easy. Here is one simple case. Let's assume we need to test another Class1 method:

```
public class Class1 {
    public int multiplyByTwo2(Class2 class2){
        return class2.getValue() * 2;
    }
}
```

To test this method, we need to make sure that the getValue() method returns a certain value, so we are going to mock this method. To do so, follow these steps:

1. Add a dependency to the Maven pom.xml configuration file:

   ```
   <dependency>
       <groupId>org.mockito</groupId>
       <artifactId>mockito-core</artifactId>
       <version>4.2.0</version>
       <scope>test</scope>
   </dependency>
   ```

2. Call the Mockito.mock() method for the class you need to simulate:

   ```
   Class2 class2Mock = Mockito.mock(Class2.class);
   ```

3. Set the value you need to be returned from a method:

   ```
   Mockito.when(class2Mock.getValue()).thenReturn(5);
   ```

4. Now, you can pass the mocked object as a parameter into the method you are testing that calls the mocked method:

```
Class1 class1 = new Class1();
int result = class1.multiplyByTwo2(class2Mock);
```

5. The mocked method returns the result you have predefined:

```
Assert.assertEquals(10, result);
```

6. The @Test method should look as follows:

```
@Test
public void multiplyByTwo2() {
    Class2 class2Mock = Mockito.mock(Class2.class);
    Mockito.when(class2Mock.getValue()).thenReturn(5);

    Class1 class1 = new Class1();
    int result = class1.multiplyByTwo2(mo);
    Assert.assertEquals(10, result);
}
```

Mockito has certain limitations. For example, you cannot mock static methods and private methods. Otherwise, it is a great way to isolate the code you are testing by reliably predicting the results of the used third-party classes.

org.apache.log4j and org.slf4j

Throughout this book, we have used System.out to display the results. In a real-life application, you can do this and redirect the output to a file, for example, for later analysis. Once you've been doing this a while, you will notice that you need more details about each output: the date and time of each statement, and the class name where the logging statement was generated, for example. As the code base grows, you will find that it would be nice to send output from different subsystems or packages to different files or turn off some messages, when everything works as expected, and turn them back on when an issue has been detected and more detailed information about code behavior is needed. And you don't want the size of the log file to grow uncontrollably.

It is possible to write code that accomplishes all this. But several frameworks do this based on the settings in a configuration file, which you can change every time you need to change the logging behavior. The two most popular frameworks that are used for this are called log4j (pronounced as LOG-FOUR-JAY) and slf4j (pronounced as S-L-F-FOUR-JAY).

These two frameworks are not rivals. The slf4j framework is a facade that provides unified access to an underlying actual logging framework; one of them can be log4j too. Such a facade is especially helpful during library development when programmers do not know what kind of logging framework will be used by the application that uses the library in advance. By writing code using slf4j, the programmers allow you to configure it later so that you can use any logging system.

So, if your code is going to be used only by the application your team develops, using just log4j is enough. Otherwise, consider using slf4j.

As in the case of any third-party library, before you can use the log4j framework, you must add a corresponding dependency to the Maven pom.xml configuration file:

```
<dependency>
    <groupId>org.apache.logging.log4j</groupId>
    <artifactId>log4j-api</artifactId>
    <version>2.17.0</version>
</dependency>
<dependency>
    <groupId>org.apache.logging.log4j</groupId>
    <artifactId>log4j-core</artifactId>
    <version>2.17.0</version>
</dependency>
```

For example, here's how the framework can be used:

```
import org.apache.logging.log4j.LogManager;
import org.apache.logging.log4j.Logger;
public class Class1 {
    static final Logger logger =
                LogManager.getLogger(Class1.class.getName());

    public static void main(String... args){
        new Class1().multiplyByTwo2(null);
```

```
    }

    public int multiplyByTwo2(Class2 class2){
        if(class2 == null){
            logger.error("The parameter should not be null");
            System.exit(1);
        }
        return class2.getValue() * 2;
    }
}
```

If we run the preceding `main()` method, we will get the following output:

```
18:34:07.672 [main] ERROR Class1 - The parameter should not be
null
Process finished with exit code 1
```

As you can see, if no log4j-specific configuration file is added to the project, log4j will provide a default configuration in the `DefaultConfiguration` class. The default configuration is as follows:

- The log message will go to a console.
- The pattern of the message is going to be `%d{HH:mm:ss.SSS} [%t] %-5level %logger{36} - %msg%n`.
- The level of logging will be `Level.ERROR` (other levels include `OFF`, `FATAL`, `WARN`, `INFO`, `DEBUG`, `TRACE`, and `ALL`).

The same result can be achieved by adding the `log4j2.xml` file to the `resources` folder (which Maven places on the classpath) with the following content:

```xml
<?xml version="1.0" encoding="UTF-8"?>
<Configuration status="WARN">
    <Appenders>
        <Console name="Console" target="SYSTEM_OUT">
            <PatternLayout pattern="%d{HH:mm:ss.SSS} [%t]
                           %-5level %logger{36} - %msg%n"/>
        </Console>
    </Appenders>
    <Loggers>
```

```
        <Root level="error">
            <AppenderRef ref="Console"/>
        </Root>
    </Loggers>
</Configuration>
```

If that is not good enough for you, it is possible to change the configuration so that it logs messages of different levels, to different files, and so on. Read the log4j documentation to learn more: `https://logging.apache.org`.

org.apache.commons

The `org.apache.commons` package is another popular library that's been developed as a project called **Apache Commons**. It is maintained by an open source community of programmers called **Apache Software Foundation**. This organization was formed by the Apache Group in 1999. The Apache Group has grown around the development of the Apache HTTP Server since 1993. The Apache HTTP Server is an open source cross-platform web server that has remained the most popular web server since April 1996.

The Apache Commons project has the following three components:

- **Commons Sandbox**: A workspace for Java component development; you can contribute to the open source work there.

- **Commons Dormant**: A repository of components that are currently inactive; you can use the code there, but you must build the components yourself since these components will probably not be released soon.

- **Commons Proper**: The reusable Java components that compose the actual `org.apache.commons` library.

We discussed the `org.apache.commons.io` package in *Chapter 5, String, Input/Output, and Files*.

In the following subsections, we will discuss three of Commons Proper's most popular packages:

- `org.apache.commons.lang3`
- `org.apache.commons.collections4`
- `org.apache.commons.codec.binary`

However, there are many more packages under `org.apache.commons` that contain thousands of classes that can easily be used to make your code more elegant and efficient.

lang and lang3

The `org.apache.commons.lang3` package is version 3 of the `org.apache.commons.lang` package. The decision to create a new package was forced by the fact that changes that were introduced in version 3 were backward-incompatible, which means that the existing applications that use the previous version of the `org.apache.commons.lang` package may stop working after the upgrade to version 3. But in the majority of mainstream programming, adding 3 to an `import` statement (as a way to migrate to the new version) typically does not break anything.

According to the documentation, the `org.apache.commons.lang3` package provides highly reusable static utility methods that are chiefly concerned with adding value to the `java.lang` classes. Here are a few notable examples:

- The `ArrayUtils` class: Allows you to search and manipulate arrays; we discussed and demonstrated this in *Chapter 6, Data Structures, Generics, and Popular Utilities.*

- The `ClassUtils` class: Provides some metadata about a class.

- The `ObjectUtils` class: Checks an array of objects for null, compares objects, and calculates the median and minimum/maximum of an array of objects in a null-safe manner; we discussed and demonstrated this in *Chapter 6, Data Structures, Generics, and Popular Utilities.*

- The `SystemUtils` class: Provides information about the execution environment.

- The `ThreadUtils` class: Finds information about currently running threads.

- The `Validate` class: Validates individual values and collections, compares them, checks for nulls and matches, and performs many other validations.

- The `RandomStringUtils` class: Generates `String` objects from the characters of various character sets.

- The `StringUtils` class: We discussed this class in *Chapter 5, String, Input/Output, and Files.*

collections4

Although the content of the `org.apache.commons.collections4` package looks quite similar to the content of the `org.apache.commons.collections` package on the surface (which is version 3 of the package), the migration to version 4 may not be as smooth as just adding 4 to the `import` statement. Version 4 removed deprecated classes and added generics and other features that are incompatible with the previous versions.

You must be hard-pressed to come up with a collection type or a collection utility that is not present in this package or one of its sub-packages. The following is just a high-level list of features and utilities that are included:

- The `Bag` interface for collections that have several copies of each object.

- A dozen classes that implement the `Bag` interface. For example, here is how the `HashBag` class can be used:

```
Bag<String> bag = new HashBag<>();
bag.add("one", 4);
System.out.println(bag);      //prints: [4:one]
bag.remove("one", 1);
System.out.println(bag);      //prints: [3:one]
System.out.println(bag.getCount("one")); //prints: 3
```

- The `BagUtils` class, which transforms `Bag`-based collections.

- The `BidiMap` interface for bidirectional maps, which allow you to retrieve not only a value by its key but also a key by its value. It has several implementations, an example of which is as follows:

```
BidiMap<Integer, String> bidi = new TreeBidiMap<>();
bidi.put(2, "two");
bidi.put(3, "three");
System.out.println(bidi);
                              //prints: {2=two, 3=three}
System.out.println(bidi.inverseBidiMap());
                              //prints: {three=3, two=2}
System.out.println(bidi.get(3));          //prints: three
System.out.println(bidi.getKey("three")); //prints: 3
bidi.removeValue("three");
System.out.println(bidi);                 //prints: {2=two}
```

- The `MapIterator` interface to provide simple and quick iteration over maps, like so:

```
IterableMap<Integer, String> map =
            new HashedMap<>(Map.of(1, "one", 2, "two"));
MapIterator it = map.mapIterator();
while (it.hasNext()) {
    Object key = it.next();
    Object value = it.getValue();
    System.out.print(key + ", " + value + ", ");
                                //prints: 2, two, 1, one,
    if(((Integer)key) == 2){
        it.setValue("three");
    }
}
System.out.println("\n" + map);
                                //prints: {2=three, 1=one}
```

- Ordered maps and sets that keep the elements in a certain order, like `List` does; for example:

```
OrderedMap<Integer, String> map = new LinkedMap<>();
map.put(4, "four");
map.put(7, "seven");
map.put(12, "twelve");
System.out.println(map.firstKey()); //prints: 4
System.out.println(map.nextKey(2)); //prints: null
System.out.println(map.nextKey(7)); //prints: 12
System.out.println(map.nextKey(4)); //prints: 7
```

- Reference maps, their keys, and/or values can be removed by the garbage collector.

- Various implementations of the `Comparator` interface.

- Various implementations of the `Iterator` interface.

- Classes that convert arrays and enumerations into collections.

- Utilities that allow you to test or create a union, intersection, or closure of collections.

- The `CollectionUtils`, `ListUtils`, `MapUtils`, and `MultiMapUtils` classes, as well as many other interface-specific utility classes.

Read the package's documentation (`https://commons.apache.org/proper/commons-collections`) for more details.

codec.binary

The `org.apache.commons.codec.binary` package provides support for Base64, Base32, binary, and hexadecimal string encoding and decoding. This encoding is necessary to make sure that the data you sent across different systems will not be changed on the way because of the restrictions on the range of characters in different protocols. Besides, some systems interpret the sent data as control characters (a modem, for example).

The following code snippet demonstrates the basic encoding and decoding capabilities of the `Base64` class of this package:

```
String encodedStr = new String(Base64
                    .encodeBase64("Hello, World!".getBytes()));
System.out.println(encodedStr);   //prints: SGVsbG8sIFdvcmxkIQ==
System.out.println(Base64.isBase64(encodedStr)); //prints: true
String decodedStr =
  new String(Base64.decodeBase64(encodedStr.getBytes()));
System.out.println(decodedStr);   //prints: Hello, World!
```

You can read more about this package on the Apache Commons project site at `https://commons.apache.org/proper/commons-codec`.

Summary

In this chapter, we provided an overview of the functionality of the most popular packages of JCL – that is, `java.lang`, `java.util`, `java.time`, `java.io`, `java.nio`, `java.sql`, `javax.sql`, `java.net`, `java.lang.math`, `java.math`, `java.awt`, `javax.swing`, and `javafx`.

The most popular external libraries were represented by the `org.junit`, `org.mockito`, `org.apache.log4j`, `org.slf4j`, and `org.apache.commons` packages. These help you avoid writing custom code in cases when such functionality already exists and can just be imported and used out of the box.

In the next chapter, we will talk about Java threads and demonstrate their usage. We will also explain the difference between parallel and concurrent processing. Then, we will show you how to create a thread and how to execute, monitor, and stop it. This will be useful not only for those who are going to write code for multi-threaded processing but also for those who would like to improve their understanding of how JVM works, which will be the topic of the following chapter.

Quiz

Answer the following questions to test your knowledge of this chapter:

1. What is the Java Class Library? Select all that apply:

    A. A collection of compiled classes

    B. Packages that come with the Java installation

    C. A `.jar` file that Maven adds to the classpath automatically

    D. Any library that's written in Java

2. What is the Java external library? Select all that apply:

    A. A `.jar` file that is not included with the Java installation

    B. A `.jar` file that must be added as a dependency in `pom.xml` before it can be used

    C. Classes not written by the authors of JVM

    D. Classes that do not belong to JCL

3. What functionality is included in the `java.lang` package? Select all that apply:

   A. It is the only package that contains Java language implementation.

   B. It contains the most often used classes of JCL.

   C. It contains the `Object` class, which is the base class for any Java class.

   D. It contains all the types listed in the Java Language Specification.

4. What functionality is included in the `java.util` package? Select all that apply:

   A. All the implementations of Java collection interfaces

   B. All the interfaces of the Java collections framework

   C. All the utilities of JCL

   D. Classes, arrays, objects, and properties

5. What functionality is included in the `java.time` package? Select all that apply:

   A. Classes that manage dates.

   B. It is the only package that manages time.

   C. Classes that represent date and time.

   D. It is the only package that manages dates.

6. What functionality is included in the `java.io` package? Select all that apply:

   A. Processing streams of binary data

   B. Processing streams of characters

   C. Processing streams of bytes

   D. Processing streams of numbers

7. What functionality is included in the `java.sql` package? Select all that apply:

   A. Supports database connection pooling

   B. Supports database statement execution

   C. Provides the capability to read/write data from/to a database

   D. Supports database transactions

8. What functionality is included in the `java.net` package? Select all that apply:

    A. Supports .NET programming

    B. Supports sockets communication

    C. Supports URL-based communication

    D. Supports RMI-based communication

9. What functionality is included in the `java.math` package? Select all that apply:

    A. Supports minimum and maximum calculations

    B. Supports big numbers

    C. Supports logarithms

    D. Supports square root calculations

10. What functionality is included in the `javafx` package? Select all that apply:

    A. Supports fax-message sending

    B. Supports fax-message receiving

    C. Supports GUI programming

    D. Supports animation

11. What functionality is included in the `org.junit` package? Select all that apply:

    A. Supports testing Java classes

    B. Supports Java units of measure

    C. Supports unit testing

    D. Supports organizational unity

12. What functionality is included in the `org.mockito` package? Select all that apply:

    A. Supports the Mockito protocol

    B. Allows you to simulate a method's behavior

    C. Supports static method simulation

    D. Generates objects that behave like third-party classes

13. What functionality is included in the `org.apache.log4j` package? Select all that apply:

   A. Supports writing messages to a file

   B. Supports reading messages from a file

   C. Supports the log4j protocol for Java

   D. Supports controlling the number and size of log files

14. What functionality is included in the `org.apache.commons.lang3` package? Select all that apply:

   A. Supports Java language version 3

   B. Complements the `java.lang` classes

   C. Contains the `ArrayUtils`, `ObjectUtils`, and `StringUtils` classes

   D. Contains the `SystemUtils` class

15. What functionality is included in the `org.apache.commons.collections4` package? Select all that apply:

   A. Various implementations of Java collections framework interfaces

   B. Various utilities for Java collections framework implementations

   C. The Vault interface and its implementations

   D. Contains the `CollectionUtils` class

16. What functionality is included in the `org.apache.commons.codec.binary` package? Select all that apply:

   A. Supports sending binary data across the network

   B. Allows you to encode and decode data

   C. Supports data encryption

   D. Contains the `StringUtils` class

8
Multithreading and Concurrent Processing

In this chapter, we will discuss ways to increase Java application performance by using workers (threads) that process data concurrently. We will explain the concept of Java threads and demonstrate their usage. We will also talk about the difference between parallel and concurrent processing and how to avoid unpredictable results caused by the concurrent modification of a shared resource.

After finishing this chapter, you will be able to write code for multithreaded processing—creating and executing threads and using a pool of threads in parallel and concurrent cases.

The following topics will be covered in this chapter:

- Thread versus process
- User thread versus daemon
- Extending the `Thread` class
- Implementing the `Runnable` interface

- Extending `Thread` versus implementing `Runnable`
- Using a pool of threads
- Getting results from a thread
- Parallel versus concurrent processing
- Concurrent modification of the same resource

Technical requirements

To be able to execute the code examples provided in this chapter, you will need the following:

- A computer with a Microsoft Windows, Apple macOS, or Linux operating system
- Java **Standard Edition** (**SE**) version 17 or later
- An **integrated development environment** (**IDE**) or your preferred code editor

Instructions on how to set up a Java SE and IntelliJ IDEA editor were provided in *Chapter 1, Getting Started with Java 17*. Files with code examples for this chapter are available on GitHub in the `https://github.com/PacktPublishing/Learn-Java-17-Programming.git` repository, in the `examples/src/main/java/com/packt/learnjava/ch08_threads` folder.

Thread versus process

Java has two units of execution—a process and a thread. A **process** usually represents the whole **Java virtual machine** (**JVM**), although an application can create another process using `java.lang.ProcessBuilder`. But since the multi-process case is outside the scope of this book, we will focus on the second unit of execution—that is, a **thread**, which is similar to a process but less isolated from other threads and requires fewer resources for execution.

A process can have many threads running and at least one thread called the **main thread**—the one that starts the application—which we use in every example. Threads can share resources, including memory and open files, which allows for better efficiency, but this comes at a price: a higher risk of unintended mutual interference, and even blocking of the execution. That is where programming skills and an understanding of concurrency techniques are required.

User thread versus daemon

There is a particular kind of thread called a daemon.

> **Note**
>
> The word *daemon* has an ancient Greek origin, meaning a divinity
> or supernatural being of nature between gods and humans and an inner
> or attendant spirit or inspiring force.

In computer science, the term *daemon* has more mundane usage and is applied
to *a computer program that runs as a background process, rather than being under the
direct control of an interactive user.* That is why there are the following two types
of threads in Java:

- User thread (default) initiated by an application (the main thread is one
  such example)

- Daemon thread that works in the background in support of user-thread activity

That is why all daemon threads exit immediately after the last user thread exits or are
terminated by the JVM after an unhandled exception.

Extending the Thread class

One way to create a thread is to extend the `java.lang.Thread` class and override its
`run()` method. Here's an example of this:

```java
class MyThread extends Thread {
    private String parameter;
    public MyThread(String parameter) {
        this.parameter = parameter;
    }
    public void run() {
        while(!"exit".equals(parameter)){
            System.out.println((isDaemon() ? "daemon"
                : "  user") + " thread " + this.getName() +
                "(id=" + this.getId() + ") parameter: " +
                                            parameter);
            pauseOneSecond();
        }
```

```
        System.out.println((isDaemon() ? "daemon"
            : "  user") + " thread " + this.getName() +
            "(id=" + this.getId() + ") parameter: " +
                                        parameter);
    }
    public void setParameter(String parameter) {
        this.parameter = parameter;
    }
}
```

If the run() method is not overridden, the thread does nothing. In our example, the thread prints its name and other properties every second, as long as the parameter is not equal to the "exit" string; otherwise, it exits.

The pauseOneSecond() method looks like this:

```
private static void pauseOneSecond(){
    try {
        TimeUnit.SECONDS.sleep(1);
    } catch (InterruptedException e) {
        e.printStackTrace();
    }
}
```

We can now use the MyThread class to run two threads—one user thread and one daemon thread, as follows:

```
public static void main(String... args) {
    MyThread thr1 = new MyThread("One");
    thr1.start();
    MyThread thr2 = new MyThread("Two");
    thr2.setDaemon(true);
    thr2.start();
    pauseOneSecond();
    thr1.setParameter("exit");
    pauseOneSecond();
    System.out.println("Main thread exists");
}
```

As you can see, the main thread creates two other threads, pauses for one second, sets the `exit` parameter on the user thread, pauses another second, and finally exits (the `main()` method completes its execution).

If we run the preceding code, we'll see something like this (the `id` thread may be different in different operating systems):

```
daemon thread Thread-1(id=14) parameter: Two
  user thread Thread-0(id=13) parameter: One
daemon thread Thread-1(id=14) parameter: Two
  user thread Thread-0(id=13) parameter: exit
Main thread exists
```

The preceding screenshot shows that the daemon thread exits automatically as soon as the last user thread (the main thread, in our example) exits.

Implementing the Runnable interface

The second way to create a thread is to use a class that implements `java.lang.Runnable`. Here is an example of such a class that has almost exactly the same functionality as the `MyThread` class:

```java
class MyRunnable implements Runnable {
    private String parameter, name;
    public MyRunnable(String name) {
        this.name = name;
    }
    public void run() {
        while(!"exit".equals(parameter)){
            System.out.println("thread " + this.name +
                            ", parameter: " + parameter);
            pauseOneSecond();
        }
        System.out.println("thread " + this.name +
                        ", parameter: " + parameter);
    }
    public void setParameter(String parameter) {
        this.parameter = parameter;
    }
}
```

The difference is that there is no `isDaemon()`, `getId()`, or any other out-of-the-box method. The `MyRunnable` class can be any class that implements the `Runnable` interface, so we cannot print whether the thread is a daemon or not. We have added the name property so that we can identify the thread.

We can use the `MyRunnable` class to create threads similar to how we have used the `MyThread` class, as follows:

```
public static void main(String... args) {
    MyRunnable myRunnable1 = new MyRunnable("One");
    MyRunnable myRunnable2 = new MyRunnable("Two");

    Thread thr1 = new Thread(myRunnable1);
    thr1.start();
    Thread thr2 = new Thread(myRunnable2);
    thr2.setDaemon(true);
    thr2.start();
    pauseOneSecond();
    myRunnable1.setParameter("exit");
    pauseOneSecond();
    System.out.println("Main thread exists");
}
```

The following screenshot proves that the behavior of the `MyRunnable` class is similar to the behavior of the `MyThread` class:

```
thread Two, parameter: null
thread One, parameter: null
thread Two, parameter: null
thread One, parameter: exit
Main thread exists
```

The daemon thread (named `Two`) exits after the last user thread exits—exactly how it happened with the `MyThread` class.

Extending Thread versus implementing Runnable

Implementation of `Runnable` has the advantage (and in some cases, the only possible option) of allowing the implementation to extend another class. It is particularly helpful when you would like to add thread-like behavior to an existing class. Implementing `Runnable` allows more flexibility in usage, but otherwise, there is no difference in functionality compared to the extending of the `Thread` class.

The `Thread` class has several constructors that allow setting the thread name and the group it belongs to. Grouping of threads helps to manage them in the case of many threads running in parallel. The `Thread` class has also several methods that provide information about the thread's status and its properties and allows us to control its behavior.

As you have seen, the thread's **identifier (ID)** is generated automatically. It cannot be changed but can be reused after the thread is terminated. Several threads, on the other hand, can be set with the same name.

The execution priority can also be set programmatically with a value between `Thread.MIN_PRIORITY` and `Thread.MAX_PRIORITY`. The smaller the value, the more time the thread is allowed to run, which means it has a higher priority. If not set, the priority value defaults to `Thread.NORM_PRIORITY`.

The state of a thread can have one of the following values:

- `NEW`: When a thread has not yet started
- `RUNNABLE`: When a thread is being executed
- `BLOCKED`: When a thread is blocked and is waiting for a monitor lock
- `WAITING`: When a thread is waiting indefinitely for another thread to perform a particular action
- `TIMED_WAITING`: When a thread is waiting for another thread to perform an action for up to a specified waiting time
- `TERMINATED`: When a thread has exited

Threads—and any objects, for that matter—can also *talk to each other* using the `wait()`, `notify()`, and `notifyAll()` methods of the `java.lang.Object` base class, but this aspect of threads' behavior is outside the scope of this book.

Using a pool of threads

Each thread requires resources—the **central processing unit** (**CPU**) and **memory**. This means the number of threads must be controlled, and one way to do that is to create a fixed number of them—a pool. Besides, creating an object incurs an overhead that may be significant for some applications.

In this section, we will look into the `Executor` interfaces and their implementations provided in the `java.util.concurrent` package. They encapsulate thread management and minimize the time an application developer spends on writing code related to threads' life cycles.

There are three `Executor` interfaces defined in the `java.util.concurrent` package, as follows:

- The base `Executor` interface: This has only one `void execute(Runnable r)` method in it.

- The `ExecutorService` interface: This extends `Executor` and adds four groups of methods that manage the life cycle of worker threads and of the executor itself, as follows:

  - `submit()` methods, which place a `Runnable` or `Callable` object in the queue for the execution (`Callable` allows the worker thread to return a value) and return an object of the `Future` interface, which can be used to access the value returned by the `Callable` object and to manage the status of the worker thread

  - `invokeAll()` methods, which place a collection of objects of the `Callable` interface in a queue for execution, which then returns a `List` interface of `Future` objects when all worker threads are complete (there is also an overloaded `invokeAll()` method with a timeout)

  - `invokeAny()` methods, which place a collection of interface `Callable` objects in the queue for the execution and return one `Future` object of any of the worker threads, which has completed (there is also an overloaded `invokeAny()` method with a timeout)

- Methods that manage worker threads' status and the service itself, as follows:

  - `shutdown()`: Prevents new worker threads from being submitted to the service.

  - `shutdownNow()`: Interrupts each worker thread that is not completed. A worker thread should be written so that it checks its own status periodically (using `Thread.currentThread().isInterrupted()`, for example) and gracefully shuts down on its own; otherwise, it will continue running even after `shutdownNow()` was called.

- `isShutdown()`: Checks whether the shutdown of the executor was initiated.

- `awaitTermination(long timeout, TimeUnit timeUnit)`: Waits until all worker threads have completed execution after a shutdown request, or a timeout occurs, or the current thread is interrupted, whichever happens first.

- `isTerminated()`: Checks whether all the worker threads have completed after the shutdown was initiated. It never returns `true` unless either `shutdown()` or `shutdownNow()` was called first.

- The `ScheduledExecutorService` interface: This extends `ExecutorService` and adds methods that allow scheduling of the execution (one-time and periodic) of worker threads

A pool-based implementation of `ExecutorService` can be created using the `java.util.concurrent.ThreadPoolExecutor` or `java.util.concurrent.ScheduledThreadPoolExecutor` class. There is also a `java.util.concurrent.Executors` factory class that covers most practical cases. So, before writing custom code for worker threads' pool creation, we highly recommend looking into using the following factory methods of the `java.util.concurrent.Executors` class:

- `newCachedThreadPool()`: Creates a thread pool that adds a new thread as needed, unless there is an idle thread created before; threads that have been idle for 60 seconds are removed from the pool

- `newSingleThreadExecutor()`: Creates an `ExecutorService` (pool) instance that executes worker threads sequentially

- `newSingleThreadScheduledExecutor()`: Creates a single-threaded executor that can be scheduled to run after a given delay, or to execute periodically

- `newFixedThreadPool(int nThreads)`: Creates a thread pool that reuses a fixed number of worker threads; if a new task is submitted when all the worker threads are still executing, it will be placed into the queue until a worker thread is available

- `newScheduledThreadPool(int nThreads)`: Creates a thread pool of a fixed size that can be scheduled to run after a given delay, or to execute periodically

- `newWorkStealingThreadPool(int nThreads)`: Creates a thread pool that uses the *work-stealing* algorithm used by `ForkJoinPool`, which is particularly useful in case the worker threads generate other threads, such as in a recursive algorithm; it also adapts to the specified number of CPUs, which you may set higher or lower than the actual CPU count on your computer

> **Work-Stealing Algorithm**
>
> A work-stealing algorithm allows threads that have finished their assigned tasks to help other tasks that are still busy with their assignments. As an example, see the description of fork/join implementation in the official Oracle Java documentation (`https://docs.oracle.com/javase/tutorial/essential/concurrency/forkjoin.html`).

Each of these methods has an overloaded version that allows passing in `ThreadFactory` that is used to create a new thread when needed. Let's see how it all works in a code sample. First, we run another version of the `MyRunnable` class, as follows:

```java
class MyRunnable implements Runnable {
    private String name;
    public MyRunnable(String name) {
        this.name = name;
    }
    public void run() {
        try {
                while (true) {
                System.out.println(this.name +
                                        " is working...");
                TimeUnit.SECONDS.sleep(1);
             }
        } catch (InterruptedException e) {
            System.out.println(this.name +
                        " was interrupted\n" + this.name +
                 " Thread.currentThread().isInterrupted()=" +
                    Thread.currentThread().isInterrupted());
        }
    }
}
```

We cannot use the `parameter` property anymore to tell the thread to stop executing because the thread life cycle is now going to be controlled by the `ExecutorService` interface, and the way it does it is by calling the `interrupt()` thread method. Also, notice that the thread we created has an infinite loop, so it will never stop executing until forced to (by calling the `interrupt()` method).

Let's write code that does the following:

- Creates a pool of three threads
- Makes sure the pool does not accept more threads
- Waits for a fixed time to let all threads finish what they're doing
- Stops (interrupts) threads that did not finish what they were doing
- Exits

The following code performs all the actions described in the preceding list:

```
ExecutorService pool = Executors.newCachedThreadPool();
String[] names = {"One", "Two", "Three"};
for (int i = 0; i < names.length; i++) {
    pool.execute(new MyRunnable(names[i]));
}
System.out.println("Before shutdown: isShutdown()=" +
            pool.isShutdown() + ", isTerminated()=" +
                            pool.isTerminated());
pool.shutdown();
            // New threads cannot be added to the pool
//pool.execute(new MyRunnable("Four"));
                        //RejectedExecutionException
System.out.println("After shutdown: isShutdown()=" +
            pool.isShutdown() + ", isTerminated()=" +
                            pool.isTerminated());
try {
  long timeout = 100;
  TimeUnit timeUnit = TimeUnit.MILLISECONDS;
  System.out.println("Waiting all threads completion for "
                    + timeout + " " + timeUnit + "...");
        // Blocks until timeout, or all threads complete
        // execution, or the current thread is
        // interrupted, whichever happens first.
  boolean isTerminated =
            pool.awaitTermination(timeout, timeUnit);
  System.out.println("isTerminated()=" + isTerminated);
  if (!isTerminated) {
```

```
        System.out.println("Calling shutdownNow()...");
        List<Runnable> list = pool.shutdownNow();
        System.out.println(list.size() + " threads running");
        isTerminated =
                     pool.awaitTermination(timeout, timeUnit);
        if (!isTerminated) {
         System.out.println("Some threads are still running");
        }
        System.out.println("Exiting");
    }
} catch (InterruptedException ex) {
    ex.printStackTrace();
}
```

The attempt to add another thread to the pool after `pool.shutdown()` is called generates `java.util.concurrent.RejectedExecutionException`.

The execution of the preceding code produces the following results:

```
One is working...
Three is working...
Two is working...
Before shutdown: isShutdown()=false, isTerminated()=false
After shutdown: isShutdown()=true, isTerminated()=false
Waiting all threads completion for 100 MILLISECONDS...
isTerminated()=false
Calling shutdownNow()...
0 threads running
One was interrupted
One Thread.currentThread().isInterrupted()=false
Two was interrupted
Two Thread.currentThread().isInterrupted()=false
Three was interrupted
Three Thread.currentThread().isInterrupted()=false
Exiting
```

Notice the `Thread.currentThread().isInterrupted()=false` message in the preceding screenshot. The thread was interrupted. We know this because the thread got an `InterruptedException` message. Why, then, does the `isInterrupted()` method return `false`? This happens because the thread state was cleared immediately after receiving the interrupt message. We're mentioning it now because it is a source of some programmer mistakes. For example, if the main thread watches the `MyRunnable` thread and calls `isInterrupted()` on it, the return value is going to be `false`, which may be misleading after the thread was interrupted.

So, in the case where another thread may be monitoring the `MyRunnable` thread, the implementation of `MyRunnable` has to be changed to this. Note in the following code snippet how the `interrupt()` method is called in the `catch` block:

```
class MyRunnable implements Runnable {
    private String name;
    public MyRunnable(String name) {
        this.name = name;
    }
    public void run() {
        try {
            while (true) {
                System.out.println(this.name + " is working...");
                TimeUnit.SECONDS.sleep(1);
            }
        } catch (InterruptedException e) {
            Thread.currentThread().interrupt();
            System.out.println(this.name +
                " was interrupted\n" + this.name +
                " Thread.currentThread().isInterrupted()=" +
                    Thread.currentThread().isInterrupted());
        }
    }
}
```

Now, if we run this thread using the same `ExecutorService` pool again, this will be the result:

```
Two is working...
Three is working...
One is working...
Before shutdown: isShutdown()=false, isTerminated()=false
After shutdown: isShutdown()=true, isTerminated()=false
Waiting all threads completion for 100 MILLISECONDS...
isTerminated()=false
Calling shutdownNow()...
0 threads running
Two was interrupted
Two Thread.currentThread().isInterrupted()=true
One was interrupted
One Thread.currentThread().isInterrupted()=true
Three was interrupted
Three Thread.currentThread().isInterrupted()=true
Exiting
```

As you can see, the value returned by the `isInterrupted()` method is now `true` and corresponds to what has happened. To be fair, in many applications, once a thread is interrupted, its status is not checked again. But setting the correct state is a good practice, especially in those cases where you are not the author of the higher-level code that creates a particular thread.

In our example, we have used a cached thread pool that creates a new thread as needed or, if available, reuses the thread already used, but which completed its job and returned to the pool for a new assignment. We did not worry about too many threads created because our demonstration application had three worker threads at the most and they were quite short-lived.

But in the case where an application does not have a fixed limit of worker threads it might need or there is no good way to predict how much memory a thread may take or how long it can execute, setting a ceiling on the worker thread count prevents an unexpected degradation of the application performance, running out of memory, or depletion of any other resources the worker threads use. If the thread behavior is extremely unpredictable, a single thread pool might be the only solution, with the option of using a custom thread-pool executor. But in the majority of cases, a fixed-size thread-pool executor is a good practical compromise between the application needs and the code complexity (earlier in this section, we listed all possible pool types created by the `Executors` factory class).

Setting the size of the pool too low may deprive the application of the chance to utilize the available resources effectively. So, before selecting the pool size, it is advisable to spend some time monitoring the application, with the goal of identifying the idiosyncrasy of the application behavior. In fact, the *deploy-monitor-adjust* cycle has to be repeated throughout the application's life cycle in order to accommodate and take advantage of changes that happened in the code or the executing environment.

The first characteristic you take into account is the number of CPUs in your system, so the thread pool size can be at least as big as the CPU count. Then, you can monitor the application and see how much time each thread engages the CPU for and how much time it uses other resources (such as **input/output (I/O)** operations). If the time spent not using the CPU is comparable with the total executing time of the thread, then you can increase the pool size by the following ratio: the time the CPU was not used divided by the total executing time, but that is in the case where another resource (disk or database) is not a subject of contention between threads. If the latter is the case, then you can use that resource instead of the CPU as the delineating factor.

Assuming the worker threads of your application are not too big or take too long executing, and belong to the mainstream population of the typical working threads that complete their job in a reasonably short period of time, you can increase the pool size by adding the (rounded-up) ratio of the desired response time and the time a thread uses the CPU or another most contentious resource. This means that, with the same desired response time, the less a thread uses the CPU or another concurrently accessed resource, the bigger the pool size should be. If the contentious resource has its own ability to improve concurrent access (such as a connection pool in a database), consider utilizing that feature first.

If the required number of threads running at the same time changes at runtime in different circumstances, you can make the pool size dynamic and create a new pool with a new size (shutting down the old pool after all its threads have completed). The recalculation of the size of a new pool might also be necessary after you add or remove the available resources. You can use `Runtime.getRuntime().availableProcessors()` to programmatically adjust the pool size based on the current count of the available CPUs, for example.

If none of the ready-to-use thread pool executor implementations that come with the **Java Development Kit (JDK)** suit the needs of a particular application, before writing the thread-managing code from scratch, try to use the `java.util.concurrent.ThreadPoolExecutor` class first. It has several overloaded constructors.

To give you an idea of its capabilities, here is the constructor with the biggest number of options:

```
ThreadPoolExecutor (int corePoolSize,
                    int maximumPoolSize,
                    long keepAliveTime,
                    TimeUnit unit,
                    BlockingQueue<Runnable> workQueue,
                    ThreadFactory threadFactory,
                    RejectedExecutionHandler handler)
```

These are the parameters of the preceding constructor:

- `corePoolSize` is the number of threads to keep in the pool, even if they are idle, unless the `allowCoreThreadTimeOut(boolean value)` method is called with a `true` value.

- `maximumPoolSize` is the maximum number of threads to allow in the pool.

- `keepAliveTime`: When the number of threads is greater than the core, this is the maximum time that excess idle threads will wait for new tasks before terminating.

- `unit` is the time unit for the `keepAliveTime` argument.

- `workQueue` is the queue to use for holding tasks before they are executed; this queue will hold only `Runnable` objects submitted by the `execute()` method.

- `threadFactory` is the factory to use when the executor creates a new thread.

- `handler` is the handler to use when the execution is blocked because the thread bounds and queue capacities are reached.

Each of the previous constructor parameters except `workQueue` can also be set via the corresponding setter after an object of the `ThreadPoolExecutor` class has been created, thus allowing more flexibility and dynamic adjustment of existing pool characteristics.

Getting results from a thread

In our examples so far, we have used the `execute()` method of the `ExecutorService` interface to start a thread. In fact, this method comes from the `Executor` base interface. Meanwhile, the `ExecutorService` interface has other methods (listed in the previous *Using a pool of threads* section) that can start threads and get back the results of thread execution.

The object that brings back the result of thread execution is of type Future—an interface that has the following methods:

- V get(): Blocks until the thread finishes; returns the result (*if available*)
- V get(long timeout, TimeUnit unit): Blocks until the thread finishes or the provided timeout is up; returns the result (if available)
- boolean isDone(): Returns true if the thread has finished
- boolean cancel(boolean mayInterruptIfRunning): Tries to cancel the execution of the thread; returns true if successful; returns false also in the case the thread had finished normally by the time the method was called
- boolean isCancelled(): Returns true if the thread execution was canceled before it had finished normally

The *if available* remark in the description of the get() method means that the result is not always available in principle, even when the get() method without parameters is called. It all depends on the method used to produce the Future object. Here is a list of all methods of ExecutorService that return a Future object(s):

- Future<?> submit(Runnable task): Submits the thread (task) for execution; returns a Future object representing the task; the get() method of the returned Future object returns null. For example, let's use the MyRunnable class that works only for 100 milliseconds, as follows:

```
class MyRunnable implements Runnable {
    private String name;
    public MyRunnable(String name) {
        this.name = name;
    }
    public void run() {
        try {
            System.out.println(this.name +
                                    " is working...");
            TimeUnit.MILLISECONDS.sleep(100);
            System.out.println(this.name + " is done");
        } catch (InterruptedException e) {
            Thread.currentThread().interrupt();
            System.out.println(this.name +
                    " was interrupted\n" + this.name +
```

```
            " Thread.currentThread().isInterrupted()=" +
                Thread.currentThread().isInterrupted());
      }
    }
}
```

And based on the code examples of the previous section, let's create a method that shuts down the pool and terminates all the threads, if necessary, as follows:

```
void shutdownAndTerminate(ExecutorService pool){
  try {
    long timeout = 100;
    TimeUnit timeUnit = TimeUnit.MILLISECONDS;
    System.out.println("Waiting all threads " +
            "completion for " + timeout + " " +
                            timeUnit + "...");
    //Blocks until timeout or all threads complete
    // execution, or the current thread is
    // interrupted, whichever happens first.
    boolean isTerminated =
          pool.awaitTermination(timeout, timeUnit);
    System.out.println("isTerminated()=" +
                                    isTerminated);
    if(!isTerminated) {
      System.out.println("Calling shutdownNow()...");
      List<Runnable> list = pool.shutdownNow();
      System.out.println(list.size() +
                            " threads running");
      isTerminated =
          pool.awaitTermination(timeout, timeUnit);
      if (!isTerminated) {
        System.out.println("Some threads are still
```

```
running");
        }
      System.out.println("Exiting");
    }
  } catch (InterruptedException ex) {
      ex.printStackTrace();
  }
}
```

We will use the preceding shutdownAndTerminate() method in a finally block to make sure no running threads were left behind. Here is the code we are going to execute:

```
ExecutorService pool = Executors.
newSingleThreadExecutor();

Future future = pool.submit(new MyRunnable("One"));
System.out.println(future.isDone());
                                            //prints: false
System.out.println(future.isCancelled());
                                            //prints: false
try{
    System.out.println(future.get());
                                            //prints: null
    System.out.println(future.isDone());
                                            //prints: true
    System.out.println(future.isCancelled());
                                            //prints: false
} catch (Exception ex){
    ex.printStackTrace();
} finally {
    shutdownAndTerminate(pool);
}
```

You can see the output of this code in the following screenshot:

```
false
false
One is working...
One is done
null
true
false
Waiting all threads completion for 100 MILLISECONDS...
isTerminated()=false
Calling shutdownNow()...
0 threads running
Exiting
```

As expected, the get() method of the Future object returns null because the run() method of Runnable does not return anything. All we can get back from the returned Future object is the information that the task was completed, or not.

- Future<T> submit(Runnable task, T result): Submits the thread (task) for execution; returns a Future object representing the task with the provided result in it; for example, we will use the following class as the result:

```java
class Result {
    private String name;
    private double result;
    public Result(String name, double result) {
        this.name = name;
        this.result = result;
    }
    @Override
    public String toString() {
        return "Result{name=" + name +
                ", result=" + result + "}";
    }
}
```

The following code snippet demonstrates how the default result is returned by the Future object returned by the submit() method:

```java
ExecutorService pool =
                    Executors.newSingleThreadExecutor();
```

```
Future<Result> future =
            pool.submit(new MyRunnable("Two"),
                        new Result("Two", 42.));
System.out.println(future.isDone());
                                        //prints: false
System.out.println(future.isCancelled());
                                        //prints: false
try{
    System.out.println(future.get());
                                        //prints: null
    System.out.println(future.isDone());
                                        //prints: true
    System.out.println(future.isCancelled());
                                        //prints: false
} catch (Exception ex){
    ex.printStackTrace();
} finally {
    shutdownAndTerminate(pool);
}
```

If we execute the preceding code, the output is going to look like this:

```
false
false
Two is working...
Two is done
Result{name=Two, result=42.0}
true
false
Waiting all threads completion for 100 MILLISECONDS...
isTerminated()=false
Calling shutdownNow()...
0 threads running
Exiting
```

As expected, the get() method of Future returns the object passed in as
a parameter.

- `Future<T> submit(Callable<T> task)`: Submits the thread (task) for execution; returns a `Future` object representing the task with the result produced and returned by the `V call()` method of the `Callable` interface, which is the only `Callable` method the interface has. Here's an example of this:

```
class MyCallable implements Callable {
    private String name;
    public MyCallable(String name) {
        this.name = name;
    }
    public Result call() {
        try {
            System.out.println(this.name +
                                        " is working...");
            TimeUnit.MILLISECONDS.sleep(100);
            System.out.println(this.name + " is done");
            return new Result(name, 42.42);
        } catch (InterruptedException e) {
            Thread.currentThread().interrupt();
            System.out.println(this.name +
                        " was interrupted\n" + this.name +
                " Thread.currentThread().isInterrupted()=" +
                    Thread.currentThread().isInterrupted());
        }
        return null;
    }
}
```

The result of the preceding code looks like this:

```
false
false
Three is working...
Three is done
Result{name=Three, result=42.42}
true
false
Waiting all threads completion for 100 MILLISECONDS...
isTerminated()=false
Calling shutdownNow()...
0 threads running
Exiting
```

As you can see, the `get()` method of the `Future` object returns the value produced by the `call()` method of the `MyCallable` class:

- `List<Future<T>> invokeAll(Collection<Callable<T>> tasks)`: Executes all `Callable` tasks of the provided collection; returns a list of `Future` objects with the results produced by the executed `Callable` objects

- `List<Future<T>> invokeAll(Collection<Callable<T>>`: Executes all `Callable` tasks of the provided collection; returns a list of `Future` objects with the results produced by the executed `Callable` objects or the timeout expires, whichever happens first

- `T invokeAny(Collection<Callable<T>> tasks)`: Executes all `Callable` tasks of the provided collection; returns the result of one that has completed successfully (meaning, without throwing an exception), if any do

- `T invokeAny(Collection<Callable<T>> tasks, long timeout, TimeUnit unit)`: Executes all `Callable` tasks of the provided collection; returns the result of one that has completed successfully (meaning, without throwing an exception), if such is available before the provided timeout expires

As you can see, there are many ways to get results from a thread. The method you choose depends on the particular needs of your application.

Parallel versus concurrent processing

When we hear about working threads executing at the same time, we automatically assume that they literally do what they are programmed to do in parallel. Only after we look under the hood of such a system do we realize that such parallel processing is possible only when the threads are each executed by a different CPU; otherwise, they time-share the same processing power. We perceive them working at the same time only because the time slots they use are very short—a fraction of the time units we use in our everyday life. When threads share the same resource, in computer science, we say they do it *concurrently*.

Concurrent modification of the same resource

Two or more threads modifying the same value while other threads read it is the most general description of one of the problems of concurrent access. Subtler problems include **thread interference** and **memory consistency** errors, both of which produce unexpected results in seemingly benign fragments of code. In this section, we are going to demonstrate such cases and ways to avoid them.

At first glance, the solution seems quite straightforward: allow only one thread at a time to modify/access the resource, and that's it. But if access takes a long time, it creates a bottleneck that might eliminate the advantage of having many threads working in parallel. Or, if one thread blocks access to one resource while waiting for access to another resource and the second thread blocks access to a second resource while waiting for access to the first one, it creates a problem called a **deadlock**. These are two very simple examples of possible challenges a programmer may encounter while using multiple threads.

First, we'll reproduce a problem caused by the concurrent modification of the same value. Let's create a `Calculator` interface, as follows:

```
interface Calculator {
    String getDescription();
    double calculate(int i);
}
```

We will use the `getDescription()` method to capture the description of the implementation. Here is the first implementation:

```
class CalculatorNoSync implements Calculator{
    private double prop;
    private String description = "Without synchronization";
    public String getDescription(){ return description; }
    public double calculate(int i){
        try {
            this.prop = 2.0 * i;
            TimeUnit.MILLISECONDS.sleep(i);
            return Math.sqrt(this.prop);
        } catch (InterruptedException e) {
            Thread.currentThread().interrupt();
            System.out.println("Calculator was interrupted");
        }
        return 0.0;
    }
}
```

As you can see, the `calculate()` method assigns a new value to the `prop` property, then does something else (we simulate it by calling the `sleep()` method), and then calculates the square root of the value assigned to the `prop` property. The `"Without synchronization"` description depicts the fact that the value of the `prop` property is changing every time the `calculate()` method is called—without any coordination or **synchronization**, as it is called in the case of coordination between threads when they concurrently modify the same resource.

We are now going to share this object between two threads, which means that the `prop` property is going to be updated and used concurrently. So, some kind of thread synchronization around the `prop` property is necessary, but we have decided that our first implementation does not do it.

Here is the method we are going to use while executing every `Calculator` implementation we are going to create:

```
void invokeAllCallables(Calculator c){
    System.out.println("\n" + c.getDescription() + ":");
    ExecutorService pool = Executors.newFixedThreadPool(2);
    List<Callable<Result>> tasks =
                            List.of(new MyCallable("One", c),
                                    new MyCallable("Two", c));
    try{
        List<Future<Result>> futures = pool.invokeAll(tasks);
        List<Result> results = new ArrayList<>();
        while (results.size() < futures.size()){
            TimeUnit.MILLISECONDS.sleep(5);
            for(Future future: futures){
                if(future.isDone()){
                    results.add((Result)future.get());
                }
            }
        }
        for(Result result: results){
            System.out.println(result);
        }
    } catch (Exception ex){
        ex.printStackTrace();
    } finally {
```

```
        shutdownAndTerminate(pool);
    }
}
```

As you can see, the preceding method does the following:

- Prints a description of the passed-in `Calculator` implementation.

- Creates a fixed-size pool for two threads.

- Creates a list of two `Callable` tasks—objects of the following `MyCallable` class:

```
class MyCallable implements Callable<Result> {
    private String name;
    private Calculator calculator;
    public MyCallable(String name,
                        Calculator calculator) {
        this.name = name;
        this.calculator = calculator;
    }
    public Result call() {
        double sum = 0.0;
        for(int i = 1; i < 20; i++){
            sum += calculator.calculate(i);
        }
        return new Result(name, sum);
    }
}
```

- A list of tasks is passed into the `invokeAll()` method of the pool, where each of the tasks is executed by invoking the `call()` method; each `call()` method applies the `calculate()` method of the passed-in `Calculator` object to every one of the 19 numbers from 1 to 20 and sums up the results. The resulting sum is returned inside the `Result` object, along with the name of the `MyCallable` object.

- Each `Result` object is eventually returned inside a `Future` object.

- The `invokeAllCallables()` method then iterates over the list of `Future` objects and checks whether each of their tasks has been completed. When a task is completed, the result is added to `List<Result> results`.

- After all tasks are completed, the `invokeAllCallables()` method then prints all elements of `List<Result> results` and terminates the pool.

Here is the result we got from one of our runs of `invokeAllCallables(new CalculatorNoSync())`:

```
Without synchronization:
Result{name=One, result=81.43661054438327}
Result{name=Two, result=83.13051012374216}
Waiting all threads completion for 100 MILLISECONDS...
isTerminated()=false
Calling shutdownNow()...
0 threads running
Exiting
```

The actual numbers are slightly different every time we run the preceding code, but the result of the `One` task never equals the result of the `Two` task. That is because, in the period between setting the value of the `prop` field and returning its square root in the `calculate()` method, the other thread managed to assign a different value to `prop`. This is a case of thread interference.

There are several ways to address this problem. We start with an atomic variable as a way to achieve thread-safe concurrent access to a property. Then, we will also demonstrate two methods of thread synchronization.

Atomic variable

An **atomic variable** can be updated only when its current value matches the expected one. In our case, this means that a `prop` value should not be used if it has been changed by another thread.

The `java.util.concurrent.atomic` package has a dozen classes that support this logic: `AtomicBoolean`, `AtomicInteger`, `AtomicReference`, and `AtomicIntegerArray`, to name a few. Each of these classes has many methods that can be used for different synchronization needs. Check the online **application programming interface (API)** documentation for each of these classes (`https://docs.oracle.com/en/java/javase/17/docs/api/java.base/java/util/concurrent/atomic/package-summary.html`). For the demonstration, we will use only two methods present in all of them, as outlined here:

- `V get()`: Returns the current value

- `boolean compareAndSet(V expectedValue, V newValue)`: Sets the value to `newValue` if the current value equals via the (`==`) operator the `expectedValue` value; returns `true` if successful or `false` if the actual value was not equal to the expected value

Here is how the `AtomicReference` class can be used to solve the problem of thread interference while accessing the `prop` property of the `Calculator` object concurrently using these two methods:

```java
class CalculatorAtomicRef implements Calculator {
    private AtomicReference<Double> prop =
                            new AtomicReference<>(0.0);
    private String description = "Using AtomicReference";
    public String getDescription(){ return description; }
    public double calculate(int i){
        try {
            Double currentValue = prop.get();
            TimeUnit.MILLISECONDS.sleep(i);
            boolean b =
              this.prop.compareAndSet(currentValue, 2.0 * i);
            //System.out.println(b);
                            //prints: true for one thread
                            //and false for another thread
            return Math.sqrt(this.prop.get());
        } catch (InterruptedException e) {
            Thread.currentThread().interrupt();
            System.out.println("Calculator was interrupted");
        }
        return 0.0;
```

```
        }
    }
```

As you can see, the preceding code makes sure that the currentValue value of the prop property does not change while the thread was sleeping. Here is a screenshot of messages produced when we run invokeAllCallables(new CalculatorAtomicRef()):

```
Using AtomicReference:
Result{name=One, result=80.88430683757149}
Result{name=Two, result=80.88430683757149}
Waiting all threads completion for 100 MILLISECONDS...|
isTerminated()=false
Calling shutdownNow()...
0 threads running
Exiting
```

Now, the results produced by the threads are the same.

The following classes of the java.util.concurrent package provide synchronization support too:

- Semaphore: Restricts the number of threads that can access a resource

- CountDownLatch: Allows one or more threads to wait until a set of operations being performed in other threads are completed

- CyclicBarrier: Allows sets of threads to wait for each other to reach a common barrier point

- Phaser: Provides a more flexible form of barrier that may be used to control phased computation among multiple threads

- Exchanger: Allows two threads to exchange objects at a rendezvous point and is useful in several pipeline designs

Synchronized method

Another way to solve the problem is to use a synchronized method. Here is another implementation of the `Calculator` interface that uses this method of solving thread interference:

```java
class CalculatorSyncMethod implements Calculator {
    private double prop;
    private String description = "Using synchronized method";
    public String getDescription(){ return description; }
    synchronized public double calculate(int i){
        try {
            //there may be some other code here
            synchronized (this) {
                this.prop = 2.0 * i;
                TimeUnit.MILLISECONDS.sleep(i);
                return Math.sqrt(this.prop);
            }
        } catch (InterruptedException e) {
            Thread.currentThread().interrupt();
            System.out.println("Calculator was interrupted");
        }
        return 0.0;
    }
}
```

We have just added the `synchronized` keyword in front of the `calculate()` method. Now, if we run `invokeAllCallables(new CalculatorSyncMethod())`, the results of both threads are always going to be the same, as we can see here:

```
Using synchronized method:
Result{name=One, result=80.88430683757149}
Result{name=Two, result=80.88430683757149}
Waiting all threads completion for 100 MILLISECONDS...
isTerminated()=false
Calling shutdownNow()...
0 threads running
Exiting
```

This is because another thread cannot enter the synchronized method until the current thread (the one that has entered the method already) has exited it. This is probably the simplest solution, but this approach may cause performance degradation if the method takes a long time to execute. In such cases, a synchronized block can be used, which only wraps several lines of code in an atomic operation.

Synchronized block

Here is an example of a synchronized block used to solve the problem of thread interference:

```java
class CalculatorSyncBlock implements Calculator {
    private double prop;
    private String description = "Using synchronized block";
    public String getDescription(){
        return description;
    }
    public double calculate(int i){
        try {
            //there may be some other code here
            synchronized (this) {
                this.prop = 2.0 * i;
                TimeUnit.MILLISECONDS.sleep(i);
                return Math.sqrt(this.prop);
            }
        } catch (InterruptedException e) {
            Thread.currentThread().interrupt();
            System.out.println("Calculator was interrupted");
        }
        return 0.0;
    }
}
```

As you can see, the synchronized block acquires a lock on the `this` object, which is shared by both threads, and releases it only after the threads exit the block. In our demonstration code, the block covers all the code of the method, so there is no difference in performance. But imagine there is more code in the method (we commented the location as `there may be some other code here`). If that is the case, the synchronized section of the code is smaller, thus having fewer chances to become a bottleneck.

If we run `invokeAllCallables(new CalculatorSyncBlock())`, the results look like this:

```
Using synchronized block:
Result{name=One, result=80.88430683757149}
Result{name=Two, result=80.88430683757149}
Waiting all threads completion for 100 MILLISECONDS...
isTerminated()=false
Calling shutdownNow()...
0 threads running
Exiting
```

As you can see, the results are exactly the same as in the previous two examples. Different types of locks for different needs and with different behavior are assembled in the `java.util.concurrent.locks` package.

Each object in Java inherits the `wait()`, `notify()`, and `notifyAll()` methods from the base object. These methods can also be used to control threads' behavior and their access to the locks.

Concurrent collections

Another way to address concurrency is to use a thread-safe collection from the `java.util.concurrent` package. Before you select which collection to use, read the *Javadoc* documentation (https://docs.oracle.com/en/java/javase/17/docs/api/index.html) to see whether the limitations of the collection are acceptable for your application. Here is a list of these collections and some recommendations:

- `ConcurrentHashMap<K,V>`: Supports full concurrency of retrievals and high-expected concurrency for updates; use it when the concurrency requirements are very demanding and you need to allow locking on the write operation but do not need to lock the element.

- `ConcurrentLinkedQueue<E>`: A thread-safe queue based on linked nodes; employs an efficient non-blocking algorithm.

- `ConcurrentLinkedDeque<E>`: A concurrent queue based on linked nodes; both `ConcurrentLinkedQueue` and `ConcurrentLinkedDeque` are an appropriate choice when many threads share access to a common collection.

- `ConcurrentSkipListMap<K,V>`: A concurrent `ConcurrentNavigableMap` interface implementation.

- `ConcurrentSkipListSet<E>`: A concurrent `NavigableSet` implementation based on the `ConcurrentSkipListMap` class. The `ConcurrentSkipListSet` and `ConcurrentSkipListMap` classes, as per the *Javadoc* documentation, "*provide expected average log(n) time cost for the contains, add, and remove operations and their variants. Ascending ordered views and their iterators are faster than descending ones*." Use them when you need to iterate quickly through elements in a certain order.

- `CopyOnWriteArrayList<E>`: A thread-safe variant of `ArrayList` in which all mutative operations (add, set, and so on) are implemented by making a fresh copy of the underlying array. As per the *Javadoc* documentation, the `CopyOnWriteArrayList` class "*is ordinarily too costly, but may be more efficient than alternatives when traversal operations vastly outnumber mutations, and is useful when you cannot or don't want to synchronize traversals, yet need to preclude interference among concurrent threads*." Use it when you do not need to add new elements at different positions and do not require sorting; otherwise, use `ConcurrentSkipListSet`.

- `CopyOnWriteArraySet<E>`: A set that uses an internal `CopyOnWriteArrayList` class for all of its operations.

- `PriorityBlockingQueue`: This is a better choice when a natural order is acceptable and you need fast adding of elements to the tail and fast removing of elements from the head of the queue. **Blocking** means that the queue waits to become non-empty when retrieving an element and waits for space to become available in the queue when storing an element.

- `ArrayBlockingQueue`, `LinkedBlockingQueue`, and `LinkedBlockingDeque` have a fixed size (bounded); other queues are unbounded.

Use these and similar characteristics and recommendations as per the guidelines, but execute comprehensive testing and performance-measuring before and after implementing your functionality. To demonstrate some of these collections' capabilities, let's use `CopyOnWriteArrayList<E>`. First, let's look in the following code snippet at how `ArrayList` behaves when we try to modify it concurrently:

```java
List<String> list = Arrays.asList("One", "Two");
System.out.println(list);
try {
    for (String e : list) {
        System.out.println(e);   //prints: One
        list.add("Three");       //UnsupportedOperationException
    }
} catch (Exception ex) {
    ex.printStackTrace();
}
System.out.println(list);        //prints: [One, Two]
```

As expected, the attempt to modify a list while iterating on it generates an exception, and the list remains unmodified.

Now, let's use `CopyOnWriteArrayList<E>` in the same circumstances, as follows:

```java
List<String> list =
        new CopyOnWriteArrayList<>(Arrays.asList("One", "Two"));
System.out.println(list);
try {
    for (String e : list) {
        System.out.print(e + " "); //prints: One Two
        list.add("Three");         //adds element Three
    }
} catch (Exception ex) {
    ex.printStackTrace();
}
System.out.println("\n" + list);
                                //prints: [One, Two, Three, Three]
```

The output this code produces looks like this:

```
[One, Two]
One Two
[One, Two, Three, Three]
```

As you can see, the list was modified without an exception, but not the currently iterated copy. That is the behavior you can use if needed.

Addressing memory consistency errors

Memory consistency errors can have many forms and causes in a multithreaded environment. They are well discussed in the *Javadoc* documentation of the java.util. concurrent package. Here, we will mention only the most common case, which is caused by a lack of visibility.

When one thread changes a property value, the other might not see the change immediately, and you cannot use the synchronized keyword for a primitive type. In such a situation, consider using the volatile keyword for the property, as this guarantees its read/write visibility between different threads.

Concurrency problems are not easy to solve, which is why it is not surprising that more and more developers are now taking a more radical approach. Instead of managing an object state, they prefer processing data in a set of stateless operations. We will see examples of such code in *Chapter 13*, *Functional Programming*, and *Chapter 14*, *Java Standard Streams*. It seems that Java and many modern languages and computer systems are evolving in this direction.

Summary

In this chapter, we talked about multithreaded processing, ways to organize it, and avoiding unpredictable results caused by concurrent modification of the shared resource. We have shown you how to create threads and execute them using pools of threads. We have also demonstrated how results can be extracted from the threads that have completed successfully and discussed the difference between parallel and concurrent processing.

In the next chapter, we will provide you with a deeper understanding of JVM and its structure and processes, and we'll discuss in detail the garbage-collection process that keeps memory from being overflown. By the end of the chapter, you will know what constitutes Java application execution, Java processes inside JVM, garbage collection, and how JVM works in general.

Quiz

1. Select all correct statements:

    A. A JVM process can have main threads.

    B. The main thread is the main process.

    C. A process can launch another process.

    D. A thread may launch another thread.

2. Select all correct statements:

    A. A daemon is a user thread.

    B. A daemon thread exits after the first user thread completes.

    C. A daemon thread exits after the last user thread completes.

    D. The main thread is a user thread.

3. Select all correct statements:

    A. All threads have `java.lang.Thread` as a base class.

    B. All threads extend `java.lang.Thread`.

    C. All threads implement `java.lang.Thread`.

    D. A daemon thread does not extend `java.lang.Thread`.

4. Select all correct statements:

    A. Any class can implement the `Runnable` interface.

    B. The `Runnable` interface implementation is a thread.

    C. The `Runnable` interface implementation is used by a thread.

    D. The `Runnable` interface has only one method.

5. Select all correct statements:

    A. A thread name has to be unique.

    B. A thread ID is generated automatically.

    C. A thread name can be set.

    D. A thread priority can be set.

6. Select all correct statements:

    A. A thread pool executes threads.

    B. A thread pool reuses threads.

    C. Some thread pools can have a fixed count of threads.

    D. Some thread pools can have an unlimited count of threads.

7. Select all correct statements:

    A. A `Future` object is the only way to get the result from a thread.

    B. A `Callable` object is the only way to get the result from a thread.

    C. A `Callable` object allows us to get the result from a thread.

    D. A `Future` object represents a thread.

8. Select all correct statements:

    A. Concurrent processing can be done in parallel.

    B. Parallel processing is possible only with several CPUs or cores available on the computer.

    C. Parallel processing is concurrent processing.

    D. Without multiple CPUs, concurrent processing is impossible.

9. Select all correct statements:

    A. Concurrent modification always leads to incorrect results.

    B. An atomic variable protects a property from concurrent modification.

    C. An atomic variable protects a property from thread interference.

    D. An atomic variable is the only way to protect a property from concurrent modification.

10. Select all correct statements:

    A. The `synchronized` method is the best way to avoid thread interference.

    B. The `synchronized` keyword can be applied to any method.

    C. The `synchronized` method can create a processing bottleneck.

    D. The `synchronized` method is easy to implement.

11. Select all correct statements:

    A. A synchronized block makes sense only when it is smaller than the method.

    B. A synchronized block requires a shared lock.

    C. Every Java object can provide a lock.

    D. A synchronized block is the best way to avoid thread interference.

12. Select all correct statements:

    A. Using a concurrent collection is preferred over using a non-concurrent one.

    B. Using a concurrent collection incurs some overhead.

    C. Not every concurrent collection fits every concurrent processing scenario.

    D. We can create a concurrent collection by calling the Collections.makeConcurrent() method.

13. Select all correct statements:

    A. The only way to avoid a memory consistency error is to declare the volatile variable.

    B. Using the volatile keyword guarantees visibility of the value change across all threads.

    C. One way to avoid concurrency is to avoid any state management.

    D. Stateless utility methods cannot have concurrency issues.

9
JVM Structure and Garbage Collection

This chapter will provide you with an overview of the structure and behavior of a **Java virtual machine** (**JVM**), which are more complex than you may expect.

A JVM executes instructions according to the coded logic. It also finds and loads the `.class` files that are requested by the application into memory, verifies them, interprets the bytecode (that is, it translates them into platform-specific binary code), and passes the resulting binary code to the central processor (or processors) for execution. It uses several service threads in addition to the application threads. One of the service threads, called **garbage collection** (**GC**), performs the important step of releasing the memory from unused objects.

By completing this chapter, you will understand what constitutes Java application execution, the Java processes inside the JVM and GC, and how the JVM works in general.

In this chapter, we will cover the following topics:

- Java application execution
- Java processes
- JVM's structure
- Garbage collection

Technical requirements

To execute the code examples provided in this chapter, you will need the following:

- A computer with Microsoft Windows, Apple macOS, or the Linux operating system
- Java SE version 17 or later
- An IDE or code editor of your choice

The instructions on how to set up a Java SE and IntelliJ IDEA editor were provided in *Chapter 1, Getting Started with Java 17*. The files that contain the code examples for this chapter are available on GitHub in the `https://github.com/PacktPublishing/Learn-Java-17-Programming.git` repository, in the `examples/src/main/java/com/packt/learnjava/ch09_jvm` folder.

Java application execution

Before we learn how the JVM works, let's review how to run an application, bearing in mind that the following statements are used as synonyms:

- Run/execute/start the main class.
- Run/execute/start the main method.
- Run/execute/start/launch an application.
- Run/execute/start/launch the JVM or a Java process.

There are also several ways to do this. In *Chapter 1, Getting Started with Java 17*, we showed you how to run the `main(String[])` method using IntelliJ IDEA. In this chapter, we will just repeat some of what has been said already and add other variations that might be helpful for you.

Using an IDE

Any IDE allows you to run the `main()` method. In IntelliJ IDEA, it can be done in three ways:

1. Click the green triangle next to the `main()` method's name:

```
 MyApplication.java
1          package com.packt.learnjava.ch09_jvm;
2
3          import com.packt.learnjava.ch09_jvm.example.
4
5    ▶     public class MyApplication {
6  ▶ @         public static void main(String... args){
7                 System.out.println("Hello, world!");
8                 for(String arg: args){
9                     System.out.print(arg + " ");
10            }
```

2. Once you have executed the `main()` method using the green triangle at least once, the name of the class will be added to the drop-down menu (on the top line, to the left of the green triangle):

3. Open the **Run** menu and select the name of the class. There are several options you can select:

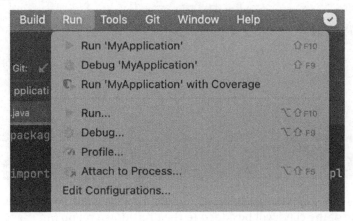

In the previous screenshot, you can also see the **Edit Configurations... option**. This can be used to set all **program arguments** that are passed to the main() method at the start, plus some other options:

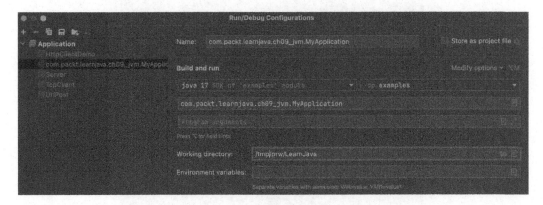

The **Program arguments** field allows for setting a parameter in the java command. For example, let's set one two three in this field:

This setting will result in the following java command:

```
java -DsomeParameter=42 -cp . \
        com.packt.learnjava.ch09_jvm.MyApplication one two three
```

We can read these parameters in the main() method:

```
public static void main(String... args){
    System.out.println("Hello, world!");
                            //prints: Hello, world!
    for(String arg: args){
        System.out.print(arg + " ");
                            //prints: one two three
    }
    String p = System.getProperty("someParameter");
    System.out.println("\n" + p);          //prints: 42
}
```

Another possible setting on the **Edit Configurations** screen is in the **Environment variables** field. The environment variables that can be accessed from the application using System.getenv(). For example, let's set the environment variables x and y , as follows:

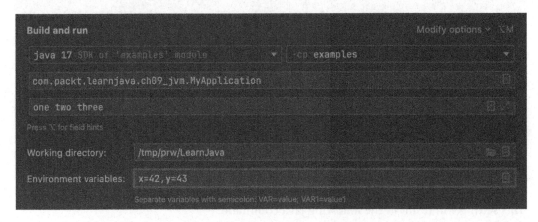

If done as shown in the preceding screenshot, the values of x and y can be read not only in the main() method, but anywhere in the application using the System.getenv("varName") method. In our case, the values of x and y can be retrieved as follows:

```
String p = System.getenv("x");
System.out.println(p);              //prints: 42
p = System.getenv("y");
System.out.println(p);              //prints: 43
```

The **VM options** field allows you to set java command options. For example, if you input -Xlog:gc, the IDE will form the following java command:

```
java -Xlog:gc -cp . com.packt.learnjava.ch09_jvm.MyApplication
```

The -Xlog:gc option requires the GC log to be displayed. We will use this option in the next section to demonstrate how GC works. The -cp . option (**cp** stands for **classpath**) indicates that the class is located in a folder on the file tree that starts from the current directory (the one where the command is entered). In our case, the .class file is located in the com/packt/learnjava/ch09_jvm folder, where com is the subfolder of the current directory. The classpath can include many locations where the JVM has to look for the .class files that are necessary for the application's execution.

Use **Modify options** link to show **VM options** as follows:

For this demonstration, let's set the value -DsomeParameter=42 in the **VM options** field as shown in the following screenshot:

Now the value of someParameter can be read not only in the main() method, but anywhere in the application code as follows:

```
String p = System.getProperty("someParameter");
System.out.println("\n" + p);
                        //prints someParameter set as VM option -D
```

There are other parameters of the java command that can be set on the **Edit Configurations** screen, too. We encourage you to spend some time on that screen and view the possible options.

Using the command line with classes

Now, let's run MyApplication from the command line. To remind you, the main class looks as follows:

```java
package com.packt.learnjava.ch09_jvm;
public class MyApplication {
    public static void main(String... args){
        System.out.println("Hello, world!");
                                //prints: Hello, world!

        for(String arg: args){
            System.out.print(arg + " ");
                                //prints all arguments
        }
        String p = System.getProperty("someParameter");
        System.out.println("\n" + p);
                        //prints someParameter set as VM option -D
    }
}
```

First, it must be compiled using the javac command. The command line looks as follows on Linux-type platforms (provided you open the Terminal window in the root of the project, in the folder where pom.xml resides):

```
javac src/main/java/com/packt/learnjava/ch09_jvm/MyApplication.
java
```

On Windows, the command looks similar:

```
javac src\main\java\com\packt\learnjava\ch09_jvm\MyApplication.
java
```

The compiled MyApplication.class file is placed in the same folder as MyApplication.java. Now, we can execute the compiled class with the java command:

```
java -DsomeParameter=42 -cp src/main/java \
  com.packt.learnjava.ch09_jvm.MyApplication one two three
```

Notice that -cp points to the src/main/java folder (the path is relative to the current folder), where the package of the main class starts. The result is as follows:

```
Hello, world!
one two three
42
4
```

We can also put both compiled classes in a .jar file and run them from there.

Using the command line with JAR files

Keeping the compiled files in a folder as .class files is not always convenient, especially when many compiled files of the same framework belong to different packages and are distributed as a single library. In such cases, the compiled .class files are usually archived together in a .jar file. The format of such an archive is the same as the format of a .zip file. The only difference is that a .jar file also includes a manifest file that contains metadata describing the archive (we will talk more about the manifest in the next section).

To demonstrate how to use it, let's create a .jar file with the ExampleClass.class file and another .jar file with MyApplication.class in it, using the following commands:

```
cd src/main/java
jar -cf myapp.jar
            com/packt/learnjava/ch09_jvm/MyApplication.class
jar -cf example.jar \
        com/packt/learnjava/ch09_jvm/example/ExampleClass.class
```

Notice that we need to run the jar command in the folder where the package of the .class file begins.

Now, we can run the application, as follows:

```
java -cp myapp.jar:example.jar \
                    com.packt.learnjava.ch09_jvm.MyApplication
```

The .jar files are in the current folder. If we would like to execute the application from another folder (let's go back to the root directory, cd ../../..), the command should look like this:

```
java -cp
src/main/java/myapp.jar:src/main/java/example.jar\
        com.packt.learnjava.ch09_jvm.MyApplication
```

Notice that every .jar file must be listed on the classpath individually. To specify just a folder where all the .jar files reside (as is the case with the .class files) is not good enough. You must add an asterisk (the wildcard symbol, *) too, as follows:

```
java -cp "src/main/java/*" \
        com.packt.learnjava.ch09_jvm.MyApplication
```

Note the quotes around the path to the folder containing the .jar files. Without quotes, this will not work.

Using the command line with an executable JAR file

It is possible to avoid specifying the main class in the command line. Instead, we can create an executable .jar file. This can be accomplished by placing the name of the main class – the one you need to run and that contains the main() method – into the manifest file. Here are the steps:

1. Create a text file called manifest.txt (the name doesn't matter, but this name makes the intent clear) that contains the following line:

    ```
    Main-Class: com.packt.learnjava.ch09_jvm.MyApplication
    ```

    There must be a space after the colon (:), and there must be an invisible newline symbol at the end, so make sure you have pressed the *Enter* key and your cursor has jumped to the beginning of the next line.

2. Execute the following command:

    ```
    cd src/main/java
    jar -cfm myapp.jar manifest.txt \
            com/packt/learnjava/ch09_jvm/*.class \
            com/packt/learnjava/ch09_jvm/example/*.class
    ```

Notice the sequence of jar command options (fm) and the sequence of the myapp.jar manifest.txt files. They must be the same because f stands for the file that the jar command is going to create, while m stands for the manifest source. If you include options with mf, then the files must be listed as manifest.txt myapp.jar.

3. Now, we can run the application using the following command:

```
java -jar myapp.jar
```

The other way to create an executable .jar file is much easier:

```
jar cfe myjar.jar
com.packt.learnjava.ch09_jvm.MyApplication \
        com/packt/learnjava/ch09_jvm/*.class\
        com/packt/learnjava/ch09_jvm/example/*.class
```

The preceding command generates a manifest with the specified main class name automatically: the c option stands for **create a new archive**, the f option stands for **archive filename**, and the e option indicates an **application entry point**.

Java processes

As you may have already guessed, JVM does not know anything about the Java language and source code. It only knows how to read bytecode. It reads the bytecode and other information from .class files, transforms (interprets) the bytecode into a sequence of binary code instructions that are specific to the current platform (where JVM is running), and passes the resulting binary code to the microprocessor that executes it. When talking about this transformation, programmers often refer to it as a **Java process** or just **process**.

The JVM is often referred to as a **JVM instance**. This is because every time a java command is executed, a new instance of JVM is launched that's dedicated to running the particular application as a separate process with its own allocated memory (the size of the memory is set as a default value or passed in as a command option). Inside this Java process, multiple threads are running, each with its own allocated memory. Some are service threads that are created by the JVM; others are application threads that are created and controlled by the application.

That is the big picture of the JVM executing the compiled code. But if you look closer and read the JVM specification, you will discover that the word *process*, concerning the JVM, is used to describe the JVM internal processes too. The JVM specification identifies several other processes running inside the JVM that are usually not mentioned by programmers, except maybe the **class loading process**.

This is because most of the time, we can successfully write and execute Java programs without knowing anything about the internal JVM processes. But once in a while, some general understanding of the JVM's internal workings helps us identify the root cause of certain issues. That is why in this section, we will provide a short overview of all the processes that happen inside the JVM. Then, in the following sections, we will discuss the JVM's memory structure and other aspects of its functionality that may be useful to a programmer.

Two subsystems run the JVM's internal processes:

- **The classloader**: This reads the `.class` file and populates a method area in JVM's memory with the class-related data:

  - Static fields

  - Method bytecode

  - Class metadata that describes the class

- **The execution engine**: This executes the bytecode using the following properties:

  - A heap area for object instantiation

  - Java and native method stacks for keeping track of the methods that have been called

  - A GC process that reclaims memory

Some of the processes that run inside the main JVM process are as follows:

- Processes that are performed by the classloader, such as the following:

  - Classloading

  - Class linking

  - Class initialization

Processes that are performed by the execution engine, such as the following:

- Class instantiation

- Method execution

- GC

- Application termination

> **The JVM Architecture**
>
> The JVM architecture can be described as having two subsystems –
> the **classloader** and the **execution engine** – that run the service processes and
> application threads using runtime data memory areas such as the method area,
> heap, and application thread stacks. **Threads** are lightweight processes that
> require less resource allocation than the JVM execution process.

This list may give you the impression that these processes are executed sequentially.
To some degree, this is true, if we're talking about one class only. It is not possible to do
anything with a class before loading it. We can only execute a method after all the previous
processes have been completed. However, GC, for example, does not happen immediately
once an object has stopped being used (see the *Garbage collection* section). Also, an
application can exit any time when an unhandled exception or some other error occurs.

Only the classloader processes are regulated by the JVM specification. The execution
engine's implementation is largely at the discretion of each vendor. It is based on
the language semantics and the performance goals that have been set by the
implementation authors.

The processes of the execution engine are in a realm that's not regulated by the JVM
specification. There is common sense, tradition, known and proven solutions, and a Java
language specification that can guide a JVM vendor's implementation decision. But there
is no single regulatory document. The good news is that the most popular JVMs use
similar solutions – or at least that's how it looks at a high level.

With this in mind, let's discuss each of the seven processes listed previously in more detail.

Classloading

According to the JVM specification, the loading phase includes finding the `.class` file by its name (in the locations listed on a classpath) and creating its representation in memory.

The first class to be loaded is the one that's passed in the command line, with the `main(String[])` method in it. The classloader reads the `.class` file, parses it, and populates the method area with static fields and method bytecode. It also creates an instance of `java.lang.Class` that describes the class. Then, the classloader links the class (see the *Class linking* section), initializes it (see the *Class initialization* section), and then passes it to the execution engine to run its bytecode.

The `main(String[])` method is an entrance door into the application. If it calls a method of another class, that class has to be found on the classpath, loaded, and initialized; only then can its method be executed too. If this – just loaded – method calls a method of another class, that class has to be found, loaded, and initialized too, and so on. That is how a Java application starts and gets going.

> **The main(String[]) Method**
>
> Every class can have a `main(String[])` method and often does. Such a method is used to run the class independently as a standalone application for testing or demonstration purposes. The presence of such a method does not make the class `main`. The class only becomes `main` if it's been identified as such in a `java` command line or a `.jar` file manifest.

That being said, let's continue discussing the loading process.

If you look in the API of `java.lang.Class`, you will not see a public constructor there. The classloader creates its instance automatically. This is the same instance that is returned by the `getClass()` method, which you can invoke on any Java object.

It does not carry the class's static data (which is maintained in the method area), nor state values (they are in an object that's created during the execution). It does not contain method bytecode either (this is stored in the method area too). Instead, the `Class` instance provides metadata that describes the class – its name, package, fields, constructors, method signatures, and so on. This metadata is useful not only for the JVM but also for the application.

> **Note**
>
> All the data that's created by the classloader in memory and maintained by the execution engine is called a **binary representation of the type**.

If the .class file contains errors or does not adhere to a certain format, the process is terminated. This means that the loaded class format and its bytecode have been validated by the loading process already. More verification follows at the beginning of the next process, called **class linking**.

Here is a high-level description of the loading process. It performs three tasks:

1. Finds and reads the .class file
2. Parses it according to the internal data structure in the method area
3. Creates an instance of java.lang.Class with the class metadata

Class linking

According to the JVM specification, class linking resolves the references of the loaded class so that the methods of the class can be executed.

Here is a high-level description of the linking process. It performs three tasks:

- **Verifies the binary representation of a class or an interface**: Although the JVM can reasonably expect that the .class file was produced by the Java compiler and all the instructions satisfy the constraints and requirements of the language, there is no guarantee that the loaded file was produced by the known compiler implementation or a compiler at all. That's why the first step of the linking process is verification. This makes sure that the binary representation of the class is structurally correct, which means the following:

  - The arguments of each method's invocation are compatible with the method descriptor.

  - The return instruction matches the return type of its method.

  - Some other checks and verification processes, which vary depending on the JVM vendor.

- **Prepares the static fields in the method area**: Once verification has been completed, the interface or class (static) variables are created in the method area and initialized to the default values of their types. The other kinds of initialization, such as the explicit assignments that are specified by a programmer and static initialization blocks, are deferred to the process called **class initialization** (see the *Class initialization* section).

- **Resolves symbolic references into concrete references that point to the method area**: If the loaded bytecode refers to other methods, interfaces, or classes, the symbolic references are resolved into concrete references that point to the method area, which is done by the resolution process. If the referred interfaces and classes haven't been loaded yet, the classloader finds and loads them as needed.

Class initialization

According to the JVM specification, initialization is accomplished by executing the class initialization methods. This happens when the programmer-defined initialization (in static blocks and static assignments) is performed, unless the class was already initialized at the request of another class.

The last part of this statement is important because the class may be requested several times by different (already loaded) methods, and also because JVM processes are executed by different threads and may access the same class concurrently. So, **coordination** (also called **synchronization**) between different threads is required, which substantially complicates the JVM implementation.

Class instantiation

This step may never happen. Technically, an instantiation process, triggered by the `new` operator, is the first step of the execution process. If the `main(String[])` method (which is static) uses only the static methods of other classes, this instantiation never happens. That's why it is reasonable to identify this process as separate from the execution.

This activity has very specific tasks:

- Allocating memory for the object (its state) in the heap area
- Initializing the instance fields to the default values
- Creating thread stacks for Java and native methods

Execution starts when the first method (not a constructor) is ready to be executed. For every application thread, a dedicated runtime stack is created, where every method call is captured in a stack frame. For example, if an exception occurs, we get data from the current stack frames when we call the `printStackTrace()` method.

Method execution

The first application thread (called the **main thread**) is created when the `main(String[])` method starts executing. It can create other application threads.

The execution engine reads the bytecode, interprets it, and sends the binary code to the microprocessor for execution. It also maintains a count of how many times and how often each method was called. If the count exceeds a certain threshold, the execution engine uses a compiler, called the **just-in-time** (**JIT**) compiler, which compiles the method bytecode into native code. This way, the next time the method is called, it will be ready without needing an interpretation. This substantially improves code performance.

The instruction that's currently being executed and the address of the next instruction are maintained in the **program counter** (**PC**) registers. Each thread has dedicated PC registers. It also improves performance and keeps track of the execution.

Garbage collection

The garbage collector identifies the objects that are not referenced anymore and can be removed from the memory.

There is a Java static method, `System.gc()`, that can be used programmatically to trigger the GC, but its immediate execution is not guaranteed. Every GC cycle affects the application's performance, so the JVM must maintain a balance between memory availability and the ability to execute the bytecode quickly enough.

Application termination

There are several ways an application can be terminated (and the JVM stopped or exited) programmatically:

- Normal termination, without an error status code

- Abnormal termination, because of an unhandled exception

- Forced programmatic exit, with or without an error status code

If there are no exceptions and infinite loops, the `main(String[])` method completes with a return statement or after its last statement is executed. As soon as this happens, the main application thread passes the control flow to the JVM and the JVM stops executing too. That is the happy ending, and many applications enjoy it in real life. Most of our examples, except those when we have demonstrated exceptions or infinite loops, have exited successfully too.

However, there are other ways a Java application can exit, some of them quite graceful too – others not so much. If the main application thread created child threads or, in other words, a programmer has written code that generates other threads, even a graceful exit may not be easy. It all depends on the kind of child threads that have been created.

If any of them is a user thread (the default), then the JVM instance continues to run even after the main thread exits. Only after all the user threads have been completed does the JVM instance stop. The main thread can request the child user thread to complete. But until it exits, the JVM continues running. And this means that the application is still running too.

But if all the child threads are daemon threads, or no child threads are running, the JVM instance stops running as soon as the main application thread exits.

How the application exits in the case of an exception depends on the code design. We touched on this in *Chapter 4, Exception Handling*, while discussing the best practices of exception handling. If the thread captures all the exceptions in a try-catch block in `main(String[])` or a similarly high-level method, then it is up to the application (and the programmer who wrote the code) to decide how best to proceed – to try to change the input data and repeat the block of code that generated the exception, to log the error and continue, or to exit. If, on the other hand, the exception remains unhandled and propagates into the JVM code, the thread (where the exception occurred) stops executing and exits. What happens next depends on the type of thread and some other conditions. The following are four possible options:

- If there are no other threads, the JVM stops executing and returns an error code and the stack trace.

- If the thread with an unhandled exception was not the main one, other threads (if present) continue running.

- If the main thread has thrown an unhandled exception and the child threads (if present) are daemons, they exit too.

- If there is at least one user child thread, the JVM continues running until all the user threads exit.

There are also ways to programmatically force the application to stop:

- `System.exit(0);`

- `Runtime.getRuntime().exit(0);`

- `Runtime.getRuntime().halt(0);`

All these methods force the JVM to stop executing any thread and exit with a status code passed in as the parameter (0, in our examples):

- Zero indicates normal termination
- A nonzero value indicates an abnormal termination

If the Java command was launched by some script or another system, the value of the status code can be used to automate the decision-making regarding the next step. But that is already outside the application and Java code.

The first two methods have identical functionality because this is how System.exit() is implemented:

```
public static void exit(int status) {
    Runtime.getRuntime().exit(status);
}
```

To see the source code in the IDE, just click on the method.

The JVM exits when some thread invokes the exit() method of the Runtime or System classes, or the halt() method of the Runtime class, and the exit or halt operation is permitted by the security manager. The difference between exit() and halt() is that halt() forces the JVM to exit immediately, while exit() performs additional actions that can be set using the Runtime.addShutdownHook() method. But these options are rarely used by mainstream programmers.

JVM's structure

The structure of the JVM can be described in terms of its runtime data structure in memory and the two subsystems that use the runtime data – the classloader and the execution engine.

Runtime data areas

Each of the runtime data areas of JVM memory belongs to one of two categories:

- **Shared areas**, which include the following:
  - **Method area**: Class metadata, static fields, and method bytecode
  - **Heap area**: Objects (states)

- **Unshared areas** that are dedicated to a particular application thread, which include the following:

  - **Java stack:** Current and caller frames, with each frame keeping the state of Java (non-native) method invocation:

    i.   Values of local variables

    ii. Method parameter values

    iii. Values of operands for intermediate calculations (operand stack)

    iv. Method return value (if any)

  - **PC register:** The next instruction to execute

  - **Native method stack:** The state of the native method invocations

We have already discussed that a programmer must be careful when using reference types and not modify the object itself unless it needs to be done. In a multi-threaded application, if a reference to an object can be passed between threads, we must be extra careful because of the possibility of the same data being modified concurrently. On the bright side, though, such a shared area can be – and often is – used as the method of communication between threads.

Classloaders

The classloader performs the following three functions:

- Reads a `.class` file

- Populates the method area

- Initializes static fields that haven't been initialized by a programmer

Execution engine

The execution engine does the following:

- Instantiates objects in the heap area

- Initializes static and instance fields using initializers written by the programmer

- Adds/removes frames to/from the Java stack

- Updates the PC register with the next instruction to execute

- Maintains the native method stack

- Keeps count of method calls and compiles popular ones

- Finalizes objects

- Runs GC

- Terminates the application

Garbage collection

Automatic memory management is an important aspect of the JVM that relieves the programmer from the need to do so programmatically. In Java, the process that cleans up memory and allows it to be reused is called **GC**.

Responsiveness, throughput, and stop-the-world

The effectiveness of GC affects two major application characteristics – **responsiveness** and **throughput**:

- **Responsiveness**: This is measured by how quickly an application responds (brings the necessary data) to the request; for example, how quickly a website returns a page, or how quickly a desktop application responds to an event. The smaller the response time, the better the user experience.

- **Throughput**: This indicates the amount of work an application can do in a unit of time; for example, how many requests a web application can serve, or how many transactions the database can support. The bigger the number, the more value the application can potentially generate and the more user requests it can support.

Meanwhile, GC needs to move data around, which is impossible to accomplish while allowing data processing to occur because the references are going to change. That's why GC needs to stop application thread execution once in a while for a while. This is called **stop-the-world**. The longer these periods are, the quicker GC does its job and the longer an application freeze lasts, which can eventually grow big enough to affect both the application's responsiveness and throughput.

Fortunately, it is possible to tune the GC's behavior using Java command options, but that is outside the scope of this book. Instead, we will provide a high-level view of the main activity of GC – inspecting objects in the heap and removing those that don't have references in any thread stack.

Object age and generation

The basic GC algorithm determines *how old* each object is. The term **age** refers to the number of collection cycles the object has survived.

When the JVM starts, the heap is empty and is divided into three sections:

- The young generation
- The old or tenured generation
- Humongous regions for holding objects that are 50% the size of a standard region or larger

The young generation has three areas:

- An Eden space
- Survivor 0 (S0)
- Survivor 1 (S1)

The newly created objects are placed in Eden. When it is filling up, a minor GC process starts. It removes the unreferred and circular referred objects and moves the others to the S1 area. During the next minor collection, S0 and S1 switch roles. The referenced objects are moved from Eden and S1 to S0.

During each of the minor collections, the objects that have reached a certain age are moved to the old generation. As a result of this algorithm, the old generation contains objects that are older than a certain age. This area is bigger than the young generation and, because of that, the GC process is more expensive and happens not as often as in the young generation. But it is checked eventually (after several minor collections). The unreferenced objects are removed and the memory is defragmented. Cleaning up the old generation is considered a major collection.

When stop-the-world is unavoidable

Some objects are collected in the old generation concurrently, while some are collected using stop-the-world pauses. The steps are as follows:

1. **Initial marking**: This marks the survivor regions (root regions) that may have references to objects in the old generation. This is done using a stop-the-world pause.
2. **Scanning**: This searches survivor regions for references to the old generation. This is done concurrently while the application continues to run.

3. **Concurrent marking**: This marks live objects over the entire heap and is done concurrently while the application continues to run.

4. **Remark**: At this stage, the live objects have been marked, which is done using a stop-the-world pause.

5. **Cleanup**: This calculates the age of live objects, frees regions (using stop-the-world), and returns them to the free list. This is done concurrently.

To help with GC tuning, the JVM provides platform-dependent default selections for the garbage collector, heap size, and runtime compiler. But fortunately, the JVM vendors improve and tune the GC process all the time, so most of the applications work just fine with the default GC behavior.

Summary

In this chapter, you learned how a Java application can be executed using an IDE or the command line. Now, you can write applications and launch them in a manner that's appropriate for the given environment. Knowledge about the JVM structure and its processes – classloading, linking, initialization, execution, GC, and application termination – provided you with better control over the application's execution and transparency regarding the performance and current state of the JVM.

In the next chapter, we will discuss and demonstrate how to manage – insert, read, update, and delete – data in a database from a Java application. We will also provide a short introduction to the SQL language and its basic database operations, including how to connect to a database, how to create the database's structure, how to write database expressions using SQL, and how to execute them.

Quiz

Answer the following questions to test your knowledge of this chapter:

1. Select all of the correct statements:

   A. An IDE executes Java code without compiling it.

   B. An IDE uses installed Java to execute the code.

   C. An IDE checks the code without using the Java installation.

   D. An IDE uses the compiler of the Java installation.

2. Select all of the correct statements:

    A. All the classes that are used by the application must be listed on the classpath.

    B. The locations of all the classes that are used by the application must be listed on the classpath.

    C. The compiler can find a class if it is in the folder that's listed on the classpath.

    D. The classes of the main package do not need to be listed on the classpath.

3. Select all of the correct statements:

    A. All the `.jar` files that are used by the application must be listed on the classpath.

    B. The locations of all the `.jar` files that are used by the application must be listed on the classpath.

    C. The JVM can only find a class if it is in the `.jar` file that's listed on the classpath.

    D. Every class can contain the `main()` method.

4. Select all of the correct statements:

    A. Every `.jar` file that contains a manifest is executable.

    B. If the `-jar` option is used by the `java` command, the classpath option is ignored.

    C. Every `.jar` file has a manifest.

    D. An executable `.jar` is a ZIP file with a manifest.

5. Select all of the correct statements:

    A. Classloading and linking can work in parallel on different classes.

    B. Classloading moves the class to the execution area.

    C. Class linking connects two classes.

    D. Class linking uses memory references.

6. Select all of the correct statements:

    A. Class initialization assigns values to instance properties.

    B. Class initialization happens every time the class is referred to by another class.

    C. Class initialization assigns values to static properties.

    D. Class initialization provides data to the instance of `java.lang.Class`.

7. Select all of the correct statements:

    A. Class instantiation may never happen.

    B. Class instantiation includes object property initialization.

    C. Class instantiation includes memory allocation on a heap.

    D. Class instantiation includes executing constructor code.

8. Select all of the correct statements:

    A. Method execution includes binary code generation.

    B. Method execution includes source code compilation.

    C. Method execution includes reusing the binary code that's produced by
       the JIT compiler.

    D. Method execution counts how many times every method was called.

9. Select all of the correct statements:

    A. Garbage collection starts immediately after the `System.gc()` method is called.

    B. The application can be terminated with or without an error code.

    C. The application exits as soon as an exception is thrown.

    D. The main thread is a user thread.

10. Select all of the correct statements:

    A. The JVM has memory areas shared across all threads.

    B. The JVM has memory areas not shared across threads.

    C. Class metadata is shared across all threads.

    D. Method parameter values are not shared across threads.

11. Select all of the correct statements:

    A. The classloader populates the method area.

    B. The classloader allocates memory on a heap.

    C. The classloader writes to the `.class` file.

    D. The classloader resolves method references.

12. Select all of the correct statements:

    A. The execution engine allocates memory on a heap.

    B. The execution engine terminates the application.

    C. The execution engine runs garbage collection.

    D. The execution engine initializes static fields that haven't been initialized by a programmer.

13. Select all of the correct statements:

    A. The number of transactions per second that a database can support is a throughput measure.

    B. When the garbage collector pauses the application, it is called stop-all-things.

    C. How slowly the website returns data is a responsiveness measure.

    D. The garbage collector clears the CPU queue of jobs.

14. Select all of the correct statements:

    A. Object age is measured by the number of seconds since the object was created.

    B. The older the object, the more probable it is going to be removed from memory.

    C. Cleaning the old generation is a major collection.

    D. Moving an object from one area of the young generation to another area of the young generation is a minor collection.

15. Select all of the correct statements:

    A. The garbage collector can be tuned by setting the parameters of the `javac` command.

    B. The garbage collector can be tuned by setting the parameters of the `java` command.

    C. The garbage collector works with its logic and cannot change its behavior based on the set parameters.

    D. Cleaning the old generation area requires a stop-the-world pause.

10
Managing Data in a Database

This chapter explains and demonstrates how to manage – that is, insert, read, update, and delete – data in a database using a Java application. It also provides a short introduction to **Structured Query Language** (**SQL**) and basic database operations, including how to connect to a database, how to create a database structure, how to write a database expression using SQL, and how to execute these expressions.

The following topics will be covered in this chapter:

- Creating a database
- Creating a database structure
- Connecting to a database
- Releasing the connection
- **Create, read, update, and delete** (**CRUD**) operations on data
- Using a shared library JAR file to access a database

By the end of the chapter, you will be able to create and use a database for storing, updating, and retrieving data as well as create and use a shared library.

Technical requirements

To be able to execute the code examples provided in this chapter, you will need the following:

- A computer with either a Microsoft Windows, Apple macOS, or Linux operating system

- Java SE version 17 or later

- An IDE or code editor you prefer

The instructions for how to set up a Java SE and IntelliJ IDEA editor were provided in *Chapter 1, Getting Started with Java 17*. The files with the code examples for this chapter are available on GitHub (`https://github.com/PacktPublishing/Learn-Java-17-Programming.git`) in the `examples/src/main/java/com/packt/learnjava/ch10_database` folder, and in the `database` folder, as a separate project of the shared library.

Creating a database

Java Database Connectivity (**JDBC**) is a Java functionality that allows you to access and modify data in a database. It is supported by the JDBC API (which includes the `java.sql`, `javax.sql`, and `java.transaction.xa` packages) and the database-specific class that implements an interface for database access (called a **database driver**), which is provided by each database vendor.

Using JDBC means writing Java code that manages data in a database using the interfaces and classes of the JDBC API and a database-specific driver, which knows how to establish a connection with the particular database. Using this connection, an application can then issue requests written in SQL.

Naturally, we are only referring to the databases that understand SQL here. They are called relational or tabular **database management systems** (**DBMSs**) and make up the vast majority of the currently used DBMSs – although some alternatives (for example, a navigational database and NoSQL) are used too.

The `java.sql` and `javax.sql` packages are included in the **Java Platform Standard Edition** (**Java SE**). The `javax.sql` package contains the `DataSource` interface that supports the statement's pooling, distributed transactions, and rowsets.

Creating a database involves the following eight steps:

1. Install the database by following the vendor instructions.

2. Open the PL/SQL terminal and create a database user, a database, a schema, tables, views, stored procedures, and anything else that is necessary to support the data model of the application.

3. Add to this application the dependency on a `.jar` file with the database-specific driver.

4. Connect to the database from the application.

5. Construct the SQL statement.

6. Execute the SQL statement.

7. Use the result of the execution as your application requires.

8. Release (that is, close) the database connection and any other resources that were opened in the process.

Steps 1 to *3* are performed only once during the database setup and before the application is run. *Steps 4* to *8* are performed by the application repeatedly as needed. In fact, *Steps 5* to *7* can be repeated multiple times with the same database connection.

For our example, we are going to use the PostgreSQL database. You will first need to perform *Steps 1* to *3* by yourself using the database-specific instructions. To create the database for our demonstration, we use the following PL/SQL commands:

```
create user student SUPERUSER;
create database learnjava owner student;
```

These commands create a `student` user that can manage all aspects of the `SUPERUSER` database, and make the `student` user an owner of the `learnjava` database. We will use the `student` user to access and manage data from the Java code. In practice, for security considerations, an application is not allowed to create or change database tables and other aspects of the database structure.

Additionally, it is a good practice to create another logical layer, called a **schema**, which can have its own set of users and permissions. This way, several schemas in the same database can be isolated, and each user (one of them is your application) can only access certain schemas. On an enterprise level, the common practice is to create synonyms for the database schema so that no application can access the original structure directly. However, we do not do this in this book for the sake of simplicity.

Creating a database structure

After the database is created, the following three SQL statements will allow you to create and change the database structure. This is done through database entities, such as a table, function, or constraint:

- The CREATE statement creates the database entity.
- The ALTER statement changes the database entity.
- The DROP statement deletes the database entity.

There are also various SQL statements that allow you to inquire about each database entity. Such statements are database-specific and, typically, they are only used in a database console. For example, in the PostgreSQL console, \d <table> can be used to describe a table, while \dt lists all the tables. Refer to your database documentation for more details.

To create a table, you can execute the following SQL statement:

```
CREATE TABLE tablename ( column1 type1, column2 type2, ... );
```

The limitations for a table name, column names, and types of values that can be used depend on the particular database. Here is an example of a command that creates the person table in PostgreSQL:

```
CREATE table person (
    id SERIAL PRIMARY KEY,
    first_name VARCHAR NOT NULL,
    last_name VARCHAR NOT NULL,
    dob DATE NOT NULL );
```

The SERIAL keyword indicates that this field is a sequential integer number that is generated by the database every time a new record is created. Additional options for generating sequential integers are SMALLSERIAL and BIGSERIAL; they differ by size and the range of possible values:

```
SMALLSERIAL: 2 bytes, range from 1 to 32,767
SERIAL: 4 bytes, range from 1 to 2,147,483,647
BIGSERIAL: 8 bytes, range from 1 to 922,337,2036,854,775,807
```

The PRIMARY_KEY keyword indicates that this is going to be the unique identifier of the record and will most probably be used in a search. The database creates an index for each primary key to make the search process faster. An index is a data structure that helps to accelerate data search in the table without having to check every table record. An index can include one or more columns of a table. If you request the description of the table, you will see all the existing indices.

Alternatively, we can make a composite PRIMARY KEY keyword using a combination of first_name, last_name, and dob:

```
CREATE table person (
    first_name VARCHAR NOT NULL,
    last_name VARCHAR NOT NULL,
    dob DATE NOT NULL,
    PRIMARY KEY (first_name, last_name, dob) );
```

However, there is a chance that there are two people who will have the same name and were born on the same day, so such a composite prim is not a good idea.

The NOT NULL keyword imposes a constraint on the field: it cannot be empty. The database will raise an error for every attempt to create a new record with an empty field or delete the value from the existing record. We did not set the size of the columns of type VARCHAR, thus allowing these columns to store string values of any length.

The Java object that matches such a record may be represented by the following Person class:

```
public class Person {
    private int id;
    private LocalDate dob;
    private String firstName, lastName;
    public Person(String firstName, String lastName,
                                        LocalDate dob){
      if (dob == null) {
        throw new RuntimeException
                            ("Date of birth cannot be null");
      }
      this.dob = dob;
      this.firstName = firstName == null ? "" : firstName;
      this.lastName = lastName == null ? "" : lastName;
    }
```

```
  public Person(int id, String firstName,
                  String lastName, LocalDate dob) {
    this(firstName, lastName, dob);
    this.id = id;
  }
  public int getId() { return id; }
  public LocalDate getDob() { return dob; }
  public String getFirstName() { return firstName;}
  public String getLastName() { return lastName; }
}
```

As you may have noticed, there are two constructors in the Person class: with and without id. We will use the constructor that accepts id to construct an object based on the existing record, while the other constructor will be used to create an object before inserting a new record.

Once created, the table can be deleted using the DROP command:

```
DROP table person;
```

The existing table can also be changed using the ALTER SQL command; for example, we can add a column address:

```
ALTER table person add column address VARCHAR;
```

If you are not sure whether such a column exists already, you can add IF EXISTS or IF NOT EXISTS:

```
ALTER table person add column IF NOT EXISTS address VARCHAR;
```

However, this possibility exists only with PostgreSQL 9.6 and later versions.

Another important consideration to take note of during database table creation is whether another index (in addition to PRIMARY KEY) has to be added. For example, we can allow a case-insensitive search of first and last names by adding the following index:

```
CREATE index idx_names on person ((lower(first_name),
lower(last_name));
```

If the search speed improves, we leave the index in place; if not, it can be removed, as follows:

```
DROP index idx_names;
```

We remove it because an index has an overhead of additional writes and storage space.

We also can remove a column from a table if we need to, as follows:

```
ALTER table person DROP column address;
```

In our examples, we follow the naming convention of PostgreSQL. If you use a different database, we suggest that you look up its naming convention and follow it, so that the names you create align with those that are created automatically.

Connecting to a database

So far, we have used a console to execute SQL statements. The same statements can be executed from Java code using the JDBC API too. But, tables are created only once, so there is not much sense in writing a program for a one-time execution.

Data management, however, is another matter. So, from now on, we will use Java code to manipulate data in a database. In order to do this, we first need to add the following dependency to the pom.xml file in the database project:

```
<dependency>
    <groupId>org.postgresql</groupId>
    <artifactId>postgresql</artifactId>
    <version>42.3.2</version>
</dependency>
```

The example project also gets access to this dependency because, in the pom.xml file of the example project, we have the following dependency on the database .jar file:

```
<dependency>
    <groupId>com.packt.learnjava</groupId>
    <artifactId>database</artifactId>
    <version>1.0-SNAPSHOT</version>
</dependency>
```

Make sure to install the database project by executing the "mvn clean install" command in the database folder before running any of the examples.

Now, we can create a database connection from the Java code, as follows:

```
String URL = "jdbc:postgresql://localhost/learnjava";
Properties prop = new Properties();
```

```
prop.put( "user", "student" );
// prop.put( "password", "secretPass123" );
try {
 Connection conn = DriverManager.getConnection(URL, prop);
} catch (SQLException ex) {
    ex.printStackTrace();
}
```

The preceding code is just an example of how to create a connection using the `java.sql.DriverManger` class. The `prop.put( "password", "secretPass123" )` statement demonstrates how to provide a password for the connection using the `java.util.Properties` class. However, we did not set a password when we created the `student` user, so we do not need it.

Many other values can be passed to `DriverManager` that configure the connection behavior. The name of the keys for the passed-in properties are the same for all major databases, but some of them are database-specific. So, read your database vendor documentation for more details.

Alternatively, for passing `user` and `password` only, we could use an overloaded `DriverManager.getConnection(String url, String user, String password)` version. It is a good practice to keep the password encrypted. We are not going to demonstrate how to do it, but there are plenty of guides available on the internet that you can refer to.

Another way of connecting to a database is to use the `javax.sql.DataSource` interface. Its implementation is included in the same `.jar` file as the database driver. In the case of `PostgreSQL`, there are two classes that implement the `DataSource` interface:

- `org.postgresql.ds.PGSimpleDataSource`
- `org.postgresql.ds.PGConnectionPoolDataSource`

We can use these classes instead of `DriverManager`. The following code is an example of creating a database connection using the `PGSimpleDataSource` class:

```
PGSimpleDataSource source = new PGSimpleDataSource();
source.setServerName("localhost");
source.setDatabaseName("learnjava");
source.setUser("student");
//source.setPassword("password");
```

```
source.setLoginTimeout(10);
try {
    Connection conn = source.getConnection();
} catch (SQLException ex) {
    ex.printStackTrace();
}
```

Using the `PGConnectionPoolDataSource` class allows you to create a pool of `Connection` objects in memory, as follows:

```
PGConnectionPoolDataSource source = new
PGConnectionPoolDataSource();
source.setServerName("localhost");
source.setDatabaseName("learnjava");
source.setUser("student");
//source.setPassword("password");
source.setLoginTimeout(10);
try {
    PooledConnection conn = source.getPooledConnection();
    Set<Connection> pool = new HashSet<>();
    for(int i = 0; i < 10; i++){
        pool.add(conn.getConnection())
    }
} catch (SQLException ex) {
    ex.printStackTrace();
}
```

This is a preferred method because creating a `Connection` object takes time. Pooling allows you to do it upfront and then reuse the created objects when they are needed. After the connection is no longer required, it can be returned to the pool and reused. The pool size and other parameters can be set in a configuration file (such as `postgresql.conf` for PostgreSQL).

However, you do not need to manage the connection pool yourself. There are several mature frameworks that can do it for you, such as HikariCP (`https://github.com/brettwooldridge/HikariCP`), Vibur (`http://www.vibur.org`), and Commons DBCP (`https://commons.apache.org/proper/commons-dbcp`) – these are reliable and easy to use.

Whatever method of creating a database connection we choose, we are going to hide it inside the getConnection() method and use it in all our code examples in the same way. With the object of the Connection class acquired, we can now access the database to add, read, delete, or modify the stored data.

Releasing the connection

Keeping the database connection alive requires a significant number of resources, such as memory and CPU, so it is a good idea to close the connection and release the allocated resources as soon as you no longer need them. In the case of pooling, the Connection object, when closed, is returned to the pool and consumes fewer resources.

Before Java 7, a connection was closed by invoking the close() method in a finally block:

```java
try {
    Connection conn = getConnection();
    //use object conn here
} finally {
    if(conn != null){
        try {
            conn.close();
        } catch (SQLException e) {
            e.printStackTrace();
        }
    }
}
```

The code inside the finally block is always executed, whether the exception inside the try block is thrown or not. However, since Java 7, the try-with-resources construct also does the job on any object that implements the java.lang.AutoCloseable or java.io.Closeable interface. Since the java.sql.Connection object does implement the AutoCloseable interface, we can rewrite the previous code snippet, as follows:

```java
try (Connection conn = getConnection()) {
    //use object conn here
} catch(SQLException ex) {
    ex.printStackTrace();
}
```

The catch clause is necessary because the AutoCloseable resource throws java.sql.SQLException.

CRUD data

There are four kinds of SQL statements that read or manipulate data in a database:

- The INSERT statement adds data to a database.

- The SELECT statement reads data from a database.

- The UPDATE statement changes data in a database.

- The DELETE statement deletes data from a database.

Either one or several different clauses can be added to the preceding statements to identify the data that is requested (such as the WHERE clause) and the order in which the results have to be returned (such as the ORDER clause).

The JDBC connection is represented by java.sql.Connection. This, among others, has the methods required to create three types of objects that allow you to execute SQL statements that provide different functionality to the database side:

- java.sql.Statement: This simply sends the statement to the database server for execution.

- java.sql.PreparedStatement: This caches the statement with a certain execution path on the database server by allowing it to be executed multiple times with different parameters in an efficient manner.

- java.sql.CallableStatement: This executes the stored procedure in the database.

In this section, we are going to review how to do it in Java code. The best practice is to test the SQL statement in the database console before using it programmatically.

The INSERT statement

The INSERT statement creates (populates) data in the database and has the following format:

```
INSERT into table_name (column1, column2, column3,...)
                values (value1, value2, value3,...);
```

Alternatively, when several records need to be added, you can use the following format:

```
INSERT into table_name (column1, column2, column3,...)
              values (value1, value2, value3,... ),
                     (value21, value22, value23,...),
                     ...;
```

The SELECT statement

The SELECT statement has the following format:

```
SELECT column_name, column_name FROM table_name
                      WHERE some_column = some_value;
```

Alternatively, when all the columns need to be selected, you can use the following format:

```
SELECT * from table_name WHERE some_column=some_value;
```

A more general definition of the WHERE clause is as follows:

```
WHERE column_name operator value
Operator:
= Equal
<> Not equal. In some versions of SQL, !=
> Greater than
< Less than
>= Greater than or equal
<= Less than or equal IN Specifies multiple possible values for
a column
LIKE Specifies the search pattern
BETWEEN Specifies the inclusive range of values in a column
```

The construct's column_name operator value can be combined using the AND and OR logical operators, and grouped by brackets, ( ).

For example, the following method brings all the first name values (separated by a whitespace character) from the person table:

```
String selectAllFirstNames() {
    String result = "";
    Connection conn = getConnection();
```

```
    try (conn; Statement st = conn.createStatement()) {
      ResultSet rs =
        st.executeQuery("select first_name from person");
      while (rs.next()) {
          result += rs.getString(1) + " ";
      }
    } catch (SQLException ex) {
        ex.printStackTrace();
    }
    return result;
}
```

The getString(int position) method of the ResultSet interface extracts the String value from position 1 (the first in the list of columns in the SELECT statement). There are similar getters for all primitive types: getInt(int position), getByte(int position), and more.

It is also possible to extract the value from the ResultSet object using the column name. In our case, it will be getString("first_name"). This method of getting values is especially useful when the SELECT statement is as follows:

```
select * from person;
```

However, bear in mind that extracting values from the ResultSet object using the column name is less efficient. The difference in performance, though, is very small and only becomes important when the operation takes place many times. Only the actual measuring and testing processes can tell whether the difference is significant to your application or not. Extracting values by column name is especially attractive because it provides better code readability, which pays off in the long run during application maintenance.

There are many other useful methods in the ResultSet interface. If your application reads data from a database, we highly recommend that you read the official documentation (www.postgresql.org/docs) of the SELECT statement and the ResultSet interface for the database version you are using.

The UPDATE statement

The data can be changed by the UPDATE statement, as follows:

```
UPDATE table_name SET column1=value1,column2=value2,... WHERE
clause;
```

We can use this statement to change the first name in one of the records from the original value, John, to a new value, Jim:

```
update person set first_name = 'Jim' where last_name = 'Adams';
```

Without the WHERE clause, all the records of the table will be affected.

The DELETE statement

To remove records from a table, use the DELETE statement, as follows:

```
DELETE FROM table_name WHERE clause;
```

Without the WHERE clause, all the records of the table are deleted. In the case of the person table, we can delete all the records using the following SQL statement:

```
delete from person;
```

Additionally, this statement only deletes the records that have a first name of Jim:

```
delete from person where first_name = 'Jim';
```

Using statements

The java.sql.Statement interface offers the following methods for executing SQL statements:

- boolean execute(String sql): This returns true if the executed statement returns data (inside the java.sql.ResultSet object) that can be retrieved using the ResultSet getResultSet() method of the java.sql. Statement interface. Alternatively, it returns false if the executed statement does not return data (for the INSERT statement or the UPDATE statement) and the subsequent call to the int getUpdateCount() method of the java.sql. Statement interface returns the number of affected rows.

- ResultSet executeQuery(String sql): This returns data as a java. sql.ResultSet object (the SQL statement used with this method is usually a SELECT statement). The ResultSet getResultSet() method of the java.sql.Statement interface does not return data, while the int getUpdateCount() method of the java.sql.Statement interface returns -1.

- `int executeUpdate(String sql)`: This returns the number of affected rows (the executed SQL statement is expected to be the UPDATE statement or the DELETE statement). The same number is returned by the `int getUpdateCount()` method of the `java.sql.Statement` interface; the subsequent call to the `ResultSet getResultSet()` method of the `java.sql.Statement` interface returns `null`.

We will demonstrate how these three methods work on each of the statements: INSERT, SELECT, UPDATE, and DELETE.

The execute(String sql) method

Let's try executing each of the statements; we'll start with the INSERT statement:

```
String sql =
    "insert into person (first_name, last_name, dob) " +
                "values ('Bill', 'Grey', '1980-01-27')";
Connection conn = getConnection();
try (conn; Statement st = conn.createStatement()) {
    System.out.println(st.execute(sql)); //prints: false
    System.out.println(st.getResultSet() == null);
                                            //prints: true
    System.out.println(st.getUpdateCount()); //prints: 1
} catch (SQLException ex) {
    ex.printStackTrace();
}
System.out.println(selectAllFirstNames()); //prints: Bill
```

The preceding code adds a new record to the `person` table. The returned `false` value indicates that there is no data returned by the executed statement; this is why the `getResultSet()` method returns `null`. But, the `getUpdateCount()` method returns 1 because one record was affected (added). The `selectAllFirstNames()` method proves that the expected record was inserted.

Now, let's execute the SELECT statement, as follows:

```
String sql = "select first_name from person";
Connection conn = getConnection();
try (conn; Statement st = conn.createStatement()) {
    System.out.println(st.execute(sql));     //prints: true
```

```
        ResultSet rs = st.getResultSet();
        System.out.println(rs == null);                    //prints: false
        System.out.println(st.getUpdateCount());     //prints: -1
        while (rs.next()) {
            System.out.println(rs.getString(1) + " ");
                                                            //prints: Bill
        }
    } catch (SQLException ex) {
        ex.printStackTrace();
    }
```

The preceding code selects all the first names from the person table. The returned true value indicates that there is data returned by the executed statement. That is why the getResultSet() method does not return null but a ResultSet object instead. The getUpdateCount() method returns -1 because no record was affected (changed). Since there was only one record in the person table, the ResultSet object contains only one result, and rs.getString(1) returns Bill.

The following code uses the UPDATE statement to change the first name in all the records of the person table to Adam:

```
String sql = "update person set first_name = 'Adam'";
Connection conn = getConnection();
try (conn; Statement st = conn.createStatement()) {
    System.out.println(st.execute(sql));   //prints: false
    System.out.println(st.getResultSet() == null);
                                            //prints: true
    System.out.println(st.getUpdateCount());   //prints: 1
} catch (SQLException ex) {
    ex.printStackTrace();
}
System.out.println(selectAllFirstNames()); //prints: Adam
```

In the preceding code, the returned false value indicates that there is no data returned by the executed statement. This is why the getResultSet() method returns null. But, the getUpdateCount() method returns 1 because one record was affected (changed) since there was only one record in the person table. The selectAllFirstNames() method proves that the expected change was made to the record.

The following DELETE statement execution deletes all records from the person table:

```
String sql = "delete from person";
Connection conn = getConnection();
try (conn; Statement st = conn.createStatement()) {
    System.out.println(st.execute(sql));   //prints: false
    System.out.println(st.getResultSet() == null);
                                            //prints: true
    System.out.println(st.getUpdateCount());   //prints: 1
} catch (SQLException ex) {
    ex.printStackTrace();
}
System.out.println(selectAllFirstNames());   //prints:
```

In the preceding code, the returned false value indicates that there is no data returned by the executed statement. That is why the getResultSet() method returns null. But, the getUpdateCount() method returns 1 because one record was affected (deleted) since there was only one record in the person table. The selectAllFirstNames() method proves that there are no records in the person table.

The executeQuery(String sql) method

In this section, we will try to execute the same statements (as a query) that we used when demonstrating the execute() method in the *The execute(String sql) method* section. We'll start with the INSERT statement, as follows:

```
String sql =
"insert into person (first_name, last_name, dob) " +
            "values ('Bill', 'Grey', '1980-01-27')";
Connection conn = getConnection();
try (conn; Statement st = conn.createStatement()) {
    st.executeQuery(sql);            //PSQLException
} catch (SQLException ex) {
    ex.printStackTrace();            //prints: stack trace
}
System.out.println(selectAllFirstNames()); //prints: Bill
```

The preceding code generates an exception with the No results were returned by the query message because the executeQuery() method expects to execute the SELECT statement. Nevertheless, the selectAllFirstNames() method proves that the expected record was inserted.

Now, let's execute the SELECT statement, as follows:

```
String sql = "select first_name from person";
Connection conn = getConnection();
try (conn; Statement st = conn.createStatement()) {
    ResultSet rs1 = st.executeQuery(sql);
    System.out.println(rs1 == null);      //prints: false
    ResultSet rs2 = st.getResultSet();
    System.out.println(rs2 == null);      //prints: false
    System.out.println(st.getUpdateCount()); //prints: -1
    while (rs1.next()) {
        System.out.println(rs1.getString(1)); //prints: Bill
    }
    while (rs2.next()) {
        System.out.println(rs2.getString(1)); //prints:
    }
} catch (SQLException ex) {
    ex.printStackTrace();
}
```

The preceding code selects all the first names from the person table. The returned false value indicates that executeQuery() always returns the ResultSet object, even when no record exists in the person table. As you can see, there appear to be two ways of getting a result from the executed statement. However, the rs2 object has no data, so, while using the executeQuery() method, make sure that you get the data from the ResultSet object.

Now, let's try to execute an UPDATE statement, as follows:

```
String sql = "update person set first_name = 'Adam'";
Connection conn = getConnection();
try (conn; Statement st = conn.createStatement()) {
    st.executeQuery(sql);              //PSQLException
} catch (SQLException ex) {
    ex.printStackTrace();              //prints: stack trace
}
System.out.println(selectAllFirstNames()); //prints: Adam
```

The preceding code generates an exception with the No results were returned by the query message because the executeQuery() method expects to execute the SELECT statement. Nevertheless, the selectAllFirstNames() method proves that the expected change was made to the record.

We are going to get the same exception while executing the DELETE statement:

```
String sql = "delete from person";
Connection conn = getConnection();
try (conn; Statement st = conn.createStatement()) {
    st.executeQuery(sql);              //PSQLException
} catch (SQLException ex) {
    ex.printStackTrace();              //prints: stack trace
}
System.out.println(selectAllFirstNames()); //prints:
```

Nevertheless, the selectAllFirstNames() method proves that all the records of the person table were deleted.

Our demonstration shows that executeQuery() should be used for SELECT statements only. The advantage of the executeQuery() method is that, when used for SELECT statements, it returns a not-null ResultSet object even when there is no data selected, which simplifies the code since there is no need to check the returned value for null.

The executeUpdate(String sql) method

We'll start demonstrating the executeUpdate() method with the INSERT statement:

```
String sql =
"insert into person (first_name, last_name, dob) " +
                "values ('Bill', 'Grey', '1980-01-27')";
Connection conn = getConnection();
try (conn; Statement st = conn.createStatement()) {
   System.out.println(st.executeUpdate(sql)); //prints: 1
   System.out.println(st.getResultSet());  //prints: null
   System.out.println(st.getUpdateCount());  //prints: 1
} catch (SQLException ex) {
    ex.printStackTrace();
}
System.out.println(selectAllFirstNames()); //prints: Bill
```

As you can see, the executeUpdate() method returns the number of affected (inserted, in this case) rows. The same number returns the int getUpdateCount() method, while the ResultSet getResultSet() method returns null. The selectAllFirstNames() method proves that the expected record was inserted.

The executeUpdate() method can't be used for executing the SELECT statement:

```
String sql = "select first_name from person";
Connection conn = getConnection();
try (conn; Statement st = conn.createStatement()) {
    st.executeUpdate(sql);     //PSQLException
} catch (SQLException ex) {
    ex.printStackTrace();     //prints: stack trace
}
```

The message of the exception is A result was returned when none was expected.

The UPDATE statement, on the other hand, is executed by the executeUpdate() method just fine:

```
String sql = "update person set first_name = 'Adam'";
Connection conn = getConnection();
try (conn; Statement st = conn.createStatement()) {
```

```
    System.out.println(st.executeUpdate(sql));   //prints: 1
    System.out.println(st.getResultSet());    //prints: null
      System.out.println(st.getUpdateCount());      //prints: 1
} catch (SQLException ex) {
    ex.printStackTrace();
}
System.out.println(selectAllFirstNames());      //prints: Adam
```

The executeUpdate() method returns the number of affected (updated, in this case) rows. The same number returns the int getUpdateCount() method, while the ResultSet getResultSet() method returns null. The selectAllFirstNames() method proves that the expected record was updated.

The DELETE statement produces similar results:

```
String sql = "delete from person";
Connection conn = getConnection();
try (conn; Statement st = conn.createStatement()) {
    System.out.println(st.executeUpdate(sql));   //prints: 1
    System.out.println(st.getResultSet());       //prints: null
    System.out.println(st.getUpdateCount());     //prints: 1
} catch (SQLException ex) {
    ex.printStackTrace();
}
System.out.println(selectAllFirstNames());       //prints:
```

By now, you have probably realized that the executeUpdate() method is better suited for INSERT, UPDATE, and DELETE statements.

Using PreparedStatement

PreparedStatement is a subinterface of the Statement interface. This means that it can be used anywhere that the Statement interface is used. The advantage of PreparedStatement is that it is cached in the database instead of being compiled every time it is invoked. This way, it is efficiently executed multiple times for different input values. It can be created by the prepareStatement() method using the same Connection object.

Since the same SQL statement can be used for creating `Statement` and `PreparedStatement`, it is a good idea to use `PreparedStatement` for any SQL statement that is called multiple times because it performs better than the `Statement` interface on the database side. To do this, all we need to change are these two lines from the preceding code example:

```
try (conn; Statement st = conn.createStatement()) {
    ResultSet rs = st.executeQuery(sql);
```

Instead, we can use the `PreparedStatement` class, as follows:

```
try (conn; PreparedStatement st = conn.prepareStatement(sql)) {
    ResultSet rs = st.executeQuery();
```

To create the `PreparedStatement` object with parameters, you can substitute the input values with the question mark symbol (`?`); for example, we can create the following method (see the `Person` class in the `database` project):

```
private static final String SELECT_BY_FIRST_NAME =
            "select * from person where first_name = ?";
static List<Person> selectByFirstName(Connection conn,
                                          String searchName) {
    List<Person> list = new ArrayList<>();
    try (PreparedStatement st =
        conn.prepareStatement(SELECT_BY_FIRST_NAME)) {
        st.setString(1, searchName);
        ResultSet rs = st.executeQuery();
        while (rs.next()) {
            list.add(new Person(rs.getInt("id"),
                    rs.getString("first_name"),
                    rs.getString("last_name"),
                    rs.getDate("dob").toLocalDate()));
        }
    } catch (SQLException ex) {
        ex.printStackTrace();
    }
    return list;
}
```

When it is used the first time, the database compiles the `PreparedStatement` object as a template and stores it. Then, when it is later used by the application again, the parameter value is passed to the template, and the statement is executed immediately without the overhead of compilation since it has been done already.

Another advantage of a prepared statement is that it is better protected from a SQL injection attack because values are passed in using a different protocol and the template is not based on the external input.

If a prepared statement is used only once, it may be slower than a regular statement, but the difference may be negligible. If in doubt, test the performance and see whether it is acceptable for your application – the increased security could be worth it.

Using CallableStatement

The `CallableStatement` interface (which extends the `PreparedStatement` interface) can be used to execute a stored procedure, although some databases allow you to call a stored procedure using either a `Statement` or `PreparedStatement` interface. A `CallableStatement` object is created by the `prepareCall()` method and can have parameters of three types:

- `IN` for an input value
- `OUT` for the result
- `IN OUT` for either an input or an output value

The `IN` parameter can be set the same way as the parameters of `PreparedStatement`, while the `OUT` parameter must be registered by the `registerOutParameter()` method of `CallableStatement`.

It is worth noting that executing a stored procedure from Java programmatically is one of the least standardized areas. PostgreSQL, for example, does not support stored procedures directly, but they can be invoked as functions that have been modified for this purpose by interpreting the `OUT` parameters as return values. Oracle, on the other hand, allows the `OUT` parameters as functions too.

This is why the following differences between database functions and stored procedures can serve only as general guidelines and not as formal definitions:

- A function has a return value, but it does not allow OUT parameters (except for some databases) and can be used in a SQL statement.

- A stored procedure does not have a return value (except for some databases); it allows OUT parameters (for most databases) and can be executed using the JDBC CallableStatement interface.

You can refer to the database documentation to learn how to execute a stored procedure.

Since stored procedures are compiled and stored on the database server, the execute() method of CallableStatement performs better for the same SQL statement than the corresponding method of the Statement or PreparedStatement interface. This is one of the reasons why a lot of Java code is sometimes replaced by one or several stored procedures that even include business logic. However, there is no one right answer for every case and problem, so we will refrain from making specific recommendations, except to repeat the familiar mantra about the value of testing and the clarity of the code you are writing:

```java
String replace(String origText, String substr1, String substr2)
{
    String result = "";
    String sql = "{ ? = call replace(?, ?, ? ) }";
    Connection conn = getConnection();
    try (conn; CallableStatement st = conn.prepareCall(sql)) {
        st.registerOutParameter(1, Types.VARCHAR);
        st.setString(2, origText);
        st.setString(3, substr1);
        st.setString(4, substr2);
        st.execute();
        result = st.getString(1);
    } catch (Exception ex){
        ex.printStackTrace();
    }
    return result;
}
```

Now, we can call this method, as follows:

```
String result = replace("That is original text",
                        "original text", "the result");
System.out.println(result);  //prints: That is the result
```

A stored procedure can be without any parameters at all, with IN parameters only, with OUT parameters only, or with both. The result may be one or multiple values, or a ResultSet object. You can find the syntax of the SQL for function creation in your database documentation.

Using a shared library JAR file to access a database

In fact, we have already started using the database project JAR file to access the database driver, set as a dependency in the pom.xml file of the database project. Now, we are going to demonstrate how to use a JAR file of the database project JAR file to manipulate data in the database. An example of such usage is presented in the UseDatabaseJar class.

To support CRUD operations, a database table often represents a class of objects. Each row of such a table contains properties of one object of a class. In the *Creating a database structure* section, we demonstrated an example of such mapping between the Person class and the person table. To illustrate how to use a JAR file for data manipulation, we have created a separate database project that has only one Person class. In addition to the properties shown in the *Creating a database structure* section, it has static methods for all CRUD operations. The following is the insert() method:

```
static final String INSERT = "insert into person " +
  "(first_name, last_name, dob) values (?, ?, ?::date)";
static void insert(Connection conn, Person person) {
   try (PreparedStatement st =
                    conn.prepareStatement(INSERT)) {
          st.setString(1, person.getFirstName());
          st.setString(2, person.getLastName());
          st.setString(3, person.getDob().toString());
          st.execute();
   } catch (SQLException ex) {
          ex.printStackTrace();
   }
}
```

The following is the `selectByFirstName()` method:

```
private static final String SELECT =
          "select * from person where first_name = ?";
static List<Person> selectByFirstName(Connection conn,
                                      String firstName) {
   List<Person> list = new ArrayList<>();
   try (PreparedStatement st = conn.prepareStatement(SELECT)) {
       st.setString(1, firstName);
       ResultSet rs = st.executeQuery();
       while (rs.next()) {
           list.add(new Person(rs.getInt("id"),
                   rs.getString("first_name"),
                   rs.getString("last_name"),
                   rs.getDate("dob").toLocalDate()));
       }
   } catch (SQLException ex) {
           ex.printStackTrace();
   }
   return list;
}
```

The following is the `updateFirstNameById()` method:

```
private static final String UPDATE =
      "update person set first_name = ? where id = ?";
public static void updateFirstNameById(Connection conn,
                            int id, String newFirstName) {
   try (PreparedStatement st = conn.prepareStatement(UPDATE)) {
           st.setString(1, newFirstName);
           st.setInt(2, id);
           st.execute();
   } catch (SQLException ex) {
           ex.printStackTrace();
   }
}
```

The following is the `deleteById()` method:

```
private static final String DELETE =
                      "delete from person where id = ?";
public static void deleteById(Connection conn, int id) {
    try (PreparedStatement st = conn.prepareStatement(DELETE)) {
            st.setInt(1, id);
            st.execute();
    } catch (SQLException ex) {
            ex.printStackTrace();
    }
}
```

As you can see, all the preceding methods accept the `Connection` object as a parameter, instead of creating and destroying it inside each method. We decided to do it like so because it allows several operations to associate with each `Connection` object in case we would like them to be committed to the database together or to be rolled back if one of them fails (read about transaction management in the documentation of the database of your choice). Besides, the JAR file (generated by the `database` project) can be used by different applications, so database connection parameters are going to be application-specific, and that is why the `Connection` object has to be created in the application that uses the JAR file. The following code demonstrates such a usage (see the `UseDatabaseJar` class).

Make sure you have executed the `mvn clean install` command in the `database` folder before running the following examples:

```
1 try(Connection conn = getConnection()){
2     cleanTablePerson(conn);
3     Person mike = new Person("Mike", "Brown",
                              LocalDate.of(2002, 8, 14));
4     Person jane = new Person("Jane", "McDonald",
                              LocalDate.of(2000, 3, 21));
5     Person jill = new Person("Jill", "Grey",
                              LocalDate.of(2001, 4, 1));
6     Person.insert(conn, mike);
7     Person.insert(conn, jane);
8     Person.insert(conn, jane);
9     List<Person> persons =
```

```
                Person.selectByFirstName(conn, jill.getFirstName());
10   System.out.println(persons.size());       //prints: 0
11   persons = Person.selectByFirstName(conn,
                                        jane.getFirstName());
12   System.out.println(persons.size());       //prints: 2
13   Person person = persons.get(0);
14   Person.updateFirstNameById(conn, person.getId(),
                                        jill.getFirstName());
15   persons = Person.selectByFirstName(conn,
                                        jane.getFirstName());
16   System.out.println(persons.size());       //prints: 1
17   persons = Person.selectByFirstName(conn,
                                        jill.getFirstName());
18   System.out.println(persons.size());       //prints: 1
19   persons = Person.selectByFirstName(conn,
                                        mike.getFirstName());
20   System.out.println(persons.size());       //prints: 1
21   for(Person p: persons){
22      Person.deleteById(conn, p.getId());
23   }
24   persons = Person.selectByFirstName(conn,
                                        mike.getFirstName());
25   System.out.println(persons.size());       //prints: 0
26 } catch (SQLException ex){
27      ex.printStackTrace();
28 }
```

Let's walk through the preceding code snippet. Lines 1 and 26 to 28 compose the try-catch block that disposes of the Connection object and catches all the exceptions that may happen inside this block during its execution.

Line 2 was included just to clean up the data from the person table before running the demo code. The following is the implementation of the cleanTablePerson() method:

```
void cleanTablePerson(Connection conn) {
   try (Statement st = conn.createStatement()) {
```

```
        st.execute("delete from person");
    } catch (SQLException ex) {
        ex.printStackTrace();
    }
}
```

In lines 3, 4, and 5, we create three objects of the Person class, then in lines 6, 7, and 8, we use them to insert records in the person table.

In line 9, we query the database for a record that has the first name taken from the jill object, and in line 10, we print out the result count, which is 0 (because we did not insert such a record).

In line 11, we query the database for a record that has the first name set to Jane, and in line 12, we print out the result count, which is 2 (because we did insert two records with such a value).

In line 13, we extract the first of the two objects returned by the previous query, and in line 14, we update the corresponding record with a different value for the first name (taken from the jill object).

In line 15, we repeat the query for a record with the first name set to Jane, and in line 16, we print out the result count, which is 1 this time (as expected, because we have changed the first name to Jill on one of the two records).

In line 17, we select all the records with the first name set to Jill, and in line 18, we print out the result count, which is 1 this time (as expected, because we have changed the first name to Jill on one of the two records that used to have the first name value Jane).

In line 19, we select all the records with the name set to Mike, and in line 20, we print out the result count, which is 1 (as expected, because we have created only one such record).

In lines 21 to 23, we delete all the retrieved records in a loop.

That is why when we select all the records with the first name Mike in line 24 again, we get a result count equal to 0 in line 25 (as expected, because there is no such record anymore).

At this point, when this code snippet is executed and the main() method of the UseDatabseJar class is completed, all the changes in the database are saved automatically.

That is how a JAR file (which allows modifying data in a database) can be used by any application that has this file as a dependency.

Summary

In this chapter, we discussed and demonstrated how the data in a database can be populated, read, updated, and deleted from a Java application. A short introduction to the SQL language described how to create a database and its structure, how to modify it, and how to execute SQL statements, using `Statement`, `PreparedStatement`, and `CallableStatement`.

Now, you can create and use a database for storing, updating, and retrieving data, and create and use a shared library.

In the next chapter, we will describe and discuss the most popular network protocols, demonstrate how to use them, and how to implement client-server communication using the latest Java HTTP Client API. The protocols reviewed include the Java implementation of a communication protocol based on TCP, UDP, and URLs.

Quiz

1. Select all the correct statements:

    A. JDBC stands for Java Database Communication.

    B. The JDBC API includes the `java.db` package.

    C. The JDBC API comes with Java installation.

    D. The JDBC API includes the drivers for all major DBMSs.

2. Select all the correct statements:

    A. A database table can be created using the `CREATE` statement.

    B. A database table can be changed using the `UPDATE` statement.

    C. A database table can be removed using the `DELETE` statement.

    D. Each database column can have an index.

3. Select all the correct statements:

    A. To connect to a database, you can use the `Connect` class.

    B. Every database connection must be closed.

    C. The same database connection may be used for many operations.

    D. Database connections can be pooled.

4. Select all the correct statements:

   A. A database connection can be closed automatically using the `try-with-resources` construct.

   B. A database connection can be closed using the `finally` block construct.

   C. A database connection can be closed using the `catch` block.

   D. A database connection can be closed without a `try` block.

5. Select all the correct statements:

   A. The INSERT statement includes a table name.

   B. The INSERT statement includes column names.

   C. The INSERT statement includes values.

   D. The INSERT statement includes constraints.

6. Select all the correct statements:

   A. The SELECT statement must include a table name.

   B. The SELECT statement must include a column name.

   C. The SELECT statement must include the WHERE clause.

   D. The SELECT statement may include the ORDER clause.

7. Select all the correct statements:

   A. The UPDATE statement must include a table name.

   B. The UPDATE statement must include a column name.

   C. The UPDATE statement may include the WHERE clause.

   D. The UPDATE statement may include the ORDER clause.

8. Select all the correct statements:

   A. The DELETE statement must include a table name.

   B. The DELETE statement must include a column name.

   C. The DELETE statement may include the WHERE clause.

   D. The DELETE statement may include the ORDER clause.

9. Select all the correct statements about the `execute()` method of the `Statement` interface:

    A. It receives a SQL statement.

    B. It returns a `ResultSet` object.

    C. The `Statement` object may return data after `execute()` is called.

    D. The `Statement` object may return the number of affected records after `execute()` is called.

10. Select all the correct statements about the `executeQuery()` method of the `Statement` interface:

    A. It receives a SQL statement.

    B. It returns a `ResultSet` object.

    C. The `Statement` object may return data after `executeQuery()` is called.

    D. The `Statement` object may return the number of affected records after `executeQuery()` is called.

11. Select all the correct statements about the `executeUpdate()` method of the `Statement` interface:

    A. It receives a SQL statement.

    B. It returns a `ResultSet` object.

    C. The `Statement` object may return data after `executeUpdate()` is called.

    D. The `Statement` object returns the number of affected records after `executeUpdate()` is called.

12. Select all the correct statements about the `PreparedStatement` interface:

    A. It extends `Statement`.

    B. An object of type `PreparedStatement` is created by the `prepareStatement()` method.

    C. It is always more efficient than `Statement`.

    D. It results in a template in the database being created only once.

13. Select all the correct statements about the `CallableStatement` interface:

   A. It extends `PreparedStatement`.

   B. An object of type `CallableStatement` is created by the `prepareCall()` method.

   C. It is always more efficient than `PreparedStatement`.

   D. It results in a template in the database being created only once.

11
Network Programming

In this chapter, we will describe and discuss the most popular network protocols – **User Datagram Protocol (UDP)**, **Transmission Control Protocol (TCP)**, **HyperText Transfer Protocol (HTTP)**, and **WebSocket** – and their support from the **Java Class Library (JCL)**. We will demonstrate how to use these protocols and how to implement client-server communication in Java code. We will also review **Uniform Resource Locator (URL)**-based communication and the latest **Java HTTP Client API**. After studying this chapter, you will be able to create server and client applications that communicate using the **UDP**, **TCP**, and **HTTP** protocols as well as **WebSocket**.

The following topics will be covered in this chapter:

- Network protocols
- UDP-based communication
- TCP-based communication
- UDP versus TCP protocols
- URL-based communication
- Using the HTTP 2 Client API
- Creating a standalone application HTTP server

By the end of the chapter, you will be able to use all the most popular protocols to send/receive messages between the client and server. You will also learn how to create a server as a separate project and how to create and use a common shared library.

Technical requirements

To be able to execute the code examples provided in this chapter, you will need the following:

- A computer with a Microsoft Windows, Apple macOS, or Linux operating system
- Java SE version 17 or later
- An IDE or code editor of your choosing

The instructions for how to set up a Java SE and IntelliJ IDEA editor were provided in *Chapter 1, Getting Started with Java 17,* of this book. The files with the code examples for this chapter are available on GitHub in the `https://github.com/PacktPublishing/Learn-Java-17-Programming.git` repository, in the `examples/src/main/java/com/packt/learnjava/ch11_network` folder, and in the `common` and `server` folders, as separate projects.

Network protocols

Network programming is a vast area. The **internet protocol (IP)** suite consists of four layers, each of which has a dozen or more protocols:

- **The link layer**: The group of protocols used when a client is physically connected to the host; three core protocols include the **Address Resolution Protocol (ARP)**, the **Reverse Address Resolution Protocol (RARP)**, and the **Neighbor Discovery Protocol (NDP)**.

- **The internet layer**: The group of inter-networking methods, protocols, and specifications used to transport network packets from the originating host to the destination host, specified by an IP address. The core protocols of this layer are **Internet Protocol version 4 (IPv4)** and **Internet Protocol version 6 (IPv6)**; IPv6 specifies a new packet format and allocates 128 bits for the dotted IP address, compared to 32 bits in IPv4. An example of an IPv4 address is `10011010.00010 111.11111110.00010001`, which results in an IP address of `154.23.254.17`. The examples in this chapter use IPv4. The industry, though, is slowly switching to IPv6. An example of an IPv6 address is `594D:1A1B:2C2D:3E3F:4D4A:5B5A:6 B4E:7FF2`.

- **The transport layer**: The group of host-to-host communication services. It includes TCP, also known as the TCP/IP protocol, and UDP (which we are going to discuss shortly). The other protocols in this group are the **Datagram Congestion Control Protocol (DCCP)** and the **Stream Control Transmission Protocol (SCTP)**.

- **The application layer**: The group of protocols and interface methods used by hosts in a communication network. It includes **Telnet, File Transfer Protocol (FTP), Domain Name System (DNS), Simple Mail Transfer Protocol (SMTP), Lightweight Directory Access Protocol (LDAP), Hypertext Transfer Protocol (HTTP), Hypertext Transfer Protocol Secure (HTTPS)**, and **Secure Shell (SSH)**.

The link layer is the lowest layer; it is used by the internet layer, which is, in turn, used by the transport layer. This transport layer is then used by the application layer in support of the protocol implementations.

For security reasons, Java does not provide access to the protocols of the link layer and the internet layer. This means that Java does not allow you to create custom transport protocols that, for example, serve as an alternative to TCP/IP. That is why, in this chapter, we will review only the protocols of the transport layer (TCP and UDP) and the application layer (HTTP). We will explain and demonstrate how Java supports them and how a Java application can take advantage of this support.

Java supports the TCP and UDP protocols with classes of the `java.net` package, while the HTTP protocol can be implemented in the Java application using the classes of the `java.net.http` package (which was introduced with Java 11).

Both the TCP and UDP protocols can be implemented in Java using *sockets*. Sockets are identified by a combination of an IP address and a port number, and they represent a connection between two applications. Since the UDP protocol is somewhat simpler than the TCP protocol, we'll start with UDP.

UDP-based communication

The UDP protocol was designed by David P. Reed in 1980. It allows applications to send messages called **datagrams** using a simple connectionless communication model with a minimal protocol mechanism such as a checksum, for data integrity. It has no handshaking dialogs and, thus, does not guarantee message delivery or preserve the order of messages. It is suitable for those cases when dropping messages or mixing up orders are preferred instead of waiting for retransmission.

A datagram is represented by the `java.net.DatagramPacket` class. An object of this class can be created using one of the six constructors; the following two constructors are the most commonly used:

- `DatagramPacket(byte[] buffer, int length)`: This constructor creates a datagram packet and is used to receive the packets; `buffer` holds the incoming datagram, while `length` is the number of bytes to be read.

- `DatagramPacket(byte[] buffer, int length, InetAddress address, int port)`: This creates a datagram packet and is used to send the packets; `buffer` holds the packet data, `length` is the packet data length, `address` holds the destination IP address, and `port` is the destination port number.

Once constructed, the `DatagramPacket` object exposes the following methods that can be used to extract data from the object or set/get its properties:

- `void setAddress(InetAddress iaddr)`: This sets the destination IP address.

- `InetAddress getAddress()`: This returns the destination or source IP address.

- `void setData(byte[] buf)`: This sets the data buffer.

- `void setData(byte[] buf, int offset, int length)`: This sets the data buffer, data offset, and length.

- `void setLength(int length)`: This sets the length for the packet.

- `byte[] getData()`: This returns the data buffer.

- `int getLength()`: This returns the length of the packet that is to be sent or received.

- `int getOffset()`: This returns the offset of the data that is to be sent or received.

- `void setPort(int port)`: This sets the destination port number.

- `int getPort()`: This returns the port number where data is to be sent or received from. Once a `DatagramPacket` object is created, it can be sent or received using the `DatagramSocket` class, which represents a connectionless socket for sending and receiving datagram packets. An object of this class can be created using one of six constructors; the following three constructors are the most commonly used:

  - `DatagramSocket()`: This creates a datagram socket and binds it to any available port on the local host machine. It is typically used to create a sending socket because the destination address (and port) can be set inside the packet (see the preceding `DatagramPacket` constructors and methods).

  - `DatagramSocket(int port)`: This creates a datagram socket and binds it to the specified port on the local host machine. It is used to create a receiving socket when any local machine address (called a **wildcard address**) is good enough.

  - `DatagramSocket(int port, InetAddress address)`: This creates a datagram socket and binds it to the specified port and the specified local address; the local port must be between 0 and 65535. It is used to create a receiving socket when a particular local machine address needs to be bound.

The following two methods of the `DatagramSocket` object are the most commonly used for sending and receiving messages (or packets):

- `void send(DatagramPacket p)`: This sends the specified packet.
- `void receive(DatagramPacket p)`: This receives a packet by filling the specified `DatagramPacket` object's buffer with the data received. The specified `DatagramPacket` object also contains the sender's IP address and the port number on the sender's machine.

Let's take a look at a code example. Here is the UDP message receiver that exits after the message has been received:

```
public class UdpReceiver {
  public static void main(String[] args) {
    try(DatagramSocket ds = new DatagramSocket(3333)) {
      DatagramPacket dp =
                       new DatagramPacket(new byte[16], 16);
      ds.receive(dp);
      for(byte b: dp.getData()) {
          System.out.print(Character.toString(b));
      }
```

```
    } catch (Exception ex){
          ex.printStackTrace();
    }
  }
}
```

As you can see, the receiver is listening for a text message (it interprets each byte as a character) on any address of the local machine on port 3333. It uses a buffer of 16 bytes only; as soon as the buffer is filled with the received data, the receiver prints its content and exits.

Here is an example of the UDP message sender:

```
public class UdpSender {
  public static void main(String[] args) {
    try(DatagramSocket ds = new DatagramSocket()){
        String msg = "Hi, there! How are you?";
        InetAddress address =
                          InetAddress.getByName("127.0.0.1");
        DatagramPacket dp = new DatagramPacket(msg.getBytes(),
                              msg.length(), address, 3333);
        ds.send(dp);
    } catch (Exception ex){
        ex.printStackTrace();
    }
  }
}
```

As you can see, the sender constructs a packet with the message, the local machine address, and the same port as the one that the receiver uses. After the constructed packet is sent, the sender exits.

We can run the sender now, but without the receiver running, there is nobody to get the message. So, we'll start the receiver first. It listens on port 3333, but there is no message coming – so it waits. Then, we run the sender and the receiver displays the following message:

```
Hi, there! How a
```

Since the buffer is smaller than the message, it was only partially received – the rest of the message is lost. That's why we increase the buffer size to 30. Also, we can create an infinite loop and let the receiver run indefinitely (see the UdpReceiver2 class):

```
public class UdpReceiver2 {
  public static void main(String[] args){
     try(DatagramSocket ds = new DatagramSocket(3333)){
       DatagramPacket dp =
                       new DatagramPacket(new byte[30], 30);
       while(true){
           ds.receive(dp);
           for(byte b: dp.getData()){
               System.out.print(Character.toString(b));
           }
           System.out.println(); //added here to have end-of-
               // line after receiving (and printing) the message
       }
     } catch (Exception ex){
           ex.printStackTrace();
     }
  }
}
```

By doing so, we can run the sender several times. Here is what the receiver UdpReceiver2 prints if we run the sender three times:

```
Hi, there! How are you?
Hi, there! How are you?
Hi, there! How are you?
```

As you can see, all three messages are received. If you run the receiver UdpReceiver2, do not forget to stop it manually after you don't need to run it anymore. Otherwise, it continues running indefinitely.

So, this is the basic idea of the UDP protocol. The sender sends a message to a certain address and port even if no socket *listens* on this address and port. It does not require establishing any kind of connection before sending the message, which makes the UDP protocol faster and more lightweight than the TCP protocol (which requires you to establish the connection first). This way, the TCP protocol takes message sending to another level of reliability by making sure that the destination exists and that the message can be delivered.

TCP-based communication

TCP was designed by the **Defense Advanced Research Projects Agency (DARPA)** in the 1970s for use in the **Advanced Research Projects Agency Network (ARPANET)**. It complements IP and, thus, is also referred to as TCP/IP. The TCP protocol, even by its name, indicates that it provides reliable (that is, error-checked or controlled) data transmission. It allows the ordered delivery of bytes in an IP network and is widely used by the web, email, secure shell, and file transfer.

An application that uses TCP/IP is not even aware of all the handshaking that takes place between the socket and the transmission details – such as network congestion, traffic load balancing, duplication, and even the loss of some IP packets. The underlying protocol implementation of the transport layer detects these problems, resends the data, reconstructs the order of the sent packets, and minimizes network congestion.

In contrast to the UDP protocol, TCP/IP-based communication is focused on accurate delivery at the expense of the delivery period. That's why it is not used for real-time applications, such as voice over IP, where reliable delivery and correct sequential ordering are required. However, if every bit needs to arrive exactly as it was sent and in the same sequence, then TCP/IP is irreplaceable.

To support such behavior, TCP/IP communication maintains a session throughout the communication. The session is identified by the client address and port. Each session is represented by an entry in a table on the server. This contains all the metadata about the session: the client IP address and port, the connection status, and the buffer parameters. However, these details are usually hidden from the application developer, so we won't go into any more detail here. Instead, we will turn to the Java code.

Similar to the UDP protocol, the TCP/IP protocol implementation in Java uses sockets. But instead of the `java.net.DatagramSocket` class that implements the UDP protocol, the TCP/IP-based sockets are represented by the `java.net.ServerSocket` and `java.net.Socket` classes. They allow messages to be sent and received between two applications, one of them being a server and the other a client.

The `ServerSocket` and `SocketClass` classes perform very similar jobs. The only difference is that the `ServerSocket` class has the `accept()` method, which *accepts* the request from the client. This means that the server has to be up and ready to receive the request first. Then, the connection is initiated by the client that creates its own socket that sends the connection request (from the constructor of the `Socket` class). The server then accepts the request and creates a local socket connected to the remote socket (on the client side).

After establishing the connection, data transmission can occur using I/O streams as described in *Chapter 5, Strings, Input/Output, and Files*. The `Socket` object has the `getOutputStream()` and `getInputStream()` methods that provide access to the socket's data streams. Data from the `java.io.OutputStream` object on the local computer appears as coming from the `java.io.InputStream` object on the remote machine.

Let's now take a closer look at the `java.net.ServerSocket` and `java.net.Socket` classes and then run some examples of their usage.

The java.net.ServerSocket class

The `java.net.ServerSocket` class has four constructors:

- `ServerSocket()`: This creates a server socket object that is not bound to a particular address and port. It requires the use of the `bind()` method to bind the socket.

- `ServerSocket(int port)`: This creates a server socket object bound to the provided port. The `port` value must be between `0` and `65535`. If the port number is specified as a value of `0`, this means that the port number needs to be bound automatically. This port number can then be retrieved by calling `getLocalPort()`. By default, the maximum queue length for incoming connections is `50`. This means that the maximum parallel incoming connections are `50` by default. Exceeding connections will be refused.

- `ServerSocket(int port, int backlog)`: This provides the same functionality as the `ServerSocket(int port)` constructor and allows you to set the maximum queue length for incoming connections by means of the `backlog` parameter.

- `ServerSocket(int port, int backlog, InetAddress bindAddr)`: This creates a server socket object that is similar to the preceding constructor, but also bound to the IP address provided. When the `bindAddr` value is `null`, it will default to accepting connections on any or all local addresses.

The following four methods of the ServerSocket class are the most commonly used, and they are essential for establishing a socket's connection:

- void bind(SocketAddress endpoint): This binds the ServerSocket object to a specific IP address and port. If the provided address is null, then the system will pick up a port and a valid local address automatically (which can be later retrieved using the getLocalPort(), getLocalSocketAddress(), and getInetAddress() methods). Additionally, if the ServerSocket object was created by the constructor without any parameters, then this method, or the following bind() method, needs to be invoked before a connection can be established.

- void bind(SocketAddress endpoint, int backlog): This acts in a similar way to the preceding method; the backlog argument is the maximum number of pending connections on the socket (that is, the size of the queue). If the backlog value is less than or equal to 0, then an implementation-specific default will be used.

- void setSoTimeout(int timeout): This sets the value (in milliseconds) of how long the socket waits for a client after the accept() method is called. If the client has not called and the timeout expires, a java.net. SocketTimeoutException exception is thrown, but the ServerSocket object remains valid and can be reused. The timeout value of 0 is interpreted as an infinite timeout (the accept() method blocks until a client calls).

- Socket accept(): This blocks until a client calls or the timeout period (if set) expires.

Other methods of the class allow you to set or get other properties of the Socket object and they can be used for better dynamic management of the socket connection. You can refer to the online documentation of the class to understand the available options in more detail.

The following code is an example of a server implementation using the ServerSocket class:

```java
public class TcpServer {
  public static void main(String[] args){
    try(Socket s = new ServerSocket(3333).accept();
      DataInputStream dis =
                  new DataInputStream(s.getInputStream());
      DataOutputStream dout =
                  new DataOutputStream(s.getOutputStream());
```

```
        BufferedReader console =
          new BufferedReader(new InputStreamReader(System.in))){
          while(true){
              String msg = dis.readUTF();
              System.out.println("Client said: " + msg);
              if("end".equalsIgnoreCase(msg)){
                  break;
              }
              System.out.print("Say something: ");
              msg = console.readLine();
              dout.writeUTF(msg);
              dout.flush();
              if("end".equalsIgnoreCase(msg)){
                  break;
              }
          }
      } catch(Exception ex) {
        ex.printStackTrace();
      }
    }
  }
```

Let's walk through the preceding code. In the try-with-resources statement, we create Socket, DataInputStream, and DataOutputStream objects based on our newly created socket, and the BufferedReader object to read the user input from the console (we will use it to enter the data). While creating the socket, the accept() method blocks until a client tries to connect to port 3333 of the local server.

Then, the code enters an infinite loop. First, it reads the bytes sent by the client as a Unicode character string encoded in a modified UTF-8 format by using the readUTF() method of DataInputStream. The result is printed with the "Client said: " prefix. If the received message is an "end" string, then the code exits the loop and the server's program exits. If the message is not "end", then the "Say something: " prompt is displayed on the console and the readLine() method blocks until a user types something and clicks *Enter*.

The server takes the input from the screen and writes it as a Unicode character string to the output stream using the `writeUtf()` method. As we mentioned already, the output stream of the server is connected to the input stream of the client. If the client reads from the input stream, it receives the message sent by the server. If the sent message is `"end"`, then the sever exits the loop and the program. If not, then the loop body is executed again.

The described algorithm assumes that the client exits only when it sends or receives the `"end"` message. Otherwise, the client generates an exception if it tries to send a message to the server afterward. This demonstrates the difference between the UDP and TCP protocols that we mentioned already – TCP is based on the session that is established between the server and client sockets. If one side drops it, the other side immediately encounters an error.

Now, let's review an example of a TCP-client implementation.

The java.net.Socket class

The `java.net.Socket` class should now be familiar to you since it was used in the preceding example. We used it to access the input and output streams of the connected sockets. Now we are going to review the `Socket` class systematically and explore how it can be used to create a TCP client. The `Socket` class has five constructors:

- `Socket()`: This creates an unconnected socket. It uses the `connect()` method to establish a connection of this socket with a socket on a server.

- `Socket(String host, int port)`: This creates a socket and connects it to the provided port on the `host` server. If it throws an exception, the connection to the server is not established; otherwise; you can start sending data to the server.

- `Socket(InetAddress address, int port)`: This acts similarly to the preceding constructor, except that the host is provided as an `InetAddress` object.

- `Socket(String host, int port, InetAddress localAddr, int localPort)`: This works similarly to the preceding constructor, except that it also allows you to bind the socket to the provided local address and port (if the program is run on a machine with multiple IP addresses). If the provided `localAddr` value is `null`, any local address is selected. Alternatively, if the provided `localPort` value is `null`, then the system picks up a free port in the bind operation.

- `Socket(InetAddress address, int port, InetAddress localAddr, int localPort)`: This acts similarly to the preceding constructor, except that the local address is provided as an `InetAddress` object.

Here are the following two methods of the `Socket` class that we have used already:

- `InputStream getInputStream()`: This returns an object that represents the source (the remote socket) and brings the data (inputs them) into the program (the local socket).

- `OutputStream getOutputStream()`: This returns an object that represents the source (the local socket) and sends the data (outputs them) to a remote socket.

Let's now examine the TCP-client code, as follows:

```java
public class TcpClient {
  public static void main(String[] args) {
    try(Socket s = new Socket("localhost",3333);
    DataInputStream dis =
                    new DataInputStream(s.getInputStream());
    DataOutputStream dout =
                    new DataOutputStream(s.getOutputStream());
    BufferedReader console =
        new BufferedReader(new InputStreamReader(System.in))){
        String prompt = "Say something: ";
        System.out.print(prompt);
        String msg;
        while ((msg = console.readLine()) != null) {
            dout.writeUTF( msg);
            dout.flush();
            if (msg.equalsIgnoreCase("end")) {
                break;
            }
            msg = dis.readUTF();
            System.out.println("Server said: " +msg);
            if (msg.equalsIgnoreCase("end")) {
                break;
            }
            System.out.print(prompt);
        }
    } catch(Exception ex){
        ex.printStackTrace();
    }
}
```

```
    }
}
```

The preceding `TcpClient` code looks almost exactly the same as the `TcpServer` code we reviewed. The only principal difference is that the `new Socket("localhost", 3333)` constructor attempts to establish a connection with the `"localhost:3333"` server immediately, so it expects that the `localhost` server is up and listening on port `3333`; the rest is the same as the server code.

Therefore, the only reason we need to use the `ServerSocket` class is to allow the server to run while waiting for the client to connect to it; everything else can be done using only the `Socket` class.

Other methods of the `Socket` class allow you to set or get other properties of the `socket` object, and they can be used for better dynamic management of the socket connection. You can read the online documentation of the class to understand the available options in more detail.

Running the examples

Let's now run the `TcpServer` and `TcpClient` programs. If we start `TcpClient` first, we get `java.net.ConnectException` with the **Connection refused** message. So, we launch the `TcpServer` program first. When it starts, no messages are displayed. Instead, it just waits until the client connects. So, we then start `TcpClient` and see the following message on the screen:

```
Say something:
```

We type `Hello!` and then press *Enter*:

```
Say something: Hello
```

Now let's look at the server-side screen:

```
Client said: Hello
Say something:
```

We type Hi! on the server-side screen and press *Enter*:

```
Client said: Hello
Say something: Hi!
```

On the client-side screen, we see the following messages:

```
Say something: Hello
Server said: Hi!
Say something:
```

We can continue this dialog indefinitely until the server or the client sends the message end. Let's make the client do it; the client says end and then exits:

```
Say something: Hello
Server said: Hi!
Say something: end

Process finished with exit code 0
```

Then, the server follows suit:

```
Client said: Hello
Say something: Hi!
Client said: end

Process finished with exit code 0
```

That's all we wanted to demonstrate while discussing the TCP protocol. Now let's review the differences between the UDP and TCP protocols.

UDP versus TCP protocols

The differences between the UDP and TCP/IP protocols can be listed as follows:

- UDP simply sends data, whether the data receiver is up and running or not. That's why UDP is better suited to sending data compared to many other clients using multicast distribution. TCP, on the other hand, requires establishing the connection between the client and the server first. The TCP client sends a special control message; the server receives it and responds with a confirmation. The client then sends a message to the server that acknowledges the server confirmation. Only after this is data transmission between the client and server possible.

- TCP guarantees message delivery or raises an error, while UDP does not, and a datagram packet may be lost.

- TCP guarantees the preservation of the order of messages on delivery, while UDP does not.

- As a result of these provided guarantees, TCP is slower than UDP.

- Additionally, protocols require headers to be sent along with the packet. The header size of a TCP packet is 20 bytes, while a datagram packet is 8 bytes. The UDP header contains Length, Source Port, Destination Port, and Checksum, while the TCP header contains Sequence Number, Ack Number, Data Offset, Reserved, Control Bit, Window, Urgent Pointer, Options, and Padding, in addition to the UDP headers.

- Different application protocols are based on the TCP or UDP protocols. The **TCP**-based protocols are **HTTP**, **HTTPS**, **Telnet**, **FTP**, and **SMTP**. The **UDP**-based protocols are **Dynamic Host Configuration Protocol (DHCP)**, DNS, **Simple Network Management Protocol (SNMP)**, **Trivial File Transfer Protocol (TFTP)**, **Bootstrap Protocol (BOOTP)**, and early versions of the **Network File System (NFS)**.

We can capture the difference between UDP and TCP in one sentence: the UDP protocol is faster and more lightweight than TCP, but less reliable. As with many things in life, you have to pay a higher price for additional services. However, not all these services will be needed in all cases, so think about the task at hand and decide which protocol to use based on your application requirements.

URL-based communication

Nowadays, it seems that everybody has some notion of a URL; those who use a browser on their computers or smartphones will see URLs every day. In this section, we will briefly explain the different parts that make up a URL and demonstrate how it can be used programmatically to request data from a website (or a file) or to send (post) data to a website.

The URL syntax

Generally speaking, the URL syntax complies with the syntax of a **Uniform Resource Identifier** (**URI**) that has the following format:

```
scheme:[//authority]path[?query][#fragment]
```

The square brackets indicate that the component is optional. This means that a URI will consist of `scheme:path` at the very least. The `scheme` component can be `http`, `https`, `ftp`, `mailto`, `file`, `data`, or another value. The `path` component consists of a sequence of path segments separated by a slash (`/`). Here is an example of a URL consisting only of `scheme` and `path`:

```
file:src/main/resources/hello.txt
```

The preceding URL points to a file on a local filesystem that is relative to the directory where this URL is used. And here are examples that you are more familiar with: `https://www.google.com`, `https://www.packtpub.com`. We will demonstrate how it works shortly.

The `path` component can be empty, but then the URL would seem useless. Nevertheless, an empty path is often used in conjunction with `authority`, which has the following format:

```
[userinfo@]host[:port]
```

The only required component of authority is `host`, which can be either an IP address (`137.254.120.50`, for example) or a domain name (`oracle.com`, for example).

The `userinfo` component is typically used with the `mailto` value of the `scheme` component, so `userinfo@host` represents an email address.

The `port` component, if omitted, assumes a default value. For example, if the `scheme` value is `http`, then the default `port` value is `80`, and if the `scheme` value is `https`, then the default `port` value is `443`.

An optional `query` component of a URL is a sequence of key-value pairs separated by a delimiter (`&`):

```
key1=value1&key2=value2
```

Finally, the optional `fragment` component is an identifier of a section of an HTML document, meaning that a browser can scroll this section into view.

> **Note**
>
> It is necessary to mention that Oracle's online documentation uses slightly different terminology:
>
> * `protocol` instead of `scheme`
> * `reference` instead of `fragment`
> * `file` instead of `path [?query] [#fragment]`
> * `resource` instead of `host [:port] path [?query] [#fragment]`

So, from the Oracle documentation perspective, the URL is composed of `protocol` and `resource` values.

Let's now take a look at the programmatic usage of URLs in Java.

The java.net.URL class

In Java, a URL is represented by an object of the `java.net.URL` class that has six constructors:

* `URL(String spec)`: This creates a URL object from the URL as a string.

* `URL(String protocol, String host, String file)`: This creates a URL object from the provided values of `protocol`, `host`, and `file` (path and query), and the default port number based on the `protocol` value provided.

* `URL(String protocol, String host, int port, String path)`: This creates a URL object from the provided values of `protocol`, `host`, `port`, and `file` (path and query). A `port` value of `-1` indicates that the default port number needs to be used based on the `protocol` value provided.

* `URL(String protocol, String host, int port, String file, URLStreamHandler handler)`: This acts in the same way as the preceding constructor and additionally allows you to pass in an object of the particular protocol handler; all the preceding constructors load default handlers automatically.

- URL(URL context, String spec): This creates a URL object that extends the URL object provided or overrides its components using the spec value provided, which is a string representation of a URL or some of its components. For example, if the scheme is present in both parameters, the scheme value from spec overrides the scheme value in context and many others.

- URL(URL context, String spec, URLStreamHandler handler): This acts in the same way as the preceding constructor and additionally allows you to pass in an object of the particular protocol handler.

Once created, a URL object allows you to get the values of various components of the underlying URL. The InputStream openStream() method provides access to the stream of data received from the URL. In fact, it is implemented as openConnection. getInputStream(). The URLConnection openConnection() method of the URL class returns a URLConnection object with many methods that provide details about the connection to the URL, including the getOutputStream() method that allows you to send data to the URL.

Let's take a look at the UrlFileReader code example that reads data from a hello. txt file, which is a local file that we created in *Chapter 5, Strings, Input/Output, and Files*. The file contains only one line: Hello!; here is the code that reads it:

```
try {
    ClassLoader classLoader =
                Thread.currentThread().getContextClassLoader();
    String file = classLoader.getResource("hello.txt").getFile();
    URL url = new URL(file);
        try(InputStream is = url.openStream()){
            int data = is.read();
            while(data != -1){
                System.out.print((char) data); //prints: Hello!
                data = is.read();
            }
        }
} catch (Exception e) {
    e.printStackTrace();
}
```

In the preceding code, we used a class loader to access the resource (hello.txt file) and construct a URL that points to it.

The rest of the preceding code is opening an input stream of data from a file and prints the incoming bytes as characters. The result is shown in the inline comment.

Now, let's demonstrate how Java code can read data from the URL that points to a source on the internet. Let's call the Google search engine with the `Java` keyword (the `UrlSiteReader` class):

```java
try {
    URL url =
        new URL("https://www.google.com/search?q=Java&num=10");
    System.out.println(url.getPath()); //prints: /search
    System.out.println(url.getFile());
                            //prints: /search?q=Java&num=10
    URLConnection conn = url.openConnection();
    conn.setRequestProperty("Accept", "text/html");
    conn.setRequestProperty("Connection", "close");
    conn.setRequestProperty("Accept-Language", "en-US");
    conn.setRequestProperty("User-Agent", "Mozilla/5.0");
    try(InputStream is = conn.getInputStream();
     BufferedReader br =
            new BufferedReader(new InputStreamReader(is))){
        String line;
        while ((line = br.readLine()) != null){
            System.out.println(line);
        }
    }
} catch (Exception e) {
    e.printStackTrace();
}
```

Here, we came up with the `https://www.google.com/search?q=Java&num=10` URL and requested the properties after some research and experimentation. There is no guarantee that it will always work, so do not be surprised if it does not return the same data we describe. Besides, it is a live search, so the result may change at any time. When it works, Google will return pages of data.

The preceding code also demonstrates the difference in the values returned by the `getPath()` and `getFile()` methods. You can view the inline comments in the preceding code example.

In comparison to the example of using a file URL, the Google search example used the URLConnection object because we need to set the request header fields:

- Accept tells the server what type of content the caller requests (understands).

- Connection tells the server that the connection will be closed after the response is received.

- Accept-Language tells the server which language the caller requests (understands).

- User-Agent tells the server information about the caller; otherwise, the Google search engine (www.google.com) responds with a 403 (forbidden) HTTP code.

The remaining code in the preceding example just reads from the input stream of data (HTML code) coming from the URL and prints it, line by line. We captured the result (copied it from the screen), pasted it into the online HTML Formatter (https://jsonformatter.org/html-pretty-print), and ran it. The result is presented in the following screenshot and this may be different when you run it since Google functionality is evolving over time:

As you can see, it looks like a typical page with the search results, except there is no Google image in the upper-left corner with the returned HTML.

> **Important Note**
>
> Beware that if you execute this code many times, Google may block your IP address.

Similarly, it is possible to send (post) data to a URL. Here is an example code:

```
try {
    URL url = new URL("http://localhost:3333/something");
    URLConnection conn = url.openConnection();
    conn.setRequestProperty("Method", "POST");
    conn.setRequestProperty("User-Agent", "Java client");
    conn.setDoOutput(true);
    OutputStream os = conn.getOutputStream()
    OutputStreamWriter osw = new OutputStreamWriter(os);
    osw.write("parameter1=value1&parameter2=value2");
    osw.flush();
    osw.close();

    InputStream is = conn.getInputStream();
    BufferedReader br =
                new BufferedReader(new InputStreamReader(is));
    String line;
    while ((line = br.readLine()) != null) {
        System.out.println(line);
    }
    br.close();
} catch (Exception e) {
    e.printStackTrace();
}
```

The preceding code expects a server running on the `localhost` server on port 3333 that can process the `POST` request with the `"/something"` path. If the server does not check the method (is it `POST` or any other HTTP method) and it does not check the `User-Agent` value, there is no need to specify any of it. So, we comment the settings out and keep them there just to demonstrate how these, and similar, values can be set if required.

Notice that we used the `setDoOutput()` method to indicate that output has to be sent; by default, it is set to `false`. Then, we let the output stream send the query parameters to the server.

Another important aspect of the preceding code is that the output stream has to be closed before the input stream is opened. Otherwise, the content of the output stream will not be sent to the server. While we did it explicitly, a better way to do it is by using the try-with-resources block that guarantees the `close()` method is called, even if an exception was raised anywhere in the block.

Here is a better version of the preceding example (using try-with-resources blocks) in the `UrlPost` class:

```
try {
    URL url = new URL("http://localhost:3333/something");
    URLConnection conn = url.openConnection();
    conn.setRequestProperty("Method", "POST");
    conn.setRequestProperty("User-Agent", "Java client");
    conn.setDoOutput(true);
    try (OutputStream os = conn.getOutputStream();
        OutputStreamWriter osw = new OutputStreamWriter(os)) {
      osw.write("parameter1=value1&parameter2=value2");
      osw.flush();
    }
    try (InputStream is = conn.getInputStream();
        BufferedReader br =
                new BufferedReader(new InputStreamReader(is)))
{
        String line;
        while ((line = br.readLine()) != null) {
            System.out.println(line);  //prints server response
        }
    }
}
```

```
} catch (Exception ex) {
   ex.printStackTrace();
}
```

As you can see, this code calls the `localhost` server on port
`3333` with the URI `something`, and the query parameters
`parameter1=value1&parameter2=value2`. Then, it immediately reads the
response from the server, prints it, and exits.

To demonstrate how this example works, we also created a simple server that listens on
port `3333` of `localhost` and has a handler assigned to process all the requests that
come with the `"/something"` path (refer to the `Server` class in a separate project in
the `server` folder):

```java
private static Properties properties;
public static void main(String[] args){
   ClassLoader classLoader =
                 Thread.currentThread().getContextClassLoader();
   properties = Prop.getProperties(classLoader,
                                             "app.properties");
   int port = Prop.getInt(properties, "port");
   try {
      HttpServer server =
              HttpServer.create(new InetSocketAddress(port), 0);
      server.createContext("/something", new PostHandler());
      server.setExecutor(null);
      server.start();
   } catch (IOException e) {
       e.printStackTrace();
   }
}
private static class PostHandler implements HttpHandler {
    public void handle(HttpExchange exch) {
       System.out.println(exch.getRequestURI());
                                          //prints: /something
       System.out.println(exch.getHttpContext().getPath());
                                          //prints: /something
       try (InputStream is = exch.getRequestBody();
```

```
            BufferedReader in =
                new BufferedReader(new InputStreamReader(is));
            OutputStream os = exch.getResponseBody()){
            System.out.println("Received as body:");
            in.lines().forEach(l -> System.out.println(
                                                 "   " + l));

            String confirm = "Got it! Thanks.";
            exch.sendResponseHeaders(200, confirm.length());
            os.write(confirm.getBytes());
        } catch (Exception ex){
            ex.printStackTrace();
        }
    }
}
```

To implement the server, we used the classes of the com.sun.net.httpserver package that comes with the JDK in the Java class library. It starts listening on port 3333 and blocks until the request comes with the "/something" path.

We used the common library (a separate project in the common folder) that includes the Prop class, which provides access to the properties file in the resources folder. Please note how references to this library are included as the dependency in the pom.xml file of the server project:

```
<dependency>
    <groupId>com.packt.learnjava</groupId>
    <artifactId>common</artifactId>
    <version>1.0-SNAPSHOT</version>
</dependency>
```

The Prop class includes two methods:

```
public static Properties getProperties(ClassLoader classLoader,
                                       String fileName)
{
    String file = classLoader.getResource(fileName).getFile();
    Properties properties = new Properties();
    try(FileInputStream fis = new FileInputStream(file)){
```

```
            properties.load(fis);
        } catch (Exception ex) {
            ex.printStackTrace();
        }
        return properties;
    }


    public static int getInt(Properties properties, String name){
        return Integer.parseInt(properties.getProperty(name));
    }
```

We use the `Prop` class to get the value of the `port` property from the `app.properties` file of the `server` project.

The implementation of the internal `PostHandler` class in the `server` project demonstrates that the URL comes without parameters: we print the URI and the path. They both have the same `"/something"` value; the parameters come from the body of the request.

After the request is processed, the server sends back the message *"Got it! Thanks."* Let's see how it works; we first run the server. This can be done in two ways:

1. Just run the `main()` method in the `Server` class using your IDE. Click any of the two green triangles, as shown in the following screenshot:

```
    public class Server {
        ± Nick Samoylov
        public static void main(String[] args){
            ClassLoader classLoader = Thread.currentThread().getCo
            Properties properties = Prop.getProperties(classLoader
            int port = Prop.getInt(properties,  name: "port");
```

2. Go to the `common` folder and execute the following Maven command:

    `mvn clean package`

    This command compiles code in the `common` project and builds the `common-1.0-SNAPSHOT.jar` file in the `target` subdirectory. Now, repeat the same command in the `server` folder and run the following command in the `server` folder:

    ```
    java -cp target/server-1.0-SNAPSHOT.jar:            \
            ../common/target/common-1.0-SNAPSHOT.jar \
            com.packt.learnjava.network.http.Server
    ```

As you can see, the preceding command lists on the classpath two `.jar` files (those we have just built) and runs the `main()` method of the `Server` class.

The outcome is that the server is waiting for the client code to call it.

Now, let's execute the client (the `UrlPost` class). We can also do this in two ways:

1. Just run the `main()` method in the `UrlPost` class using your IDE. Click any of the two green triangles, as shown in the following screenshot:

2. Go to the `examples` folder and execute the following Maven command:

    `mvn clean package`

    This command compiles code in the `examples` project and builds a `examples-1.0-SNAPSHOT.jar` file in the `target` subdirectory.

    Now, run the following command in the `examples` folder:

    ```
    java -cp target/examples-1.0-SNAPSHOT.jar:            \
            com.packt.learnjava.ch11_network.UrlPost
    ```

After running the client code, observe the following output on the server-side screen:

```
/something
/something
Received as body:
    parameter1=value1&parameter2=value2
```

As you can see, the server received the parameters (or any other message for that matter) successfully. Now it can parse them and use them as needed.

If we look at the client-side screen, we will see the following output:

```
Got it! Thanks.

Process finished with exit code 0
```

This means that the client received the message from the server and exited as expected.

Notice that the server in our example does not exit automatically and has to be stopped manually.

Other methods of the URL and URLConnection classes allow you to set/get other properties and can be used for more dynamic management of the client-server communication. There is also the HttpUrlConnection class (and other classes) in the java.net package that simplifies and enhances URL-based communication. You can read the online documentation of the java.net package to understand the available options better.

Using the HTTP 2 Client API

The HTTP Client API was introduced with Java 9 as an incubating API in the jdk.incubator.http package. In Java 11, it was standardized and moved to the java.net.http package. It is a far richer and easier-to-use alternative to the URLConnection API. In addition to all the basic connection-related functionality, it provides non-blocking (asynchronous) requests and responses using CompletableFuture and supports both HTTP 1.1 and HTTP 2.

HTTP 2 added the following new capabilities to the HTTP protocol:

- The ability to send data in a binary format rather than textual format; the binary format is more efficient for parsing, more compact, and less susceptible to various errors.

- It is fully multiplexed, thus allowing multiple requests and responses to be sent concurrently using just one connection.

- It uses header compression, thus reducing the overhead.

- It allows a server to push a response to the client's cache if the client indicates that it supports HTTP 2.

The package contains the following classes:

- HttpClient: This is used to send requests and receive responses both synchronously and asynchronously. An instance can be created using the static newHttpClient() method with default settings or by using the HttpClient. Builder class (returned by the static newBuilder() method) that allows you to customize the client configuration. Once created, the instance is immutable and can be used multiple times.

- HttpRequest: This creates and represents an HTTP request with the destination URI, headers, and other related information. An instance can be created using the HttpRequest.Builder class (returned by the static newBuilder() method). Once created, the instance is immutable and can be sent multiple times.

- HttpRequest.BodyPublisher: This publishes a body (for the POST, PUT, and DELETE methods) from a certain source, such as a string, a file, an input stream, or a byte array.

- HttpResponse: This represents an HTTP response received by the client after an HTTP request has been sent. It contains the origin URI, headers, message body, and other related information. Once created, the instance can be queried multiple times.

- HttpResponse.BodyHandler: This is a functional interface that accepts the response and returns an instance of HttpResponse.BodySubscriber that can process the response body.

- HttpResponse.BodySubscriber: This receives the response body (its bytes) and transforms it into a string, a file, or a type.

The `HttpRequest.BodyPublishers`, `HttpResponse.BodyHandlers`, and `HttpResponse.BodySubscribers` classes are factory classes that create instances of the corresponding classes. For example, the `BodyHandlers.ofString()` method creates a `BodyHandler` instance that processes the response body bytes as a string, while the `BodyHandlers.ofFile()` method creates a `BodyHandler` instance that saves the response body in a file.

You can read the online documentation of the `java.net.http` package to learn more about these and other related classes and interfaces. Next, we will take a look at and discuss some examples of HTTP API usage.

Blocking HTTP requests

The following code is an example of a simple HTTP client that sends a GET request to an HTTP server (see the `get()` method in the `HttpClientDemo` class):

```
HttpClient httpClient = HttpClient.newBuilder()
        .version(HttpClient.Version.HTTP_2) // default
        .build();
HttpRequest req = HttpRequest.newBuilder()
        .uri(URI.create("http://localhost:3333/something"))
        .GET()          // default
        .build();
try {
  HttpResponse<String> resp =
            httpClient.send(req, BodyHandlers.ofString());
  System.out.println("Response: " +
                resp.statusCode() + " : " + resp.body());
} catch (Exception ex) {
    ex.printStackTrace();
}
```

We created a builder to configure an `HttpClient` instance. However, since we used default settings only, we can do it with the same result, as follows:

```
HttpClient httpClient = HttpClient.newHttpClient();
```

To demonstrate the client's functionality, we will use the same `Server` class that we used already. As a reminder, this is how it processes the client's request and responds with `"Got it! Thanks.":`

```
try (InputStream is = exch.getRequestBody();
     BufferedReader in =
            new BufferedReader(new InputStreamReader(is));
     OutputStream os = exch.getResponseBody()){
  System.out.println("Received as body:");
  in.lines().forEach(l -> System.out.println("   " + l));

  String confirm = "Got it! Thanks.";
  exch.sendResponseHeaders(200, confirm.length());
  os.write(confirm.getBytes());
  System.out.println();
} catch (Exception ex){
   ex.printStackTrace();
}
```

If we launch this server and run the preceding client's code, the server prints the following message on its screen:

```
Received as body:
```

The client did not send a message because it used the HTTP GET method. Nevertheless, the server responds, and the client's screen shows the following message:

```
Response: 200 : Got it! Thanks.
```

The `send()` method of the `HttpClient` class is blocked until the response has come back from the server.

Using the HTTP POST, PUT, or DELETE methods produces similar results; let's run the following code now (see the `post()` method in the `HttpClientDemo` class):

```
HttpClient httpClient = HttpClient.newBuilder()
        .version(Version.HTTP_2)  // default
        .build();
```

```
HttpRequest req = HttpRequest.newBuilder()
        .uri(URI.create("http://localhost:3333/something"))
        .POST(BodyPublishers.ofString("Hi there!"))
        .build();
try {
    HttpResponse<String> resp =
                httpClient.send(req, BodyHandlers.ofString());
    System.out.println("Response: " +
                    resp.statusCode() + " : " + resp.body());
} catch (Exception ex) {
    ex.printStackTrace();
}
```

As you can see, this time the client posts the message `Hi there!` and the server's screen shows the following:

```
Received as body:
     Hi there!
```

The `send()` method of the `HttpClient` class is blocked until the same response has come back from the server:

```
Response: 200 : Got it! Thanks.
```

So far, the demonstrated functionality was not much different from the URL-based communication that we saw in the previous section. Now we are going to use the `HttpClient` methods that are not available in the URL streams.

Non-blocking (asynchronous) HTTP requests

The `sendAsync()` method of the `HttpClient` class allows you to send a message to a server without blocking. To demonstrate how it works, we will execute the following code (see the `getAsync1()` method in the `HttpClientDemo` class):

```
HttpClient httpClient = HttpClient.newHttpClient();
HttpRequest req = HttpRequest.newBuilder()
        .uri(URI.create("http://localhost:3333/something"))
        .GET()    // default
        .build();
```

```
CompletableFuture<Void> cf = httpClient
        .sendAsync(req, BodyHandlers.ofString())
        .thenAccept(resp -> System.out.println("Response: " +
                    resp.statusCode() + " : " + resp.body()));
System.out.println("The request was sent asynchronously...");
try {
    System.out.println("CompletableFuture get: " +
                               cf.get(5, TimeUnit.SECONDS));
} catch (Exception ex) {
    ex.printStackTrace();
}
System.out.println("Exit the client...");
```

In comparison to the example with the send() method (which returns the HttpResponse object), the sendAsync() method returns an instance of the CompletableFuture<HttpResponse> class. If you read the documentation of the CompletableFuture<T> class, you will see that it implements the java.util. concurrent.CompletionStage interface, which provides many methods that can be chained and allows you to set various functions to process the response.

To give you an idea, here is the list of the methods declared in the CompletionStage interface: acceptEither, acceptEitherAsync, acceptEitherAsync, applyToEither, applyToEitherAsync, applyToEitherAsync, handle, handleAsync, handleAsync, runAfterBoth, runAfterBothAsync, runAfterBothAsync, runAfterEither, runAfterEitherAsync, runAfterEitherAsync, thenAccept, thenAcceptAsync, thenAcceptAsync, thenAcceptBoth, thenAcceptBothAsync, thenAcceptBothAsync, thenApply, thenApplyAsync, thenApplyAsync, thenCombine, thenCombineAsync, thenCombineAsync, thenCompose, thenComposeAsync, thenComposeAsync, thenRun, thenRunAsync, thenRunAsync, whenComplete, whenCompleteAsync, and whenCompleteAsync.

We will talk about functions and how they can be passed as parameters in *Chapter 13, Functional Programming*. For now, we will just mention that the resp -> System. out.println("Response: " + resp.statusCode() + " : " + resp. body()) construction represents the same functionality as the following method:

```
void method(HttpResponse resp){
    System.out.println("Response: " +
```

```
                            resp.statusCode() + " : " + resp.body());
  }
```

The `thenAccept()` method applies the passed-in functionality to the result returned by the previous method of the chain.

After the `CompletableFuture<Void>` instance is returned, the preceding code prints `The request was sent asynchronously...` message and blocks it on the `get()` method of the `CompletableFuture<Void>` object. This method has an overloaded version `get(long timeout, TimeUnit unit)`, with two parameters, `TimeUnit unit` and `long timeout`, which specify the number of the units, indicating how long the method should wait for the task that is represented by the `CompletableFuture<Void>` object to complete. In our case, the task is to send a message to the server and to get back the response (and process it using the function provided). If the task is not completed in the allotted time, the `get()` method is interrupted (and the stack trace is printed in the `catch` block).

The `Exit the client...` message should appear on the screen either in 5 seconds (in our case) or after the `get()` method returns.

If we run the client, the server's screen shows the following message again with the blocking HTTP `GET` request:

```
Received as body:
```

The client's screen displays the following message:

```
The request was sent asynchronously...
Response: 200 : Got it! Thanks.
CompletableFuture get: null
Exit the client...
```

As you can see, **The request was sent asynchronously...** message appears before the response came back from the server. This is the point of an asynchronous call; the request to the server was sent and the client is free to continue to do anything else. The passed-in function will be applied to the server response. At the same time, you can pass the `CompletableFuture<Void>` object around and call it at any time to get the result. In our case, the result is `void`, so the `get()` method simply indicates that the task was completed.

We know that the server returns the message, and so we can take advantage of it by using another method of the `CompletionStage` interface. We have chosen the `thenApply()` method, which accepts a function that returns a value:

```
CompletableFuture<String> cf = httpClient
                .sendAsync(req, BodyHandlers.ofString())
                .thenApply(resp -> "Server responded: " +
                . resp.body());
```

Now, the `get()` method returns the value produced by the `resp -> "Server responded: " + resp.body()` function, so it should return the server message body; let's run this code (see the `getAsync2()` method in the `HttpClientDemo` class) and see the result:

```
The request was sent asynchronously...
CompletableFuture get: Server responded: Got it! Thanks.
Exit the client...
```

Now, the `get()` method returns the server's message as expected, and it is presented by the function and passed as a parameter to the `thenApply()` method.

Similarly, we can use the HTTP POST, PUT, or DELETE methods for sending a message (see the `postAsync()` method in the `HttpClientDemo` class):

```
HttpClient httpClient = HttpClient.newHttpClient();
HttpRequest req = HttpRequest.newBuilder()
        .uri(URI.create("http://localhost:3333/something"))
        .POST(BodyPublishers.ofString("Hi there!"))
        .build();
CompletableFuture<String> cf = httpClient
        .sendAsync(req, BodyHandlers.ofString())
        .thenApply(resp -> "Server responded: " + resp.body());
System.out.println("The request was sent asynchronously...");
try {
    System.out.println("CompletableFuture get: " +
                                cf.get(5, TimeUnit.SECONDS));
} catch (Exception ex) {
    ex.printStackTrace();
}
System.out.println("Exit the client...");
```

The only difference from the previous example is that the server now displays the received client's message:

```
Received as body:
Hi there!
```

The client's screen displays the same message as in the case of the GET method:

```
The request was sent asynchronously...
CompletableFuture get: Server responded: Got it! Thanks.
Exit the client...
```

The advantage of asynchronous requests is that they can be sent quickly and without needing to wait for each of them to complete. The HTTP 2 protocol supports it by multiplexing; for example, let's send three requests as follows (see the postAsyncMultiple() method in the HttpClientDemo class):

```
HttpClient httpClient = HttpClient.newHttpClient();
List<CompletableFuture<String>> cfs = new ArrayList<>();
List<String> nums = List.of("1", "2", "3");
for(String num: nums){
    HttpRequest req = HttpRequest.newBuilder()
            .uri(URI.create("http://localhost:3333/something"))
            .POST(BodyPublishers.ofString("Hi! My name is "
                                        + num + "."))
            .build();
    CompletableFuture<String> cf = httpClient
            .sendAsync(req, BodyHandlers.ofString())
            .thenApply(rsp -> "Server responded to msg " + num +
                ": " + rsp.statusCode() + " : " + rsp.body());
    cfs.add(cf);
}
System.out.println("The requests were sent asynchronously...");
try {
    for(CompletableFuture<String> cf: cfs){
        System.out.println("CompletableFuture get: " +
                                    cf.get(5, TimeUnit.SECONDS));
    }
```

```
  } catch (Exception ex) {
      ex.printStackTrace();
  }
  System.out.println("Exit the client...");
```

The server's screen shows the following messages:

```
Received as body:
   Hi! My name is 2.

Received as body:
   Hi! My name is 3.

Received as body:
   Hi! My name is 1.
```

Notice the arbitrary sequence of the incoming requests; this is because the client uses a pool of Executors.newCachedThreadPool() threads to send the messages. Each message is sent by a different thread, and the pool has its own logic for using the pool members (threads). If the number of messages is large, or if each of them consumes a significant amount of memory, it may be beneficial to limit the number of threads run concurrently.

The HttpClient.Builder class allows you to specify the pool that is used for acquiring the threads that send the messages (see the postAsyncMultipleCustomPool() method in the HttpClientDemo class):

```
ExecutorService pool = Executors.newFixedThreadPool(2);
HttpClient httpClient = HttpClient.newBuilder().executor(pool).
build();
List<CompletableFuture<String>> cfs = new ArrayList<>();
List<String> nums = List.of("1", "2", "3");
for(String num: nums){
    HttpRequest req = HttpRequest.newBuilder()
            .uri(URI.create("http://localhost:3333/something"))
            .POST(BodyPublishers.ofString("Hi! My name is "
                                              + num + "."))
            .build();
    CompletableFuture<String> cf = httpClient
            .sendAsync(req, BodyHandlers.ofString())
            .thenApply(rsp -> "Server responded to msg " + num +
```

```
                           ": " + rsp.statusCode() + " : " + rsp.body());
        cfs.add(cf);
    }
    System.out.println("The requests were sent asynchronously...");
    try {
        for(CompletableFuture<String> cf: cfs){
            System.out.println("CompletableFuture get: " +
                                        cf.get(5, TimeUnit.SECONDS));
        }
    } catch (Exception ex) {
        ex.printStackTrace();
    }
    System.out.println("Exit the client...");
```

If we run the preceding code, the results will be the same, but the client will use only two threads to send messages. The performance may be a bit slower (in comparison to the previous example) as the number of messages grows. So, as is often the case in a software system design, you need to balance the amount of memory used and the performance.

Similar to the executor, several other objects can be set on the HttpClient object to configure the connection to handle authentication, request redirection, cookie management, and more.

Server push functionality

The second (after multiplexing) significant advantage of the HTTP 2 protocol over HTTP 1.1 is allowing the server to push the response into the client's cache if the client indicates that it supports HTTP 2. Here is the client code that takes advantage of this feature (see the push() method in the HttpClientDemo class):

```
HttpClient httpClient = HttpClient.newHttpClient();
HttpRequest req = HttpRequest.newBuilder()
    .uri(URI.create("http://localhost:3333/something"))
    .GET()
    .build();
CompletableFuture cf = httpClient
    .sendAsync(req, BodyHandlers.ofString(),
        (PushPromiseHandler) HttpClientDemo::applyPushPromise);
```

```
System.out.println("The request was sent asynchronously...");
try {
    System.out.println("CompletableFuture get: " +
                                    cf.get(5, TimeUnit.SECONDS));
} catch (Exception ex) {
    ex.printStackTrace();
}
System.out.println("Exit the client...");
```

Notice the third parameter of the sendAsync() method. It is a function that handles the push response if one comes from the server. It is up to the client developer to decide how to implement this function; here is one possible example:

```
void applyPushPromise(HttpRequest initReq, HttpRequest pushReq,
  Function<BodyHandler, CompletableFuture<HttpResponse>>
  acceptor){
  CompletableFuture<Void> cf =
   acceptor.apply(BodyHandlers.ofString())
  .thenAccept(resp -> System.out.println("Got pushed response "
                                    + resp.uri()));
  try {
        System.out.println("Pushed completableFuture get: " +
                                cf.get(1, TimeUnit.SECONDS));
  } catch (Exception ex) {
        ex.printStackTrace();
  }
  System.out.println("Exit the applyPushPromise function...");
}
```

This implementation of the function does not do much. It just prints out the URI of the push origin. But, if necessary, it can be used to receive the resources from the server (for example, images that support the provided HTML) without requesting them. This solution saves the round-trip request-response model and shortens the time of the page loading. It also can be used for updating the information on the page.

You can find many code examples of a server that sends push requests; all major browsers support this feature too.

WebSocket support

HTTP is based on the request-response model. A client requests a resource, and the server provides a response to this request. As we have demonstrated several times, the client initiates the communication. Without it, the server cannot send anything to the client. To get over this limitation, the idea was first introduced as a TCP connection in the HTML5 specification and, in 2008, the first version of the WebSocket protocol was designed.

It provides a full-duplex communication channel between the client and the server. After the connection is established, the server can send a message to the client at any time. Together with JavaScript and HTML5, the WebSocket protocol support allows web applications to present a far more dynamic user interface.

The WebSocket protocol specification defines WebSocket (`ws`) and WebSocket Secure (`wss`) as two schemes that are used for unencrypted and encrypted connections, respectively. The protocol does not support fragmentation, but allows all the other URI components described in the *URL syntax* section.

All the classes that support the WebSocket protocol for a client are located in the `java. net` package. To create a client, we need to implement the `WebSocket.Listener` interface, which has the following methods:

- `onText()`: Invoked when textual data has been received
- `onBinary()`: Invoked when binary data has been received
- `onPing()`: Invoked when a ping message has been received
- `onPong()`: Invoked when a pong message has been received
- `onError()`: Invoked when an error has happened
- `onClose()`: Invoked when a close message has been received

All the methods of this interface are `default`. This means that you do not need to implement all of them, but only those that the client requires for a particular task (see the private `WsClient` class in the `HttpClientDemo` class):

```
class WsClient implements WebSocket.Listener {
    @Override
    public void onOpen(WebSocket webSocket) {
```

```
            System.out.println("Connection established.");
            webSocket.sendText("Some message", true);
            Listener.super.onOpen(webSocket);
        }
        @Override
        public CompletionStage onText(WebSocket webSocket,
                                CharSequence data, boolean last) {
            System.out.println("Method onText() got data: " +
                                                            data);
            if(!webSocket.isOutputClosed()) {
                webSocket.sendText("Another message", true);
            }
            return Listener.super.onText(webSocket, data, last);
        }
        @Override
        public CompletionStage onClose(WebSocket webSocket,
                                int statusCode, String reason) {
            System.out.println("Closed with status " +
                            statusCode + ", reason: " + reason);
            return Listener.super.onClose(webSocket,
                                            statusCode, reason);
        }
    }
}
```

A server can be implemented in a similar way, but server implementation is beyond the scope of this book. To demonstrate the preceding client code, we are going to use a WebSocket server provided by the echo.websocket.events website. It allows a WebSocket connection and sends the received message back; such a server is typically called an **echo server**.

We expect that our client will send the message after the connection is established. Then, it will receive (the same) message from the server, display it, and send back another message, and so on, until it is closed. The following code invokes the client that we created (see the webSocket() method in the HttpClientDemo class):

```
HttpClient httpClient = HttpClient.newHttpClient();
WebSocket webSocket = httpClient.newWebSocketBuilder()
    .buildAsync(URI.create("ws://echo.websocket.events"),
```

```
                                new WsClient()).join();
System.out.println("The WebSocket was created and ran
asynchronously.");
try {
    TimeUnit.MILLISECONDS.sleep(200);
} catch (InterruptedException ex) {
    ex.printStackTrace();
}
webSocket.sendClose(WebSocket.NORMAL_CLOSURE, "Normal closure")
        .thenRun(() -> System.out.println("Close is sent."));
```

The preceding code creates a `WebSocket` object using the `WebSocket.Builder` class. The `buildAsync()` method returns the `CompletableFuture` object. The `join()` method of the `CompletableFuture` class returns the result value when complete, or throws an exception. If an exception is not generated, then, as we mentioned already, the `WebSocket` communication continues until either side sends a **Close** message. That is why our client waits for 200 milliseconds, and then sends the **Close** message and exits. If we run this code, we will see the following messages:

```
Connection established.
The WebSocket was created and ran asynchronously.
Method onText() got data: echo.websocket.events sponsored by Lob.com
Method onText() got data: Some message
Method onText() got data: Another message
Method onText() got data: Another message
Method onText() got data: Another message
Close is sent.
```

As you can see, the client behaves as expected. To finish our discussion, we would like to mention the fact that all modern web browsers support the WebSocket protocol.

Summary

In this chapter, you were presented with a description of the most popular network protocols: UDP, TCP/IP, and WebSocket. The discussion was illustrated with code examples using JCL. We also reviewed URL-based communication and the latest Java HTTP 2 Client API.

Now you can use the basic internet protocols to send/receive messages between client and server, and also know how to create a server as a separate project and how to create and use a common shared library.

The next chapter provides an overview of Java GUI technologies and demonstrates a GUI application using JavaFX, including code examples with control elements, charts, CSS, FXML, HTML, media, and various other effects. You will learn how to use JavaFX to create a GUI application.

Quiz

1. Name five network protocols of the application layer.
2. Name two network protocols of the transport layer.
3. Which Java package includes classes that support the HTTP protocol?
4. Which protocol is based on exchanging datagrams?
5. Can a datagram be sent to the IP address where there is no server running?
6. Which Java package contains classes that support UDP and TCP protocols?
7. What does TCP stand for?
8. What is common between the TCP and TCP/IP protocols?
9. How is a TCP session identified?
10. Name one principal difference between the functionality of `ServerSocket` and `Socket`.
11. Which is faster, TCP or UDP?
12. Which is more reliable, TCP or UDP?
13. Name three TCP-based protocols.
14. Which of the following are the components of a URI? Select all that apply:

    A. Fragment

    B. Title

    C. Authority

    D. Query

15. What is the difference between `scheme` and `protocol`?
16. What is the difference between a URI and a URL?

17. What does the following code print?

```
URL url = new URL("http://www.java.com/
something?par=42");
  System.out.print(url.getPath());
  System.out.println(url.getFile());
```

18. Name two new features that HTTP 2 has that HTTP 1.1 does not.

19. What is the fully qualified name of the `HttpClient` class?

20. What is the fully qualified name of the `WebSocket` class?

21. What is the difference between `HttpClient.newBuilder().build()` and `HttpClient.newHttpClient()`?

22. What is the fully qualified name of the `CompletableFuture` class?

12
Java GUI Programming

This chapter provides an overview of Java **graphical user interface** (**GUI**) technologies and demonstrates how the JavaFX kit can be used to create a GUI application. The latest versions of JavaFX not only provide many helpful features but also allow for the preserving and embedding of legacy implementations and styles.

In a certain respect, the GUI is the most important part of an application. It directly interacts with the user. If the GUI is inconvenient, unappealing to the eye, or confusing, even the best backend solution might not persuade the user to use this application. By contrast, a well-thought-out, intuitive, and nicely designed GUI helps to retain users, even if the application does not do the job as well as its competitors.

The agenda of the chapter requires us to cover the following topics:

- Java GUI technologies
- JavaFX fundamentals
- HelloWorld with JavaFX
- Control elements
- Charts
- Applying CSS

- Using FXML
- Embedding HTML
- Playing media
- Adding effects

By the end of the chapter, you will be able to create a user interface using Java GUI technologies, as well as creating and using a user interface project as a standalone application.

Technical requirements

To be able to execute the code examples provided in this chapter, you will need the following:

- A computer with a Microsoft Windows, Apple macOS, or Linux operating system
- Java SE version 17 or later
- An IDE or code editor of your choice

The instructions for how to set up Java SE and the IntelliJ IDEA editor were provided in *Chapter 1, Getting Started with Java 17*. The files with the code examples for this chapter are available on GitHub at `https://github.com/PacktPublishing/Learn-Java-17-Programming.git` in the `examples/src/main/java/com/packt/learnjava/ch12_gui` folder and in the `gui` folder, which contains a standalone GUI application.

Java GUI technologies

The name **Java Foundation Classes** (**JFC**) may be a source of much confusion. It implies *the classes that are at the foundation of Java*, while, in fact, JFC includes only classes and interfaces related to the GUI. To be precise, JFC is a collection of three frameworks: the **Abstract Window Toolkit** (**AWT**), Swing, and Java 2D.

JFC is part of **Java Class Library** (**JCL**), although the name JFC came into being only in 1997, while AWT was part of JCL from the very beginning. At that time, Netscape developed a GUI library called **Internet Foundation Classes** (**IFC**), and Microsoft created **Application Foundation Classes** (**AFC**) for GUI development, too. So, when Sun Microsystems and Netscape decided to form a new GUI library, they inherited the word *Foundation* and created JFC. The Swing framework took over the Java GUI programming from AWT and was successfully used for almost two decades.

A new GUI programming toolkit, JavaFX, was added to JCL in Java 8. It was removed from JCL in Java 11, and since then, has resided as an open source project supported by the company Gluon as a downloadable module in addition to the JDK. JavaFX uses a somewhat different approach to GUI programming than AWT and Swing. It presents a more consistent and simpler design and has a good chance of being a winning Java GUI-programming toolkit.

JavaFX fundamentals

Cities such as New York, London, Paris, and Moscow have many theaters, and people who live there cannot avoid hearing about new plays and productions released almost every week. It makes them inevitably familiar with theater terminology, in which the terms *stage*, *scene*, and *event* are probably used most often. These three terms are at the foundation of a JavaFX application structure, too.

The top-level container in JavaFX that holds all other components is represented by the `javafx.stage.Stage` class. So, you can say that, in the JavaFX application, everything happens on a *stage*. From a user perspective, it is a display area or window where all the controls and components perform their actions (like actors in a theater). And, similar to the actors in a theater, they do it in the context of a *scene*, represented by the `javafx.scene.Scene` class. So, a JavaFX application, like a play in a theater, is composed of `Scene` objects presented inside the `Stage` object one at a time. Each `Scene` object contains a graph that defines the positions of the scene actors (called **nodes**) in JavaFX: controls, layouts, groups, shapes, and so on. Each of them extends the abstract class, `javafx.scene.Node`.

Some of the nodes' controls are associated with *events*: a button clicked or a checkbox checked, for example. These events can be processed by the event handler associated with the corresponding control element.

The main class of a JavaFX application has to extend the abstract `java.application.Application` class, which has several life cycle methods. We list them in the sequence of the invocation: `launch()`, `init()`, `notifyPreloader()`, `start()`, and `stop()`. It looks like quite a few to remember. But, most probably, you need to implement only one method, `start()`, where the actual GUI is constructed and executed. Nevertheless, we will review all the life cycle methods just for completeness:

- `static void launch(Class<? extends Application> appClass, String... args)`: This launches the application and is often called the `main` method; it does not return until `Platform.exit()` is called or all the application windows close. The `appClass` parameter must be a public subclass of the `Application` class with a public no-argument constructor.

- `static void launch(String... args)`: The same as the preceding method, assuming that the public subclass of the `Application` class is the immediately enclosing class. This is the method most often used to launch the JavaFX application; we are going to use it in our examples, too.

- `void init()`: This method is called after the `Application` class is loaded; it is typically used for some kind of resource initialization. The default implementation does nothing, and we are not going to use it.

- `void notifyPreloader(Preloader.PreloaderNotification info)`: This can be used to show progress when the initialization takes a long time; we are not going to use it.

- `abstract void start(Stage primaryStage)`: The method we are going to implement. It is called after the `init()` method returns, and after the system is ready to do the main job. The `primaryStage` parameter is the stage where the application is going to present its scenes.

- `void stop()`: This is called when the application should stop, and can be used to release the resources. The default implementation does nothing, and we are not going to use it.

The API of the JavaFX toolkit can be found online (`https://openjfx.io/javadoc/18//`). As of the time of writing, the latest version is *18*. Oracle provides extensive documentation and code examples, too (`https://docs.oracle.com/javafx/2//`). The documentation includes the description and user manual of Scene Builder (a development tool that provides a visual layout environment and lets you quickly design a user interface for the JavaFX application without writing any code). This tool may be useful for creating a complex and intricate GUI, and many people use it all the time. In this book though, we will concentrate on JavaFX code writing without using this tool.

To be able to do it, the following are the necessary steps:

1. Add the following dependency to the `pom.xml` file:

```
<dependency>
    <groupId>org.openjfx</groupId>
    <artifactId>javafx-controls</artifactId>
    <version>18</version>
</dependency>
<dependency>
    <groupId>org.openjfx</groupId>
```

```
    <artifactId>javafx-fxml</artifactId>
    <version>18</version>
</dependency>
```

2. Download the JavaFX SDK for your OS from `https://gluonhq.com/products/javafx/` (the `openjfx-18_osx-x64_bin-sdk.zip` file, as of the time of writing) and unzip it in any directory.

3. Assuming you have unzipped the JavaFX SDK into the `/path/javafx-sdk/` folder, add the following options to the Java command, which will launch your JavaFX application on the Linux platform:

    ```
    --module-path /path/javafx-sdk/lib
    --add-modules=javafx.controls,javafx.fxml
    ```

    On Windows, the same options look as follows:

    ```
    --module-path C:\path\javafx-sdk\lib
    --add-modules=javafx.controls,javafx.fxml
    ```

    `/path/JavaFX/` and `C:\path\JavaFX\` are the placeholders that you need to substitute with the actual path to the folder that contains the JavaFX SDK.

Assuming that the application's main class is `HelloWorld`, in the case of IntelliJ, enter the preceding options into the `VM options` field, as follows (the example is for Linux):

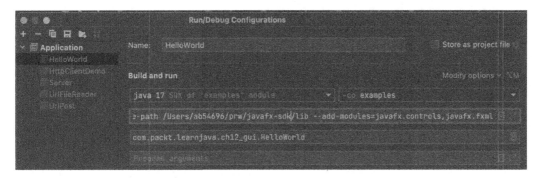

These options have to be added to `Run/Debug Configurations` of the `HelloWorld`, `BlendEffect`, and `OtherEffects` classes of the `ch12_gui` package of the source code. If you prefer a different IDE or have a different OS, you can find recommendations on how to set it in the `openjfx.io` documentation (`https://openjfx.io/openjfx-docs`).

To run the `HelloWorld`, `BlendEffect`, and `OtherEffects` classes from the command line, use the following commands on the Linux platform in the project root directory (where the `pom.xml` file is located):

```
mvn clean package

java --module-path /path/javafx-sdk/lib                      \
     --add-modules=javafx.controls,javafx.fxml               \
     -cp target/examples-1.0-SNAPSHOT.jar:target/libs/* \
      com.packt.learnjava.ch12_gui.HelloWorld

java --module-path /path/javafx-sdk/lib                      \
     --add-modules=javafx.controls,javafx.fxml               \
     -cp target/examples-1.0-SNAPSHOT.jar:target/libs/*  \
      com.packt.learnjava.ch12_gui.BlendEffect

java --module-path /path/javafx-sdk/lib                      \
     --add-modules=javafx.controls,javafx.fxml               \
     -cp target/examples-1.0-SNAPSHOT.jar:target/libs/*  \
      com.packt.learnjava.ch12_gui.OtherEffects
```

On Windows, the same commands look as follows:

```
mvn clean package

java --module-path C:\path\javafx-sdk\lib                    \
     --add-modules=javafx.controls,javafx.fxml               \
     -cp target\examples-1.0-SNAPSHOT.jar;target\libs\*  \
      com.packt.learnjava.ch12_gui.HelloWorld

java --module-path C:\path\javafx-sdk\lib                    \
     --add-modules=javafx.controls,javafx.fxml               \
     -cp target\examples-1.0-SNAPSHOT.jar;target\libs\*   \
      com.packt.learnjava.ch12_gui.BlendEffect

java --module-path C:\path\javafx-sdk\lib                    \
     --add-modules=javafx.controls,javafx.fxml               \
```

```
    -cp target\examples-1.0-SNAPSHOT.jar;target\libs\*       \
    com.packt.learnjava.ch12_gui.OtherEffects
```

Each of the `HelloWorld`, `BlendEffect`, and `OtherEffects` classes has two
`start()` methods: `start1()` and `start2()`. After you run the class once, rename
`start()` as `start1()`, and `start1()` as `start()`, and run the preceding commands
again. Then, rename `start()` as `start2()`, and `start2()` as `start()`, and run the
previous commands yet again. And so on, until all the `start()` methods are executed.
This way you will see the results of all the examples in this chapter.

This concludes the high-level presentation of JavaFX. With that, we move to the most
exciting (for any programmer) part: writing code.

HelloWorld with JavaFX

Here is the `HelloWorld` JavaFX application that shows the `Hello, World!` and
`Exit` text:

```java
import javafx.application.Application;
import javafx.application.Platform;
import javafx.scene.control.Button;
import javafx.scene.layout.Pane;
import javafx.scene.text.Text;
import javafx.scene.Scene;
import javafx.stage.Stage;

public class HelloWorld extends Application {
  public static void main(String... args) {
      launch(args);
  }
  @Override
  public void start(Stage primaryStage) {
    Text txt = new Text("Hello, world!");
    txt.relocate(135, 40);

    Button btn = new Button("Exit");
    btn.relocate(155, 80);
    btn.setOnAction(e:> {
        System.out.println("Bye! See you later!");
```

```
            Platform.exit();
    });


    Pane pane = new Pane();
    pane.getChildren().addAll(txt, btn);


    primaryStage
        .setTitle("The primary stage (top-level container)");
    primaryStage.onCloseRequestProperty()
        .setValue(e:> System.out.println(
                                    "Bye! See you later!"));
    primaryStage.setScene(new Scene(pane, 350, 150));
    primaryStage.show();
    }

}
```

As you can see, the application is launched by calling the `Application.`
`launch(String... args)` static method. The `start(Stage primaryStage)`
method creates a `Text` node with the message **Hello, World!** located at the absolute
position 135 (horizontally) and 40 (vertically). Then, it creates another node, `Button`,
with the text `Exit` located at the absolute position 155 (horizontally) and 80 (vertically).
The action, assigned to `Button` (when it is clicked), prints **Bye! See you later!** on
a screen and forces the application to exit using the `Platform.exit()` method. These
two nodes are added as children to the layout pane, which allows absolute positioning.

The `Stage` object is assigned the title of `The primary stage (top-level`
`container)`. It is also assigned an action on clicking the close-the-window symbol (the
x button) in the window's upper corner: top left on the Linux system and top right on the
Windows system.

While creating actions, we have used a Lambda expression, which we are going to discuss
in *Chapter 13, Functional Programming*.

The created layout pane is set on a `Scene` object. The scene size is set to 350 pixels
horizontally and 150 pixels vertically. The `Scene` object is placed on the stage. Then,
the stage is displayed by calling the `show()` method.

If we run the preceding application (the `start()` method of the `HellowWorld` class), the following window will pop up:

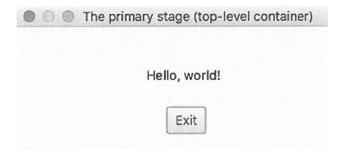

Clicking on the **Exit** button results in the expected message being displayed:

```
Bye! See you later!
```

But, if you need to do something else after the **x** button is clicked and the window closes, you can add an implementation of the `stop()` method to the `HelloWorld` class. In this example it looks as follows:

```
@Override
public void stop(){
    System.out.println(
                "Doing what has to be done before closing");}
```

If you click the **x** button or the **Exit** button, the display will show the following:

```
Bye! See you later!
Doing what has to be done before closing
```

This example gives you a sense of how JavaFX works. From now on, while reviewing the JavaFX capabilities, we will present only the code in the `start()` method.

The toolkit has a huge number of packages, each with many classes, and each class having many methods. We won't be able to discuss all of them. Instead, we are going to present just an overview of all the major areas of the JavaFX functionality in the most simple and straightforward way we can.

Control elements

The **control elements** are included in the `javafx.scene.control` package (`https://openjfx.io/javadoc/11/javafx.controls/javafx/scene/control/package-summary.html`). There are more than 80 of them, including a button, text field, checkbox, label, menu, progress bar, and scroll bar, to name a few. As we have mentioned already, each control element is a subclass of `Node` that has more than 200 methods. So, you can imagine how rich and fine-tuned a GUI can be when built using JavaFX. However, the scope of this book allows us to cover only a few elements and their methods.

We have already implemented a button in the example in the preceding section. Let's now use a label and a text field to create a simple form with input fields (first name, last name, and age) and a **Submit** button. We will build it in steps. All the following code snippets are sequential sections of another `start()` method in the `HelloWorld` class (rename the previous `start()` method `start1()`, and rename the `start2()` method `start()`).

First, let's create controls:

```
Text txt = new Text("Fill the form and click Submit");
TextField tfFirstName = new TextField();
TextField tfLastName = new TextField();
TextField tfAge = new TextField();
Button btn = new Button("Submit");
btn.setOnAction(e:> action(tfFirstName, tfLastName, tfAge));
```

As you can guess, the text will be used as the form instructions. The rest is quite straightforward and looks very similar to what we have seen in the `HelloWorld` example. `action()` is a function implemented as the following method:

```
void action(TextField tfFirstName,
                TextField tfLastName, TextField tfAge ) {
    String fn = tfFirstName.getText();
    String ln = tfLastName.getText();
    String age = tfAge.getText();
    int a = 42;
    try {
        a = Integer.parseInt(age);
    } catch (Exception ex){}
    fn = fn.isBlank() ? "Nick" : fn;
    ln = ln.isBlank() ? "Samoylov" : ln;
```

```
        System.out.println("Hello, "+fn+" "+ln + ", age " +
                                                a + "!");

    Platform.exit();
}
```

This function accepts three parameters (the `javafx.scene.control.TextField` objects), then gets the submitted input values and just prints them. The code makes sure that there are always some default values available for printing, and that entering a non-numeric value of `age` does not break the application.

With the controls and action in place, we then put them into a grid layout using the `javafx.scene.layout.GridPane` class:

```
GridPane grid = new GridPane();
grid.setAlignment(Pos.CENTER);
grid.setHgap(15);
grid.setVgap(5);
grid.setPadding(new Insets(20, 20, 20, 20));
```

The `GridPane` layout pane has rows and columns that form cells in which the nodes can be set. Nodes can span columns and rows. The `setAlignment()` method sets the position of the grid to the center of a scene (the default position is the top left of a scene). The `setHgap()` and `setVgap()` methods set the spacing (in pixels) between the columns (horizontally) and rows (vertically). The `setPadding()` method adds some space along the borders of the grid pane. The `Insets()` object sets the values (in pixels) in the order of top, right, bottom, and left.

Now, we are going to place the created nodes in the corresponding cells (arranged in two columns):

```
int i = 0;
grid.add(txt,    1, i++, 2, 1);
GridPane.setHalignment(txt, HPos.CENTER);
grid.addRow(i++, new Label("First Name"), tfFirstName);
grid.addRow(i++, new Label("Last Name"),  tfLastName);
grid.addRow(i++, new Label("Age"), tfAge);
grid.add(btn,    1, i);
GridPane.setHalignment(btn, HPos.CENTER);
```

The add() method accepts either three or five parameters:

- The node, the column index, and the row index
- The node, the column index, the row index, how many columns to span, and how many rows to span

The columns and rows indices start from 0.

The setHalignment() method sets the position of the node in the cell. The HPos enum has values LEFT, RIGHT, and CENTER. The addRow(int i, Node... nodes) method accepts the row index and the varargs of nodes. We use it to place the Label and TextField objects.

The rest of the start() method is very similar to the HelloWorld example (only the title and size have changed):

```
primaryStage.setTitle("Simple form example");
primaryStage.onCloseRequestProperty()
    .setValue(e -> System.out.println("Bye! See you later!"));
primaryStage.setScene(new Scene(grid, 300, 200));
primaryStage.show();
```

If we run the newly implemented start() method, the result will be as follows:

We can fill the data as follows, for example:

After you click the **Submit** button, the following message is displayed and the application exits:

```
Hello, John Grant, age 35!
```

To help visualize the layout, especially in the case of a more complex design, you can use the `setGridLinesVisible(boolean v)` grid method to make the grid lines visible. It helps to see how the cells are aligned. We can add (uncomment) the following line to our example:

```
grid.setGridLinesVisible(true);
```

We run it again, and the result will be as follows:

As you can see, the layout is now outlined explicitly, which helps us to visualize the design.

The `javafx.scene.layout` package includes 24 layout classes such as `Pane` (we saw it in the `HelloWorld` example), `StackPane` (allows us to overlay nodes), `FlowPane` (allows the positions of nodes to flow as the size of the window changes), and `AnchorPane` (preserves the nodes' position relative to their anchor point), to name a few. The `VBox` layout will be demonstrated in the next section, *Charts*.

Charts

JavaFX provides the following chart components for data visualization in the `javafx.scene.chart` package:

- `LineChart`: Adds a line between the data points in a series. Typically used to present the trends over time.

- `AreaChart`: Similar to `LineChart`, but fills the area between the line that connects the data points and the axis. Typically used for comparing cumulated totals over time.

- `BarChart`: Presents data as rectangular bars. Used for visualization of discrete data.

- `PieChart`: Presents a circle divided into segments (filled with different colors), each segment representing a value as a proportion of the total. We will demonstrate it in this section.

- `BubbleChart`: Presents data as two-dimensional oval shapes called bubbles, which allow presenting three parameters.

- `ScatterChart`: Presents the data points in a series as is. Useful to identify the presence of a clustering (data correlation).

The following example (the `start3()` method of the `HellowWorld` class) demonstrates how the result of testing can be presented as a pie chart. Each segment represents the number of tests succeeded, failed, or ignored:

```
Text txt = new Text("Test results:");

PieChart pc = new PieChart();
pc.getData().add(new PieChart.Data("Succeed", 143));
pc.getData().add(new PieChart.Data("Failed" ,  12));
pc.getData().add(new PieChart.Data("Ignored",  18));
```

```
VBox vb = new VBox(txt, pc);
vb.setAlignment(Pos.CENTER);
vb.setPadding(new Insets(10, 10, 10, 10));

primaryStage.setTitle("A chart example");
primaryStage.onCloseRequestProperty()
        .setValue(e:> System.out.println("Bye! See you later!"));
primaryStage.setScene(new Scene(vb, 300, 300));
primaryStage.show();
```

We have created two nodes—Text and PieChart—and placed them in the cells of the VBox layout, which sets them in a column, one above another. We have added the padding of 10 pixels around the edges of the VBox pane. Notice that VBox extends the Node and Pane classes, as other panes do, too. We have also positioned the pane in the center of the scene using the setAlignment() method. The rest is the same as all other previous examples, except the scene title and size.

If we run this example (rename the previous start() method start2(), and rename the start3() method start()), the result will be as follows:

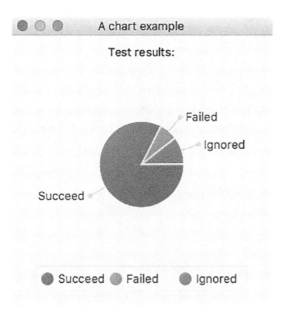

The PieChart class, as well as any other chart, has several other methods that can be useful for presenting more complex and dynamic data in a user-friendly manner.

Now, let's discuss how you can enrich the look and feel of your application by using the power of **Cascading Style Sheets** (CSS).

Applying CSS

By default, JavaFX uses the style sheet that comes with the distribution JAR file. To override the default style, you can add a style sheet to the scene using the `getStylesheets()` method:

```
scene.getStylesheets().add("/mystyle.css");
```

The `mystyle.css` file has to be placed in the `src/main/resources` folder. Let's do it, and add the `mystyle.css` file with the following content to the `HelloWorld` example:

```
#text-hello {
   :fx-font-size: 20px;
   -fx-font-family: "Arial";
   -fx-fill: red;
}
.button {
   -fx-text-fill: white;
   -fx-background-color: slateblue;
}
```

As you can see, we would like to style the `Button` node and the `Text` node that has a `text-hello` ID in a certain way. We also have to modify the `HelloWorld` example by adding the ID to the `Text` element and the style sheet file to the scene (the `start4()` method):

```
Text txt = new Text("Hello, world!");
txt.setId("text-hello");
txt.relocate(115, 40);

Button btn = new Button("Exit");
btn.relocate(155, 80);
btn.setOnAction(e -> {
    System.out.println("Bye! See you later!");
    Platform.exit();
```

```
});

Pane pane = new Pane();
pane.getChildren().addAll(txt, btn);

Scene scene = new Scene(pane, 350, 150);
scene.getStylesheets().add("/mystyle.css");

primaryStage.setTitle("The primary stage (top-level
container)");
primaryStage.onCloseRequestProperty()
    .setValue(e -> System.out.println("\nBye! See you later!"));
primaryStage.setScene(scene);
primaryStage.show();
```

If we run this code (rename the previous `start()` method `start3()` and rename the `start4()` method `start()`), the result will be as follows:

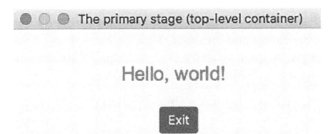

Alternatively, an inline style can be set on any node that will be used to overwrite the file style sheet, default or not. Let's add (uncomment) the following line to the latest version of the `HelloWorld` example:

```
btn.setStyle("-fx-text-fill: white; -fx-background-color:
red;");
```

If we run the example again, the result will be as follows:

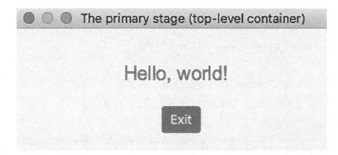

Look through the JavaFX CSS reference guide (`https://docs.oracle.com/javafx/2/api/javafx/scene/doc-files/cssref.html`) to get an idea of the variety and possible options for custom styling.

Now, let's discuss an alternative way of building a user interface for an FX application, without writing Java code, by using **FX Markup Language** (**FXML**).

Using FXML

FXML is an XML-based language that allows building a user interface and maintaining it independently of the application (business) logic (as far as the look and feel are concerned, or other presentation-related changes). Using FXML, you can design a user interface without even writing one line of Java code.

FXML does not have a schema, but its capabilities reflect the API of the JavaFX objects used to build a scene. This means you can use the API documentation to understand what tags and attributes are allowed in the FXML structure. Most of the time, JavaFX classes can be used as tags and their properties as attributes.

In addition to the FXML file (the view), the controller (Java class) can be used for processing the model and organizing the page flow. The model consists of domain objects managed by the view and the controller. It also allows using all the power of CSS styling and JavaScript. But, in this book, we will be able to demonstrate only the basic FXML capabilities. The rest you can find in the FXML introduction (`https://docs.oracle.com/javafx/2/api/javafx/fxml/doc-files/introduction_to_fxml.html`) and many good tutorials available online.

To demonstrate FXML usage, we are going to reproduce the simple form we created in the *Control elements* section and then enhance it by adding the page flow. Here's how our form, with first name, last name, and age, can be expressed in FXML:

```
<?xml version="1.0" encoding="UTF-8"?>
<?import javafx.scene.Scene?>
<?import javafx.geometry.Insets?>
<?import javafx.scene.text.Text?>
<?import javafx.scene.control.Label?>
<?import javafx.scene.control.Button?>
<?import javafx.scene.layout.GridPane?>
<?import javafx.scene.control.TextField?>
<Scene fx:controller="com.packt.learnjava.ch12_gui.
HelloWorldController"
        xmlns:fx="http://javafx.com/fxml"
        width="350" height="200">
    <GridPane alignment="center" hgap="15" vgap="5">
        <padding>
            <Insets top="20" right="20" bottom="20" left="20"/>
        </padding>
        <Text id="textFill" text="Fill the form and click
          Submit" GridPane.rowIndex="0" GridPane.columnSpan="2">
            <GridPane.halignment>center</GridPane.halignment>
        </Text>
        <Label text="First name"
                GridPane.columnIndex="0" GridPane.rowIndex="1"/>
        <TextField fx:id="tfFirstName"
                GridPane.columnIndex="1" GridPane.rowIndex="1"/>
        <Label text="Last name"
                GridPane.columnIndex="0" GridPane.rowIndex="2"/>
        <TextField fx:id="tfLastName"
                GridPane.columnIndex="1" GridPane.rowIndex="2"/>
        <Label text="Age"
                GridPane.columnIndex="0" GridPane.rowIndex="3"/>
        <TextField fx:id="tfAge"
                GridPane.columnIndex="1" GridPane.rowIndex="3"/>
        <Button text="Submit"
```

```
                    GridPane.columnIndex="1" GridPane.rowIndex="4"
                    onAction="#submitClicked">
                <GridPane.halignment>center</GridPane.halignment>
            </Button>
        </GridPane>
    </Scene>
```

As you can see, it expresses the desired scene structure, familiar to you already, and specifies the controller class, HelloWorldController, which we are going to see shortly. As we have mentioned already, the tags match the class names we have been using to construct the same GUI with Java only. We put the preceding FXML code (as the helloWorld.fxml file) into the resources folder.

Now, let's look at the start5() method (rename it start()) of the HelloWorld class that uses the helloWorld.fxml file:

```
try {
    ClassLoader classLoader =
                Thread.currentThread().getContextClassLoader();
    String file =
            classLoader.getResource("helloWorld.fxml").getFile();
    FXMLLoader lder = new FXMLLoader();
    lder.setLocation(new URL("file:" + file));
    Scene scene = lder.load();

    primaryStage.setTitle("Simple form example");
    primaryStage.setScene(scene);
    primaryStage.onCloseRequestProperty().setValue(e ->
                    System.out.println("\nBye! See you later!"));
    primaryStage.show();
} catch (Exception ex){
    ex.printStackTrace();
}
```

The start() method just loads the helloWorld.fxml file and sets the stage, the latter being done exactly as in our previous examples.

Now, let's look at the `HelloWorldController` class. If need be, we could launch the application having only the following:

```
public class HelloWorldController {
    @FXML
    protected void submitClicked(ActionEvent e) {
    }
}
```

The form would be presented, but the button click would do nothing. That is what we meant while talking about the user interface development independent of the application logic. Notice the @FXML annotation. It binds the method and properties to the FXML tags using their IDs. Here is how the full controller implementation looks:

```
@FXML
private TextField tfFirstName;
@FXML
private TextField tfLastName;
@FXML
private TextField tfAge;
@FXML
protected void submitClicked(ActionEvent e) {
    String fn = tfFirstName.getText();
    String ln = tfLastName.getText();
    String age = tfAge.getText();
    int a = 42;
    try {
        a = Integer.parseInt(age);
    } catch (Exception ex) {
    }
    fn = fn.isBlank() ? "Nick" : fn;
    ln = ln.isBlank() ? "Samoylov" : ln;
    String hello = "Hello, " + fn + " " + ln + ", age " +
                                                        a + "!";
    System.out.println(hello);
    Platform.exit();
}
```

It should look very familiar to you for the most part. The only difference is that we refer to the fields and their values not directly (as previously), but using binding marked with the @FXML annotation. If we run the HelloWorld class now (don't forget to rename the start5() method as start()), the page appearance and behavior will be exactly the same as we described in the *Control elements* section:

If the **x** button in the upper corner is clicked, the following output appears on the screen:

```
Bye! See you later!
Doing what has to be done before closing

Process finished with exit code 0
```

If the **Submit** button is clicked, the output shows the following message:

```
Hello, Joe Blow, age 23!
Doing what has to be done before closing

Process finished with exit code 0
```

Now, let's look at the standalone GUI application with two pages implemented as a separate project in the gui folder:

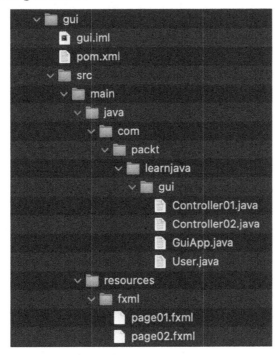

As you can see, this application consists of the main GuiApp class, two Controller classes, the User class, and two pages (the .fxml files). Let us start from the .fxml files. To make it simple, the page01.fxml file has almost exactly the same content as the helloWorld.fxml file described in the preceding section. The only difference is that it refers to the Controller01 class, which has the start() method implemented exactly as the start5() method described previously, too. The main GuiApp class looks very simple:

```
public class GuiApp extends Application {
    public static void main(String... args) {
        launch(args);
    }
    @Override
    public void stop(){
        System.out.println("Doing what has to be done...");
    }
    public void start(Stage primaryStage) {
```

```
            Controller01.start(primaryStage);
    }
}
```

As you can see, it just invokes the `start()` method in the `Controller01` class, which in turn displays the familiar page to your form:

After the form is filled and the **Submit** button is clicked, the submitted values are processed in the `Controller01` class and then passed to the `Controller02` class, using the `submitClicked()` method of the `Controller01` class:

```
@FXML
protected void submitClicked(ActionEvent e) {
    String fn = tfFirstName.getText();
    String ln = tfLastName.getText();
    String age = tfAge.getText();
    int a = 42;
    try {
        a = Integer.parseInt(age);
    } catch (Exception ex) {
    }
    fn = fn.isBlank() ? "Nick" : fn;
    ln = ln.isBlank() ? "Samoylov" : ln;
    Controller02.goToPage2(new User(a, fn, ln));

    Node source = (Node) e.getSource();
```

```
            Stage stage = (Stage) source.getScene().getWindow();
            stage.close();
        }
```

The `Controller02.goToPage2()` method looks as follows:

```java
public static void goToPage2(User user) {
    try {
        ClassLoader classLoader =
                Thread.currentThread().getContextClassLoader();
        String file = classLoader.getResource("fxml" +
                    File.separator + "page02.fxml").getFile();
        FXMLLoader loader = new FXMLLoader();
        loader.setLocation(new URL("file:" + file));
        Scene scene = loader.load();

        Controller02 c = loader.getController();
        String hello = "Hello, " + user.getFirstName() + " " +
            user.getLastName() + ", age " + user.getAge() + "!";
        c.textHello.setText(hello);

        Stage primaryStage = new Stage();
        primaryStage.setTitle("Second page of GUI App");
        primaryStage.setScene(scene);
        primaryStage.onCloseRequestProperty()
            .setValue(e -> {
                            System.out.println("\nBye!");
                            Platform.exit();
                        });
        primaryStage.show();
    } catch (Exception ex) {
        ex.printStackTrace();
    }
}
```

The second page just presents the received data. Here is how its FXML looks (the `page2.fxml` file):

```xml
<?xml version="1.0" encoding="UTF-8"?>
<?import javafx.scene.Scene?>
<?import javafx.geometry.Insets?>
<?import javafx.scene.text.Text?>
<?import javafx.scene.layout.GridPane?>


<Scene fx:controller="com.packt.lernjava.gui.Controller02"
       xmlns:fx="http://javafx.com/fxml"
       width="350" height="150">
    <GridPane alignment="center" hgap="15" vgap="5">
        <padding>
            <Insets top="20" right="20" bottom="20" left="20"/>
        </padding>
        <Text fx:id="textHello"
              GridPane.rowIndex="0" GridPane.columnSpan="2">
            <GridPane.halignment>center</GridPane.halignment>
        </Text>
        <Text id="textDo" text="Do what has to be done here"
              GridPane.rowIndex="1" GridPane.columnSpan="2">
            <GridPane.halignment>center</GridPane.halignment>
        </Text>
    </GridPane>
</Scene>
```

As you can see, the page has only two read-only `Text` fields. The first one (with `id="textHello"`) shows the data passed from the previous page. The second just shows the message, `Do what has to be done here`. This is not very sophisticated, but it demonstrates how the flow of data and pages can be organized.

If we execute the `GuiApp` class, we will see the familiar form and can fill it with data:

After we click the **Submit** button, this window will be closed and the new one will appear:

Now, we can click the **x** button in the upper-left corner (or in the upper-right corner on Windows) and see the following message:

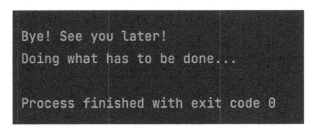

The `stop()` method worked as expected.

With that, we conclude our presentation of FXML and move to the next topic of adding HTML to the JavaFX application.

Embedding HTML

To add HTML to JavaFX is easy. All you have to do is to use the `javafx.scene.web.`
`WebView` class, which provides a window where the added HTML is rendered similar to
how it happens in a browser. The `WebView` class uses WebKit, the open source browser
engine, and thus supports full browsing functionality.

Like all other JavaFX components, the `WebView` class extends the `Node` class and can
be treated in the Java code as such. In addition, it has its own properties and methods
that allow adjusting the browser window to the encompassing application by setting
the window size (maximum, minimum, and preferred height and width), font scale,
zoom rate, adding CSS, enabling the context (right-click) menu, and similar. The
`getEngine()` method returns a `javafx.scene.web.WebEngine` object associated
with it. It provides the ability to load HTML pages, navigate them, apply different styles
to the loaded pages, access their browsing history and the document model, and execute
JavaScript.

To start using the `javafx.scene.web` package, two steps have to be taken first:

1. Add the following dependency to the `pom.xml` file:

   ```
   <dependency>
       <groupId>org.openjfx</groupId>
       <artifactId>javafx-web</artifactId>
       <version>11.0.2</version>
   </dependency>
   ```

   The version of `javafx-web` typically stays abreast with the Java version, but at the
   time of writing, version 12 of `javafx-web` has not yet been released, so we are
   using the latest available version, *11.0.2*.

2. Since `javafx-web` uses the `com.sun.*` packages, which have been removed
   from Java 9 (`https://docs.oracle.com/javase/9/migrate/toc.`
   `htm#JSMIG-GUID-F7696E02-A1FB-4D5A-B1F2-89E7007D4096`), to access
   the `com.sun.*` packages from Java 9+, set the following VM options in addition
   to `--module-path` and `--add-modules`, described in the JavaFX fundamentals
   section in `Run/Debug Configuration` of the `HtmlWebView` class of the
   `ch12_gui` package (for Windows, change the slash sign to the backward slash):

   ```
   --add-exports javafx.graphics/com.sun.javafx.
   sg.prism=ALL-UNNAMED
   --add-exports javafx.graphics/com.sun.javafx.scene=ALL-
   ```

```
UNNAMED

--add-exports javafx.graphics/com.sun.javafx.util=ALL-
UNNAMED

--add-exports javafx.base/com.sun.javafx.logging=ALL-
UNNAMED

--add-exports javafx.graphics/com.sun.prism=ALL-UNNAMED

--add-exports javafx.graphics/com.sun.glass.ui=ALL-
UNNAMED

--add-exports javafx.graphics/com.sun.javafx.geom.
transform=ALL-UNNAMED

--add-exports javafx.graphics/com.sun.javafx.tk=ALL-
UNNAMED

--add-exports javafx.graphics/com.sun.glass.utils=ALL-
UNNAMED

--add-exports javafx.graphics/com.sun.javafx.font=ALL-
UNNAMED

--add-exports javafx.graphics/com.sun.javafx.
application=ALL-UNNAMED

--add-exports javafx.controls/com.sun.javafx.scene.
control=ALL-UNNAMED

--add-exports javafx.graphics/com.sun.javafx.scene.
input=ALL-UNNAMED

--add-exports javafx.graphics/com.sun.javafx.geom=ALL-
UNNAMED

--add-exports javafx.graphics/com.sun.prism.paint=ALL-
UNNAMED

--add-exports javafx.graphics/com.sun.scenario.
effect=ALL-UNNAMED

--add-exports javafx.graphics/com.sun.javafx.text=ALL-
UNNAMED

--add-exports javafx.graphics/com.sun.javafx.iio=ALL-
UNNAMED

--add-exports javafx.graphics/com.sun.scenario.effect.
impl.prism=ALL-UNNAMED

--add-exports javafx.graphics/com.sun.javafx.scene.
text=ALL-UNNAMED
```

3. To execute the `HtmlWebView` class from the command line, go to the `examples` folder and use the following command for Unix/Linux/macOS systems (don't forget to substitute `/path/JavaFX` with the actual path to the folder that contains the JavaFX SDK):

```
mvn clean package

java --module-path /path/javaFX/lib --add-modules=javafx.
controls,javafx.fxml --add-exports javafx.graphics/
com.sun.javafx.sg.prism=ALL-UNNAMED --add-exports
javafx.graphics/com.sun.javafx.scene=ALL-UNNAMED
--add-exports javafx.graphics/com.sun.javafx.util=ALL-
UNNAMED --add-exports javafx.base/com.sun.javafx.
logging=ALL-UNNAMED --add-exports javafx.graphics/com.
sun.prism=ALL-UNNAMED --add-exports javafx.graphics/
com.sun.glass.ui=ALL-UNNAMED --add-exports javafx.
graphics/com.sun.javafx.geom.transform=ALL-UNNAMED
--add-exports javafx.graphics/com.sun.javafx.tk=ALL-
UNNAMED --add-exports javafx.graphics/com.sun.glass.
utils=ALL-UNNAMED  --add-exports javafx.graphics/com.sun.
javafx.font=ALL-UNNAMED  --add-exports javafx.graphics/
com.sun.javafx.application=ALL-UNNAMED --add-exports
javafx.controls/com.sun.javafx.scene.control=ALL-
UNNAMED --add-exports javafx.graphics/com.sun.javafx.
scene.input=ALL-UNNAMED --add-exports javafx.graphics/
com.sun.javafx.geom=ALL-UNNAMED  --add-exports javafx.
graphics/com.sun.prism.paint=ALL-UNNAMED  --add-exports
javafx.graphics/com.sun.scenario.effect=ALL-UNNAMED
--add-exports javafx.graphics/com.sun.javafx.text=ALL-
UNNAMED --add-exports javafx.graphics/com.sun.javafx.
iio=ALL-UNNAMED --add-exports javafx.graphics/com.sun.
scenario.effect.impl.prism=ALL-UNNAMED --add-exports
javafx.graphics/com.sun.javafx.scene.text=ALL-
UNNAMED  -cp target/examples-1.0-SNAPSHOT.jar com.packt.
learnjava.ch12_gui.HtmlWebView
```

4. On Windows, the same command looks as follows (don't forget to substitute `C:\ path\JavaFX` with the actual path to the folder that contains the JavaFX SDK):

```
mvn clean package

java --module-path C:\path\JavaFX\lib
--add-modules=javafx.controls,javafx.fxml --add-exports
javafx.graphics\com.sun.javafx.sg.prism=ALL-UNNAMED
```

```
--add-exports javafx.graphics\com.sun.javafx.scene=ALL-
UNNAMED --add-exports javafx.graphics\com.sun.javafx.
util=ALL-UNNAMED --add-exports javafx.base\com.sun.
javafx=ALL-UNNAMED --add-exports javafx.base\com.sun.
javafx.logging=ALL-UNNAMED --add-exports javafx.graphics\
com.sun.prism=ALL-UNNAMED --add-exports javafx.graphics\
com.sun.glass.ui=ALL-UNNAMED --add-exports javafx.
graphics\com.sun.javafx.geom.transform=ALL-UNNAMED
--add-exports javafx.graphics\com.sun.javafx.tk=ALL-
UNNAMED --add-exports javafx.graphics\com.sun.glass.
utils=ALL-UNNAMED  --add-exports javafx.graphics\com.sun.
javafx.font=ALL-UNNAMED  --add-exports javafx.graphics\
com.sun.javafx.application=ALL-UNNAMED --add-exports
javafx.controls\com.sun.javafx.scene.control=ALL-
UNNAMED --add-exports javafx.graphics\com.sun.javafx.
scene.input=ALL-UNNAMED --add-exports javafx.graphics\
com.sun.javafx.geom=ALL-UNNAMED  --add-exports javafx.
graphics\com.sun.prism.paint=ALL-UNNAMED  --add-exports
javafx.graphics\com.sun.scenario.effect=ALL-UNNAMED
--add-exports javafx.graphics\com.sun.javafx.text=ALL-
UNNAMED --add-exports javafx.graphics\com.sun.javafx.
iio=ALL-UNNAMED --add-exports javafx.graphics\com.sun.
scenario.effect.impl.prism=ALL-UNNAMED --add-exports
javafx.graphics\com.sun.javafx.scene.text=ALL-
UNNAMED  -cp target\examples-1.0-SNAPSHOT.jar com.packt.
learnjava.ch12_gui.HtmlWebView
```

The `HtmlWebView` class contains several `start()` methods too. Rename and execute them one by one, as described in the *JavaFX fundamentals* section.

Let's look at a few examples now. We create a new application, `HtmlWebView`, and set VM options for it with the VM options (`--module-path`, `--add-modules`, and `--add-exports`) we have described. Now, we can write and execute code that uses the `WebView` class.

First, here is how simple HTML can be added to the JavaFX application (the `start()` method in the `HtmlWebView` class):

```
WebView wv = new WebView();
WebEngine we = wv.getEngine();
String html =
        "<html><center><h2>Hello, world!</h2></center></html>";
we.loadContent(html, "text/html");
Scene scene = new Scene(wv, 200, 60);
```

```
primaryStage.setTitle("My HTML page");
primaryStage.setScene(scene);
primaryStage.onCloseRequestProperty()
        .setValue(e -> System.out.println("Bye! See you later!"));
primaryStage.show();
```

The preceding code creates a `WebView` object, gets the `WebEngine` object from it, uses the acquired `WebEngine` object to load the HTML, sets the `WebView` object on the scene, and configures the stage. The `loadContent()` method accepts two strings: the content and its mime type. The content string can be constructed in the code or created from reading the `.html` file.

If we run the `HtmlWebView` class, the result will be as follows:

Hello, world!

If necessary, you can show other JavaFX nodes along with the `WebView` object in the same window. For example, let's add a `Text` node above the embedded HTML (the `start2()` method in the `HtmlWebView` class):

```
Text txt = new Text("Below is the embedded HTML:");

WebView wv = new WebView();
WebEngine we = wv.getEngine();
String html =
        "<html><center><h2>Hello, world!</h2></center></html>";
we.loadContent(html, "text/html");

VBox vb = new VBox(txt, wv);
vb.setSpacing(10);
vb.setAlignment(Pos.CENTER);
vb.setPadding(new Insets(10, 10, 10, 10));

Scene scene = new Scene(vb, 300, 120);
primaryStage.setScene(scene);
primaryStage.setTitle("JavaFX with embedded HTML");
primaryStage.onCloseRequestProperty()
```

```
        .setValue(e -> System.out.println("Bye! See you later!"));
  primaryStage.show();
```

As you can see, the WebView object is not set on the scene directly, but on the layout object instead, along with a txt object. Then, the layout object is set on the scene. The result of the preceding code is as follows:

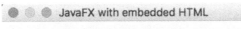

Below is the embedded HTML:

Hello, world!

With a more complex HTML page, it is possible to load it from the file directly, using the load() method. To demonstrate this approach, let's create a form.html file in the resources folder with the following content:

```
<!DOCTYPE html>
<html lang="en">
<head>
    <meta charset="UTF-8">
    <title>The Form</title>
</head>
<body>
<form action="http://someServer:port/formHandler"
method="post">
  <table>
    <tr>
      <td><label for="firstName">First name:</label></td>
      <td><input type="text" id="firstName" name="firstName">
      </td>
    </tr>
    <tr>
      <td><label for="lastName">Last name:</label></td>
      <td><input type="text" id="lastName" name="lastName">
      </td>
    </tr>
```

```
        <tr>
          <td><label for="age">Age:</label></td>
          <td><input type="text" id="age" name="age"></td>
        </tr>
        <tr>
          <td></td>
          <td align="center">
              <button id="submit" name="submit">Submit</button>
          </td>
        </tr>
      </table>
  </form>
  </body>
  </html>
```

This HTML presents a form similar to the one we have created in the *Using FXML* section. After the **Submit** button is clicked, the form data is posted to a server to the \formHandler URI (see the <form> HTML tag). To present this form inside a JavaFX application, the following code can be used:

```
ClassLoader classLoader =
                Thread.currentThread().getContextClassLoader();
String file = classLoader.getResource("form.html").getFile();


Text txt = new Text("Fill the form and click Submit");


WebView wv = new WebView();
WebEngine we = wv.getEngine();
File f = new File(file);
we.load(f.toURI().toString());


VBox vb = new VBox(txt, wv);
vb.setSpacing(10);
vb.setAlignment(Pos.CENTER);
vb.setPadding(new Insets(10, 10, 10, 10));
```

```
Scene scene = new Scene(vb, 300, 200);

primaryStage.setScene(scene);
primaryStage.setTitle("JavaFX with embedded HTML");
primaryStage.onCloseRequestProperty()
        .setValue(e -> System.out.println("Bye! See you later!"));
primaryStage.show();
```

As you can see, the difference from our other examples is that we now use the `File` class and its `toURI()` method to access the HTML in the `src/main/resources/form.html` file directly, without converting the content to a string first. If you run the `start3()` method (renamed `start()`) of the `HtmlWebView` class, the result looks as follows:

This solution is useful when you need to send a request or post data from your JavaFX application. But, when the form you would like a user to fill is already available on the server, you can just load it from the URL.

For example, let's incorporate a Google search in the JavaFX application. We can do it by changing the parameter value of the `load()` method to the URL of the page we would like to load (the `start4()` method of the `HtmlWebView` class):

```
Text txt = new Text("Enjoy searching the Web!");

WebView wv = new WebView();
WebEngine we = wv.getEngine();
we.load("http://www.google.com");
```

```
VBox vb = new VBox(txt, wv);
vb.setSpacing(20);
vb.setAlignment(Pos.CENTER);
vb.setStyle("-fx-font-size: 20px;-fx-background-color:
lightblue;");
vb.setPadding(new Insets(10, 10, 10, 10));

Scene scene = new Scene(vb,750,500);
primaryStage.setScene(scene);
primaryStage.setTitle(
                "JavaFX with the window to another server");
primaryStage.onCloseRequestProperty()
    .setValue(e -> System.out.println("Bye! See you later!"));
primaryStage.show();
```

We have also added a style to the layout in order to increase the font and add color to the background, so we can see the outline of the area where the rendered HTML is embedded. When we run this example (don't forget to rename the start4() method start()), the following window appears:

In this window, you can perform all the aspects of a search that you usually access via the browser.

And, as we have mentioned already, you can zoom into the rendered page. For example, if we add the wv.setZoom(1.5) line to the preceding example, the result will be as follows:

Similarly, we can set the scale for the font and even the style from a file:

```
wv.setFontScale(1.5);
we.setUserStyleSheetLocation("mystyle.css");
```

Notice, though, that we set the font scale on the WebView object, while we set the style in the WebEngine object.

We can also access (and manipulate) the DOM object of the loaded page using the WebEngine class method, getDocument():

```
Document document = we.getDocument();
```

And, we can access the browsing history, get the current index, and move the history backward and forward:

```
WebHistory history = we.getHistory();
int currInd = history.getCurrentIndex();
history.go(-1);
history.go( 1);
```

For each entry of the history, we can extract its URL, title, or last-visited date:

```
WebHistory history = we.getHistory();
ObservableList<WebHistory.Entry> entries =
                                        history.getEntries();
for(WebHistory.Entry entry: entries){
    String url = entry.getUrl();
    String title = entry.getTitle();
    Date date = entry.getLastVisitedDate();
}
```

Read the documentation of the `WebView` and `WebEngine` classes to get more ideas about how you can take advantage of their functionality.

Playing media

Adding an image to a scene of the JavaFX application does not require the `com.sun.*` packages, so the `--add-export` VM options listed in the *Embedding HTML* section are not needed. But, it doesn't hurt to have them anyway, so leave the `--add-export` options in place if you have added them already.

An image can be included in a scene using the `javafx.scene.image.Image` and `javafx.scene.image.ImageView` classes. To demonstrate how to do it, we are going to use the Packt logo, `packt.png`, located in the `resources` folder. Here is the code that does it (the `start6()` method of the `HelloWorld` class):

```
ClassLoader classLoader =
            Thread.currentThread().getContextClassLoader();
String file = classLoader.getResource("packt.png").getFile();

Text txt = new Text("What a beautiful image!");

FileInputStream input = new FileInputStream(file);
Image image = new Image(input);
ImageView iv = new ImageView(image);

VBox vb = new VBox(txt, iv);
vb.setSpacing(20);
vb.setAlignment(Pos.CENTER);
```

```
vb.setPadding(new Insets(10, 10, 10, 10));

Scene scene = new Scene(vb, 300, 200);
primaryStage.setScene(scene);
primaryStage.setTitle("JavaFX with embedded HTML");
primaryStage.onCloseRequestProperty()
     .setValue(e -> System.out.println("Bye! See you later!"));
primaryStage.show();
```

If we run the preceding code, the result will be as follows:

What a beautiful image!

The currently supported image formats are BMP, GIF, JPEG, and PNG. Look through the API of the Image and ImageView classes (https://openjfx.io/javadoc/11/javafx.graphics/javafx/scene/image/package-summary.html) to learn the many ways an image can be formatted and adjusted as needed.

Now, let's see how to use other media files in a JavaFX application. Playing an audio or movie file requires the --add-export VM options listed in the *Embedding HTML* section.

The currently supported encodings are as follows:

- AAC: **Advanced Audio Coding** audio compression
- H.264/AVC: H.264/MPEG-4 Part 10 / **AVC (Advanced Video Coding)** video compression
- MP3: Raw MPEG-1, 2, and 2.5 audio; layers I, II, and III
- PCM: Uncompressed, raw audio samples

You can see a more detailed description of the supported protocols, media containers, and metadata tags in the API documentation (`https://openjfx.io/javadoc/11/ javafx.media/javafx/scene/media/package-summary.html`).

The following three classes allow constructing a media player that can be added to a scene:

```
javafx.scene.media.Media;
javafx.scene.media.MediaPlayer;
javafx.scene.media.MediaView;
```

The `Media` class represents the source of the media. The `MediaPlayer` class provides all the methods that control the media playback: `play()`, `stop()`, `pause()`, `setVolume()`, and similar. You can also specify the number of times that the media should be played. The `MediaView` class extends the `Node` class and can be added to a scene. It provides a view of the media being played by the media player and is responsible for a media appearance.

For the demonstration, let's run the `start5()` method of the `HtmlWebView` class, which plays the `jb.mp3` file located in the `resources` folder:

```
Text txt1 = new Text("What a beautiful music!");
Text txt2 =
    new Text("If you don't hear music, turn up the volume.");

ClassLoader classLoader =
                Thread.currentThread().getContextClassLoader();
String file = classLoader.getResource("jb.mp3").getFile();
File f = new File(file);
Media m = new Media(f.toURI().toString());
MediaPlayer mp = new MediaPlayer(m);
MediaView mv = new MediaView(mp);

VBox vb = new VBox(txt1, txt2, mv);
vb.setSpacing(20);
vb.setAlignment(Pos.CENTER);
vb.setPadding(new Insets(10, 10, 10, 10));

Scene scene = new Scene(vb, 350, 100);
primaryStage.setScene(scene);
primaryStage.setTitle("JavaFX with embedded media player");
```

```
primaryStage.onCloseRequestProperty()
        .setValue(e -> System.out.println("Bye! See you later!"));
primaryStage.show();


mp.play();
```

Notice how a Media object is constructed based on the source file. The MediaPlayer object is constructed based on the Media object and then set as a property of the MediaView class constructor. The MediaView object is set on the scene along with two Text objects. We use the VBox object to provide the layout. Finally, after the scene is set on the stage and the stage becomes visible (after the show() method completes), the play() method is invoked on the MediaPlayer object. By default, the media is played once.

If we execute this code, the following window will appear and the jb.m3 file will be played:

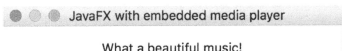

We could add controls to stop, pause, and adjust the volume, but it would require much more code, and that would go beyond the scope of this book. You can find a guide on how to do it in the Oracle online documentation (https://docs.oracle.com/javafx/2/media/jfxpub-media.htm).

A sea.mp4 movie file can be played similarly (the start6() method of the HtmlWebView class):

```
Text txt = new Text("What a beautiful movie!");


ClassLoader classLoader =
                Thread.currentThread().getContextClassLoader();
String file = classLoader.getResource("sea.mp4").getFile();
File f = new File(file);
Media m = new Media(f.toURI().toString());
MediaPlayer mp = new MediaPlayer(m);
MediaView mv = new MediaView(mp);
```

```
VBox vb = new VBox(txt, mv);
vb.setSpacing(20);
vb.setAlignment(Pos.CENTER);
vb.setPadding(new Insets(10, 10, 10, 10));

Scene scene = new Scene(vb, 650, 400);
primaryStage.setScene(scene);
primaryStage.setTitle("JavaFX with embedded media player");
primaryStage.onCloseRequestProperty()
     .setValue(e -> System.out.println("Bye! See you later!"));
primaryStage.show();

mp.play();
```

The only difference is the different sizes of the scene needed to show the full frame of this particular clip. We figured out the necessary size after several trial-and-error adjustments. Alternatively, we could use the `MediaView` methods (`autosize()`, `preserveRatioProperty()`, `setFitHeight()`, `setFitWidth()`, `fitWidthProperty()`, `fitHeightProperty()`, and similar) to adjust the size of the embedded window and to match the size of the scene automatically. If we execute the preceding example, the following window will pop up and play the clip:

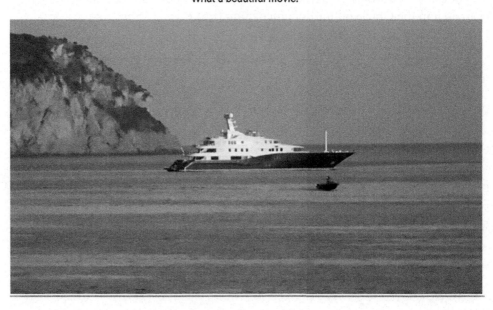

We can even combine playing both audio and video files in parallel, and thus provide a movie with a soundtrack (the start7() method of the HtmlWebView class):

```
Text txt1 = new Text("What a beautiful movie and sound!");
Text txt2 = new Text("If you don't hear music, turn up the
volume.");

ClassLoader classLoader =
                Thread.currentThread().getContextClassLoader();
String file = classLoader.getResource("jb.mp3").getFile();
File fs = new File(file);
Media ms = new Media(fs.toURI().toString());
MediaPlayer mps = new MediaPlayer(ms);
MediaView mvs = new MediaView(mps);

File fv =
     new File(classLoader.getResource("sea.mp4").getFile());
Media mv = new Media(fv.toURI().toString());
MediaPlayer mpv = new MediaPlayer(mv);
MediaView mvv = new MediaView(mpv);

VBox vb = new VBox(txt1, txt2, mvs, mvv);
vb.setSpacing(20);
vb.setAlignment(Pos.CENTER);
vb.setPadding(new Insets(10, 10, 10, 10));

Scene scene = new Scene(vb, 650, 500);
primaryStage.setScene(scene);
primaryStage.setTitle("JavaFX with embedded media player");
primaryStage.onCloseRequestProperty()
     .setValue(e -> System.out.println("Bye! See you later!"));
primaryStage.show();

mpv.play();
mps.play();
```

It is possible to do this because each of the players is executed by its own thread.

For more information about the `javafx.scene.media` package, read the API and the developer guide online, links to which are provided here:

- `https://openjfx.io/javadoc/11/javafx.media/javafx/scene/media/package-summary.html` for the API of the `javafx.scene.media` package

- `https://docs.oracle.com/javafx/2/media/jfxpub-media.htm` for a tutorial on the usage of the `javafx.scene.media` package

Adding effects

The `javafx.scene.effects` package contains many classes that allow the adding of various effects to the nodes:

- `Blend`: Combines pixels from two sources (typically images) using one of the pre-defined `BlendModes`

- `Bloom`: Makes the input image brighter, so that it appears to glow

- `BoxBlur`: Adds blur to an image

- `ColorAdjust`: Allows adjustments of hue, saturation, brightness, and contrast to an image

- `ColorInput`: Renders a rectangular region that is filled with the given paint

- `DisplacementMap`: Shifts each pixel by a specified distance

- `DropShadow`: Renders a shadow of the given content behind the content

- `GaussianBlur`: Adds blur using a particular (Gaussian) method

- `Glow`: Makes the input image appear to glow

- `InnerShadow`: Creates a shadow inside the frame

- `Lighting`: Simulates a light source shining on the content and makes flat objects look more realistic

- `MotionBlur`: Simulates the given content seen in motion

- `PerspectiveTransform`: Transforms the content as seen in a perspective

- `Reflection`: Renders a reflected version of the input below the actual input content

- `SepiaTone`: Produces a sepia tone effect, similar to the appearance of antique photographs

- `Shadow`: Creates a monochrome duplicate of the content with blurry edges

All effects share a parent, the `Effect` abstract class. The `Node` class has the `setEffect(Effect e)` method, which means that any of the effects can be added to any node. That is the main way of applying effects to the nodes—the actors that produce a scene on a stage (if we recall our analogy introduced at the beginning of this chapter).

The only exception is the `Blend` effect, which makes its usage more complicated than the use of other effects. In addition to using the `setEffect(Effect e)` method, some of the `Node` class children also have the `setBlendMode(BlendMode bm)` method, which allows regulating how the images blend into one another when they overlap. So, it is possible to set different blend effects in different ways that override one another and produce an unexpected result that may be difficult to debug. That is what makes the `Blend` effect usage more complicated, and that is why we are going to start the overview with how the `Blend` effect can be used.

Three aspects regulate the appearance of the area where two images overlap (we use two images in our examples to make it simpler, but, in practice, many images can overlap):

- **The value of the opacity property**: This defines how much can be seen through the image; the opacity value 0.0 means the image is fully transparent, while the opacity value 1.0 means nothing behind it can be seen.

- **The alpha value and strength of each color**: This defines the transparency of the color as a double value in the range 0.0-1.0 or 0-255.

- **The blending mode, defined by the BlendMode enum value**: Depending on the mode, opacity, and alpha value of each color, the result might also depend on the sequence in which the images were added to the scene; the first added image is called a bottom input, while the second of the overlapping images is called a top input. If the top input is completely opaque, the bottom input is hidden by the top input.

The resulting appearance of the overlapping area is calculated based on the opacity, the alpha values of the colors, the numeric values (strength) of the colors, and the blending mode, which can be one of the following:

- ADD: The color and alpha components from the top input are added to those from the bottom input.

- BLUE: The blue component of the bottom input is replaced with the blue component of the top input; the other color components are unaffected.

- COLOR_BURN: The inverse of the bottom input color components is divided by the top input color components, all of which is then inverted to produce the resulting color.

- COLOR_DODGE: The bottom input color components are divided by the inverse of the top input color components to produce the resulting color.

- DARKEN: The darker of the color components from the two inputs is selected to produce the resulting color.

- DIFFERENCE: The darker of the color components from the two inputs is subtracted from the lighter one to produce the resulting color.

- EXCLUSION: The color components from the two inputs are multiplied and doubled, and then subtracted from the sum of the bottom input color components, to produce the resulting color.

- GREEN: The green component of the bottom input is replaced with the green component of the top input; the other color components are unaffected.

- HARD_LIGHT: The input color components are either multiplied or screened, depending on the top input color.

- LIGHTEN: The lighter of the color components from the two inputs is selected to produce the resulting color.

- MULTIPLY: The color components from the first input are multiplied by those from the second input.

- OVERLAY: The input color components are either multiplied or screened, depending on the bottom input color.

- RED: The red component of the bottom input is replaced with the red component of the top input; the other color components are unaffected.

- SCREEN: The color components from both of the inputs are inverted, multiplied with each other, and that result is again inverted to produce the resulting color.

- SOFT_LIGHT: The input color components are either darkened or lightened, depending on the top input color.

- SRC_ATOP: The part of the top input lying inside the bottom input is blended with the bottom input.

- SRC_OVER: The top input is blended over the bottom input.

To demonstrate the Blend effect, let's create another application, called BlendEffect. It does not require the com.sun.* packages, so the --add-export VM options are not needed. Only the --module-path and --add-modules options, described in the *JavaFX fundamentals* section, have to be set for compilation and execution.

The scope of this book does not allow us to demonstrate all possible combinations, so we will create a red circle and a blue square (see the `BlendEffect` class):

```
Circle createCircle(){
    Circle c = new Circle();
    c.setFill(Color.rgb(255, 0, 0, 0.5));
    c.setRadius(25);
    return c;
}

Rectangle createSquare(){
    Rectangle r = new Rectangle();
    r.setFill(Color.rgb(0, 0, 255, 1.0));
    r.setWidth(50);
    r.setHeight(50);
    return r;
}
```

We used the `Color.rgb(int red, int green, int blue, double alpha)` method to define the colors of each of the figures, but there are many more ways to do it. Read the `Color` class API documentation for more details (`https://openjfx.io/javadoc/11/javafx.graphics/javafx/scene/paint/Color.html`).

To overlap the created circle and square, we will use the `Group` node:

```
Node c = createCircle();
Node s = createSquare();
Node g = new Group(s, c);
```

In the preceding code, the square is a bottom input. We will also create a group where the square is a top input:

```
Node c = createCircle();
Node s = createSquare();
Node g = new Group(c, s);
```

The distinction is important because we defined the circle as half-opaque, while the square was completely opaque. We will use the same settings throughout all our examples.

Let's compare the two modes, MULTIPLY and SRC_OVER. We will set them on the groups, using the setEffect() method, as follows:

```
Blend blnd = new Blend();
blnd.setMode(BlendMode.MULTIPLY);
Node c = createCircle();
Node s = createSquare();
Node g = new Group(s, c);
g.setEffect(blnd);
```

In the start() method of the called BlendEffect class, for each mode, we create two groups, one with the input where the circle is on top of the square, and another with the input where the square is on top of the circle, and we put the four created groups in a GridPane layout (see the source code for details). If we run the BlendEffect application, the result will be as follows:

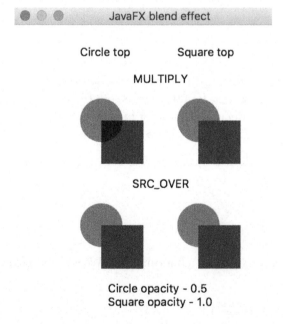

As was expected, when the square is on the top (the two images on the right), the overlapping area is completely taken by the opaque square. But, when the circle is a top input (the two images on the left), the overlapped area is somewhat visible and calculated based on the blend effect.

However, if we set the same mode directly on the group, the result will be slightly different. Let's run the same code but with the mode set on the group:

```
Node c = createCircle();
Node s = createSquare();
Node g = new Group(c, s);
g.setBlendMode(BlendMode.MULTIPLY);
```

Locate the following code in the start() method:

```
Node[] node = setEffectOnGroup(bm1, bm2);
//Node[] node = setModeOnGroup(bm1, bm2);
```

And change it to the following:

```
//Node[] node = setEffectOnGroup(bm1, bm2);
Node[] node = setModeOnGroup(bm1, bm2);
```

If we run the BlendEffect class again, the result will look as follows:

As you can see, the red color of the circle has slightly changed and there is no difference between the MULTIPLY and SRC_OVER modes. That is the issue with the sequence of adding the nodes to the scene we mentioned at the beginning of the section.

The result also changes depending on which node the effect is set on. For example, instead of setting the effect on the group, let's set the effect on the circle only:

```
Blend blnd = new Blend();
blnd.setMode(BlendMode.MULTIPLY);
Node c = createCircle();
Node s = createSquare();
c.setEffect(blnd);
Node g = new Group(s, c);
```

Locate the following code in the start() method:

```
Node[] node = setModeOnGroup(bm1, bm2);
//Node[] node = setEffectOnCircle(bm1, bm2);
```

And change it to the following:

```
//Node[] node = setModeOnGroup(bm1, bm2);
Node[] node = setEffectOnCircle(bm1, bm2);
```

We run the application and see the following:

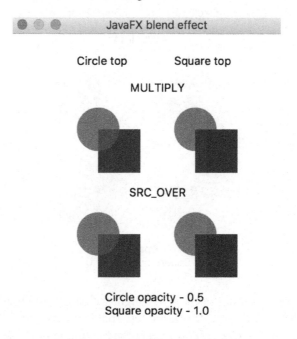

The two images on the right remain the same as in all the previous examples, but the two images on the left show the new colors of the overlapping area. Now, let's set the same effect on the square instead of the circle, as follows:

```
Blend blnd = new Blend();
blnd.setMode(BlendMode.MULTIPLY);
Node c = createCircle();
Node s = createSquare();
s.setEffect(blnd);
Node g = new Group(s, c);
```

Locate the following code in the start() method:

```
        Node[] node = setEffectOnCircle(bm1, bm2);
        //Node[] node = setEffectOnSquare(bm1, bm2);
```

And change it to the following:

```
        //Node[] node = setEffectOnCircle(bm1, bm2);
        Node[] node = setEffectOnSquare(bm1, bm2);
```

The result will slightly change again and will look as presented in the following screenshot:

There is no difference between the MULTIPLY and SRC_OVER modes, but the red color is different than it was when we set the effect on the circle.

We can change the approach again and set the blend mode directly on the circle only, using the following code:

```
Node c = createCircle();
Node s = createSquare();
c.setBlendMode(BlendMode.MULTIPLY);
```

Locate the following code in the start() method:

```
Node[] node = setEffectOnSquare(bm1, bm2);
//Node[] node = setModeOnCircle(bm1, bm2);
```

And change it to this:

```
//Node[] node = setEffectOnSquare(bm1, bm2);
Node[] node = setModeOnCircle(bm1, bm2);
```

The result changes again:

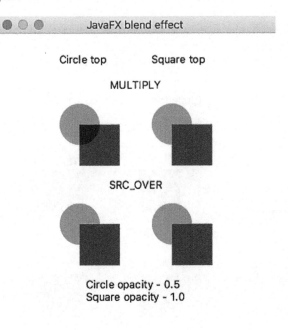

Setting the blend mode on the square only removes the difference between the MULTIPLY and SRC_OVER modes again.

Locate the following code in the start() method:

```
Node[] node = setModeOnCircle(bm1, bm2);
//Node[] node = setModeOnSquare(bm1, bm2);
```

And change it to the following:

```
//Node[] node = setModeOnCircle(bm1, bm2);
Node[] node = setModeOnSquare(bm1, bm2);
```

The result is as follows:

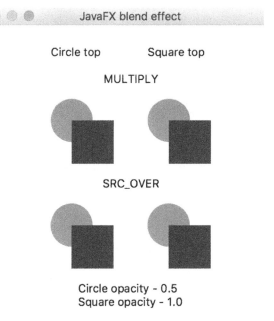

To avoid confusion and make the results of the blending more predictable, you have to watch the sequence in which the nodes are added to the scene and the consistency of the way the blend effect is applied.

In the source code provided with this book, you will find examples for all effects included in the `javafx.scene.effects` package. They are all demonstrated by running side-by-side comparisons. Here is one example:

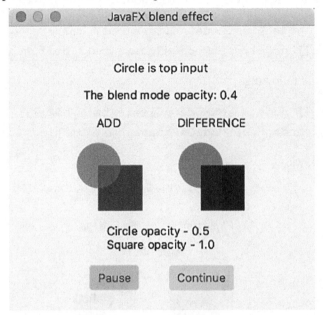

For your convenience, there are **Pause** and **Continue** buttons provided that allow you to pause the demonstration and review the result for different values of opacity set on the blend effect.

To demonstrate all other effects, we have created yet another application, called `OtherEffects`, which also doesn't require the `com.sun.*` packages, so the `--add-export` VM options are not needed. The effects demonstrated include `Bloom`, `BoxBlur`, `ColorAdjust`, `DisplacementMap`, `DropShadow`, `Glow`, `InnerShadow`, `Lighting`, `MotionBlur`, `PerspectiveTransform`, `Reflection`, `ShadowTone`, and `SepiaTone`. We have used two images to present the result of applying each of the effects (the Packt logo and a mountain lake view):

```
ClassLoader classLoader =
            Thread.currentThread().getContextClassLoader();
String file = classLoader.getResource("packt.png").getFile();
FileInputStream inputP = new FileInputStream(file);
Image imageP = new Image(inputP);
ImageView ivP = new ImageView(imageP);
```

```
String file2 = classLoader.getResource("mount.jpeg").getFile();
FileInputStream inputM = new FileInputStream(file2);
Image imageM = new Image(inputM);
ImageView ivM = new ImageView(imageM);
ivM.setPreserveRatio(true);
ivM.setFitWidth(300);
```

We also have added two buttons that allow you to pause and continue the demonstration (it iterates over the effect and the values of their parameters):

```
Button btnP = new Button("Pause");
btnP.setOnAction(e1 -> et.pause());
btnP.setStyle("-fx-background-color: lightpink;");

Button btnC = new Button("Continue");
btnC.setOnAction(e2 -> et.cont());
btnC.setStyle("-fx-background-color: lightgreen;");
```

The et object is the object of the EffectsThread thread:

```
EffectsThread et = new EffectsThread(txt, ivM, ivP);
```

The thread goes through the list of the effects, creates a corresponding effect 10 times (with 10 different effects' parameter values), and, every time, sets the created Effect object on each of the images, then sleeps for 1 second to give you an opportunity to review the result:

```
public void run(){
    try {
        for(String effect: effects){
            for(int i = 0; i < 11; i++){
                double d = Math.round(i * 0.1 * 10.0) / 10.0;
                Effect e = createEffect(effect, d, txt);
                ivM.setEffect(e);
                ivP.setEffect(e);
                TimeUnit.SECONDS.sleep(1);
                if(pause){
                    while(true){
                        TimeUnit.SECONDS.sleep(1);
```

```
                            if(!pause){
                                break;
                            }
                        }
                    }
                }
            }
            Platform.exit();
        } catch (Exception ex){
            ex.printStackTrace();
        }
    }
}
```

We will show how each effect is created next, under the screenshot with the effect's result. To present the result, we have used the GridPane layout:

```
GridPane grid = new GridPane();
grid.setAlignment(Pos.CENTER);
grid.setVgap(25);
grid.setPadding(new Insets(10, 10, 10, 10));

int i = 0;
grid.add(txt,    0, i++, 2, 1);
GridPane.setHalignment(txt, HPos.CENTER);
grid.add(ivP,    0, i++, 2, 1);
GridPane.setHalignment(ivP, HPos.CENTER);
grid.add(ivM,    0, i++, 2, 1);
GridPane.setHalignment(ivM, HPos.CENTER);
grid.addRow(i++, new Text());
HBox hb = new HBox(btnP, btnC);
hb.setAlignment(Pos.CENTER);
hb.setSpacing(25);
grid.add(hb,     0, i++, 2, 1);
GridPane.setHalignment(hb, HPos.CENTER);
```

And, finally, the created `GridPane` object was passed to the scene, which in turn was placed on a stage familiar to you from our earlier examples:

```
Scene scene = new Scene(grid, 450, 500);
primaryStage.setScene(scene);
primaryStage.setTitle("JavaFX effect demo");
primaryStage.onCloseRequestProperty()
     .setValue(e3 -> System.out.println("Bye! See you later!"));
primaryStage.show();
```

The following screenshots depict examples of the effects of each of the 13 parameter values. Under each screenshot, we present the code snippet from the `createEffect(String effect, double d, Text txt)` method that created this effect:

- Effect of parameter value 1:

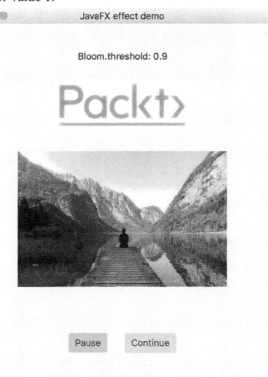

```
//double d = 0.9;
txt.setText(effect + ".threshold: " + d);
Bloom b = new Bloom();
b.setThreshold(d);
```

- Effect of parameter value 2:

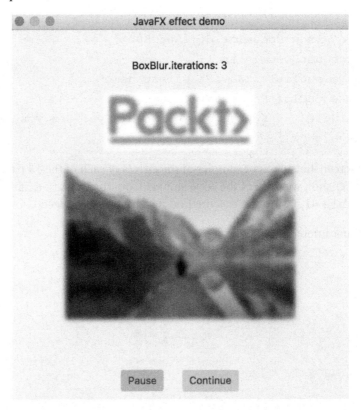

```
// double d = 0.3;
int i = (int) d * 10;
int it = i / 3;
txt.setText(effect + ".iterations: " + it);
BoxBlur bb = new BoxBlur();
bb.setIterations(i);
```

- Effect of parameter value 3:

```
double c = Math.round((-1.0 + d * 2) * 10.0) / 10.0;        // 0.6
txt.setText(effect + ": " + c);
ColorAdjust ca = new ColorAdjust();
ca.setContrast(c);
```

- Effect of parameter value 4:

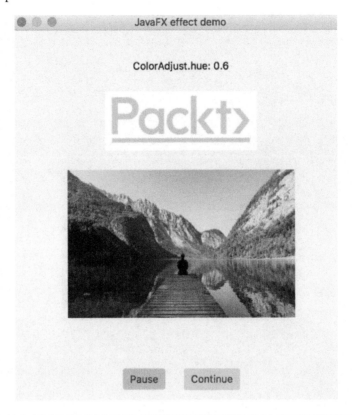

```
double h = Math.round((-1.0 + d * 2) * 10.0) / 10.0;      // 0.6
txt.setText(effect + ": " + h);
ColorAdjust ca1 = new ColorAdjust();
ca1.setHue(h);
```

- Effect of parameter value 5:

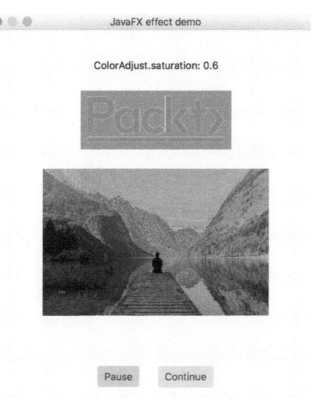

```
double st = Math.round((-1.0 + d * 2) * 10.0) / 10.0;    // 0.6
txt.setText(effect + ": " + st);
ColorAdjust ca3 = new ColorAdjust();
ca3.setSaturation(st);
```

- Effect of parameter value 6:

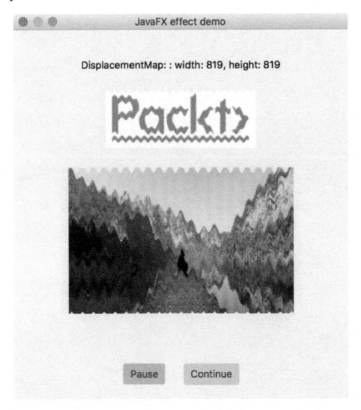

```
int w = (int)Math.round(4096 * d);  //819
int h1 = (int)Math.round(4096 * d); //819
txt.setText(effect + ": " + ": width: " + w + ", height: " +
                                                            h1);
DisplacementMap dm = new DisplacementMap();
FloatMap floatMap = new FloatMap();
floatMap.setWidth(w);
floatMap.setHeight(h1);
for (int k = 0; k < w; k++) {
    double v = (Math.sin(k / 20.0 * Math.PI) - 0.5) / 40.0;
    for (int j = 0; j < h1; j++) {
        floatMap.setSamples(k, j, 0.0f, (float) v);
    }
}
dm.setMapData(floatMap);
```

- Effect of parameter value 7:

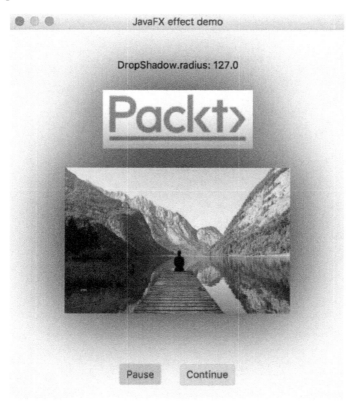

```
double rd = Math.round(((127.0 * d) * 10.0) / 10.0; // 127.0
System.out.println(effect + ": " + rd);
txt.setText(effect + ": " + rd);
DropShadow sh = new DropShadow();
sh.setRadius(rd);
```

- Effect of parameter value 8:

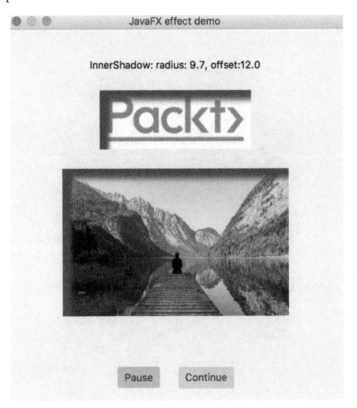

```
double rad = Math.round(12.1 * d *10.0)/10.0;      // 9.7
double off = Math.round(15.0 * d *10.0)/10.0;      // 12.0
txt.setText("InnerShadow: radius: " + rad + ", offset:" + off);
InnerShadow is = new InnerShadow();
is.setColor(Color.web("0x3b596d"));
is.setOffsetX(off);
is.setOffsetY(off);
is.setRadius(rad);
```

- Effect of parameter value 9:

```
double sS = Math.round((d * 4)*10.0)/10.0;        // 0.4
txt.setText(effect + ": " + sS);
Light.Spot lightSs = new Light.Spot();
lightSs.setX(150);
lightSs.setY(100);
lightSs.setZ(80);
lightSs.setPointsAtX(0);
lightSs.setPointsAtY(0);
lightSs.setPointsAtZ(-50);
lightSs.setSpecularExponent(sS);
Lighting lSs = new Lighting();
lSs.setLight(lightSs);
lSs.setSurfaceScale(5.0);
```

- Effect of parameter value 10:

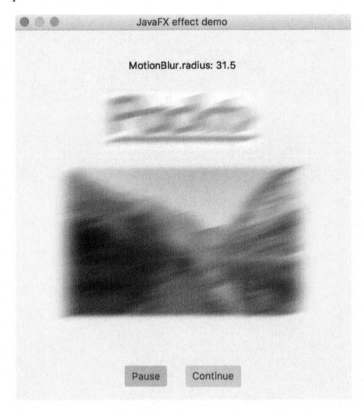

```
double r = Math.round((63.0 * d)*10.0) / 10.0;       // 31.5
txt.setText(effect + ": " + r);
MotionBlur mb1 = new MotionBlur();
mb1.setRadius(r);
mb1.setAngle(-15);
```

- Effect of parameter value 11:

```
// double d = 0.9;
txt.setText(effect + ": " + d);
PerspectiveTransform pt =
        new PerspectiveTransform(0., 1. + 50.*d, 310., 50. -
      50.*d, 310., 50. + 50.*d + 1., 0., 100. - 50. * d + 2.);
```

- Effect of parameter value 12:

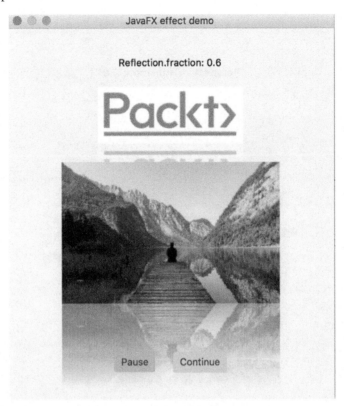

```
// double d = 0.6;
txt.setText(effect + ": " + d);
Reflection ref = new Reflection();
ref.setFraction(d);
```

- Effect of parameter value 13:

```
// double d = 1.0;
txt.setText(effect + ": " + d);
SepiaTone sep = new SepiaTone();
sep.setLevel(d);
```

The full source code of this demonstration is provided with the book and is available on GitHub.

Summary

In this chapter, you were introduced to the JavaFX kit, its main features, and how it can be used to create a GUI application. The topics covered included an overview of Java GUI technologies, the JavaFX control elements, charts, using CSS, FXML, embedding HTML, playing media, and adding effects.

Now, you can create a user interface using Java GUI technologies, as well as creating and using a user interface project as a standalone application.

The next chapter is dedicated to functional programming. It provides an overview of functional interfaces that come with JDK, explains what a Lambda expression is, and how to use a functional interface in a Lambda expression. It also explains and demonstrates how to use method references.

Quiz

1. What is the top-level content container in JavaFX?

2. What is the base class of all the scene participants in JavaFX?

3. Name the base class of a JavaFX application.

4. What is one method of the JavaFX application that has to be implemented?

5. Which Application method has to be called by the main method to execute a JavaFX application?

6. Which two VM options are required to execute a JavaFX application?

7. Which Application method is called when the JavaFX application window is closed using the **x** button in the upper corner?

8. Which class has to be used to embed HTML?

9. Name three classes that have to be used to play media.

10. What is the VM option required to be added in order to play media?

11. Name five JavaFX effects.

Part 3: Advanced Java

This section will expand on some advance concepts in Java Programming while building a sample project that is being created at the end of the previous section. By the end of this section, the readers will have a standalone project built using the concepts covered in this section..

This section contains the following chapters:

13
Functional Programming

This chapter brings you into the world of functional programming. It explains what a functional interface is, provides an overview of the functional interfaces that come with JDK, and defines and demonstrates Lambda expressions and how to use them with functional interfaces, including using **method reference**.

The following topics will be covered in this chapter:

- What is functional programming?
- Standard functional interfaces
- Functional pipelines
- Lambda expression limitations
- Method reference

By the end of the chapter, you will be able to write functions and use them for Lambda expressions in order to pass them as method parameters.

Technical requirements

To be able to execute the code examples provided in this chapter, you will need the following:

- A computer with a Microsoft Windows, Apple macOS, or Linux operating system
- Java SE version 17 or later
- An IDE or any code editor you prefer

The instructions for how to set up a Java SE and IntelliJ IDEA editor were provided in *Chapter 1, Getting Started with Java 17*. The files with the code examples for this chapter are available on GitHub at `https://github.com/PacktPublishing/Learn-Java-17-Programming.git` in the `examples/src/main/java/com/packt/learnjava/ch13_functional` folder.

What is functional programming?

Before we provide the definition, let us revisit the code with elements of functional programming that we have used already in the preceding chapters. All these examples give you a pretty good idea of how a function can be constructed and passed around as a parameter.

In *Chapter 6, Data Structures, Generics, and Popular Utilities*, we talked about the `Iterable` interface and its `default void forEach (Consumer<T> function)` method, and provided the following example:

```
Iterable<String> list = List.of("s1", "s2", "s3");
System.out.println(list);                 //prints: [s1, s2, s3]
list.forEach(e -> System.out.print(e + " "));//prints: s1 s2 s3
```

You can see how a `Consumer e -> System.out.print(e + " ")` function is passed into the `forEach()` method and applied to each element flowing into this method from the list. We will discuss the `Consumer` function shortly.

We also mentioned two methods of the `Collection` interface that accept a function as a parameter too:

- The `default boolean remove(Predicate<E> filter)` method attempts to remove all the elements that satisfy the given predicate from the collection; a `Predicate` function accepts an element of the collection and returns a Boolean value.

- The default `T[] toArray(IntFunction<T[]> generator)` method returns an array of all the elements of the collection, using the provided `IntFunction` generator function to allocate the returned array.

In the same chapter, we also mentioned the following method of the `List` interface:

- `default void replaceAll(UnaryOperator<E> operator)`: This replaces each element of the list with the result of applying the provided `UnaryOperator` to that element; `UnaryOperator` is one of the functions we are going to review in this chapter.

We described the `Map` interface, its `default V merge(K key, V value, BiFunction<V,V,V> remappingFunction)` method, and how it can be used for concatenating the `String` values: `map.merge(key, value, String::concat)`. `BiFunction<V,V,V>` takes two parameters of the same type and returns the value of the same type as well. The `String::concat` construct is called a **method reference** and will be explained in the *Method references* section.

We provided the following example of passing a `Comparator` function:

```
list.sort(Comparator.naturalOrder());
Comparator<String> cmp =
                (s1, s2) -> s1 == null ? -1 : s1.compareTo(s2);
list.sort(cmp);
```

It takes two `String` parameters, then compares the first one to `null`. If the first parameter is `null`, the function returns `-1`; otherwise, it compares the first parameter and the second one using the `compareTo()` method.

In *Chapter 11*, *Network Programming*, we looked at the following code:

```
HttpClient httpClient = HttpClient.newBuilder().build();
HttpRequest req = HttpRequest.newBuilder()
  .uri(URI.create("http://localhost:3333/something")).build();
try {
   HttpResponse<String> resp =
                httpClient.send(req, BodyHandlers.ofString());
   System.out.println("Response: " +
                resp.statusCode() + " : " + resp.body());
} catch (Exception ex) {
```

```
        ex.printStackTrace();
}
```

The `BodyHandler` object (a function) is generated by the `BodyHandlers`.
`ofString()` factory method and passed into the `send()` method as a parameter. Inside
the method, the code calls its `apply()` method:

```
BodySubscriber<T> apply(ResponseInfo responseInfo)
```

Finally, in *Chapter 12, Java GUI Programming*, we used an `EventHandler` function
as a parameter in the following code snippet:

```
btn.setOnAction(e -> {
                System.out.println("Bye! See you later!");
                Platform.exit();
            });
primaryStage.onCloseRequestProperty()
    .setValue(e -> System.out.println("Bye! See you later!"));
```

The first function is `EventHandler<ActionEvent>`. This prints a message and forces
the application to exit. The second is the `EventHandler<WindowEvent>` function.
This just prints the message.

This ability to pass a function as a parameter constitutes functional programming. It is
present in many programming languages and does not require the managing of object
states. The function is stateless. Its result depends only on the input data, no matter how
many times it is called. Such coding makes the outcome more predictable, which is the
most attractive aspect of functional programming.

The area that benefits the most from such a design is parallel data processing. Functional
programming allows for shifting the responsibility for parallelism from the client code to
the library. Before that, in order to process elements of Java collections, the client code had
to iterate over the collection and organize the processing. In Java 8, new (default) methods
were added that accept a function as a parameter and then apply it to each element of the
collection, in parallel or not, depending on the internal processing algorithm. So, it is the
library's responsibility to organize parallel processing.

What is a functional interface?

When we define a function, we provide an implementation of an interface that has only one abstract method. That is how the Java compiler knows where to put the provided functionality. The compiler looks at the interface (`Consumer`, `Predicate`, `Comparator`, `IntFunction`, `UnaryOperator`, `BiFunction`, `BodyHandler`, and `EventHandler` in the preceding examples), sees only one abstract method there, and uses the passed-in functionality as the method implementation. The only requirement is that the passed-in parameters must match the method signature. Otherwise, the compile-time error is generated.

That is why any interface that has only one abstract method is called a **functional interface**. Please note that the requirement of having **only one abstract method** includes the method inherited from the parent interface. For example, consider the following interfaces:

```
@FunctionalInterface
interface A {
    void method1();
    default void method2(){}
    static void method3(){}
}

@FunctionalInterface
interface B extends A {
    default void method4(){}
}

@FunctionalInterface
interface C extends B {
    void method1();
}

//@FunctionalInterface
interface D extends C {
    void method5();
}
```

The A interface is a functional interface because it has only one abstract method, method1(). The B interface is a functional interface too because it has only one abstract method—the same one inherited from the A interface. The C interface is a functional interface because it has only one abstract method, method1(), which overrides the abstract method of the parent interface, A. The D interface cannot be a functional interface because it has two abstract methods—method1() from the parent interface, A, and method5().

To help avoid runtime errors, the @FunctionalInterface annotation was introduced in Java 8. It tells the compiler about the intent so the compiler can check and see whether there is truly only one abstract method in the annotated interface. This annotation also warns a programmer, who reads the code, that this interface has only one abstract method intentionally. Otherwise, a programmer may waste time adding another abstract method to the interface only to discover at runtime that it cannot be done.

For the same reason, the Runnable and Callable interfaces, which have existed in Java since its early versions, were annotated in Java 8 as @FunctionalInterface. This distinction is made explicit and serves as a reminder to users that these interfaces can be used to create a function:

```
@FunctionalInterface
interface Runnable {
    void run();
}


@FunctionalInterface
interface Callable<V> {
    V call() throws Exception;
}
```

As with any other interface, the functional interface can be implemented using the anonymous class:

```
Runnable runnable = new Runnable() {
    @Override
    public void run() {
        System.out.println("Hello!");
    }
};
```

An object created this way can later be used as follows:

```
runnable.run();    //prints: Hello!
```

If we look closely at the preceding code, we notice that there is unnecessary overhead. First, there is no need to repeat the interface name, because we declared it already as the type for the object reference. And, second, in the case of a functional interface that has only one abstract method, there is no need to specify the method name that has to be implemented. The compiler and Java runtime can figure it out. All we need is to provide the new functionality. The Lambda expressions were introduced especially for this purpose.

What is a Lambda expression?

The term **Lambda** comes from *lambda calculus*—a universal model of computation that can be used to simulate any Turing machine. It was introduced by mathematician Alonzo Church in the 1930s. A **Lambda expression** is a function, implemented in Java as an anonymous method. It also allows for the omitting of modifiers, return types, and parameter types. That makes for a very compact notation.

The syntax of the Lambda expression includes the list of parameters, an arrow token (->), and a body. The list of parameters can be empty, such as (), without parentheses (if there is only one parameter), or a comma-separated list of parameters surrounded by parentheses. The body can be a single expression or a statement block inside braces ({}). Let's look at a few examples:

- `()  ->  42;` always returns 42.

- `x  ->  x*42  +  42;` multiplies the x value by 42, then adds 42 to the result and returns it.

- `(x,  y)  ->  x  *  y;` multiplies the passed-in parameters and returns the result.

- `s  ->  "abc".equals(s);` compares the value of the s variable and literal "abc"; it returns a Boolean result value.

- `s  ->  System.out.println("x=" + s);` prints the s value with the prefix "x=".

- `(i,  s)  ->  {  i++;  System.out.println(s + "=" + i);  };` increments the input integer and prints the new value with the prefix s + "=", with s being the value of the second parameter.

Without functional programming, the only way to pass some functionality as a parameter in Java would be by writing a class that implements an interface, creating its object, and then passing it as a parameter. But even the least-involved style using an anonymous class requires writing too much boilerplate code. Using functional interfaces and Lambda expressions makes the code shorter, clearer, and more expressive.

For example, Lambda expressions allow us to reimplement our preceding example with the Runnable interface, as follows:

```
Runnable runnable = () -> System.out.println("Hello!");
```

As you can see, creating a functional interface is easy, especially with Lambda expressions. But before doing that, consider using one of the 43 functional interfaces provided in the java.util.function package. This will not only allow you to write less code but will also help other programmers who are familiar with the standard interfaces to understand your code better.

The local variable syntax for Lambda parameters

Until the release of Java 11, there were two ways to declare parameter types—explicitly and implicitly. Here is an explicit version:

```
BiFunction<Double, Integer, Double> f =
                        (Double x, Integer y) -> x / y;
System.out.println(f.apply(3., 2)); //prints: 1.5
```

The following is an implicit parameter type definition:

```
BiFunction<Double, Integer, Double> f = (x, y) -> x / y;
System.out.println(f.apply(3., 2));    //prints: 1.5
```

In the preceding code, the compiler infers the type of the parameters from the interface definition.

In Java 11, another method of parameter type declaration was introduced using the var type holder, which is similar to the var local variable type holder introduced in Java 10 (see *Chapter 1, Getting Started with Java 17*).

The following parameter declaration is syntactically exactly the same as the implicit one before Java 11:

```
BiFunction<Double, Integer, Double> f =
                                (var x, var y) -> x / y;
    System.out.println(f.apply(3., 2));    //prints: 1.5
```

The new local variable-style syntax allows us to add annotations without defining the parameter type explicitly. Let's add the following dependency to the pom.xml file:

```
<dependency>
    <groupId>org.jetbrains</groupId>
    <artifactId>annotations</artifactId>
    <version>22.0.0</version>
</dependency>
```

It allows us to define passed-in variables as non-null:

```
import javax.validation.constraints.NotNull;
import java.util.function.BiFunction;
import java.util.function.Consumer;


BiFunction<Double, Integer, Double> f =
                       (@NotNull var x, @NotNull var y) -> x / y;
System.out.println(f.apply(3., 2));     //prints: 1.5
```

An annotation communicates to the compiler the programmer's intent, so it can warn the programmer during compilation or execution if the declared intent is violated. For example, we have tried to run the following code:

```
BiFunction<Double, Integer, Double> f = (x, y) -> x / y;
System.out.println(f.apply(null, 2));
```

It failed with NullPointerException at runtime. Then, we have added the annotation as follows:

```
BiFunction<Double, Integer, Double> f =
        (@NotNull var x, @NotNull var y) -> x / y;
System.out.println(f.apply(null, 2));
```

The result of running the preceding code looks like this:

```
Exception in thread "main" java.lang.IllegalArgumentException:
Argument for @NotNull parameter 'x' of
com/packt/learnjava/ch13_functional/LambdaExpressions
.lambda$localVariableSyntax$1 must not be null
at com.packt.learnjava.ch13_functional.LambdaExpressions
.$$$reportNull$$$0(LambdaExpressions.java)
```

```
at com.packt.learnjava.ch13_functional.LambdaExpressions
.lambda$localVariableSyntax$1(LambdaExpressions.java)
at com.packt.learnjava.ch13_functional.LambdaExpressions
.localVariableSyntax(LambdaExpressions.java:59)
at com.packt.learnjava.ch13_functional.LambdaExpressions
.main(LambdaExpressions.java:12)
```

The Lambda expression was not even executed.

The advantage of the local variable syntax in the case of Lambda parameters becomes clear if we need to use annotations when the parameters are the objects of a class with a really long name. Before Java 11, the code might have looked like the following:

```
BiFunction<SomeReallyLongClassName,
AnotherReallyLongClassName, Double> f =
        (@NotNull SomeReallyLongClassName x,
    @NotNull AnotherReallyLongClassName y) -> x.doSomething(y);
```

We had to declare the type of the variable explicitly because we wanted to add annotations, and the following implicit version would not even compile:

```
BiFunction<SomeReallyLongClassName,
AnotherReallyLongClassName, Double> f =
        (@NotNull x, @NotNull y) -> x.doSomething(y);
```

With Java 11, the new syntax allows us to use the implicit parameter type inference using the var type holder:

```
BiFunction<SomeReallyLongClassName,
AnotherReallyLongClassName, Double> f =
        (@NotNull var x, @NotNull var y) -> x.doSomething(y);
```

That is the advantage of and the motivation behind introducing the local variable syntax for the Lambda parameter's declaration. Otherwise, consider staying away from using var. If the type of the variable is short, using its actual type makes the code easier to understand.

Standard functional interfaces

Most of the interfaces provided in the java.util.function package are specializations of the following four interfaces: Consumer<T>, Predicate<T>, Supplier<T>, and Function<T,R>. Let's review them and then look at a short overview of the other 39 standard functional interfaces.

Consumer<T>

By looking at the Consumer<T> interface definition, <indexentry content="standard functional interfaces:Consumer">, you can already guess that this interface has an abstract method that accepts a parameter of type T and does not return anything. Well, when only one type is listed, it may define the type of the return value, as in the case of the Supplier<T> interface. But the interface name serves as a clue: the consumer name indicates that the method of this interface just takes the value and returns nothing, while supplier returns the value. This clue is not precise but helps to jog the memory.

The best source of information about any functional interface is the java.util.function package API documentation (https://docs.oracle.com/en/java/javase/12/docs/api/java.base/java/util/function/package-summary.html). If we read it, we learn that the Consumer<T> interface has one abstract and one default method:

- void accept(T t): Applies the operation to the given argument
- default Consumer<T> andThen(Consumer<T> after): Returns a composed Consumer function that performs, in sequence, the current operation followed by the after operation

It means that, for example, we can implement and then execute it as follows:

```
Consumer<String> printResult =
                    s -> System.out.println("Result: " + s);
printResult.accept("10.0");    //prints: Result: 10.0
```

We can also have a factory method that creates the function, for example:

```
Consumer<String> printWithPrefixAndPostfix(String pref, String
postf){
    return s -> System.out.println(pref + s + postf);
}
```

Now, we can use it as follows:

```
printWithPrefixAndPostfix("Result: ",
                          " Great!").accept("10.0");
                                    //prints: Result: 10.0 Great!
```

To demonstrate the andThen() method, let's create the Person class:

```
public class Person {
    private int age;
    private String firstName, lastName, record;
    public Person(int age, String firstName, String lastName) {
        this.age = age;
        this.lastName = lastName;
        this.firstName = firstName;
    }
    public int getAge() { return age; }
    public String getFirstName() { return firstName; }
    public String getLastName() { return lastName; }
    public String getRecord() { return record; }
    public void setRecord(String fullId) {
                                    this.record = record; }
}
```

You may have noticed that record is the only property that has a setting. We will use it to set a personal record in a consumer function:

```
String externalData = "external data";
Consumer<Person> setRecord =
    p -> p.setFullId(p.getFirstName() + " " +
    p.getLastName() + ", " + p.getAge() + ", " + externalData);
```

The `setRecord` function takes the values of the `Person` object properties and some data from an external source and sets the resulting value as the `record` property value. Obviously, it could be done in several other ways, but we do it for demo purposes. Let's also create a function that prints the `record` property:

```
Consumer<Person> printRecord = p -> System.out.println(
                                           p.getRecord());
```

The composition of these two functions can be created and executed as follows:

```
Consumer<Person> setRecordThenPrint = setRecord.
                                     andThen(printPersonId);
setRecordThenPrint.accept(new Person(42, "Nick", "Samoylov"));
                //prints: Nick Samoylov, age 42, external data
```

This way, it is possible to create a whole processing pipe of the operations that transform the properties of an object that is passed through the pipe.

Predicate\<T\>

This functional interface, `Predicate<T>`, has one abstract method, five defaults, and a static method that allows predicates chaining:

- `boolean test(T t)`: Evaluates the provided parameter to see whether it meets the criteria or not
- `default Predicate<T> negate()`: Returns the negation of the current predicate
- `static <T> Predicate<T> not(Predicate<T> target)`: Returns the negation of the provided predicate
- `default Predicate<T> or(Predicate<T> other)`: Constructs a logical OR from this predicate and the provided one
- `default Predicate<T> and(Predicate<T> other)`: Constructs a logical AND from this predicate and the provided one
- `static <T> Predicate<T> isEqual(Object targetRef)`: Constructs a predicate that evaluates whether or not two arguments are equal according to `Objects.equals(Object, Object)`

The basic use of this interface is pretty straightforward:

```
Predicate<Integer> isLessThan10 = i -> i < 10;
System.out.println(isLessThan10.test(7));        //prints: true
System.out.println(isLessThan10.test(12));       //prints: false
```

We can also combine it with the previously created
`printWithPrefixAndPostfix(String pref, String postf)` function:

```
int val = 7;
Consumer<String> printIsSmallerThan10 =
printWithPrefixAndPostfix("Is " + val + " smaller than 10? ",
                                                " Great!");
printIsSmallerThan10.accept(String.valueOf(isLessThan10.
                                                test(val)));
                    //prints: Is 7 smaller than 10? true Great!
```

The other methods (also called **operations**) can be used for creating operational chains
(also called **pipelines**), and can be seen in the following examples:

```
Predicate<Integer> isEqualOrGreaterThan10 = isLessThan10.
                                                negate();
System.out.println(isEqualOrGreaterThan10.test(7));
                                                //prints: false
System.out.println(isEqualOrGreaterThan10.test(12));
                                                //prints: true

isEqualOrGreaterThan10 = Predicate.not(isLessThan10);
System.out.println(isEqualOrGreaterThan10.test(7));
                                                //prints: false
System.out.println(isEqualOrGreaterThan10.test(12));
                                                //prints: true

Predicate<Integer> isGreaterThan10 = i -> i > 10;
Predicate<Integer> is_lessThan10_OR_greaterThan10 =
                            isLessThan10.or(isGreaterThan10);
System.out.println(is_lessThan10_OR_greaterThan10.test(20));
                                                // true
```

```
System.out.println(is_lessThan10_OR_greaterThan10.test(10));
                                                    // false


Predicate<Integer> isGreaterThan5 = i -> i > 5;
Predicate<Integer> is_lessThan10_AND_greaterThan5 =
                isLessThan10.and(isGreaterThan5);
System.out.println(is_lessThan10_AND_greaterThan5.test(3));
                                                    // false
System.out.println(is_lessThan10_AND_greaterThan5.test(7));
                                                    // true


Person nick = new Person(42, "Nick", "Samoylov");
Predicate<Person> isItNick = Predicate.isEqual(nick);
Person john = new Person(42, "John", "Smith");
Person person = new Person(42, "Nick", "Samoylov");
System.out.println(isItNick.test(john));
                                        //prints: false
System.out.println(isItNick.test(person));
                                        //prints: true
```

The predicate objects can be chained into more complex logical statements and include all necessary external data, as was demonstrated before.

Supplier<T>

This functional interface, Supplier<T>, has only one abstract method, T get(), which returns a value. The basic usage can be seen as follows:

```
Supplier<Integer> supply42 = () -> 42;
System.out.println(supply42.get());  //prints: 42
```

It can be chained with the functions discussed in the preceding sections:

```
int input = 7;
int limit = 10;
Supplier<Integer> supply7 = () -> input;
Predicate<Integer> isLessThan10 = i -> i < limit;
Consumer<String> printResult = printWithPrefixAndPostfix("Is "
        + input + " smaller than " + limit + "? ", " Great!");
```

```
printResult.accept(String.valueOf(isLessThan10.test(
                                         supply7.get())));
               //prints: Is 7 smaller than 10? true Great!
```

The `Supplier<T>` function is typically used as an entry point of data going into a processing pipeline.

Function<T, R>

The notation of this and other functional interfaces that return values includes the listing of the return type as the last in the list of generics (R in this case) and the type of the input data in front of it (an input parameter of type T in this case). So, the `Function<T, R>` notation means that the only abstract method of this interface accepts an argument of type T and produces a result of type R. Let's look at the online documentation (`https://docs.oracle.com/en/java/javase/12/docs/api/java.base/java/util/function/Function.html`).

The `Function<T, R>` interface has one abstract method, `R apply(T)`, and two methods for operations chaining:

- `default <V> Function<T,V> andThen(Function<R, V> after)`: Returns a composed function that first applies the current function to its input, and then applies the `after` function to the result

- `default <V> Function<V,R> compose(Function<V, T> before)`: Returns a composed function that first applies the `before` function to its input, and then applies the current function to the result

There is also an `identity()` method:

- `static <T> Function<T,T> identity()`: Returns a function that always returns its input argument

Let's review all these methods and how they can be used. Here is an example of the basic usage of the `Function<T, R>` interface:

```
Function<Integer, Double> multiplyByTen = i -> i * 10.0;
System.out.println(multiplyByTen.apply(1));    //prints: 10.0
```

We can also chain it with all the functions we have discussed in the preceding sections:

```
Supplier<Integer> supply7 = () -> 7;
Function<Integer, Double> multiplyByFive = i -> i * 5.0;
Consumer<String> printResult =
            printWithPrefixAndPostfix("Result: ", " Great!");
printResult.accept(multiplyByFive.
    apply(supply7.get()).toString());
                              //prints: Result: 35.0 Great!
```

The andThen() method allows constructing a complex function from simpler ones. Notice the divideByTwo.andThen() line in the following code:

```
Function<Double, Long> divideByTwo =
                    d -> Double.valueOf(d / 2.).longValue();
Function<Long, String> incrementAndCreateString =
                              l -> String.valueOf(l + 1);
Function<Double, String> divideByTwoIncrementAndCreateString =
                divideByTwo.andThen(incrementAndCreateString);
printResult.accept(divideByTwoIncrementAndCreateString.
                                              apply(4.));
                              //prints: Result: 3 Great!
```

It describes the sequence of the operations applied to the input value. Notice how the return type of the divideByTwo() function (Long) matches the input type of the incrementAndCreateString() function.

The compose() method accomplishes the same result, but in reverse order:

```
Function<Double, String> divideByTwoIncrementAndCreateString =
                incrementAndCreateString.compose(divideByTwo);
printResult.accept(divideByTwoIncrementAndCreateString.
                                              apply(4.));
                              //prints: Result: 3 Great!
```

Now, the sequence of composition of the complex function does not match the sequence of the execution. It may be very convenient in the case where the `divideByTwo()` function is not created yet and you would like to create it in-line. Then, the following construct will not compile:

```
Function<Double, String> divideByTwoIncrementAndCreateString =
        (d -> Double.valueOf(d / 2.).longValue())
                    .andThen(incrementAndCreateString);
```

The following line will compile just fine:

```
Function<Double, String> divideByTwoIncrementAndCreateString =
        incrementAndCreateString
        .compose(d -> Double.valueOf(d / 2.).longValue());
```

It allows for more flexibility while constructing a functional pipeline, so you can build it in a fluent style without breaking the continuous line when creating the next operations.

The `identity()` method is useful when you need to pass in a function that matches the required function signature but does nothing. But, it can substitute only a function that returns the same type as the input type, as shown in this example:

```
Function<Double, Double> multiplyByTwo = d -> d * 2.0;
System.out.println(multiplyByTwo.apply(2.));  //prints: 4.0

multiplyByTwo = Function.identity();
System.out.println(multiplyByTwo.apply(2.));  //prints: 2.0
```

To demonstrate its usability, let's assume we have the following processing pipeline:

```
Function<Double, Double> multiplyByTwo = d -> d * 2.0;
System.out.println(multiplyByTwo.apply(2.));  //prints: 4.0

Function<Double, Long> subtract7 = d -> Math.round(d - 7);
System.out.println(subtract7.apply(11.0));    //prints: 4

long r = multiplyByTwo.andThen(subtract7).apply(2.);
System.out.println(r);                        //prints: -3
```

Then, we decide that, under certain circumstances, the `multiplyByTwo()` function should do nothing. We could add to it a conditional close that turns it on/off. But, if we want to keep the function intact or if this function is passed to us from third-party code, we can just do the following:

```
Function<Double, Double> multiplyByTwo = d -> d * 2.0;
System.out.println(multiplyByTwo.apply(2.));  //prints: 4.0

Function<Double, Long> subtract7 = d -> Math.round(d - 7);
System.out.println(subtract7.apply(11.0));    //prints: 4

long r = multiplyByTwo.andThen(subtract7).apply(2.);
System.out.println(r);                          //prints: -3

multiplyByTwo = Function.identity();
System.out.println(multiplyByTwo.apply(2.)); //prints: 2.0;

r = multiplyByTwo.andThen(subtract7).apply(2.);
System.out.println(r);                          //prints: -5
```

As you can see, the `multiplyByTwo()` function now does nothing, and the final result is different.

Other standard functional interfaces

The other 39 functional interfaces in the `java.util.function` package are variations of the four interfaces we have just reviewed. These variations are created in order to achieve one or any combination of the following:

- Better performance by avoiding autoboxing and unboxing via the explicit usage of `int`, `double`, or `long` primitives
- Allowing two input parameters and/or a shorter notation

Here are just a few examples:

- `IntFunction<R>` with the `R apply(int)` method provides a shorter notation (without generics for the input parameter type) and avoids autoboxing by requiring the primitive `int` as a parameter.

- `BiFunction<T,U,R>` with the `R apply(T,U)` method allows two input parameters; `BinaryOperator<T>` with the `T apply(T,T)` method allows two input parameters of type `T` and returns a value of the same type, `T`.

- `IntBinaryOperator` with the `int applAsInt(int,int)` method accepts two parameters of the `int` type and returns the value of the `int` type, too.

If you are going to use functional interfaces, we encourage you to study the API of the interfaces of the `java.util.functional` package (`https://docs.oracle.com/en/java/javase/12/docs/api/java.base/java/util/function/package-summary.html`).

Lambda expression limitations

There are two aspects of a Lambda expression that we would like to point out and clarify:

- If a Lambda expression uses a local variable created outside it, this local variable has to be final or effectively final (not reassigned in the same context).

- The `this` keyword in a Lambda expression refers to the enclosing context, not the Lambda expression itself.

As in an `anonymous` class, the variable created outside and used inside a Lambda expression becomes effectively final and cannot be modified. The following is an example of an error caused by the attempt to change the value of an initialized variable:

```
int x = 7;
//x = 3; //compilation error
Function<Integer, Integer> multiply = i -> i * x;
```

The reason for this restriction is that a function can be passed around and executed in different contexts (different threads, for example), and an attempt to synchronize these contexts would defeat the original idea of the stateless function and the evaluation of the expression, depending only on the input parameters, not on the context variables. That is why all the local variables used in the Lambda expression have to be effectively final, meaning that they can either be *declared* final explicitly or *become* final by virtue of not changing the value.

There is one possible workaround for this limitation though. If the local variable is of a reference type (but not a `String` or primitive wrapping type), it is possible to change its state, even if this local variable is used in the Lambda expression:

```
List<Integer> list = new ArrayList();
list.add(7);
int x = list.get(0);
System.out.println(x);   // prints: 7
list.set(0, 3);
x = list.get(0);
System.out.println(x);   // prints: 3
Function<Integer, Integer> multiply = i -> i * list.get(0);
```

This workaround should be used with care because of the danger of unexpected side effects if this Lambda is executed in a different context.

The `this` keyword inside an `anonymous` class refers to the instance of the `anonymous` class. By contrast, inside the Lambda expression, the `this` keyword refers to the instance of the class that surrounds the expression, also called an **enclosing instance**, **enclosing context**, or **enclosing scope**.

Let's create a `ThisDemo` class that illustrates the difference:

```
class ThisDemo {
    private String field = "ThisDemo.field";

    public void useAnonymousClass() {
        Consumer<String> consumer = new Consumer<>() {
            private String field = "Consumer.field";
            public void accept(String s) {
                System.out.println(this.field);
            }
        };
        consumer.accept(this.field);
    }

    public void useLambdaExpression() {
        Consumer<String> consumer = consumer = s -> {
            System.out.println(this.field);
```

```
        };
        consumer.accept(this.field);
    }
}
```

If we execute the preceding methods, the output will be as shown in the following code comments:

```
ThisDemo d = new ThisDemo();
d.useAnonymousClass();      //prints: Consumer.field
d.useLambdaExpression();    //prints: ThisDemo.field
```

As you can see, the this keyword inside the anonymous class refers to the anonymous class instance, while this in a Lambda expression refers to the enclosing class instance. A Lambda expression just does not (and cannot) have a field. A Lambda expression is not a class instance and cannot be referred to by this. According to Java's specifications, such an approach *allows more flexibility for implementations* by treating this the same as the surrounding context.

Method references

So far, all our functions were short one-liners. Here is another example:

```
Supplier<Integer> input = () -> 3;
Predicate<Integer> checkValue = d -> d < 5;
Function<Integer, Double> calculate = i -> i * 5.0;
Consumer<Double> printResult = d -> System.out.println(
                                            "Result: " + d);

if(checkValue.test(input.get())){
    printResult.accept(calculate.apply(input.get()));
} else {
    System.out.println("Input " + input.get() +
                                        " is too small.");
}
```

If the function consists of two or more lines, we could implement them as follows:

```
Supplier<Integer> input = () -> {
    // as many line of code here as necessary
```

```
        return 3;
};
Predicate<Integer> checkValue = d -> {
    // as many line of code here as necessary
    return d < 5;
};
Function<Integer, Double> calculate = i -> {
    // as many lines of code here as necessary
    return i * 5.0;
};
Consumer<Double> printResult = d -> {
    // as many lines of code here as necessary
    System.out.println("Result: " + d);
};
if(checkValue.test(input.get())){
    printResult.accept(calculate.apply(input.get()));
} else {
    System.out.println("Input " + input.get() +
                                        " is too small.");
}
```

When the size of a function implementation grows beyond several lines of code, such a code layout may not be easy to read. It may obscure the overall code structure. To avoid this issue, it is possible to move the function implementation into a method and then refer to this method in the Lambda expression. For example, let's add one static and one instance method to the class where the Lambda expression is used:

```
private int generateInput(){
    // Maybe many lines of code here
    return 3;
}
private static boolean checkValue(double d){
    // Maybe many lines of code here
    return d < 5;
}
```

Also, to demonstrate the variety of possibilities, let's create another class, with one static method and one instance method:

```java
class Helper {
    public double calculate(int i){
        // Maybe many lines of code here
        return i* 5;
    }
    public static void printResult(double d){
        // Maybe many lines of code here
        System.out.println("Result: " + d);
    }
}
```

Now, we can rewrite our last example as follows:

```java
Supplier<Integer> input = () -> generateInput();
Predicate<Integer> checkValue = d -> checkValue(d);
Function<Integer, Double> calculate = i -> new Helper().
calculate(i);
Consumer<Double> printResult = d -> Helper.printResult(d);

if(checkValue.test(input.get())){
    printResult.accept(calculate.apply(input.get()));
} else {
    System.out.println("Input " + input.get() +
                                        " is too small.");
}
```

As you can see, even if each function consists of many lines of code, such a structure keeps the code easy to read. Yet, when a one-line Lambda expression consists of a reference to an existing method, it is possible to further simplify the notation by using a method reference without listing the parameters.

The syntax of the method reference is Location::methodName, where Location indicates in which object or class the methodName method belongs, and the two colons (::) serve as a separator between the location and the method name. Using method reference notation, the preceding example can be rewritten as follows:

```
Supplier<Integer> input = this::generateInput;
Predicate<Integer> checkValue =
MethodReferenceDemo::checkValue;
Function<Integer, Double> calculate = new Helper()::calculate;
Consumer<Double> printResult = Helper::printResult;

if(checkValue.test(input.get())){
    printResult.accept(calculate.apply(input.get()));
} else {
    System.out.println("Input " + input.get() +
                                        " is too small.");
}
```

You have probably noticed that we have intentionally used different locations, two instance methods, and two static methods in order to demonstrate the variety of possibilities. If it feels like too much to remember, the good news is that a modern IDE (IntelliJ IDEA is one example) can do it for you and convert the code you are writing to the most compact form. You just have to accept the IDE's suggestion.

Summary

This chapter introduced you to functional programming by explaining and demonstrating the concept of functional interfaces and Lambda expressions. The overview of standard functional interfaces that comes with JDK helps you to avoid writing custom code, while the method reference notation allows you to write well-structured code that is easy to understand and maintain.

Now, you are able to write functions and use them for Lambda expressions in order to pass them as a method parameter.

In the next chapter, we will talk about data stream processing. We will define what data streams are, and look at how to process their data and how to chain stream operations in a pipeline. Specifically, we will discuss the streams' initialization and operations (methods), how to connect them in a fluent style, and how to create parallel streams.

Quiz

1. What is a functional interface? Select all that apply:

   A. A collection of functions

   B. An interface that has only one method

   C. Any interface that has only one abstract method

   D. Any library written in Java

2. What is a Lambda expression? Select all that apply:

   A. A function, implemented as an anonymous method without modifiers, return types, and parameter types

   B. A functional interface implementation

   C. Any implementation in a Lambda calculus style

   D. A notation that includes the list of parameters, an arrow token (->), and a body that consists of a single statement or a block of statements

3. How many input parameters does the implementation of the `Consumer<T>` interface have?

4. What is the type of the return value in the implementation of the `Consumer<T>` interface?

5. How many input parameters does the implementation of the `Predicate<T>` interface have?

6. What is the type of the return value in the implementation of the `Predicate<T>` interface?

7. How many input parameters does the implementation of the `Supplier<T>` interface have?

8. What is the type of the return value in the implementation of the `Supplier<T>` interface?

9. How many input parameters does the implementation of the `Function<T,R>` interface have?

10. What is the type of the return value in the implementation of the `Function<T,R>` interface?

11. In a Lambda expression, what does the `this` keyword refer to?

12. What is method reference syntax?

14
Java Standard Streams

In this chapter, we will talk about processing data streams, which are different from the I/O streams we reviewed in *Chapter 5, Strings, Input/Output, and Files*. We will define what data streams are, how to process their elements using methods (operations) of the `java.util.stream.Stream` object, and how to chain (connect) stream operations in a pipeline. We will also discuss stream initialization and how to process streams in parallel.

The following topics will be covered in this chapter:

- Streams as a source of data and operations

- Stream initialization

- Operations (methods)

- Numeric stream interfaces

- Parallel streams

- Creating a standalone stream-processing application

By the end of the chapter, you will be able to write code that processes streams of data as well as create a stream-processing application as a standalone project.

Technical requirements

To be able to execute the code examples provided in this chapter, you will need the following:

- A computer with a Microsoft Windows, Apple macOS, or Linux operating system

- Java SE version 17 or later

- An IDE or code editor of your choice

The instructions for how to set up a Java SE and IntelliJ IDEA editor were provided in *Chapter 1, Getting Started with Java 17*. The files with the code examples for this chapter are available on the GitHub repository at `https://github.com/PacktPublishing/Learn-Java-17-Programming.git` in the `examples/src/main/java/com/packt/learnjava/ch14_streams` folder and the `streams` folder, which contains a standalone stream-processing application.

Streams as a source of data and operations

Lambda expressions, described and demonstrated in the previous chapter, together with functional interfaces add a powerful functional programming capability to Java. They allow passing behavior (functions) as parameters to libraries optimized for the performance of data processing. This way, an application programmer can concentrate on the business aspects of a developed system, leaving the performance aspects to the specialists – the authors of the library. One example of such a library is `java.util.stream`, which is going to be the focus of this chapter.

In *Chapter 5, Strings, Input/Output, and Files*, we talked about I/O streams as a source of data, but beyond that, they are not of much help for further processing of data. Also, they are byte- or character-based, not object-based. You can create a stream of objects only after objects have been programmatically created and serialized first. The I/O streams are just connections to external resources, mostly files, and not much else. However, sometimes it is possible to make a transition from an I/O stream to `java.util.stream.Stream`. For example, the `BufferedReader` class has the `lines()` method that converts the underlying character-based stream into a `Stream<String>` object.

On the other hand, the streams of the `java.util.stream` package are oriented toward processing collections of objects. In *Chapter 6, Data Structures, Generics, and Popular Utilities*, we described two methods of the `Collection` interface that allow you to read collection elements as elements of a stream: `default Stream<E> stream()` and `default Stream<E> parallelStream()`. We also mentioned the `stream()` method of `java.util.Arrays`. It has the following eight overloaded versions that convert an array or part of it into a stream of the corresponding data types:

- `static DoubleStream stream(double[] array)`
- `static DoubleStream stream(double[] array, int startInclusive, int endExclusive)`
- `static IntStream stream(int[] array)`
- `static IntStream stream(int[] array, int startInclusive, int endExclusive)`
- `static LongStream stream(long[] array)`
- `static LongStream stream(long[] array, int startInclusive, int endExclusive)`
- `static <T> Stream<T> stream(T[] array)`
- `static <T> Stream<T> stream(T[] array, int startInclusive, int endExclusive)`

Let's now look closer at the streams of the `java.util.stream` package. The best way to understand what a stream is is to compare it with a collection. The latter is a data structure stored in memory. Every collection element is computed before being added to the collection. By contrast, an element emitted by a stream exists somewhere else, in the source, and is computed on demand. So, a collection can be a source for a stream.

A `Stream` object is an implementation of the `Stream` interface, `IntStream`, `LongStream`, or `DoubleStream`; the last three are called **numeric streams**. The methods of the `Stream` interface are also available in numeric streams. Some of the numeric streams have a few extra methods, such as `average()` and `sum()`, which are specific numeric values. In this chapter, we are going to speak mostly about the `Stream` interface and its methods, but everything we will cover is equally applicable to numeric streams too.

A stream *produces* (or *emits*) stream elements as soon as a previously emitted element has been processed. It allows declarative presentation of methods (operations) that can be applied to the emitted elements, also in parallel. Today, when the machine learning requirements of large dataset processing are becoming ubiquitous, this feature reinforces the position of Java as one of the few modern programming languages of choice.

Will all that said, we will start with a stream initialization.

Stream initialization

There are many ways to create and initialize a stream – an object of type `Stream` or any of the numeric interfaces. We grouped them by classes and interfaces that have stream-creating methods. We did it for your convenience so that it would be easier for you to remember and find them if need be.

Stream interface

This group of `Stream` factories is composed of static methods that belong to the `Stream` interface.

empty()

The `Stream<T>` `empty()` method creates an empty stream that does not emit any element:

```
Stream.empty().forEach(System.out::println);    //prints nothing
```

The `forEach()` `Stream` method acts similarly to the `forEach()` `Collection` method and applies the passed-in function to each of the stream elements:

```
new ArrayList().forEach(System.out::println);   //prints nothing
```

The result is the same as creating a stream from an empty collection:

```
new ArrayList().stream().forEach(System.out::println);
                                                //prints nothing
```

Without any element emitted, nothing happens. We will discuss the `forEach()` `Stream` method in the *Terminal operations* subsection.

of(T... values)

The `of(T... values)` method accepts varargs and can also create an empty stream:

```
Stream.of().forEach(System.out::print);          //prints nothing
```

However, it is most often used for initializing a non-empty stream:

```
Stream.of(1).forEach(System.out::print);              //prints: 1
Stream.of(1,2).forEach(System.out::print);            //prints: 12
Stream.of("1 ","2").forEach(System.out::print);    //prints: 1 2
```

Note the method reference used for the invocation of the `println()` and `print()` methods.

Another way to use the `of(T... values)` method is as follows:

```
String[] strings = {"1 ", "2"};
Stream.of(strings).forEach(System.out::print);    //prints: 1 2
```

If there is no type specified for the `Stream` object, the compiler does not complain if the array contains a mix of types:

```
Stream.of("1 ", 2).forEach(System.out::print);    //prints: 1 2
```

Adding generics that declare the expected element type causes an exception when at least one of the listed elements has a different type:

```
//Stream<String> stringStream = Stream.of("1 ", 2);
                                                 //compile error
```

Generics help a programmer to avoid many mistakes, so they should be added wherever possible.

The `of(T... values)` method can also be used for the concatenation of multiple streams. Let's assume, for example, that we have the following four streams that we would like to concatenate into one:

```
Stream<Integer> stream1 = Stream.of(1, 2);
Stream<Integer> stream2 = Stream.of(2, 3);
Stream<Integer> stream3 = Stream.of(3, 4);
Stream<Integer> stream4 = Stream.of(4, 5);
```

We would like to concatenate them into a new stream that emits the $1,2,2,3,3,4,4,5$ values. First, we try the following code:

```
Stream.of(stream1, stream2, stream3, stream4)
   .forEach(System.out::print);
     //prints: java.util.stream.ReferencePipeline$Head@58ceff1j
```

It does not do what we hoped for. It treats each stream as an object of the `java.util.stream.ReferencePipeline` internal class that is used in the `Stream` interface implementation. So, we need to add the `flatMap()` operation to convert each stream element into a stream (which we will describe in the *Intermediate operations* subsection):

```
Stream.of(stream1, stream2, stream3, stream4)
  .flatMap(e -> e).forEach(System.out::print);
                                              //prints: 12233445
```

The function we passed into `flatMap()` as a parameter (`e -> e`) looks like it's doing nothing, but that is because each element of the stream is a stream already, so there is no need to transform it. By returning an element as the result of the `flatMap()` operation, we tell the pipeline to treat the return value as a `Stream` object.

ofNullable(T t)

The `ofNullable(T t)` method returns `Stream<T>`, emitting a single element if the passed-in `t` parameter is not `null`; otherwise, it returns an empty `Stream`. To demonstrate the usage of the `ofNullable(T t)` method, we create the following method:

```
void printList1(List<String> list){
    list.stream().forEach(System.out::print);
}
```

We execute this method twice – with the parameter list equal to `null` and a `List` object. Here are the results:

```
//printList1(null);                    //NullPointerException
List<String> list = List.of("1 ", "2");
printList1(list);                      //prints: 1 2
```

Note how the first call to the `printList1()` method generates
`NullPointerException`. To avoid the exception, we can implement the method
as follows:

```
void printList1(List<String> list){
    (list == null ? Stream.empty() : list.stream())
                        .forEach(System.out::print);
}
```

The same result can be achieved with the `ofNullable(T t)` method:

```
void printList2(List<String> list){
    Stream.ofNullable(list).flatMap(l -> l.stream())
                        .forEach(System.out::print);
}
```

Note how we have added `flatMap()` because, otherwise, the `Stream` element that
flows into `forEach()` would be a `List` object. We will talk more about the `flatMap()`
method in the *Intermediate operations* subsection. The function passed into the
`flatMap()` operation in the preceding code can be expressed as a method reference too:

```
void printList4(List<String> list){
    Stream.ofNullable(list).flatMap(Collection::stream)
                        .forEach(System.out::print);
}
```

Iterate (Objectand UnaryOperator)

Two static methods of the `Stream` interface allow you to generate a stream of values
using an iterative process similar to the traditional `for` loop, as follows:

- `Stream<T> iterate(T seed, UnaryOperator<T> func)`: This creates
  an infinite sequential stream based on the iterative application of the second
  parameter, the `func` function, to the first `seed` parameter, producing a stream of
  values: `seed, f(seed), f(f(seed))`, and so on.

- `Stream<T> iterate(T seed, Predicate<T> hasNext, UnaryOperator<T> next)`: This creates a finite sequential stream based on the iterative application of the third parameter, the `next` function, to the first `seed` parameter, producing a stream of values: `seed`, `f(seed)`, `f(f(seed))`, and so on, as long as the third parameter, the `hasNext` function, returns `true`.

The following code demonstrates the usage of these methods, as follows:

```
Stream.iterate(1, i -> ++i).limit(9)
        .forEach(System.out::print);    //prints: 123456789


Stream.iterate(1, i -> i < 10, i -> ++i)
        .forEach(System.out::print);    //prints: 123456789
```

Note that we were forced to add an intermediate operator, `limit(int n)`, to the first pipeline to avoid generating an infinite number of generated values. We will talk more about this method in the *Intermediate operations* subsection.

concat (stream a and stream b)

The `Stream<T> concat(Stream<> a, Stream<T> b)` static method of the `Stream` interface creates a stream of values based on two streams, a and b, passed in as parameters. The newly created stream consists of all the elements of the first parameter, a, followed by all the elements of the second parameter, b. The following code demonstrates this method:

```
Stream<Integer> stream1 = List.of(1, 2).stream();
Stream<Integer> stream2 = List.of(2, 3).stream();
Stream.concat(stream1, stream2)
  .forEach(System.out::print); //prints: 1223
```

Note that the 2 element is present in both original streams and consequently is emitted twice by the resulting stream.

generate (Supplier)

The `Stream<T> generate(Supplier<T> supplier)` static method of the `Stream` interface creates an infinite stream, where each element is generated by the provided `Supplier<T>` function. The following are two examples:

```
Stream.generate(() -> 1).limit(5)
  .forEach(System.out::print);      //prints: 11111


Stream.generate(() -> new Random().nextDouble()).limit(5)
    .forEach(System.out::println);  //prints: 0.38575117472619247
                                    //          0.5055765386778835
                                    //          0.6528038976983277
                                    //          0.4422354489467244
                                    //          0.06770955839148762
```

If you run this code, you will probably get different results because of the random (pseudo-random) nature of the generated values.

Since the created stream is infinite, we have added a `limit(int n)` operation that allows only the specified number of stream elements to flow through. We will talk more about this method in the *Intermediate operations* subsection.

The Stream.Builder interface

The `Stream.Builder<T> builder()` static method returns an internal (located inside the `Stream` interface) `Builder` interface that can be used to construct a `Stream` object. The interface `Builder` extends the `Consumer` interface and has the following methods:

- `default Stream.Builder<T> add(T t)`: This calls the `accept(T)` method and returns the `Builder` object, thus allowing you to chain the add `(T t)` methods in a fluent dot-connected style.

- `void accept(T t)`: This adds an element to the stream (this method comes from the `Consumer` interface).

- `Stream<T> build()`: This transitions this builder from the constructing state to the `built` state. After this method is called, no new elements can be added to this stream.

The usage of the add(T t) method is straightforward:

```
Stream.<String>builder().add("cat").add(" dog").add(" bear")
    .build().forEach(System.out::print);  //prints: cat dog bear
```

Note how we have added the <String> generics in front of the builder() method. This way, we tell the builder that the stream we are creating will have String-type elements. Otherwise, it will add the elements as Object types and not make sure that the added elements are of the String type.

The accept(T t) method is used when the builder is passed as a parameter of the Consumer<T> type or when you do not need to chain the methods that add the elements. The following is a code example:

```
Stream.Builder<String> builder = Stream.builder();
List.of("1", "2", "3").stream().forEach(builder);
builder.build().forEach(System.out::print);     //prints: 123
```

The forEach(Consumer<T> consumer) method accepts a Consumer function that has the accept(T t) method. Every time an element is emitted by the stream, the forEach() method receives it and passes it to the accept(T t) method of the Builder object. Then, when the build() method is called in the next line, the Stream object is created and starts emitting the elements added earlier by the accept(T t) method. The emitted elements are passed to the forEach() method, which then prints them one by one.

Here is an example of an explicit usage of the accept(T t) method:

```
List<String> values = List.of("cat", " dog", " bear");
Stream.Builder<String> builder = Stream.builder();
for(String s: values){
    if(s.contains("a")){
        builder.accept(s);
    }
}
builder.build().forEach(System.out::print);  //prints: cat bear
```

This time, we decided not to add all the list elements to the stream but only those that contain the a character. As expected, the created stream contains only the cat and bear elements. Also, note how we use <String> generics to make sure that all the stream elements are of the String type.

Other classes and interfaces

In Java 8, two default methods were added to the `java.util.Collection` interface, as follows:

- `Stream<E> stream()`: This returns a stream of the elements of this collection.

- `Stream<E> parallelStream()`: This returns (possibly) a parallel stream of the elements of this collection – we say *possibly*, because the JVM attempts to split the stream into several chunks and process them in parallel (if there are several CPUs) or virtually parallel (using CPU time-sharing). However, it is not always possible and depends, in part, on the nature of the requested processing.

This means that all the collection interfaces that extend this interface, including `Set` and `List`, have these methods, as shown in this example:

```
List.of("1", "2", "3").stream().forEach(builder);
List.of("1", "2", "3").parallelStream().forEach(builder);
```

We will talk about parallel streams in the *Parallel streams* section.

We described eight static overloaded `stream()` methods of the `java.util.Arrays` class at the beginning of the *Streams as a source of data and operations* section. Here is an example of another way of creating a stream, using the subset of an array:

```
int[] arr = {1, 2, 3, 4, 5};
Arrays.stream(arr, 2, 4).forEach(System.out::print);
                                              //prints: 34
```

The `java.util.Random` class allows you to create numeric streams of pseudo-random values, as follows:

- `DoubleStream doubles()`: Creates an unlimited stream of `double` values between 0 (inclusive) and 1 (exclusive)

- `IntStream ints()` and `LongStream longs()`: Creates an unlimited stream of corresponding type values

- `DoubleStream doubles(long streamSize)`: Creates a stream (of the specified size) of `double` values between 0 (inclusive) and 1 (exclusive)

- `IntStream ints(long streamSize)` and `LongStream longs(long streamSize)`: Creates a stream of the specified size of the corresponding type values

- `IntStream ints(int randomNumberOrigin, int randomNumberBound)`: Creates an unlimited stream of `int` values between `randomNumberOrigin` (inclusive) and `randomNumberBound` (exclusive)

- `LongStream longs(long randomNumberOrigin, long randomNumberBound)`: Creates an unlimited stream of `long` values between `randomNumberOrigin` (inclusive) and `randomNumberBound` (exclusive)

- `DoubleStream doubles(long streamSize, double randomNumberOrigin, double randomNumberBound)`: Creates a stream of the specified size of `double` values between `randomNumberOrigin` (inclusive) and `randomNumberBound` (exclusive)

Here is an example of one of the preceding methods:

```
new Random().ints(5, 8).limit(5)
            .forEach(System.out::print);    //prints: 56757
```

Due to the use of `random`, every execution may (and probably will) generate a different result.

The `java.nio.file.Files` class has six static methods creating streams of lines and paths, as follows:

- `Stream<String> lines(Path path)`: Creates a stream of lines from the file specified by the provided path

- `Stream<String> lines(Path path, Charset cs)`: Creates a stream of lines from the file specified by the provided path; bytes from the file are decoded into characters using the provided `charset`

- `Stream<Path> list(Path dir)`: Creates a stream of files and directories in the specified directory

- `Stream<Path> walk(Path start, FileVisitOption... options)`: Creates a stream of files and directories of the file tree that starts with `Path start`

- `Stream<Path> walk(Path start, int maxDepth, FileVisitOption... options)`: Creates a stream of files and directories of the file tree that starts with `Path start`, down to the specified `maxDepth` depth

- `Stream<Path> find(Path start, int maxDepth, BiPredicate<Path, BasicFileAttributes> matcher, FileVisitOption... options)`: Creates a stream of files and directories (that match the provided predicate) of the file tree that starts with `Path start`, down to the specified depth, specified by the `maxDepth` value

Other classes and methods that create streams include the following:

- The `java.util.BitSet` class has the `IntStream stream()` method, which creates a stream of indices, for which this `BitSet` contains a bit in the `set` state.

- The `java.io.BufferedReader` class has the `Stream<String> lines()` method, which creates a stream of lines from this `BufferedReader` object, typically from a file.

- The `java.util.jar.JarFile` class has the `Stream<JarEntry> stream()` method that creates a stream of ZIP file entries.

- The `java.util.regex.Pattern` class has the `Stream<String> splitAsStream(CharSequence input)` method, which creates a stream from the provided sequence around matches of this pattern.

A `java.lang.CharSequence` interface has two methods, as follows:

- `default IntStream chars()`: Creates a stream of int, zero-extending the char values

- `default IntStream codePoints()`: Creates a stream of code point values from this sequence

There is also a `java.util.stream.StreamSupport` class that contains static low-level utility methods for library developers. However, we won't be reviewing it, as this is outside the scope of this book.

Operations (methods)

Many methods of the `Stream` interface, including those that have a functional interface type as a parameter, are called **operations** because they are not implemented as traditional methods. Their functionality is passed into a method as a function. The operations are just shells that call a method of the functional interface, assigned as the type of the `parameter` method.

For example, let's look at the `Stream<T> filter (Predicate<T> predicate)` method. Its implementation is based on the call to the `test (T t)` method Boolean of the `Predicate<T>` function. So, instead of saying, *we use the* `filter ()` *method of the* `Stream` *object to select some of the stream elements and skip others*, programmers prefer to say, *we apply an operation filter that allows some of the stream elements to get through and skip others*. It describes the nature of the action (operation), not the particular algorithm, which is unknown until the method receives a particular function. There are two groups of operations in the `Stream` interface, as follows:

- **Intermediate operations**: Instance methods that return a `Stream` object

- **Terminal operations**: Instance methods that return some type other than `Stream`

Stream processing is organized typically as a pipeline, using a fluent (dot-connected) style. A `Stream`-creating method or another stream source starts such a pipeline. A terminal operation produces the final result or a side effect and eponymously ends the pipeline. An intermediate operation can be placed between the originating `Stream` object and the terminal operation.

An intermediate operation processes stream elements (or not, in some cases) and returns the modified (or not) `Stream` object, so the next intermediate or terminal operation can be applied. Examples of intermediate operations are the following:

- `Stream<T> filter(Predicate<T> predicate)`: Selects only elements matching a criterion.

- `Stream<R> map(Function<T,R> mapper)`: Transforms elements according to the passed-in function. Note that the type of the returned `Stream` object may be quite different from the input type.

- `Stream<T> distinct()`: Removes duplicates.

- `Stream<T> limit(long maxSize)`: Limits a stream to the specified number of elements.

- `Stream<T> sorted()`: Arranges the stream elements in a certain order.

We will discuss some other intermediate operations in the *Intermediate operations* section.

The processing of the stream elements actually begins only when a terminal operation starts executing. Then, all the intermediate operations (if present) start processing in sequence. As soon as the terminal operation has finished execution, the stream closes and cannot be reopened.

Examples of terminal operations are `forEach()`, `findFirst()`, `reduce()`, `collect()`, `sum()`, `max()`, and other methods of the `Stream` interface that do not return the `Stream` object. We will discuss them in the *Terminal operations* subsection.

All the `Stream` operations support parallel processing, which is especially helpful in the case of a large amount of data processed on a multi-core computer. We will discuss it in the *Parallel streams* subsection.

Intermediate operations

As we mentioned already, an intermediate operation returns a `Stream` object that emits the same or modified values and may even be of a different type than the stream source.

The intermediate operations can be grouped by their functionality into four categories of operations that perform **filtering**, **mapping**, **sorting**, or **peeking**.

Filtering

This group includes operations that remove duplicates, skip some of the elements, limit the number of processed elements, and select for further processing only those that pass certain criteria, as follows:

- `Stream<T> distinct()`: Compares stream elements using `Object.equals(Object)` method and skips duplicates

- `Stream<T> skip(long n)`: Ignores the provided number of stream elements that are emitted first

- `Stream<T> limit(long maxSize)`: Allows only the provided number of stream elements to be processed

- `Stream<T> filter(Predicate<T> predicate)`: Allows only those elements to be processed that result in `true` when processed by the provided `Predicate` function

- `default Stream<T> dropWhile(Predicate<T> predicate)`: Skips those first elements of the stream that result in `true` when processed by the provided `Predicate` function

- `default Stream<T> takeWhile(Predicate<T> predicate)`: Allows only those first elements of the stream to be processed that result in `true` when processed by the provided `Predicate` function

The following is code that demonstrates how the operations just described work:

```java
Stream.of("3", "2", "3", "4", "2").distinct()
                .forEach(System.out::print);      //prints: 324

List<String> list = List.of("1", "2", "3", "4", "5");
list.stream().skip(3).forEach(System.out::print);  //prints: 45

list.stream().limit(3).forEach(System.out::print);
                                                  //prints: 123

list.stream().filter(s -> Objects.equals(s, "2"))
            .forEach(System.out::print);          //prints: 2

list.stream().dropWhile(s -> Integer.valueOf(s) < 3)
            .forEach(System.out::print);          //prints: 345

list.stream().takeWhile(s -> Integer.valueOf(s) < 3)
            .forEach(System.out::print);          //prints: 12
```

Note that we were able to reuse the source List<String> object but could not reuse the Stream object. Once a Stream object is closed, it cannot be reopened.

Mapping

This group includes arguably the most important intermediate operations. They are the only intermediate operations that modify the elements of the stream. They **map** (transform) the original stream element value to a new one, as follows:

- Stream<R> map(Function<T, R> mapper): Applies the provided function to each element of type T of the stream and produces a new element value of type R

- IntStream mapToInt(ToIntFunction<T> mapper): Applies the provided function to each element of type T of the stream and produces a new element value of type int

- LongStream mapToLong(ToLongFunction<T> mapper): Applies the provided function to each element of type T of the stream and produces a new element value of type long

- `DoubleStream mapToDouble(ToDoubleFunction<T> mapper)`: Applies the provided function to each element of type `T` of the stream and produces a new element value of type `double`

- `Stream<R> flatMap(Function<T, Stream<R>> mapper)`: Applies the provided function to each element of type `T` of the stream and produces a `Stream<R>` object that emits elements of type R

- `IntStream flatMapToInt(Function<T, IntStream> mapper)`: Applies the provided function to each element of type `T` of the stream and produces a `IntStream` object that emits elements of type `int`

- `LongStream flatMapToLong(Function<T, LongStream> mapper)`: Applies the provided function to each element of type `T` of the stream and produces a `LongStream` object that emits elements of type `long`

- `DoubleStream flatMapToDouble(Function<T, DoubleStream> mapper)`: Applies the provided function to each element of type `T` of the stream and produces a `DoubleStream` object that emits elements of type `double`

The following are examples of the usage of these operations, as follows:

```
List<String> list = List.of("1", "2", "3", "4", "5");
list.stream().map(s -> s + s)
            .forEach(System.out::print);  //prints: 1122334455

list.stream().mapToInt(Integer::valueOf)
            .forEach(System.out::print);  //prints: 12345

list.stream().mapToLong(Long::valueOf)
            .forEach(System.out::print);  //prints: 12345

list.stream().mapToDouble(Double::valueOf)
        .mapToObj(Double::toString)
        .map(s -> s + " ")
        .forEach(System.out::print);
                                //prints: 1.0 2.0 3.0 4.0 5.0

list.stream().mapToInt(Integer::valueOf)
    .flatMap(n -> IntStream.iterate(1, I -> i < n, i -> ++i))
```

```
    .forEach(System.out::print);                //prints: 1121231234

list.stream().map(Integer::valueOf)
    .flatMapToInt(n -> IntStream.iterate(1, i->i<n, i -> ++i))
    .forEach(System.out::print);                //prints: 1121231234

list.stream().map(Integer::valueOf)
    .flatMapToLong(n -> LongStream.iterate(1, i->i<n,i -> ++i))
    .forEach(System.out::print);                //prints: 1121231234

list.stream().map(Integer::valueOf)
  .flatMapToDouble(n -> DoubleStream.iterate(1,i->i<n,i -> ++i))
    .mapToObj(Double::toString)
    .map(s -> s +"""")
    .forEach(System.out::print);
                //prints: 1.0 1.0 2.0 1.0 2.0 3.0 1.0 2.0 3.0 4.0
```

In the last example, by converting the stream to DoubleStream, we transformed each numeric value to a String object and added white space, so the result can be printed with whitespace between the numbers. These examples are very simple – just conversion with minimal processing. But in real life, each map() or flatMap() operation typically accepts a more complex function that does something more useful.

Sorting

The following two intermediate operations sort the stream elements, as follows:

- Stream<T> sorted(): Sorts stream elements in natural order (according to their Comparable interface implementation)

- Stream<T> sorted(Comparator<T> comparator): Sorts stream elements in order according to the provided Comparator<T> object

Naturally, these operations cannot be finished until all the elements are emitted, so such processing creates a lot of overhead, slows down performance, and has to be used for small streams.

Here is some demo code:

```
List<String> list = List.of("2", "1", "5", "4", "3");
list.stream().sorted().forEach(System.out::print);
                                            //prints: 12345
list.stream().sorted(Comparator.reverseOrder())
             .forEach(System.out::print);    //prints: 54321
```

Peeking

An intermediate `Stream<T> peek(Consumer<T> action)` operation applies the provided `Consumer<T>` function to each stream element but does not change the stream values (`Consumer<T>` returns `void`). This operation is used for debugging. The following code shows how it works:

```
List<String> list = List.of("1", "2", "3", "4", "5");
list.stream()
  .peek(s -> System.out.print("3".equals(s) ? 3 : 0))
  .forEach(System.out::print); //prints: 0102330405
```

Terminal operations

Terminal operations are the most important operations in a stream pipeline. It is possible to accomplish everything in them without using any other operations.

We have already used the `forEach(Consumer<T>)` terminal operation to print each element. It does not return a value, thus it is used for its side effects. However, the `Stream` interface has many more powerful terminal operations that do return values.

Chief among them is the `collect()` operation, which has two forms, as follows:

- `R collect(Collector<T, A, R> collector)`

- `R collect(Supplier<R> supplier, BiConsumer<R, T> accumulator, BiConsumer<R, R> combiner)`

This allows you to compose practically any process that can be applied to a stream. The classic example is as follows:

```
List<String> list = Stream.of("1", "2", "3", "4", "5")
                          .collect(ArrayList::new,
                                   ArrayList::add,
```

```
                                      ArrayList::addAll);
  System.out.println(list);   //prints: [1, 2, 3, 4, 5]
```

This example is used in such a way as to be suitable for parallel processing. The first parameter of the `collect()` operation is a function that produces a value based on the stream element. The second parameter is the function that accumulates the result. The third parameter is the function that combines the accumulated results from all the threads that processed the stream.

However, having only one such generic terminal operation will force programmers to write the same functions repeatedly. That is why the API authors added the `Collectors` class, which generates many specialized `Collector` objects without the need to create three functions for every `collect()` operation.

In addition to that, the API authors added to the `Stream` interface various even more specialized terminal operations that are much simpler and easier to use. In this section, we will review all the terminal operations of the `Stream` interface and, in the `Collect` subsection, look at the plethora of `Collector` objects produced by the `Collectors` class. We will start with the most simple terminal operation that allows you to process each element of this stream one at a time.

In our examples, we are going to use the following class, `Person`:

```java
public class Person {
    private int age;
    private String name;
    public Person(int age, String name) {
        this.age = age;
        this.name = name;
    }
    public int getAge() {return this.age; }
    public String getName() { return this.name; }
    @Override
    public String toString() {
        return "Person{" + "name='" + this.name + "'" +
                                    ", age=" + age + "}";
    }
}
```

Processing each element

There are two terminal operations in this group, as follows:

- `void forEach(Consumer<T> action)`: Applies the provided action for each element of this stream

- `void forEachOrdered(Consumer<T> action)`: Applies the provided action for each element of this stream in the order defined by the source, regardless of whether the stream is sequential or parallel

If the order in which you need the elements to be processed is important and has to be the order in which values are arranged at the source, use the second method, especially if you can foresee that it is possible your code is going to be executed on a computer with several CPUs. Otherwise, use the first one, as we did in all our examples.

Let's see an example of the `forEach()` operation in use for reading comma-separated values (age and name) from a file and creating `Person` objects. We have placed the following `persons.csv` file (**csv** stands for **comma-separated values**) file in the `resources` folder:

```
23 , Ji m
   2 5 , Bob
  15 , Jill
17 , Bi ll
```

We have added spaces inside and outside the values in order to take this opportunity to show you some simple but very useful tips for working with real-life data.

First, we will just read the file and display its content line by line, but only those lines that contain the letter J (adjust the path value or set it to `absolute` if the code cannot find the `persons.csv` file):

```
Path path = Paths.get("src/main/resources/persons.csv");
try (Stream<String> lines = Files.newBufferedReader(path).
lines()) {
    lines.filter(s -> s.contains("J"))
         .forEach(System.out::println);
                                //prints: 23 , Ji m 15 , Jill
} catch (IOException ex) {
    ex.printStackTrace();
}
```

That is a typical way of using the `forEach()` operation – processing each element independently. This code also provides an example of a try-with-resources construct that closes the `BufferedReader` object automatically.

The following is how an inexperienced programmer might write code that reads the stream elements from the `Stream<String>` lines object and creates a list of `Person` objects:

```java
List<Person> persons = new ArrayList<>();
lines.filter(s -> s.contains("J")).forEach(s -> {
    String[] arr = s.split(",");
    int age = Integer.valueOf(StringUtils.remove(arr[0], ' '));
    persons.add(new Person(age, StringUtils.remove(arr[1],
                                                      ' ')));
});
```

You can see how the `split()` method is used to break each line by a comma that separates the values and how the `org.apache.commons.lang3.StringUtils.remove()` method removes spaces from each value. Although this code works well in small examples on a single-core computer, it might create unexpected results with a long stream and parallel processing.

This is the reason that lambda expressions require all variables to be final or effectively final – so that the same function can be executed in a different context.

The following is a correct implementation of the preceding code:

```java
List<Person> persons = lines.filter(s -> s.contains("J"))
    .map(s -> s.split(","))
    .map(arr -> {
        int age = Integer.valueOf(StringUtils.remove(arr[0],
                                                      ' '));
        return new Person(age, StringUtils.remove(arr[1], ' '));
    }).collect(Collectors.toList());
```

To improve readability, we can create a method that does the job of mapping:

```java
private Person createPerson(String[] arr){
    int age = Integer.valueOf(StringUtils.remove(arr[0], ' '));
    return new Person(age, StringUtils.remove(arr[1], ' '));
}
```

Now, we can use it as follows:

```
List<Person> persons = lines.filter(s -> s.contains("J"))
                            .map(s -> s.split(","))
                            .map(this::createPerson)
                            .collect(Collectors.toList());
```

As you can see, we have used the `collect()` operator and the `Collector` function created by the `Collectors.toList()` method. We will see more functions created by the `Collectors` class in the *Collect* subsection.

Counting all elements

The `long count()` terminal operation of the `Stream` interface looks straightforward and benign. It returns the number of elements in this stream. Those who are used to working with collections and arrays may use the `count()` operation without thinking twice. The following code snippet demonstrates a caveat:

```
long count = Stream.of("1", "2", "3", "4", "5")
                    .peek(System.out::print)
                    .count();
System.out.print(count);            //prints: 5
```

If we run the preceding code, the result will look as follows:

```
5
```

As you see, the code that implements the `count()` method was able to determine the stream size without executing all the pipelines. The `peek()` operation did not print anything, which proves that elements were not emitted. So, if you expected to see the values of the stream printed, you might be puzzled and expect that the code has some kind of defect.

Another caveat is that it is not always possible to determine the stream size at the source. Besides, the stream may be infinite. So, you have to use `count()` with care.

Another possible way to determine the stream size is by using the `collect()` operation:

```
long count = Stream.of("1", "2", "3", "4", "5")
                    .peek(System.out::print)       //prints: 12345
                    .collect(Collectors.counting());
System.out.println(count);                         //prints: 5
```

The following screenshot shows what happens after the preceding code example has been run:

As you can see, the `collect()` operation does not calculate the stream size at the source. That is because the `collect()` operation is not as specialized as the `count()` operation. It just applies the passed-in collector to the stream. The collector just counts the elements provided to it by the `collect()` operation.

Match all, any, or none

There are three seemingly very similar terminal operations that allow us to assess whether all, any, or none of the stream elements have a certain value, as follows:

- `boolean allMatch(Predicate<T> predicate)`: Returns `true` when each of the stream elements returns `true` when used as a parameter of the provided `Predicate<T>` function

- `boolean anyMatch(Predicate<T> predicate)`: Returns `true` when one of the stream elements returns `true` when used as a parameter of the provided `Predicate<T>` function

- `boolean noneMatch(Predicate<T> predicate)`: Returns `true` when none of the stream elements return `true` when used as a parameter of the provided `Predicate<T>` function

The following are examples of their usage:

```
List<String> list = List.of("1", "2", "3", "4", "5");
boolean found = list.stream()
                .peek(System.out::print)      //prints: 123
                .anyMatch(e -> "3".equals(e));
System.out.println(found);                        //prints: true


boolean noneMatches = list.stream()
                    .peek(System.out::print) //prints: 123
                    .noneMatch(e -> "3".equals(e));
System.out.println(noneMatches);                  //prints: false


boolean allMatch = list.stream()
```

```
                            .peek(System.out::print)      //prints: 1
                            .allMatch(e -> "3".equals(e));
    System.out.println(allMatch);                    //prints: false
```

Please note that all these operations are optimized so as not to process all the stream elements if the result can be determined early.

Find any or first

The following terminal operations allow you to find any element or the first element of the stream correspondingly, as follows:

- `Optional<T> findAny()`: Returns `Optional` with the value of any element of the stream, or an empty `Optional` if the stream is empty

- `Optional<T> findFirst()`: Returns an `Optional` with the value of the first element of the stream, or an empty `Optional` if the stream is empty

The following examples illustrate these operations:

```
List<String> list = List.of("1", "2", "3", "4", "5");
Optional<String> result = list.stream().findAny();
System.out.println(result.isPresent());    //prints: true
System.out.println(result.get());          //prints: 1

result = list.stream()
             .filter(e -> "42".equals(e))
             .findAny();
System.out.println(result.isPresent());    //prints: false
//System.out.println(result.get());        //NoSuchElementException

result = list.stream().findFirst();
System.out.println(result.isPresent());    //prints: true
System.out.println(result.get());          //prints: 1
```

In the first and third of the preceding examples, the `findAny()` and `findFirst()` operations produce the same result – they both find the first element of the stream. But in parallel processing, the result may be different.

When the stream is broken into several parts for parallel processing, the `findFirst()` operation always returns the first element of the stream, while the `findAny()` operation returns the first element only in one of the processing threads.

Now, let's talk about `class java.util.Optional` in more detail.

Optional class

The object of `java.util.Optional` is used to avoid returning `null` (as it may cause `NullPointerException`). Instead, an `Optional` object provides methods that allow you to check for the presence of a value and substitute it with a predefined value if the return value is `null`, as shown in the following example:

```java
List<String> list = List.of("1", "2", "3", "4", "5");
String result = list.stream()
                    .filter(e -> "42".equals(e))
                    .findAny()
                    .or(() -> Optional.of("Not found"))
                    .get();
System.out.println(result);                 //prints: Not found


result = list.stream()
             .filter(e -> "42".equals(e))
             .findAny()
             .orElse("Not found");
System.out.println(result);                 //prints: Not found


Supplier<String> trySomethingElse = () -> {
    //Code that tries something else
    return "43";
};
result = list.stream()
             .filter(e -> "42".equals(e))
             .findAny()
             .orElseGet(trySomethingElse);
System.out.println(result);                 //prints: 43


list.stream()
    .filter(e -> "42".equals(e))
```

```
.findAny()
.ifPresentOrElse(System.out::println,
   () -> System.out.println("Not found"));
                                    //prints: Not found
```

As you can see, if the `Optional` object is empty, then the following applies, as follows:

- The `or()` method of the `Optional` class allows you to return an alternative `Optional` object.

- The `orElse()` method allows you to return an alternative value.

- The `orElseGet()` method allows you to provide the `Supplier` function, which returns an alternative value.

- The `ifPresentOrElse()` method allows you to provide two functions – one that consumes the value from the `Optional` object, and another one that does something else if the `Optional` object is empty.

Minimum and maximum

The following terminal operations return the minimum or maximum value of stream elements, if present, as follows:

- `Optional<T> min(Comparator<T> comparator)`: Returns the minimum element of this stream using the provided `Comparator` object

- `Optional<T> max(Comparator<T> comparator)`: Returns the maximum element of this stream using the provided `Comparator` object

The following code demonstrates this:

```
List<String> list = List.of("a", "b", "c", "c", "a");
String min = list.stream()
               .min(Comparator.naturalOrder())
               .orElse("0");
System.out.println(min);      //prints: a

String max = list.stream()
 .max(Comparator.naturalOrder())
               .orElse("0");
System.out.println(max);      //prints: c
```

As you can see, in the case of non-numerical values, the minimum element is the one that is first when ordered from left to right, according to the provided comparator. The maximum, accordingly, is the last element. In the case of numeric values, the minimum and maximum are just that – the smallest and biggest numbers among the stream elements:

```java
int mn = Stream.of(42, 77, 33)
              .min(Comparator.naturalOrder())
              .orElse(0);
System.out.println(mn);      //prints: 33


int mx = Stream.of(42, 77, 33)
              .max(Comparator.naturalOrder())
              .orElse(0);
System.out.println(mx);      //prints: 77
```

Let's look at another example, using the `Person` class. The task is to find the oldest person in the following list:

```java
List<Person> persons = List.of(new Person(23, "Bob"),
  new Person(33, "Jim"),
  new Person(28, "Jill"),
  new Person(27, "Bill"));
```

In order to do that, we can create the following `Comparator<Person>` that compares `Person` objects only by age:

```java
Comparator<Person> perComp = (p1, p2) -> p1.getAge() -
p2.getAge();
```

Then, using this comparator, we can find the oldest person:

```java
Person theOldest = persons.stream()
                         .max(perComp)
                         .orElse(null);
System.out.println(theOldest);
                         //prints: Person{name='Jim', age=33}
```

To array

The following two terminal operations generate an array that contains stream elements, as follows:

- `Object[] toArray()`: Creates an array of objects; each object is an element of the stream

- `A[] toArray(IntFunction<A[]> generator)`: Creates an array of stream elements using the provided function

Let's look at some examples:

```
List<String> list = List.of("a", "b", "c");
Object[] obj = list.stream().toArray();
Arrays.stream(obj).forEach(System.out::print);     //prints: abc


String[] str = list.stream().toArray(String[]::new);
Arrays.stream(str).forEach(System.out::print);     //prints: abc
```

The first example is straightforward. It converts elements to an array of the same type. As for the second example, the representation of `IntFunction` as `String[]::new` is probably not obvious, so let's walk through it. `String[]::new` is a method reference that represents the `i -> new String[i]` lambda expression because the `toArray()` operation receives from the stream not the elements but their count:

```
String[] str = list.stream().toArray(i -> new String[i]);
```

We can prove it by printing an `i` value:

```
String[] str = list.stream()
                   .toArray(i -> {
                           System.out.println(i);     //prints: 3
                           return new String[i];
                   });
```

The `i -> new String[i]` expression is `IntFunction<String[]>` that, according to its documentation, accepts an `int` parameter and returns the result of the specified type. It can be defined using an anonymous class, as follows:

```
IntFunction<String[]> intFunction = new IntFunction<String[]>()
{
```

```
        @Override
        public String[] apply(int i) {
            return new String[i];
        }
};
```

The `java.util.Collection` interface has a very similar method that converts
a collection to an array:

```
List<String> list = List.of("a", "b", "c");
String[] str = list.toArray(new String[lits.size()]);
Arrays.stream(str).forEach(System.out::print);      //prints: abc
```

The only difference is that `toArray()` of the `Stream` interface accepts a function, while
the `toArray()` of the `Collection` interface takes an array.

Reduce

This terminal operation is called `reduce` because it processes all the stream elements and
produces one value, thus reducing all the stream elements to one value. However, this is
not the only operation that does it. The `collect` operation reduces all the values of the
stream element to one result as well. In a way, all terminal operations are reductive.
They produce one value after processing many elements.

So, you can view `reduce` and `collect` as synonyms that help to add structure
and classification to many operations available in the `Stream` interface. Also,
operations in the `reduce` group can be viewed as specialized versions of the `collect`
operation because `collect()` can be tailored to provide the same functionality as the
`reduce()` operation.

With all that said, let's look at a group of `reduce` operations, as follows:

- `Optional<T> reduce(BinaryOperator<T> accumulator)`: Reduces the
  elements of the stream using the provided associative function that aggregates the
  elements; returns an `Optional` with the reduced value if available

- `T reduce(T identity, BinaryOperator<T> accumulator)`: Provides
  the same functionality as the previous `reduce()` version but with the identity
  parameter used as the initial value for an accumulator or a default value if a stream
  is empty

- U reduce(U identity, BiFunction<U,T,U> accumulator, BinaryOperator<U> combiner): Provides the same functionality as the previous reduce() versions but, in addition, uses the combiner function to aggregate the results when this operation is applied to a parallel stream; if the stream is not parallel, the combiner function is not used

To demonstrate the reduce() operation, we are going to use the same Person class we have used before and the same list of Person objects as the source for our stream examples:

```
List<Person> persons = List.of(new Person(23, "Bob"),
                               new Person(33, "Jim"),
                               new Person(28, "Jill"),
                               new Person(27, "Bill"));
```

Let's find the oldest person in this list using the reduce() operation:

```
Person theOldest = list.stream()
        .reduce((p1, p2) -> p1.getAge() > p2.getAge() ? p1 : p2)
          .orElse(null);
System.out.println(theOldest);
                          //prints: Person{name='Jim', age=33}
```

The implementation is somewhat surprising, isn't it? The reduce() operation takes an accumulator, but it seems it did not accumulate anything. Instead, it compares all stream elements. Well, the accumulator saves the result of the comparison and provides it as the first parameter for the next comparison (with the next element). You can say that the accumulator, in this case, accumulates the results of all previous comparisons.

Let's now accumulate something explicitly. Let's assemble all the names from a list of persons in one comma-separated list:

```
String allNames = list.stream()
                      .map(p -> p.getName())
                      .reduce((n1, n2) -> n1 + ", " + n2)
                      .orElse(null);
System.out.println(allNames);     //prints: Bob, Jim, Jill, Bill
```

The notion of accumulation, in this case, makes a bit more sense, doesn't it?

Now, let's use the `identity` value to provide some initial value:

```
String all = list.stream()
             .map(p -> p.getName())
             .reduce("All names: ", (n1, n2) -> n1 + ", " + n2);
System.out.println(all);
                    //prints: All names: , Bob, Jim, Jill, Bill
```

Note that this version of the `reduce()` operation returns `value`, not the `Optional` object. That is because, by providing the initial value, we guarantee that at least this value will be present in the result if the stream turns out to be empty. But the resulting string does not look as pretty as we hoped. Apparently, the provided initial value is treated as any other stream element, and a comma is added after it by the accumulator we have created. To make the result look pretty again, we can use the first version of the `reduce()` operation again and add the initial value this way:

```
String all = "All names: " + list.stream()
                              .map(p -> p.getName())
                              .reduce((n1, n2) -> n1 + ", " + n2)
                              .orElse(null);
System.out.println(all);
                    //prints: All names: Bob, Jim, Jill, Bill
```

Alternatively, we can use a space as a separator instead of a comma:

```
String all = list.stream()
             .map(p -> p.getName())
             .reduce("All names:", (n1, n2) -> n1 + " " + n2);
System.out.println(all);
                        //prints: All names: Bob Jim Jill Bill
```

Now, the result looks better. While demonstrating the `collect()` operation in the next subsection, we will show a better way to create a comma-separated list of values with a prefix.

Meanwhile, let's continue to review the reduce() operation and look at its third form – the one with three parameters: identity, accumulator, and combiner. Adding combiner to the reduce() operation does not change the result:

```
String all = list.stream()
                  .map(p -> p.getName())
                  .reduce("All names:", (n1, n2) -> n1 + " " + n2,
                                        (n1, n2) -> n1 + " " + n2 );
System.out.println(all);
                          //prints: All names: Bob Jim Jill Bill
```

This is because the stream is not parallel and the combiner is used only with a parallel stream. If we make the stream parallel, the result changes:

```
String all = list.parallelStream()
                  .map(p -> p.getName())
                  .reduce("All names:", (n1, n2) -> n1 + " " +
n2, (n1, n2) -> n1 + " " + n2 );
System.out.println(all);
                      //prints: All names: Bob All names: Jim
                      //All names: Jill All names: Bill
```

Apparently, for a parallel stream, the sequence of elements is broken into subsequences, each processed independently, and their results aggregated by the combiner. While doing that, the combiner adds the initial value (identity) to each of the results. Even if we remove the combiner, the result of the parallel stream processing remains the same because a default combiner behavior is provided:

```
String all = list.parallelStream()
                  .map(p -> p.getName())
                  .reduce("All names:", (n1, n2) -> n1 + " " + n2);
System.out.println(all);
                      //prints: All names: Bob All names: Jim
                      //All names: Jill All names: Bill
```

In the previous two forms of the `reduce()` operations, the identity value was used by the accumulator. In the third form, the `identity` value is used by the combiner (note that the U type is the combiner type). To get rid of the repetitive `identity` value in the result, we have decided to remove it (and the trailing space) from the second parameter in the combiner:

```
String all = list.parallelStream().map(p->p.getName())
                .reduce("All names:", (n1, n2) -> n1 + " " + n2,
  (n1, n2) -> n1 + " " + StringUtils.remove(n2, "All names: "));
System.out.println(all); //prints: All names: Bob Jim Jill Bill
```

The result is as expected.

In our string-based examples so far, the identity has not just been an initial value. It also served as an identifier (a label) in the resulting string. However, when the elements of the stream are numeric, the identity looks more like just an initial value. Let's look at the following example:

```
List<Integer> ints = List.of(1, 2, 3);
int sum = ints.stream()
                .reduce((i1, i2) -> i1 + i2)
                .orElse(0);
System.out.println(sum);                              //prints: 6
sum = ints.stream()
            .reduce(Integer::sum)
            .orElse(0);
System.out.println(sum);                              //prints: 6
sum = ints.stream()
            .reduce(10, Integer::sum);
System.out.println(sum);                              //prints: 16
sum = ints.stream()
            .reduce(10, Integer::sum, Integer::sum);
System.out.println(sum);                              //prints: 16
```

The first two of the pipelines are exactly the same, except that the second pipeline uses a method reference. The third and fourth pipelines have the same functionality too. They both use an initial value of 10. Now, the first parameter makes more sense as the initial value than the identity, doesn't it? In the fourth pipeline, we added a combiner, but it is not used because the stream is not parallel. Let's make it parallel and see what happens:

```
List<Integer> ints = List.of(1, 2, 3);
int sum = ints.parallelStream()
              .reduce(10, Integer::sum, Integer::sum);
System.out.println(sum);                         //prints: 36
```

The result is 36 because the initial value of 10 was added three times, with each partial result. Apparently, the stream was broken into three subsequences. However, it is not always the case, as the number of subsequences changes as the stream grows and the number of CPUs on the computer increases. This is why you cannot rely on a certain fixed number of subsequences, and it is better to not use a non-zero initial value with parallel streams:

```
List<Integer> ints = List.of(1, 2, 3);
int sum = ints.parallelStream()
              .reduce(0, Integer::sum, Integer::sum);
System.out.println(sum);                         //prints: 6
sum = 10 + ints.parallelStream()
               .reduce(0, Integer::sum, Integer::sum);
System.out.println(sum);                         //prints: 16
```

As you can see, we have set the identity to 0, so every subsequence will get it, but the total is not affected when the result from all the processing threads is assembled by the combinator.

Collect

Some of the usages of the collect() operation are very simple and can be easily mastered by any beginner, while other cases can be complex and not easy to understand, even for a seasoned programmer. Together with the operations discussed already, the most popular cases of collect() usage we present in this section are more than enough for all the needs a beginner may have and will cover most of the needs of a more experienced professional. Together with the operations of numeric streams (see the *Numeric stream interfaces* section), they cover all the needs a mainstream programmer will ever have.

As we have mentioned already, the `collect()` operation is very flexible and allows us to customize stream processing. It has two forms, as follows:

- `R collect(Collector<T, A, R> collector)`: Processes the stream elements of type `T` using the provided `Collector` and produces the result of type `R` via an intermediate accumulation of type `A`

- `R collect(Supplier<R> supplier, BiConsumer<R, T> accumulator, BiConsumer<R, R> combiner)`: Processes the stream elements of type `T` using the provided functions:

  - `Supplier<R> supplier`: Creates a new result container

  - `BiConsumer<R, T> accumulator`: A stateless function that adds an element to the result container

  - `BiConsumer<R, R> combiner`: A stateless function that merges two partial result containers – it adds the elements from the second result container to the first result container

Let's look at the second form of the `collect()` operation first. It is very similar to the `reduce()` operation with the three parameters we have just demonstrated: `supplier`, `accumulator`, and `combiner`. The biggest difference is that the first parameter in the `collect()` operation is not an identity or the initial value but instead the container, an object, that is going to be passed between functions and which maintains the state of the processing.

Let's demonstrate how it works by selecting the oldest person from the list of `Person` objects. For the following example, we are going to use the familiar `Person` class as the container but add to it a constructor without parameters with two setters:

```
public Person(){}
public void setAge(int age) { this.age = age;}
public void setName(String name) { this.name = name; }
```

Adding a constructor without parameters and setters is necessary because the `Person` object as a container should be creatable at any moment without any parameters and should be able to receive and keep the partial results: the `name` and `age` of the person who is the oldest, so far. The `collect()` operation will use this container while processing each element and, after the last element is processed, contain the name and age of the oldest person.

We will use again the same list of persons:

```
List<Person> list = List.of(new Person(23, "Bob"),
                            new Person(33, "Jim"),
                            new Person(28, "Jill"),
                            new Person(27, "Bill"));
```

Here is the `collect()` operation that finds the oldest person in the list:

```
BiConsumer<Person, Person> accumulator = (p1, p2) -> {
    if(p1.getAge() < p2.getAge()){
        p1.setAge(p2.getAge());
        p1.setName(p2.getName());
    }
};
BiConsumer<Person, Person> combiner = (p1, p2) -> {
    System.out.println("Combiner is called!");
    if(p1.getAge() < p2.getAge()){
        p1.setAge(p2.getAge());
        p1.setName(p2.getName());
    }
};
Person theOldest = list.stream()
                    .collect(Person::new, accumulator, combiner);
System.out.println(theOldest);
                            //prints: Person{name='Jim', age=33}
```

We tried to inline the functions in the operation call, but it looked a bit difficult to read, so we decided to create functions first and then use them in the `collect()` operation. The container, a `Person` object, is created only once before the first element is processed. In this sense, it is similar to the initial value of the `reduce()` operation. Then, it is passed to the accumulator, which compares it to the first element. The age field in the container was initialized to the default value of zero, and thus the age and name of the first element were set in the container as the parameters of the oldest person, so far. When the second stream element (the `Person` object) is emitted, its age value is compared to the age value currently stored in the container, and so on, until all elements of the stream are processed. The result is shown in the previous comments.

When the stream is sequential, the combiner is never called. But when we make it parallel (`list.parallelStream()`), the **Combiner is called!** message is printed three times. As in the case of the `reduce()` operation, the number of partial results may vary, depending on the number of CPUs and the internal logic of the `collect()` operation implementation. So, the **Combiner is called!** message can be printed any number of times.

Now, let's look at the first form of the `collect()` operation. It requires an object of the class that implements the `java.util.stream.Collector<T,A,R>` interface, where `T` is the stream type, `A` is the container type, and `R` is the result type. You can use one of the following `of()` methods (from the `Collector` interface) to create the necessary `Collector` object:

```
static Collector<T,R,R> of(Supplier<R> supplier,
                BiConsumer<R,T> accumulator,
                BinaryOperator<R> combiner,
                Collector.Characteristics... characteristics)
```

Alternatively, you can use this:

```
static Collector<T,A,R> of(Supplier<A> supplier,
                BiConsumer<A,T> accumulator,
                BinaryOperator<A> combiner,
                Function<A,R> finisher,
                Collector.Characteristics... characteristics).
```

The functions you have to pass to the preceding methods are similar to those we have demonstrated already. But we are not going to do this, for two reasons. First, it is more involved and pushes us beyond the scope of this book, and, second, before doing that, you have to look in the `java.util.stream.Collectors` class, which provides many ready-to-use collectors.

As we have mentioned already, together with the operations discussed so far and the numeric streams operations we are going to present in the next section, ready-to-use collectors cover the vast majority of processing needs in mainstream programming, and there is a good chance you will never need to create a custom collector.

Collectors

The `java.util.stream.Collectors` class provides more than 40 methods that create `Collector` objects. We are going to demonstrate only the simplest and most popular ones, as follows:

- `Collector<T,?,List<T>> toList()`: Creates a collector that generates a `List` object from stream elements

- `Collector<T,?,Set<T>> toSet()`: Creates a collector that generates a `Set` object from stream elements

- `Collector<T,?,Map<K,U>> toMap (Function<T,K> keyMapper, Function<T,U> valueMapper)`: Creates a collector that generates a `Map` object from stream elements

- `Collector<T,?,C> toCollection (Supplier<C> collectionFactory)`: Creates a collector that generates a `Collection` object of the type provided by `Supplier<C> collectionFactory`

- `Collector<CharSequence,?,String> joining()`: Creates a collector that generates a `String` object by concatenating stream elements

- `Collector<CharSequence,?,String> joining (CharSequence delimiter)`: Creates a collector that generates a delimiter-separated `String` object from stream elements

- `Collector<CharSequence,?,String> joining (CharSequence delimiter, CharSequence prefix, CharSequence suffix)`: Creates a collector that generates a delimiter-separated `String` object from the stream elements and adds the specified `prefix` and `suffix`

- `Collector<T,?,Integer> summingInt (ToIntFunction<T>)`: Creates a collector that calculates the sum of the results generated by the provided function applied to each element; the same method exists for `long` and `double` types

- `Collector<T,?,IntSummaryStatistics> summarizingInt (ToIntFunction<T>)`: Creates a collector that calculates the sum, minimum, maximum, count, and average of the results generated by the provided function applied to each element; the same method exists for `long` and `double` types

- `Collector<T,?,Map<Boolean,List<T>>> partitioningBy (Predicate<? super T> predicate)`: Creates a collector that separates the elements using the provided `Predicate` function

- `Collector<T,?,Map<K,List<T>>> groupingBy(Function<T,U>)`: Creates a collector that groups elements into `Map` with keys generated by the provided function

The following demo code shows how to use the collectors created by the methods listed earlier. First, we will demonstrate usage of the `toList()`, `toSet()`, `toMap()`, and `toCollection()` methods:

```java
List<String> ls = Stream.of("a", "b", "c")
                        .collect(Collectors.toList());
System.out.println(ls);                    //prints: [a, b, c]


Set<String> set = Stream.of("a", "a", "c")
                        .collect(Collectors.toSet());
System.out.println(set);                   //prints: [a, c]


List<Person> list = List.of(new Person(23, "Bob"),
                            new Person(33, "Jim"),
                            new Person(28, "Jill"),
                            new Person(27, "Bill"));
Map<String, Person> map = list.stream()
                        .collect(Collectors
                          .toMap(p -> p.getName() + "-" +
                                 p.getAge(), p -> p));
System.out.println(map);
            //prints: {Bob-23=Person{name='Bob', age:23},
            //         Bill-27=Person{name='Bill', age:27},
            //         Jill-28=Person{name='Jill', age:28},
            //         Jim-33=Person{name='Jim', age:33}}


Set<Person> personSet = list.stream()
                        .collect(Collectors
                          .toCollection(HashSet::new));
System.out.println(personSet);
            //prints: [Person{name='Bill', age=27},
            //         Person{name='Jim', age=33},
            //         Person{name='Bob', age=23},
            //         Person{name='Jill', age=28}]
```

The `joining()` method allows you to concatenate the `Character` and `String` values in a delimited list with `prefix` and `suffix`:

```
List<String> list1 = List.of("a", "b", "c", "d");
String result = list1.stream()
                       .collect(Collectors.joining());
System.out.println(result);                   //prints: abcd


result = list1.stream()
                .collect(Collectors.joining(", "));
System.out.println(result);                   //prints: a, b, c, d


result = list1.stream()
         .collect(Collectors.joining(", ", "The result: ", ""));
System.out.println(result);    //prints: The result: a, b, c, d


result = list1.stream()
  .collect(Collectors.joining(", ", "The result: ",
                                      ". The End."));
System.out.println(result);
                 //prints: The result: a, b, c, d. The End.
```

Now, let's turn to the `summingInt()` and `summarizingInt()` methods. They create collectors that calculate the sum and other statistics of the `int` values produced by the provided functions applied to each element:

```
List<Person> list2 = List.of(new Person(23, "Bob"),
                             new Person(33, "Jim"),
                             new Person(28, "Jill"),
                             new Person(27, "Bill"));
int sum = list2.stream()
               .collect(Collectors.summingInt(Person::getAge));
System.out.println(sum);                   //prints: 111


IntSummaryStatistics stats = list2.stream()
          .collect(Collectors.summarizingInt(Person::getAge));
System.out.println(stats); //prints: IntSummaryStatistics{
        //count=4, sum=111, min=23, average=27.750000, max=33}
```

```
System.out.println(stats.getCount());      //prints: 4
System.out.println(stats.getSum());        //prints: 111
System.out.println(stats.getMin());        //prints: 23
System.out.println(stats.getAverage());    //prints: 27.750000
System.out.println(stats.getMax());        //prints: 33
```

There are also the `summingLong()`, `summarizingLong()`, `summingDouble()`, and `summarizingDouble()` methods.

The `partitioningBy()` method creates a collector that groups the elements by the provided criteria and put the groups (lists) in a `Map` object, with a Boolean value as the key:

```
Map<Boolean, List<Person>> map2 = list2.stream()
      .collect(Collectors.partitioningBy(p -> p.getAge() > 27));
System.out.println(map2); //prints: {false=[Person{name='Bob',
//age=23}, Person{name='Bill', age=27}, true=[Person{name='Jim',
//age=33}, Person{name='Jill', age=28}]}
```

As you can see, using the `p.getAge() > 27` criteria, we were able to put all the persons in two groups: one is below or equal to 27 years of `age` (the key is `false`), and another is above 27 (the key is `true`).

Finally, the `groupingBy()` method allows you to group elements by a value and put the groups (lists) in a `Map` object, with this value as a key:

```
List<Person> list3 = List.of(new Person(23, "Bob"),
                             new Person(33, "Jim"),
                             new Person(23, "Jill"),
                             new Person(33, "Bill"));
Map<Integer, List<Person>> map3 = list3.stream()
               .collect(Collectors.groupingBy(Person::getAge));
System.out.println(map3);
//prints: {33=[Person{name='Jim', age=33}, Person{name='Bill',
//age=33}], 23=[Person{name='Bob', age=23}, Person{name='Jill',
//age=23}]}
```

To be able to demonstrate this method, we changed our list of `Person` objects by setting age on each of them to either 23 or 33. The result is two groups ordered by their age.

There are also overloaded `toMap()`, `groupingBy()`, and `partitioningBy()` methods as well as the following, often overloaded, methods that create corresponding `Collector` objects, as follows:

- `counting()`
- `reducing()`
- `filtering()`
- `toConcurrentMap()`
- `collectingAndThen()`
- `maxBy()`, `minBy()`
- `mapping()`, `flatMapping()`
- `averagingInt()`, `averagingLong()`, `averagingDouble()`
- `toUnmodifiableList()`, `toUnmodifiableMap()`, `toUnmodifiableSet()`

If you cannot find the operation you need among those discussed in this book, search the `Collectors` API first, before building your own `Collector` object.

Numeric stream interfaces

As we have mentioned already, all three numeric interfaces, `IntStream`, `LongStream`, and `DoubleStream`, have methods similar to the methods in the `Stream` interface, including the methods of the `Stream.Builder` interface. This means that everything we have discussed so far in this chapter equally applies to any numeric stream interfaces. That is why, in this section, we will only talk about those methods that are not present in the `Stream` interface, as follows:

- The `range(lower,upper)` and `rangeClosed(lower,upper)` methods in the `IntStream` and `LongStream` interfaces allow you to create a stream from the values in the specified range.
- The `boxed()` and `mapToObj()` intermediate operations convert a numeric stream to `Stream`
- The `mapToInt()`, `mapToLong()`, and `mapToDouble()` intermediate operations convert a numeric stream of one type to a numeric stream of another type.

- The `flatMapToInt()`, `flatMapToLong()`, and `flatMapToDouble()` intermediate operations convert a stream to a numeric stream.

- The `sum()` and `average()` terminal operations calculate the sum and average of numeric stream elements.

Creating a stream

In addition to the methods of the `Stream` interface that create streams, the `IntStream` and `LongStream` interfaces allow you to create a stream from the values in the specified range.

range() and rangeClosed()

The `range(lower, upper)` method generates all values sequentially, starting from the `lower` value and ending with the value just before `upper`:

```
IntStream.range(1, 3).forEach(System.out::print);   //prints: 12
LongStream.range(1, 3).forEach(System.out::print); //prints: 12
```

The `rangeClosed(lower, upper)` method generates all the values sequentially, starting from the `lower` value and ending with the `upper` value:

```
IntStream.rangeClosed(1, 3).forEach(System.out::print);
                                                    //prints: 123
LongStream.rangeClosed(1, 3).forEach(System.out::print);
                                                    //prints: 123
```

Intermediate operations

In addition to the intermediate operations of the `Stream` interface, the `IntStream`, `LongStream`, and `DoubleStream` interfaces also have number-specific intermediate operations: `boxed()`, `mapToObj()`, `mapToInt()`, `mapToLong()`, `mapToDouble()`, `flatMapToInt()`, `flatMapToLong()`, and `flatMapToDouble()`.

boxed() and mapToObj()

The `boxed()` intermediate operation converts (boxes) elements of the primitive numeric type to the corresponding wrapper type:

```
//IntStream.range(1, 3).map(Integer::shortValue)
                                                //comp error
```

```
//                      .forEach(System.out::print);

IntStream.range(1, 3)
        .boxed()
        .map(Integer::shortValue)
        .forEach(System.out::print);          //prints: 12

//LongStream.range(1, 3).map(Long::shortValue)
                                              //compile error
//                      .forEach(System.out::print);

LongStream.range(1, 3)
         .boxed()
         .map(Long::shortValue)
         .forEach(System.out::print);         //prints: 12

//DoubleStream.of(1).map(Double::shortValue)
                                              //compile error
//                   .forEach(System.out::print);

DoubleStream.of(1)
          .boxed()
          .map(Double::shortValue)
          .forEach(System.out::print);        //prints: 1
```

In the preceding code, we have commented out the lines that generate compilation errors because the elements generated by the range() method are primitive types. The boxed() operation converts a primitive value to the corresponding wrapping type, so it can be processed as a reference type. The mapToObj() intermediate operation does a similar transformation, but it is not as specialized as the boxed() operation and allows you to use an element of primitive type to produce an object of any type:

```
IntStream.range(1, 3)
        .mapToObj(Integer::valueOf)
        .map(Integer::shortValue)
        .forEach(System.out::print);          //prints: 12

IntStream.range(42, 43)
```

```
.mapToObj(i -> new Person(i, "John"))
.forEach(System.out::print);
                            //prints: Person{name='John', age=42}


LongStream.range(1, 3)
        .mapToObj(Long::valueOf)
        .map(Long::shortValue)
        .forEach(System.out::print);        //prints: 12


DoubleStream.of(1)
         .mapToObj(Double::valueOf)
         .map(Double::shortValue)
         .forEach(System.out::print);       //prints: 1
```

In the preceding code, we have added the map() operation just to prove that the mapToObj() operation does the job and creates an object of the wrapping type, as expected. Also, by adding the pipeline that produces Person objects, we have demonstrated how the mapToObj() operation can be used to create an object of any type.

mapToInt(), mapToLong(), and mapToDouble()

The mapToInt(), mapToLong(), and mapToDouble() intermediate operations allow you to convert a numeric stream of one type to a numeric stream of another type. For the sake of example, we will convert a list of String values to a numeric stream of different types by mapping each String value to its length:

```
List<String> list = List.of("one", "two", "three");
list.stream()
    .mapToInt(String::length)
    .forEach(System.out::print);        //prints: 335


list.stream()
    .mapToLong(String::length)
    .forEach(System.out::print);        //prints: 335


list.stream()
  .mapToDouble(String::length)
  .forEach(d -> System.out.print(d + " "));
```

```
                                        //prints: 3.0 3.0 5.0

list.stream()
    .map(String::length)
    .map(Integer::shortValue)
    .forEach(System.out::print);        //prints: 335
```

The elements of the created numeric streams are of the primitive type:

```
//list.stream().mapToInt(String::length)
//               .map(Integer::shortValue) //compile error
//               .forEach(System.out::print);
```

As we are on this topic, if you would like to convert elements to a numeric wrapping type, the intermediate map() operation is the way to do it (instead of mapToInt()):

```
list.stream().map(String::length)
        .map(Integer::shortValue)
    .forEach(System.out::print);        //prints: 335
```

flatMapToInt(), flatMapToLong(), and flatMapToDouble()

The flatMapToInt(), flatMapToLong(), and flatMapToDouble() intermediate operations produce a numeric stream of the following corresponding type:

```
List<Integer> list = List.of(1, 2, 3);
list.stream()
    .flatMapToInt(i -> IntStream.rangeClosed(1, i))
    .forEach(System.out::print);        //prints: 112123

list.stream()
    .flatMapToLong(i -> LongStream.rangeClosed(1, i))
    .forEach(System.out::print);        //prints: 112123

list.stream()
    .flatMapToDouble(DoubleStream::of)
    .forEach(d -> System.out.print(d + " "));
                                        //prints: 1.0 2.0 3.0
```

As you can see in the preceding code, we have used `int` values in the original stream, but it can be a stream of any type:

```
List.of("one", "two", "three")
    .stream()
    .flatMapToInt(s -> IntStream.rangeClosed(1, s.length()))
    .forEach(System.out::print);          //prints: 12312312345
```

Terminal operations

Numeric-specific terminal operations are pretty straightforward. There are two of them, as follows:

- `sum()`: Calculates the sum of numeric stream elements
- `average()`: Calculates the average of numeric stream elements

sum() and average()

If you need to calculate a sum or an average of the values of numeric stream elements, the only requirement for the stream is that it should not be infinite. Otherwise, the calculation never finishes. The following are examples of these operational usages:

```
int sum = IntStream.empty().sum();
System.out.println(sum);       //prints: 0

sum = IntStream.range(1, 3).sum();
System.out.println(sum);       //prints: 3

double av = IntStream.empty().average().orElse(0);
System.out.println(av);        //prints: 0.0

av = IntStream.range(1, 3).average().orElse(0);
System.out.println(av);        //prints: 1.5

long suml = LongStream.range(1, 3).sum();
System.out.println(suml);      //prints: 3

double avl = LongStream.range(1, 3).average().orElse(0);
```

```
System.out.println(avl);      //prints: 1.5


double sumd = DoubleStream.of(1, 2).sum();
System.out.println(sumd);     //prints: 3.0


double avd = DoubleStream.of(1, 2).average().orElse(0);
System.out.println(avd);      //prints: 1.5
```

As you can see, using these operations on an empty stream is not a problem.

Parallel streams

We have seen that changing from a sequential stream to a parallel stream can lead to incorrect results if code was not written and tested to process a parallel stream. The following are a few more considerations related to parallel streams.

Stateless and stateful operations

There are **stateless operations**, such as `filter()`, `map()`, and `flatMap()`, which do not keep data around (do not maintain state) while moving processing from one stream element to the next. Also, there are stateful operations, such as `distinct()`, `limit()`, `sorted()`, `reduce()`, and `collect()`, that can pass a state from previously processed elements to the processing of the next element.

Stateless operations usually do not pose a problem while switching from a sequential stream to a parallel one. Each element is processed independently, and the stream can be broken into any number of substreams for independent processing. With stateful operations, the situation is different. To start with, using them for an infinite stream may never finish processing. Also, while discussing the `reduce()` and `collect()` stateful operations, we have demonstrated how switching to a parallel stream can produce a different result if the initial value (or identity) is set without parallel processing in mind.

There are performance considerations too. Stateful operations often require you to process all the stream elements in several passes, using buffering. For large streams, it may tax JVM resources and slow down, if not completely shut down, an application.

This is why a programmer should not take switching from sequential to parallel streams lightly. If stateful operations are involved, code has to be designed and tested to be able to perform parallel stream processing without negative effects.

Sequential or parallel processing?

As we indicated in the previous section, parallel processing may or may not produce better performance. You have to test every use case before deciding on using parallel streams. Parallelism can yield better performance, but code has to be designed and possibly optimized to do it. Also, each assumption has to be tested in an environment that is as close to production as possible.

However, there are a few considerations you can take into account while deciding between sequential and parallel processing, as follows:

- Small streams are typically processed faster sequentially (although, what is *small* for your environment should be determined through testing and by measuring performance).

- If stateful operations cannot be replaced with stateless ones, carefully design your code for parallel processing or just avoid it.

Consider parallel processing for procedures that require extensive calculations, but think about bringing the partial results together for the final result. Look in the streams folder. It contains a standalone stream-processing application. To simulate a stream of data, we created an input.csv file that contains a header and 14 lines, each line representing data of one person: first name, last name, age, street address, city, state, and zip code.

The application reads this file as a stream of lines, skips the first line (header), and processes the rest of the lines by converting each of them to a Person class object:

```
List<Person> getInputPersonList(File file) throws IOException {
  return Files.lines(file.toPath())
            .skip(1)
          .parallel()
          .map(Main::validLine)
          .map(l -> {
              Person person =
                  new Person(Integer.parseInt(l.get(2)),
                                  l.get(0), l.get(1));
              person.setAddress(l.get(3), l.get(4),
                  l.get(5), Integer.parseInt(l.get(6)));
              return person;
          }).toList();
}
```

Since the sequence of processing the lines does not affect the result, we can process the stream of lines in parallel. Also, note that we stop processing (by throwing an exception) if a line does not have enough data or some data does not match the expected format:

```java
List<String> validLine(String line){
    String[] arr = line.split(",");
    if(arr.length != 7){
      throw new RuntimeException(EXPECTED + " 7 column: " +
                                                        line);

    }

    List<String> values = Arrays.stream(arr)
      .parallel()
      .map(s -> {
            String val = s.trim();
            if(val.isEmpty()){
                throw new RuntimeException(EXPECTED +
                                " only non-empty values: " + line);

            }
            return val;
    }).toList();

    try {
          Integer.valueOf(values.get(2));
          Integer.valueOf(values.get(6));
    } catch (Exception e) {
      throw new RuntimeException(EXPECTED +
                          " numbers in columns 3 and 7: " + line);

    }
    if(values.get(6).length() != 5){
      throw new RuntimeException(EXPECTED +
                                " zip code 5 digits only: " + line);

    }
    return values;
}
```

Then, we process the resulting list of `Person` class objects as follows:

```
Set<String> cities = new HashSet<>();
Set<String> states = new HashSet<>();
Set<Integer> zips = new HashSet<>();
Map<Integer, Integer> oldestByZip = new HashMap<>();
Map<Integer, String> oldestNameByZip = new HashMap<>();


URL url = Main.class.getClassLoader().getResource(
                                        "input.csv");
File file = new File(url.toURI());


List<Person> list = getInputPersonList(file);
list.stream()
    .forEach(p -> {
            cities.add(p.getCity());
            states.add(p.getState());
            zips.add(p.getZip());
            int age = oldestByZip.getOrDefault(p.getZip(), 0);
            if(p.getAge() > age){
              oldestByZip.put(p.getZip(), p.getAge());
              oldestNameByZip.put(p.getZip(),
                            p.getAge() + ": " + p.getName());
            } else if (p.getAge() == age){
              oldestNameByZip.put(p.getZip(),
                    oldestNameByZip.get(p.getZip()) +
                                        ", " + p.getName());
            }
    });
```

In the preceding code, we create the `Set` and `Map` objects that contain results that we print later, as follows:

```
System.out.println("cities: " +
  cities.stream().sorted().collect(Collectors.joining(", ")));
System.out.println("states: " +
  states.stream().sorted().collect(Collectors.joining(", ")));
```

```
System.out.println("zips: " + zips.stream().sorted()
                              .map(i -> String.valueOf(i))
                      .collect(Collectors.joining(", ")));
System.out.println("Oldest in each zip: " +
            oldestNameByZip.keySet().stream().sorted()
          .map(i -> i + "=>" + oldestNameByZip.get(i))
                      .collect(Collectors.joining("; ")));
```

The output is demonstrated in the following screenshot:

```
cities: Coal, Denver, Prost, Young
states: AZ, CO
zips: 12345, 12346, 22345, 32345
Oldest in each zip: 12345=>35: Bob Blow; 12346=>25: Ben Hill; 22345=>38: Rick Meadows; 32345=>28: Fred Grant
```

As you can see, it shows in alphabetical order all the cities, all the states, and all the zip codes listed in the input.csv file, as well as the oldest person for each zip code.

The same result can be achieved by using a for-loop instead of each stream in this application, so using Java standard streams is more a matter of style than necessity. We prefer using streams because it allows for more compact code. In *Chapter 15, Reactive Programming*, we will present and discuss another type of stream (called a *reactive stream*) that cannot be replaced by for-loops, at least not easily. Reactive streams are used primarily for asynchronous processing, which will also be explored in the next chapter.

Summary

In this chapter, we have talked about data-stream processing, which is different from processing the I/O streams we reviewed in *Chapter 5, Strings, Input/Output, and Files*. We defined what data streams are, how to process their elements using stream operations, and how to chain (connect) stream operations in a pipeline. We also discussed stream initialization and how to process streams in parallel.

Now, you know how to write code that processes streams of data, as well as create a stream-processing application as a standalone project.

In the next chapter, you will be introduced to the **Reactive Manifesto**, its purpose, and examples of its implementations. We will discuss the difference between reactive and responsive systems and what **asynchronous** and **non-blocking** processing are. We will also talk about **Reactive Streams** and **RxJava**.

Quiz

1. What is the difference between I/O streams and `java.util.stream.Stream`? Select all that apply:

   A. I/O streams are oriented toward data delivery, while `Stream` is oriented toward data processing.

   B. Some I/O streams can be transformed into `Stream`.

   C. I/O streams can read from a file, while `Stream` cannot.

   D. I/O streams can write to a file, while `Stream` cannot.

2. What do the `empty()` and `of(T... values)` `Stream` methods have in common?

3. What type are the elements emitted by the `Stream.ofNullable(Set.of(1,2,3 )` stream?

4. What does the following code print?

   ```
   Stream.iterate(1, i -> i + 2)
           .limit(3)
           .forEach(System.out::print);
   ```

5. What does the following code print?

   ```
   Stream.concat(Set.of(42).stream(),
                 List.of(42).stream()).limit(1)
                            .forEach(System.out::print);
   ```

6. What does the following code print?

   ```
   Stream.generate(() -> 42 / 2)
           .limit(2)
           .forEach(System.out::print);
   ```

7. Is `Stream.Builder` a functional interface?

8. How many elements does the following stream emit?

   ```
   new Random().doubles(42).filter(d -> d >= 1)
   ```

9. What does the following code print?

   ```
   Stream.of(1,2,3,4)
           .skip(2)
   ```

```
               .takeWhile(i -> i < 4)
               .forEach(System.out::print);
```

10. What is the value of d in the following code?

```
double d = Stream.of(1, 2)
                      .mapToDouble(Double::valueOf)
                      .map(e -> e / 2)
                      .sum();
```

11. What is the value of the s string in the following code?

```
String s = Stream.of("a","X","42").sorted()
  .collect(Collectors.joining(","));
```

12. What is the result of the following code?

```
List.of(1,2,3).stream()
                      .peek(i -> i > 2 )
                      .forEach(System.out::print);
```

13. How many stream elements does the peek() operation print in the following code?

```
List.of(1,2,3).stream()
                      .peek(System.out::println)
                      .noneMatch(e -> e == 2);
```

14. What does the or() method return when the Optional object is empty?

15. What is the value of the s string in the following code?

```
String s = Stream.of("a","X","42")
  .max(Comparator.naturalOrder())
  .orElse("12");
```

16. How many elements does the IntStream.rangeClosed(42, 42) stream emit?

17. Name two stateless operations.

18. Name two stateful operations.

15
Reactive Programming

In this chapter, you will be introduced to the **Reactive Manifesto** and the world of reactive programming. We start with defining and discussing the main concepts of reactive programming – asynchronous, non-blocking, and responsive. Using them, we then define and discuss reactive programming, the main reactive frameworks, and talk about **RxJava** in more detail.

In this chapter, we will cover the following topics:

- Asynchronous processing
- Non-blocking APIs
- Reactive – responsive, resilient, elastic, and message-driven systems
- Reactive streams
- RxJava

By the end of the chapter, you will be able to write code for asynchronous processing using reactive programming.

Technical requirements

To be able to execute the code examples that are provided in this chapter, you will need the following:

- A computer with an operating system: Microsoft Windows, Apple macOS, or Linux

- Java SE version 17 or later

- Any IDE or code editor you prefer

The instructions for how to set up a Java SE and IntelliJ IDEA editor were provided in *Chapter 1*, *Getting Started with Java 17*, of this book. The files and the code examples for this chapter are available from the GitHub repository at `https://github.com/PacktPublishing/Learn-Java-17-Programming.git`. You can locate them in the `examples/src/main/java/com/packt/learnjava/ch15_reactive` folder.

Asynchronous processing

Asynchronous means that the requestor gets the response immediately, but the result is not there. Instead, the requestor waits until the result is sent to them, saved in the database, or, for example, presented as an object that allows you to check whether the result is ready. If the latter is the case, the requestor calls a certain method to this object periodically and, when the result is ready, retrieves it using another method on the same object. The advantage of asynchronous processing is that the requestor can do other things while waiting.

In *Chapter 8*, *Multithreading and Concurrent Processing*, we demonstrated how a child thread can be created. Such a child thread then sends a non-asynchronous (blocking) request and waits for its return doing nothing. Meanwhile, the main thread continues executing and periodically calls the child thread object to see whether the result is ready. That is the most basic of asynchronous processing implementations. In fact, we already used it when we used parallel streams.

The parallel stream operations that work behind the scenes to create the child threads break the stream into segments, assign each segment to a dedicated thread for processing, and then aggregate the partial results from all the segments into the final result. In the previous chapter, we even wrote functions that did the aggregating job. As a reminder, the function was called **combiner**.

Let's compare the performance of sequential and parallel streams using an example.

Sequential and parallel streams

To demonstrate the difference between sequential and parallel processing, let's imagine a system that collects data from 10 physical devices (such as sensors) and calculates an average. The following is the `get()` method, which collects a measurement from a sensor identified by its ID:

```
double get(String id){
    try{
        TimeUnit.MILLISECONDS.sleep(100);
    } catch(InterruptedException ex){
        ex.printStackTrace();
    }
    return id * Math.random();
}
```

We have included a delay of 100 ms to imitate the time it takes to collect the measurement from the sensor. As for the resulting measurement value, we use the `Math.random()` method. We are going to call this `get()` method using an object of the `MeasuringSystem` class, which is where the method belongs.

Then, we are going to calculate an average to offset the errors and other idiosyncrasies of individual devices:

```
void getAverage(Stream<Integer> ids) {
    LocalTime start = LocalTime.now();
    double a = ids.mapToDouble(id -> new MeasuringSystem()
                    .get(id))
                .average()
                .orElse(0);
    System.out.println((Math.round(a * 100.) / 100.) + " in " +
        Duration.between(start, LocalTime.now()).toMillis() +
                                            "ms");
}
```

Notice how we convert the stream of IDs into `DoubleStream` using the `mapToDouble()` operation so that we can apply the `average()` operation. The `average()` operation returns an `Optional<Double>` object, and we call its `orElse(0)` method, which returns either the calculated value or zero (for example, if the measuring system could not connect to any of its sensors and returned an empty stream).

The last line of the `getAverage()` method prints the result and the time it took to calculate it. In real code, we would return the result and use it for other calculations. However, for demonstration purposes, we will just print it.

Now we can compare the performance of sequential stream processing with the performance of parallel processing (see the `MeasuringSystem` class and the `compareSequentialAndParallelProcessing()` method):

```
List<Integer> ids = IntStream.range(1, 11)
                             .mapToObj(i -> i)
                             .collect(Collectors.toList());
getAverage(ids.stream());            //prints: 2.99 in 1030 ms
getAverage(ids.parallelStream());   //prints: 2.34 in  214 ms
```

The results might be different if you run this example because, as you might recall, we simulate the collected measurements as random values.

As you can see, the processing of a parallel stream is five times faster than the processing of a sequential stream. The results are different because the measurement produces a slightly different result each time.

Although the parallel stream uses asynchronous processing behind the scenes, this is not what programmers have in mind when talking about the asynchronous processing of requests. From the application's perspective, it is just parallel (also called concurrent) processing. It is faster than sequential processing, but the main thread has to wait until all the calls are made and the data has been retrieved. If each call takes at least 100 ms (as it is in our case), then the processing of all the calls cannot be completed in less time, even when each call is made by a dedicated thread.

Of course, we can create a service that uses a child thread to make all the calls, while the main thread does something else. Later, the main thread can call the service again and get the result or pick it up from a previously agreed location. That truly would be the asynchronous processing programmers are talking about.

But before writing such code, let's look at the `CompletableFuture` class located in the `java.util.concurrent` package. It does everything described and more.

Using the CompletableFuture object

Using the `CompletableFuture` object, we can separate sending the request to the measuring system from getting the result from the `CompletableFuture` object. That is exactly the scenario we described while explaining what asynchronous processing was. Let's demonstrate it in the code (see the `MeasuringSystem` class and the `completableFuture()` method):

```
List<CompletableFuture<Double>> list = ids.stream()
    .map(id -> CompletableFuture.supplyAsync(() ->
  new MeasuringSystem().get(id))).collect(Collectors.toList());
```

The `supplyAsync()` method does not wait for the call to the measuring system to return. Instead, it immediately creates a `CompletableFuture` object and returns it. This is so that a client can use this object any time later on to retrieve the result returned by the measuring system. The following code takes the list of `CompletableFuture` objects and iterates over it, retrieving the result from each object and calculating the average value:

```
LocalTime start = LocalTime.now();
double a = list.stream()
              .mapToDouble(cf -> cf.join().doubleValue())
              .average()
              .orElse(0);
System.out.println((Math.round(a * 100.) / 100.) + " in " +
  Duration.between(start, LocalTime.now()).toMillis() + " ms");
                                            //prints: 2.92 in 6 ms
```

Additionally, some methods allow you to check whether the value was returned at all, but that is not the point of this demonstration, which is to show how the `CompletableFuture` class can be used to organize asynchronous processing.

The created list of `CompletableFuture` objects can be stored anywhere and processed very quickly (in our case, in 6 ms), provided that the measurements have been received already (all the `get()` methods were invoked and returned values). After creating the list of `CompletableFuture` objects and before processing it, the system is not blocked and can do something else. That is the advantage of asynchronous processing.

The `CompletableFuture` class has many methods and is supported by several other classes and interfaces. For example, a fixed-size thread pool can be added to limit the number of threads (see the `MeasuringSystem` class and the `threadPool()` method):

```
ExecutorService pool = Executors.newFixedThreadPool(3);
List<CompletableFuture<Double>> list = ids.stream()
        .map(id -> CompletableFuture.supplyAsync(() ->
                        new MeasuringSystem().get(id), pool))
        .collect(Collectors.toList());
```

There is a variety of such pools for different purposes and different performances. But using a pool does not change the overall system design, so we omit such a detail.

As you can see, the power of asynchronous processing is great. There is also a variation of the asynchronous API called a **non-blocking API**. We are going to discuss this in the next section.

Non-blocking APIs

The client of a non-blocking API gets the results without being blocked for a significant amount of time, thus allowing the client to do something else during the period when the results are being prepared. So, the notion of a non-blocking API implies a highly responsive application. The processing of the request (that is, getting the results) can be done synchronously or asynchronously – it does not matter to the client. In practice, though, typically, the application uses asynchronous processing to facilitate an increased throughput and improved performance of the API.

The term **non-blocking** came into use with the `java.nio` package. The **non-blocking input/output** (**NIO**) provides support for intensive **input/output** (**I/O**) operations. It describes how the application is implemented: it does not dedicate an execution thread to each of the requests but provides several lightweight worker threads that do the processing asynchronously and concurrently.

The java.io package versus the java.nio package

Writing and reading data to and from external memory (for example, a hard drive) is a much slower operation than processing in memory only. Initially, the already-existing classes and interfaces of the `java.io` package worked well, but once in a while, they would create a performance bottleneck. The new `java.nio` package was created to provide more effective I/O support.

The `java.io` implementation is based on I/O stream processing. As we saw in the previous section, essentially, this is a blocking operation even if some kind of concurrency is happening behind the scenes. To increase speeds, the `java.nio` implementation was introduced based on the reading/writing to/from a buffer in the memory. Such a design allowed it to separate the slow process of filling/emptying the buffer and quickly reading/writing from/to it.

In a way, it is similar to what we have done in our example of `CompletableFuture` usage. The additional advantage of having data in a buffer is that it is possible to inspect the data, going there and back along with the buffer, which is impossible while reading sequentially from the stream. It has provided more flexibility during data processing. In addition, the `java.nio` implementation introduced another middleman process called a **channel** for bulk data transfers to and from a buffer.

The reading thread is getting data from a channel and only receives what is currently available or nothing at all (if no data is in the channel). If data is not available, the thread, instead of remaining blocked, can do something else–for example, reading/writing to/from other channels in the same way the main thread in our `CompletableFuture` example was free to do whatever had to be done while the measuring system was getting data from its sensors.

This way, instead of dedicating a thread to one I/O process, a few worker threads can serve many I/O processes. Such a solution was eventually called NIO and was later applied to other processes, the most prominent being the *event processing in an event loop*, which is also called a **run loop**.

The event/run loop

Many non-blocking systems are based on the **event** (or **run**) loop – a thread that is continually executed. It receives events (requests and messages) and then dispatches them to the corresponding event handlers (workers). There is nothing special about event handlers. They are just methods (functions) dedicated by the programmer for the processing of the particular event type.

Such a design is called a **reactor design pattern**. It is constructed around processing events and service requests concurrently. Also, it gives the name to the **reactive programming** and **reactive systems** that *react* to events and process them concurrently.

Event loop-based design is widely used in operating systems and graphical user interfaces. It has been available in Spring WebFlux since Spring 5 and can be implemented in JavaScript and the popular executing environment, Node.js. The latter uses an event loop as its processing backbone. The toolkit, Vert.x, is built around the event loop, too.

Before the adoption of an event loop, a dedicated thread was assigned to each incoming request – much like in our demonstration of stream processing. Each of the threads required the allocation of a certain amount of resources that were not request-specific, so some of the resources – mostly memory allocation – were wasted. Then, as the number of requests grew, the CPU needed to switch its context from one thread to another more frequently to allow more or less concurrent processing of all the requests. Under the load, the overhead of switching the context is substantial enough to affect the performance of an application.

Implementing an event loop has addressed these two issues. It has eliminated the waste of resources by avoiding the creation of a thread for each request and removed the overhead of switching the context. With an event loop in place, a much smaller memory allocation is needed for each request to capture its specifics, which makes it possible to keep many more requests in memory so that they can be processed concurrently. The overhead of the CPU context-switching has become far smaller too because of the diminishing context size.

The non-blocking API is a way of processing requests so that systems are able to handle a much bigger load while remaining highly responsive and resilient.

Reactive

Usually, the term **reactive** is used in the context of reactive programming and reactive systems. Reactive programming (which is also called Rx programming) is based on asynchronous data streams (which is also called **reactive streams**). It was introduced as a **Reactive Extension** (**RX**) of Java, which is also called **RxJava** (`http://reactivex.io`). Later, RX support was added to Java 9 in the `java.util.concurrent` package. It allows a `Publisher` to generate a stream of data to which a `Subscriber` can asynchronously subscribe.

One principal difference between reactive streams and standard streams (which are also called **Java 8 streams** and are located in the `java.util.stream` package) is that a source (publisher) of the reactive stream pushes elements to subscribers at its own rate, while in standard streams, a new element is pulled and emitted only after the previous one has been processed (in fact, it acts like a `for` loop).

As you have seen, we were able to process data asynchronously even without this new API by using `CompletableFuture`. But after writing such code a few times, you might notice that most of the code is just plumbing, so you get the feeling that there has to be an even simpler and more convenient solution. That's how the reactive streams initiative (`http://www.reactive-streams.org`) was born. The scope of the effort was defined as follows:

The scope of Reactive Streams is to find a minimal set of interfaces, methods, and protocols that will describe the necessary operations and entities to achieve the goal – asynchronous streams of data with non-blocking back pressure.

The term **non-blocking backpressure** refers to one of the problems of asynchronous processing: coordinating the speed rate of the incoming data with the ability of the system to process them without the need for stopping (blocking) the data input. The solution is to inform the source that the consumer has difficulty keeping up with the input. Also, processing should react to the change in the rate of the incoming data in a more flexible manner than just blocking the flow, hence the name *reactive*.

Several libraries already implement the reactive streams API: RxJava (`http://reactivex.io`), Reactor (`https://projectreactor.io`), Akka Streams (`https://akka.io/docs`), and Vert.x (`https://vertx.io/`) are among the most well known. Writing code using RxJava or another library of asynchronous streams constitutes *reactive programming*. It realizes the goal declared in the Reactive Manifesto (`https://www.reactivemanifesto.org`) by building reactive systems that are *responsive*, *resilient*, *elastic*, and *message-driven*.

Responsive

This term is relatively self-explanatory. The ability to respond in a timely manner is one of the primary qualities of any system. There are many ways to achieve it. Even a traditional blocking API supported by enough servers and other infrastructure can achieve decent responsiveness under a growing load.

Reactive programming helps to do this using less hardware. It comes at a price, as reactive code requires changing the way we think about control flow. But after some time, this new way of thinking becomes as natural as any other familiar skill.

In the following sections, we will see quite a few examples of reactive programming.

Resilient

Failures are inevitable. The hardware crashes, the software has defects, unexpected data is received, or an untested execution path has been taken – any of these events, or a combination of them, can happen at any time. *Resilience* is the ability of a system to continue delivering the expected results under unexpected circumstances.

For example, it can be achieved using redundancy of the deployable components and hardware, using isolation of parts of the system so the domino effect becomes less probable, by designing the system with automatically replaceable parts, or by raising an alarm so that qualified personnel can interfere. Additionally, we have talked about distributed systems as a good example of resilient systems by design.

A distributed architecture eliminates a single point of failure. Also, breaking the system into many specialized components that talk to one another using messages allows better tuning for the duplication of the most critical parts and creates more opportunities for their isolation and potential failure containment.

Elastic

Usually, the ability to sustain the biggest possible load is associated with **scalability**. But the ability to preserve the same performance characteristics under a varying load, not just under the growing one, is called **elasticity**.

The client of an elastic system should not notice any difference between the idle periods and the periods of peak load. A non-blocking reactive style of implementation facilitates this quality. Also, breaking the program into smaller parts and converting them into services that can be deployed and managed independently allows for the fine-tuning of resource allocation.

Such small services are called microservices, and many of them together can comprise a reactive system that can be both scalable and elastic. We will talk about such architecture, in more detail, in the following sections and the next chapter.

Message-driven

We have already established that component isolation and system distribution are two aspects that help to keep the system responsive, resilient, and elastic. Loose and flexible connections are important conditions that support these qualities, too. And the asynchronous nature of the reactive system simply does not leave the designer any other choice but to build communication between the components and the messages.

It creates breathing space around each component without which the system would become a tightly coupled monolith that was susceptible to all kinds of problems, not to mention a maintenance nightmare.

In the next chapter, we are going to look at an architectural style that can be used to build an application as a collection of loosely coupled microservices that communicate using messages.

Reactive streams

The reactive streams API, which was introduced in Java 9, consists of the following four interfaces:

```
@FunctionalInterface
public static interface Flow.Publisher<T> {
    public void subscribe(Flow.Subscriber<T> subscriber);
}
public static interface Flow.Subscriber<T> {
    public void onSubscribe(Flow.Subscription subscription);
    public void onNext(T item);
    public void onError(Throwable throwable);
    public void onComplete();
}
public static interface Flow.Subscription {
    public void request(long numberOfItems);
    public void cancel();
}
public static interface Flow.Processor<T,R>
                extends Flow.Subscriber<T>, Flow.Publisher<R> {
}
```

A `Flow.Subscriber` object can be passed, as a parameter, into the `subscribe()` method of `Flow.Publisher<T>`. Then, the publisher calls the subscriber's `onSubscribe()` method and passes to it a `Flow.Subscription` object as a parameter. Now, the subscriber can call `request(long numberOfItems)` on the subscription object to request data from the publisher. That is the way the **pull model** can be implemented, which leaves it up to a subscriber to decide when to request another item for processing. The subscriber can unsubscribe from the publisher services by calling the `cancel()` method on the subscription.

In return, the publisher can pass a new item to the subscriber by calling the subscriber's `onNext()` method. When no more data will be coming (that is, all the data from the source was emitted) the publisher calls the subscriber's `onComplete()` method. Also, by calling the subscriber's `onError()` method, the publisher can tell the subscriber that it has encountered a problem.

The `Flow.Processor` interface describes an entity that can act as both a subscriber and a publisher. It allows you to create chains (or pipelines) of such processors, so a subscriber can receive an item from a publisher, transform it, and then pass the result to the next subscriber or processor.

In a push model, the publisher can call `onNext()` without any request from the subscriber. If the rate of processing is lower than the rate of the item being published, the subscriber can use various strategies to relieve the pressure. For example, it can skip the items or create a buffer for temporary storage with the hope that the item production will slow down and the subscriber will be able to catch up.

This is the minimal set of interfaces that the reactive streams initiative has defined in support of the asynchronous data streams with non-blocking backpressure. As you can see, it allows the subscriber and publisher to talk to each other and coordinate the rate of incoming data; therefore, it makes possible a variety of solutions for the backpressure problem that we discussed in the *Reactive* section.

There are many ways to implement these interfaces. Currently, in JDK 9, there is only one implementation of one of the interfaces: the `SubmissionPublisher` class implements `Flow.Publisher`. The reason for this is that these interfaces are not supposed to be used by an application developer. It is a **Service Provider Interface (SPI)** that is used by the developers of the reactive streams libraries. If needed, use one of the already-existing toolkits to implement the reactive streams API that we mentioned earlier: RxJava, Reactor, Akka Streams, Vert.x, or any other library of your preference.

RxJava

In our examples, we will use **RxJava 2.2.21** (`http://reactivex.io`). It can be added to the project using the following dependency:

```
<dependency>
    <groupId>io.reactivex.rxjava2</groupId>
    <artifactId>rxjava</artifactId>
    <version>2.2.21</version>
</dependency>
```

First, let's compare two implementations of the same functionality using the `java.util.stream` package and the `io.reactivex` package. The sample program is going to be very simple:

- Create a stream of integers: 1, 2, 3, 4, and 5.
- Only filter the even numbers (that is, 2 and 4).

- Calculate the square root of each of the filtered numbers.

- Calculate the sum of all the square roots.

Here is how it can be implemented using the `java.util.stream` package (see the `ObservableIntro` class and the `squareRootSum()` method):

```
double a = IntStream.rangeClosed(1, 5)
                    .filter(i -> i % 2 == 0)
                    .mapToDouble(Double::valueOf)
                    .map(Math::sqrt)
                    .sum();
System.out.println(a);           //prints: 3.414213562373095
```

Additionally, the same functionality implemented with RxJava looks like this:

```
Observable.range(1, 5)
       .filter(i -> i % 2 == 0)
       .map(Math::sqrt)
       .reduce((r, d) -> r + d)
       .subscribe(System.out::println);
                               //prints: 3.414213562373095
```

RxJava is based on the `Observable` object (which plays the role of `Publisher`) and `Observer` that subscribes to the `Observable` object and waits for the data to be emitted.

In contrast to the `Stream` functionality, `Observable` has significantly different capabilities. For example, a stream, once closed, cannot be reopened, while an `Observable` object can be used again. Here is an example (see the `ObservableIntro` class and the `reuseObservable()` method):

```
Observable<Double> observable = Observable.range(1, 5)
       .filter(i -> i % 2 == 0)
       .doOnNext(System.out::println)      //prints 2 and 4 twice
       .map(Math::sqrt);

observable
       .reduce((r, d) -> r + d)
       .subscribe(System.out::println);
```

```
                                           //prints: 3.414213562373095

observable
      .reduce((r, d) -> r + d)
      .map(r -> r / 2)
      .subscribe(System.out::println);
                                       //prints: 1.7071067811865475
```

In the preceding example, as you can see from the comments, the `doOnNext()` operation was called twice, which means the observable object also emitted values twice, once for each processing pipeline:

```
reuseObservable():
2
4
3.414213562373095
2
4
1.7071067811865475
```

If we do not want `Observable` to run twice, we can cache its data, by adding the `cache()` operation (see the `ObservableIntro` class and the `cacheObservableData()` method):

```
Observable<Double> observable = Observable.range(1,5)
      .filter(i -> i % 2 == 0)
      .doOnNext(System.out::println)   //prints 2 and 4 only once
      .map(Math::sqrt)
      .cache();

observable
      .reduce((r, d) -> r + d)
      .subscribe(System.out::println);
                                       //prints: 3.414213562373095

observable
      .reduce((r, d) -> r + d)
      .map(r -> r / 2)
```

```
            .subscribe(System.out::println);
                                //prints: 1.7071067811865475
```

As you can see, the second usage of the same `Observable` object took advantage of the cached data, thus allowing for better performance:

```
cacheObservableData():
2
4
3.414213562373095
1.7071067811865475
```

RxJava provides such a rich functionality that there is no way we can review it all in this book. Instead, we will try to cover the most popular functionality. The API describes the methods available for invocation using an `Observable` object. Such methods are also called **operations** (as in the case with the standard Java 8 streams) or **operators** (this term is mostly used in connection to reactive streams). We will use these three terms – methods, operations, and operators – interchangeably as synonyms.

Observable types

Talking about the RxJava 2 API (notice that is it quite different from RxJava 1), we will use the online documentation, which can be found at `http://reactivex.io/RxJava/2.x/javadoc/index.html`.

An observer subscribes to receive values from an observable object, which can behave as one of the following types:

- **Blocking**: This waits until the result is returned.

- **Non-blocking**: This processes the emitted elements asynchronously.

- **Cold**: This emits an element at the observer's request.

- **Hot**: This emits elements whether an observer has subscribed or not.

An observable object can be an object of one of the following classes of the `io.reactivex` package:

- `Observable<T>`: This can emit none, one, or many elements; it does not support backpressure.

- `Flowable<T>`: This can emit none, one, or many elements; it supports backpressure.

- `Single<T>`: This can emit either one element or an error; the notion of backpressure does not apply.

- `Maybe<T>`: This represents a deferred computation. It can emit either no value, one value, or an error; the notion of backpressure does not apply.

- `Completable`: This represents a deferred computation without any value. This indicates the completion of a task or an error; the notion of backpressure does not apply.

An object of each of these classes can behave as a blocking, non-blocking, cold, or hot observable. They differ from each other by the number of values that can be emitted, their ability to defer the returning of the result or returning the flag of the task completion only, and their ability to handle backpressure.

Blocking versus non-blocking

To demonstrate this behavior, we create an observable that emits five sequential integers, starting with 1 (see the `BlockingOperators` class and the `observableBlocking1()` method):

```
Observable<Integer> obs = Observable.range(1,5);
```

All the blocking methods (operators) of `Observable` start with the "blocking." For example, the `blockingLast()` operator blocks the pipeline until the last elements are emitted:

```
Double d2 = obs.filter(i -> i % 2 == 0)
               .doOnNext(System.out::println)   //prints 2 and 4
               .map(Math::sqrt)
               .delay(100, TimeUnit.MILLISECONDS)
               .blockingLast();
System.out.println(d2);                          //prints: 2.0
```

In this example, we only select even numbers, print the selected element, and then calculate the square root and wait for 100 ms (imitating a long-running calculation). The result of this example is as follows:

```
observableBlocking1():
2
4
2.0
```

The non-blocking version of the same functionality is as follows (see the
BlockingOperators class and the second half of the observableBlocking1()
method):

```
List<Double> list = new ArrayList<>();
obs.filter(i -> i % 2 == 0)
    .doOnNext(System.out::println)   //prints 2 and 4
    .map(Math::sqrt)
    .delay(100, TimeUnit.MILLISECONDS)
    .subscribe(d -> {
        if(list.size() == 1){
            list.remove(0);
        }
        list.add(d);
    });
System.out.println(list);                //prints: []
```

We use the List object to capture the result because, as you might remember, the lambda
expression does not allow us to use the non-final variables.

As you can see, the resulting list is empty. That is because the pipeline calculations are
performed without blocking (asynchronously). We set a delay of 100 ms (to simulate
processing, which takes a long time), but there is no blocking operation, so the control
goes down to the next line that prints the list content, which is still empty.

To prevent the control from going to this line too early, we can set a delay in front of it
(see the BlockingOperators class and the observableBlocking2() method):

```
try {
    TimeUnit.MILLISECONDS.sleep(250);
} catch (InterruptedException e) {
    e.printStackTrace();
}
System.out.println(list);    //prints: [2.0]
```

Note that the delay has to be 200 ms at least because the pipeline processes two elements,
each with a delay of 100 ms. Now you can see the list contains an expected value of 2.0.

Esentially, that is the difference between blocking and non-blocking operators. Other classes that represent an observable have similar blocking operators. Here are some examples of blocking Flowable, Single, and Maybe (see the BlockingOperators class and the flowableBlocking(), singleBlocking(), and maybeBlocking() methods):

```
Flowable<Integer> obs = Flowable.range(1,5);
Double d2 = obs.filter(i -> i % 2 == 0)
        .doOnNext(System.out::println)   //prints 2 and 4
        .map(Math::sqrt)
        .delay(100, TimeUnit.MILLISECONDS)
        .blockingLast();
System.out.println(d2);                        //prints: 2.0


Single<Integer> obs2 = Single.just(42);
int i2 = obs2.delay(100, TimeUnit.MILLISECONDS).blockingGet();
System.out.println(i2);                        //prints: 42


Maybe<Integer> obs3 = Maybe.just(42);
int i3 = obs3.delay(100, TimeUnit.MILLISECONDS).blockingGet();
System.out.println(i3);                        //prints: 42
```

The Completable class has blocking operators that allow us to set a timeout (see the BlockingOperators class and the second half of the completableBlocking() method):

```
(1) Completable obs = Completable.fromRunnable(() -> {
        System.out.println("Run");                //prints: Run
        try {
            TimeUnit.MILLISECONDS.sleep(200);
        } catch (InterruptedException e) {
            e.printStackTrace();
        }
    });
(2) Throwable ex = obs.blockingGet();
(3) System.out.println(ex);                        //prints: null


//(4) ex = obs.blockingGet(15, TimeUnit.MILLISECONDS);
```

```
// java.util.concurrent.TimeoutException:
//        The source did not signal an event for 15 milliseconds.

(5)  ex = obs.blockingGet(150, TimeUnit.MILLISECONDS);
(6)  System.out.println(ex);                          //prints: null

(7)  obs.blockingAwait();
(8)  obs.blockingAwait(15, TimeUnit.MILLISECONDS);
```

The result of the preceding code is presented in the following screenshot:

The first Run message comes from line 2 in response to the call of the blocking blockingGet() method. The first null message comes from line 3. Line 4 throws an exception because the timeout was set to 15 ms, while the actual processing was set to a delay of 100 ms. The second Run message comes from line 5 in response to the blockingGet() method call. This time, the timeout is set to 150 ms, which is more than 100 ms, so the method is able to return before the timeout was up.

The last two lines, 7 and 8, demonstrate the usage of the blockingAwait() method with and without a timeout. This method does not return a value but allows the observable pipeline to run its course. Interestingly, it does not break with an exception even when the timeout is set to a smaller value than the time the pipeline takes to finish. Apparently, it starts waiting after the pipeline has finished processing unless it is a defect that will be fixed later (the documentation is not clear regarding this point).

Although blocking operations do exist (and we will review more of them while talking about each observable type in the following sections), they are and should only be used in cases when it is not possible to implement the required functionality of using non-blocking operations only. The main thrust of reactive programming is to strive to process all requests asynchronously in a non-blocking style.

Cold versus hot

So far, all the examples we have seen have only demonstrated a cold observable, which only provides the next value at the request of the processing pipeline after the previous value has been processed. Here is another example (see the ColdObservable class and the main() method):

```
Observable<Long> cold =
        Observable.interval(10, TimeUnit.MILLISECONDS);
cold.subscribe(i -> System.out.println("First: " + i));
pauseMs(25);
cold.subscribe(i -> System.out.println("Second: " + i));
pauseMs(55);
```

We have used the interval() method to create an Observable object that represents a stream of sequential numbers emitted at every specified interval (in our case, every 10 ms). Then, we subscribe to the created object, wait 25 ms, subscribe again, and wait another 55 ms. The pauseMs() method is as follows:

```
void pauseMs(long ms){
    try {
        TimeUnit.MILLISECONDS.sleep(ms);
    } catch (InterruptedException e) {
        e.printStackTrace();
    }
}
```

If we run the preceding example, the output will look similar to the following:

```
First: 0
First: 1
First: 2
First: 3
Second: 0
Second: 1
First: 4
Second: 2
First: 5
First: 6
Second: 3
Second: 4
First: 7
```

As you can see, each of the pipelines processed every value emitted by the cold observable.

To convert the *cold* observable into a *hot* one, we use the `publish()` method, which converts the observable into a `ConnectableObservable` object that extends the `Observable` object (see the `HotObservable` class and the `hot1()` method):

```
ConnectableObservable<Long> hot =
        Observable.interval(10, TimeUnit.MILLISECONDS).publish();
hot.connect();
hot.subscribe(i -> System.out.println("First: " + i));
pauseMs(25);
hot.subscribe(i -> System.out.println("Second: " + i));
pauseMs(55);
```

As you can see, we have to call the `connect()` method so that the `ConnectableObservable` object starts emitting values. The output looks similar to the following:

```
hot1():
First: 0
First: 1
First: 2
First: 3
Second: 3
First: 4
Second: 4
First: 5
Second: 5
First: 6
Second: 6
First: 7
Second: 7
First: 8
Second: 8
```

The preceding output shows that the second pipeline did not receive the first three values because it was subscribed to the observable later on. So, the observable emits values independent of the ability of the observers to process them. If the processing falls behind, and new values keep coming while the previous ones are not fully processed yet, the `Observable` class puts them into a buffer. If this buffer grows large enough, the JVM can run out of memory because, as we mentioned earlier, the `Observable` class is not capable of backpressure management.

For such cases, the `Flowable` class is a better candidate for the observable because it does have the ability to handle backpressure. Here is an example (see the `HotObservable` class and the `hot2()` method):

```
PublishProcessor<Integer> hot = PublishProcessor.create();
hot.observeOn(Schedulers.io(), true)
    .subscribe(System.out::println, Throwable::printStackTrace);
for (int i = 0; i < 1_000_000; i++) {
    hot.onNext(i);
}
```

The `PublishProcessor` class extends `Flowable` and has an `onNext(Object o)` method that forces it to emit the passed-in object. Before calling it, we have subscribed to the observable using the `Schedulers.io()` thread. We will talk about schedulers in the *Multithreading (scheduler)* section.

The `subscribe()` method has several overloaded versions. We decided to use the one that accepts two `Consumer` functions: the first one processes the passed-in value, and the second one processes an exception if it was thrown by any of the pipeline operations (it works similar to a `Catch` block).

If we run the preceding example, it will successfully print the first 127 values and then throw `MissingBackpressureException`, as shown in the following screenshot:

```
126
127
io.reactivex.exceptions.MissingBackpressureException Create breakpoint : Could not emit value due to lack of requests
    at io.reactivex.processors.PublishProcessor$PublishSubscription.onNext(PublishProcessor.java:364)
    at io.reactivex.processors.PublishProcessor.onNext(PublishProcessor.java:243)
    at com.packt.learnjava.ch15_reactive.HotObservable.hot2(HotObservable.java:38)
    at com.packt.learnjava.ch15_reactive.HotObservable.main(HotObservable.java:13)
```

The message in the exception provides a clue: `Could not emit value due to lack of requests`. Apparently, the rate of emitting values is higher than the rate of consuming them, while an internal buffer can only keep 128 elements. If we add a delay (to simulate a longer processing time), the result will be even worse (see the `HotObservable` class and the `hot3()` method):

```
PublishProcessor<Integer> hot = PublishProcessor.create();
hot.observeOn(Schedulers.io(), true)
    .delay(10, TimeUnit.MILLISECONDS)
    .subscribe(System.out::println, Throwable::printStackTrace);
```

```
for (int i = 0; i < 1_000_000; i++) {
    hot.onNext(i);
}
```

Even the first 128 elements will not get through and the output will only have
MissingBackpressureException.

To address this issue, a backpressure strategy has to be set. For example, let's drop every
value that the pipeline did not manage to process (see the HotObservable class and the
hot4() method):

```
PublishProcessor<Integer> hot = PublishProcessor.create();
hot.onBackpressureDrop(v -> System.out.println("Dropped: "+ v))
    .observeOn(Schedulers.io(), true)
    .subscribe(System.out::println, Throwable::printStackTrace);
for (int i = 0; i < 1_000_000; i++) {
    hot.onNext(i);
}
```

Notice that the strategy has to be set before the observeOn() operation, so it will be
picked up by the created Schedulers.io() thread.

The output shows that many of the emitted values were dropped. Here is an
output fragment:

```
391673
391674
391675
391676
391677
391678
Dropped: 391850
Dropped: 391851
Dropped: 391852
```

We will talk about other backpressure strategies in the *Operators* section when
we overview the corresponding operators.

Disposable

Notice that a `subscribe()` method actually returns a `Disposable` object that can be queried to check whether the pipeline processing has been completed and disposed of (see the `DisposableUsage` class and the `disposable1()` method):

```
Observable<Integer> obs = Observable.range(1,5);
List<Double> list = new ArrayList<>();
Disposable disposable =
    obs.filter(i -> i % 2 == 0)
        .doOnNext(System.out::println)       //prints 2 and 4
        .map(Math::sqrt)
        .delay(100, TimeUnit.MILLISECONDS)
        .subscribe(d -> {
            if(list.size() == 1){
                list.remove(0);
            }
            list.add(d);
        });
System.out.println(disposable.isDisposed()); //prints: false
System.out.println(list);                    //prints: []

try {
    TimeUnit.MILLISECONDS.sleep(200);
} catch (InterruptedException e) {
    e.printStackTrace();
}
System.out.println(disposable.isDisposed());  //prints: true
System.out.println(list);                     //prints: [2.0]
```

Also, it is possible to enforce the disposing of a pipeline, thus effectively canceling the processing (see the `DisposableUsage` class and the `disposable2()` method):

```
Observable<Integer> obs = Observable.range(1,5);
List<Double> list = new ArrayList<>();
Disposable disposable =
    obs.filter(i -> i % 2 == 0)
        .doOnNext(System.out::println)       //prints 2 and 4
        .map(Math::sqrt)
```

```
        .delay(100, TimeUnit.MILLISECONDS)
        .subscribe(d -> {
            if(list.size() == 1){
                list.remove(0);
            }
            list.add(d);
        });
System.out.println(disposable.isDisposed()); //prints: false
System.out.println(list);                     //prints: []
disposable.dispose();
try {
    TimeUnit.MILLISECONDS.sleep(200);
} catch (InterruptedException e) {
    e.printStackTrace();
}
System.out.println(disposable.isDisposed()); //prints: true
System.out.println(list);                     //prints: []
```

As you can see, by adding the call to disposable.dispose(), we have stopped processing, so even after a delay of 200 ms, the list remains empty (see the last line of the preceding example).

This method of forced disposal can be used to make sure that there are no runaway threads. Each created Disposable object can be disposed of in the same way that resources are released in a finally block. The CompositeDisposable class helps us to handle multiple Disposable objects in a coordinated manner.

When an onComplete or onError event happens, the pipeline is disposed of automatically.

For example, you can use the add() method and add a newly created Disposable object to the CompositeDisposable object. Then, when necessary, the clear() method can be invoked on the CompositeDisposable object. It will remove the collected Disposable objects and call the dispose() method on each of them.

Creating an observable

You have already seen a few methods of how to create an observable in our examples. There are many other factory methods, including `Observable`, `Flowable`, `Single`, `Maybe`, and `Completable`. However, not all of the following methods are available in each of these interfaces (see the comments; *all* means that all of the listed interfaces have it):

- `create()`: This creates an `Observable` object by providing the full implementation (all).

- `defer()`: This creates a new `Observable` object every time a new `Observer` subscribes (all).

- `empty()`: This creates an empty `Observable` object that completes immediately upon subscription (all, except for `Single`).

- `never()`: This creates an `Observable` object that does not emit anything and does nothing at all; it does not even complete (all).

- `error()`: This creates an `Observable` object that emits an exception immediately upon subscription (all).

- `fromXXX()`: This creates an `Observable` object, where *XXX* can be *Callable*, *Future* (all), *Iterable*, *Array*, *Publisher* (`Observable` and `Flowable`), *Action*, or *Runnable* (`Maybe` and `Completable`); this means it creates an `Observable` object based on the provided function or object.

- `generate()`: This creates a cold `Observable` object that generates values based on the provided function or object (`Observable` and `Flowable` only).

- `range()`, `rangeLong()`, `interval()`, `intervalRange()`: This creates an `Observable` object that emits sequential `int` or `long` values, which may or may not be limited by the specified range and spaced by the specified time interval (`Observable` and `Flowable` only).

- `just()`: This creates an `Observable` object based on the provided object or a set of objects (all, except for `Completable`).

- `timer()`: This creates an `Observable` object that, after the specified time, emits an `0L` signal (all) and then completes for `Observable` and `Flowable`.

There are also many other helpful methods, such as `repeat()`, `startWith()`, and more. We just do not have enough space to list all of them. Refer to the online documentation (`http://reactivex.io/RxJava/2.x/javadoc/index.html`).

Let's look at an example of the `create()` method usage. The `create()` method of `Observable` is as follows:

```
public static Observable<T> create(ObservableOnSubscribe<T>
source)
```

The passed-in object has to be an implementation of the `ObservableOnSubscribe<T>` functional interface, which only has one abstract method, `subscribe()`:

```
void subscribe(ObservableEmitter<T> emitter)
```

The `ObservableEmitter<T>` interface contains the following methods:

- `boolean isDisposed()`: This returns `true` if the processing pipeline was disposed of or the emitter was terminated.

- `ObservableEmitter<T> serialize()`: This provides the serialization algorithm used by the calls to `onNext()`, `onError()`, and `onComplete()`, located in the `Emitter` base class.

- `void setCancellable(Cancellable c)`: This sets, on this emitter, a `Cancellable` implementation (that is, a functional interface that has only one method, `cancel()`).

- `void setDisposable(Disposable d)`: This sets, on this emitter, a `Disposable` implementation (which is an interface that has two methods: `isDispose()` and `dispose()`).

- `boolean tryOnError(Throwable t)`: This handles the error condition, attempts to emit the provided exception, and returns `false` if the emission is not allowed.

To create an observable, all the preceding interfaces can be implemented as follows (see the `CreateObservable` class and the `main()` method):

```
ObservableOnSubscribe<String> source = emitter -> {
    emitter.onNext("One");
    emitter.onNext("Two");
    emitter.onComplete();
};
Observable.create(source)
        .filter(s -> s.contains("w"))
        .subscribe(v -> System.out.println(v),
```

```
                    e -> e.printStackTrace(),
              () -> System.out.println("Completed"));
pauseMs(100);
```

Let's take a closer look at the preceding example. We created an `ObservableOnSubscribe` function as `source` and implemented the emitter: we told the emitter to emit `One` at the first call to `onNext()`, to emit `Two` at the second call to `onNext()`, and then to call `onComplete()`. We passed the `source` function to the `create()` method and built the pipeline to process all of the emitted values.

To make it more interesting, we added the `filter()` operator, which only allows you to further propagate the values with the *w* character. Additionally, we chose the `subscribe()` method version with three parameters: the `Consumer onNext`, `Consumer onError`, and `Action onComplete` functions. The first is called every time a next value reached the method, the second is called when an exception was emitted, and the third is called when the source emits an `onComplete()` signal. After creating the pipeline, we paused for 100 ms to give the asynchronous process a chance to finish. The result is as follows:

If we remove the `emitter.onComplete()` line from the emitter implementation, only the message `Two` will be displayed.

So, those are the basics of how the `create()` method can be used. As you can see, it allows for full customization. In practice, it is rarely used because there are far simpler ways to create an observable. We will review them in the following sections.

Additionally, you will see examples of other factory methods that are used in our examples throughout other sections of this chapter.

Operators

There are literally hundreds (if we count all of the overloaded versions) of operators available in each of the observable interfaces, `Observable`, `Flowable`, `Single`, `Maybe`, and `Completable`.

In the `Observable` and `Flowable` interfaces, the number of methods goes beyond 500. That is why, in this section, we are going to provide just an overview and a few examples that will help you to navigate the maze of possible options.

We have grouped all the operators into 10 categories: transforming, filtering, combining, converting from XXX, exceptions handling, life cycle events handling, utilities, conditionals and Booleans, backpressure, and connectable.

Please note that these are not all of the operators that are available. You can see more in the online documentation (`http://reactivex.io/RxJava/2.x/javadoc/index.html`).

Transforming

The following operators transform the values emitted by an observable:

- `buffer()`: This collects the emitted values into bundles according to the provided parameters or by using the provided functions. It periodically emits these bundles one at a time.

- `flatMap()`: This produces observables based on the current observable and inserts them into the current flow; it is one of the most popular operators.

- `groupBy()`: This divides the current `Observable` object into groups of observables (`GroupedObservables` objects).

- `map()`: This transforms the emitted value using the provided function.

- `scan()`: This applies the provided function to each value in combination with the value produced as the result of the previous application of the same function to the previous value.

- `window()`: This emits groups of values similar to `buffer()` but as observables, each of which emits a subset of values from the original observable and then terminates with `onCompleted()`.

The following code demonstrates the use of `map()`, `flatMap()`, and `groupBy()` (see the `NonBlockingOperators` class and the `transforming()` method):

```
Observable<String> obs = Observable.fromArray("one", "two");

obs.map(s -> s.contains("w") ? 1 : 0)
    .forEach(System.out::print);              //prints: 01
System.out.println();
List<String> os = new ArrayList<>();
List<String> noto = new ArrayList<>();
obs.flatMap(s -> Observable.fromArray(s.split("")))
        .groupBy(s -> "o".equals(s) ? "o" : "noto")
```

```
        .subscribe(g -> g.subscribe(s -> {
            if (g.getKey().equals("o")) {
                os.add(s);
            } else {
                noto.add(s);
            }
        }));
System.out.println(os);                        //prints: [o, o]
System.out.println(noto);                      //prints: [n, e, t, w]
```

Filtering

The following operators (and their multiple overloaded versions) select which of the values will continue to flow through the pipeline:

- debounce(): This emits a value only when a specified span of time has passed without the observable emitting another value.

- distinct(): This selects unique values only.

- elementAt(long n): This emits only one value with the specified n position in the stream.

- filter(): This emits only the values that match the specified criteria.

- firstElement(): This emits the first value only.

- ignoreElements(): This does not emit values; only the onComplete() signal goes through.

- lastElement(): This emits the last value only.

- sample(): This emits the most recent value emitted within the specified time interval.

- skip(long n): This skips the first n values.

- take(long n): This only emits the first n values.

The following code showcases examples of some of the uses of the preceding operators (see the NonBlockingOperators class and the filtering() method):

```
Observable<String> obs = Observable.just("onetwo")
        .flatMap(s -> Observable.fromArray(s.split("")));
// obs emits "onetwo" as characters
obs.map(s -> {
```

```
                 if("t".equals(s)){
                     NonBlockingOperators.pauseMs(15);
                 }
                 return s;
             })
             .debounce(10, TimeUnit.MILLISECONDS)
             .forEach(System.out::print);                    //prints: eo
obs.distinct().forEach(System.out::print);          //prints: onetw
obs.elementAt(3).subscribe(System.out::println);    //prints: t
obs.filter(s -> s.equals("o"))
    .forEach(System.out::print);                     //prints: oo
obs.firstElement().subscribe(System.out::println); //prints: o
obs.ignoreElements().subscribe(() ->
        System.out.println("Completed!"));  //prints: Completed!
Observable.interval(5, TimeUnit.MILLISECONDS)
    .sample(10, TimeUnit.MILLISECONDS)
    .subscribe(v -> System.out.print(v + " "));
                                            //prints: 1 3 4 6 8
pauseMs(50);
```

Combining

The following operators (and their multiple overloaded versions) create a new observable using multiple source observables:

- `concat(src1, src2)`: This creates an `Observable` object that emits all values of `src1` and then all values of `src2`.

- `combineLatest(src1, src2, combiner)`: This creates an `Observable` object that emits a value emitted by either of the two sources combined with the latest value emitted by each source using the provided `combiner` function.

- `join(src2, leftWin, rightWin, combiner)`: This combines the values emitted by two observables during the `leftWin` and `rightWin` time windows according to the `combiner` function.

- `merge()`: This combines multiple observables into one; in contrast to `concat()`, it might interleave them, whereas `concat()` never interleaves the emitted values from different observables.

- `startWith(T item)`: This adds the specified value before emitting values from the source observable.

- `startWith(Observable<T> other)`: This adds the values from the specified observable before emitting values from the source observable.

- `switchOnNext(Observable<Observable> observables)`: This creates a new `Observable` object that emits the most-recently emitted values of the specified observables.

- `zip()`: This combines the values of the specified observables using the provided function.

The following code demonstrates the use of some of these operators (see the `NonBlockingOperators` class and the `combined()` method):

```
Observable<String> obs1 = Observable.just("one")
            .flatMap(s -> Observable.fromArray(s.split("")));
Observable<String> obs2 = Observable.just("two")
            .flatMap(s -> Observable.fromArray(s.split("")));
Observable.concat(obs2, obs1, obs2)
        .subscribe(System.out::print);    //prints: twoonetwo
Observable.combineLatest(obs2, obs1, (x,y) -> "("+x+y+")")
        .subscribe(System.out::print); //prints: (oo)(on)(oe)
System.out.println();
obs1.join(obs2, i -> Observable.timer(5,
            TimeUnit.MILLISECONDS),i -> Observable.timer(5,
            TimeUnit.MILLISECONDS), (x,y) -> "("+x+y+")")
                            .subscribe(System.out::print);
            //prints: (ot)(nt)(et)(ow)(nw)(ew)(oo)(no)(eo)
Observable.merge(obs2, obs1, obs2)
        .subscribe(System.out::print);
                    //prints: twoonetwo obs1.startWith("42")
    .subscribe(System.out::print);        //prints: 42one
Observable.zip(obs1, obs2, obs1,  (x,y,z) -> "("+x+y+z+")")
        .subscribe(System.out::print);
                            //prints: (oto)(nwn)(eoe)
```

Converting from XXX

These operators are pretty straightforward. Here is a list of from-XXX operators of the `Observable` class:

- `fromArray(T... items)`: This creates an `Observable` object from a varargs.

- `fromCallable(Callable<T> supplier)`: This creates an `Observable` object from a `Callable` function.

- `fromFuture(Future<T> future)`: This creates an `Observable` object from a `Future` object.

- `fromFuture(Future<T> future, long timeout, TimeUnit unit)`: This creates an `Observable` object from a `Future` object with the timeout parameters applied to the `future`.

- `fromFuture(Future<T> future, long timeout, TimeUnit unit, Scheduler scheduler)`: This creates an `Observable` object from a `Future` object with the timeout parameters applied to the `future` and the scheduler (note that `Schedulers.io()` is recommended; please see the *Multithreading (scheduler)* section).

- `fromFuture(Future<T> future, Scheduler scheduler)`: This creates an `Observable` object from a `Future` object on the specified scheduler (note that `Schedulers.io()` is recommended; please see the *Multithreading (scheduler)* section).

- `fromIterable(Iterable<T> source)`: This creates an `Observable` object from an iterable object (for example, `List`).

- `fromPublisher(Publisher<T> publisher)`: This creates an `Observable` object, for example from a `Publisher` object.

Exceptions handling

The `subscribe()` operator has an overloaded version that accepts the `Consumer<Throwable>` function, which handles exceptions raised anywhere in the pipeline. It works in a similar way to the all-embracing `try-catch` block. If you have this function passed into the `subscribe()` operator, you can be sure that is the only place where all exceptions will end up.

However, if you need to handle the exceptions in the middle of the pipeline, the values flow can be recovered and processed by the rest of the operators, that is, after the operator has thrown the exception. The following operators (and their multiple overloaded versions) can help with that:

- `onErrorXXX()`: This resumes the provided sequence when an exception was caught; XXX indicates what the operator does: `onErrorResumeNext()`, `onErrorReturn()`, or `onErrorReturnItem()`.

- `retry()`: This creates an `Observable` object that repeats the emissions emitted from the source; it resubscribes to the source `Observable` if it calls `onError()`.

The demo code appears as follows (see the `NonBlockingOperators` class and the `exceptions()` method):

```
Observable<String> obs = Observable.just("one")
            .flatMap(s -> Observable.fromArray(s.split("")));
Observable.error(new RuntimeException("MyException"))
  .flatMap(x -> Observable.fromArray("two".split("")))
  .subscribe(System.out::print,
      e -> System.out.println(e.getMessage())
                                        //prints: MyException
  );
Observable.error(new RuntimeException("MyException"))
        .flatMap(y -> Observable.fromArray("two".split("")))
        .onErrorResumeNext(obs)
        .subscribe(System.out::print);          //prints: one
Observable.error(new RuntimeException("MyException"))
        .flatMap(z -> Observable.fromArray("two".split("")))
        .onErrorReturnItem("42")
        .subscribe(System.out::print);          //prints: 42
```

Life cycle events handling

These operators are each invoked on a certain event that happened anywhere in the pipeline. They work similarly to the operators described in the *Exceptions handling* section.

The format of these operators is doXXX(), where XXX is the name of the event: onComplete, onNext, onError, and similar. Not all of them are available in all the classes, and some of them are slightly different in Observable, Flowable, Single, Maybe, or Completable. However, we do not have space to list all the variations of all these classes and will limit our overview to a few examples of the life cycle events-handling operators of the Observable class:

- doOnSubscribe(Consumer<Disposable> onSubscribe): This executes when an observer subscribes.

- doOnNext(Consumer<T> onNext): This applies the provided Consumer function when the source observable calls onNext.

- doAfterNext(Consumer<T> onAfterNext): This applies the provided Consumer function to the current value after it is pushed downstream.

- doOnEach(Consumer<Notification<T>> onNotification): This executes the Consumer function for each emitted value.

- doOnEach(Observer<T> observer): This notifies an Observer object for each emitted value and the terminal event it emits.

- doOnComplete(Action onComplete): This executes the provided Action function after the source observable generates the onComplete event.

- doOnDispose(Action onDispose): This executes the provided Action function after the pipeline was disposed of downstream.

- doOnError(Consumer<Throwable> onError): This executes when the onError event is sent.

- doOnLifecycle(Consumer<Disposable> onSubscribe, Action onDispose): This calls the corresponding onSubscribe or onDispose function for the corresponding event.

- doOnTerminate(Action onTerminate): This executes the provided Action function when the source observable generates the onComplete event or an exception (the onError event) is raised.

- doAfterTerminate(Action onFinally): This executes the provided Action function after the source observable generates the onComplete event or an exception (the onError event) is raised.

- doFinally(Action onFinally): This executes the provided Action function after the source observable generates the onComplete event or an exception (the onError event) is raised, or the pipeline was disposed of downstream.

Here is demo code (see the `NonBlockingOperators` class and the `events()` method):

```
Observable<String> obs = Observable.just("one")
           .flatMap(s -> Observable.fromArray(s.split("")));


obs.doOnComplete(() -> System.out.println("Completed!"))
       .subscribe(v -> {
           System.out.println("Subscribe onComplete: " + v);
       });
pauseMs(25);
```

If we run this code, the output will be as follows:

```
events():
Subscribe onNext: o
Subscribe onNext: n
Subscribe onNext: e
Completed!
```

You will also see other examples of these operators' usage in the *Multithreading (scheduler)* section.

Utilities

Various useful operators (and their multiple overloaded versions) can be used for controlling the pipeline behavior:

- `delay()`: This delays the emission for a specified period.
- `materialize()`: This creates an `Observable` object that represents both the emitted values and the notifications sent.
- `dematerialize()`: This reverses the result of the `materialize()` operator.
- `observeOn()`: This specifies the `Scheduler` (thread) on which the `Observer` should observe the `Observable` object (see the *Multithreading (scheduler)* section).
- `serialize()`: This forces the serialization of the emitted values and notifications.
- `subscribe()`: This subscribes to the emissions and notifications from an observable; various overloaded versions accept callbacks used for a variety of events, including `onComplete` and `onError`; only after `subscribe()` is invoked do the the values start flowing through the pipeline.

- subscribeOn(): This subscribes the Observer to the Observable object asynchronously using the specified Scheduler (see the *Multithreading (scheduler)* section).

- timeInterval(), timestamp(): This converts an Observable<T> class that emits values into Observable<Timed<T>>, which, in turn, emits the amount of time elapsed between the emissions or the timestamp correspondingly.

- timeout(): This repeats the emissions of the source Observable; it generates an error if no emissions happen after the specified period of time.

- using(): This creates a resource that is disposed of automatically along with the Observable object; it works similarly to the try-with-resources construct.

The following code contains examples of some of these operators being used in a pipeline (see the NonBlockingOperators class and the utilities() method):

```
Observable<String> obs = Observable.just("one")
        .flatMap(s -> Observable.fromArray(s.split("")));
obs.delay(5, TimeUnit.MILLISECONDS)
    .subscribe(System.out::print);              //prints: one
pauseMs(10);
System.out.println(); //used here just to break the line
Observable source = Observable.range(1,5);
Disposable disposable = source.subscribe();
Observable.using(
  () -> disposable,
  x -> source,
  y -> System.out.println("Disposed: " + y)
                                  //prints: Disposed: DISPOSED
)
.delay(10, TimeUnit.MILLISECONDS)
.subscribe(System.out::print);              //prints: 12345
pauseMs(25);
```

If we run all these examples, the output will appear as follows:

```
utilities():
one
Disposed: DISPOSED
12345
```

As you can see, when completed, the pipeline sends the `DISPOSED` signal to the `using` operator (the third parameter), so the `Consumer` function we pass as the third parameter can dispose of the resources used by the pipeline.

Conditional and Boolean

The following operators (and their multiple overloaded versions) allow you to the evaluate one or more observables or emitted values and change the logic of the processing accordingly:

- `all(Predicate criteria)`: This returns `Single<Boolean>` with a `true` value, that is, if all the emitted values match the provided criteria.

- `amb()`: This accepts two or more source observables and emits values from only the first of them that starts emitting.

- `contains(Object value)`: This returns `Single<Boolean>` with `true`, that is, if the observable emits the provided value.

- `defaultIfEmpty(T value)`: This emits the provided value if the source `Observable` does not emit anything.

- `sequenceEqual()`: This returns `Single<Boolean>` with `true`, that is, if the provided sources emit the same sequence; an overloaded version allows us to provide the equality function used for comparison.

- `skipUntil(Observable other)`: This discards emitted values until the provided `Observable other` emits a value.

- `skipWhile(Predicate condition)`: This discards emitted values as long as the provided condition remains `true`.

- `takeUntil(Observable other)`: This discards emitted values after the provided `Observable other` emits a value.

- `takeWhile(Predicate condition)`: This discards emitted values after the provided condition becomes `false`.

The following code contains a few demo examples (see the `NonBlockingOperators` class and the `conditional()` method):

```
Observable<String> obs = Observable.just("one")
                .flatMap(s -> Observable.fromArray(s.split("")));
Single<Boolean> cont = obs.contains("n");
System.out.println(cont.blockingGet());              //prints: true
obs.defaultIfEmpty("two")
```

```
        .subscribe(System.out::print);              //prints: one
Observable.empty().defaultIfEmpty("two")
        .subscribe(System.out::print);              //prints: two

Single<Boolean> equal = Observable.sequenceEqual(obs,
                            Observable.just("one"));
System.out.println(equal.blockingGet());            //prints: false

equal = Observable.sequenceEqual(Observable.just("one"),
                            Observable.just("one"));
System.out.println(equal.blockingGet());            //prints: true

equal = Observable.sequenceEqual(Observable.just("one"),
                            Observable.just("two"));
System.out.println(equal.blockingGet());            //prints: false
```

Backpressure

So, we discussed and demonstrated the **backpressure** effect and the possible drop strategy in the *Cold versus hot* section. The other strategy might be as follows:

```
Flowable<Double> obs = Flowable.fromArray(1.,2.,3.);
obs.onBackpressureBuffer().subscribe();
//or
obs.onBackpressureLatest().subscribe();
```

The buffering strategy allows you to define the buffer size and provide a function that can be executed if the buffer overflows. The latest strategy tells the values producer to pause (when the consumer cannot process the emitted values on time) and emit the next value on request.

Note that the backpressure operators are available only in the `Flowable` class.

Connectable

The operators of this category allow us to connect observables and, thus, achieve more precisely controlled subscription dynamics:

- `publish()`: This converts an `Observable` object into a `ConnectableObservable` object.

- `replay()`: This returns a `ConnectableObservable` object that repeats all the emitted values and notifications every time a new `Observer` subscribes.

- `connect()`: This instructs a `ConnectableObservable` object to begin emitting values to the subscribers.

- `refCount()`: This converts a `ConnectableObservable` object into an `Observable` object.

We have demonstrated how `ConnectableObservable` works in the *Cold versus hot* section. One principal difference between `ConnectableObservable` and `Observable` is that `ConnectableObservable` does not start emitting values until its `connect` operator has been called.

Multithreading (scheduler)

By default, RxJava is single-threaded. This means that the source observable and all its operators notify the observers on the same thread that the `subscribe()` operator is called.

There are two operators, `observeOn()` and `subscribeOn()`, that allow you to move the execution of individual actions to a different thread. These methods take a `Scheduler` object as an argument that, well, schedules the individual actions to be executed on a different thread.

The `subscribeOn()` operator declares which scheduler should emit the values.

The `observeOn()` operator declares which scheduler should observe and process values.

The `Schedulers` class contains factory methods that create `Scheduler` objects with different life cycles and performance configurations:

- `computation()`: This creates a scheduler based on a bounded thread pool with a size up to the number of available processors; it should be used for CPU-intensive computations. Use `Runtime.getRuntime().availableProcessors()` to avoid using more of these types of schedulers than available processors; otherwise, the performance might become degraded because of the overhead of the thread-context switching.

- `io()`: This creates a scheduler based on an unbounded thread pool used for I/O-related work, such as working with files and databases in general when the interaction with the source is blocking by nature; avoid using it otherwise because it might spin too many threads and negatively affect performance and memory usage.

- `newThread()`: This creates a new thread every time and does not use any pool; it is an expensive way to create a thread, so you are expected to know exactly what the reason is for using it.

- `single()`: This creates a scheduler based on a single thread that executes all the tasks sequentially; this is useful when the sequence of the execution matters.

- `trampoline()`: This creates a scheduler that executes tasks in a first-in-first-out manner; this is useful for executing recursive algorithms.

- `from(Executor executor)`: This creates a scheduler based on the provided executor (thread pool), which allows for better control over the max number of threads and their life cycles.

In *Chapter 8*, *Multithreading and Concurrent Processing*, we talked about thread pools. To remind you, here are the pools we discussed:

```
Executors.newCachedThreadPool();
Executors.newSingleThreadExecutor();
Executors.newFixedThreadPool(int nThreads);
Executors.newScheduledThreadPool(int poolSize);
Executors.newWorkStealingPool(int parallelism);
```

As you can see, some of the other factory methods of the `Schedulers` class are backed by one of these thread pools, and they serve as just a simpler and shorter expression of a thread pool declaration. To make the examples simpler and more comparable, we are only going to use a `computation()` scheduler. Let's look at the basics of parallel/concurrent processing in RxJava.

The following code is an example of delegating CPU-intensive calculations to dedicated threads (see the `Scheduler` class and the `parallel1()` method):

```
Observable.fromArray("one","two","three")
        .doAfterNext(s -> System.out.println("1: " +
            Thread.currentThread().getName() + " => " + s))
        .flatMap(w -> Observable.fromArray(w.split("")))
                    .observeOn(Schedulers.computation())
            //.flatMap(s -> {
```

```
//         CPU-intensive calculations go here
// }
    .doAfterNext(s -> System.out.println("2: " +
    Thread.currentThread().getName() + " => " + s))
)
    .subscribe(s -> System.out.println("3: " + s));
pauseMs(100);
```

In this example, we decided to create a sub-flow of characters from each emitted word and let a dedicated thread process the characters of each word. The output of this example appears as follows:

```
parallel1():
3: o
2: RxComputationThreadPool-1 => o
1: main => one
3: n
2: RxComputationThreadPool-1 => n
3: e
2: RxComputationThreadPool-1 => e
1: main => two
3: t
2: RxComputationThreadPool-2 => t
3: w
2: RxComputationThreadPool-2 => w
3: o
2: RxComputationThreadPool-2 => o
1: main => three
3: t
2: RxComputationThreadPool-3 => t
3: h
2: RxComputationThreadPool-3 => h
3: r
2: RxComputationThreadPool-3 => r
3: e
2: RxComputationThreadPool-3 => e
3: e
2: RxComputationThreadPool-3 => e
```

As you can see, the main thread was used to emit the words, and the characters of each word were processed by a dedicated thread. Please note that although in this example the sequence of the results coming to the subscribe() operation corresponds to the sequence the words and characters were emitted, in real-life cases, the calculation time of each value will not be the same. So, there is no guarantee that the results will come in the same sequence.

If needed, we can put each word emission on a dedicated non-main thread too, so the main thread can be free to do anything else. For example, note the following (see the `Scheduler` class and the `parallel2()` method):

```
Observable.fromArray("one","two","three")
        .observeOn(Schedulers.computation())
        .doAfterNext(s -> System.out.println("1: " +
                Thread.currentThread().getName() + " => " + s))
        .flatMap(w -> Observable.fromArray(w.split(""))
                .observeOn(Schedulers.computation())
                .doAfterNext(s -> System.out.println("2: " +
                Thread.currentThread().getName() + " => " + s))
        )
        .subscribe(s -> System.out.println("3: " + s));
pauseMs(100);
```

The output of this example is as follows:

```
3: o
2: RxComputationThreadPool-2 => o
1: RxComputationThreadPool-1 => one
3: n
2: RxComputationThreadPool-2 => n
3: e
2: RxComputationThreadPool-2 => e
1: RxComputationThreadPool-1 => two
3: t
2: RxComputationThreadPool-3 => t
3: w
2: RxComputationThreadPool-3 => w
1: RxComputationThreadPool-1 => three
3: o
2: RxComputationThreadPool-3 => o
3: t
2: RxComputationThreadPool-4 => t
3: h
2: RxComputationThreadPool-4 => h
3: r
2: RxComputationThreadPool-4 => r
3: e
2: RxComputationThreadPool-4 => e
3: e
2: RxComputationThreadPool-4 => e
```

As you can see, the main thread no longer emits the words.

In RxJava 2.0.5, a new, simpler way of parallel processing was introduced, similar to parallel processing in the standard Java 8 streams. Using `ParallelFlowable`, the same functionality can be achieved as follows (see the `Scheduler` class and the `parallel3()` method):

```
ParallelFlowable src =
            Flowable.fromArray("one","two","three").parallel();
src.runOn(Schedulers.computation())
    .doAfterNext(s -> System.out.println("1: " +
                Thread.currentThread().getName() + " => " + s))
    .flatMap(w -> Flowable.fromArray(((String)w).split("")))
    .runOn(Schedulers.computation())
    .doAfterNext(s -> System.out.println("2: " +
                Thread.currentThread().getName() + " => " + s))
    .sequential()
    .subscribe(s -> System.out.println("3: " + s));
pauseMs(100);
```

As you can see, the `ParallelFlowable` object is created by applying the `parallel()` operator to the regular `Flowable` operator. Then, the `runOn()` operator tells the created observable to use the `computation()` scheduler to emit the values. Please note that there is no need to set another scheduler (for processing the characters) inside the `flatMap()` operator. It can be set outside it – just in the main pipeline, which makes the code simpler. The result looks like this:

```
1: RxComputationThreadPool-2 => two
1: RxComputationThreadPool-3 => three
1: RxComputationThreadPool-1 => one
2: RxComputationThreadPool-3 => t
2: RxComputationThreadPool-1 => o
2: RxComputationThreadPool-3 => h
2: RxComputationThreadPool-1 => n
2: RxComputationThreadPool-3 => r
2: RxComputationThreadPool-1 => e
2: RxComputationThreadPool-3 => e
2: RxComputationThreadPool-3 => e
3: t
3: o
3: t
3: n
3: h
3: e
3: r
3: e
3: e
2: RxComputationThreadPool-2 => t
3: w
2: RxComputationThreadPool-2 => w
3: o
2: RxComputationThreadPool-2 => o
```

As for the subscribeOn() operator, its location in the pipeline does not play any role. Wherever it is placed, it still tells the observable which scheduler should emit the values. Here is an example (see the Scheduler class and the subscribeOn1() method):

```
Observable.just("a", "b", "c")
        .doAfterNext(s -> System.out.println("1: " +
            Thread.currentThread().getName() + " => " + s))
        .subscribeOn(Schedulers.computation())
        .subscribe(s -> System.out.println("2: " +
            Thread.currentThread().getName() + " => " + s));
pauseMs(100);
```

The result looks like this:

```
2: RxComputationThreadPool-1 => a
1: RxComputationThreadPool-1 => a
2: RxComputationThreadPool-1 => b
1: RxComputationThreadPool-1 => b
2: RxComputationThreadPool-1 => c
1: RxComputationThreadPool-1 => c
```

Even if we change the location of the `subscribeOn()` operator, as shown in the following example, the result does not change (see the `Scheduler` class and the `subscribeOn2()` method):

```
Observable.just("a", "b", "c")
        .subscribeOn(Schedulers.computation())
        .doAfterNext(s -> System.out.println("1: " +
            Thread.currentThread().getName() + " => " + s))
        .subscribe(s -> System.out.println("2: " +
            Thread.currentThread().getName() + " => " + s));
pauseMs(100);
```

Finally, here is the example with both operators (see the `Scheduler` class and the `subscribeOnAndObserveOn()` method):

```
Observable.just("a", "b", "c")
        .subscribeOn(Schedulers.computation())
        .doAfterNext(s -> System.out.println("1: " +
            Thread.currentThread().getName() + " => " + s))
        .observeOn(Schedulers.computation())
        .subscribe(s -> System.out.println("2: " +
            Thread.currentThread().getName() + " => " + s));
pauseMs(100);
```

Now the result shows that two threads are used: one for subscribing and another for observing:

```
1: RxComputationThreadPool-1 => a
2: RxComputationThreadPool-2 => a
1: RxComputationThreadPool-1 => b
2: RxComputationThreadPool-2 => b
1: RxComputationThreadPool-1 => c
2: RxComputationThreadPool-2 => c
```

This concludes our short overview of RxJava, which is a big and still-growing library with a lot of possibilities, many of which we just did not have space in this book to review. We encourage you to try and learn it because it seems that reactive programming is the way modern data processing is heading.

In the following chapters, we will demonstrate how to build reactive applications (microservices) using Spring Boot and Vert.x.

Summary

In this chapter, you learned what reactive programming is and what its main concepts are: asynchronous, non-blocking, responsive, and more. Reactive streams were introduced and explained in simple terms, along with the RxJava library, which is the first solid implementation that supports reactive programming principles.

Now you can write code for asynchronous processing using reactive programming.

In the next chapter, we will talk about microservices as the foundation for creating reactive systems, and we will review another library that successfully supports reactive programming: **Vert.x**. We will use it to demonstrate how various microservices can be built.

Quiz

1. Select all the correct statements:

    A. Asynchronous processing always provides results later.

    B. Asynchronous processing always provides responses quickly.

    C. Asynchronous processing can use parallel processing.

    D. Asynchronous processing always provides results faster than a blocking call.

2. Can `CompletableFuture` be used without using a thread pool?

3. What does the *nio* in `java.nio` stand for?

4. Is an `event` loop the only design that supports a non-blocking API?

5. What does the *Rx* in RxJava stand for?

6. Which Java package of the **Java Class Library** (**JCL**) supports reactive streams?

7. Select all classes from the following list that can represent an observable in a reactive stream:

   A. `Flowable`

   B. `Probably`

   C. `CompletableFuture`

   D. `Single`

8. How do you know that a particular method (operator) of the `Observable` class is blocking?

9. What is the difference between a cold and a hot observable?

10. The `subscribe()` method of `Observable` returns a `Disposable` object. What happens when the `dispose()` method is called on this object?

11. Select all the names of the methods that create an `Observable` object:

    A. `interval()`

    B. `new()`

    C. `generate()`

    D. `defer()`

12. Name two transforming `Observable` operators.

13. Name two filtering `Observable` operators.

14. Name two backpressure-processing strategies.

15. Name two `Observable` operators that allow you to add threads to the pipeline processing.

16
Java Microbenchmark Harness

In this chapter, you will learn about a **Java Microbenchmark Harness (JMH)** project that allows measuring various code performance characteristics. If performance is an important issue for your application, this tool can help you to identify bottlenecks with precision—up to the method level.

In addition to theoretical knowledge, you will have a chance to run JMH using practical demo examples and recommendations.

The following topics will be covered in this chapter:

- What is JMH?
- Creating a JMH benchmark
- Running the benchmark
- Using the IDE plugin
- JMH benchmark parameters
- JMH usage examples

By the end of the chapter, you will be able to not only measure the average execution time of an application and other performance values (such as throughput, for example) but also to do it in a controlled manner—with or without the JVM optimizations, warm-up runs, and so on.

Technical requirements

To be able to execute the code examples provided in this chapter, you will need the following:

- A computer with a Microsoft Windows, Apple macOS, or Linux operating system
- Java SE version 17 or later
- The IDE or code editor you prefer

The instructions for how to set up a Java SE and IntelliJ IDEA editor were provided in *Chapter 1, Getting Started with Java 17*. The files with the code examples for this chapter are available on GitHub in the https://github.com/PacktPublishing/Learn-Java-17-Programming.git repository in the examples/src/main/java/com/packt/learnjava/ch16_microbenchmark folder.

What is JMH?

According to the Oxford English Dictionary, a **benchmark** is *a standard or point of reference against which things may be compared or assessed*. In programming, it is the way to compare the performance of applications, or just methods. The **micro preface** is focused on the latter—smaller code fragments rather than an application as a whole. JMH is a framework for measuring the performance of a single method.

That may appear to be very useful. Can we not just run a method 1,000 or 100,000 times in a loop, measure how long it took, and then calculate the average of the method's performance? We can. The problem is that JVM is a much more complicated program than just a code-executing machine. It has optimization algorithms focused on making the application code run as fast as possible.

For example, let's look at the following class:

```java
class SomeClass {
    public int someMethod(int m, int s) {
        int res = 0;
        for(int i = 0; i < m; i++){
            int n = i * i;
```

```
            if (n != 0 && n % s == 0) {
                res =+ n;
            }
        }
        return res;
    }
}
```

We filled the `someMethod()` method with code that does not make much sense but keeps the method busy. To test the performance of this method, it is tempting to copy the code into a test method and run it in a loop:

```
public void testCode() {
    StopWatch stopWatch = new StopWatch();
    stopWatch.start();
    int xN = 100_000;
    int m = 1000;
    for(int x = 0; i < xN; x++) {
        int res = 0;
        for(int i = 0; i < m; i++){
            int n = i * i;
            if (n != 0 && n % 250_000 == 0) {
                res += n;
            }
        }
    }
    System.out.println("Average time = " +
            (stopWatch.getTime() / xN /m) + "ms");
}
```

However, JVM will see that the `res` result is never used and qualify the calculations as **dead code** (a code section that is never executed). So, why bother executing this code at all?

You may be surprised to see that the significant complication or simplification of the algorithm does not affect the performance. That is because, in every case, the code is not actually executed.

You may change the test method and pretend that the result is used by returning it:

```java
public int testCode() {
    StopWatch stopWatch = new StopWatch();
    stopWatch.start();
    int xN = 100_000;
    int m = 1000;
    int res = 0;
    for(int x = 0; i < xN; x++) {
        for(int i = 0; i < m; i++) {
            int n = i * i;
            if (n != 0 && n % 250_000 == 0) {
                res += n;
            }
        }
    }
    System.out.println("Average time = " +
            (stopWatch.getTime() / xN / m) + "ms");
    return res;
}
```

This may convince JVM to execute the code every time, but it is not guaranteed. JVM may notice that the input into the calculations does not change and this algorithm produces the same result every run. Since the code is based on constant input, this optimization is called **constant folding**. The result of this optimization is that this code may be executed only once and the same result is assumed for every run, without actually executing the code.

In practice though, the benchmark is often built around a method, not a block of code. For example, the test code may look as follows:

```java
public void testCode() {
    StopWatch stopWatch = new StopWatch();
    stopWatch.start();
    int xN = 100_000;
    int m = 1000;
    SomeClass someClass = new SomeClass();
    for(int x = 0; i < xN; x++) {
        someClass.someMethod(m, 250_000);
```

```
    }
    System.out.println("Average time = " +
        (stopWatch.getTime() / xN / m) + "ms");
}
```

But even this code is susceptible to the same JVM optimization we have just described.

JMH was created to help to avoid this and similar pitfalls. In the *JMH usage examples* section, we will show you how to use JMH to work around the dead code and constant folding optimization, using the @State annotation and the Blackhole object.

Besides, JMH allows for measuring not only average execution time but also throughput and other performance characteristics.

Creating a JMH benchmark

To start using JMH, the following dependencies have to be added to the pom.xml file:

```
<dependency>
    <groupId>org.openjdk.jmh</groupId>
    <artifactId>jmh-core</artifactId>
    <version>1.21</version>
</dependency>
<dependency>
    <groupId>org.openjdk.jmh</groupId>
    <artifactId>jmh-generator-annprocess</artifactId>
    <version>1.21</version>
</dependency>
```

The name of the second .jar file, annprocess, provides a hint that JMH uses annotations. If you guessed so, you were correct. Here is an example of a benchmark created for testing the performance of an algorithm:

```
public class BenchmarkDemo {
    public static void main(String... args) throws Exception{
        org.openjdk.jmh.Main.main(args);
    }
    @Benchmark
    public void testTheMethod() {
        int res = 0;
```

```
        for(int i = 0; i < 1000; i++){
            int n = i * i;
            if (n != 0 && n % 250_000 == 0) {
                res += n;
            }
        }
    }
}
```

Please notice the @Benchmark annotation. It tells the framework that this method's performance has to be measured. If you run the preceding main() method, you will see an output similar to the following:

```
# Run progress: 0.00% complete, ETA 06:31:40
# Fork: 1 of 5
# Warmup Iteration   1: 0.001 ops/ns
# Warmup Iteration   2: 0.001 ops/ns
# Warmup Iteration   3: 0.001 ops/ns
# Warmup Iteration   4: 0.001 ops/ns
# Warmup Iteration   5: 0.001 ops/ns
Iteration   1: 0.001 ops/ns
Iteration   2: 0.001 ops/ns
Iteration   3: 0.001 ops/ns
Iteration   4: 0.001 ops/ns
Iteration   5: 0.001 ops/ns
```

This is only one segment of an extensive output that includes multiple iterations under different conditions with the goal being to avoid or offset the JVM optimization. It also takes into account the difference between running the code once and running it multiple times. In the latter case, JVM starts using the just-in-time compiler, which compiles the often-used bytecodes' code into native binary code and does not even read the bytecodes. The warm-up cycles serve this purpose—the code is executed without measuring its performance as a dry run that *warms up* the JVM.

There are also ways to tell the JVM which method to compile and use as binary directly, which method to compile every time, and to provide similar instructions to disable certain optimization. We will talk about this shortly.

Let's now see how to run the benchmark.

Running the benchmark

As you have probably guessed, one way to run a benchmark is just to execute the `main()` method. It can be done using the `java` command directly or using the IDE. We talked about it in *Chapter 1, Getting Started with Java 17*. Yet there is an easier and more convenient way to run a benchmark: by using an IDE plugin.

Using an IDE plugin

All major Java-supporting IDEs have such a plugin. We will demonstrate how to use the plugin for IntelliJ installed on a macOS computer, but it is equally applicable to Windows systems.

Here are the steps to follow:

1. To start installing the plugin, press the *command* key and comma (,) together, or just click the wrench symbol (with the hover text **Preferences**) in the top horizontal menu:

2. It will open a window with the following menu in the left pane:

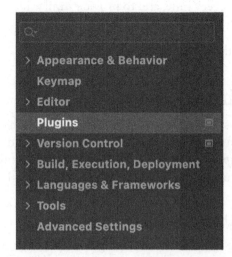

3. Select **Plugins**, as shown in the preceding screenshot, and observe the window with the following top horizontal menu:

4. Select **Marketplace**, type JMH in the **Search plugins in marketplace** input field, and press *Enter*. If you have an internet connection, it will show you a **JMH plugin** symbol, similar to the one shown in the following screenshot:

5. Click the **Install** button and then, after it turns into **Restart IDE**, click it again:

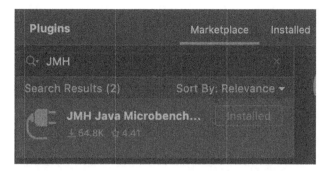

6. After the IDE restarts, the plugin is ready to be used. Now you can not only run the `main()` method but you can also pick and choose which of the benchmark methods to execute if you have several methods with the `@Benchmark` annotation. To do this, select **Run...** from the **Run** drop-down menu:

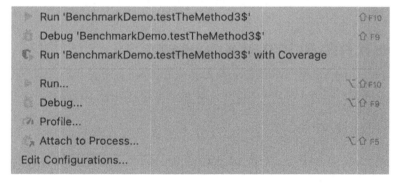

7. It will bring up a window with a selection of methods you can run:

8. Select the one you would like to run and it will be executed. After you have run a method at least once, you can just right-click on it and execute it from the pop-up menu:

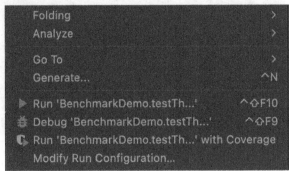

9. You can also use the shortcuts shown to the right of each menu item.

Now let's review the parameters that can be passed to the benchmark.

JMH benchmark parameters

There are many benchmark parameters that allow for fine-tuning the measurements for the particular needs of the task at hand. We are going to present only the major ones.

Mode

The first set of parameters defines the performance aspect (mode) the particular benchmark has to measure:

-   `Mode.AverageTime`: Measures the average execution time
-   `Mode.Throughput`: Measures the throughput by calling the benchmark method in an iteration
-   `Mode.SampleTime`: Samples the execution time, instead of averaging it; allows us to infer the distributions, percentiles, and so on
-   `Mode.SingleShotTime`: Measures the single method invocation time; allows for the testing of a cold startup without calling the benchmark method continuously

These parameters can be specified in the annotation @BenchmarkMode, for example:

```
@BenchmarkMode(Mode.AverageTime)
```

It is possible to combine several modes:

```
@BenchmarkMode({Mode.Throughput, Mode.AverageTime, Mode.
SampleTime, Mode.SingleShotTime}
```

It is also possible to request all of them:

```
@BenchmarkMode(Mode.All)
```

The described parameters and all the parameters we are going to discuss later in this chapter can be set at the method and/or class level. The method-level set value overrides the class-level value.

Output time unit

The unit of time used for presenting the results can be specified using the @OutputTimeUnit annotation:

```
@OutputTimeUnit(TimeUnit.NANOSECONDS)
```

The possible time units come from the java.util.concurrent.TimeUnit enum.

Iterations

Another group of parameters defines the iterations used for the warm-ups and measurements, for example:

```
@Warmup(iterations = 5, time = 100,
                        timeUnit =  TimeUnit.MILLISECONDS)
@Measurement(iterations = 5, time = 100,
                        timeUnit = TimeUnit.MILLISECONDS)
```

Forking

While running several tests, the @Fork annotation allows you to set each test to be run in a separate process, for example:

```
@Fork(10)
```

The passed-in parameter value indicates how many times the JVM can be forked into independent processes. The default value is -1. Without it, the test's performance can be mixed if you use several classes implementing the same interface in tests and they affect each other.

The warmups parameter is another one that can be set to indicate how many times the benchmark has to execute without collecting measurements:

```
@Fork(value = 10, warmups = 5)
```

It also allows you to add Java options to the java command line, for example:

```
@Fork(value = 10, jvmArgs = {"-Xms2G", "-Xmx2G"})
```

The full list of JMH parameters and examples of how to use them can be found in the openjdk project (http://hg.openjdk.java.net/code-tools/jmh/file/tip/jmh-samples/src/main/java/org/openjdk/jmh/samples). For example, we did not mention @Group, @GroupThreads, @Measurement, @Setup, @Threads, @Timeout, @TearDown, or @Warmup.

JMH usage examples

Let's now run a few tests and compare them. First, we run the following test method:

```
@Benchmark
@BenchmarkMode(Mode.All)
@OutputTimeUnit(TimeUnit.NANOSECONDS)
public void testTheMethod0() {
    int res = 0;
    for(int i = 0; i < 1000; i++){
        int n = i * i;
        if (n != 0 && n % 250_000 == 0) {
            res += n;
        }
    }
}
```

As you can see, we have requested to measure all the performance characteristics and to use nanoseconds while presenting the results. On our system, the test execution took around 20 minutes and the final result summary looked like this:

```
Benchmark                                                  Mode     Cnt        Score        Error   Units
BenchmarkDemo.testTheMethod0                               thrpt     25        0.001  ±     0.001  ops/ns
BenchmarkDemo.testTheMethod0                               avgt      25      879.400  ±    23.350  ns/op
BenchmarkDemo.testTheMethod0                               sample 8614070    964.566  ±    13.584  ns/op
BenchmarkDemo.testTheMethod0:testTheMethod0·p0.00          sample           549.000              ns/op
BenchmarkDemo.testTheMethod0:testTheMethod0·p0.50          sample           881.000              ns/op
BenchmarkDemo.testTheMethod0:testTheMethod0·p0.90          sample           960.000              ns/op
BenchmarkDemo.testTheMethod0:testTheMethod0·p0.95          sample           962.000              ns/op
BenchmarkDemo.testTheMethod0:testTheMethod0·p0.99          sample          1352.000              ns/op
BenchmarkDemo.testTheMethod0:testTheMethod0·p0.999         sample         13136.000              ns/op
BenchmarkDemo.testTheMethod0:testTheMethod0·p0.9999        sample         33408.000              ns/op
BenchmarkDemo.testTheMethod0:testTheMethod0·p1.00          sample      24641536.000              ns/op
BenchmarkDemo.testTheMethod0                               ss         5     23350.800  ± 4108.800  ns/op
```

Let's now change the test as follows:

```
@Benchmark
@BenchmarkMode(Mode.All)
@OutputTimeUnit(TimeUnit.NANOSECONDS)
public void testTheMethod1() {
    SomeClass someClass = new SomeClass();
    int i = 1000;
    int s = 250_000;
    someClass.someMethod(i, s);
}
```

If we run the testTheMethod1() now, the results will be slightly different:

```
Benchmark                                                  Mode     Cnt        Score          Error   Units
BenchmarkDemo.testTheMethod1                               thrpt     25        0.001  ±       0.001  ops/ns
BenchmarkDemo.testTheMethod1                               avgt      25      925.099  ±      26.689  ns/op
BenchmarkDemo.testTheMethod1                               sample 8105111   1215.290  ±      57.860  ns/op
BenchmarkDemo.testTheMethod1:testTheMethod1·p0.00          sample           846.000                ns/op
BenchmarkDemo.testTheMethod1:testTheMethod1·p0.50          sample           881.000                ns/op
BenchmarkDemo.testTheMethod1:testTheMethod1·p0.90          sample           961.000                ns/op
BenchmarkDemo.testTheMethod1:testTheMethod1·p0.95          sample          1028.000                ns/op
BenchmarkDemo.testTheMethod1:testTheMethod1·p0.99          sample          1576.000                ns/op
BenchmarkDemo.testTheMethod1:testTheMethod1·p0.999         sample         19712.000                ns/op
BenchmarkDemo.testTheMethod1:testTheMethod1·p0.9999        sample        347636.531                ns/op
BenchmarkDemo.testTheMethod1:testTheMethod1·p1.00          sample      72482816.000                ns/op
BenchmarkDemo.testTheMethod1                               ss         5   1351110.400  ± 9370596.601  ns/op
```

The results are mostly different around sampling and single-shot running. You can play with these methods and change the forking and number of warm-ups.

Using the @State annotation

This JMH feature allows you to hide the source of the data from JVM, thus preventing dead code optimization. You can add a class as the source of the input data as follows:

```
@State(Scope.Thread)
public static class TestState {
    public int m = 1000;
    public int s = 250_000;
}


@Benchmark
@BenchmarkMode(Mode.All)
@OutputTimeUnit(TimeUnit.NANOSECONDS)
public int testTheMethod3(TestState state) {
    SomeClass someClass = new SomeClass();
    return someClass.someMethod(state.m, state.s);
}
```

The Scope value is used for sharing data between tests. In our case, with only one test using the TestCase class object, we do not have a need for sharing. Otherwise, the value can be set to Scope.Group or Scope.Benchmark, which means we could add setters to the TestState class and read/modify it in other tests.

When we ran this version of the test, we got the following results:

```
Benchmark                     Mode  Cnt     Score     Error  Units
BenchmarkDemo.testTheMethod3  avgt   25  2657.405 ± 93.749  ns/op
```

The data has changed again. Notice that the average time for execution has increased three-fold, which indicates that more JVM optimization was not applied.

Using the Blackhole object

This JMH feature allows for simulating result usage, thus preventing JVM from implementing folding constants optimization:

```
@Benchmark
@BenchmarkMode(Mode.All)
@OutputTimeUnit(TimeUnit.NANOSECONDS)
public void testTheMethod4(TestState state,
                                     Blackhole blackhole){
  SomeClass someClass = new SomeClass();
  blackhole.consume(someClass.someMethod(state.m, state.s));
}
```

As you can see, we have just added a parameter `Blackhole` object and called the `consume()` method on it, thus pretending that the result of the tested method is used.

When we ran this version of the test, we got the following results:

Benchmark	Mode	Cnt	Score	Error	Units
BenchmarkDemo.testTheMethod4	thrpt	25	≈ 10⁻³		ops/ns
BenchmarkDemo.testTheMethod4	avgt	25	2849.015 ±	674.026	ns/op
BenchmarkDemo.testTheMethod4	sample	5630034	2828.607 ±	23.264	ns/op
BenchmarkDemo.testTheMethod4:testTheMethod4·p0.00	sample		2528.000		ns/op
BenchmarkDemo.testTheMethod4:testTheMethod4·p0.50	sample		2656.000		ns/op
BenchmarkDemo.testTheMethod4:testTheMethod4·p0.90	sample		2964.000		ns/op
BenchmarkDemo.testTheMethod4:testTheMethod4·p0.95	sample		2976.000		ns/op
BenchmarkDemo.testTheMethod4:testTheMethod4·p0.99	sample		4144.000		ns/op
BenchmarkDemo.testTheMethod4:testTheMethod4·p0.999	sample		17536.000		ns/op
BenchmarkDemo.testTheMethod4:testTheMethod4·p0.9999	sample		44288.000		ns/op
BenchmarkDemo.testTheMethod4:testTheMethod4·p1.00	sample		35454976.000		ns/op
BenchmarkDemo.testTheMethod4	ss	5	311340.000 ±	380514.997	ns/op

This time, the results look not that different. Apparently, the constant folding optimization was neutralized even before the `Blackhole` usage was added.

Using the @CompilerControl annotation

Another way to tune up the benchmark is to tell the compiler to compile, inline (or not), and exclude (or not) a particular method from the code. For example, consider the following class:

```java
class SomeClass{
    public int oneMethod(int m, int s) {
        int res = 0;
        for(int i = 0; i < m; i++){
            int n = i * i;
            if (n != 0 && n % s == 0) {
                res = anotherMethod(res, n);
            }
        }
        return res;
    }

    @CompilerControl(CompilerControl.Mode.EXCLUDE)
    private int anotherMethod(int res, int n){
        return res +=n;
    }

}
```

Assuming we are interested in how the method `anotherMethod()` compilation/inlining affects the performance, we can set the `CompilerControl` mode on it to the following:

- `Mode.INLINE`: To force method inlining

- `Mode.DONT_INLINE`: To avoid method inlining

- `Mode.EXCLUDE`: To avoid method compiling

Using the @Param annotation

Sometimes, it is necessary to run the same benchmark for a different set of input data. In such a case, the `@Param` annotation is very useful.

@Param is a standard Java annotation used by various frameworks, for example, JUnit. It identifies an array of parameter values. The test with the @Param annotation will be run as many times as there are values in the array. Each test execution picks up a different value from the array.

Here is an example:

```
@State(Scope.Benchmark)
public static class TestState1 {
    @Param({"100", "1000", "10000"})
    public int m;
    public int s = 250_000;
}


@Benchmark
@BenchmarkMode(Mode.All)
@OutputTimeUnit(TimeUnit.NANOSECONDS)
public void testTheMethod6(TestState1 state,
                                        Blackhole blackhole){
  SomeClass someClass = new SomeClass();
  blackhole.consume(someClass.someMethod(state.m, state.s));
}
```

The testTheMethod6() benchmark is going to be used with each of the listed values of the parameter m.

A word of caution

The described harness takes away most of the worries of the programmer who measures the performance. And yet, it is virtually impossible to cover all the cases of JVM optimization, profile sharing, and similar aspects of JVM implementation, especially if we take into account that JVM code evolves and differs from one implementation to another. The authors of JMH acknowledge this fact by printing the following warning along with the test results:

```
REMEMBER: The numbers below are just data. To gain reusable insights, you need to follow up on
why the numbers are the way they are. Use profilers (see -prof, -lprof), design factorial
experiments, perform baseline and negative tests that provide experimental control, make sure
the benchmarking environment is safe on JVM/OS/HW level, ask for reviews from the domain experts.
Do not assume the numbers tell you what you want them to tell.
```

The description of the profilers and their usage can be found in the `openjdk` project (`http://hg.openjdk.java.net/code-tools/jmh/file/tip/jmh-samples/src/main/java/org/openjdk/jmh/samples`). Among the same samples, you will encounter a description of the code generated by JMH, based on the annotations.

If you would like to get really deep into the details of your code execution and testing, there is no better way to do it than to study the generated code. It describes all the steps and decisions JMH makes in order to run the requested benchmark. You can find the generated code in `target/generated-sources/annotations`.

The scope of this book does not allow for going into too many details on how to read it, but it is not very difficult, especially if you start with a simple case of testing one method only. We wish you all the best in this endeavor.

Summary

In this chapter, you have learned about the JMH tool and were able to use it for your applications. You have learned how to create and run a benchmark, how to set the benchmark parameters, and how to install IDE plugins if needed. We have also provided practical recommendations and references for further reading.

Now you are able to not only measure the average execution time of an application and other performance values (such as throughput, for example) but to do it in a controlled manner—with or without JVM optimizations, warm-up runs, and so on.

In the next chapter, you will learn useful practices for designing and writing application code. We will talk about Java idioms, their implementation and usage, and provide recommendations for implementing `equals()`, `hashCode()`, `compareTo()`, and `clone()` methods. We will also discuss the difference between the usage of the `StringBuffer` and `StringBuilder` classes, how to catch exceptions, best design practices, and other proven programming practices.

Quiz

1.   Select all the correct statements:

   A. JMH is useless since it runs methods outside the production context.

   B. JMH is able to work around some JVM optimizations.

   C. JMH allows for measuring not only average performance time but other performance characteristics too.

   D. JMH can be used to measure the performance of small applications too.

2. Name two steps necessary to start using JMH.

3. Name four ways JMH can be run.

4. Name two modes (performance characteristics) that can be used (measured) with JMH.

5. Name two of the time units that can be used to present JMH test results.

6. How can data (results, state) be shared between JMH benchmarks?

7. How do you tell JMH to run the benchmark for the parameter with the enumerated list of values?

8. How can the compilation of a method be forced or turned off?

9. How can the JVM's constant folding optimization be turned off?

10. How can Java command options be provided programmatically for running a particular benchmark?

17
Best Practices for Writing High-Quality Code

When programmers talk to each other, they often use jargon that cannot be understood by non-programmers, or is vaguely understood by the programmers of different programming languages. But those who use the same programming language understand each other just fine. Sometimes, it may also depend on how knowledgeable a programmer is. A novice may not understand what an experienced programmer is talking about, while a seasoned colleague nods and responds in kind. This chapter is designed to fill this gap and improve the understanding between programmers of different levels. In this chapter, we will discuss some Java programming jargon – the Java idioms that describe certain features, functionality, design solutions, and so on. You will also learn about the most popular and useful practices for designing and writing application code.

The following topics will be covered in this chapter:

- Java idioms, their implementation, and their usage
- The `equals()`, `hashCode()`, `compareTo()`, and `clone()` methods
- The `StringBuffer` and `StringBuilder` classes

- The `try`, `catch`, and `finally` clauses

- Best design practices

- Code is written for people

- Use well-established frameworks and libraries

- Testing is the shortest path to quality code

By the end of this chapter, you will have a solid understanding of what other Java programmers are talking about while discussing their design decisions and the functionality they use.

Technical requirements

To execute the code examples provided in this chapter, you will need the following:

- A computer with either Microsoft Windows, Apple macOS, or Linux

- Java SE version 17 or later

- An IDE or code editor of your choice

The instructions for how to set up a Java SE and IntelliJ IDEA editor were provided in *Chapter 1, Getting Started with Java 17*. The files containing the code examples for this chapter are available on GitHub at `https://github.com/PacktPublishing/Learn-Java-17-Programming.git` in the `examples/src/main/java/com/packt/learnjava/ch17_bestpractices` folder and in the `spring` and `reactive` folders.

Java idioms, their implementation, and their usage

In addition to serving as a means of communication among professionals, programming idioms are also proven programming solutions and common practices not directly derived from the language specification but born out of the programming experience. In this section, we are going to discuss the ones that are used most often. You can find and study the full list of idioms in the official Java documentation (`https://docs.oracle.com/javase/tutorial`).

The equals() and hashCode() methods

The default implementation of the equals() and hashCode() methods in the java. lang.Object class looks as follows:

```java
public boolean equals(Object obj) {
    return (this == obj);
}
/**
* Whenever it is invoked on the same object more than once
during
* an execution of a Java application, the hashCode method
* must consistently return the same integer...
* As far as is reasonably practical, the hashCode method
defined
* by class Object returns distinct integers for distinct
objects.
*/
@HotSpotIntrinsicCandidate
public native int hashCode();
```

As you can see, the default implementation of the equals() method only compares memory references that point to the addresses where the objects are stored. Similarly, as you can see from the comments (quoted from the source code), the hashCode() method returns the same integer for the same object and a different integer for different objects. Let's demonstrate this using the Person class:

```java
public class Person {
    private int age;
    private String firstName, lastName;
    public Person(int age, String firstName, String lastName){
        this.age = age;
        this.lastName = lastName;
        this.firstName = firstName;
    }
    public int getAge() { return age; }
    public String getFirstName() { return firstName; }
    public String getLastName() { return lastName; }
}
```

Here is an example of how the default equals() and hashCode() methods behave:

```
Person person1 = new Person(42, "Nick", "Samoylov");
Person person2 = person1;
Person person3 = new Person(42, "Nick", "Samoylov");
System.out.println(person1.equals(person2)); //prints: true
System.out.println(person1.equals(person3)); //prints: false
System.out.println(person1.hashCode());
                                        //prints: 777874839
System.out.println(person2.hashCode());
                                        //prints: 777874839
System.out.println(person3.hashCode());
                                        //prints: 596512129
```

The output in your system might be slightly different.

The person1 and person2 references and their hash codes are equal because they point to the same object (the same area of memory and the same address), while the person3 reference points to another object.

In practice, though, as we described in *Chapter 6, Data Structures, Generics, and Popular Utilities*, we would like the equality of the object to be based on the value of all or some of the object properties. So, here is a typical implementation of the equals() and hashCode() methods:

```
@Override
public boolean equals(Object o) {
    if (this == o) return true;
    if (o == null) return false;
    if(!(o instanceof Person)) return false;
    Person person = (Person)o;
    return getAge() == person.getAge() &&
        Objects.equals(getFirstName(), person.getFirstName()) &&
            Objects.equals(getLastName(), person.getLastName());
}
@Override
public int hashCode() {
  return Objects.hash(getAge(), getFirstName(), getLastName());
}
```

It used to be more involved, but using `java.util.Objects` utilities makes it much easier, especially if you notice that the `Objects.equals()` method handles `null` too.

Here, we have added the described implementation of the `equals()` and `hashCode()` methods to the `Person1` class and executed the same comparisons:

```
Person1 person1 = new Person1(42, "Nick", "Samoylov");
Person1 person2 = person1;
Person1 person3 = new Person1(42, "Nick", "Samoylov");
System.out.println(person1.equals(person2)); //prints: true
System.out.println(person1.equals(person3)); //prints: true
System.out.println(person1.hashCode());
                                        //prints: 2115012528
System.out.println(person2.hashCode());
                                        //prints: 2115012528
System.out.println(person3.hashCode());
                                        //prints: 2115012528
```

As you can see, the change we have made not only makes the same objects equal but makes two different objects with the same values of the properties equal too. Furthermore, the hash code value is now based on the values of the same properties as well.

In *Chapter 6, Data Structures, Generics, and Popular Utilities*, we explained why it is important to implement the `hasCode()` method while implementing the `equals()` method.

The same set of properties must be used for establishing equality in the `equals()` method and for the hash calculation in the `hashCode()` method.

Having the `@Override` annotation in front of these methods assures that they override the default implementation in the `Object` class. Otherwise, a typo in the method's name may create the illusion that the new implementation is being used when it isn't. Debugging such cases has proved much more difficult and costly than just adding the `@Override` annotation, which generates an error if the method does not override anything.

The compareTo() method

In *Chapter 6, Data Structures, Generics, and Popular Utilities*, we used the `compareTo()` method (the only method of the `Comparable` interface) extensively and pointed out that the order that is established based on this method (its implementation by the elements of a collection) is called a **natural order**.

To demonstrate this, we created the `Person2` class:

```java
public class Person2 implements Comparable<Person2> {
  private int age;
  private String firstName, lastName;
  public Person2(int age, String firstName, String lastName)
  {
      this.age = age;
      this.lastName = lastName;
      this.firstName = firstName;
  }
  public int getAge() { return age; }
  public String getFirstName() { return firstName; }
  public String getLastName() { return lastName; }
  @Override
  public int compareTo(Person2 p) {
      int result = Objects.compare(getFirstName(),
                  p.getFirstName(), Comparator.naturalOrder());
      if (result != 0) {
          return result;
      }
      result = Objects.compare(getLastName(),
                  p.getLastName(), Comparator.naturalOrder());
      if (result != 0) {
          return result;
      }
      return Objects.compare(age, p.getAge(),
                                  Comparator.naturalOrder());
  }
  @Override
  public String toString() {
```

```
        return firstName + " " + lastName + ", " + age;
    }
}
```

Then, we composed a list of `Person2` objects and sorted it:

```
Person2 p1 = new Person2(15, "Zoe", "Adams");
Person2 p2 = new Person2(25, "Nick", "Brook");
Person2 p3 = new Person2(42, "Nick", "Samoylov");
Person2 p4 = new Person2(50, "Ada", "Valentino");
Person2 p6 = new Person2(50, "Bob", "Avalon");
Person2 p5 = new Person2(10, "Zoe", "Adams");
List<Person2> list =
        new ArrayList<>(List.of(p5, p2, p6, p1, p4, p3));
Collections.sort(list);
list.stream().forEach(System.out::println);
```

The result looks as follows:

```
Ada Valentino, 50
Bob Avalon, 50
Nick Brook, 25
Nick Samoylov, 42
Zoe Adams, 10
Zoe Adams, 15
```

There are three things worth noting:

- According to the `Comparable` interface, the `compareTo()` method must return a negative integer, zero, or a positive integer if the object is less than, equal to, or greater than another object. In our implementation, we returned the result immediately if the values of the same property of two objects were different. We already know that this object is *bigger* or *smaller*, regardless of what the other properties are. But the sequence in which you compare the properties of two objects, affects the final result. It defines the precedence in which the property value affects the order.

- We have put the result of `List.of()` into a new `ArrayList()` object. We did so because, as we mentioned in *Chapter 6, Data Structures, Generics, and Popular Utilities*, the collection that's created by the `of()` factory method is unmodifiable. No elements can be added or removed from it and the order of the elements cannot be changed either, while we need to sort the created collection. We only used the `of()` method because it is more convenient and provides a shorter notation.

- Finally, using `java.util.Objects` for comparing properties makes the implementation much easier and more reliable than custom coding.

While implementing the `compareTo()` method, it is important to make sure that the following rules are not violated:

- `obj1.compareTo(obj2)` returns the same value as `obj2.compareTo(obj1)`, but only when the returned value is 0.

- If the returned value is not 0, `obj1.compareTo(obj2)` has the opposite sign of `obj2.compareTo(obj1)`.

- If `obj1.compareTo(obj2) > 0` and `obj2.compareTo(obj3) > 0`, then `obj1.compareTo(obj3) > 0`.

- If `obj1.compareTo(obj2) < 0` and `obj2.compareTo(obj3) < 0`, then `obj1.compareTo(obj3) < 0`.

- If `obj1.compareTo(obj2) == 0`, then `obj2.compareTo(obj3)` and `obj1.compareTo(obj3) > 0` have the same sign.

- Both `obj1.compareTo(obj2)` and `obj2.compareTo(obj1)` throw the same exceptions, if any.

It is also recommended, but not always required, that if `obj1.equals(obj2)`, then `obj1.compareTo(obj2) == 0` and, at the same time, if `obj1.compareTo(obj2) == 0`, then `obj1.equals(obj2)`.

The clone() method

The `clone()` method's implementation in the `java.lang.Object` class looks like this:

```
@HotSpotIntrinsicCandidate
protected native Object clone() throws
CloneNotSupportedException;
```

The comment shown in the preceding code states the following:

```
/**
 * Creates and returns a copy of this object.   The precise
 * meaning of "copy" may depend on the class of the object.
 ***/
```

The default result of this method returns a copy of the object fields as-is, which is fine if the values are of primitive types. However, if an object property holds a reference to another object, only the reference itself will be copied, not the referred object. That is why such a copy is called a **shallow copy**. To get a **deep copy**, you must override the `clone()` method and clone each of the object properties that refers to an object.

In any case, to be able to clone an object, it must implement the `Cloneable` interface and make sure that all the objects along the inheritance tree (and the properties that are objects) implement the `Cloneable` interface too (except the `java.lang.Object` class). The `Cloneable` interface is just a marker interface that tells the compiler that the programmer made a conscious decision to allow this object to be cloned (whether it's because the shallow copy was good enough or because the `clone()` method was overridden). An attempt to call `clone()` on an object that does not implement the `Cloneable` interface will result in a `CloneNotSupportedException`.

It looks complex already, but in practice, there are even more pitfalls. For example, let's say that the `Person` class has an `address` property of the `Address` type. The shallow copy, p2, of the `Person` object, p1, will refer to the same object of `Address` so that `p1.address == p2.address`. Here is an example. The `Address` class looks as follows:

```
class Address {
  private String street, city;
  public Address(String street, String city) {
      this.street = street;
      this.city = city;
  }
  public void setStreet(String street){
                                  this.street = street; }
  public String getStreet() { return street; }
  public String getCity() { return city; }
}
```

The `Person3` class uses it like this:

```java
class Person3 implements Cloneable{
  private int age;
  private Address address;
  private String firstName, lastName;

  public Person3(int age, String firstName,
                          String lastName, Address address) {
      this.age = age;
      this.address = address;
      this.lastName = lastName;
      this.firstName = firstName;
  }
  public int getAge() { return age; }
  public Address getAddress() { return address; }
  public String getLastName() { return lastName; }
  public String getFirstName() { return firstName; }
  @Override
  public Person3 clone() throws CloneNotSupportedException{
      return (Person3) super.clone();
  }
}
```

Notice that the `clone()` method does a shallow copy because it does not clone the `address` property. Here is the result of using such a `clone()` method implementation:

```java
Person3 p1 = new Person3(42, "Nick", "Samoylov",
                  new Address("25 Main Street", "Denver"));
Person3 p2 = p1.clone();
System.out.println(p1.getAge() == p2.getAge());
                                                    // true
System.out.println(p1.getLastName() == p2.getLastName());
                                                    // true
System.out.println(p1.getLastName().equals(p2.getLastName()));
                                                    // true
System.out.println(p1.getAddress() == p2.getAddress());
                                                    // true
```

```
System.out.println(p2.getAddress().getStreet());
                                    //prints: 25 Main Street
p1.getAddress().setStreet("42 Dead End");
System.out.println(p2.getAddress().getStreet());
                                    //prints: 42 Dead End
```

As you can see, after the cloning is complete, the change that was made to the `address` property of the source object is reflected in the same property of the clone. That isn't very intuitive, is it? While cloning, we expected an independent copy, didn't we?

To avoid sharing the `Address` object, you must clone it explicitly too. To do so, you must make the `Address` object cloneable, as follows:

```
public class Address implements Cloneable{
   private String street, city;
   public Address(String street, String city) {
       this.street = street;
       this.city = city;
   }
   public void setStreet(String street){
                                   this.street = street; }
   public String getStreet() { return street; }
   public String getCity() { return city; }
   @Override
   public Address clone() throws CloneNotSupportedException {
       return (Address)super.clone();
   }
}
```

With that implementation in place, we can now add the `address` property for cloning:

```
class Person4 implements Cloneable{
   private int age;
   private Address address;
   private String firstName, lastName;
   public Person4(int age, String firstName,
                       String lastName, Address address) {
       this.age = age;
       this.address = address;
```

```
        this.lastName = lastName;
        this.firstName = firstName;
    }
    public int getAge() { return age; }
    public Address getAddress() { return address; }
    public String getLastName() { return lastName; }
    public String getFirstName() { return firstName; }
    @Override
    public Person4 clone() throws CloneNotSupportedException{
        Person4 cl = (Person4) super.clone();
        cl.address = this.address.clone();
        return cl;
    }
}
```

Now, if we run the same test, the results are going to be as we expected them originally:

```
Person4 p1 = new Person4(42, "Nick", "Samoylov",
                    new Address("25 Main Street", "Denver"));
Person4 p2 = p1.clone();
System.out.println(p1.getAge() == p2.getAge());          // true
System.out.println(p1.getLastName() == p2.getLastName());
                                                          // true
System.out.println(p1.getLastName().equals(p2.getLastName()));
                                                          // true
System.out.println(p1.getAddress() == p2.getAddress());
                                                          // false
System.out.println(p2.getAddress().getStreet());
                                       //prints: 25 Main Street
p1.getAddress().setStreet("42 Dead End");
System.out.println(p2.getAddress().getStreet());
                                       //prints: 25 Main Street
```

So, if the application expects all the properties to be deeply copied, all the objects involved must be cloneable. That is fine so long as none of the related objects, whether it's a property in the current object or the parent class (and their properties and parents), do not acquire a new object property without making them cloneable and are cloned explicitly in the `clone()` method of the container object. This last statement is complex. The reason for its complexity is due to the underlying complexity of the cloning process. That is why programmers often stay away from making objects cloneable.

Instead, they prefer to clone the object manually, if need be, as shown in the following code:

```
Person4 p1 = new Person4(42, "Nick", "Samoylov",
                      new Address("25 Main Street", "Denver"));
Address address = new Address(p1.getAddress().getStreet(),
                                 p1.getAddress().getCity());
Person4 p2 = new Person4(p1.getAge(), p1.getFirstName(),
                            p1.getLastName(), address);
System.out.println(p1.getAge() == p2.getAge());
                                                      // true
System.out.println(p1.getLastName() == p2.getLastName());
                                                      // true
System.out.println(p1.getLastName().equals(p2.getLastName()));
                                                      // true
System.out.println(p1.getAddress() == p2.getAddress());// false
System.out.println(p2.getAddress().getStreet());
                                       //prints: 25 Main Street
p1.getAddress().setStreet("42 Dead End");
System.out.println(p2.getAddress().getStreet());
                                       //prints: 25 Main Street
```

This approach still requires code changes if another property is added to any related object. However, it provides more control over the result and has less chance of unexpected consequences.

Fortunately, the `clone()` method is not used very often. You may never encounter a need to use it.

The StringBuffer and StringBuilder classes

We talked about the difference between the `StringBuffer` and `StringBuilder` classes in *Chapter 6*, *Data Structures, Generics, and Popular Utilities*. We are not going to repeat this here. Instead, we will just mention that, in a single-threaded process (which is the vast majority of cases), the `StringBuilder` class is the preferred choice because it is faster.

The try, catch, and finally clauses

Chapter 4, *Exception Handling*, is dedicated to using the `try`, `catch`, and `finally` clauses, so we are not going to repeat this here. We would like to repeat that using a `try-with-resources` statement is the preferred way to release resources (traditionally done in a `finally` block). Deferring the library makes the code simpler and more reliable.

Best design practices

The term *best* is often subjective and context-dependent. That is why we would like to disclose that the following recommendations are based on the vast majority of cases in mainstream programming. However, they should not be followed blindly and unconditionally because there are cases when some of these practices, in some contexts, are useless or even wrong. Before following them, try to understand the motivation behind them and use it as a guide for your decisions. For example, size matters. If the application is not going to grow beyond a few thousand lines of code, a simple monolith with laundry-list-style code is good enough. But if there are complicated pockets of code and several people working on it, breaking the code into specialized pieces would be beneficial for code understanding, maintenance, and even scaling, if one particular code area requires more resources than others.

We will start with higher-level design decisions in no particular order.

Identifying loosely coupled functional areas

These design decisions can be made very early on, based just on the general understanding of the main parts of the future system, their functionality, and the data they produce and exchange. There are several benefits of doing this:

- You can identify the structure of the future system, which has bearings on the further design steps and implementation
- You can specialize in and analyze parts deeply
- You can develop parts in parallel
- You can have a better understanding of the data flow

Breaking the functional area into traditional tiers

With each functional area in place, specializations based on the technical aspects and technologies can be used. The traditional separation of technical specialization is as follows:

- The frontend (user graphic or web interface)
- The middle tier with extensive business logic
- The backend (data storage or data source)

The benefits of doing this include the following:

- You can deploy and scale by tiers
- You can gain programmer specialization based on your expertise
- You can develop parts in parallel

Coding to an interface

The specialized parts, based on the decisions described in the previous two subsections, must be described in an interface that hides the implementation details. The benefits of such a design lie in the foundations of **object-oriented programming** (**OOP**) and were described in detail in *Chapter 2, Java Object-Oriented Programming (OOP)*, so we are not going to repeat this here.

Using factories

We talked about this in *Chapter 2, Java Object-Oriented Programming (OOP)*, too. An interface, by definition, does not and cannot describe the constructor of a class that implements the interface. Using factories allows you to close this gap and expose just an interface to a client.

Preferring composition over inheritance

Originally, OOP focused on inheritance as a way to share the common functionality between objects. Inheritance is even one of the four OOP principles, as we have described in *Chapter 2, Java Object-Oriented Programming (OOP)*. In practice, however, this method of functionality sharing creates too much dependency between classes included in the same inheritance line. The evolution of application functionality is often unpredictable, and some of the classes in the inheritance chain start to acquire functionality that's unrelated to the original purpose of the class chain. We can argue that there are design solutions that allow us not to do this and keep the original classes intact. But, in practice, such things happen all the time, and the subclasses may suddenly change behavior just because they acquired new functionality through inheritance. We cannot choose our parents, can we? Besides, it breaks encapsulation this way, which is another foundational principle of OOP.

Composition, on the other hand, allows us to choose and control which functionality of the class to use and which to ignore. It also allows the object to stay light and not be burdened by the inheritance. Such a design is more flexible, extensible, and predictable.

Using libraries

Throughout this book, we have mentioned that using the **Java Class Library** (**JCL**) and external (to the **Java Development Kit** (**JDK**)) Java libraries makes programming much easier and produces code of higher quality. *Chapter 7, Java Standard and External Libraries*, contains an overview of the most popular Java libraries. People who create libraries invest a lot of time and effort, so you should take advantage of them any time you can.

In *Chapter 13, Functional Programming*, we described standard functional interfaces that reside in the `java.util.function` package of JCL. That is another way to take advantage of a library – by using its set of well-known and shared interfaces, instead of defining your own.

This last statement is a good segue to the next topic about writing code that can easily be understood by other people.

Code is written for people

The first decades of programming required writing machine commands so that electronic devices could execute them. Not only was it a tedious and error-prone endeavor, but it also required you to write the instructions in a manner that yielded the best performance possible. This is because the computers were slow and did not do much code optimization, if at all.

Since then, we have made a lot of progress in terms of both hardware and programming. The modern compiler went a long way toward making the submitted code work as fast as possible, even when a programmer did not think about it. We talked about this with specific examples in the previous chapter.

It allowed programmers to write more lines of code without thinking much about optimization. But tradition and many books about programming continued to call for it, and some programmers still worry about their code performance – more so than the results it produces. It is easier to follow tradition than to break away from it. That is why programmers tend to pay more attention to the way they write code than to the business they automate, although good code that implements incorrect business logic is useless.

However, back to the topic. With modern JVM, the need for code optimization by a programmer is not as pressing as it used to be. Nowadays, a programmer must pay attention mostly to the big picture, to avoid structural mistakes that lead to poor code performance and to code that is used multiple times. The latter becomes less pressing as the JVM becomes more sophisticated, observing the code in real time, and just returning the results (without execution) when the same code block is called several times with the same input.

That leaves us with the only conclusion possible – while writing code, you must make sure it is easy to read and understand for a human, not for a computer. Those who have worked in the industry for some time have been puzzled over code they wrote a few years prior. You can improve your code-writing style via clarity and the transparency of its intent.

Now, let's discuss the need for comments. We do not need comments that echo what the code does, as shown in the following example:

```
//Initialize variable
int i = 0;
```

The comments that explain the intent are much more valuable:

```
// In case of x > 0, we are looking for a matching group
// because we would like to reuse the data from the account.
// If we find the matching group, we either cancel it and
```

```
// clone, or add the x value to the group, or bail out.
// If we do not find the matching group,
// we create a new group using data of the matched group.
```

The commented code can be very complex. Good comments explain the intent and provide guidance that helps us understand the code. Yet, programmers often do not bother to write comments. The argument against writing comments typically includes two statements:

- Comments must be maintained and evolve along with the code; otherwise, they may become misleading. However, no tool can prompt the programmer to adjust the comments along with changing the code. Thus, comments are dangerous.

- The code itself must be written (including name selection for variables and methods) so that no extra explanation is needed.

Both statements are true, but it is also true that comments can be very helpful, especially those that capture the intent. Besides, such comments tend to require fewer adjustments because the code intent doesn't change often, if ever.

Use well-established frameworks and libraries

Programmers are not always given a chance to select the framework and libraries to develop the software. Often, the company prefers to stay with the set of software and development tools they have already used for other projects. But when you get such a possibility of choosing, the variety of available products may be overwhelming. It may also be tempting to select the latest new offer that is trending in the programming community. Nevertheless, experience proves time and again that the best course of action would be to select something well–established and proven to be production-strong. Besides, using solid software with a long history requires typically writing less boilerplate code.

To demonstrate this point, we created two projects:

- Using the Spring Boot framework
- Using the **Vert.x** toolkit

We start with Spring Boot. It is an open source Java-based framework, developed by the Pivotal Team for building standalone production-strong applications. By default, it does not need an external web server, because it embeds a web server (Tomcat or Netty). As a result, the Spring Boot user does not need to write any non-business code. You don't need even to create configuration, as in Spring. You just define which non-business features you need (such as health check, metrics, or swagger doc, for example) using the properties file and tune them using annotation.

Naturally, because there is so much implemented behind the scenes, Spring Boot is very opinionated. But you would be hard-pressed to find a case when it cannot be used to produce a solid efficient application. Most probably, limitations of Spring Boot will manifest themselves in large-scale projects. The best approach for using Spring Boot is to embrace its way to do things, because by doing this you will save a lot of time and will get a robust and well-optimized solution.

To simplify dependency management, Spring Boot provides the required third-party dependencies for each type of application in the so-called `starter` JAR file. For example, spring-boot-starter-web brings into the project all the libraries necessary for Spring MVC (Model-View-Controller) and the Tomcat web server. Based on the selected starter package, Spring Boot automatically configures the application.

You can find comprehensive and well-written information for programmers of all levels – from beginners to experienced professionals – at `https://spring.io/projects/ spring-boot`. If you plan to use Spring Boot in your line of work, we encourage you to read it.

To demonstrate Spring Boot capabilities and advantages, we created a project in the `spring` folder. To run this sample application, you need the database, created in *Chapter 10, Managing Data in a Database,* of this book, up and running. The sample application manages (creates, reads, updates, deletes) records of persons in the database. This functionality is accessible via the UI (HTML pages), which is human-oriented. In addition, we implemented access to the same functionality via RESTful services, which can be used by other applications.

You can run the application from an IDE by executing the `Application` class. Alternatively, you can start the application from the command line. There are two command files in the `spring` folder: mvnw (for Unix/Linux/Mac systems) and `mvnw. cmd` (for Windows). They can be used to launch the application as follows:

- For Unix/Linux/Mac systems:

```
./mvnw spring-boot:run
```

- For Windows:

```
.\mvnw.cmd spring-boot:run
```

When you do it the first time, you may get an error:

```
java.lang.ClassNotFoundException: org.apache.maven.wrapper.
MavenWrapperMain
```

If that happens, install the Maven wrapper by executing the following command:

```
mvn -N io.takari:maven:wrapper
```

Alternatively, you can build the executable .jar file:

- For Unix/Linux/Mac systems:

```
./mvnw clean package
```

- For Windows:

```
.\mvnw.cmd clean package
```

Then you can put the created .jar file on any computer that has Java 17 installed and run it, using the following command:

```
java -jar target/spring-0.0.1-SNAPSHOT.jar
```

After the application is running, execute the following command:

```
curl -XPOST localhost:8083/ws/new                    \
     -H 'Content-Type: application/json'             \
     -d '{"dob":"2002-08-14",                        \
         "firstName":"Mike","lastName":"Brown"}'
```

The curl command requires the application to create a new person record. The expected response looks as follows (the id value will be different every time you run this command):

```
Person{id=42, dob=2002-08-14, firstName='Mike',
                     lastName='Brown'} successfully updated.
```

To see the HTTP code in the response, add the option -v to the command. The HTTP code 200 indicates successful processing of the request.

Now let's execute the update command:

```
curl -XPUT localhost:8083/ws/update                    \
   -H 'Content-Type: application/json'                 \
   -d '{"id":42,"dob":"2002-08-14",                    \
          "firstName":"Nick","lastName":"Brown"}'
```

The application responds to this command as follows:

```
Person{id=42, dob=2002-08-14, firstName='Nick',
                    lastName='Brown'} successfully updated.
```

Notice that not all fields in the payload have to be populated. Only the id value is required and has to match with one of the existing records. The application retrieves the current Person record by the provided id value and updates only those properties that are provided.

The delete endpoint is similarly constructed. The difference is that the data (the Person record identity number id) is passed as part of the URL. Now let's execute the following command:

```
curl localhost:8083/ws/delete/1
```

The application responds to this command with the following message:

```
Person{id=42, dob=2002-08-14, firstName='Nick',
                    lastName='Brown'} successfully deleted.
```

The list of all the existing records can be retrieved with the following command:

```
curl localhost:8083/ws/list
```

All the preceding functionalities can be accessed via the UI. Type in the browser the URL http://localhost:8083/ui/list and click the corresponding links.

You can also type `http://localhost:8083` in the browser URL and access the following page:

Welcome to Spring Boot application!

Start with <u>Home</u> or <u>All persons</u> page

Then again, click any of the available links. The Home page presents information about the current application version and its heath. The `http://localhost:8083/swagger-ui.html` URL brings up the list of all the application endoints.

We highly encourage you to study the application code and read the Spring Boot documentation on the `https://spring.io/projects/spring-boot` website.

Now let us look in the project in the `reactive` folder. It demonstrates the reactive methods of communication, using Vert.x, which is an event-driven non-blocking lightweight polyglot toolkit. It allows you to write components in Java, JavaScript, Groovy, Ruby, Scala, Kotlin, and Ceylon. It supports an asynchronous programming model and a distributed event bus that reaches into the JavaScript browser, thus allowing the creation of real-time web applications. However, because of the focus of this book, we are going to use Java only.

To demonstrate how a reactive system of microservices may look if implemented using the **Vert**.x toolkit, we have created an HTTP server that can accept a REST-based request to the system, send an EventBus-based message to another *verticle* (the fundamental processing unit in the **Vert**.x toolkit that can be deployed), receive a reply, and send the response back to the original request.

We created two verticles:

- `HttpServerVert`, which acts as a server and receives HTTP messages, which then sends them to a particular address via the EventBus(a lightweight distributed messaging system)

- `MessageRcvVert`, which listens messages on a particular event-bus address

Now we can deploy them as follows:

```
public class ReactiveSystemDemo {
    public static void main(String... args) {
        Vertx vertx = Vertx.vertx();
        RxHelper.deployVerticle(vertx,
                    new MessageRcvVert("1", "One"));
        RxHelper.deployVerticle(vertx,
```

```
                  new MessageRcvVert("2", "One"));
    RxHelper.deployVerticle(vertx,
                  new MessageRcvVert("3", "Two"));
    RxHelper.deployVerticle(vertx,
                  new HttpServerVert(8082));
  }
}
```

To execute this code, run the `ReactiveSystemDemo` class. The result is expected to be as follows:

```
MessageRcvVert(vert.x-eventloop-thread-2, 3, Two) is waiting...
MessageRcvVert(vert.x-eventloop-thread-1, 2, One) is waiting...
MessageRcvVert(vert.x-eventloop-thread-0, 1, One) is waiting...
HttpServerVert(vert.x-eventloop-thread-3, localhost:8082) is waiting...
```

Let's now start sending HTTP requests to our system. First, let's send the same HTTP GET request three times:

```
demo>
demo> curl localhost:8082/some/path/Nick/One/someValue
MessageRcvVert(vert.x-eventloop-thread-0, 1, One) got message 'Nick called with value someValue'. Thank you.
demo>
demo> curl localhost:8082/some/path/Nick/One/someValue
MessageRcvVert(vert.x-eventloop-thread-1, 2, One) got message 'Nick called with value someValue'. Thank you.
demo>
demo> curl localhost:8082/some/path/Nick/One/someValue
MessageRcvVert(vert.x-eventloop-thread-0, 1, One) got message 'Nick called with value someValue'. Thank you.
demo>
```

If there are several verticles registered with the same address (as it is in our case: we have registered two verticles with the same `One` address), the system uses a round-robin algorithm to select the verticle that should receive the next message.

The first request went to the receiver with `ID="1"`, the second request went to the receiver with `ID="2"`, and the third request went to the receiver with `ID="1"` again.

We get the same results using the HTTP POST request for the /some/path/send path:

```
demo>
demo> curl -X POST localhost:8082/some/path/send -d '{"name":"Nick","address":"One","anotherParam":"someValue"}'
MessageRcvVert(vert.x-eventloop-thread-1, 2, One) got message 'Nick called with value someValue'. Thank you.
demo>
demo> curl -X POST localhost:8082/some/path/send -d '{"name":"Nick","address":"One","anotherParam":"someValue"}'
MessageRcvVert(vert.x-eventloop-thread-0, 1, One) got message 'Nick called with value someValue'. Thank you.
demo>
demo> curl -X POST localhost:8082/some/path/send -d '{"name":"Nick","address":"One","anotherParam":"someValue"}'
MessageRcvVert(vert.x-eventloop-thread-1, 2, One) got message 'Nick called with value someValue'. Thank you.
demo>
```

Again, the receiver of the message is rotated using the round-robin algorithm. Now, let's publish a message to our system twice.

Since the receiver's reply cannot propagate back to the system user, we need to take a look at the messages that are logged on the backend:

```
HttpServerVert(vert.x-eventloop-thread-3, localhost:8082): got payload
    {"name":"Nick","address":"One","anotherParam":"someValue"}
MessageRcvVert(vert.x-eventloop-thread-0, 1, One) got message 'Nick called with value someValue'.
MessageRcvVert(vert.x-eventloop-thread-1, 2, One) got message 'Nick called with value someValue'.

HttpServerVert(vert.x-eventloop-thread-3, localhost:8082): got payload
    {"name":"Nick","address":"One","anotherParam":"someValue"}
MessageRcvVert(vert.x-eventloop-thread-1, 2, One) got message 'Nick called with value someValue'.
MessageRcvVert(vert.x-eventloop-thread-0, 1, One) got message 'Nick called with value someValue'.
```

As you can see, the publish() method sends the message to all verticles that are registered to the specified address. And note that the verticle with ID="3" (registered with the Two address) never received a message.

Before we wrap up this reactive system demonstration, it is worth mentioning that the **Vert.x** toolkit allows you to easily cluster verticles. You can read about this feature in the **Vert.x** documentation at https://vertx.io/docs/vertx-core/java.

These two examples demonstrated how little code you have to write in order to create a complete web application if you use a well-established framework. It does not mean that you cannot explore the latest and greatest of frameworks. By any means, you can and should do it to stay abreast with progress in your industry. Just keep in mind that it takes some time for a new product to mature and become reliable and helpful enough for creating a production-strong software solution.

Testing is the shortest path to quality code

The last best practice we will discuss is this statement: *testing is not an overhead or a burden; it is the programmer's guide to success*. The only question is when to write the test.

There is a compelling argument that requires writing a test before any line of code is written. If you can do it, that is great. We are not going to try and talk you out of it. But if you do not do it, try to start writing a test after you have written one, or all, the lines of code you have been tasked to write.

In practice, many experienced programmers find it helpful to start writing testing code after some of the new functionality is implemented. This is because that is when the programmer understands better how the new code fits into the existing context. They may even try and hardcode some values to see how well the new code is integrated with the code that calls the new method. After making sure the new code is well integrated, the programmer can continue implementing and tuning it, all while testing the new implementation against the requirements in the context of the calling code.

One important qualification must be added – while writing the test, it is better if the input data and the test criteria are set not by you, but by the person who assigned you the task or the tester. Setting the test according to the results the code produces is a well-known programmer's trap. Objective self-assessment is not easy, if at all possible.

Summary

In this chapter, we discussed the Java idioms that a mainstream programmer encounters daily. We also discussed the best design practices and related recommendations, including code-writing styles and testing.

You also learned about the most popular Java idioms related to certain features, functionalities, and design solutions. These idioms were demonstrated with practical examples, where you learned how to incorporate them into your code and the professional language that's used to communicate with other programmers.

This chapter concludes this book about Java 17 and its usage for writing effective application code. If you have read all of it, then you should have a very good overview of this topic and acquired valuable programming knowledge and skills you can immediately apply professionally. If you found this material valuable, then it makes us happy to know that we have achieved our goal. Thank you for reading.

Quiz

Answer the following questions to test your knowledge of this chapter:

1. Select all the correct statements:

   A. Idioms can be used to communicate the code's intent.

   B. Idioms can be used to explain what the code does.

   C. Idioms can be misused and obscure the topic of conversation.

   D. Idioms should be avoided to express the idea clearly.

2. Is it necessary to implement `hasCode()` every time `equals()` is implemented?

3. If `obj1.compareTo(obj2)` returns a negative value, what does this mean?

4. Does the deep copy notion apply to a primitive value during cloning?

5. Which is faster, `StringBuffer` or `StringBuilder`?

6. What are the benefits of coding to an interface?

7. What are the benefits of using composition versus inheritance?

8. What is the advantage of using libraries versus writing your own code?

9. Who is the target audience of your code?

10. Is testing required?

Assessments

Chapter 1 – Getting Started with Java 17

1. c) Java Development Kit

2. b) Java Class Library

3. d) Java Standard Edition

4. b) Integrated Development Environment

5. a) Project building, b) Project configuration, c) Project documentation

6. a) boolean, b) numeric

7. a) long, c) short, d) byte

8. d) Value representation

9. a) \\ , b) 2_0 , c) 2__0f , d) \f

10. a) % , c) & , d) ->

11. a) 0

12. b) false, false

13. d) 4

14. c) Compilation error

15. b) 2

16. a), c), d)

17. d) 20 -1

18. c) The x value is within the 11 range

19. c) result = 32

20. a) A variable can be declared, b) A variable can be assigned

21. b) A selection statement, d) An increment statement

Chapter 2 – Java Object-Oriented Programming (OOP)

1. a), d)
2. b), c), d)
3. a), b), c)
4. a), c), d)
5. d)
6. c), d)
7. a), b)
8. b), d)
9. d)
10. b)
11. a), c)
12. b), c), d)
13. a), b)
14. b), c)
15. b), c), d)
16. b), c)
17. c)
18. a), b), c)
19. b), c), d)
20. a), c)
21. a), c), d)

Chapter 3 – Java Fundamentals

1. a), d)
2. c), d)
3. a), b), d)
4. a), c), d)
5. a), c)

6. a), b), d)

7. a), b), c), d)

8. c), d)

9. d)

10. c)

11. b)

12. c)

Chapter 4 – Exception Handling

1. a), b), c)

2. b)

3. c)

4. a), b), c), d)

5. a)

6. a), c)

7. d)

Chapter 5 – Strings, Input/Output, and Files

1. b)

2. c)

3. b)

4. a)

5. d)

6. a), c), d)

7. c)

8. d)

9. a), b), c)

10. c), d) (notice the usage of the `mkdir()` method, instead of `mkdirs()`)

Chapter 6 – Data Structures, Generics, and Popular Utilities

1. d)
2. b), d)
3. a), b), c), d)
4. a), b), c), d)
5. a), b), d)
6. a), b), c)
7. c)
8. a), b), c), d)
9. b), d)
10. b)
11. b), c)
12. a)
13. c)
14. d)
15. b)
16. c)
17. a)
18. b)
19. c)

Chapter 7 – Java Standard and External Libraries

1. a), b), c)
2. a), b), d)
3. b), c)
4. b), d)
5. a), c)
6. a), b), c), d)

7. b), c), d)

8. b), c)

9. b)

10. c), d)

11. a), c)

12. b), d)

13. a), d)

14. b), c), d)

15. a), b), d)

16. b), d)

Chapter 8 – Multithreading and Concurrent Processing

1. a), c), d)

2. b), c), d)

3. a)

4. a), c), d)

5. b), c), d)

6. a), b), c), d)

7. c), d)

8. a), b), c)

9. b), c)

10. b), c), d)

11. a), b), c)

12. b), c)

13. b), c)

Chapter 9 – JVM Structure and Garbage Collection

1. b), d)
2. c)
3. d)
4. b), c)
5. a), d)
6. c)
7. a), b), c), d)
8. a), c), d)
9. b), d)
10. a), b), c), d)
11. a)
12. a), b), c)
13. a), c)
14. a), c), d)
15. b), d)

Chapter 10 – Managing Data in a Database

1. c)
2. a), d)
3. b), c), d)
4. a), b), c), d)
5. a), b), c)
6. a), d)
7. a), b), c)
8. a), c)
9. a), c), d)
10. a), b)
11. a), d)
12. a), b), d)
13. a), b), c)

Chapter 11 – Network Programming

1. The correct answer may include FTP, SMTP, HTTP, HTTPS, WebSocket, SSH, Telnet, LDAP, DNS, or some other protocols

2. The correct answer may include UDP, TCP, SCTP, DCCP, or some other protocols

3. `java.net.http`

4. UDP

5. Yes

6. `java.net`

7. Transmission Control Protocol

8. They are synonyms

9. The TCP session is identified by IP address and port of the source and IP address and port of the destination

10. `ServerSocket` can be used without the client running. It just listens on the specified port

11. UDP

12. TCP

13. The correct answers may include HTTP, HTTPS, Telnet, FTP, or SMTP

14. a), c), d)

15. They are synonyms

16. They are synonyms

17. `/something/something?par=42`

18. The correct answer may include binary format, header compression, multiplexing, or push capability

19. `java.net.http.HttpClient`

20. `java.net.http.WebSocket`

21. No difference

22. `java.util.concurrent.CompletableFuture`

Chapter 12 – Java GUI Programming

1. Stage
2. Node
3. Application
4. `void start(Stage pm)`
5. `static void launch(String... args)`
6. `--module-path` and `--add-modules`
7. `void stop()`
8. `WebView`
9. `Media`, `MediaPlayer`, `MediaView`
10. `--add-exports`
11. Any five from the following list: `Blend`, `Bloom`, `BoxBlur`, `ColorAdjust`, `DisplacementMap`, `DropShadow`, `Glow`, `InnerShadow`, `Lighting`, `MotionBlur`, `PerspectiveTransform`, `Reflection`, `ShadowTone`, and `SepiaTone`

Chapter 13 – Functional Programming

1. c)
2. a), d)
3. One
4. void
5. One
6. `boolean`
7. None
8. `T`
9. One
10. `R`
11. The enclosing context
12. `Location::methodName`

Chapter 14 – Java Standard Streams

1. a), b)

2. `of ()`, without parameters, produces an empty stream

3. `java.util.Set`

4. 135

5. 42

6. 2121

7. No, but it extends the functional interface `Consumer` and can be passed around as such

8. None

9. 3

10. 1.5

11. 42, X, a

12. Compilation error, because `peek ()` cannot return anything

13. 2

14. An alternative `Optional` object

15. a

16. One

17. Any of `filter ()`, `map ()`, and `flatMap ()`

18. Any of `distinct ()`, `limit ()`, `sorted ()`, `reduce ()`, and `collect ()`

Chapter 15 – Reactive Programming

1. a), b), c)

2. Yes

3. Non-Blocking Input/Output

4. No

5. Reactive eXtension

6. `java.util.concurrent`

7. a), d)

8. The blocking operator name starts with **blocking**

9. A hot observable emits values at its own pace. A cold observable emits the next value after the previous one has reached the Terminal operator

10. The observable stops emitting values and the pipeline stops operating

11. a), c), d)

12. For example, any two from the following: `buffer()`, `flatMap()`, `groupBy()`, `map()`, `scan()`, and `window()`

13. For example, any two from the following: `debounce()`, `distinct()`, `elementAt(long n)`, `filter()`, `firstElement()`, `ignoreElements()`, `lastElement()`, `sample()`, `skip()`, and `take()`

14. Drop excessive values, take the latest, use buffer

15. `subscribeOn()`, `observeOn()`, `fromFuture()`

Chapter 16 – Java Microbenchmark Harness

1. b), c), d)

2. Add a dependency on JMH to the project (or classpath, if run manually) and add the annotation `@Benchmark` to the method you would like to test for performance

3. As the main method using a Java command with an explicitly named main class, as the main method using a java command with an executable `.jar` file, and using an IDE running as the main method or using a plugin and running an individual method

4. Any two of the following: `Mode.AverageTime`, `Mode.Throughput`, `Mode.SampleTime`, and `Mode.SingleShotTime`

5. Any two of the following: `TimeUnit.NANOSECONDS`, `TimeUnit.MICROSECONDS`, `TimeUnit.MILLISECONDS`, `TimeUnit.SECONDS`, `TimeUnit.MINUTES`, `TimeUnit.HOURS`, and `TimeUnit.DAYS`

6. Using an object of a class with the annotation `@State`

7. Using the annotation `@Param` in front of the `state` property

8. Using the annotation `@CompilerConrol`

9. Using a parameter of the type `Blackhole` that consumes the produced result

10. Using the annotation `@Fork`

Chapter 17 – Best Practices for Writing High-Quality Code

1. a), b), c)

2. Generally, it is recommended but not required. It is required for certain situations, for example, an when object of the class is going to be placed and searched inside a hash-based data structure

3. `obj1` is less than `obj2`

4. No

5. `StringBuilder`

6. Allowing the implementation to change without changing the client code

7. More control over the code evolution and code flexibility for accommodating a change

8. More reliable code, quicker to write, less testing, easier for other people to understand

9. Other programmers that are going to maintain your code and you some time later

10. No, but it is very helpful to you

Index

Packt>

Other Books You May Enjoy

If you enjoyed this book, you may be interested in these other books by Packt:

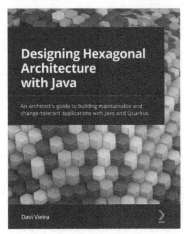

Designing Hexagonal Architecture with Java

Davi Vieira

ISBN: 9781801816489

- Find out how to assemble business rules algorithms using the specification design pattern

- Combine domain-driven design techniques with hexagonal principles to create powerful domain models

- Employ adapters to make the system support different protocols such as REST, gRPC, and WebSocket

- Create a module and package structure based on hexagonal principles

- Use Java modules to enforce dependency inversion and ensure isolation between software components

- Implement Quarkus DI to manage the life cycle of input and output ports

The Complete Coding Interview Guide in Java

Anghel Leonard

ISBN: 9781839212062

- Solve the most popular Java coding problems efficiently
- Tackle challenging algorithms that will help you develop robust and fast logic
- Practice answering commonly asked non-technical interview questions that can make the difference between a pass and a fail
- Get an overall picture of prospective employers' expectations from a Java developer
- Solve various concurrent programming, functional programming, and unit testing problems

Packt is searching for authors like you

If you're interested in becoming an author for Packt, please visit `authors.packtpub.com` and apply today. We have worked with thousands of developers and tech professionals, just like you, to help them share their insight with the global tech community. You can make a general application, apply for a specific hot topic that we are recruiting an author for, or submit your own idea.

Share Your Thoughts

Now you've finished *Learn Java 17 Programming*, we'd love to hear your thoughts! Scan the QR code below to go straight to the Amazon review page for this book and share your feedback or leave a review on the site that you purchased it from.

https://packt.link/r/1-803-24143-8

Your review is important to us and the tech community and will help us make sure we're delivering excellent quality content.

Made in the USA
Las Vegas, NV
25 November 2022

60255103R00411